KISS	Keep It Short and Simple
LEAA	Law Enforcement Assistance Administration
LESTN	Law Enforcement Satellite Training Network
LETN	Law Enforcement Television Network
MBO	Management by Objective
MIS	Management Information System
MMPI	Minnesota Multiphasic Personality Inventory
MPO	Master Patrol Officer
NAFTO	National Association of Field Training Officers
NAPO	National Association of Police Organizations
NIJ	National Institute of Justice
NLRB	National Labor Relations Board
OCFAF	Open Case Fired Ammunition Files
OJT	On-the-Job Training
PDM	Participatory Decision Making
PERF	Police Executive Research Forum (Foundation)
PIN	Pager Information Network
PMP	Patrol Management Program
PODSCORB	Planning, Organizing, Directing, Staffing, Coordinating, Reporting and Budgeting
POP	Problem-Oriented Policing
POST	Peace Officer Standards and Training
PPBS	Planning-Programming-Budgeting System
PTSD	Post-Traumatic Stress Disorder
Q & A	Question and answer
QID	Qualified individual with a disability
QPP	Quality Performance Plan
QUID	Quantified Interpersonal Decision Making
QUOD	Quantified Organizational Decision Making
QWL	Quality of Work Life
RFP	Request for Proposal
SHARK	Skim, highlight, assess, reread, keep
SMART	Specific, measurable, attainable, relevant, trackable
TEAM	Traffic Enforcement and Management System
TQM	Total Quality Management
ZBB	Zero-Based Budgeting

www.wadsworth.com

wadsworth.com is the World Wide Web site for Wadsworth and is your direct source to dozens of online resources.

At *wadsworth.com* you can find out about supplements, demonstration software, and student resources. You can also send email to many of our authors and preview new publications and exciting new technologies.

wadsworth.com
Changing the way the world learns®

Management and Supervision in Law Enforcement

Third Edition

Wayne Bennett
Former Chief of Police
Edina, Minnesota
Boulder City, Nevada

Kären M. Hess, PhD
Normandale Community College
Bloomington, Minnesota

WADSWORTH
™
THOMSON LEARNING

Australia • Canada • Mexico • Singapore
Spain • United Kingdom • United States

WADSWORTH

THOMSON LEARNING

Executive Editor, Criminal Justice: Sabra Horne
Development Editor: Terri Edwards
Assistant Editor: Ann Tsai
Editorial Assistant: Cortney Bruggink
Marketing Manager: Jennifer Somerville
Project Editor: Jennie Redwitz
Print Buyer: Karen Hunt
Permissions Editor: Bob Kauser
Production Service Coordinator: Andrea Bednar,
                         Shepherd, Incorporated

Text Designer: Carolyn Deacy
Photo Researcher: Mary Reeg
Copy Editor: Carol Hoke
Illustrator: Jim Brimeyer
Cover Designer: Harold Burch
Cover Image: Stock Boston / © A. Ramey
Cover Printer: Phoenix Color Corporation
Compositor: Shepherd, Incorporated
Printer: R. R. Donnelley, Crawfordsville
Index: Christine M. H. Orthmann

Library of Congress Cataloging-in-Publication Data
Bennett, Wayne.
    Management and supervision in law enforcement /
Wayne Bennett, Kären M. Hess.—3rd ed.
      p.   cm.
    Includes indexes.
    ISBN 0-534-55431-8
    1. Police—Personnel management 2. Policy—
United States—Personnel management.
    I. Hess, Kären M., 1939– II. Title

    HV7936.P47 B47 2000
    363.2'068'3—dc21   00-042868

Wadsworth/Thomson Learning
10 Davis Drive
Belmont, CA 94002-3098
USA

For more information about our products, contact us:
Thomson Learning Academic Resource Center
1-800-423-0563
http://www.wadsworth.com

International Headquarters
Thomson Learning
International Division
290 Harbor Drive, 2nd Floor
Stamford, CT 06902-7477
USA

UK/Europe/Middle East/South Africa
Thomson Learning
Berkshire House
168-173 High Holborn
London WC1V 7AA
United Kingdom

Asia
Thomson Learning
60 Albert Street, #15-01
Albert Complex
Singapore 189969

Canada
Nelson Thomson Learning
1120 Birchmount Road
Toronto, Ontario M1K 5G4
Canada

Contents in Brief

Contents

SECTION II

3 Basic Management/Personal Skills

Communication: A Critical Management Skill, 75

6 Budgeting and Managing Costs Creatively, 169

9   Promoting Growth and Development, 279

10   Motivation and Morale, 315

SECTION IV   **Managing Problems**

11 Discipline and Problem Behaviors, 355

SECTION V   Getting the Job Done . . . Through Others

15   Deploying Law Enforcement Resources and Improving Productivity, 465

16   Performance Appraisals and Evaluation, 513

Foreword

As a former employee of Wayne Bennett's in the 1960s at the Edina, Minnesota, Police Department, I went on to lead my own police departments in Burnsville, Minnesota, and Madison, Wisconsin. I am especially pleased to introduce *Management and Supervision in Law Enforcement,* Third Edition.

This text is about law enforcement managers and supervisors, their jobs and the complicated interrelationships with all members of the law enforcement team and with the communities they serve. It is also about leadership, the important role of clarifying values, creating the vision, asking, listening, rewarding and coaching excellence to align an organization's work to achieve the vision. Being an effective supervisor and manager is first having the competency to do your job well. Then the job of being a leader begins—being a leader goes far beyond technical competency into the areas of energizing others and removing the barriers in systems that prevent employees from doing the quality job they would like to do.

The text illustrates the best known methods and practices of police leadership and management today, while keeping an eye on what will be needed tomorrow. We are in an age of rapid change. This rapid change may lead to conflict in our society. At the turn of the last century, the transition from an agrarian to industrial society was extremely conflict-ridden. We can expect the same as we enter the information age. Futurists tell us by the year 2050, 90% of the knowledge we have today will be outmoded. Even today, the half-life of an engineer's job knowledge is five years. Technological changes in society, and internally within the law enforcement profession, must be counterbalanced by a genuine concern for people, regardless of their economic level, race, creed, sexual preference, gender or other individual characteristics. We must recognize today that people are our most important organizational resource. We are a diverse society that needs leaders who can enjoin and empower people to work together to achieve commonly shared goals. Humanitarian concerns within law enforcement between leaders and their employees are as important as concerns for a society as a whole.

Throughout the years, we have learned few lessons about organizational change. We still think we can order people to be what we want them to be and tell them what we want them to do without their input and participation. If leaders today use an authoritarian leadership style to get work done, they will find it is as ineffective as it is immoral. Some leaders think they can be service-oriented outside of the organization without changing the inside first. Michael Eisner of the Disney Corporation says he believes the treatment of customers will improve if leaders first improve the treatment of their employees. Quality improvement expert Dr. W. Edwards Deming decried the authoritarian style by telling leaders to drive fear out of the workplace, empower employees and create joy in work.

We seem to know that healthy employees—physically, mentally and emotionally—mean greater productivity, but we also get higher productivity from employees who love their work, who find joy in their jobs. Leaders have a moral responsibility and obligation to foster joy in work, to have a positive outlook about work and to generate excitement in others. It is the job of leaders today to enable the growth and development of their employees—continuously and forever. It is important and vital work, but it will be a difficult journey for some leaders to switch from being a dictator to becoming a coach.

This text provides a comprehensive overview of the responsibilities of leaders in law enforcement. The first emphasis is on the organization: what the leader's role is in the organizational structure and how it has evolved from authoritarian to leader. The second emphasis is on the interpersonal skills successful leaders have: communicating effectively, listening, and providing feedback to others, planning, budgeting, problem solving and empowering others.

A third emphasis is on how leaders develop themselves and their subordinates, how they educate, motivate and coach others to reach their full potential. A fourth emphasis is on dealing with the problems and conflicts that inevitably arise within any organization; the ability to smooth out troubles; dealing with problem behaviors, complaints and grievances. The text concludes with how leaders can actually accomplish these tasks through empowering others; that is, sharing the problem with those who are doing the job. This text emphasizes a proactive approach to law enforcement; looking forward, not back, and anticipating the future.

Three themes will be found throughout the text. The first theme is the need for participatory leadership—empowering all personnel to become contributing members in the law enforcement team. A second theme is the need for viewing citizens as "customers," much like business people do—asking their opinions, listening, considering their beliefs and expectations and asking them to help us make their community safe. The third theme is the need to understand and accept change as inevitable and an opportunity for us as we move from an authoritarian, old military model to a more humanistic, participatory model. The key to all of this is to develop police leadership capable of moving forward. Today's and tomorrow's leaders must be people who, according to military historian B. H. Liddell Hart, have a profound understanding of human nature, a knack of smoothing out troubles, can win affection while communicating energy, are able to move ahead with ruthless determination when appropriate and generate an electrifying current while keeping a cool head.

David C. Couper
Former Chief of Police
Madison, Wisconsin

Preface

Welcome to the Third Edition of *Management and Supervision in Law Enforcement*. Based on feedback from students and instructors, we have made several changes in this edition, perhaps the most important of which are the consolidation of some chapters and a reduction in the overall length. Early 1990s sources have been replaced by late 1990s sources, and all statistics have been updated.

In addition, we have added or expanded several important topics, including the following: the evolution of law enforcement, use of focus groups, decision making, news conferences, the Internet as a resource, technological aids including using computers to enhance productivity, the crime triangle, the cone of resolution, hot spots, the Law Enforcement Officers' Bill of Rights, Garrity protection, racial profiling, scheduling and shift work, fitness for duty evaluations and research.

Although significant changes have been made, three themes continue from previous editions. First, managers and supervisors need to move from an authoritative style to a participative leadership style that empowers all personnel to become contributing team members. Second, community policing and problem solving are key to preserving the peace and fighting crime. Citizens can become allies in both. Law enforcement cannot go it alone any longer. Third, change must be viewed as an opportunity rather than as something to resist. Not only must managers help their people grow and develop, they themselves must continuously grow and develop, looking for new and better ways to accomplish their mission. Futurist Alvin Toffler asserts: "The illiterate of the 21st century will not be those who cannot read and write, but those who cannot learn, unlearn and relearn." This text is a beginning toward opening your mind to new ways of thinking and doing.

Section I, Management and Supervision: An Overview, takes a broad look at management, beginning with the law enforcement organization itself and the challenges this organization presents (Chapter 1). Next the role of the manager; the various levels of management, including first-line managers or supervisors; and the specific skills required at each level are examined. This is followed by a discussion of the evolving role of managers as leaders and a participatory management style and what this challenge means for law enforcement agencies (Chapter 2).

Section II, Basic Management/Personal Skills, focuses on basic skills that affect everything done by law enforcement managers at all levels. A critical basic skill that can "make or break" a law enforcement manager is communication. Effective communication is at the core of effective management (Chapter 3). The manager's role, by definition, includes problem solving and decision making (Chapter 4). How decisions are made and by whom are vital management questions. Among the most important decisions are those involving how time will be spent—the time of individual managers, officers and the agency as a whole (Chapter 5). Other important decisions involve how resources other than time can be most effectively managed, that is, the ongoing task of budgeting, which has a direct effect on what individual managers, their officers and ultimately the agency can accomplish (Chapter 6). The second section concludes with a discussion of the selection process and suggestions on dealing with unions (Chapter 7).

Section III, Managers and the Skills of Others, focuses on how managers can develop their subordinates' numerous talents through participatory leadership. It first explains the importance of training (Chapter 8) and then suggests ways managers can go beyond training to fully develop the potential of all personnel (Chapter 9). Managers must not only build on the strengths of their people and accommodate their weaknesses but also motivate their officers to be as effective as possible. Research has shown that tangible rewards such as pay raises and fringe benefits are not necessarily the most motivating influences. In fact, they are often thought of as "givens," making managing much more challenging. Managers who can develop and motivate their team members will make a tremendous contribution to the department and to accomplishing its goals and objectives. In addition, many concepts basic to motivation are directly related to keeping morale high. Attending to employees' motivation and morale is critical to being an effective manager (Chapter 10).

Section IV, Managing Problems, discusses problems that may occur in any law enforcement organization. They are an inevitable part of the challenge of accomplishing work through others. Managers must recognize problem behaviors and use an appropriate combination of constructive criticism, discipline and incentives to correct the problems (Chapter 11). In addition, supervisors and managers will be faced with numerous complaints and grievances from their subordinates, their superiors and the public they serve. They or their officers may in fact be the objects of civil lawsuits. Effectively handling such matters requires great skill in communication (Chapter 12). Conflicts, disagreements, differences of opinion and outright confrontations may also occur and must be dealt with diplomatically by law enforcement managers (Chapter 13). Finally, all the preceding, plus the challenges inherent in law enforcement work itself, can result in extreme stress for supervisors, managers and subordinates. Reducing such stress is a critical role of administrators (Chapter 14).

Section V, Getting the Job Done . . . Through Others, focuses on getting the job done through effective leadership. (People would rather be led than "managed.") Personnel must be effectively deployed and their productivity enhanced (Chapter 15). Evaluation should be continuous and include both formal and informal evaluation. The results should be used to help employees continue to grow and develop and to make the department more effective as well (Chapter 16). The section concludes with a discussion of the need for managers to be forward looking, considering what the future of law enforcement and the entire criminal justice system may hold (Chapter 17).

How to Use This Book

Management and Supervision in Law Enforcement, Third Edition, is a planned learning experience. It uses triple-strength learning, presenting all key concepts at least three times within a chapter. The more actively you participate, the better your learning will be. You will learn and remember more if you first familiarize yourself with the total scope of the subject. Read and think about the table of contents, for it provides an outline of the many facets of law enforcement management and supervision. Then follow these steps as you study each chapter:

1. Read the objectives at the beginning of the chapter. These are stated as "Do You Know?" questions. Assess your current knowledge of the content of each question, and examine preconceptions you may hold.

2. Read the list of key terms and think about their possible meanings.

3. Read the chapter, underlining, highlighting or taking notes if that is your preferred study style. Pay special attention to all information highlighted as follows:

Sources of stress can be found in a person's daily living, personality and job.

Also pay special attention to all words in bold print—these are the chapter's key terms.

4. When you have finished reading a chapter, reread the "Do You Know?" questions to make sure you can give an educated response to each. If you find yourself stumped by one, find the appropriate section in the chapter and review it. Also define each key term. If you find yourself stumped, either find the term in the chapter or look it up in the glossary.

5. Read the discussion questions and be prepared to contribute to a class discussion of the ideas presented in the chapter.

6. Complete the InfoTrack College Edition Assignment and be prepared to share your findings with the class.

7. Periodically review the "Do You Know?" questions, key terms and chapter summaries.

By following these steps, you will learn more, understand it better and remember it longer. Good learning!

Acknowledgments

We would like to thank Dorothy Bennett for her assistance with photographs and Christine M. H. Orthmann for her careful editing, indexing and preparation of the *Instructor's Manual*. We would also acknowledge the assistance of and extend our thanks to M. John Velier, FBI Management Science Unit; Professor Robert Moore, University of Nevada at Las Vegas; and Chief Robert Lowrie, former chief of police, Boulder City Police Department. A special thank you goes to Michael Bennett, Imagemakers International Inc., who provided many photographs at no charge.

A heartfelt thanks to the reviewers of the past editions of the text for their valuable suggestions: Timothy Apolito, University of Dayton; Tom Barker, Jacksonville State University; A. J. Bartok, Regional Law Enforcement Academy, Colorado; Lloyd Bratz, Cuyahoga Community College; Gib H. Bruns, Arizona State University; David Carter, Michigan State University; Dana Dewitt, Cadron State College;

Larry Gould, Northern Arizona University; Joseph J. Hanrahan, Westfield State College; Robert G. Huckabee, Indiana State University; Alan Lawson, Ferris State University, Michigan; Muriel Lembright, Wichita State University; William McCamey, Western Illinois University; Robert L. Marsh, Boise State University; Robert G. May, Waubonsee Community College; John Maxwell, Community College of Philadelphia; Dennis M. Payne, Michigan State University; Carroll S. Price, Penn Valley Community College; Lawrence G. Stephens, Columbus State Community College; W. Fred Wegener, Indiana University of Pennsylvania; Stanley W. Wisnoski, Jr., Broward Community College; and Solomon Zhao, University of Nebraska, Omaha.

And special thanks to the reviewers for the Third Edition: Tom Barker, Jacksonville State University; Lloyd L. Bratz, Cuyahoga Community College; David L. Carter, Michigan State University; Dana C. DeWitt, Chadron State College; Joseph J. Hanrahan, Westfield State College; William McCamey, Western Illinois University; Jihong Zhao, University of Nebraska at Omaha.

Finally, a special thanks to our executive editor, Sabra Horne; our assistant editor, Ann Tsai; our permissions editor, Bob Kauser; and our production editor, Jennie Redwitz, at Wadsworth and to our product service coordinator at Shepherd, Inc., Andrea Bednar.

About the Authors

Wayne W. Bennett is a graduate of the FBI National Police Academy, holds an LLB degree in law and has served as the Director of Public Safety for the Edina, Minnesota, Police Department as well as Chief of Police of the Boulder City, Nevada, Police Department. He is coauthor of *Criminal Investigation,* sixth edition, and is currently working on an *Introduction to Criminal Justice* text for Wadsworth Publishing Company.

Kären M. Hess holds a PhD in English from the University of Minnesota and a PhD in criminal justice from Pacific Western University. Other Wadsworth texts Dr. Hess has coauthored are *Corrections in the 21ˢᵗ Century: A Practical Approach, Criminal Investigation* (Sixth Edition), *Criminal Procedure, Introduction to Law Enforcement and Criminal Justice* (Sixth Edition), *Introduction to Private Security* (Fourth Edition), *Juvenile Justice* (Third Edition), *The Police in the Community: Strategies for the 21st Century* (Second Edition), *Police Operations* and *Seeking Employment in Criminal Justice and Related Fields* (Third Edition).

The content of this text is based on the practical experience of Wayne W. Bennett, who has spent 45 years in law enforcement and has taught various aspects of management and supervision over the past 30 years, as well as the research and experience of Kären M. Hess, PhD, who has been developing instructional programs for over 30 years. The text itself has been reviewed by several experts in management and supervision in law enforcement. Any errors, however, are the sole responsibility of the authors.

| Chapter | 1 | The Law Enforcement Organization |

Good organizations are living bodies that
grow new muscles to meet challenges.
—Robert Townsend, corporate consultant

Do You Know?

- How law enforcement agencies were traditionally organized?
- What three eras of policing have been identified?
- What should drive an organization?
- How goals differ from objectives and work plans?
- What line and staff personnel are?
- What advantages and disadvantages are associated with specialization?
- What the chain of command is?
- What unity of command refers to?
- What the span of control is?
- What authority should be coupled with?
- What management tools help coordination?
- What type of organization law enforcement managers should recognize?
- What needs to be reexamined?
- What community policing and problem-solving policing (COPPS) are viewed as?

Can You Define?

accountability
administrative services
authority
bifurcated society
chain of command
channels of
    communication
community era
community policing
coordination
decentralization
delegation
empowered
field services
flat organization
formal organization
generalists

goals
guiding philosophy
hierarchy
informal organization
key result areas
line personnel
mission
mission statement
objectives
organization
organizational chart
paradigm
paradigm shift
political era
proactive
problem-solving
    policing

professional model
pyramid of authority
reactive
reform era
responsibility
scuttlebutt
span of control
specialists
spoils system
staff personnel
stakeholders
unity of command
values
Wolf Pack syndrome
work plans

INTRODUCTION

An **organization** is an artificial structure created to coordinate either people or groups and resources to achieve a mission or goal. Organizations exist for many different reasons. One important reason is that a group can accomplish things an individual could never do alone. For example, no single individual could have put a person on the moon, but an organization—NASA—was successful.

The need for organizing has been recognized for centuries. Since recorded time people have banded together into societies. Within these societies they have sought ways to protect themselves from nature and from those who would harm them or their possessions. They made rules, set up ways to enforce these rules and provided swift punishment to those who did not obey. Modern-day law enforcement agencies are an outgrowth of this need for "law and order."

To understand the present, it is often helpful to look at the past—where traditions and the status quo originated. Therefore, the chapter begins with a brief history of the development of law enforcement agencies and the organizational structure that became typical. It examines the traditional military, pyramid-style structure and the generalists and specialists usually found within this organization. The chapter next looks at the mission of law enforcement agencies and the functions they serve. The effect of this mission on an organization's goals, objectives and work plans is then described. This is followed by a discussion of the importance of coordination, not only within the formal organization but externally and within the informal organization found in any agency. The chapter concludes with a glimpse at the law enforcement organization of the future and the changes to be anticipated.

Evolution of Law Enforcement Organizations

Most agencies have an organization with a rich tradition going back to the 1800s in England. In England the Industrial Revolution changed the country from a rural to an urban society, with the accompanying problems of unemployment, poverty and crime. One result was the founding of the Metropolitan Police in London in 1829. The fundamental principles on which this police force rested were set forth by Sir Robert Peel, often called the "Father of Modern Policing." They included the following:

- Police must be stable, efficient and organized militarily.
- Police must be under governmental control.
- The deployment of police strength by both time and area is essential.
- Public security demands that every police officer be given a number.
- Police headquarters should be centrally located and easily accessible.

Peel's principles for reform called for local responsibility for law and order; appointed, paid civilians to assume this responsibility and standards for these individuals' conduct and organizations.

Police organizations developed in a similar manner in the United States. New York City established the first modern American city police force in 1844, modeled after London's Metropolitan Police Department. In 1874 the Texas Rangers were commissioned as police officers and became the first agency similar to our present-day state police. Federal agencies were also established, with the FBI created in 1908. In addition to these, many jurisdictions established county law enforcement agencies. These early organizations were modeled after the military, with ranks, levels of command and uniforms. Just as the military has a commander in chief, law enforcement agencies also have chiefs (or sheriffs). Likewise, just as the commander in chief is ultimately responsible to the citizens of the United States, law enforcement chiefs are ultimately responsible to the citizens of the political entity their department serves.

The typical law enforcement organizational design is that of a pyramid-shaped hierarchy based on a military model.

Law enforcement agencies provide their services to the political entity from which they derive their authority and responsibility. Providing services is their sole reason for existence. It is highly likely that newly created municipalities would expect *someone* to respond to their needs for the many services provided by police. Americans have come to expect and demand reasonably safe communities, so they demand law enforcement organizations. As such organizations develop, they resemble those already in existence in other communities because tradition and experience are enduring.

Further, most present-day law enforcement managers "inherited" their organization when they assumed their positions. Most have perpetuated the traditional organization, diagrammed in Figure 1.1, because it has worked.

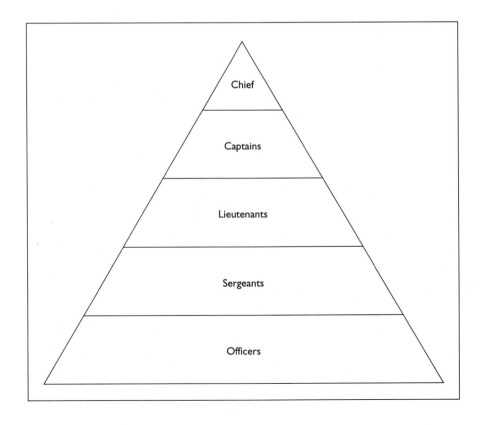

Figure 1.1
The Pyramid of Authority— Organizational Hierarchy

The Traditional Law Enforcement Organization

Pre–World War II law enforcement agencies followed the industry pattern by placing maximum emphasis on the job and minimum attention on the human interrelationships of people filling the positions. Rigid rules and regulations were used excessively, along with frequent use and abuse of the threat of firing. Individual needs were almost totally ignored. Early law enforcement management was characterized by the general attitude of, "If you don't like the job, plenty of others want it."

Law enforcement organizations were simple. The typical **pyramid of authority** predominated with its **hierarchy** of authoritative management. Command officers and supervisors had complete authority over subordinates, and there was little tolerance for departmental appeal except through the courts. Communication flowed downward. Little or no specialization existed, and training was nonexistent or minimal. Selection was based largely on physical qualifications, and most applicants had military experience.

The majority of personnel were assigned to foot patrol. Police radio communications systems and other technology were virtually nonexistent. University- or college-level training, programs and even courses were unheard of. Ten-hour days and six-day weeks were common, accompanied by extremely low salaries. Flexibility was nonexistent, and fringe benefits were few. As a line in the operetta *The Mikado* puts it: "A policeman's lot was not a happy one."

Three Eras of Policing

Policing has evolved in the way it views itself, its responsibilities and the most effective means of meeting those responsibilities.

Three distinct eras of policing have been identified: the political era, the reform era and the community era.

The Political Era (1840–1930)

In the **political era,** policing was characterized by police authority coming from politicians and the law, a broad social service function, decentralized organization, an intimate relationship with the community and extensive use of foot patrol. Because of the close tie between police authority and politics during this era, corruption was a common problem. One factor underlying this corruption was the prevalent **spoils system,** whose motto, "To the victor go the spoils," resulted in political interference with policing. The prevailing party believed its members should be immune from arrest and receive other special privileges. Furthermore, the spoils system encouraged politicians to reward their friends by giving them key positions in police departments. A major step toward reducing corruption within police departments occurred in 1883, when Congress passed the Pendleton Act, which created the civil service system and made it unlawful to fire or demote a government employee for political reasons.

During the political era police served a broad social service function, with some even running soup lines. Police were also close to their community, with foot patrol bringing beat officers into contact with the people.

In 1929 President Herbert Hoover appointed the National Commission on Law Observance and Enforcement to examine the American criminal justice system. The commission, named after chairman George Wickersham, devoted two reports to the police. Report 11, *Lawlessness in Law Enforcement,* described the problem of police brutality, concluding that "the third degree—the inflicting of pain, physical or mental, to extract confessions or statements—is extensively practiced." Report 14, *The Police,* focused on police administration and called for expert leadership, centralized administrative control and higher personnel standards. In other words, Report 14 called for police professionalism, which led to the second era.

The Reform Era (1930–1980)

The reform era developed in reaction to the political. During the **reform era** policing was characterized by police authority coming from the law and professionalism, crime control as the primary function, a centralized and efficient organization, a professional remoteness from the community and an emphasis on preventive motorized patrol and rapid response to crime.

As early as the 1920s, August Vollmer, often called the father or dean of modern police administration, was calling for reforms in policing. He developed the first degree-granting program in law enforcement at San Jose State College and advocated that police function as social service workers and act to prevent crime. A Vollmer protégé, O. W. Wilson, became the main architect of the reform era and the style of policing known as the **professional model.** Like Vollmer, Wilson advocated police efficiency through scientific techniques. His classic text, *Police Administration,* was considered the bible of police administration during the 1950s and outlined specific ways to use one-officer patrol cars, to deploy personnel and to discipline officers. In 1947 Wilson founded the first professional school of criminology.

Reformers who sought to disassociate policing from politics advocated professional law enforcement officers charged with enforcing the law fairly and impartially. The social service function so prevalent during the political era became less important, even nonexistent in some departments, as police turned greater attention to fighting a war on crime. Two key strategies in this war were preventive automobile patrol and rapid response to calls. This style of policing is what most Americans are familiar with and have come to expect.

Reform that had begun during the 1930s and thrived during the 1950s and 1960s began to erode during the 1970s. One event in 1972 had a great impact on eroding the reform strategy. The classic Kansas City Preventive Patrol Experiment called into question the effectiveness of preventive patrol and rapid response—the two central strategies of the reform era. Wrobleski and Hess (2000, p. 31) remark:

> The professional model faced many challenges including the inability of "traditional" police approaches to decrease crime; the rapidly escalating drug problem; the pressing problems associated with the deinstitutionalization of thousands of mentally ill, many of whom became homeless; dealing with thousands of immigrants, some legal, some illegal, many speaking no English; and the breakdown of the family unit.

To meet these challenges, many departments turned to community-oriented policing—COP.

The Community Era (1980–Present)

Following changes occurring in corporate America, many police departments became "customer-oriented," viewing citizens as consumers of police services. Policing during the **community era** is characterized by police authority coming from community support, law and professionalism; provision of a broad range of services, including crime control; decentralized organization with greater authority given to patrol officers; an intimate relationship with the community; and the use of foot patrol and a problem-solving approach.

Community policing is discussed in greater depth later in this chapter and throughout the text, as it affects all aspects of the police organization and function. Table 1.1 summarizes the distinguishing characteristics of the three eras of policing.

Other Influences on the Evolution of Police Management

Management principles evolving in the business world have directly influenced how police executives have managed their forces. Such changes have taken police management and leadership philosophies from a strict control approach to an approach that delegates increased responsibility to the line officer. Breen (1999, p. 61) observes:

> The first modern efforts to enhance productivity in industry stemmed from the research of Frederick Taylor, an industrial engineer who applied what he called "scientific management" to the operations of manufacturing enterprises early in the 20th century. . . .
>
>   Scientific management called for a small span of control, clear chain of command, tall organizational hierarchy and centralized decision making, enforced through procedure-based directives. This militarily modeled organization and

Table 1.1 The Three Eras of Policing

	Political Era 1840 to 1930	Reform Era 1930 to 1980	Community Era 1980 to Present
Authorization	Politicians and law	Law and professionalism	Community support (political), law and professionalism
Function	Broad social services	Crime control	Broad provision of services
Organizational Design	Decentralized	Centralized, classical	Decentralized, task forces
Relationship to Community	Intimate	Professional, remote	Intimate
Tactics and Technology	Foot patrol	Preventive patrol and rapid response to calls	Foot patrol, problem solving, public relations
Outcome	Citizen, political satisfaction	Crime control	Quality of life and citizen satisfaction

Source: Linda S. Miller and Kären M. Hess. *The Police in the Community: Strategies for the 21st Century,* 2nd ed. West/Wadsworth Publishing, 1998, p. 17. Reprinted by permission. (Summarized from George L. Kelling and Mark H. Moore, "From Political to Reform to Community: The Evolving Strategy of Police." In *Community Policing: Rhetoric or Reality.* Edited by Jack R. Green and Stephen D. Mastrofski, New York: Praeger Publishers, 1991, pp. 6, 14–15, 22–23.)

conformant management style, which was standard police management custom, reached its zenith in the 1970s. . . .

[However, during] the 1940s, Peter Drucker was asserting that productivity is enhanced when workers are required to take responsibility for their own productivity and exercise control over it. . . .

Throughout the 1960s and 1970s, Peter Drucker maintained that management technology had to move beyond the stick-and-carrot approach and decrease its reliance on classic organization control-oriented practices. He again suggested that genuine productivity meant workers who were self-starting, self-directed and accepting of responsibility.

Such is the approach taken with today's community-oriented policing philosophy. In a sense all police become leaders and managers of their own policing mission. Breen (p. 63) concludes: "Leadership training is essential for our leadership mission. As responsibility is continually pushed to the bottom of flatter hierarchies, leadership will be required of police officers of all ranks."

Mission and Goals

The primary purpose of most law enforcement agencies is to provide specialized services to specific political entities 24 hours a day, 7 days a week, 365 days a year. This is their **mission.** Although this broad mission is generally understood, it is often not clearly articulated or put into writing.

A **mission statement** is a management tool often reflected in a slogan. Major United States companies, as well as those of government agencies, have such slogans, for example, the Army's "Be all that you can be."

> The mission statement, the organization's overriding purpose, should be the driving force of any organization, including law enforcement.

Mission statements articulate the rationale for an organization's existence. A mission statement can be the most powerful underlying influence in law enforcement, affecting organizational and individual attitudes, conduct and performance. Mission statements are best developed by an appointed committee, representative but not too large for individual participation. Developing the statement is only the first step. It must then be distributed, explained, understood and accepted by all department members. A mission statement is not automatically implemented or effective. It must be practiced in everyday actions and decision making by management and field personnel.

The mission statement of a law enforcement agency should be:

- Believable.
- Worthy of support.
- Widely known.
- Shared.
- Exciting to key stakeholders.

Who are "key stakeholders"? **Stakeholders** are those affected *by* the organization and those in a position to *affect it.* In a law enforcement organization, stakeholders include everyone in the jurisdiction. Two key questions to answer are:

- What do the stakeholders *want?*
- What do the stakeholders *need?*

What people want and what they need are *not* necessarily the same. Stakeholders should, however, have input into what is provided for them.

An example of an effective mission statement is that of the Charlotte (North Carolina) Police Department:

Mission: The Charlotte Police Department is committed to fairness, compassion, and excellence while providing police services in accordance with the law and sensitive to the priorities and needs of the people.

A mission statement such as this can both guide and drive an organization. Mission statements are usually part of an organization's overall guiding philosophy.

An Organization's Guiding Philosophy and Values

A **guiding philosophy** consists of an organization's mission statement *and* its basic **values,** the beliefs, principles or standards considered worthwhile or desirable. Consider, for example, the values set forth by the International Association of Chiefs of Police (IACP):[1]

The members of IACP are committed to the values that are reflected in the association's constitution, member Code of Ethics and Strategic Plan. These include:

A commitment to fair and impartial enforcement of laws and ordinances and respect for fundamental human rights.

A commitment to advancing the principles of respect for individual dignity and respect for constitutional rights of all persons with whom their departments come into contact.

A commitment to the highest ideals of honor and integrity to maintain the respect and confidence of their governmental officials, subordinates, the public and their fellow police executives.

A dedication to innovative and participative management, at all times seeking to improve their departments, increase productivity and remain responsive to the needs of their jurisdiction.

A commitment to friendly and courteous service by striving to improve communications with all members of the public, at all times seeking improvement in the quality and image of public service.

A dedication to improve their personal knowledge and abilities and those of their colleagues through independent study, courses, meetings and seminars.

A reverence for the value of human life and commitment to conduct themselves so as to maintain public confidence in their profession, the department and their performance of the public trust.

[1]Reprinted from *The Police Chief,* Vol. LXI, No. 11, November 1993, p. 14. Copyright held by The International Association of Chiefs of Police, Inc., 515 N. Washington St., Alexandria, Virginia 22314, U.S.A. Further reproduction without express written permission from IACP is strictly prohibited.

You may be thinking that mission statements and value statements are fine but are simply words. How do such words get translated into action?

Our Declaration of Independence was a statement of the guiding philosophy of our country, but it did not establish how the United States should be structured or governed. This was accomplished through our Constitution and Bill of Rights. A statement of philosophy is meaningless without a plan or blueprint for accomplishing it. Goals, objectives and work plans provide this blueprint.

Goals, Objectives and Work Plans

Goals, objectives and work plans are interdependent. All three are needed to carry out an organization's mission.

Goals are broad, general, desired outcomes. **Objectives** are specific, measurable ways to accomplish the goals. **Work plans** are the precise activities that contribute to accomplishing objectives.

Goals

Goals are visionary, projected achievements. They provide guidelines for planning efforts. They are what in business would be called the **key result areas.** Goals provide the foundation for objectives and ultimately for work plans. Among the commonly agreed-upon goals of most law enforcement agencies are:

- Enforcing laws.
- Preventing crime.
- Preserving the peace.
- Protecting civil rights and civil liberties.
- Providing services.

Few people would argue about the value of these goals. The disagreements arise over which are most important and how resources should be apportioned. For example, how much service and of what kind, compared with how much enforcing of laws? It is also often difficult to determine which objectives might accomplish the goals.

Objectives

Objectives are needed before work plans can be developed. They are much more specific than goals and usually have a time line. Objectives are critical to planning, assigning tasks and evaluating performance.

Following are the objectives developed under the direction of the chief of police of the Boulder City (Nevada) Police Department for the patrol division for one year:

- Continue to strive for a safe community with a low crime rate and keep Boulder City a "Safe Place to Live."
- Maintain and monitor a professional Traffic Enforcement program.
- Provide professional and competent Animal Control services.
- Provide the city with up-to-date Reserve Officer and Police Explorer programs.

- Provide the members of the Department with timely, cost-effective, quality law enforcement training.
- Keep the momentum of the Department and Patrol at its high level. The Supervisors, Sergeants, Watch Commanders and Division Commander must continue to develop leadership qualities and motivational techniques.

Some departments spell out their objectives much more specifically. For example:

- Reduce Part I crimes by 5 percent.

- Reduce accidents by 10 percent.

- Reduce overtime by 7 percent.

Good objectives are clear and understandable, especially to those who will be responsible for carrying them out. They are also practical; that is, they are realistic and achievable. Personnel must have the knowledge, skill and resources to accomplish their objectives. Effective objectives deal with important matters. They should motivate and energize each person to perform not only at a high level individually but also as a team member.

Law enforcement managers are obligated to support the objectives of both the organization and the employees. Regardless of position all employees must act responsibly toward the organization and each other. Good objectives provide the basis for a department's work plans.

Work Plans

Work plans, sometimes called *tactical* and *strategic plans,* are the detailed steps needed to accomplish objectives. They are tied to a time line and are an effective way to evaluate an organization's performance. Recall that the first objective of the Boulder City Police Department's patrol division was to "continue to strive for a safe community with a low crime rate and keep Boulder City a 'Safe Place to Live.' " The department's work plan for this first objective has seven very specific activities, the first three of which follow:

- Continue monitoring and encouraging each officer's activity in the areas of (1) patrol, (2) vacant house checks and (3) field interview forms.
- Complete incident reports referring to community problems observed which are to be handled by other City Departments: (1) street lights out, (2) signs down/old/missing, (3) junk cars, (4) unsafe action/condition, e.g., refrigerator left or trash or debris on roadways, (5) graffiti on public property.
- Provide Community Service activity to include Criminal Justice program, expand Business Alert, Neighborhood Watch, Senior Adult Safety Check program, etc.

Although these work plans are very specific, they also leave room for flexibility. In the third item, for example, the "etc." leaves room to add services whose need may become apparent during the year. Similar work plans are established for each division within the organization. Jensen and Hsieh (1999, p. 1) assert:

> Law enforcement professionals face more challenges today than ever before. Not since the advent of modern policing have agencies sought so arduously to examine and refine their missions, goals, and strategies to deal with increasingly ill-defined purposes. To make matters more difficult, this examination comes during a time of decreasing budgets, increasing legal and media scrutiny, and often-uncertain public relations.

After a law enforcement agency has determined its goals and objectives and developed work plans, these plans must be put into action—by people organized to do so.

The Formal Organization

The **formal organization** is put together by design and rational plan. The essential elements of a formal organization are:

- A clear statement of mission, goals, objectives and values.
- A division of labor among specialists.
- A rational organization or design.
- A hierarchy of authority and responsibility.

The first element has been discussed.

Typical Divisions in Law Enforcement Agencies

Law enforcement agencies typically are divided into field and administrative services, with personnel designated as line and staff personnel.

> **Field services** using **line personnel** *directly* help accomplish the goals of the department. **Administrative services** using **staff personnel** *support* the line organization.

Field services' main division is the uniformed patrol. Larger agencies may have other divisions as well, such as investigations, narcotics, vice and juvenile. Line personnel fulfill the goals and objectives of the organization. This is what most people think of as law enforcement—the uniformed police officer on the street.

Field service divisions are typically further broken into shifts to provide service within a framework of geographical space and extended time. Continuity of service must be provided between areas and shifts. Larger departments may divide the political entity they serve into distinct *precincts* or *district stations*, geographical areas served by a given portion of the officers, essentially forming a number of smaller organizations subject to overall administration and operational command. Time is typically divided into three eight-hour shifts so that service can be provided continuously. Officers frequently rotate through these shifts. Personnel assigned to specific divisions and shifts varies depending on the community's size and service needs.

Administrative services, which are usually centralized, include recruitment and training, records and communications, planning and research, and technical services. Staff personnel assist line personnel, including supervisors. The laboratory staff, for example, assists line personnel, acting as liaison, specialist or advisory personnel. They are technical experts who provide specialized information.

Legal staff (city, county or district attorneys) act as legal advisors to all members of the agency. Technical communications personnel are staff operatives, assisting the entire operation.

Conflicts can and do arise between line and staff, particularly when staff attempts to act in a capacity beyond advisory or informational. Line personnel are concerned with providing direct community services. Staff personnel help by providing better communications, evidence examination, improved equipment, better patrol vehicles, safety equipment such as armored vests, advanced records systems and data analysis and so on. Both line and staff are necessary components of the law enforcement organization. They must, however, be coordinated and controlled to achieve department goals.

Division of Labor—Generalists and Specialists

Law enforcement agencies, despite their organizational hierarchy, are basically decentralized units, with most decisions made at the level of the patrol, detective, juvenile and narcotics officers and that of the first-line supervisor. Even the authority to arrest is made at the lowest level of the organization. Most arrests are made by patrol officers, detectives and juvenile officers.

Law enforcement agencies cannot function without division of work and, often, specialization. Neither can they function without maximum coordination of these **generalists** and **specialists.** As the organization grows in size, specialization develops to meet the needs of the community. The extent of specialization is a management decision.

Specialization occurs when the organizational structure is divided into units with specific tasks to perform. The patrol unit is assigned the majority of personnel and provides the greatest variety of tasks and services. Even though specialized units are formed, the patrol division often still performs some tasks of these units.

For example, patrol officers may investigate a crime scene up to a point at which they must leave their shift or area to continue the investigation. Or they may investigate only to the point of protecting the scene and keeping witnesses present, or making an immediate arrest of a suspect. At this point they may complete their report on tasks performed relating to the specific crime and either turn it over to another shift of patrol officers or to the investigative unit. Regardless of the division of tasks performed by generalist or specialist units, close communication about cases must occur or problems develop.

Specialization creates a potential for substantially increased levels of expertise, creativity and innovation. The more completely an employee can perform a task or set of tasks, the more job satisfaction the employee will experience. When specialization is not practical, people must understand why the division of labor is necessary. It must also be clear where patrol's responsibility ends and that of the investigative unit begins.

The greater the specialization, necessary as it is, the greater the difficulties of coordination, communication, control and employee relationships. Conflicts and jealousies may arise: "Let the expert do it, if he or she is going to get the credit."

Officers in a small agency must perform all tasks. They cannot afford the luxury of specialization. However, with more standardized training requirements and accreditation, all officers have similar backgrounds for performing tasks, regardless of the size of the agency. The major difference is the frequency of opportunity.

As with all organizational specialization, there are disadvantages, such as taking personnel away from tasks performed by generalists. Further, increased problems of communication may cause division not only physically but also mentally, emotionally and psychologically. Command must be coordinated, as must information to other interested units or personnel. In addition, employees in specialized divisions may not have as much opportunity for advancement because they are highly trained in a specific area and, subsequently, out of the mainstream.

Specialization can enhance a department's effectiveness and efficiency, but overspecialization can impede the organizational purpose.

Overspecialization fragments opportunity to achieve the organizational purpose of providing courteous, competent, expeditious law enforcement services. The more specialized an agency becomes, the more attention must be paid to interrelationships and coordination.

Rational Organization and Hierarchy of Authority

The structure of most police departments, as noted, is typically a semimilitary, pyramid-shaped hierarchy with authority flowing from the narrow apex down to the broad base. This hierarchical pyramid is often graphically represented in an organizational chart.

The Organizational Chart

An **organizational chart** visually depicts how personnel are organized within an agency and might also illustrate how the agency fits into the community's political structure. Figure 1.2 shows the organization of the police department of Boulder City, Nevada, a community with a population over 13,000 and a police department of 25. This is typical of how police departments are organized in smaller cities. The figure also shows how the police department fits into the city's organizational structure.

This formal organization is generally supported in writing by rules and regulations, department operational manuals and job descriptions. All provide control and a foundation from which actions can be taken.

The larger the agency and the jurisdiction it serves, the more complex the organization and the chart depicting it. Figure 1.3, which is a chart of the Minneapolis Police Department, shows how a large police department is organized.

Figure 1.2
A Typical Small Police Department Organizational Chart

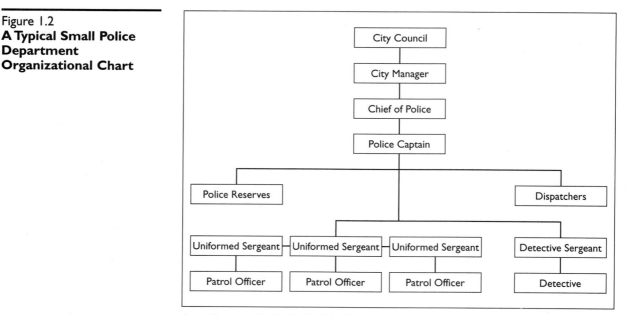

Source: Courtesy of the Boulder City Police Department.

Chain of Command

The **chain of command** is the order of authority. It begins at the top of the pyramid with the chief or sheriff and flows downward to the next level or *echelon*. The chain of command flows down through the commissioned ranks in the agency—from deputy chief to captain to lieutenant to sergeant and finally to the patrol officer.

The chain of command establishes definite lines of authority and **channels of communication.**

Each level must forward communications to the next higher or lower level. Channels of communication are the official paths through which orders flow from management to workers. Most companies set up these channels carefully and for good reasons. They are the "highways" for orders and communications to follow and as such keep everyone aware of events. They coordinate the organization into a whole unit instead of a series of parts. When an individual leaves these channels and takes a shortcut, he or she is apt to run into problems. For example, a patrol officer who takes a complaint directly to the chief rather than to the sergeant would probably fall out of favor in the department.

Sometimes in law enforcement work, however, emergencies exist that cannot wait to send information through the expected channels. This is one of the challenges of police work.

Unity of Command

Another important part of sound organizational design is unity of command.

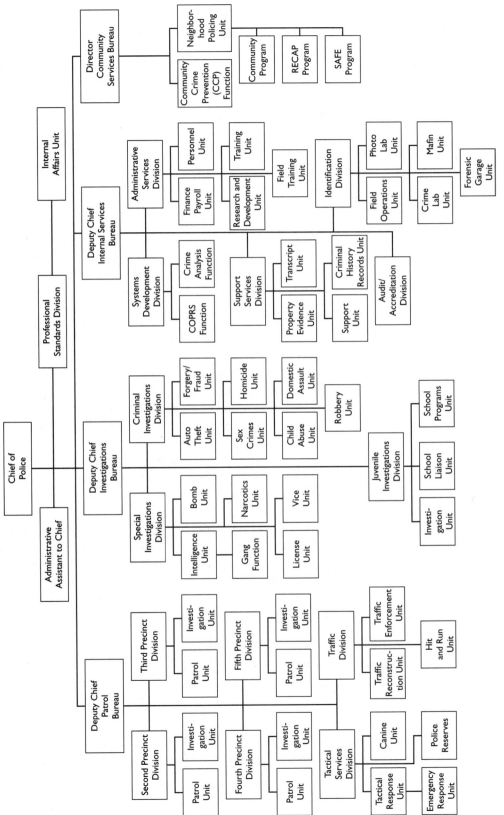

Figure 1.3
**A Typical Large Police
Department
Organizational Chart**

Source: Courtesy of the Minneapolis Police Department.

> **Unity of command** means that every individual in the organization has only one immediate superior or supervisor.

Unity of command is extremely important and needs to be ensured in most instances. Each individual, unit and situation should be under the control of one—and only one—person.

Span of Control

Another critical factor in most law enforcement organizations is the number of people one individual manages or supervises.

> The **span of control** refers to the number of people or units supervised by one manager.

Participants in management classes frequently ask, "What is a reasonable number of people for one person to supervise or manage?" No absolute answer exists. Historically three or four people were considered the maximum that could be effectively managed in a law enforcement agency. However, because of technological advances such as communications with personnel in the field, higher levels of education and training and the extent of the empowerment and flattening of the organization, this number may rise. The span of control also depends on the department's size, the supervisors' and subordinates' abilities, crime rates, community expectations and the political environment. Often the greater the span of control, the less effective the management or supervision.

Do not confuse span of control with how many people one person has authority over. The chief, for example, has authority over everyone in the department, but the chief's span of control extends to only those who report directly to him or her.

The span of control must be realistic. If too few people report to a manager, that manager is not earning his or her salary. If too many people report to a manager, that manager cannot do a good job with all of them. Within a law enforcement agency, the more levels in the pyramid, the smaller the span of control. A number of factors must be considered:

- Distance in space and time between manager and subordinate.
- Difficulty of the tasks performed.
- Types of assistance available to the manager.
- Extent of direction subordinates need.
- Extent of subordinates' skill and experience.

Each factor must be considered as personnel are assigned. Other important considerations are who has authority, who has responsibility and what can be delegated.

Authority,
Responsibility
and Delegation

Authority, responsibility and delegation are key factors in any organization. Without them organizations could not exist.

Authority is the power to enforce laws, exact obedience and command. **Responsibility** is the state of being answerable, liable or accountable. Thus, managers have the authority to give commands, and subordinates have the responsibility of carrying out the commands. This is very much in keeping with the militaristic model.

The third concept, **delegation,** is also crucial in any organization. Organizations exist because they can accomplish what no one person can accomplish. That single person, the chief, must be able to assign (delegate) tasks to others, who may, in turn, further delegate.

When authority is delegated, it should be coupled with responsibility.

This concept is *key* for all managers, at whatever their level within the police organization, for this is how **accountability** can be ensured. Accountability makes people responsible for tasks assigned to them. Accountability is needed because all the tasks specified in the agency's work plans must be accomplished by someone if the organization is to fulfill its mission. The tasks are successfully carried out through the efficient coordination of labor.

Coordination

Coordination ensures that each individual unit performs harmoniously with the total effort to achieve the department's mission.

Management tools for coordination include:

- A clear chain of command and unity of command.
- Clear channels of communication and strict adherence to them.
- Clear, specific job descriptions.
- Clear, specific goals, objectives and work plans.
- Standard operating procedures for routine tasks.
- An agency regulation guidebook.
- Meetings and roll calls.
- Informational bulletins, newsletters and memos.

Coordinating efforts should be a part of an agency's work plan as shown in the plan developed for the Boulder City Police Department. Included within the strategic plan for the investigative division is the directive to work closely with the patrol division in investigating all crimes committed in Boulder City and to work closely with the Clark County District Attorney's office.

As important as the formal organization of a police department is, as in any group, an informal structure also exists.

Figure 1.4
**Formal and Informal
Organizational Charts**

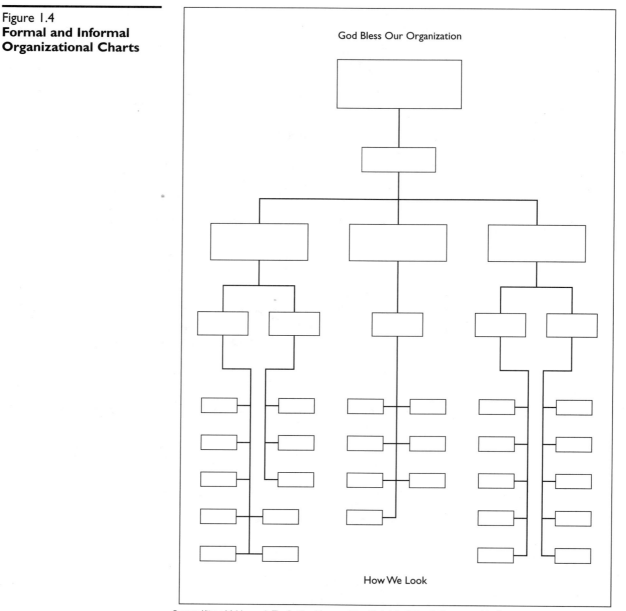

God Bless Our Organization

How We Look

Source: Kären M. Hess, ed., *The Positive Manager.* New York: John Wiley & Sons, copyright ©
1984. Reprinted by permission of John Wiley & Sons, Inc.

The Informal Organization

The formal organization groups people by task and responsibility and clearly delineates the chain of command and channels of communication. The **informal organization** exists side-by-side with this formal organization and may in fact be a truer representation of the way the department actually functions (Figure 1.4). Within any organization some people may emerge as leaders, regardless of whether they are in a leadership position. In addition, within any organization people will form their own groups—people who enjoy being together and perhaps working together.

Figure 1.4
continued

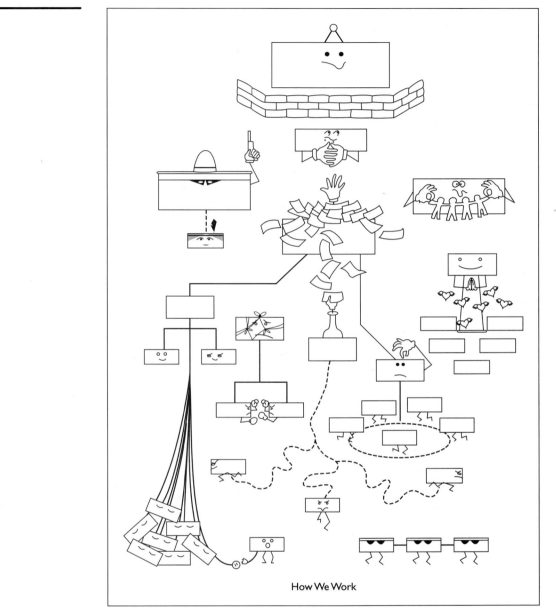

How We Work

Managers should recognize the informal organization that exists within any law enforcement agency.

The informal organization operates without official sanctions, but it influences agency performance. It may help or harm the goals of the formal organization, and it may support the organization or cause dissention.

Inasmuch as informal organizations are going to exist regardless of whether the supervisor likes them, it might be wise to view them as a positive force and use them to facilitate the work of the department. This can be done by thinking of the informal leader not as a "ringleader" but as a person "in on things," one whose talents can benefit the whole group.

One aspect of the informal organization is **scuttlebutt,** that is, gossip or rumors. Scuttlebutt can undermine morale and reduce productivity. Also of importance is the **Wolf Pack syndrome,** thought by some to be a vestige of primitive male hunting groups. Within these groups no weaknesses were tolerated because the deficiency of one individual could have dire consequences for all. Any weak member was attacked by the others. Such aggressive behavior helped ensure that the group would be strong when it faced danger. For example, if one police officer sees another's unoccupied squad car with its window open, the officer may put all the police gear in the car on the unsecured squad's hood and then hide to watch the errant officer return to the very visible evidence of his mistake.

The Emerging Law Enforcement Organization

Business and industry are undergoing sweeping changes in organization and management styles to remain competitive. Law enforcement agencies are also facing the need for change to meet the competition of private policing. Harr and Hess (2000, p. 71) note: "Private security is the nation's primary protective resource today, outspending public law enforcement by more than 73 percent and employing nearly three times the workforce."

Police departments and other law enforcement agencies not only must compete with private police but also must compete for the bright, young college graduates now entering the work force. No longer will law enforcement agencies be recruiting a majority of candidates with a military background. Instead they will be recruiting college graduates who will not accept authority blindly.

In addition, like businesses, many police departments are turning to a flat organization, one with fewer lieutenants and captains, fewer staff departments, fewer staff assistants, more sergeants and more patrol officers. Typical pyramid organization charts will have the top pushed down and the sides expanded at the base. Some police departments are beginning to experiment with alternative organization designs. One example of such experimentation places the patrol officers at the top with everyone under them playing a supporting role (Figure 1.5).

Byrne (1997, p. 43) notes results of a reorganization effort by the Green Bay, Wisconsin, Police Department that included:

> . . . elimination of the ranks of assistant chief, deputy chief, inspector and sergeant, reduction of administrative and supervisory staff by 21%, reinvestment of department resources in field police services, and decentralization of field police services.
>
> The reorganization increased the number of officers on the street from 135 to 151—and it was all accomplished without any increase in the department's budget.

Figure 1.5
**The Inverted Pyramid
of Authority—
Organizational Hierarchy**

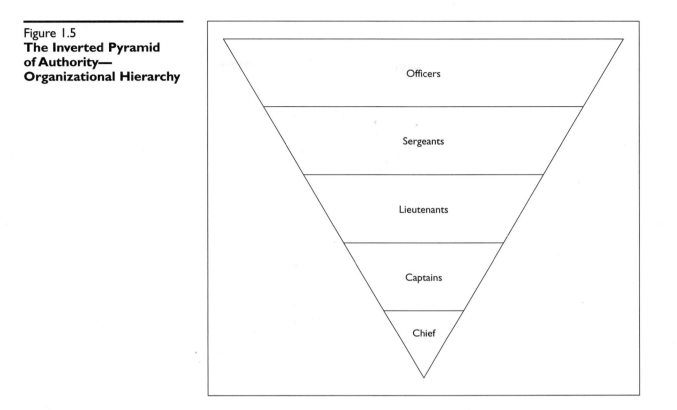

*The Empowered
Organization*

Top-heavy organizational structures are no longer tolerated in business. Progressive firms are flattening their structure, restructuring top-heavy organizations, and pushing authority and decision making down as low as possible. Successful businesses concentrate on soliciting ideas from everyone in their organization about every facet of their operation. This approach should be applied to policing, especially small departments. If officer retention is to be maintained and loyalty and morale preserved and heightened, officers must be **empowered.** Maguire (1997, p. 547) notes:

> The organizational structures of large municipal police departments in the United States have changed substantially . . . . Precinct-based police organizations employing only sworn police officers have been transformed into highly centralized, specialized, formal organizations with tall hierarchies and large administrative units. Community policing reformers have attempted to reverse this progression toward more "bureaucratic" organizational forms. They argue that police should thin out their administrative components to cut red tape and to focus more resources on the goals of the organization; deformalize, eliminating unnecessary rules and policies; despecialize, to encourage departmentwide problem solving; "delayerize," to enhance communications and decision making by flattening the organizational hierarchy.

Mastrofski (1999, p. 8) adds: "National surveys of departments of over 100 sworn [officers] . . . found that between 1987 and 1993 there was very little change in the structure of police organizations." However, from 1993 to 1999, decision making has become more decentralized, geographic command and authority have become more popular and organizational hierarchies are flattening (p. 8). **Decentralization** according to Turner (2000, p. 50) generally refers to a department's organizational structure and operations: "It is an operating principle that encourages flattening of the organization and places decision-making authority and autonomy at the level where information is plentiful. In police organizations, this is usually at the level of the patrol officer, where officers interacting with the public need the freedom to exercise discretion within predetermined parameters." A **flat organization** empowers line personnel.

Reiter (1999, p. 8) states: "By inverting the organizational pyramid, law enforcement agencies take a bold and symbolic step toward becoming empowered." Blanchard (1996, p. 85) explains that inverting the pyramid—placing the chief at the bottom and the patrol officers at the top—symbolizes that the chief serves the organization and is responsible for its leadership. Under this structure officers gain responsibilities and leadership. Reiter (p. 10) concludes: "Trust is the essence of leadership in an empowered organization. Empowered leaders push decision making down to the officer level because they have confidence in their officers' abilities and believe that many decisions are best made at that level."

Why the Need to Change?

Some readers may be thinking, "If it ain't broke, don't fix it. What's wrong with the way the law enforcement agencies are organized? They have worked fine for the past two hundred years."

However, law enforcement must now deal with disruptive social, demographic and technological changes. America is becoming increasingly diverse, with more minorities and more elderly people. Hawley (1999, p. 28) states: "Thousands of people—many from south of the border—stream into the country every day in defiance of federal law. For law enforcement, this circumstance poses unique challenges and occasional dilemmas."

America is also becoming a **bifurcated society** with more wealth, more poverty and a shrinking middle class. The gap between the "haves" and the "have nots" is widening. Data from the Congressional Budget Office reveal ("Gap between Rich . . . ," 1999, p. A11):

> The gap between rich and poor has grown into an economic chasm so wide that this year the richest 2.7 Americans, the top 1 percent, will have as much after-tax money to spend as the bottom 100 million. . . .
>
> The data show that income disparity has grown so much that four out of five households, or about 217 million people, are taking home a thinner slice of the economic pie today than in 1977.

Other social and cultural changes include the weakening influence of family, church and school.

Technology is also forcing policing to change. Domash (1998, p. 31) notes how computer technology has revolutionized the law enforcement industry, having an impact on everything from crime scene investigations and photography to law enforcement gear, public safety products and police vehicles: "The law enforcement industry has faced many changes in recent years. But none have been as evident as the impact of computer technology and advanced communications systems."

> The challenges facing not only law enforcement but our entire country necessitate reexamining our public organizations, including law enforcement.

Change may require a **paradigm shift.** A **paradigm** is a model, theory or frame of reference.

Covey (1989, p. 23) shows by analogy how understanding a situation can result in a simple paradigm shift. He describes a situation on a subway in New York. People are minding their own business, some reading, some dozing, others gazing into space. The tranquility of the scene is broken when a man with small children boards the subway and the children begin running, yelling and throwing things. The man ignores the children. A passenger becomes increasingly annoyed at the children's behavior and at the indifference of the adult accompanying them. Finally the passenger confronts the man, suggesting that the children are disturbing everyone else and that he keep them under control. As if coming out of a daze, the man responds: "Oh, you're right. I guess I should do something about it. We just came from the hospital where their mother died about an hour ago. I don't know what to think, and I guess they don't know how to handle it either." In that instant the passenger's paradigm—his belief about how children should be acting—changed dramatically.

It is important that law enforcement managers at all levels reexamine past assumptions, consider future projections and think very carefully about the future of policing, law enforcement and the entire criminal justice system, including the move toward community involvement in every aspect of policing, courts and corrections.

Community Policing and Problem-Solving Policing (COPPS)

Miller and Hess (1998, p. 594) define **community policing** as: "A philosophy or orientation that emphasizes working with citizens to solve crime-related problems and prevent crime." They note (p. xxii):

> Community policing offers one avenue for making neighborhoods safer. Community policing is not a program or a series of programs. It is a philosophy, a belief that working together, the police and the community can accomplish what neither can accomplish alone. The *synergy* that results from community policing can be powerful. It is like the power of a finely tuned athletic team, with each member contributing to the total effort. Occasionally heroes may emerge, but victory depends on a team effort.

Hall (1998, p. 6) notes:

> A recent investigative report by the Hudson Institute, showing crime dropping in "cities where humane, economical community policy" is being practiced was not a surprise. . . .
>
> Most observers acknowledge that the national trend toward community policing has been a key catalyst in the decrease.

Oakland, California, police have instituted a program called "Code 33," named after the police code for "emergency, clear the air." This program is focused on police listening to the concerns of Oakland's youths, thereby improving their relationship with them. Here a "Code 33" participant jokes with a police officer during a meeting.

Neubauer (1999, p. 6) echoes: "Over the past decade, communities throughout the United States have witnessed a remarkable decline in the rate of crime. . . . No factor has been more crucial to the reduction in crime levels than the partnership between law enforcement agencies and the communities they serve." Fishbein (1998, p. 1) concurs:

> Indeed, the community represents a major, often-untapped crime prevention resource. Residents can provide an essential information base greater than that of police departments with limited personnel and resources. . . . Police work then becomes comprehensive, problem solving and proactive as opposed to solely reactive.

This problem-solving element is a critical aspect of community policing, as Miller and Hess (p. 88) note: "**Problem-solving policing** involves identifying problems and making decisions about how best to deal with them. . . . A basic characteristic of community policing is that it is proactive rather than reactive. Being **proactive** involves recognizing problems and seeking the underlying cause(s) of the problems." This is in contrast to the traditional **reactive** approach of simply responding to calls for service.

Community-oriented policing and **problem-solving** (COPPS) may offer an answer to more effective law enforcement for the future.

The COPS program (Office of Community Oriented Policing Services) was an important part of the Violent Crime Control and Law Enforcement Act of 1994. Weiss and Dresser (1999, p. 26) explain that COPS was designed to:

- Increase the number of community policing officers on the beat by 100,000.
- Promote the implementation of department-wide community policing in law enforcement agencies across the country.

- Help develop an infrastructure to institutionalize and sustain community policing after federal funding has ended.
- Demonstrate and evaluate the viability of agencies practicing community policing to significantly improve the quality of life by reducing the levels of violence, crime and disorder in communities.

Table 1.2 compares traditional policing with community policing.

What has worked in policing in the past may not work today or tomorrow. The chapters that follow reflect this reality and how COPPS is affecting all aspects of law enforcement.

Table 1.2
Comparison of Traditional Policing and Community Policing

Question	Traditional Policing	Community Policing
Who are the police?	A government agency principally responsible for law enforcement.	Police are the public and the public are the police: the police officers are those who are paid to give full-time attention to the duties of every citizen.
What is the relationship of the police force to public service departments?	Priorities often conflict	The police are one department among many responsible for improving the quality of life.
What is the role of the police?	Focusing on solving crimes.	A broader problem-solving approach.
How is police efficiency measured?	By detection and arrest rates.	By the absence of crime and disorder.
What are the highest priorities?	Crimes that are high value (e.g., bank robberies) and those involving violence.	Whatever problems disturb the community most.
What, specifically, do police deal with?	Incidents.	Citizens' problems and concerns.
What determines the effectiveness of police?	Response times.	Public cooperation.
What view do police take of service calls?	Deal with them only if there is no real police work to do.	Vital function and great opportunity.
What is police professionalism?	Swift, effective response to serious crime.	Keeping close to the community.
What kind of intelligence is most important?	Crime intelligence (study of particular crimes or series of crimes).	Criminal intelligence (information about the activities of individuals or groups).
What is the essential nature of police accountability?	Highly centralized; governed by rules, regulations and policy directives; accountable to the law.	Emphasis on local accountability to community needs.
What is the role of headquarters?	To provide the necessary rules and policy directives.	To preach organizational values.
What is the role of the press liaison department?	To keep the "heat" off operational officers so they can get on with the job.	To coordinate an essential channel of communication with the community.
How do the police regard prosecutions?	As an important goal.	As one tool among many.

Source: Malcolm K. Sparrow. *Implementing Community Policing*, U.S. Department of Justice, National Institute of Justice, November 1988, pp 8–9.

Summary

Managers need to understand the organizational structure within which most law enforcement agencies function. The typical organizational design is that of a pyramid-shaped hierarchy based on a military model. Three distinct eras of policing have been identified: The political era, the reform era and the community era.

The mission statement should be the driving force of any organization, including law enforcement agencies. This mission statement can direct the development of meaningful goals and objectives and realistic work plans. Goals are broad, general, desired outcomes. Objectives are specific, measurable ways to accomplish the goals. Work plans are the precise activities that contribute to accomplishing objectives. Along with a mission statement, goals, objectives and work plans, a formal organization of personnel to accomplish the tasks is mandatory.

One aspect of an agency's organizational structure is division into field services with line personnel and administrative services with staff personnel. *Line* personnel *directly* help accomplish the goals of the department. *Staff* personnel *support* the line organization.

An organization typically relies on a chain of command, unity of command, a span of control and set channels of communication. The chain of command establishes definite lines of authority and channels of communication. Unity of command means that every individual in the organization has only one immediate superior or supervisor. The span of control refers to the number of people or units supervised by one manager.

These organizational features are necessary to ensure the efficient delegation of tasks. The delegation of authority should go hand-in-hand with responsibility.

As agencies become larger, they often become specialized. Specialization can enhance an agency's effectiveness and efficiency, but overspecialization can impede the organizational purpose. Specialization also requires a higher degree of coordination, although coordination is critical for any department, large or small, specialized or not. Management tools for coordination include:

- A clear chain of command and unity of command.
- Clear channels of communication and strict adherence to them.
- Clear, specific job descriptions.
- Clear, specific goals, objectives and work plans.
- Standard operating procedures for routine tasks.
- An agency regulation guidebook.
- Meetings and roll calls.
- Informational bulletins, newsletters and memos.

In addition to the formal organization depicted in an organizational chart, any law enforcement agency also has an informal organization that managers should recognize. The informal organization can help or hinder accomplishment of the agency's mission.

The challenges facing not only law enforcement but our entire country necessitate reexamining our public organizations, including law enforcement. Community policing and problem-oriented policing (COPPS) may offer an answer to more effective law enforcement for the future.

Discussion Questions

1. Who is a law enforcement manager?
2. Is there a difference between the terms *pyramidal structure* and *hierarchy?*
3. What is the difference between unity of command and chain of command?
4. What are staff positions in a typical police department?
5. What is the purpose of law enforcement management?
6. What does *delegation* mean? Can you delegate authority? Responsibility?
7. What does an organizational chart indicate?
8. How could you reorganize to force decision making downward? Is this desirable?
9. What is an informal organization?
10. What changes do you foresee in law enforcement agencies in the twenty-first century?

InfoTrac College Edition Assignment

Find two journal articles on *strategic planning* and summarize them. Include the full reference citation along with your summary. Be prepared to share your findings with the class.

References

Blanchard, Ken. "Turning the Organizational Pyramid Upside Down." In *The Leader of the Future*, edited by F. Hesselbein, M. Goldsmith and R. Beckard. San Francisco: Jossey-Bass, 1996, p. 85.

Breen, Michael D. "Today's Leadership Challenge for Police Executives." *The Police Chief,* Vol. LXVI, No. 3, March 1999, pp. 61–63.

Byrne, Edward C. "Putting Police Work Back on the Street." *Law and Order,* Vol. 45, No. 5, May 1997, pp. 43–45.

Covey, Stephen R. *The Seven Habits of Highly Effective People: Restoring the Character Ethic.* New York: Simon and Schuster, 1989.

Domash, Shelly Feuer. "Technological Change Spurs Growth in Police Industry." *Police,* Vol. 22, No. 8, August 1998, pp. 24–31.

Fishbein, Diana. "The Comprehensive Care Model: Providing a Framework for Community Policing." *FBI Law Enforcement Bulletin,* Vol. 67, No. 5, May 1998, pp. 1–5.

"Gap between Rich and Poor Has Become More Substantial." (Minneapolis/St. Paul) *Star Tribune,* September 5, 1999, p. A11.

Hall, Dennis. "More Evidence to Enlist Your Town in Fight against Crime." *Police,* Vol. 22, No. 6, June 1998, p. 6.

Harr, J. Scott and Hess, Kären M. *Seeking Employment in Criminal Justice and Related Fields,* 3rd ed. Belmont, CA: Wadsworth Publishing Company, 2000.

Hawley, Donna L. "Police Action against Illegal Immigration: Where Does It Stand?" *Police,* Vol. 23, No. 6, June 1999, pp. 28–34.

International Association of Chiefs of Police. "Value Statement." *The Police Chief,* November 1993, p. 14.

Jensen, Carl J. and Hsieh, Yvonne. "Law Enforcement and the Millennialist Vision: A Behavioral Approach." *FBI Law Enforcement Bulletin,* Vol. 68, No. 9, September 1999, pp. 1–6.

Maguire, Edward R. "Structural Change in Large Municipal Police Organizations during the Community Policing Era." *Justice Quarterly,* Vol. 14, No. 3, September 1997, pp. 547–576.

Mastrofski, Steven. "Thinking Out Loud: How Far Has CJ Research Come in 10 Years?" *Law Enforcement News,* June 15, 1999, pp. 8–10.

Miller, Linda S. and Hess, Kären M. *The Police in the Community: Strategies for the 21ˢᵗ Century,* 2nd ed. Belmont, CA: West/Wadsworth Publishing Company, 1998.

Neubauer, Ronald S. "Community Partnership—The Key to Maintaining Safe Communities." *The Police Chief,* Vol. LXVI, No. 5, May 1999, p. 6.

Reiter, Michael S. "Empowered Policing." *FBI Law Enforcement Bulletin,* Vol. 68, No. 2, February 1999, pp. 7–11.

Turner, Yvonne C. " 'Decentralizing' the Specialized Unit Function in Small Police Agencies." *The Police Chief,* Vol. LXVII, No. 2, February 2000, pp. 50–51.

Weiss, Jim and Dresser, Mary. "COP: The Policing Revolution at Work in the Real World." *Police,* Vol. 23, No. 8, August 1999, pp. 26–31.

Wrobleski, Henry M. and Hess, Kären M. *An Introduction to Law Enforcement and Criminal Justice,* 6th ed. Belmont, CA: Wadsworth Publishing Company, 2000.

Chapter 2

The Role of the Manager and Leadership in Law Enforcement

> The watchwords of the new leadership paradigm are coach, inspire, gain commitment, empower, affirm, flexibility, responsibility, self-management, shared power, autonomous teams and entrepreneurial units.
>
> —Donald C. Witham, Chief, FBI Strategic Planning Unit

Do You Know?

- How authority and power are alike? How they differ?
- What basic management skills are important?
- What four tools successful managers use?
- What management by objectives (MBO) involves?
- What Theory X/Theory Y, the Four-System Approach, the Mature Employee Theory and the Managerial/Leadership Grid say about management style?
- What management style is best suited for law enforcement work?
- What typical levels of management exist in law enforcement?
- What essential functions chief executives perform?
- How strategic and tactical planning differ?
- With whom law enforcement chief executives typically interact?
- What three management problems are common?
- What basic difference exists between managers and leaders?
- What theories of leadership have been researched?
- What types of leadership styles have been identified and what their main characteristics are?
- What constitutes effective leadership training?
- What the attributes of a high-performing team are?

Can You Define?

administrative skills
aligned on purpose
authority
Authority-Compliance
   Management
autocratic leadership
chief executive officer
   (CEO)
conceptual skills
consideration structure
consultative leadership

Country Club
   Management
creative talents
delegation
democratic leadership
executive manager
facilitators
first-line managers
focused on task
Four-System Approach
free-rein leadership

future focused
high communication
holistic management
Impoverished
   Management
initiating structure
interactors
interfacers
laissez-faire leadership
leader
leadership

manage
management
management by
    objectives (MBO)
Managerial/Leadership
    Grid
managers
Mature Employee
    Theory
middle management
Middle-of-the-Road
    Management
participative leadership
people skills

power
rapid response
roll call
sea gull management
shared responsibility
situational leadership
SMART goals and
    objectives
strategic planning
supervision
supervisors
synergism
tactical planning
Task Management

team
Team Management
technical skills
Theory X/Theory Y
Total Quality
    Management
    (TQM)
trait theorists
traits
transformational
    leadership
Wallenda Effect

INTRODUCTION

The organizational chart discussed in the preceding chapter is inanimate, similar to a house without people. The form and foundation exist and are necessary, but it is in no sense vital or exciting. Vitality and excitement come when the boxes in the chart are filled with people, men and women patrol officers, investigators, sergeants, lieutenants, captains and chiefs interacting, working together to accomplish their mission—"to serve and protect." The organization accomplishes its mission through managers directing and guiding employees and resources, both internal and external to the organization.

Managers in law enforcement face unique problems because of the extended period of service (24 hours a day, 365 days a year). The chief executive officer (CEO) of the law enforcement agency obviously cannot be physically present for this extended period and must therefore rely on the organizational structure to permit other members to perform administrative and operational functions. In addition, challenges facing today's law enforcement administrators are huge, including strained budgets and cutbacks, greater citizen demands and expectations for service and an increasingly diverse society in general.

This chapter examines the complex role of the law enforcement manager, the challenges presented by management and the relationship between authority and power. This is followed by an overview of the basic skills and tools required of an effective manager. Contributions to management from the business world, including management by objective and total quality management, are the next area of discussion, followed by an analysis of the various management styles currently operating. The chapter then examines the levels of management typically found within law enforcement agencies, the responsibilities of each level, the management problems most commonly encountered and a look into law enforcement management as a career. Next is a discussion of the differences between managing and leading and a review of key characteristics of leaders. This is followed by a review of research on and theories related to leadership and various leadership styles. A description of the team approach is presented next, followed by a discussion of the implications of the research and the apparent need for change within bureaucratic law enforcement organizations. The chapter concludes with a look at leadership training and development, new skills required and guidelines for effective leadership.

Managers and Management

Manage means to control and direct, to administer, to take charge of. Those who undertake these activities are called **managers. Management** is the process of using resources to achieve organizational goals.

Managers and supervisors control and direct people and operations to achieve organizational objectives. Managers and supervisors are also jointly involved in planning, organizing, staffing and budgeting. In fact, many gray areas exist in what managers and supervisors do. This is increasingly true in organizations that have been "flattened" by eliminating some middle-management positions and empowering employees at the lowest level.

Law enforcement management is a process of deciding goals and objectives, adopting a work plan to accomplish them, obtaining and wisely using resources and making decisions that result in a high level of performance and productivity.

Managers must also support the development of *individual* responsibility, permitting all employees to achieve maximum potential while simultaneously supporting organizational needs. The sum total of individual member energy is transferred to organizational energy needed for success.

Authority and Power

Authority, responsibility and accountability were discussed in the preceding chapter. Consider now the relationship between the authority and the power of police managers.

Authority is the ability to get things done through others by influencing behavior. **Power,** on the other hand, is the ability to get things done with or without legal right. Authority uses force; power uses persuasion. It has been said: "Authority or force is the use of 10,000 armed troops. Power is a wink." Power is the ability to persuade people to do something they might not otherwise do. Law enforcement executive managers have both authority and power.

Authority is generally granted by law or an order. Power is the influence of a person or group, without benefit of law or order. However, managers should have both authority and personal power. When it is necessary to take charge of a situation, authority is a legitimate use of power.

> Authority and power both imply the ability to coerce compliance, that is, to *make* subordinates carry out orders. Both are important to managers at all levels. However, authority relies on force or on some law or order, whereas power relies on persuasion and lacks the support of law or rule.

In a democracy authority and power are not always regarded as desirable. Even though managers may use both and employees recognize management's right to use both, a limitation exists in the mind-set of employees as to how much is acceptable. They expect some freedom of choice.

Managers should never manipulate employees but should use formal and informal authority and power with people and groups to benefit the total organization. They should also avoid **sea gull management.** According to management guru Ken Blanchard: "[Seagull managers] hear something's wrong, so they fly in, make a lot of noise, crap on everybody and fly away" (Smith, 2000, p. 18).

Delegation

Transferring of authority, called **delegation,** is a necessary and often difficult aspect of management because it requires placing trust in others to do the job as well as, or better than, you would do yourself.

Theodore Roosevelt once said: "The best executive is the one who has enough sense to pick good people to do what he wants done, and self-restraint enough to keep from meddling with them while they do it." Yet many managers fail to delegate effectively because they believe, "If you want something done right, you have to do it yourself." Pollar (1996, p. 76) lists five common reasons people fail to delegate:

- Nobody does it better—I know how to do it right.
- Guilt—It's my responsibility to get it done.
- Insecurity—Uncertainty about the project's goals, worry that someone else will do a better job and upstage me, worry that someone else will do a terrible job which will reflect negatively on me.
- Lack of trust—I'm not confident someone else will do a good job.
- Takes time—It's faster if I do it myself rather than trying to explain it to someone else.

Pollar (pp. 76–77) further suggests that delegation is *not* passing the buck, giving up control, refusing to make a decision by assigning it to another, shirking personal responsibility for a task or dumping unpleasant tasks onto someone else.

Many managers are uncertain whether they delegate appropriately. To assess delegation effectiveness, Pollar (pp. 77–78) suggests managers ask themselves the following questions:

1. When you come back from a trip or a vacation, is your "In" basket too full?
2. When you are away from the office, is your trip shadowed by worry? Do you wonder what is going wrong in your absence?
3. Are you still handling the same activities and problems that you did before your last promotion?
4. Are you constantly interrupted with questions and requests for guidance from your staff and associates?
5. Are you continually finding it harder to stay on top of your work because you are bogged down by too many routine details?

Managers who answer "yes" to most of these questions are probably not delegating effectively or often enough. Pollar (p. 78) offers specific steps for efficient delegation:

- State a clear objective.
- Determine guidelines for the project.

- Set necessary limitations or constraints.
- Grant the person the authority to carry out the assignment.
- Set the deadline for its completion.
- Decide the best means for the person to provide you with regular progress reports.

Basic Management Skills and Tools

To be effective, managers at all levels must be skilled at planning, organizing, coordinating, reporting and budgeting. Equally critical, however, are people skills such as communicating, motivating and leading, as will be discussed throughout the book.

Basic management skills include technical skills, administrative skills, conceptual skills and people skills.

Technical skills include all the procedures necessary to be a "good cop": interviewing and interrogating, searching, arresting, gathering evidence and so on. Police officers often become sergeants because of their technical skills.

Administrative skills include organizing, delegating and directing the work of others. They also include writing proposals, formulating work plans and developing budgets.

Conceptual skills include the ability to problem solve, plan and see the "big picture" and how all the pieces within it fit. Managers must be able to think in terms of the future, synthesize great amounts of data, make decisions on complex matters and have broad, even national, perspectives. They must see the organization as a whole, yet existing within society. They must also have a sensitivity to the spirit—not just the letter—of the law.

People skills include being able to communicate clearly, to motivate, to discipline appropriately and to inspire. People skills also include working effectively with managers up the chain of command, as well as with the general public. The higher the management position, the more important people skills become.

A Balance

Successful managers balance these skills and more, as illustrated in the Wheel of Managerial Success (Figure 2.1).

Basic Tools

According to management guru Blanchard (1988, p. 14): "Successful managers use four tools to accomplish their goals."

Successful managers have:

- Clear goals.
- A commitment to excellence.
- Feedback.
- Support.

"Good performance," says Blanchard, "starts with clear goals." The importance of goals cannot be overemphasized. Just as important, however, are the

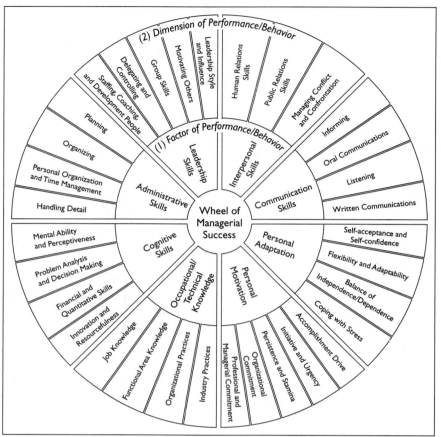

Figure 2.1
The Wheel of Managerial Success

Source: Joy Fisher Hazucha and Robert J. Schneider, Personnel Decisions, Inc. *The Wheel of Managerial Success.* Copyright © 1982 by Personnel Decisions, Inc. Reprinted by permission.

objectives developed to meet the goals. According to Blanchard, **SMART goals and objectives** are:

Specific.

Measurable.

Attainable.

Relevant.

Trackable.

For example, to say that you want to lose 50 pounds in two months is specific and measurable, but it probably is not attainable. To say that you want to lose two pounds a week, however, meets the criteria for a SMART objective.

The Role of Self-Confidence

Most police supervisors and managers have been promoted into their positions because they possessed or had learned the necessary skills and tools. But with the excitement and pride of promotion often comes an instinctive tinge of self-doubt. Taking on a new level of management is a major challenge and involves risk. Even though initially daunting, change can serve as a catalyst for growth.

Change frequently requires that a person use already acquired skills in a new context, which can be threatening. Asking a person to walk across a six-inch-wide board on the ground poses no threat. Put it 40 feet in the air, and the person is unlikely to take even the first step. To maintain self-confidence, seek the support of your peers, set goals for yourself in mastering the skills you need and get feedback.

Lessons Learned from Business

Law enforcement management has followed the lead of business in some important ways, including management by objectives (MBO) and Total Quality Management (TQM).

Management by Objectives

Management theorist Peter Drucker is credited with first using the term **management by objectives (MBO)** in the early 1950s. It has been popular for almost 50 years.

> Management by objectives involves managers and subordinates setting goals and objectives together and then tracking performance to ensure that the objectives are met.

The key to the MBO system is to get workers to participate in deciding and setting goals, both individually and in work groups. The performance achieved is then compared to these agreed-upon goals.

Total Quality Management

The pioneer in **Total Quality Management (TQM)** was W. Edwards Deming, a management guru who assisted Japanese businesses in recovering and prospering. Hishmeh (1998, p. 92) explains: "Total Quality Management refers to a management process and set of disciplines that are coordinated to ensure that the organization consistently meets and exceeds customer requirements." A recent survey of 250 leading U.S. companies revealed that 68 percent were using TQM to address quality and continuous improvement issues (Hishmeh, p. 92). Although Deming's famous "14 Points" were originally aimed at business, several are applicable to the public sector as well—including law enforcement:

- Create constancy of purpose for improvement of product and service.
- Adopt the new philosophy.
- Improve constantly.
- Institute modern methods of training on the job.
- Institute modern methods of supervision.
- Drive fear from the workplace.
- Break down barriers between staff areas.
- Eliminate numerical goals for the work force.
- Remove barriers that rob people of pride of workmanship.
- Institute a vigorous program of education and training (Deming, 1982, p. 17).

Hishmeh (p. 92) notes that TQM should result in reduced cost and bring high quality through efficiency, improved morale and stronger employee loyalty. Working continually for improvement in measurable steps is at the heart of TQM.

Management Styles

Just as different managers use different types of authority and power, they also have varied personalities and management styles. Managers at any level may be sociable and friendly, firm and hard driving or analytical and detail oriented. Several theories regarding management style have been developed, including those of McGregor, Likert, Argyris, and Blake and Mouton. Within each theory "pure" or ideal types are described, but in reality management style should be viewed as a continuum, with "pure" types at the opposing ends.

Theory X/Theory Y— McGregor

This theory from the 1960s is concerned with why workers work and how management views them and their work. Douglas McGregor claimed that how workers were regarded was largely due to two approaches to management, which he labeled Theory X and Theory Y.

In **Theory X,** the organization managed with the following assumptions:

- Workers need control by coercion, threats and punishment.
- The average worker frequently has an aversion to work.
- Management makes all decisions and directs employees to carry them out.
- Workers are dull and lazy.
- Workers desire secure jobs above all else.

Under Theory X, management's responsibility is to provide constant employee supervision. Employees do not want responsibility. They are primarily interested in wages, fringe benefits and avoiding punishment.

Theory Y, in contrast, operates under these assumptions:

- Employees can be trusted to do a good job.
- Employees are willing workers.
- Employees can be given reasonable goals to accomplish.
- Employees should share in decision making.

McGregor favored the humanistic approach reflected in Theory Y. He believed management should encourage self-motivation and fewer outside controls. Decisions could be delegated. Employees would be responsive to management's goals if management set the proper environment for work. Theory X might have worked in the past, but with better-educated workers, it could create hostility.

McGregor's Theory X/Theory Y says that managers act toward subordinates in relation to the views they have of them. Theory X views employees as lazy and motivated by pay. Theory Y views employees as committed and motivated by growth and development.

Table 2.1 summarizes McGregor's assumptions of Theory X and Theory Y.

Table 2.1
McGregor's Assumptions of Theory X and Theory Y

Theory X	Theory Y
1. The average person inherently dislikes work and will avoid it when possible.	1. The expenditure of physical and mental effort in work is as natural as the expenditure of physical and mental exertion in play or rest.
2. Most people must be coerced, controlled, directed, or threatened with punishment to get them to put forth adequate energy in achieving organizational goals.	2. An employee will exercise self-direction and self-control in the service of objectives to which he or she is committed.
3. The average person prefers to be directed, wishes to avoid responsibility, and has relatively little ambition; he or she wants security above all.	3. Commitment to objectives is a function of the rewards associated with their achievement.
4. The average person is inherently self-centered and indifferent to organizational needs.	4. The average person learns, under proper conditions, not only to accept but also to seek responsibility.
5. The average person is by nature resistant to change.	5. The capacity to exercise high degrees of imagination, ingenuity, and creativity in solving organizational problems is widely, not narrowly, distributed in the population.
6. The average person is gullible, not very bright, the ready dupe of the charlatan and the demagogue.	6. The intellectual potentialities of the average person are only partially utilized under the conditions of modern industrial life.
	7. The essential task of management is to arrange organizational conditions and methods of operation so people can achieve their own goals best by directing their own efforts toward organizational goals.

Source: Douglas McGregor, *The Human Side of Enterprise.* © 1960 McGraw-Hill Book Company, New York. Reprinted by permission.

The Four-System Approach—Likert

Rensis Likert divided managerial approaches into four different systems. System 1, similar to McGregor's Theory X, is the *traditional,* dictatorial approach to managing people. In this system, which generally exploited employees, coercion and a few economic rewards would suffice.

System 2 is similar to System 1, except that economic rewards replace coercion. Some information on organizational development is permitted but not in opposition to management's control.

System 3, which is more liberal, uses employee initiative and gives employees more responsibility. System 4 is participative management, which is the complete opposite of System 1. Participative management is closely allied with the democratic approach except that employees do not vote. Final decisions are made by management but only after employees have added their input.

System 4 also includes team management, which is widely used today. The participative approach encourages support of employees because decisions are made partially on their suggestions. It is easier to support your own suggestion or someone else's if you have a part in it. System 4 draws on the thoughts and backgrounds of all members associated with a particular problem area.

> Likert's **Four-System Approach** to management goes from System 1, which is a traditional, authoritarian style, to System 4, which is a participative management style.

The characteristics of Likert's System 1 and System 4, the two extremes, are compared in Table 2.2.

Table 2.2
Likert's System 1 and System 4 Compared

System 1 (Traditional)	System 4 (Participative)
Leadership is not based on confidence and trust. Subordinates don't feel free to discuss ideas with managers, and managers don't use subordinates' opinions in decision making.	**Leadership** is based on confidence and trust in subordinates. Subordinates discuss their ideas with managers, and their ideas and opinions are used in decision making.
Motivation is based on fear, threat, punishment, and some rewards. Responsibility for achieving goals decreases down the hierarchy.	**Motivation** is through economic rewards and involvement in setting goals. People at all levels feel a responsibility for reaching goals.
Communication flows downward from the top of the hierarchy and is viewed with suspicion. There is little feedback.	**Communication** flows freely throughout the organization. There is much feedback.
Interaction between managers and employees is minimal and is viewed with fear and distrust. There is little teamwork.	**Interaction** between managers and employees is extensive, friendly, and based on a high degree of confidence and trust. There is a great deal of teamwork.
Decision making takes place primarily at the top of the hierarchy with little subordinate involvement. Acceptance of the decision is usually not considered.	**Decision making** is dispersed but linked through teamwork. Subordinates are fully involved in decisions relating to their work.
Goals are set at the top of the organization. Goals are resisted. Performance goals are relatively low.	**Goals** are set through participation at the level where they will be achieved. Goals are accepted. Performance goals are high.
Controls are concentrated in top management and are used in a punitive way.	**Controls** are widespread and are used for self-guidance and for coordinated problem solving.

Source: Rensis Likert, *The Human Organization: Its Management and Values.*
© 1967 McGraw-Hill Book Company. New York. Reprinted with permission.

The Mature Employee Theory—Argyris

Another approach to management is the **Mature Employee Theory,** devised by Chris Argyris. This theory emphasizes employees' growth and development as a means of increasing their contributions to the job. Argyris analyzed the relationship between the demands of the organization and those of the individual members, believing that both have an effect on the end result. He determined that the work force has energy to be released if management recognizes it.

> Argyris' Mature Employee Theory views employees and their organization as *interdependent.*

Organizations and individuals exist for a purpose. If organizations keep employees dependent, subordinate and restrained, employees cannot help the organization meet its objectives. Both are interdependent: Organizations provide jobs and people perform them.

As individuals develop, they mature from passive to active and from dependent to interdependent. Individuals and organizations need to develop together in much the same way. They need to grow and mature together to be of mutual benefit. Organizations tend to restrict individuals, which results in frustration, failure, short-term perspectives and conflict. A comparison of immature and mature behaviors is contained in Table 2.3.

Argyris concluded that management frequently behaves inconsistently, does not help others with their ideas and is not open to ideas or concerned about others' ideas.

Table 2.3 **Argyris's Seven Development Dimensions**	Childlike Behaviors	Mature, Adult Behaviors
	Passiveness	Activeness
	Dependent upon others	Relatively independent
	Few reactive behaviors	Many reactive behaviors
	Shallow, brief, erratic interests	Intense, long-term, coherent commitments
	Engages in brief, unconnected jobs	Seeks long-term challenges that link the past and the future
	Satisfied with low status	Seeks advancement
	Low self-awareness, impulsive	Self-aware and self-controlled

Source: Paul R. Timm. *Supervision,* 2nd ed. St. Paul, MN: West Publishing Company, 1992, p. 119. Reprinted by permission. All rights reserved.

The Managerial/ Leadership Grid Theory—Blake and Mouton

In the 1960s Dr. Robert R. Blake and Dr. Jane S. Mouton designed the **Managerial Grid** behavioral model, which has also gained wide acceptance. The Managerial Grid, republished as the **Leadership Grid** figure in 1991, identifies different managerial styles and seeks to bring management's needs and the individual's needs closer together for mutual benefit. Manager behavior patterns are placed on a square grid (Figure 2.2).

Blake-Mouton's Managerial/Leadership Grid describes five management styles: Authority-Compliance Management, Country Club Management, Impoverished Management, Middle-of-the-Road Management and Team Management.

In the lower right is the **Authority-Compliance Management** style, the early autocratic, authoritarian approach. The manager is a no-nonsense taskmaster. Concern is for manager authority, status and operation of the organization. Employees have little say and less influence, and production is the only concern. This is also known as **Task Management.**

The upper left corner is the opposite, the **Country Club Management** style. Managers are overly concerned with keeping employees happy at the expense of reasonable productivity. The work atmosphere is friendly and comfortable. Concern for employees is utmost; concern for productivity is limited.

The lower left corner illustrates the **Impoverished Management** style, which permits workers to do just enough to get by. Managers and employees put in their time and look ahead to retirement. Little real concern exists for employees or management. Little is expected and little is given. Minimal effort is made. Ignore problems and they will go away.

In the middle is the **Middle-of-the-Road Management** style, with the manager showing some concern for both employees and management but in a low key manner that is not really productive. The manager is a fence straddler, appeasing both sides, avoiding conflict and satisfying no one.

The upper right corner is the **Team Management** approach, suggested as the ideal. The manager works with employees as a team, providing information, caring about their feelings and concerns, assisting, advising and coaching. Managers encourage employees to be creative and share suggestions for improvement. Employees are committed to their jobs and organization through a mutual relationship of trust and respect. Goals are achieved as a team.

Figure 2.2
**The Leadership Grid®
Figure, the Paternalism/
Maternalism Figure and
the Opportunism Figure.**
The grid can also be used to
demonstrate opportunism
and paternalism/maternalism
as shown in the figure.

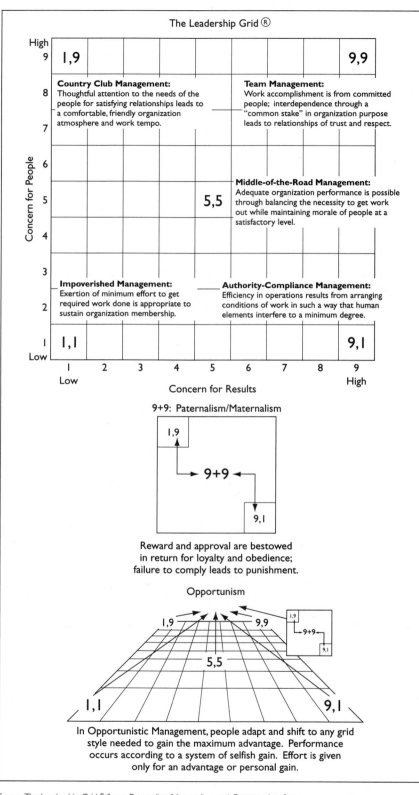

The Leadership Grid®

Country Club Management:
Thoughtful attention to the needs of the people for satisfying relationships leads to a comfortable, friendly organization atmosphere and work tempo.

Team Management:
Work accomplishment is from committed people; interdependence through a "common stake" in organization purpose leads to relationships of trust and respect.

Middle-of-the-Road Management:
Adequate organization performance is possible through balancing the necessity to get work out while maintaining morale of people at a satisfactory level.

Impoverished Management:
Exertion of minimum effort to get required work done is appropriate to sustain organization membership.

Authority-Compliance Management:
Efficiency in operations results from arranging conditions of work in such a way that human elements interfere to a minimum degree.

Concern for People — High 9, 8, 7, 6, 5, 4, 3, 2, 1 Low

Concern for Results — Low 1 2 3 4 5 6 7 8 9 High

9+9: Paternalism/Maternalism

Reward and approval are bestowed in return for loyalty and obedience; failure to comply leads to punishment.

Opportunism

In Opportunistic Management, people adapt and shift to any grid style needed to gain the maximum advantage. Performance occurs according to a system of selfish gain. Effort is given only for an advantage or personal gain.

Source: The Leadership Grid® figure, Paternalism/Maternalism and Opportunism from *Leadership Dilemmas—Grid Solutions,* by Robert R. Blake and Anne Adams McCanse. (Formerly the Managerial Grid figure by Robert R. Blake and Jane S. Mouton) Houston: Gulf Publishing Company (Grid Figure: p. 29, Paternalism Figure: p. 30, Opportunism Figure: p. 31). Copyright © 1991 by Scientific Methods, Inc. Reproduced by permission of the owners.

People-Minded Management

Another contemporary management style finding its way into law enforcement is people-minded management, the near opposite of autocratic management. Jones (1998a, p. 32) states: "The people-minded philosophy emphasizes respect, competence and fairness." He expands on this description further (pp. 32–36):

> People-minded supervisors
> - Treat employees with respect. They consider officers adults and trust them to carry out instruction.
> - Are fair and consistent in dispensing awards, discipline, pay, promotions, assignment and benefits. They develop standards and make sure these are known and understood by all concerned.
> - Praise officers in public and reprimand them in private. They know that rewards should always be given in front of supervisors, peers and subordinates.
> - Listen to officers, even when they disagree.
> - Provide development opportunities and encourage growth.
> - Keep officers informed about things which effect them.
> - Explain desired results, without offering apologies, then get out of the officers' way and let them perform.

Which Management Style to Select?

The management style you select depends on the individuals involved, the tasks to be accomplished and any emergency the organization is facing, such as a hostage incident, a multiple-alarm fire or an officer down.

> No one management style is more apt than another to achieve the agency's mission. The selected style must match individual personalities and situations.

It was once thought that fist-pounding, authoritarian managers were the greatest achievers. People now believe that many styles of management or combinations of several can be effective.

Now turn your attention to some specific functions performed at the three basic levels of management, beginning with the first-line, supervisory level.

Levels of Managers

The organizational chart depicts the number of management levels of the agency. (Figure 2.3).

> Management typically has three levels:
> - The top level or CEO (chief, sheriff).
> - The middle level (captains, lieutenants).
> - The first-line level (sergeants).

First-Line Managers

The critical importance of first-line supervisors is well stated in the adage: "Generals win battles but sergeants win wars." Most **first-line managers** or **supervisors** are sergeants, who are responsible to the next highest rank in the organization unless their position is specialized. Management philosopher Drucker says: "Supervisors are, so to speak, the ligaments, the tendons and sinews of an organization. They provide the articulation. Without them, no joint can move."

Figure 2.3
**The Levels
of Management**

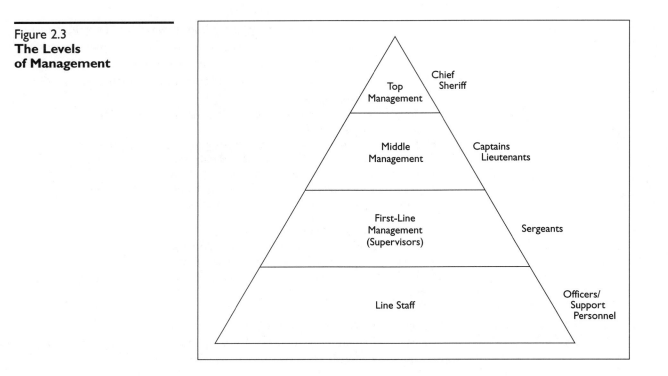

Supervisors' fundamental responsibility is to ensure that what needs to be accomplished in any given shift *is* accomplished effectively and legally. They are concerned with **supervision** of the day-to-day concerns of law enforcement officers, that is, overseeing the activities of all nonranking employees in the agency. Among their functions are:

- Managing line personnel in the field.
- Supervising patrol activities.
- Conducting inspections.
- Maintaining discipline.
- Enforcing rules and regulations.
- Conducting roll call.
- Managing field operations.

Roll call is the meeting of officers before each shift when officers check in and receive a briefing before going on duty.

Weaver (1990, p. 47) notes that rookies are easy to supervise because they are so enthusiastic, positive and eager to be accepted into the "police family." It is much harder to supervise veteran officers. Weaver gives four specific suggestions for supervising veteran officers—suggestions equally applicable to rookies.

First, *earn the right to supervise.* Weaver (pp. 47–49) says: "Promotion to sergeant no more makes a cop a supervisor than walking in a hangar makes him [or her] a pilot." Techniques to follow include:

- Allow officer input in decision-making processes.
- Communicate with employees openly and honestly.
- Refrain from unnecessary demonstrations of authority.
- Share credit for good work.

Second, *give specific, measurable assignments.* Techniques to follow include:

- Be conscious of time periods (i.e., how long it will take an officer to accomplish the task).
- Talk in terms of numbers (i.e., four arrests or ten traffic contacts).
- Ask officers to repeat the instructions if necessary.
- Write down assignment requirements. Do not rely on memory.
- Follow up during the shift to ensure compliance.

Third, *be reasonable in your expectations.* Techniques to follow include:

- Always set the work example. Do not demand something you yourself are not willing to do.
- Provide motivation and training to encourage improvement.
- Remember that everyone has a bad day from time to time.
- Do not be stingy with public praise.
- Do not overload the good worker just to compensate for the underachiever.

Fourth, *immediately reward positive behavior.* It has been said that a good supervisor is a lot like a cross-eyed javelin thrower—he or she does not win many medals but certainly keeps the crowd alert.

Supervisors frequently are not trained in the new skills they need. Initial training should concentrate on the "people activities" performed by supervisors, with particular emphasis on motivating others.

Middle Management

Middle management usually includes captains and lieutenants. Captains have authority over all officers of the agency below the chief or sheriff and are responsible only to the chief or sheriff.

Lieutenants are second in rank to captains. They are in charge of sergeants and all officers within their assigned responsibility, and they report to captains. Captains and lieutenants may perform the following functions:

- Inspecting assigned operations
- Reviewing and making recommendations on reports
- Helping develop plans
- Preparing work schedules
- Overseeing records and equipment

*The Top Level—
The Executive
Manager*

The **executive manager,** or the **chief executive officer** (**CEO**), is the top official in any law enforcement agency. The title may be chief of police, director, superintendent or sheriff, but the authority and responsibility of the position are similar. The executive manager is either elected or appointed by the city council, the county commission or the city manager, subject to approval of the city council.

Executive managers have full authority and responsibility as provided by the charter provisions of their local jurisdictions. People appointed to this position are to enforce the applicable laws of the United States, as well as state and local jurisdiction and all rules and regulations established by local government or the civil service commission.

Executive managers are responsible for planning, organizing and managing the agency's resources, including its employees. They are responsible for preserving the peace and enforcing laws and ordinances. The duties and responsibilities of executive managers often include:

- Developing a mission statement.
- Formulating goals and objectives.
- Preparing an annual budget.
- Preparing and periodically reviewing agency rules and regulations, and general and specific agency orders.
- Developing strategic long-term and tactical short-term plans for organizational operations.
- Attending designated meetings of the city council or other organizations.
- Preparing required reports to the governing authority or person.
- Coordinating with other law enforcement agencies.
- Participating in emergency preparedness plans and operations.
- Developing public relations liaisons with the press.
- Administering ongoing, operational financial processes.
- Developing training programs to meet local needs.
- Acting as liaison with community agencies.

Texts on management often convey the image of an executive working at an uncluttered desk in a spacious office. The executive is rationally planning, organizing, coordinating and controlling the organization. After careful analysis the executive makes critical decisions and has competent, motivated subordinates readily available to offer insightful input. The executive has a full schedule but no unexpected interruptions. Time lines are met without problem.

Several studies, however, indicate that this is *not* a realistic portrayal. In fact, most executives work at an unrelenting pace, are frequently interrupted and are often more oriented to reacting to crises than to planning and executing.

The executive manager's roles in law enforcement may differ from other levels of managers. Executive managers are responsible for the "big picture," for

As a CEO, the police chief meets with the city council to discuss the police budget and other police issues.

not only accomplishing the department's mission through goals and objectives but also for interacting with the community, its leaders, organizations and individual citizens.

Essential Functions of Law Enforcement Executives

Acting in a *managerial* capacity, law enforcement executives serve as:

- Planners.
- Facilitators.
- Interfacers.
- Interactors.

Planners

Law enforcement managers must possess basic skills for planning, that is, the ability to set goals and objectives and to develop work plans to meet them. Whether managers personally formulate these goals and objectives or seek assistance from their staff, plans are essential. Law enforcement organizations cannot function efficiently without tactical and strategic planning.

Tactical planning is short-term planning. **Strategic planning** is long-term planning.

Tactical planning is short-term, present or everyday operational planning. It includes the year's work plans. Strategic planning, on the other hand, is long-term, large-scale, futuristic planning.

Some people may use the term *tactical* in an operational or military sense to refer to unusual situations in which combat might be expected. In law enforcement this might include serving warrants, conducting drug raids, dealing with hostage situations and the like. In this context tactical planning would mean planning designed to carry out a tactical operation.

Tactical planning is most often necessary to provide the flexibility needed for change; determine personnel needs; determine objectives and provide organizational control; handle large incidents such as drug raids and special events such as sports competitions, popular concerts, large conventions and parades. According to Jones (1998b, p. 82):

> Planning is perhaps the most tedious aspect of any tactical operation. . . .
>
> A tactical plan is a dynamic concept involving team safety and logistics, that ensures the mission is commensurate with the team's capabilities. It lessens vicarious liability, delineates responsible entities, enhances courtroom testimony, identifies tactical responsibilities and fosters a "can do" attitude. . . .
>
> Planning is not just a leadership task. It requires subordinate participation as well. The team leader needs to take into account time constraints, information overload, and limited thinking. Through team involvement, the plan takes on the identity of a team plan instead of just the plan.

A meeting of line and staff personnel can determine the events for which tactical planning is necessary. Special problems can then be resolved and personnel needs assessed and assigned. A review of similar past events may require assistance from other police agencies in the area or state or federal aid. Tactical planning should be flexible because of changing conditions such as the number of people involved.

Strategic plans, in contrast, focus on the future and on setting priorities. A department might decide to place more emphasis on the use of technological advances, including communications and technology training. It might decide to continue the same emphasis on the level of recruitment and in-service training for sworn personnel and to place less emphasis on the use of sworn personnel for nonsworn duties. In addition it might identify new activities such as developing accurate job descriptions and career paths for all employees and eliminating other activities such as free services that most agencies charge for (e.g., fingerprinting, alarms and computer entry).

Withham (1998, p. 23) suggests several essential elements of strategic planning for law enforcement:

- *A manage-for-results orientation*—requires people to distance themselves somewhat from their daily duties and think about the big picture.

- *Environmental analysis*—primary activities here are data gathering and analysis of relevant trends.

- *Organizational assessment*—determines an organization's capabilities (strengths and weaknesses) in light of its mission. Resource assessment (e.g., human, facilities, budget and financial) is conducted. The product of this step should be a precise listing of all the organization's competencies and shortcomings.

Figure 2.4 contains a sample worksheet for an action plan.

OBJECTIVE: _____

_____

_____

STRATEGY: _____

_____

_____

WHAT IS KNOWN ABOUT THE SITUATION (+'s and −'s): _____

_____

_____

What will be done (Tasks)	Who will do it (Persons)	When will it be done	Resources needed	Evidence of accomplishment

Figure 2.4
Action Plan Sample Worksheet

Both tactical and strategic planning are essential. In the country's war on drugs, for example, the federal government has developed a strategic plan. States, counties and municipal levels of government must develop tactical plans to put the strategic plan into practical operation.

Facilitators

Facilitators assist others in performing their duties. Law enforcement managers at any level do not personally bring the agency goals, objectives and work plans to fruition. This is accomplished through a joint agency effort, as well as with the assistance of others external to the agency.

Rules, regulations, personal rapport, communications, standards, guidelines, logic, basic principles and direction all assist others in performing their duties.

Once they have directed subordinates on what to do and how, managers should let people carry out their duties independently. Trust, honesty and integrity are important in the manager-subordinate work relationship.

Operating within this environment is constant change. All levels of management must recognize change and be flexible enough to adapt to its demands.

Interfacers

Law enforcement executive managers must be **interfacers** who communicate with all segments of the agency, from chief deputy to patrol officer. They must have knowledge of communications and specialized staff activities and relationships, and must understand the division of labor and the allocations of personnel.

They must set agency goals and work plans with input from all agency members. They are the interfacers between all actions of agency personnel and all other people and agencies in contact with these personnel. Like good drivers they can look toward the horizon without losing sight of immediate concerns.

Interactors

Law enforcement managers also must be **interactors** who work effectively with a number of groups. They act as the department's official representative to the press, other local government departments, the business community, schools and numerous community committees and organizations.

Figure 2.5 illustrates the interactions of a typical law enforcement executive and, to some extent, all law enforcement managers. This diagram shows that only one-fifth of the executive manager's role is with the law enforcement organization. Executive managers have political, community, interorganizational and media roles as well.

Each organization with whom the executive interacts sees the importance and conduct of the position from different viewpoints. Law enforcement managers must determine these varied expectations and develop goals and work plans to meet them effectively.

Law enforcement executives typically interact with politicians, community groups, the media, executives of other law enforcement organizations, as well as individuals and groups within the agency itself.

Attendance at intergovernmental staff meetings is mandatory. Law enforcement agencies need services and information exchange from engineering, finance, planning, building inspections and other departments, just as other departments need the services of the police department.

Although media communications have some undesirable aspects, if reporters and law enforcement personnel establish honest, forthright rapport, they can establish generally good working relationships. Law enforcement needs the media as much as the media need it. (Dealing effectively with the media is discussed in depth in Chapter 3.) Personal contact with representatives of all groups develops an atmosphere of trust, integrity and respect for each other's duties and responsibilities.

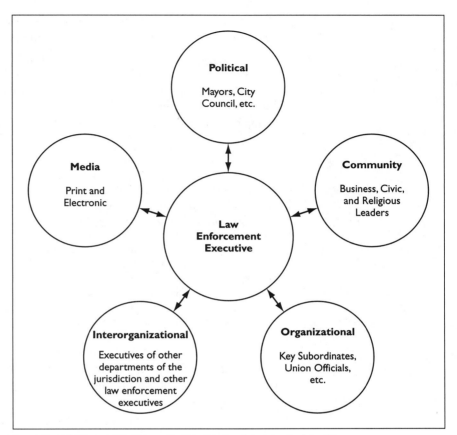

Figure 2.5
Typical Role Set of a Law Enforcement Executive

Source: Donald Witham and Paul Watson, *The Role of the Law Enforcement Executive.* FBI Management Science Unit, 1983. Reprinted by permission.

On Becoming an Executive Manager

When a person first becomes a chief of police, whether selected from within the department or as an outsider, many rumors concerning the appointment will precede the new chief's first day on the job. New chiefs should call a department meeting as soon as possible. At this meeting they should openly state that they understand the officers' concerns and past loyalties but expect to earn their respect. They should also describe the working relationships they seek. Such an open meeting will help allay fears, squelch rumors, decrease suspicions and establish an early rapport with the staff and line personnel.

A chief's management style should be adjusted to the department's needs. Some important changes should be made as soon as possible, but lesser changes should be instituted slowly. Change is stressful for an organization as well as individuals. People will have different opinions about the need for change. A participative approach that invites input from all employees usually works best, as discussed later in the chapter. Decisions should be based on what is good for the community and the department, not on what pleases specific individuals or interest groups.

Whether the department is small or large, the chief of police holds a powerful position in the governmental structure and in the community. The position is also challenging, exciting and filled with barriers and pitfalls. Chiefs should allow time for contemplation, innovation and creative thinking. They must be both managers and leaders. Their responsibilities are heavy, but their rewards are great.

A two-day conference for police executives offered some useful advice to those facing twenty-first-century police leadership ("Police Leadership for . . .," 1999, p. 60):

- Bring passion to the job.
- Understand yourself and your personal vision.
- Lead change throughout government.
- Create an environment of partnerships.
- Continually evaluate change forces.
- Foster debate and innovation.
- Approach the thinking process collaboratively.
- Concentrate on leadership development.
- Allow others to be recognized.
- Fashion a diverse organization.
- Master the vital art of communication.
- Do not allow yourself to bog down.

If chiefs adopt a coequal management approach with the department's formal and informal leaders, they may find that their organizational philosophy will be accepted more readily, thus enabling the organizational changes to occur with less resistance.

A major goal of chief executive officers should be to establish an environment in which success is expected and excellence is desired. Ideally, the chief of police is also a leader within the community, particularly in interactions with the city council and the city manager.

Weinblatt (1997, p. 26) observes: "Two common downsides of wearing the gold-adorned uniform are the politics and the consistent time drain." Indeed, as Robert Frost once said: "By working faithfully eight hours a day, you may eventually get to be boss and work twelve hours a day!" Weinblatt further notes (p. 27): "With beepers, cellular phones and other modern technological advances, it's just not possible to get away from the chief job."

Politics

Being forced to operate in a political environment is another stressor for chiefs. Weinblatt (p. 28) states: "The mark of a good chief is the ability to find a balance between divergent groups, to resolve conflicts, to represent the department to the public and to have an impeccable professional and private life." According to Sharp (1995, p. 44):

Law enforcement administrators . . . are forced to become politicians as part of their job responsibilities. . . .

Playing politics is part of their jobs, like it or not—and most do not. . . .

Roughly 80% of the administrators responding to a recent poll said they knew beforehand that politics was intertwined with their duties. . . .

However, as [one] chief . . . pointed out . . . , "Politics is not always negative." . . . In his eyes, politics can be defined as "the ability to get along, having the personal contact through which allies are able to use their abilities of persuasion to accomplish the task at hand." . . .

[Of the poll respondents], a majority (68%) said it is part of their jobs to act politically to make sure their departments receive the financial and public support they need to serve their communities.

Other results from the poll (p. 47) showed the biggest complaint regarding politics and its role in police administration is that it interferes with routine tasks, with 91 percent reporting politics interferes with day-to-day administrative duties to some extent. Also, more than half (59 percent) of the respondents believe administrators will need to become more involved in politics in the future.

The political nature of police administrative positions also requires chiefs to keep abreast of changes in legislation. According to Cameron (1997, p. 1): "[The police chief] must constantly be aware of restrictions put upon the police by new laws, regulations, codes, statutes, decrees, ordinances, rulings, and mandates. These come from the President, Congress, Supreme Court, Governor, State Legislature, the Mayor, and all the various and numerous federal, state and local councils and regulatory bodies that apply." Neubauer (1999, p. 6) explains how police administrators must become proactive in the legislative process to best serve their departments and communities:

As law enforcement executives, our responsibility to serve and protect the public extends beyond simply enforcing laws and maintaining order. It is our duty to ensure that the laws and regulations we enforce allow us to operate in the safest, most efficient and most effective manner. This means that we must get involved in the legislative process and provide our political leaders with the insight on law enforcement matters that we have gained through our experience.

The IACP provides us with the ideal forum to accomplish this vital task.

Hughes (1999, p. 63) adds: "Direct involvement in the development of legislation concerning law enforcement . . . is vital to the police service." He notes:

Some problems created by state legislation may simply be an attempt to solve a real or perceived problem by a legislator so interested in passage of a bill that he failed to ask law enforcement officials if it could be implemented the way it was drafted. . . .

[Some legislators] . . . don't understand the limited financial resources or practical problems that might exist when police have not had input on a related issue.

In addition, Weinblatt (1999, p. 49) stresses: "Chiefs need to understand not just what their officers, command staff and the public thinks, they also need to anticipate what their direct boss—the city council, mayor or manager—wants."

What City Managers Expect from the Chief of Police

Many police chiefs operate under the city manager form of government and report directly to the city manager, not to the city council. In fact, the city manager acts as a buffer between the chief and the council. The chief expects loyalty from his or her personnel, and the city manager expects loyalty from the chief of police. If city managers change during a chief's tenure, the chief should request a meeting to establish a new working relationship. The chief should not expect that the new manager's policies and procedures will be the same as those of the previous city manager. Trust, loyalty and integrity are essential elements for good rapport. The governing philosophy of the city manager and the chief of police must be within acceptable working parameters. However, the city manager is in charge, and flexibility may be required of the chief of police if philosophical differences arise. The chief should determine what the city manager's expectations are:

- What kinds and frequency of reports? Written or oral?
- Who should the chief notify immediately of serious events or incidents?
- What circumstances should the chief deal with directly?
- Should the chief attend city council meetings?
- Should disciplinary actions be reported?

The city manager and the police chief should get together both formally and informally. The chief might invite the city manager to inservice training sessions, roll calls, ride-alongs, stakeouts and the like. The chief should also learn just what the city manager expects from the police department and its chief. A chief's success—indeed, the chief's very job—may depend on an effective relationship with the city manager. To be continually at odds with the city manager is a form of career suicide.

Common Management Problems

Three important management problems for law enforcement are:

- Administering the budget.
- Maintaining effective community relations.
- Establishing and administering personnel systems and procedures, including recruitment selection, training and discipline of key employees.

Each decade has its unique changes and challenges. Police chiefs must be constantly alert to the following areas of major concern:

- Employees—Chiefs must evaluate their employees but also be aware that employees are evaluating them.
- Conflict—This must be resolved as soon as possible.
- Politics—Although it is impossible to remain aloof from politics, chiefs should remain objective.
- Communication—Chiefs should keep their department members, their superiors, the media and the community informed.
- Priorities—Few chiefs have sufficient time for everything. They must establish priorities wisely and learn to delegate.
- Street wisdom—Chiefs should get out in the community, ride with officers occasionally, talk with staff, get to know the informal as well as the formal organization.
- Personal conduct—Chiefs are constantly under scrutiny and must perform professionally at all times.

Indicators of Organizational Problems

The following indicators of organizational problems and possible underlying causes are each addressed in depth at appropriate places later in the text.

The manager at higher levels has to make too many decisions. Even though managers are decision makers, decisions should be made at the lowest level practicable. First-line managers should encourage subordinates in the field to exercise independent decision making.

Failure to achieve organizational goals and objectives may be caused by unrealistic goals and objectives or by inadequate manager review or follow-up. *Ineffective, inefficient use of resources* is usually due to a poor organizational design. It may have too little or too much specialization, too many or too few managers, poor division of work load, poor communications flow or a combination of these factors. *Failure to be aware of technology that would improve operations* is usually due to insufficient attention devoted to research and development. *Failure to provide adequate services* is usually due to administrative and operational failures.

Duplication of services or tasks frequently happens with a lack of planning and coordination at the command level. *Lack of coordination between management and subordinates or between work shifts or specialized divisions* is usually due to failure to exercise command responsibility.

Excessive conflict not due to personality clashes indicates low morale and lack of proper communication throughout the organization. *Low morale* problems are indicated by increases in subordinate complaints, grievances, absenteeism, unvalidated sick leave or work performance and productivity decreases. Department meetings should be held to determine the needs of individuals and the organization. Emphasis should be on performance, with proper recognition when it is achieved. *Lack of opportunity for creativity and innovation* is usually due to lack of proper support and recognition for new ideas. Brainstorming sessions are needed.

Law Enforcement Management as a Career

Deciding to become a law enforcement officer is an exciting career choice, but becoming a manager in law enforcement is even more challenging. It is an opportunity to develop personally and a responsibility to develop others. You can become a successful law enforcement manager in many ways.

Prepare and develop yourself for promotion. Study, attend training programs, take correspondence courses, read trade journals, attend academic courses, use the public library and the law enforcement agency's library and listen to contemporaries. Be ready when opportunity arises.

Be available. Once prepared, you become a valuable resource to the law enforcement organization. Assert yourself at appropriate times. Support your organization's goals and objectives. Participate in work programs. Volunteer to do more than others. Become so valuable to the organization's future that it cannot do without you. Become an information source who is willing to selflessly share information.

Support your manager. An old adage advises: "If you want your manager's job, praise and support him or her because soon that person will move up the ladder. Be derogatory to your manager and he or she will be there forever." Complaining, continually finding fault, being negative or nonsupportive—all are fast tracks to organizational oblivion. You may accomplish a short-term goal, but in the long run you will destroy your career. Be supportive; if you criticize, make it constructive criticism. Be positive. Praise the good things happening.

Select an advisor or mentor. These are people within or outside the police organization who can assist and counsel you. Advisors can point you in the right direction. They can be a sounding board.

Be positive at and toward work. Either like what you do or change to another job. Rarely can you excel at something you hate. Work longer, more diligently and more competently than anyone else in the organization. Before you know it, you will be an expert.

Nurture interpersonal relationships. Management is getting things done through others. This is impossible to do without treating others as important. Working with others is one of the keys to success. Working alone is a long, hard road. Develop your interpersonal relationships. Combine their strengths with your weaknesses and their weaknesses with your strengths.

Management and Leadership

Leadership has been defined as "working with and through individuals and groups to accomplish organizational goals" (Hersey and Blanchard); "a process of achieving goals through managerial principles, which can be subdivided into three basic areas: establishing direction, motivating and inspiring, and influencing others to complete the task at hand as effectively and efficiently as possible" (Pomerenke, 1994, p. 37); and "power governed by principle, directed toward raising people to their highest level of personal motive and social morality and tested by achieving of results measured by original purpose. Power manipulates people as they are; leadership as they could be. Power manages; leadership mobilizes. Power tends to corrupt; leadership to create. Great leadership requires great followership. Leaders mobilize the best in their followers who in turn demand more from their leaders" (Burns, 1978).

Buchholz and Roth (1987, p. 29) report that when people are asked why leaders want to become leaders, certain answers come up routinely: (1) to get power, (2) to take control and (3) to be served (get money, respect, recognition, prestige, etc.). But when you think about leaders you respect, you will find they got to be leaders for exactly opposite reasons (p. 30): "In most instances, leaders ultimately get power, control and are served by doing just the *opposite*. Effective leaders tend to *empower* their people, to *free* them up, and to *serve* them." Leaders lead by pulling rather than pushing.

Managing vs. Leading

According to Ramirez (1995, p. 177):

> True effective leadership is a phenomenon that is difficult to define, but easy to recognize when you experience it. The best measure of leadership then should be the effect that is exhibited by those who are being led ultimately toward organizational goals. . . .
>
> This may have been best stated long ago by Lao Tsu: . . . *The good leader is he who the people revere. The great leader is he whose people say, "We did it ourselves."*

Bennis (1989) draws some helpful distinctions between managers and leaders:

Managers administer; leaders innovate.

Managers focus on systems and structure; leaders, on people.

Managers rely on control; leaders inspire trust.

Managers have short-range views; leaders, long-range perspectives.

Managers always eye the bottom line; leaders eye the horizon.

Managers accept the status quo; leaders challenge it.

Managers do things right; leaders do the right thing.

This same concern for "doing things right" was observed by Peter Drucker over 20 years ago in a study of the Los Angeles Police Department requested by the chief. Among Drucker's findings was: "You police are so concerned with doing things right that you fail to do the right things." In other words the administration was so concerned with managing that they failed to lead. He also said: "Police are so concerned with doing things right [that] you promote for the absence of wrongdoing rather than for the presence of initiative, innovation and leadership."

Table 2.4 presents some striking differences between management and leadership.

A basic difference between managers and leaders is that managers focus on tasks, whereas leaders focus on people.

Table 2.4
Management vs. Leadership

Management	Leadership
Does the thing right	Does the right thing
Tangible	Intangible
Referee	Cheerleader
Directs	Coaches
What you do	How you do it
Pronounces	Facilitates
Responsible	Responsive
Has a view of the mission	Has vision of mission
Views world from inside	Views world from outside
Chateau leadership	Front-line leadership
What you say	How you say it
No gut stake in enterprise	Gut stake in enterprise
Preserving life	Passion for life
Driven by constraints	Driven by goals
Looks for things done wrong	Looks for things done right
Runs a cost center	Runs an effort center
Quantitative	Qualitative
Initiates programs	Initiates an ongoing process
Develops programs	Develops people
Concerned with programs	Concerned with people
Concerned with efficiency	Concerned with efficacy
Sometimes plays the hero	Plays the hero no more

Source: Bill Westfall. "Leadership: Caring for the Organizational Spirit." *Knight Line USA*, May-June 1993, p. 9. Leaders Care for the Spirit reprinted with permission of *Executive Excellence*, Provo, Utah. September 1992, p. 11.

A manager operates in the status quo, but a leader takes risks. Police administrators must be both skilled managers and effective leaders. The distinctions between managing and leading are also noted by Braiden (1994, p. 14):

> The most basic difference between leaders and managers is this: Managers think it is their job to run the organization well. That is why, more often than not, managers give themselves ulcers trying to know and control everything. Leaders know it is their job to make sure the organization is run well by others. Leaders concentrate on having the right people, in the right places, doing the right things. Leaders are comfortable sharing authority and responsibility, successes and failures, with other leaders.

Farr (1998, p. 4) notes: "Management deals with *things* (work flow, cash flow, inventory, etc.) and keeps your business running smoothly. Leadership deals with *change* (new technology, new processes, new strategies, etc.) and involves guiding your people, their perceptions and their motivations." Fulton (1998a, p. 82) says: "Leaders do what managers don't." Leaders solve problems, maximize potential with competent associates, take safe risks, take responsibility, move forward, lead by example and have vision. Fulton adds:

> Although the principles of leadership are consistent over time, the ability to lead is an ability sought by many but achieved by few. Being a successful leader in police work requires many skills and abilities. But the satisfaction of being a true leader far exceeds the safety of being a mediocre manager.

Managers may or may not be leaders, and leaders do not have to be managers. A true leader has the potential to influence from any position in the organization, formal or informal.

Characteristics of Leaders

A **leader** in the purest sense influences others by example. This characteristic of leadership was recognized in the sixth century B.C. by Chinese philosopher Lao-Tzu when he wrote:

> The superior leader gets things done
> With very little motion.
> He imparts instruction not through many words
> But through a few deeds.
> He keeps informed about everything
> But interferes hardly at all.
> He is a catalyst,
> And although things wouldn't get done as well
> If he weren't there,
> When they succeed he takes no credit.
> And because he takes no credit
> Credit never leaves him.

Leadership creates a special bond that has to be earned. To build and maintain credibility, it is necessary to clarify values, identify the wishes of the community and employees, build a consensus, communicate shared values, stand up for beliefs and lead by example. Farr (p. 4) believes the hallmark of a good leader is motivation and asserts that strong leaders are good communicators, outgoing, persistent yet patient, sensitive, trustworthy, appreciative of others, optimistic, people oriented, realistic, organized and prepared. Fulton (1998b, p. 82) adds other traits successful leaders must possess: honesty, courage, dependability, creativity, confidence, personal energy, loyalty, tact and humility.

A good leader knows being the boss does not mean bossing. Rather it means giving employees the resources, training and coaching they need and providing them with information so they can see their organization's mission.

Research on and Theories Related to Leadership

Leadership has been studied over the past several decades from many different perspectives.

Theories about leadership include the study of traits, the classic studies conducted at Michigan and Ohio State Universities, the Managerial/Leadership Grid and situational leadership.

Trait Theorists

The first group of researchers, the **trait theorists,** examined the individual. They looked at leaders in industry and government to determine what special characteristics or **traits** these people possessed. They found that most leaders are *goal oriented,* stimulating employees to achieve goals by following rather than being forced or commanded to achieve. Leaders are *motivated* and expect the same of those they work for and with. They are *planners and prioritizers* who consider alternatives and variations and lay out realistic courses of action according to the circumstances.

Leaders are *intelligent,* having sufficient knowledge to make decisions. They are *observant,* absorbing information that may not be immediately usable and retaining it for future use. They are also *inquisitive,* delving, probing, pondering and searching. They question everything and do not accept things as they are simply because "that's the way we've always done it."

Leaders are *able to seek out problems.* They foresee problems and prevent them. They are proactive rather than reactive. They are also *creative and innovative thinkers,* spending a certain portion of their time "contemplating their navels," that is, sitting back, thinking and dreaming, yet being practical and realistic. Like Walt Disney, they believe: "If you can dream it, you can do it." Leaders look at everything they do and ask: "How can I do this differently? Better?" When they discover the answer, they do it.

Leaders are *persevering,* determined, yielding only when proven wrong. Leaders are *risk takers.* They do not want to make mistakes but accept that doers will make mistakes, learn from them, and move forward. Remember the saying, "The person who makes no mistakes usually makes nothing." Consider the example of Tom Watson, founder of IBM. When Watson learned that a promising young junior executive had entered into a risky business venture that lost over $10 million dollars, Watson called the man into his office. When the junior executive asked whether Watson wanted him to resign, Watson replied, "You can't be serious. We've just spent $10 million dollars educating you."

Although by definition leaders need others to be followers, most leaders are not governed or unduly influenced by others. They are *independent* and confident in their choices. Leaders are also *effective communicators,* having above-average verbal and written skills. They are *people oriented* because they recognize that they accomplish things *through* others. Ability is important, but the ability to discover ability in others and then help them develop it is the true test of leadership. To accomplish goals with the help of others, leaders need a *high level of personal strength, energy and good health.*

Leaders *know their own limitations.* They neither underestimate nor overestimate their potential. Leaders *live by personal principles and values.* They must have a guiding philosophy similar to that of their organization. Truly effective leaders are *visionary,* working creatively and innovatively, with a clear idea of where they are going and how they are going to get there.

Leaders are *honest* people who are role models in integrity. Although they know their own limitations, they are also *self-confident* and *optimistic.* A graphic example of the consequences of a lack of self-confidence is the death of tightrope aerialist Karl Wallenda. In 1968 Wallenda said: "Being on the tightrope is living; everything else is waiting." He loved his "work" and had total confidence in himself. Ten years later he fell to his death. His wife, also an aerialist, said that he had recently been worried about falling. This was in total contrast to his earlier years, when all his energy was focused on succeeding.

The **Wallenda Effect** is readily seen in sports when a team that is ahead starts playing simply to keep its lead rather than to increase it. Such a team, playing not to lose rather than to win, often loses its momentum and can be defeated.

Although many traits were identified, none dominate. Leadership trait theory was highly popular because it simplified the process of selecting leaders. Guaranteed leadership through possession of specific traits, however, was never fully realized because of the number of traits identified and the fact that no single person possessed them all. No criteria determined which traits were more desirable than others. Even possession of all the traits did not guarantee leadership success.

After many studies and experiments, trait theorists could not empirically document leadership characteristics. Researchers in the 1940s and 1950s turned their attention to the situations in which leaders actually functioned.

The Michigan and Ohio Studies

Research conducted at Michigan State University and Ohio State University also provides insights into effective leadership. These studies determined that leaders must provide an environment that motivates employees to accomplish organizational goals.

The Michigan State study looked at how leaders motivated individuals or groups to achieve organizational goals. They determined that leaders must have a sense of the task to be accomplished and the most favorable work environment. Three principles of leadership behavior emerged from the Michigan State study:

- Leaders must give task direction to their followers.
- Closeness of supervision directly affects employee production. High-producing units had less direct supervision; highly supervised units had

lower production. Conclusion: Employees need some freedom to make choices. Given this, they produce at a higher rate.

- Leaders must be employee oriented. It is the leader's responsibility to facilitate employees' accomplishment of goals.

The Ohio State study on leadership behavior used similar methods. This research focused on two dimensions: initiating structure and consideration structure.

Initiating structure looked at the leader's behavior in assigning *tasks*. It included whether leaders assigned employees to specific tasks and asked them to follow standard rules and regulations. **Consideration structure** looked at establishing the *relationship* between the group and the leader. It included whether the leader found time to listen to employees, was willing to make changes and was friendly and approachable.

The Ohio study used these two variables—focus on task and focus on relationships—to develop a management quadrant describing leadership behavior.

The Managerial Grid from a Leadership Perspective

Blake and Mouton developed their Managerial Grid from the studies done at Ohio State University and the Group Dynamics Leadership studies. As Figure 2.2 shows, the grid illustrates five types of management or leadership styles based on concern for production (task) versus concern for people (relationship).

Hersey and Blanchard (1977, p. 96) summarized the attitudinal preferences of each management style in several areas, including their basic production-people beliefs, guiding slogans, decision making, conflict with superiors and peers, conflict with subordinates, creativity and promotion of creative effort (Table 2.5).

Situational Leadership

The next development in leadership theory was that of Hersey and Blanchard. They viewed leadership as an interplay between the amount of direction (task behavior) a leader gives, combined with the amount of relationship behavior a leader provides (the Managerial/ Leadership Grid) *and* the readiness level that followers exhibit on a specific task the leader is attempting to accomplish through the individual or group.

Situational leadership specifies that initially workers need support and direction. As they become more task ready, they need less direction and more support, up to the point where even support can be reduced. The basic premise of situational leadership theory is that as the followers' readiness level in relation to task increases, leaders should begin to lessen their direction or task behavior and simultaneously increase their relationship behavior. This would be the leaders' strategy until individuals or groups reach a moderate level of task readiness.

As followers or groups move into an above-average level of readiness, leaders would decrease both their task behavior and their relationship behavior. At this point followers would be ready not only from the task point of view but also from the amount of relationship behavior they need.

Once a follower or group reaches this level of readiness, close supervision is reduced and delegation is increased, indicating the leader's trust and confidence.

Table 2.5
**Attitudinal Preferences
of Various Management
Styles**

	Authority-Compliance Management	Country Club Management	Middle-of-the-Road Management	Impoverished Management	Team Management
Basic Production–People Beliefs	Sees good relationships as incidental to high production. Supervisors achieve production goals by planning, directing and controlling all work.	Sees production as incidental to good relations. Supervisors establish a pleasant work atmosphere and harmonious relationships between people.	Sees high production and sound relations in conflict. Supervisors stay neutral and carry out established procedures.	Seeks a balance between high production and good human relations. Supervisors find a middle ground so a reasonable degree of production can be achieved without destroying morale.	Sees production resulting from integrating task and human requirements. Good relationships and high production are both attainable. Supervisors get effective production through participation and involvement of people and their ideas.
Guiding Slogans	Produce or perish.	Try to win friends and influence people.	Don't rock the boat.	Be firm but fair.	People support what they help create.
Decision Making	Inner-directed, depending on own skills, knowledge, attitudes and beliefs in approaching problems and making decisions.	Other-directed, eager to find solutions that reflect the ideas and opinions of others so solutions are accepted.	Avoids problems or defers them to others.	Samples opinions, manipulates participation, compromises and then sells the final solution.	Seeks emergent solutions as the result of debate, deliberation and experimentation by those with relevant facts and knowledge.
Conflict with Superiors and Peers	Takes a win-lose approach, fighting to win its own points as often as possible.	Avoids conflict by conforming to the thinking of the boss or peers.	Keeps its mouth shut and does not express dissent.	Expresses opinions and then tries to find reasonable compromises.	Confronts conflict directly, communicating feelings and facts as a basis to work through conflict.
Conflict with Subordinates	Suppresses conflict through authority.	Smooths over and tries to release tension by appeals to the "goodness of people."	Does not get involved with conflict. It usually avoids issues that might give rise to conflict by simply not discussing them with subordinates.	Deals with surface tensions and symptoms only, letting conflict situations "cool off" for a while, working for a blending of different positions so a somewhat acceptable solution is reached.	Confronts conflict directly and works through it at the time it arises. Conflict is accepted so the clash of ideas and people can generate creative solutions to problems. Those involved are brought together to work through differences.
Creativity	Considers ideas the responsibility of the few, not expected of the majority.	Expects no one to be creative, but a creative person is congratulated.	Sometimes has good ideas "pop up," but ideas are usually unrelated to company goals or morale.	Values creativity and seeks it from everyone, usually under nonthreatening conditions that will not disturb staff or the authority structure.	Expects those interested in and able to tackle a problem to do so. A high degree of interplay of ideas exists. Experimentation is the rule rather than the exception. Innovations further shared goals and solve important problems.
Promotion of Creative Effort	Promotes innovation by rewards and promotions. When a conflict of ideas arises, it is "survival of the fittest."	Encourages innovations by accepting all ideas uncritically. Ideas that will generate conflicts are side-stepped.	Discourages creativity. Ideas are not discussed on the job, so conflicts are unlikely.	Encourages innovation under controlled conditions. Brainstorming and "idea of the month" campaigns are used.	Uses feedback of results of experiments as a basis for further development and thinking. Open expression of differences and mature conflict are accepted. Everyone encourages innovations by defining and communicating problems.

Source: Adapted from Hershey and Blanchard (1977).

Transformational Leadership

The most recent form of leadership to be recognized is **transformational leadership,** which treats employees as the organization's most valuable asset. It is employee-centered and focused on empowerment.

An important aspect of transformational leadership is its employee-orientation. Transformational leadership seeks to empower people to make the fullest possible contribution to the organization. What is often lacking, however, is a model for effective *followership.* A leader cannot simply tell people they are empowered and expect them to instantly know how to perform. Employees need training, resources and authority if they are to be "empowered."

The focus on leadership rather than management complements the move toward community-oriented, problem-solving policing because it stresses resolving problems and not simply reacting to incidents. It encourages experimenting with new ways and allows honest mistakes to encourage creativity.

Ford et al. (1999, p. 14) have developed a road map for making the change to community policing through transformational leadership. They suggest:

> A leader needs three things to build this road map: an understanding of the stages one must go through to make transformational change happen in an organization; an understanding of the underlying elements for change in the move to community policing; and an understanding of key challenges a leader must face in any transformational change effort.

Their road map is shown in Table 2.6.

Leadership Styles

Management literature has identified many leadership styles, several of which can be found in police organizations.

Leadership styles include autocratic, democratic or participative and laissez-faire.

Autocratic Leadership

Autocratic leadership is most frequently mentioned in connection with early history. Many early leaders inherited their positions. They were members of the aristocracy, and through the centuries positions of leadership were passed down to family members.

In early industrial production efforts, the boss was often a domineering figure. He (and bosses were invariably men) was specifically chosen because he displayed traits associated with autocratic leadership. His authority was uncontested, and employees did what they were told or else. This style of management emerged in response to the demands of the Industrial Revolution, when masses of illiterate workers used expensive machinery and needed to follow explicit orders.

Managers who used autocratic leadership made decisions without participant input. They were completely authoritative and showed little or no concern for subordinates. Rules were rules, without exception. Certain circumstances may call for autocratic leadership.

Table 2.6
Community Policing: A Road Map for Change

			TIME LINE		
Exploration	Commitment	Planning	Implementation	Monitoring and Revision	Institutionalization
	Concept	Action Items/ Bench Marking Recommendations	New Knowledge and Implementation	Movement and Impact Data	Examples of Practices
Organizational Structure	Roles and Responsibilities	Blend specialist CPO's into overall patrol units. Define those task areas requiring specialization department-wide and train accordingly. Develop teams utilizing a combination of specialists whenever possible. Review other best practices.	■ Redo job descriptions ■ Redefine relationships across functions and work groups ■ Reduce reporting lines	■ Identify key "generalist" roles and evaluate the number of personnel who participate in this role ■ Track the efficiency of services/systems likely to be affected by a more generalist role and evaluate whether improvements are made as a result of new rules ■ Evaluate the amount of extra work that is avoided through generalist approach (fewer call backs, fewer referrals, etc.)	*Baltimore, MD*—Over the past decade, the agency has evolved from specialized community policing units with a rather narrow focus to a department-wide community policing mandate. Every facet of the agency is geared toward meeting the goals of community policing. Relationships throughout the department have been restructured to allow information, guidance, and authority to flow through the organization without supervisory barriers or traditional "chain-of-command" restraints.
	Divisional Alignment	Geographic subdivisions developed, with internal and external input for assignment of personnel. Reporting lines tailored to activity and geographic area of accountability, rather than function. Review other best practices.	■ Assign areas of geographic responsibility for all personnel ■ Study feasibility of organization for better accountability ■ Decentralize organization into geographic areas as appropriate ■ Assign cross functional teams to areas	■ Evaluate departmental effectiveness in key roles/geographical areas and note improvements as well as areas of weakness ■ Identify key problems unique to each area and track improvements over time (e. g. , less crime, fewer complaints, quality of life issues)	*Grand Rapids, MI*—One centralized agency is in the process of moving into five district areas. Officers are responsible for a geographical area within their district. *Lansing, MI*—Decentralized the department in top problem solving areas and made officers accountable for a specific area. Two new precincts were created to decentralize services. *St. Petersburg, FL*—The city was divide into geographic regions and all employees are accountable for activities in the area to which they are assigned.
	Organizational Accountability to Community	Expand measures beyond crime statistics and response times to include citizen perceptions of safety and security (quality of life). Review other best practices.	■ Create atmosphere soliciting public input ■ Survey community ■ Add citizens to internal planning processes	■ Send customer satisfaction survey following interaction with department to obtain feedback ■ Survey citizen perceptions of safety and quality of life in neighborhood ■ Develop systems for community input, suggestions, and feedback (e. g. , toll-free line, web page, surveys, suggestion box)	*Sagamore Hills, OH*—An agency serving a rural community initiated their change to community policing by surveying residents. Based on survey, strategies for decreasing residents' fear of crime were developed.

Source: Ford et al. "Transformational Leadership and Community Policing: A Road Map for Change." *The Police Chief,* Vol. LXVI, No. 12, December 1999, p. 19. Reprinted by permission.

Consultative, Democratic or Participative Leadership

Consultative, democratic or **participative leadership** has been evolving since the 1930s and 1940s. Democratic leadership does not mean that every decision is made only after discussion and a vote. It means rather that management welcomes employees' ideas and input. Employees are encouraged to be innovative. Management development of a strong sense of individual achievement and responsibility is a necessary ingredient of participative or consultative leadership.

Democratic or participative managers are interested in their subordinates and their problems and welfare. Management still makes the final decisions but takes into account the input from employees.

Laissez-Faire Leadership

Laissez-faire leadership implies nonintervention and is almost a contradiction in terms. Let everything run itself without direction from the leader, who exerts little or no control. This style arises from the concept that employees are adults, should know as well as the manager what is right and wrong and will automatically do what is right for themselves and the organization.

Laissez-faire leaders want employees to be happy and believe that if employees are happy, they will be more productive. Employees *should* feel comfortable and good about their work, but this should be because they participate. Even when they participate, employees must still do the job and meet the organization's goals and objectives. Leaderless management, sometimes called **free-rein leadership,** may result in low morale, inefficiency, lack of discipline and low productivity.

Ineffective Management Styles

Despite copious volumes written on the subject of effective management and leadership, many supervisors continue to hold on to practices that simply do not work. According to McDevitt (1999b, p. 144): "Their approach may have worked with some consistency in the past, however, these managers are usually so far into their 'comfort zone' that they don't realize they're losing an opportunity for real leadership." McDevitt (1999b, pp. 144–146) describes three styles of ineffective management and the reasons managers continue to use them:

- *"Beholding" Style of Management*—This style is based on the theory that when a subordinate is somehow "beholding" to a manager, the manager will receive the best work product and loyalty in return.

- *"Past Glory" Style of Management*—Managers believe that because "it worked in the past, it will work for me now." An example is the manager who stubbornly resists automation of tasks by computerization.

- *"Creative Dissatisfaction" Style of Management*—The manager who practices this style of management intentionally maintains dissatisfaction among subordinates by allowing them to focus their anger on minor issues or even turning employees against each other. Incompetent managers often practice this style of management in an effort to divert attention from the root of the problem, which is their own inability to manage.

Figure 2.6 shows the continuum of leadership styles.

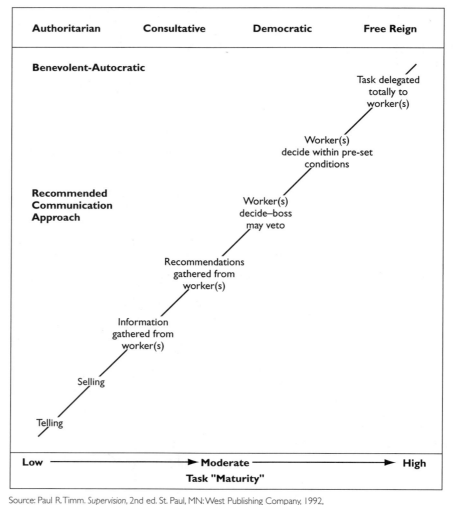

Figure 2.6
Continuum of Leadership Styles

Implications

Research on leaders and leadership is abundant. Each theory offers something to the law enforcement manager. However, no one type of leader or leadership style will suffice in all situations.

Internationally, leaders have been recognized because of the leadership abilities they displayed for a particular time, place and need. Put into another situation and time, they might not have become leaders.

Leaders must often be autocratic in one situation and democratic or participatory in another. They must know when to make an immediate decision and when to make a decision only after input, discussion and consideration.

Emergency situations rarely permit the opportunity for democratic or participatory decision making. Employees in nonemergency situations rarely respond well to autocratic leadership for routine task performance over the long term.

Leaders know what to do, how to do it, when to do it and with what type of employee, according to the demands of the individual situation.

Leadership—A Call for Change

Managers must pay attention to the new ideas and trends emerging from America's businesses: a commitment to people, the development of a people-oriented workplace, and the belief that leadership can and does make a difference. Leadership in law enforcement historically depended on a strong, authoritarian chief. However, this style of leadership neglects everything known about people and their behavior. Coercion discourages creativity and risk taking and often causes people to rebel.

President Eisenhower used to demonstrate this aspect of leadership with a simple piece of string. He would put the string on a table and say: "Pull it and it'll follow wherever you wish. Push it and it'll go nowhere at all." It is the same with people: "I don't mind being pushed as long as I can steer."

Managers must shift from telling and controlling the people they work with to developing and enhancing them. They must ask for their input before making critical decisions that affect them. They must also listen to their customers—the citizens—in new and more open ways. Managers must stop reacting to incidents and begin solving problems. They must permit risk taking and tolerate honest mistakes to encourage creativity and achieve innovation. To better understand this change in leadership style, compare the key concepts from each, summarized in Table 2.7.

Cunningham (1994, p. 74) suggests that administrators need to shift from the traditional "power-at-the-top" organization to a "power-sharing, empowered philosophy." They can accomplish this by taking two important steps: "Flattening the organizational structure/hierarchy and increasing communication." The benefits of employee empowerment are numerous (Cunningham, p. 76):

> Empowerment offers a win-win-win proposition: By empowering the members of [an] organization, the leader enhances his [or her] own ability to lead; agency personnel are able to use their minds, demonstrate their capabilities and grow both personally and professionally; and the public receives more responsive service, customized to meet its specific need.

**Table 2.7
Reform and New Style Leadership Compared**

Reform (Authoritarian) Style	New Style
Response to incidents	Problem solving
Individual effort and competitiveness	Teamwork
Professional expertise	Community orientation; ask customers what they want
Go by the "book"; decisions by emotion	Use data-based decision making
Tell subordinates	Ask and listen to employees
Boss as patriarch and order giver	Boss as coach and teacher
Maintain status quo	Create, innovate, experiment
Control and watch employees	Trust employees
Reliance on scientific investigation and technology rather than people	Reliance on skilled employees—a better resource than machines
When things go wrong, blame employees	Errors mean failed systems/processes—improve them
Organization is closed to outsiders	Organization is open

Changing from autocratic management to any other style is a slow, evolutionary process. Developing a new corporate culture for an organization can take years. Part of the challenge is the bureaucracy within most law enforcement agencies.

Bureaucracy

At the heart of the difficulty in changing leadership style is the bureaucratic nature of most law enforcement agencies. As Cunningham (p. 72) notes:

> In law enforcement, the organizational culture is based on the paramilitary rank structure, which stresses strict obedience to directives from above. . . .
>
> The paramilitary and bureaucratic structure that is typical of American law enforcement is its own barrier to innovation and change. . . .
>
> With the dampening effect of the bureaucratic nature of law enforcement organizations, it is not surprising that innovation, communication, initiative and participation are virtually nonexistent.

Leadership Training and Development

An appointment to fill a position on an organizational chart does not automatically make one a leader. By the same token, relatively few leaders are able to simply step into the role without needing to develop and refine their leadership skills and abilities. As McDevitt (1999a, p. 95) states:

> One need not be a "charismatic" leader in the mold of a John F. Kennedy or even an Adolf Hitler. So-called "born" leaders (if there really are any) are probably few and far between. Any reasonably intelligent person with enough confidence in himself to develop his abilities and talents can learn and practice some basic leadership principles.

Leaders who have adopted a specific leadership style can change that style through training. They can turn their weaknesses into strengths through studying, working with mentors or observing other leaders in action. Leaders are not born; they are developed. Task-oriented leaders can become people-oriented leaders.

Leadership training before appointment is highly desirable. If not possible, it should happen soon after appointment. Each leader must be an individual, not a mirror image of the predecessor. Bergner (1998, p. 16) asserts:

> Departments need to understand that developing and training officers into competent leaders begins at the beginning, on the very first day of an officer's career. Developing leaders has everything to do with administrators knowing what kinds of qualities make for good leaders, and then structuring a department that recognizes, encourages, rewards and trains those individuals who have the characteristics of good leadership.

Breen (1999, p. 63) adds:

> Leadership training is essential for our professional mission. As responsibility is continually pushed to the bottom of flatter hierarchies, leadership will be required of police officers of all ranks. It is necessary to the creation of what our communities and officers are both demanding: quality, broad-based service implemented in such a way that it is rewarding to the citizen as well as the officer.

According to Bushey (1999, p. 71): "The development of subordinate leaders is among the most important and solemn responsibilities facing a law enforcement administrator."

Table 2.8
Skill Layers for Managers

A	B	C
When used alone, these skills are suited to a rigidly traditional workplace.	Combined with the skills in column A, the skills below are needed in today's progressive workplace.	Combined with columns A and B, these skills are needed to build and maintain a team environment.
Direct people.	Involve people.	Develop self-motivated people.
Get people to understand ideas.	Get people to generate ideas.	Get groups of diverse people to generate and implement their own best ideas.
Manage one-to-one.	Encourage teamwork.	Build teams that manage more of their own day-to-day work.
Maximize the department's performance.	Build relationships with other departments.	Champion cross-functional efforts to improve quality, service and productivity.
Implement changes from above.	Initiate changes within the department.	Anticipate, initiate and respond to changes dictated by forces outside the organization.

© 1991 Achieve Global (formerly Zenger-Miller)

Source: John H. Zenger et al., "Leadership in a Team Environment." *Security Management*, September 1992, p. 29. Reprinted with permission from Achieve Global. Copyright © MCMXCI Achieve Global, Inc. All rights reserved. Not for resale.

> Leadership can be developed through comprehensive training programs, including participative management and team building theory, motivational theory, communications and decision making.

Required Leadership Skills

Table 2.8 summarizes the skill layers for law enforcement managers. McKenna (1993) stresses the need for what Tom Peters called "Management by Wandering Around" (MBWA). He gives as an example Abraham Lincoln, "America's quintessential leader," because he got into the trenches with his troops and managed directly.

Guidelines for Effective Leadership

- Know your work and those you manage.
- Know how to get and maintain cooperation.
- Learn as much as possible about decision making.
- Learn as much as possible about how to be a leader.
- Learn how to give praise and constructive criticism.
- Learn to think positively; create rather than destroy.
- Learn to handle bad situations as well as good ones.
- Know when to discipline and when to be authoritarian or democratic/participatory.
- Help your employees improve themselves. Doing so will in turn improve you. Give them responsibility, tell them your expectations and provide instructions.

- Be honest with yourself and your officers. Expect honesty from them. Maintain integrity in yourself and demand it in others.

- Use your employees' abilities. They can provide new approaches to problems. Establish two-way communication to capture the vast amount of information contained within the group. Use participation to achieve more acceptance of decisions.

- Do not oversupervise. Employees do not like managers constantly breathing down their necks.

- Remember that you are part of management, and never downgrade management or managers. If a problem exists, help solve it rather than creating a worse one.

- Keep your perception of your leadership abilities in line with subordinates' perceptions. Ask them what you can do better for them.

- If you call a meeting, make it worthwhile. Excessive meetings only to provide a façade of participation are worse than no meetings. Every meeting should produce a result.

- Treat employee's mistakes as a teaching responsibility, not a punitive opportunity.

- Develop officers who differ with you, rather than clones. Develop officers who can compensate for your own weaknesses. (The tendency is to do the opposite.)

- Be consistent. Be direct. Be honest. Be fair.

- Listen. Lead by example.

- Develop people skills.

- Be a risk taker.

Holistic Management

Police officers feel a high sense of peer identification—no call has higher priority than a fellow officer in danger. Police officers also receive an ego boost by the fact that they are readily identified by their uniforms and have certain powers above and beyond those of the average citizen.

The police manager is responsible for ensuring that the officer does not lose this feeling of ego satisfaction (e.g., after a citizen has flashed an obscene gesture to the officer) and continues to develop this sense of belonging to a unique profession geared toward helping one's fellow human beings. The **holistic management** approach views law enforcement officers and support personnel as total individuals who make up a *team*.

The Team Approach

A **team** consists of two or more people who must coordinate their activities regularly to accomplish a common task. A more in-depth definition is given by team-building experts Francis and Young (Pollar, 1997, p. 87), who state that a team is "an energetic group of people who are committed to achieving common objectives, who work well together, and who produce high-quality results." The team approach builds on the concept of **synergism,** that the group can channel individual energies to accomplish together what no individual could possibly accomplish alone—that the whole is greater than the sum of its parts (for example, when 2 + 2 = 5).

Synergism is all around us. Athletics provides countless examples of how a team, working together, can defeat a "superstar." Examples of synergism also come from the music world. Consider the power and energy produced by a top-notch marching band or symphony orchestra. Every musician must know his or her part. Individual players may have solos, but ultimately what is important is how it all sounds together.

The Wilson Learning Corporation has identified eight attributes of high-performing teams (Buchholz and Roth, p. 14).

Attributes of high-performing teams are:
- **Participative leadership**—creating an interdependency by empowering, freeing up and serving others.
- **Shared responsibility**—establishing an environment in which all team members feel as responsible as the manager for the performance of the work unit.
- **Aligned on purpose**—having a sense of common purpose about why the team exists and the function it serves.
- **High communication**—creating a climate of trust and open, honest communication.
- **Future focused**—seeing change as an opportunity for growth.
- **Focused on task**—keeping meetings focused on results.
- **Creative talents**—applying individual talents and creativity.
- **Rapid response**—identifying and acting on opportunities.

Although Buchholz and Roth were speaking of teams in the business world, the same eight attributes are likely to be present in a high-performing law enforcement agency. In addition, administrators and their subordinates can learn some lessons about teamwork from nature, for example, from geese ("The Lessons from Geese," 1994):

Fact: As each goose flaps its wings, it creates an uplift for the birds that follow. By flying in a "V" formation, the whole flock adds 71% greater flying range than if each bird flew alone. *Lesson:* People who share common directions and sense of community get where they are going quicker and easier because they are traveling on the thrust of one another.

Fact: When a goose falls out of formation, it suddenly feels the drag and resistance of flying alone. It quickly moves back into formation to take advantage of the lifting power of the bird immediately in front of it. *Lesson:* If we have as much sense as a goose, we stay in formation with those headed where we want to go. We are willing to accept their help and give help to others.

Fact: When the lead goose tires, it rotates back into formation and another goose flies to the point position. *Lesson:* It pays to take turns doing the hard tasks and sharing the leadership. As with geese, people are dependent on each others' skills, capabilities and unique arrangement of gifts, talents and resources.

Fact: The geese flying in formation honk to encourage those up front to continue their speed. *Lesson:* We need to make sure our honking is encouraging.

In groups where there is encouragement, the production is much greater. The power of encouragement (to stand by one's heart or core values or encourage the others) is the greatest quality of honking we seek.

Fact: When a goose gets sick, wounded, or shot down, two geese drop out of formation and follow it down to help and protect it. They stay with it until it dies or is able to fly again. Then they launch out with another formation or catch up with the flock. *Lesson:* If we have as much sense as geese, we will stand by each other in difficulties as well as when we are strong.

True leaders are not intimidated by outstanding team members. They do not fear for their jobs. They develop followers who will surpass them. Athletes, for example, will become coaches and train other athletes who will break their records. Advocating a gentle approach to power, Lee ("A Gentle Approach . . . ," 1998, p. 40) notes: "Power does not come from coercion or compromise. True leaders—such as Mahatma Gandhi, Nelson Mandela, and Dwight D. Eisenhower—inspire loyalty, trust, admiration, and honor, creating . . . principle-centered power."

One way to initiate action is to encourage employees at the lowest level to work together to solve their problems, with or without manager involvement. These are not highly organized, trained teams but rather groups of employees with a common problem who band together. They are organized informally from anywhere in the organization to focus on a specific problem or project. They are usually self-formed, self-managed and highly productive. When they have met the need the group dissolves.

Self-Directed Work Teams

In a classic study known as the Hawthorne Experiment, researchers proved that when management paid attention to employees and gave them a say in workplace practices and policies, overall workplace productivity increased.

A team approach is becoming more popular in departments across the country. Here officers brainstorm solutions to crime problems identified in their precinct.

Ramirez (1999, p. 21) asserts that such "empowerment" creates self-directed work teams:

> A self-directed work team consists of a group of highly trained individuals with the responsibility and authority for completing a well-defined project. . . . Top management basically leaves the teams alone as long as they meet or exceed established goals. . . .
>
> Self-directed work teams can identify opportunities, find solutions, and implement actions quickly. . . . [They] represent an important part of an organization's overall strategy for a number of reasons. First, those closest to the work know best how to perform and improve their jobs. Second, most employees want to feel "ownership" in their jobs, that they are contributing to the organization in a meaningful way. Finally, the autonomy teams enjoy provides opportunities for empowerment that individual employees usually do not have.

Leadership and COPPS

Linskey (1998, p. 3) states: "Because a cornerstone of community policing is direct involvement with people both within and outside the organization, the need for leadership ability is all the more important." DeParis (1998, p. 68) adds:

> Organizational change requires a top-down approach. Despite all the literature and anecdotes relating to the "people side" of the change equation, a fundamental element is the boss. Without executive-level commitment to the COPPS vision, and the willingness to initiate the wide-ranging structural modifications needed to initiate and sustain organizational change, the effort will fail. . . . Police leaders must be mindful that such efforts thrive only in a highly supportive environment that is created by the strategic actions of the executive, not the tactical actions of the workforce.

DeParis (p. 68) advocates that police executives take strategic steps to initiate and sustain the organizational change cycle, specifically:

- Adopt transformational leadership rather than transactional leadership.
- Move the organizational structure from the bureaucratic to the organic.
- Change the culture from risk-averse to risk-tolerant.

Engelson (1999, pp. 64, 67) suggests: "Today's law enforcement leaders have a tremendous opportunity to position their organizations to solve problems proactively, rather than to simply react. Resourceful leaders can establish value-centered organizational goals that have the support of employees and community members alike."

Summary

Managers have authority and power, which both imply the ability to coerce compliance, that is, to *make* subordinates carry out orders. Both are important to managers at all levels. However, authority relies on force or on some law or order, whereas power relies on persuasion and lacks the support of law and rule.

Basic management skills include technical skills, administrative skills, conceptual skills and people skills. Successful managers have clear goals and a commitment to excellence, feedback and support. Management by objectives

(MBO) involves managers and subordinates setting goals and objectives together and then tracking performance to ensure that the objectives are met.

Several management theories have evolved over time. McGregor's Theory X/Theory Y says that managers act toward subordinates in relation to the views they have of them. Theory X views employees as lazy and motivated by pay. Theory Y views employees as committed and motivated by growth and development. Likert's Four-System Approach to management goes from System 1, which is a traditional, authoritarian style, to System 4, which is a participative management style. Argyris's Mature Employee Theory views employees and their organization as interdependent. Blake-Mouton's Managerial/Leadership Grid describes five management styles: Authority-Compliance, Country Club, Impoverished, Middle-of-the-Road and Team Management. No one style is more apt to achieve the department's mission than another. The selected style must be matched to individual personalities.

Management typically has three levels: the top level (chief, sheriff), the middle level (captains, lieutenants) and the first-line level (sergeants).

Law enforcement executives are planners, facilitators, interfacers and interactors. They are responsible for both tactical and strategic planning. *Tactical planning* is short-term planning. *Strategic planning* is long-term planning. In addition to these roles and responsibilities, law enforcement executives typically interact with politicians, community groups, the media, executives of other law enforcement organizations and individuals and groups within the law enforcement agency itself.

Three important management problems for law enforcement are administering the budget, maintaining effective community relations and establishing and administering personnel systems and procedures, including recruitment selection, training and discipline of key employees.

The basic difference between managers and leaders is that managers focus on tasks, whereas leaders focus on people. A leader in the purest sense influences others by example. Theories about leadership include the study of traits, the classic studies conducted at Michigan and Ohio State Universities, the Managerial Grid, situational leadership and transformational leadership.

Trait theorists identified characteristics leaders possessed. The Michigan and Ohio studies determined that leaders must provide an environment that motivates employees to accomplish organizational goals. Situational leadership specifies that initially workers need support and direction. As they mature they need less direction and more support, up to the point where even support can be reduced. Transformational leadership treats employees as the organization's most valuable asset. It is employee-centered and focused on empowerment. Research has also identified several leadership styles, including autocratic, consultative, democratic or participative and laissez-faire.

Leadership can be developed through comprehensive training programs, including participative management and team building theory, communications and decision making.

Attributes of high-performing teams are participative leadership, shared responsibility, aligned on purpose, high communication, future focused, focused on task, creative talents and rapid response. Leaders must balance the need for synergism and the need for survival of the organization.

Discussion Questions

1. Who should be responsible for law enforcement planning? How should it be accomplished?
2. Why is coordination important? What are some examples?
3. What are the main problem areas of the different levels of law enforcement managers?
4. How do you develop yourself to be a law enforcement manager?
5. What is your definition of leadership?
6. What traits do you attribute to successful law enforcement leaders? If you had to select one most important characteristic of a law enforcement leader, what would you select?
7. Which style of leadership do you prefer? Which style do you perceive you use most of the time?
8. What are the merits of the holistic approach to leadership?
9. What direction should law enforcement leaders take for the future?
10. What leadership traits do you possess? What leadership traits do you need to develop?

InfoTrac College Edition Assignment

Find one journal article on *decentralization in the business world* and one journal article on *decentralization in law enforcement*. Compare the advantages each article sets forth for this change in management. Be sure to include the full reference citation along with your information. Be prepared to share your findings with the class.

References

Bennis, Warren. *Why Leaders Can't Lead: The Unconscious Conspiracy Continues.* San Francisco: Jossey-Bass, 1989.

Bergner, Laurie L. "Developing Leaders Begins at the Beginning." *The Police Chief,* Vol. LXV, No. 11, November 1998, pp. 16–23.

Blanchard, Ken. "Getting Back to Basics." *Today's Office,* January 1988, pp. 14, 19.

Braiden, Chris. "Leadership: Not What (or Where) We Think." *Law Enforcement News,* April 15, 1994, pp. 14, 16.

Breen, Michael D. "Today's Leadership Challenge for Police Executives." *The Police Chief,* Vol. LXVI, No. 3, March 1999, pp. 61–63.

Buchholz, Steve and Roth, Thomas. *Creating the High-Performance Team.* New York: John Wiley and Sons, 1987.

Burns, James MacGregor. *Leadership.* New York: Harper & Row, 1978.

Bushey, Keith D. "The Unproductive Executive." *The Police Chief,* Vol. LXVI, No. 3, March 1999, p. 71.

Cameron, Bruce. "Do You Really Want to Be a Police Chief?" *Law and Order,* Vol. 45, No. 4, April 1997, p. 1.

Cunningham, Scott A. "The Empowering Leader and Organizational Change." *The Police Chief,* August 1994, pp. 72–76.

Deming, W. Edwards. *Quality, Productivity, and Competitive Position.* Cambridge, MA: Institute of Technology, Center for Advanced Engineering Study, 1982.

DeParis, Richard J. "Organizational Leadership and Change Management: Removing Systems Barriers to Community-Oriented Policing and Problem Solving." *The Police Chief,* Vol. LXV, No. 12, December 1998, pp. 68–76.

Engelson, Wade. "Leadership Challenges in the Information Age." *The Police Chief,* Vol. LXVI, No. 3, March 1999, pp. 64–67.

Farr, James N. "Where You Lead, Will They Follow?" *Norwest Business Advantage Magazine,* Fall/Winter 1998, p. 4.

Ford, J. Kevin; Boles, Jerome G.; Plamondon, Kevin E.; and White, Jane P. "Transformational Leadership and Community Policing: A Road Map for Change." *The Police Chief,* Vol. LXVI, No. 12, December 1999, pp. 14–22.

Fulton, Roger. "Leaders Do What Managers Don't." *Law Enforcement Technology,* Vol. 25, No. 8, August 1998a, p. 82.

Fulton, Roger. "10 Leadership Traits You Should Possess." *Law Enforcement Technology,* Vol. 25, No. 9, September 1998b, p. 82.

"A Gentle Approach to Power." *Successful Meetings,* February 1998, p. 40.

Hersey, Paul and Blanchard, Kenneth H. *Management of Organizational Behavior,* 3rd ed. Englewood Cliffs, NJ: Prentice–Hall, 1977.

Hishmeh, Sam. "Total Quality Management." *Law and Order,* Vol. 46, No. 4, April 1998, pp. 92–95.

Hughes, Carroll J. "Legislative Programs Need Police Input." *Law and Order,* Vol. 47, No. 5, May 1999, pp. 63–66.

Jones, Tony L. "Autocratic vs. People-Minded Supervisors." *Law and Order,* Vol. 46, No. 5, May 1998a, pp. 32–36.

Jones, Tony. "Tactical Planning and Warning Order Use." *Law and Order,* Vol. 46, No. 3, March 1998b, pp. 82–84.

"The Lessons from Geese." Sioux Falls, SD, Central Plains Clinic, Ltd. , Employee Newsletter *Vital Sign,* January 14, 1994.

Linskey, Joseph P. "Separating the Leaders from the Managers." *Community Policing Exchange,* Phase 4, #23, November/December 1998, p. 3.

McDevitt, Daniel S. "Common Sense Leadership." *Law and Order,* Vol. 47, No. 8, August 1999a, pp. 95–96.

McDevitt, Daniel S. "Ineffective Management Strategies and Why Managers Use Them." *Law and Order,* Vol. 47, No. 7, July 1999b, pp. 143–146.

McKenna, Joseph F. "Close Encounters of the Executive Kind." *Industry Week,* September 6, 1993, pp. 13–18.

Neubauer, Ronald S. "The Role of Law Enforcement Leaders in the Legislative Process." *The Police Chief,* Vol. LXVI, No. 3, March 1999, p. 6.

"Police Leadership for the 21st Century." *The Police Chief,* Vol. LXVI, No. 3, March 1999, pp. 57–60.

Pollar, Odette. "Giving Up Control." *Successful Meetings,* January 1996, pp. 75–79.

Pollar, Odette. "Sticking Together." *Successful Meetings,* January 1997, pp. 87–90.

Pomerenke, Russ J. "Practical Applications for Developing Leadership Skills." *The Police Chief,* April 1994, pp. 36–41.

Ramirez, Stephen M. "Black Orchid Leadership." *Law and Order,* Vol. 43, No. 9, September 1995, pp. 177–179.

Ramirez, Stephen M. "Self-Directed Work Teams." *FBI Law Enforcement Bulletin,* Vol. 68, No. 8, August 1999, pp. 20–24.

Sharp, Arthur G. "Was e.e. cummings Right?" *Law and Order,* Vol. 43, No. 10, October 1995, pp. 44–47.

Smith, Scott. S. "Pulse: Talking with Ken Blanchard." *Entrepreneur,* January 2000, p. 18.

Weaver, Jim. "Supervising the Veteran Officer." *The Police Chief,* February 1990, pp. 47–49.

Weinblatt, Richard B. "So . . .You Wanna Be a Police Chief." *Police,* Vol. 21, No. 10, October 1997, pp. 26–33.

Weinblatt, Richard B. "The Shifting Landscape of Chief's Jobs: What's Changed and How to Forge a Path." *Law and Order,* Vol. 27, No. 10, October 1999, pp. 49–51.

Withham, John. "Strategic Planning for Law Enforcement." *The Police Chief,* Vol. LXV, No. 3, March 1998, pp. 23–28.

Chapter 3

Communication: A Critical Management Skill

Language is the picture and counterpart of thought.

—Mark Hopkins, builder of Central Pacific and Southern Pacific Railroads

Do You Know?

- How communication is defined?
- What the communication process involves?
- What the KISS principle is?
- What percentage of a message is conveyed by body language and tone of voice rather than words?
- What the critical factors in selecting a channel are?
- What the weakest link in the communication process is?
- How much faster people can think and listen than they can talk?
- What active listening is?
- What feedback is?
- What directions communication can flow?
- What barriers can hinder communication?
- What behaviors can discourage communication? Encourage communication?
- What four kinds of meetings are typically held?
- How to make meetings efficient and productive?

Can You Define?

abstract words
active listening
agenda
body language
channels of
   communication
communication
communication
   barriers
communication
   enhancers
communication process
decode
downward
   communication

encode
external communication
feedback
gender barrier
grapevine
horizontal
   communication
internal communication
jargon
KISS principle
lateral communication
lines of communication
news media echo effect
nonverbal
   communication

perp walk
rumor mill
standard English
tone
two-way
   communication
upward
   communication
verbal channels of
   communication
vertical
   communication
written
   communication

INTRODUCTION

Administrators are in the communication business. Of all the skills a manager/leader/supervisor needs to be effective, skill in communicating is *the* most vital. In fact, more than 50 percent of a law enforcement manager's time is spent in some form of communication. First-line supervisors usually spend about 15 percent of their time with superiors, 50 percent with subordinates and 35 percent with other managers and duties. These estimates vary, but they emphasize the importance of communication in everyday law enforcement operations.

Early law enforcement communication consisted of blowing whistles or firing weapons to attract attention. Some departments used a system of red lights on the corners of the highest structures in the community. These were turned on by the dispatcher or the local telephone operator when an officer was needed. Observing the red lights, the officer on foot or vehicle patrol then phoned the station. Officers set times to meet at certain locations on their beat to transfer information. Vehicle telecommunication and personal hand radios did not exist in those days. Technologically, law enforcement communication has come a long way.

Communication, however, is much more encompassing than messages to and from the dispatching center. Technical communications are essential to law enforcement operations, especially in emergencies. Equally important, however, are all the other kinds of communication occurring every minute.

Consider how much of a person's day is occupied with communication. Conversations, television, radio, memos, letters, e-mails, faxes, phone calls, meetings, newspapers—the list is long. Even private thoughts are communication. Every waking hour, people's minds are filled with ideas and thoughts even when they cannot communicate them. Psychologists say that nearly 100,000 thoughts pass through our minds every day, conveyed by a multitude of media.

Although technological advances have greatly expanded our communication capability, the communication process has not changed. This chapter examines that process and its variables as well as the crucial need for effective communication. This is followed by a discussion of lines of communication, including both downward and upward communication, and problems that result from poor communication. Next specific types of internal communication, including newsletters and meetings, are examined. The chapter concludes with external communication, including dealing with the media and communicating with outside agencies and the public.

Communication Defined

Communication is the complex process through which information *and understanding* are transferred from one person to another.

This process may involve written or spoken words or signs and gestures. Communication involves more than sending an idea. Successful communication occurs when the receiver's understanding of the message is the same as the sender's intent. Sounds simple enough, but often it just does not happen. People who have played the telephone game, sending a whispered message around a circle, have witnessed first hand how often messages are *not* communicated. To understand how messages can become so muddled, consider the process of communication.

The Communication Process

The basic parts of the communication process are the message, sender and receiver. The process, however, is much more complex than this, as illustrated in Figure 3.1.

A message originates in a sender's mind. The sender, having a unique knowledge base and set of values, must **encode** the message into words or gestures. The code is sent through some channel (which may distort the code). A receiver, also having a unique knowledge base and set of values, must **decode** or translate the message. The receiver may or may not provide **feedback** to the sender, that is, an indication that the message is or is not understood.

Successful communication occurs only if (1) the sender can correctly encode the message, (2) the channel is free of distortion and (3) the receiver can correctly decode the message.

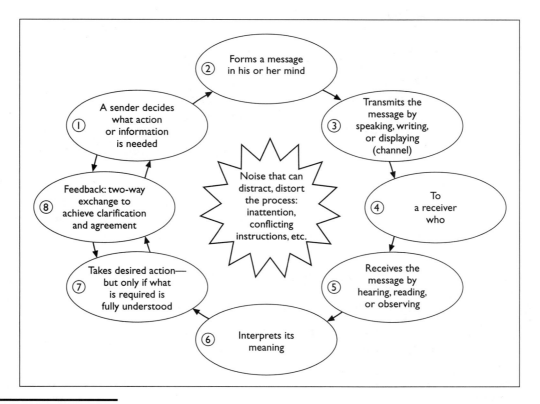

Figure 3.1
The Communication Process

The **communication process** involves a message, a sender, a channel and a receiver. It may include feedback.

Often the sender is unaware that the encoding of the message may be inappropriate. For example, a physician might refer to a person using the abbreviation "S.O.B." To medical people this quite naturally means "short of breath." Laypeople, however, would likely decode it to mean something far different.

Problems that arise from encoding and decoding from one language to another can prove quite humorous. For example, several years ago Sol Linowitz, ambassador to the Organization of American States and former chairman of Xerox Corporation, met with some Central American presidents. One president asked through an interpreter what the Xerox company did, and Linowitz gave him a very brief explanation, which the interpreter translated into Spanish. Linowitz watched with concern as the listening presidents rolled their eyes, shook their heads and then suddenly became quiet, looking at him with awe. Hastily he asked the interpreter what he had told the presidents. The interpreter replied, "I told them exactly what you said—that Xerox is a company that has invented a new method of reproduction."

The problem of translating from one language to another is illustrated by the computer translation of the familiar English phrase "out of sight, out of mind" into Russian for "invisible idiot." Another example is found in Mexico, where an "H" on the water faucet means "helado"—cold—and a "C" means "caliente"—hot.

One of the most striking examples of the devastating effects of miscommunication occurred in 1945. The Emperor of Japan and his cabinet were almost ready to accept the Allies' ultimatum to give up or be crushed. However, they wanted more time to discuss the specific terms, so they sent a message saying they were following a "mokusatsu" policy, meaning "no comment" yet. The translation, however, said that they had *ignored* the surrender demand. The result was bombs on Hiroshima and Nagasaki!

Messages do indeed often get lost in translation. Imagine that thoughts could be color coded. You color code your thoughts blue, and the person you are talking to color codes his or her thoughts yellow. What will happen to the message? It may be a mixture of sender *and* receiver preconceptions and a totally different color—green.

In other words, effective communication takes into consideration not only the message and channel but also the sender and receiver. How effectively messages are conveyed depends on the following:

- Communication skills of the sender
- Clarity of purpose
- Effectiveness of the message itself
- Appropriateness of the channel used
- Receptivity of the receiver
- Communication skills of the receiver
- Feedback

Shared frames of reference such as language, experience and cultural heritage are extremely important in communication. The smaller the shared frames of reference, the more likely miscommunication and misunderstanding will occur.

Consider the parable of the six blind men and the elephant. Each man felt a single, different part of the animal, and each came to a very different conclusion about what an elephant was like. One man felt only the sturdy side and compared the elephant to a wall; one felt only the tusk and thought an elephant was like a spear; one felt only the trunk and believed the elephant to be like a snake; one felt only a leg and envisioned a tree trunk; one felt only an ear and thought an elephant resembled a fan; and one felt only the tail and exclaimed an elephant to be like a rope. By experiencing only an isolated part of the whole creature, each man came to a very different—and very incorrect—conclusion as to what the whole beast appeared to be.

The Sender of the Message

Communication begins with a person (or group) with a message to relay. The sender of the message will have characteristics such as age, sex, educational level and past experience that may affect the message. The purpose of the message should be clearly understood. Communication usually has one or more of the following purposes: to inform, entertain, persuade or be understood.

Once the purpose is clear, the message itself must be put into language, which may be verbal (spoken or written) or nonverbal. An effective communicator has developed the basic message "sending" skills of speaking and writing, as well as the message "receiving" skills of listening and reading. The most effective communication is a two-way exchange.

The Message

The message should be in simple, **standard English,** that is, it follows the grammatical rules of American English. Whether spoken or written, the message should avoid **jargon** (the specialized language of a field) and evasive or "impressive" language. All too often people attempt to avoid an issue or to *impress* rather than *express.*

Jargon from the military illustrates this tendency. Imagine yourself the receiver of the following phrases and see whether you can decode the message in each:

- Tactical redeployment
- Manually operated impact device
- Operate in a target-rich environment
- Controlled flight into terrain

Tactical redeployment is simply retreating. A manually operated impact device is a hammer. Troops operating in a target-rich environment are outnumbered. Controlled flight into terrain is a plane crash.

The business world also uses such jargon. For example, employee theft is referred to as "inventory shrinkage" and losing money as having a "net profit revenue deficiency." Law enforcement too has its share of jargon: aforesaid, alleged perpetrator, a party later identified as John Doe, said officer proceeded to exit his squad.

The general rule is to keep it conversational and follow the KISS principle.

The **KISS principle** means: Keep It Short and Simple.

Use familiar words with only one or two syllables when possible. For example:

Prefer this:	To this:
let	afford an opportunity
find out	ascertain
end	terminate
use	utilize

Use prepositional phrases sparingly. For example:

Prefer this:	To this:
because	due to the fact that
if	in the event that
now	at the present time
today	as of this date

Omit all "empty words" and redundancies. For example:

Prefer this:	To this:
planning	advanced planning
asked	asked the question
blue	blue in color
square	square in shape
February	month of February
shrugged	shrugged his shoulders

Be especially careful of how you use modifiers. They can result in embarrassing statements such as the following:

Three cars were reported stolen by our police department yesterday.
This memo offers suggestions for handling obscene phone calls from the chief.
Stress and anxiety can be emotionally destructive to line personnel. We must get rid of them.

Tone, or the emotional effect of certain words, is another factor that greatly influences the message. Some words carry negative connotations, for example, *dirtbag, snitch, soused* and *slammer.* Be aware of such words and avoid using them when communicating professionally.

Abstract words and generalities may blur messages and result in miscommunication. A department policy that prohibits *long hair,* for example, is subject to misinterpretation because it is not sufficiently specific. The sender needs to be precise. What does *at your earliest convenience* mean? It would be clearer to give the date by which you would like something done. What does *contact me* suggest? That the person write, telephone, come in for a visit, physically bump into you or perhaps try to reach you through ESP? Be as specific as possible to ensure that your meaning is communicated clearly.

Nonverbal Messages and Body Language

Nonverbal communication is how messages may be transferred without words. Mimes, for example, use facial expressions and hand and body motions to convey their messages. Entire books are written about **body language** and interpreting the mannerisms of other people, including eye contact or lack of it, facial expressions, leg and arm movements and so on.

The majority of communication between two people comes from body language and tone of voice.

Only 7 percent comes from the words used.

Eye contact, for example, is considered by many communication experts to be one of the most important skills a person can develop. According to Giuliano (1999b, p. 104): "This ability does more than focus your eyes—it also focuses your thoughts and your presence." He (p. 104) lists the following benefits of eye contact:

- Instantly inspires trust
- Automatically bestows confidence
- Quickly buys you time
- Quietly keeps control
- Deftly wields power
- Effortlessly puts others at ease

Many nonverbal messages are obvious: A frown, a smile, a shrug, a yawn, tapping fingers, rolling eyes and so forth. Consider what the following nonverbal cues tell about a person:

- Walking—fast, slow, stomping
- Posture—rigid, relaxed
- Facial expression—wink, smile, frown
- Eye contact—direct, indirect, shifting
- Gestures—nod, shrug, finger point
- Physical spacing—close, distant
- Appearance—well groomed, unkempt

Use caution, however, when interpreting body language. For example, a trial lawyer was trying to "read" the jury just before they went to deliberation and was very concerned that one man's posture—arms folded in front of him—spelled trouble for his client. However, after the verdict was read in favor of his client, the lawyer approached the juror and explained that he had expected a different response, given the man's folded arms. The juror simply replied, "I've got a big belly. A man's gotta put his arms somewhere."

Channels of Communication

Technology has expanded the **channels of communication,** or the means by which messages are conveyed.

Critical factors to consider in selecting a channel include speed and opportunity for feedback. Expense is also important.

Verbal Channels

Among the most common **verbal channels of communication** are one-on-one conversations, telephone conversations, radio dispatch, interviews, meetings, news conferences and speeches. Verbal channels are often selected because they are fast and they allow for feedback and are relatively inexpensive.

One-on-one conversations are usually the most common form of communication in a law enforcement agency. Verbal communication is often used for reprimanding employees because it is more personal and allows for feedback. Such reprimands may be followed up by a written memo or report.

The *telephone* is effective where feedback is needed immediately. It is a readily available, **two-way communication** with feedback occurring during the process. On the other hand, telephone conversations are usually not recorded and may involve excessive time. Further, one person may have interrupted the other. Finally, the message may be misunderstood because it is only auditory. Important visual clues are missing.

Cellular phones (CPs) have improved the convenience and immediate availability of verbal communication channels. Schuiteman (1999, p. 52) notes: "CPs increase officer/deputy work efficiency and productivity, provide a secure means of transmitting sensitive information, and increase the sense of security that officers/deputies have while working." As with other phone communication, however, valuable visual clues are absent.

Meetings and *seminars* also provide for two-way communication. These channels allow for an open exchange of information and ideas and for feedback. However, the timing may be bad for some, meetings and seminars may consume an inordinate amount of time, and sometimes a few individuals dominate. Conducting effective meetings is discussed later in this chapter.

A disadvantage of two-way verbal channels is that they are temporary: There is no permanent record of them. This disadvantage can be negated by taping the communication. In fact, most law enforcement agencies record all calls that come into the dispatcher.

One-way verbal communication includes audiocassettes, videos and television. Such channels are well suited to conveying information—training, for example—but are limited in that they do not allow feedback.

Written Channels

Written communication includes notes, memos, letters, e-mails, faxes, reports, manuals, bulletins, policies and the like. Written communication has the advantage of being permanent but the disadvantage of being slower and usually more expensive. The primary disadvantage of written communication, however, is lack of immediate feedback.

Reports can be prepared at the convenience of the sender, allowing time to organize and select the appropriate words. Reports can also be widely disseminated. On the other hand, they are one-way communication, impersonal, fairly expensive and may be misinterpreted.

Memos are more immediate and less expensive, provide a permanent record and can be widely disseminated. Like reports, however, they are impersonal, one-way communication.

The *fax* machine has greatly enhanced the efficiency of written communication. Fax messages are rapid, can be acknowledged and allow for feedback almost as rapidly as in verbal communication.

E-mail is another means of rapid communication. In fact, e-mail is quickly becoming the most popular form of communication in the business world because it enhances the lines of communication between managers and employees and between co-workers of all levels. Dees (1999, p. 65) states: "Electronic mail (e-mail) has become such an essential part of business and personal communications that someone without an e-mail address is branded as a Luddite, and the absence of this information on a business card is like failing to include a telephone number." Sharp (1999, p. 79) adds: "E-mail provides some great opportunities for law enforcement. It can improve internal and inter-department communications, enhance contacts with citizens and vendors, and ultimately lead to improved service to the public."

E-mail is not without its perils, however, as Field (2000, p. 49) cautions: "If implemented with no guiding principles or organizational agreement, electronic mail can be a potential minefield for leaders." How so? Field explains:

> Electronic mail represents a step on the path to virtual human relations. Electronic communications are seductive and will distance people from one another unless organizations assume control with specific plans and organization-based agendas. If organizations fail to preserve traditional internal communications, they risk the disappearance of critical, traditional organizational dynamics.

The Receiver of the Message

A key factor in any communication is the receiver of the message. Like the sender, the receiver has certain characteristics that influence the way in which the message is received, including age, sex, educational level and past experiences.

First, consider the receiver from the sender's perspective. Who is the message for? How receptive is the receiver likely to be? What distractions may have to be overcome? Does the receiver have the necessary background and ability to understand/act on the message? What prejudices or values might hinder or enhance the communication?

Next, consider the receiver from the receiver's perspective. The most important responsibility the receiver of a verbal message has is to *listen*. Unfortunately, listening is one of the most neglected yet most important skills in communication.

Listening

Ryan (1999, p. 30) maintains:

> Each of us has a deep and innate desire to be listened to. It is a need so fundamental that when it is consistently denied in either adults or children it can lead to mental illness. Conversely, when our desire to be heard and understood is fulfilled, we are energized, uplifted, more creative and significantly more productive.

As important as listening is, many people lack good listening skills. Jenkins (1999, p. 59) reports that "75 percent of what we hear is heard incorrectly; and of the remaining 25 percent, we forget 75 percent within weeks."

The weakest link in the communication process is *listening*.

It is much more difficult to listen to a recorded message than to listen to someone speaking directly to you. For example, a secretary typing a letter dictated by the chief of police began the final paragraph with the sentence: "I hardly agree with your decision." Unfortunately, what the chief had said was: "I heartily agree with your decision." Even more unfortunately, the chief did not proofread the letter but simply signed it. A totally incorrect message was delivered.

Unfortunately, few people have ever taken a course in listening. We were taught to speak, read and write, but we simply *assume* we know how to listen. Yet most people are *not* good listeners. One of the main reasons is the gap between speaking and listening rates. The average person speaks at a rate of approximately 125 words per minute but listens at about 400 words per minute. This gap lets people daydream or begin to think about other topics.

People listen and think four times faster than they talk.

Preoccupation is another common problem. People often "hear" the sounds but do not "listen" to the message; instead, they evaluate what they are hearing and concentrate on how they are going to respond. It is almost impossible to think, speak and listen at the same time.

Poor listening habits are practiced and become entrenched. Other factors that affect listening include the person's attitude toward the speaker and/or the topic, the location, the time available, noise and other distractions and lack of interest or boredom.

A Test of Listening Skills

University of Minnesota professor and listening expert Ralph Nichols suggests 10 questions to test listening skills. Answer *yes* or *no* to each of the following:

1. Do you try to make others think you are listening to them, whether you are or not?

2. Are you easily distracted from what a person is saying?

3. Do you take notes on what a person is saying?

4. Do you assess the quality of what a person will say by appearance or how the person talks?

5. We know that a person thinks four times as fast as another person talks. Do you use this excess time to think about other things, such as your reply?

6. Are you receptive to facts and figures rather than concepts and ideas in a speech?

7. Do certain words or phrases "turn you off" so that you cannot listen clearly to what is being said?

8. If you do not understand or are annoyed by what a speaker is saying, do you question the speaker?

9. Do you try to avoid hearing something that you decide would take too much time and trouble to figure out?

10. If you decide that a speaker is not going to say anything worthwhile, do you "tune out" and think about other things?

Each *no* scores 10 points. A score of 80 is excellent.

To be an effective listener, look at the speaker. Jenkins (p. 62) asserts: "Listening is sometimes inseparable from looking. Being attuned to the non-verbal clues of a speaker's delivery and attitude can help you understand the total message of a conversation or a speech." Think about the words and the implied message. Ask questions to clarify, but do not interrupt, and remain objective.

It is often said that everyone talks, but few listen. The results when people do *not* listen can be disastrous.

The Importance of Listening

Law enforcement officers need to receive information more than they need to give it. A major portion of their time is spent receiving information for forms and reports, taking action in arrests, eliciting information in interviews and interrogations and many other duties requiring careful listening. According to Keller (1999, p. 72):

> Listening is a fundamental aspect of effective communication. . . . When 282 members of the Academy of Certified Administrative Managers were asked to list the skills most crucial for managerial ability, "active listening" was rated number one and placed in the "supercritical" category.

Excellent listening skills are required for officers who interview witnesses to accidents. Confusion usually abounds at such scenes, making listening very difficult.

Active listening includes concentration, full attention and thought.

Listening skill *can* be improved. Opportunities for practice occur daily. Pay attention to those with whom you are speaking, show appropriate responses to what they are saying, listen for feelings as well as the content, look at and listen to body language, and respond directly to what is being said. Active listening is hard work, but it pays off.

Recognize that in communication, receivers and senders of messages constantly switch roles. The effective communicator is skilled not only at speaking (or writing) but also at listening (and reading).

Feedback

I know that you believe that you understand what you think I said, BUT I am not sure you realize that what you heard is not what I meant! Without feedback, communication is one way.

Feedback is the process by which the sender knows if the receiver has understood the message.

Two people may talk and yet neither may understand what the other is saying. Most feedback is direct and oral. Two people discuss something, one makes a statement, and the other responds. Head nodding or shaking, smiling, grimacing, raised eyebrows, yawns—all are forms of feedback. The better the feedback, the better the communication.

Internal Lines of Communication

Lines of communication are inherent in an organizational structure. Just as authority flows downward and outward, so can communication. However, communication should also flow upward.

Communication may be downward, upward (vertical) or lateral (horizontal). It may also be internal or external. Most effective communication is two way.

Downward communication includes directives from managers and supervisors, either spoken or written. When time is limited and an emergency exists, communication often *must* flow downward and one way. In such cases, subordinates must listen and act on the communication.

Top-level law enforcement managers issue orders, policies, rules and regulations, memos, orders of the day and so on. These communications are delivered primarily downward and sometimes laterally. Communication from this level filters down and is understood by receivers according to personal knowledge, training, competence and experience.

Middle-level management and the on-line supervisors also issue directives, roll-call information, explanations of directives from higher-level managers, information for department newsletters or roll-call bulletins, letters, memos and instructions. Again, such communication is distributed downward and laterally.

Upward communication includes requests from subordinates to their superiors. It should also include input on important decisions affecting subordinates. Effective managers give all subordinates a chance to contribute ideas, opinions and values as decisions are made.

Another critical form of upward communication is found in operational reports. The major portion of law enforcement operations is in the field at the lowest level of the hierarchy. Most investigations, traffic citations, arrests, form completion and other activity is at this basic level. These actions eventually travel both from the bottom up and laterally throughout the organization. Communication may take the form of reports, charts, statistics, daily summaries or logs. All are extremely important.

Downward and upward communication are also called **vertical communication**. **Lateral** or **horizontal communication** includes communication among managers on the same level and among subordinates on the same level. **Internal communication** includes all of the preceding as well as messages from dispatch to officers in the field—among the most important communication of any law enforcement agency.

Subordinate Communication

Communicating with subordinates is an essential managerial responsibility. Managers and supervisors accomplish organizational goals through their subordinates. Employees want to know what is going on in the organization, to be "in the know." If employees do not know what the administration expects, they cannot support organizational goals and objectives.

The Grapevine

In addition to the formal channels of communication established by an organization, informal channels also exist. Commonly referred to as the **grapevine,** these informal channels frequently hinder cooperation and teamwork.

Keller (p. 73) cautions: "Never lose sight of the power of the grapevine. If you fail to keep your word with an employee, other employees are likely to find out about it quickly, resulting in a severe blow to your credibility." Managers and supervisors must realize that even if they *wanted* to stop the grapevine, they could not. In fact, directing people not to talk about an issue often ensures that the word will spread more quickly. Thus it is important for managers to make the grapevine work for them rather than against them.

The term **rumor mill,** commonly applied to the grapevine, suggests some of the problems associated with informal channels of communication. The grapevine is strongest in organizations in which information is not openly shared. Employees begin to guess and speculate when they do not know—hence the rumors. One way to positively influence the grapevine is to provide staff with *all* information needed to function efficiently, effectively and happily. This includes letting people know the bad as well as the good. Do not let the grapevine beat you to informing people of bad news that affects them.

The Importance of Communication Skills to Managers

As Keller (p. 72) sums up: "Clearly, communication is the most important tool a leader has at his disposal; effective, accurate communication touches all aspects of leadership."

It happens to everyone at some time—"sticking your foot in your mouth." Giuliano (1999a, p. 96) offers some actions to help minimize the effects of such verbal faux pas:

- Forethought—To avoid the blunder in the first place, think before you speak.
- Apologize—Say you are sorry and "What was I thinking?"
- Redirect—Immediately change the subject, yet maintain eye contact to help you focus on the new conversation and help others in the room feel more comfortable.
- Move on—You blew it, you apologized, and you relieved the embarrassment of others as quickly as you could. Put it behind you, relax, and continue.

Lack of communication is often an obstacle to correcting problems. Without effective communication, people do not know what is expected of them or how well they are doing. Managers and subordinates may not be able to agree on the quality of services they provide. Equipment needs may not be revealed. Animosities may fester.

Consequences of not communicating well include low morale, increased union disputes, reduced work quality and quantity and sometimes even lawsuits. The list is endless.

Barriers to Communication

Communication barriers include:

- Time.
- Volume of information.
- Tendency to say what we think others want to hear.
- Failure to select the best word.
- Prejudices (sender and/or receiver).
- Strained sender-receiver relationships.

Time is important to everyone, especially law enforcement officers and managers. Communication systems have greatly enhanced the ability to pass information from one person or organization to another. On the other hand, computers, fax machines, copiers and other devices have deluged subordinates and managers alike with information. To cope, managers must be selective in what they personally take action on and what they delegate to others.

Another obstruction to communication is the tendency to say what we think others want to hear. This is especially true when the information is negative and can be dangerous because the person may form opinions or act on insufficient information. State all the facts about a situation so the receiver can correctly interpret them.

A third obstacle is the varied meanings words may have. For example, the word *victim* may arouse concern and empathy, but it may also arouse annoyance and pity. Select your words carefully to convey precisely what you mean. In one department a police chief sent a memo to all officers asking for suggestions on how to improve retention. He received numerous ideas on how to help officers improve their memories. What he wanted, however, was thoughts on how to keep officers from quitting the department.

Another important obstacle to communications is prejudice. Bias against a certain race, religion, nationality, gender, sexual preference or disability can create tremendous communication barriers.

Strained sender-receiver relationships can seriously hinder communication. For example, a rookie's suggestion to a field training officer of a "better" way of searching a suspect based on the latest research is not likely to be well received. It will in fact probably be cut short with a comment such as, "Who's teaching who here?"

The Gender Barrier

Much attention is now focusing on significant differences in how men and women communicate. Such differences often create a **gender barrier.** Table 3.1 summarizes gender differences in communication.

Table 3.1
Conversational Styles: Gender Tendencies

Listening	
Male	**Female**
Irregular eye contact	Uninterrupted eye contact
Infrequent nodding	Frequent nodding
Infrequent humming sounds	Frequent humming sounds
May continue another activity while speaking	Usually stops other activities while speaking
Interrupts in order to speak	Waits for pauses in order to speak
Questions are designed to analyze speaker's information	Questions are designed to elicit more information

Speaking	
Male	**Female**
Few pauses	Frequent pauses
May abruptly change topic	Connects information to previous speaker's information
Speaks until interrupted	Stops speaking when information delivered
Speaks louder than previous speaker	Uses same volume as previous speaker
Frequent use of "I" and "me"	Frequent use of "us" and "we"
Personal self-disclosure rarely included	Personal self-disclosure often included
Humor delivered as separate jokes or anecdotes	Humor interwoven into discussion content
Humor often based on kidding or making fun of others	Humor rarely based on kidding or making fun of others

Source: Peg Meier and Ellen Foley, "War of the Words." Minneapolis/St. Paul. *Star Tribune, First Sunday,* January 6, 1991. Reprinted with permission of the *Star Tribune.*

According to Meyers (1999, p. 46): "The dynamics of gender and the problems that arise from male/female differences have grabbed the attention of men and women everywhere." Noting that although the business world has made much progress with regard to gender equity, Meyers states that men and women are still worlds apart in the way they communicate (p. 48):

> Men and women use language as a means to accomplish different goals: Men use talk primarily to preserve independence and negotiate and maintain status in a hierarchical social order, while women tend to use the language of conversation as a means for establishing connections and negotiating relationships. . . .
>
> Men tend to rely on factual information, speak in direct, solution-oriented terms, and draw the group's focus to themselves to establish their place in the group. . . .
>
> Because most men are comfortable being direct, they tend to interrupt others, especially women, more than women interrupt them. . . .
>
> An interruption may not even be intended, and yet it creates anger and tension.

Obstacles within the Process

Recall that the communication process consists of a sender, a channel, a receiver and, ideally, feedback. Problems can arise within any aspect of this process.

The *message* may be *improperly encoded.* The sender must translate or *encode* the message accurately, unambiguously and precisely, avoiding complex language. It must get past the sender's prejudices, limitations and values. Nonverbal cues must support, not contradict, the message.

Further, the sender must not *misuse communication channels.* An obvious example is the department bulletin board, a potentially powerful communication channel. All too often, however, material is posted and simply left, long past its effective "life." Cluttered bulletin boards lose their communicating power. Other examples are dull, one-way meetings and department newsletters that do little more than report sports news and social events.

A more critical example is one-on-one communication between managers and subordinates that becomes one-way and primarily negative/disciplinary. Most one-on-one communication should be *positive.* It should not be limited to official business but should also include more personal or casual topics to let subordinates know they are important as both individuals and employees.

"Noise in the channel" may seriously interfere with communication. This may be actual physical noise, such as an airplane flying overhead, a phone ringing or more than one person talking at once. An uncomfortable room—too hot, too cold, unpleasant odors—can also detract from communication.

Written communication can be hindered by poor copy quality, messy copy with lots of cross-through and write-overs, illegible handwriting, faint print and so on. Such "noise" in the channel not only interferes physically with the message, but it often annoys the receiver, further hindering effective communication.

Poor timing is another common obstacle. If the receiver is upset, angry, rushed, tired, hurt, preoccupied or unprepared, the message may not be communicated.

The *message* may be *improperly decoded.* The receiver must translate or *decode* the message accurately and precisely. The encoded message must pass through not only the personality screen of the sender but also the perception screen of the receiver.

Poor *listening* habits are a prime factor in improperly decoding messages. The criticality of listening in communication has already been discussed. It bears repeating. Poor listening habits are a *major* cause of communication breakdowns. Listeners may be defensive, too emotionally involved or distracted.

Closely related to poor listening habits are *lack of trust, credibility* and *candor.* If people feel they cannot believe what someone tells them, they may misinterpret or ignore messages. For example, if a manager tells subordinates that they will be getting new uniforms and they do not, the subordinates will be less likely to believe the next "promise" and question the motive behind the promise as well. Another common example is the lack of credibility people may place in some politicians. What they say to get elected and what they actually do are often quite different.

Behavioral Obstacles to Communication

Six behaviors tend to stop communication: judging, superiority, certainty, controlling, manipulation and indifference (Buchholz and Roth, 1987, pp. 80–82).

Buchholz and Roth note: "These behavior modes are often engaged in innocently and unconsciously, certainly not deliberately, by well-meaning people."

Judging seriously interferes with listening. "You're wrong." Rather than focusing on the potential of what someone is saying, the person who judges focuses on discrediting what the speaker is presenting.

In a hierarchical organization, *superiority* or an "I'm-more-important-than-you" attitude can seriously hinder communication. This may occur not only between managers and subordinates but also between certain divisions, such as detectives and patrol. One-upsmanship or flaunting a position of authority hinders communication.

Certainty or the inability to recognize a possible mistake is common with the person who is positive of the truth or accuracy of his or her information. "My mind's made up. Don't confuse me with the facts."

This is illustrated by the young man who went to see a psychiatrist to learn to cope with being dead. This young man was certain he was dead, but no one would believe him. The psychiatrist, eager to help the man, asked him, "Do dead people bleed?"

When the young man answered, "Of course not," the psychiatrist asked for the young man's hand and for permission to stick his finger with a pin. The young man consented and, as the psychiatrist expected, the finger bled. Amazed, the young man exclaimed, "I'll be darned, dead people do bleed!"

Logic seldom works on those who are certain of the "facts." As an old saying astutely notes: "It ain't the things you don't know what gets you into trouble; it's the things you know for sure what ain't so."

Controlling also hinders communication: "Let me tell you how to do your job." Many managers believe their role is to tell their subordinates what to do and how. Few people appreciate such control.

Manipulation is characterized by the "gotcha" mentality. Manipulation involves communicating with hidden motives to get people to unknowingly agree or act in a certain way. The manipulator "uses" people.

Indifference often accompanies a feeling of superiority and a lack of concern for others. "You're not important. What you think doesn't matter." You can unwittingly convey this attitude by a simple act such as answering a phone call while talking with another person.

According to Buchholz and Roth (p. 82), other behaviors that inhibit communication include "facial expressions such as frowning or raising eyebrows, shaking the head, yawning, sighing, leaning back, avoiding eye contact, gazing around the room, taking irrelevant notes, or changing the subject."

Communication Enhancers

Communication enhancers are often the opposite of actions that cause the obstruction. To overcome the obstacle of communication overload, establish priorities. Not all communications need to be available to all employees. The main criteria should be whether the employees need the information to perform assigned tasks and whether it would improve morale. Overloading with immaterial communications will restrict employees' performance and productivity.

If a message promises further information, follow through. Use and encourage free and open two-way communication whenever possible. Emphasize brevity and accuracy.

Obstacles to communication are difficult to eliminate, but many can be minimized by concentrating on what you say and write. Communicating openly and clearly reduces informal communications such as the grapevine and rumor mill. When you look at the barriers within the communication process itself, certain guidelines become obvious.

Properly encode messages. Say what you mean (and mean what you say). Watch word choice. Consider the receiver of the message. Match nonverbal communication with the verbal message. Make sure messages are accurate and timely. Always be open, candid, honest and sincere. Such information can do much to eliminate rumors.

Select the best communication channel. Focus on one-on-one, face-to-face communication, which is the most powerful channel available. Although this takes more time than a bulletin or memo, it is decidedly more effective.

Behaviors That Encourage Communication

Just as barriers within the communication process suggest guidelines for effective communication, the six behaviors that inhibit communication have counterparts: describing, equality, openness, problem-orientation, positive intent and empathy (Buchholz and Roth, pp. 82–85).

Describing is the opposite of judging: "I see it like this." "I hear you saying . . . ." The speaker presents feelings or perceptions that do not judge others.

Equality is the opposite of superiority: "We're on the same team. We're in this together." People's differences are acknowledged as providing strength through diversity.

Openness is the opposite of certainty: "What do you think? Who has an idea? You've got a good point there. You may be right!" Investigating options rather than steadfastly clinging to *the* solution greatly enhances communication.

People work together toward solutions rather than choosing up sides. In effect people agree to disagree without being disagreeable.

Problem orientation is the opposite of controlling: "We're going to have to work this out. We're on the spot and need to come up with an answer." Encourage people to share their perspectives on an issue.

Positive intent is the opposite of manipulation: "Here's why I'm asking you to do this." People react positively to situations they believe are accurately represented. They resent being used or subjected to hidden agendas.

Empathy is the opposite of indifference: "I understand how you feel. I appreciate your concern. I care." The person with empathy can identify with other people's problems, share their feelings and accept their reaction.

Other behaviors that can enhance communication, according to Buchholz and Roth (p. 85), are "leaning forward, smiling, nodding, having direct eye contact, sticking to the subject under discussion, and paying full attention."

Communication at Meetings

It has been said that meetings are gatherings where minutes are kept and hours are lost. The 3M Meeting Management Institute has developed a matrix by which managers can determine the cost of their meetings (see Table 3.2).

According to McArthur (1999, p. 51): "Meetings—at least some of them—are necessary. Ideally, they can be an efficient way to get people with differing points of view or areas of expertise to exchange information and ideas." Imperato (1999, p. D6) adds: "There is a legitimate social component to meetings. You should never overlook the social side of work rituals—even in meetings that are 'all business.'" Indeed:

> A good meeting brings people together, facilitates decision making, helps others take responsibility, energizes participants and helps build strong work teams ("Meeting Magic," 1998, p. 5).

Yet too many meetings are held simply because they are part of the weekly routine or because other options (such as sending e-mails or memos) are ignored. As San Francisco 49ers head coach Steve Mariucci ("From the Top,"

Table 3.2
Hourly Cost of a Meeting

How much employees make per hour, multiplied by the number of employees attending a meeting, yields the price of the conference.

Annual Salary of Attendees	Number of Attendees				
	6	8	10	15	20
$100,000	$600	$800	$1,000	$1,500	$2,000
$80,000	480	640	800	1,200	1,600
$60,000	360	480	600	900	1,200
$40,000	240	320	400	600	800
$20,000	120	160	200	300	400

Source: 3M Meeting Management Institute. Reproduced by permission of and copyrighted by Minnesota Mining and Mfg. Co.

1999, p. 59) explains: "I think variety is very important when it comes to leading meetings. One thing I don't do, though, is meet with people every single day. Meeting too much is overkill, and sessions can become boring and predictable."

Meetings do serve an important function and need not be time wasters. The keys are planning and effective communication. Departments typically have four types of meetings.

Types of meetings:

- Informational
- Opinion seeking
- Problem solving
- New-idea seeking

Knowing what type of meeting to plan helps to set appropriate goals for the meeting. Every meeting should have a clearly defined purpose and anticipated outcome. Some meetings serve two or more purposes. Before scheduling a meeting, however, explore alternatives: Is group action needed? Could the desired results be accomplished by one-on-one interactions? A phone call? A memo? E-mail?

Meeting Preparation

One key to successful meetings is a carefully prepared **agenda** or outline, usually given to participants *before* the meeting. The agenda should have a time frame, including beginning and ending. Ideally, the ending time will make it difficult to stay beyond what is scheduled, for example, the end of a shift. Put the most important items first in case time runs out. Commenting on the benefits of advanced agenda distribution, McDonald (1999, p. 29) notes:

> What you do with attendees *before* a meeting is as important as what happens at the get-together. Here's why: The more you crank up their thinking before they get to the event, the better prepared they are to grab information during the event.

In addition to creating an agenda, do the following to ensure a smooth, efficient meeting:

- Schedule the meeting room.
- Prepare handouts and visuals.
- Make name tents and arrange seating if appropriate.
- Check the room arrangement and temperature.
- Check audiovisual equipment to be used.

The meeting room should be large enough, well lit and free of distractions. Handouts and visual aids should look professional. Seating is usually most effective in a U- or an O-shape. Do not overlook the potential value of assigning seats. Name tents are especially helpful if not all participants know each other. Be sure audiovisual equipment is functioning properly. Focus the overhead projector. Be sure flipcharts have ample paper and that colored pens are available.

Conducting the Meeting

Start on time. End on time. Starting on time is a must. People quickly learn when a manager does not begin meetings promptly and will tend to come late as a result. To counteract lateness, close the door so that those arriving late will be obvious. Some managers go so far as to lock the door.

Assign someone to take minutes or tape-record the meeting. At the beginning of the meeting, ask whether the agenda and schedule are acceptable. Make adjustments if necessary and then stick to the agenda and time schedule.

Agree on whether to allow smoking or interruptions and whether to provide refreshments or a break, and agree on task needs versus social needs.

To facilitate open communication and group participation, first be aware of bad habits people may display at meetings, including speechifying, repeating the same points, interrupting, speaking without being recognized by the chair, never contributing, acting as a know-it-all or as the "we tried it and it didn't work" historian each time an idea is presented, sidetracking and changing issues.

Both the chair and participants can change such counterproductive behavior in several ways. Determine norms about how meetings will proceed. Require recognition from the chair. Outlaw personal attacks. Read the preceding list of counterproductive behaviors and ask everyone to refrain from them. Talk to the worst disrupters before the meeting and ask for their cooperation. Give disrupters special tasks or roles, such as taking minutes.

Induce discussion of the meeting process during the meeting. Discuss only behavior, never personalities. Ask the "Yes, but . . ." disrupter to give positive answers and solutions rather than objections. Stop the meeting and ask people who are engaged in side conversations to share their discussions with the entire group. Try to draw out those who do not voluntarily contribute to discussions. Smile and be reassuring.

A Model for Action

Group process theorists have created many models to explain group dynamics. The models explain the roles different individuals play in making a meeting work. In these models titles are attached to the roles, such as the *initiator* who gets things started, the *harmonizer* who smooths disputes and the *summarizer* who pulls together the pieces so everyone can understand them.

Another model views participants at a meeting as builders. The *cranes* are the people who get ideas and who lift people up. Their ideas are sometimes lofty, but they help the group reach new heights. The *bulldozers* are those people who make things happen. They are able to overcome obstacles so the group can move ahead. The *backhoes* are those who carry a lot of weight and move things around to new places. They look forward while still making changes in the present. The *dump trucks* are those people who remove the rubble and debris from a project. They are willing to carry burdens others do not want and to haul them away. The *graders* are the people who smooth the surface. They apply the final polish to ideas and level the path to progress. The *shovel-leaners* are those who are part of the crew but do not do much. They like to be included and to watch but are not interested in helping. Finally, there is the *chief,* the manager, the one who assigns the tasks and keeps everyone on task, encouraging, praising and motivating.

Ending the Meeting

One part of meetings that is often overlooked is the windup. Before closing a meeting, summarize the main points discussed. Review new ideas, assign tasks and set deadlines. Following the meeting, prepare the minutes and distribute them as soon as practical.

Keys for effective meetings:

- Prepare in advance—have an agenda.
- Start and stop on time.
- Stick to the agenda.
- Facilitate open communication and participation.

Newsletter

Newsletters can be an important form of interdepartmental communication. A newsletter can address the personal side of policing. For instance, it can focus on achievements of people within the department, sworn and civilian, acknowledge and welcome new employees and cover topics such as weddings, births, deaths and community activities and contributions.

External Communication

External communication includes all interactions with agencies and people outside the department, including the news media and citizen contacts. Law enforcement agencies must effectively interact with other components of the criminal justice system, that is, the courts and correctional services. Law enforcement agencies must also interface with other social services, as well as with other departments of the jurisdiction they serve, as noted in Chapter 2.

Communication with the Media

Brooks (1999, p. 22) notes: "The news media have a distinct role in a democracy to oversee the actions of the traditional three branches of government and thereby prevent abuses of power by those branches." Consequently, the media can be friend or foe, depending on the effectiveness of the channels of communication.

Difficulties in dealing with the press usually arise from the need to balance the public's right to know, the First Amendment right to freedom of the press, and the need of law enforcement agencies to protect the Sixth Amendment rights of those accused of crimes, as well as the privacy of crime victims. Nonetheless, Rosenthal (1999b, p. 16) notes: "Law enforcement can and *should* work *with* the media, so the media don't work *on* law enforcement. Cooperation works. Confrontation doesn't." Hall (1998, p. 24) echoes the need for police administrators to "manage the press in a crisis before the press manages them." As one media consultant to law enforcement puts it: "We can't control what the news media does, so we need to do the best job we can. We need to invite reporters into our offices and educate them about law enforcement" (Hoffmann, 1998, p. 97).

Some law enforcement agencies have a policy that line officers and supervisors are not to issue statements or opinions about any activities or conditions related to their duties to newspaper reporters or radio or television stations.

Such requests are to be referred to middle management, who may in turn refer them to a public relations department. Other law enforcement executives claim that every officer is a "public information officer."

Whatever decisions you make regarding communication with the media, you must clearly define policies and procedures, such as those the New York City Police Department uses (Table 3.3). Clearly formulated policies and procedures for communicating with the media are necessary to effectively conduct agency business as well as for a sound public relations/community relations program. Woodall (1998, p. 72) states:

> A complete media Standard Operating Procedure will establish authority, delegate responsibility and define the rules to be followed when dealing with reporters and photographers from newspapers, radio and television. A solid media SOP will be a valuable asset, particularly when the agency must confront a high-visibility case and intense media coverage.

It is also helpful to know about media ethics codes. Rosenthal (1999a, p. 26) lists the four main principles of the *Society of Professional Journalists Code of Ethics* as: "Seek truth and report it; minimize harm; act independently; be accountable." The implications for law enforcement are that: "If you know more about the media's ethical standards, you'll be in a better position to insist that they play by those rules—*their* rules—and give you the fair shake that you're entitled to."

Table 3.3
New York City Police Department's Press Release Policy

Guidelines in Criminal Cases

The following information should be made available for publication, when and after an arrest is made:

(a) The accused's name, age, residence, employment, marital status and similar background information.

(b) The substance or text of the charge such as a complaint, indictment, information and, where appropriate, the identity of the complainant.

(c) The identity of the investigating and arresting agency and length of the investigation.

(d) The circumstances immediately surrounding the arrest, including the time and place of arrest, resistance, pursuit, possession and use of weapons and a description of items seized at the time of arrest.

NOTE: P.G. 116-22 prohibits disclosure of identity of children under 16 who are arrested or complainants. Victims of sex crimes should likewise not be identified to the press.

Pretrial disclosure of the following information may cause substantial risk of prejudice to a defendant and thereby adversely affect a case. For that reason, the following information SHOULD NOT be released without first clearing with the Public Information Division.

(a) Statements as to the character or reputation of an accused person or prospective witness.

(b) Admissions, confessions or the contents of a statement or alibi attributable to an accused person.

(c) The performance or results of tests or the refusal of the accused to take a test.

(d) Statements concerning the credibility or anticipated testimony of prospective witnesses.

(e) The possibility of a plea of guilty to the offense charged or to a lesser offense, or other disposition.

(f) Opinions concerning evidence or argument in the case, whether or not it is anticipated that such evidence or argument will be used at trial.

Source: Courtesy of the New York City Police Department.

Sometimes media involvement alters the way law enforcement performs. For example, intense media coverage of high-profile cases may have far-reaching effects on other, more low-profile incidents and, consequently, affect how the entire criminal justice system handles such matters. As Surette (1999, pp. 601-602) explains:

> In high-profile trials, media attention affects the actions of attorneys, witnesses, judges, jurors, and the audience involved with the publicized case. High-profile trials also influence the everyday practices of law enforcement and adjudication, and affect the outcomes of numerous low-profile cases. . . . When the media or public makes noise about certain problems such as prostitution and gambling, the police and prosecution respond, at least for awhile, but sooner or later the patterns of law enforcement return to normal.
>
> This effect, herein termed a **news media echo effect,** therefore, occurs when a highly publicized criminal case results in a shift in processing for similarly charged but nonpublicized cases [boldface added].

Parrish (1993, pp. 91–93) maintains that officers should be aware of the pitfalls of meeting the press at the scene of a crime or other police incident. Even if the department has a public information officer or the chief meets the press later, the media at the scene will want information. Following are 10 tips Parrish suggests for dealing with the media, no matter what size the department:

1. Be aware of cameras. Just because you do not see one does not mean they are not present. Citizens with video cameras are prevalent, hoping to catch something they can sell to the media.

2. Notify supervisors of any negative camera pictures taken. This will give supervisors time to prepare an answer.

3. Do not use the cop-out, "No comment." Learn to say the same thing creatively. If a reporter asks if a serial killer is on the loose, respond by saying that the investigation is just starting. You are not refusing to talk; you are just not giving any information.

4. Explain your actions. If you cannot give an answer, explain why: it may compromise the integrity of the investigation.

5. Learn to say, "I don't know." Maybe you just arrived at the scene a few minutes ahead of the press and honestly do not know. But provide information as to when or where the information can be obtained later.

6. Be aware of media deadlines. The media lives by deadlines.

7. Be careful of live TV shots. Live shots may compromise the location of a SWAT team at the scene. Live shots may catch you in an embarrassing moment.

8. The media should have the same access as the public. If the media is obeying the law, let them take pictures. However, be aware that pictures may show only part of the incident, the part unfavorable to the police. The picture may only show officers wrestling a person to the ground and not show what led up to the arrest, but that can be explained.

A Virginia State Police sergeant holds a news conference regarding the crash of a small plane in a remote, mountainous section of the George Washington National Forest in July 1999. The crash killed at least one person and scattered wreckage over a large area. What would be the challenges of handling a press conference like this?

9. Do not lie to the press. The lie will be discovered, and you will pay the penalty on the next news story.

10. Try trusting the press or some members of the press. You don't have to have an "us versus them" relationship. Trust can be built between law enforcement and the press. Police need sources of information, and so do the press. Cultivate a working relationship between police and the press. Deal with the media fairly and openly.

News Conferences

Communication during news conferences is also of vital importance to any police department. Scoville (1998, p. 21) offers the following recommendations for dealing with the media:

- Prepare a list of key messages you wish to convey.

- As in court, think "evidence"—facts that prove your messages and make them credible (though not at the possible expense of the case itself).

- Think of tough topics or sensitive questions you might be asked and formulate answers that include your key messages.

- Take the initiative. Be prepared to give information. Answer a question and go on with the kinds of comments you've practiced, but be cautious about making them sound pre-packaged.

- Be honest, never hedge, and never, never lie to the press.

- Be personal, not too stiff, too smooth or overbearing.

- Use positive words and phrases when you answer questions.

- Be aware of body language. Look the reporter in the eye; don't swing your legs around or slump in your chair.

- Assume that everything you say can be used as a quote.
- Be energetic. An expressive face, a well-modulated, lively voice and appropriate gestures will help maintain the interviewer's interest.
- Offer your phone number and work schedule to the reporter in case he/she has further questions.
- Always be gracious, even if the interview was challenging or even non-productive.
- Finally, if you're asked a question and don't know the answer, don't speculate.

Further suggestions for giving a news conference include limiting your opening statement to 10 minutes or less; then open the floor for questions. Repeat each question after it is asked to help those in the audience who may not have heard it. Also make sure you understand the question before attempting to answer it. Keep your responses short and to the point, avoiding legalese and jargon. Do not allow questions that stray from the subject of the conference; explain that you will answer extraneous questions later. Furthermore, let the audience know whether copies of your prepared statement are available. From start to finish, treat every microphone as "live" and every camera as "on." Finally, to better prepare for the next time, critique your news conferences objectively.

Actively strive to make reporting good news easier for the media. One media consultant to law enforcement advises: "To get good reporting, we in law enforcement have to contribute to it. If we don't talk to the media we are inviting their suspicions" (Hoffmann, p. 97).

Using the Media

As you have seen, the media and law enforcement may both benefit through cooperation. In fact, in some instances, law enforcement and media collaboration is quite deliberate. Consider, for example, the **perp walk,** "a law enforcement tradition in which suspects are paraded before the hungry eyes of the news media" ("Putting the Hobbles . . . ," 1999, p. 1). Brandon (1999, p. 99) describes the activity:

> It's a recurring scene for news reporters, photographers and camera crews; a handcuffed figure, often wearing a jail uniform, is escorted through a crowd of news media people by a group of law enforcement officers. Reporters shout questions as the cameras roll. . . .
>
> There is seldom a legitimate reason to move the suspect through an area of public access where the media is located. It is simply done for the publicity provided by the news media.
>
> Journalists and law enforcement officers don't agree about a lot of things, but they both benefit from "perp walks." The media get the pictures they need for the evening news and the morning's paper. Officers get a chance to take a public bow for their work.

However, recent criticism has fallen on this practice, and several courts across the country are now considering whether perp walks may violate suspects' rights to privacy. A federal court judge in New York has already handed down a ruling forcing the NYPD to suspend its perp walks after a burglary suspect was led out of the station house in handcuffs, placed in a squad car, driven around the block and then brought back into the station, all at the request of a local news station who wanted footage of the man for their newscast.

Law enforcement may engage the media to help its mission in other ways. According to Rosenthal (1998a, p. 21):

> The best way to get some positive stories out is through a three-step process that I call "The Power of Pro-Activity."
>
> *Step One* . . . is for each agency to build good relationships with members of the media. . . .
>
> *Step Two* . . . is to build on those relationships by providing the news media with stories you know they want. . . . the stories that "sizzle," such as SWAT team training, a drug raid or a wolf-pack DUI sweep. . . .
>
> *Step Three* . . . is getting reporters to cover the positive stories you want them to cover.

Law enforcement may also use the media for news releases, to "get the word out." In these instances Rosenthal (1998b, p. 22) recommends:

> For less important stories, consider using a simple fact sheet. Write down—in this order— the six basic questions you need to answer: What; Who; Where; When; How and Why. Then answer those questions with the available facts. . . .
>
> By providing this simple fact sheet you'll get the basic information to the media (and the public) and save yourself a lot of time and effort in the process. . . .
>
> Fact sheets will work in many routine situations; the full-dress news release can be saved for larger, more important stories.

Some police departments are using the media in a more direct way by actually hosting their own television programs on the cable company's local access channel. According to Young (1997, p. 21): "As the most visible arm of the municipal government, the police department can work with the cable company to provide a wealth of public service programming." Keith (1998, p. 5) describes one such program airing in Oxnard, California, called *StreetBeat:*

> The program . . . offers residents the chance to learn more about their police department, find out about crime trends in their neighborhoods, and learn crime prevention techniques that could help them avoid becoming a victim. The program is extremely well-received and is the cable channel's most watched program. . . .
>
> There is no cost to the police department to produce the program because the cable company pays all production costs. In fact, the program produces a profit. The advertising revenues are divided between the cable company and the department. The department's share, well over $20,000 a year, funds crime prevention efforts. . . .
>
> The department plans to continue to use the technology available through cable television—it is simply an avenue too important to ignore.

Other agencies have found that developing working partnerships with the local media outlets can be extremely beneficial. In Louisville, Kentucky, for example, the police chief's efforts to build a solid relationship with local media has greatly strengthened the city's community policing initiatives. As Riggs (1998, p. 4) notes: "Building a working relationship with the media proved to be difficult and time consuming, but the results were worth the effort. Currently, crime and the fear of crime are down, while arrests and calls for service have actually increased."

Communication with the Broader Community

Outside Agencies

Police officers frequently work with outside agencies to accomplish their goals. Fulton (1993, p. 50) observes: "Whether it involves problems in getting junk cars removed from a drug-infested neighborhood, releasing sensitive records from social services for a homicide investigation, or conflict over traffic control at fire scenes, your management skills will be tested." To minimize problems, Fulton offers three suggestions:

> *Understand their perspective. . . .* Your agency works around the clock, seven days a week; theirs may only work regular business hours. You have an overtime budget; many agencies don't. Your agency is paramilitary; theirs is strictly civilian. You have strict procedural guidelines; theirs may be very loose.
>
> *Sell! Don't Tell. . . .* Taking [a paramilitary approach] in dealing with another agency will probably get you nowhere. . . . Being demanding or officious will probably not get the results you want since the members of the other agency don't work "for" you.
>
> *Stay calm, be reasonable.* Before the situation or problem ever got to you, chances are that someone else had tried unsuccessfully to get the job done. In doing so, they may have muddied the waters and turned the whole situation into a power struggle or an emotionally charged issue. Try to make your own entry into the situation as calm and rational as possible. Avoid getting caught up in the emotional firestorm that may have forced it to your level in the first place.

Annual Reports

One effective way to keep the public informed about the operations of a police department is to publish an annual report. Long recognized as effective business communication tools, annual reports can also serve law enforcement agencies. They might include the department's mission statement; a brief biographical overview of department members with names, academic degrees, dates of hire, dates of most recent promotion and special duties; departmental information and statistics; a summary of projects and projected programs; a budget statement; an outline of ongoing interaction with the fire service, emergency medical care providers, scuba and rescue units, or any emergency support group in your community; and a closing, which may include statements of appreciation and remarks on the "state of the department."

The Internet

Boba (1999, p. 7) asserts: "One part of a police department's role in the community is to provide criminal activity information to its citizens." To accomplish this task, no tool is currently more efficient and effective than the Internet. D'Arcy (1997, p. 15) adds: "Experts estimate that nearly one-third of the families in the United States have access to the Internet." And the numbers are increasing every year.

This type of external communication can be extremely beneficial to departments that are willing to invest the time and minimal expense to devise a web site. D'Arcy (p. 15) states: "In one sense, an Internet home page is very much like a traditional brochure, providing useful information to the public. The great benefit of a computerized home page is that it's so easy to change." According to Boba (p. 9): "The Web page can provide such community-oriented information as crime rates or crime patterns." It can also be used to obtain feedback and crime tips from citizens in the community, often allowing them to remain anonymous. Paynter (1998, p. 29) elaborates:

> At the Phoenix Police Department, the need to disseminate information on fugitives and their crimes for its Silent Witness program was the main reason it established an Internet site. . . . The idea behind it was "somebody, somewhere, saw something" and that "something" could be information the police need to solve a crime.

Paynter (pp. 31–32) also reports:

> The Nashville PD puts interactive crime reports on its site. This allows visitors to look at what's happening in their neighborhood. . . .
> The Nashville site provides valuable public safety information as well as a number of entertaining sections designed to generate interest.

Goodman (1997, p. 48) observes: "Perhaps the most popular law enforcement site on the Web today is that of the FBI—accessed over 3.6 million times each month. . . . The FBI's online presence provides the equivalent of 300 additional public contacts each month for every one of the bureau's 11,000 special agents."

The Internet can also help law enforcement and security professionals communicate more effectively with each other, by posting sites where valuable information may be accessed and shared. According to Uttenweiler (1999, p. 75): "Security professionals can wield the Web as a tool that helps them do their jobs more efficiently. . . . The Internet offers a way to reduce the clutter [of paperwork on your desk] and still conduct the requisite research in a more time-efficient and organized manner."

Paynter (p. 32) offers suggestions for developing a successful Internet page:

- Survey the department and the public to see what should be included on the site.

- Use a separate computer system and phoneline from your mainframe computer and computer databases to prevent visitors to your site from getting into your computer databases.

- Put information on the site that entertains and generates interest.

- Update it frequently.

- Charge several employees with maintaining and updating the site, or hire an Internet provider to do it.

Other Modes of External Communications

Although the Internet may be the latest wave of technology to help law enforcement spread valuable information, other communication networks are also being implemented, such as basic phones, faxes and pagers. Estrada (1998, p. B3) describes a communication system called Community Watch, which significantly reduces the time required to notify people when the need arises:

> The system uses a series of phone lines and modems to call, fax or page up to 700 people per hour and alert them to such things as missing children, wanted criminals, check or credit-card fraud, hazardous materials spills, suspicious activity and emergency situations.

The system . . . can fine-tune the notifications to call individuals, a single block or every volunteer for a radius of several miles or more. . . .

And it has outbound and inbound message capabilities, which makes it ideal for keeping large numbers of people informed and updated. Block club captains, for example, can punch in members' numbers and have them called automatically to let them know about meetings or suspicious activity.

Likewise, such businesses as banks, malls and stores can be notified of criminal activity in an area. Investigators also can analyze the pattern and in some cases anticipate a criminal suspect's next moves and alert businesses even as the crimes happen.

External Communications as Public Relations

Every contact with the public is a public relations contact. It is critical that all members of the agency, especially those in positions of authority, present a positive image and communicate effectively.

This is true no matter whether officers are giving directions or answering a call from a citizen with a raccoon in the chimney. It is true whether traffic officers are issuing a ticket or the chief of police is addressing the Rotary or the local PTA.

Summary

Effective communication is the lifeblood of a law enforcement agency, whether it is written, spoken, downward, upward, lateral, informal or formal, internal or external.

Communication is the complex process through which information is transferred from one person to another. The communication process involves a message, a sender, a channel and a receiver, and it may include feedback. Effective communication should follow the KISS principle, that is, Keep It Short and Simple. Words themselves, however, are only a small part of the message. Ninety-three percent of communication between two people comes from body language and tone of voice.

Critical factors to consider in selecting a channel include speed, opportunity for feedback and expense. The weakest link in the communication process is *listening*. People listen and think four times faster than they talk. Active listening includes concentration, full attention and thought. Feedback is the process by which the sender knows whether the receiver has understood the message.

Communication may be downward, upward (vertical) or lateral (horizontal). It may also be internal or external. Most effective communication is two way.

Communication barriers include time, volume of information, tendency to say what we think others want to hear, failure to select the best word, prejudices (of the sender and/or receiver) and strained sender-receiver relationships. Certain behaviors discourage communication: judging, superiority, certainty, controlling, manipulation and indifference. Other behaviors encourage communication: describing, equality, openness, problem orientation, positive intent and empathy.

Communication is an important part of the law enforcement job, including meetings. Meetings may be informational, opinion seeking, problem solving or new-idea seeking. For more effective meetings: (1) prepare in advance—have an agenda, (2) start and stop on time, (3) stick to the agenda and (4) facilitate open communication and participation.

Discussion Questions

1. Why is communication ability important to law enforcement managers?
2. How would you compare and contrast the various channels of communication?
3. Which is more difficult, written or spoken communication? Why? Which do you prefer?
4. What are the main obstacles to communication in your agency?
5. What types of communication exist in your agency? What is the value of each?
6. What types of feedback are available in a typical law enforcement agency?
7. How is nonverbal communication used in law enforcement? How is such nonverbal communication depicted on television programs about law enforcement?
8. What methods do you use as an active listener?
9. What is the key role of the first-line supervisor as a communicator in a law enforcement agency?
10. What public figures do you consider to be effective communicators? What characteristics make them so?

InfoTrac College Edition Assignment

Select an area of *communication* of interest to you and research it in at least three journals, one of which should be from the criminal justice field. You might select topics such as gender differences, nonverbal communication, the impact of technology on communication or any other area you would like to know more about. Write a brief (one- to two-page) summary of your findings. Include the full reference citation for each source, and be prepared to share your findings with the class.

References

Boba, Rachel. "Using the Internet to Disseminate Crime Information." *FBI Law Enforcement Bulletin,* Vol. 68, No. 10, October 1999, pp. 6–9.

Brandon, Craig. " 'Perp Walks' Questioned." *Law and Order,* Vol. 47, No. 9, September 1999, pp. 99–102.

Brooks, Michael E. "The Ethics of Intentionally Deceiving the Media." *FBI Law Enforcement Bulletin,* Vol. 68, No. 5, May 1999, pp. 22–26.

Buchholz, Steve and Roth, Thomas. *Creating the High-Performance Team.* New York: John Wiley and Sons, 1987.

D'Arcy, Stephen. "Plugging Into the Net." *The Police Chief,* Vol. LXIV, No. 2, February 1997, p. 15.

Dees, Tim. "Your E-Mail Can Hurt You." *Law and Order,* Vol. 47, No. 9, September 1999, pp. 65–69.

Estrada, Márquez. "Network Helps Town Spread the Word when Problem Arises." (Minneapolis/St. Paul) *Star Tribune,* June 7, 1998, p. B3.

Field, Mark W. "Organizational Dynamics in a Technology-Driven World: The Impact of E-mail on Law Enforcement." *The Police Chief,* Vol. LXVII, No. 2, February 2000, pp. 45–49.

"From the Top." *Successful Meetings,* October 1999, pp. 59–60.

Fulton, Roger V. "Avoiding the Emotional Firestorm When Working with Outside Agencies." Vol. 20, No. 6, *Law Enforcement Technology,* June 1993, pp. 50–51.

Giuliano, Peter. "Did I Say That?" *Successful Meetings,* March 1999a, p. 96.

Giuliano, Peter. "Seven Benefits of Eye Contact." *Successful Meetings,* August 1999b, p. 104.

Goodman, Max. "Working the Net." *The Police Chief,* Vol. LXIV, No. 8, August 1997, pp. 48–53.

Hall, Dennis. "Don't Get Into a Urinating Contest with Someone Who Uses Blue Ink." *Police,* Vol. 22, No. 12, December 1998, pp. 24–25.

Hoffmann, John. "Why the Media Gets It Wrong." *Law and Order,* Vol. 46, No. 8, August 1998, pp. 95–97.

Imperato, Gina. "3M Expert Tells How to Run Meetings that Really Work." (Minneapolis/St. Paul) *Star Tribune,* May 23, 1999, p. D6.

Jenkins, Tom. "Prick Up Your Ears." *Successful Meetings,* November 1999, pp. 59–62.

Keith, David. "Cable Television: A Medium too Important to Ignore." *Community Policing Exchange,* July/August 1998, p. 5.

Keller, Michael A. "Leadership and Perception." *The Police Chief,* Vol. LXVI, No. 3, March 1999, pp. 72–73.

McArthur, Jerie. "Meeting!! A Last Resort." *Minnesota Business and Opportunities,* March 1999, p. 51.

McDonald, Tom. "Turbo-Charged Meetings." *Successful Meetings,* August 1999, p. 29.

"Meeting Magic." *Norwest Business Advantage Magazine,* Fall/Winter 1998, p. 5.

Meyers, Caryn. "Mars and Venus in the Meeting Room." *Successful Meetings,* April 1999, pp. 46–50.

Parrish, Penny. "Media Alert." *Law and Order,* Vol. 41, No. 9, September 1993, pp. 91–93.

Paynter, Ronnie L. "Internet Connections." *Law Enforcement Technology,* Vol. 25, No. 8, August 1998, pp. 28–32.

"Putting the Hobbles on Perp Walks?" *Law Enforcement News,* Vol. XXV, No. 509, April 15, 1999, pp. 1, 10.

Riggs, Troy. "Media Outlets Broadcast Fugitive Profiles, Capture Criminals." *Community Policing Exchange,* July/August 1998, p. 4.

Rosenthal, Rick. "Answers to Media Relations Questions: Part II." *Law and Order,* Vol. 46, No. 4, April 1998a, pp. 21–22.

Rosenthal, Rick. "More Answers to Media Relations Questions." *Law and Order,* Vol. 46, No. 8, August 1998b, pp. 22–24.

Rosenthal, Rick. "More Media Ethics Codes." *Law and Order,* Vol. 47, No. 9, September 1999a, pp. 26–28.

Rosenthal, Rick. "The Quill and Badge Award." *Law and Order,* Vol. 47, No. 1, January 1999b, pp. 16–18.

Ryan, Anita. "Are You Listening?" *Talking Business,* March/April 1999, p. 30.

Schuiteman, John G. "Cellular Phones and Pagers for Police." *Law and Order,* Vol. 47, No. 6, June 1999, pp. 51–53.

Scoville, Dean. " 'Any-City' Confidential: Here's the Story on Cop-Media Relations." *Police,* Vol. 22, No. 5, May 1998, pp. 18–25.

Sharp, Arthur G. "E-Mail: A New Way of Getting the Message." *Law and Order,* Vol. 47, No. 5, May 1999, pp. 79–83.

Surette, Ray. "Media Echoes: Systemic Effects of News Coverage." *Justice Quarterly,* Vol. 16, No. 3, September 1999, pp. 601–631.

Uttenweiler, William L. "Working the Web." *Security Management,* Vol. 43, No. 10, October 1999, pp. 75–78.

Woodall, Elliott. "Why Have a Written Media Relations Policy?" *The Police Chief,* Vol. LXV, No. 6, June 1998, pp. 72–73.

Young, Theresa. "Public Access: Reaching the Community through Cable TV." *FBI Law Enforcement Bulletin,* Vol. 66, No. 6, June 1997, pp. 20–26.

4

Problem Solving
and Decision Making

Imagination is more important than
knowledge. For knowledge is limited, whereas
imagination embraces the entire world.
—Albert Einstein

Do You Know?

- What levels of decision making exist?
- What kinds of decisions managers must make?
- What functions may be served by the brain's left and right sides?
- What creativity is?
- What common thinking traps exist? Mental locks?
- What "killer phrases" are and how to deal with them?
- What methods are commonly used to make decisions or solve problems?
- What levels of the agency benefit from group participation in decision making?
- What groupthink is?
- What the steps are in the seven-step problem-solving/decision-making process?
- What force-field analysis is? The nominal group technique? The Delphi technique?
- How brainstorming can be most effective?
- What other considerations decision making includes?
- What the SARA problem-solving process includes?

Can You Define?

administrative decision
brainstorming
command decision
consensus decision
consultative decision
convergent thinking
creative procrastination
creativity
decision-making process
Delphi technique
divergent thinking
driving forces
equilibrium
focus groups

force-field analysis
GIGO
groupthink
innovation
intelligence
intuition
killer phrases
left-brain thinking
management
    information systems
    (MIS)
mental locks
modified Delphi
    technique

nominal group
    technique
operational decision
participatory decision
    making (PDM)
problem-oriented
    policing (POP)
restraining forces
right-brain thinking
snap decisions
thinking traps
whole-brain thinking

INTRODUCTION

Problem solving and decision making are primary responsibilities of law enforcement managers at all levels. A problem is a deviation from what is desired, a difficulty. A decision is a judgment or conclusion. It is the act of making up one's mind or settling a dispute.

Most law enforcement managers developed their decision-making skills in the field as patrol officers. They made important decisions constantly, but their decisions were usually based on clear department policies and procedures. The decision to arrest someone, for example, was made many times. If something new occurred, the first-line supervisor might be directed to the scene for a decision. Even this decision was comparatively easy because standards existed and the supervisor had to consider only alternatives to the established procedure.

Because of the discretion they had as patrol officers, most law enforcement managers are comfortable making decisions as long as guidelines exist. There is little time to problem solve if someone is shooting at you. Often, however, law enforcement managers encounter unique problems that call for problem-solving/decision-making skills. Martinez (1998, p. 605) defines problem solving as: "The process of moving toward a goal when the path to that goal is uncertain." He also observes that errors are an inherent part of problem solving (p. 606):

> There is no formula for true problem solving. If we know exactly how to get from point A to point B, then reaching point B does not involve problem solving. Think of problem solving as working your way through a maze. In negotiating a maze, you make your way toward your goal step by step, making some false moves but gradually moving closer toward the intended end point. What guides your choices? Perhaps a rule like this: choose the path that seems to result in *some* progress toward the goal. Such a rule is one example of a *heuristic*. A heuristic is a rule of thumb. It is a strategy that is powerful and general, but not absolutely guaranteed to work. Heuristics are crucial because they are *the* tools by which problems are solved.

This chapter begins by describing the kinds of decisions managers must make. Next the chapter examines research on how the human brain processes information and on how creativity and innovation help in solving problems. Specific methods for making decisions or solving problems are described, as is participatory decision making. This is followed by several specific approaches to problem solving, including a seven-step decision-making process, force-field analysis, the nominal group technique and the Delphi technique. Important in all these approaches is brainstorming. Next is a look at common mistakes in decision making/problem solving, and criteria for making decisions. The chapter concludes with a brief discussion of problem-oriented and community-oriented policing, problem solving and focus groups.

Kinds of Decisions

Decisions may deal with problems that are trivial or critical, short term or long term, personal or organizational. They may also be categorized by the level in the organizational hierarchy at which they are made. The executive level mainly deals with conceptual problems and alternatives, middle management most frequently makes administrative decisions and first-line supervisors most frequently make operational decisions.

Decisions may be **strategic**—executive level; **administrative**—middle-management level or **operational**—first-line level.

Decisions at all levels involve individual skills, organizational policies, different managerial styles and a certain amount of risk taking. Decisions may also be categorized by who carries them out.

Decisions may be command, consultative or consensual.

A **command decision** is one that managers make on their own, with little or no input from others. For example, the chief of police decides to give an award to an officer.

A **consultative decision,** in contrast, is one that uses input and opinions from others. The final decision is still made by the one in charge but only after considering the input of others. For example, a lieutenant in charge of organizing a Neighborhood Watch program might ask for ideas from other officers and from citizens and consult other agencies that already have such a program. The lieutenant then makes decisions about the program based on this input. Managers will gain greater acceptance of and support for their decisions if they seek input from all levels and weigh that input before making their final decisions.

A **consensus decision** is made democratically by a group. It is a joint decision often made by members of a committee. For example, training priorities for the year might be decided by a committee established for this purpose. This committee might operate independently or seek input from others in the organization. Blanchard, Carlos and Randolph (1999, p. 35) assert: "For a company [or agency] to prosper and [succeed], it needs to take advantage of the full brain power of its entire work force, not just its management-level staff. . . . If managers want employees to make responsible decisions, they must share information and establish a trusting relationship." To help boost the collective brain power of an agency, they (pp. 35–39) suggest managers give useful data, be straightforward, make information meaningful, act on input, take mistakes in stride and praise progress because even little changes that signal that people are taking responsibility must be noticed.

Law enforcement organizations regularly make all three kinds of decisions. One key to effectiveness is that the individuals involved know what kind of decision they are making. For example, a situation in which a manager makes it very clear that he or she alone is going to decide an issue is quite different from a situation in which the manager *appears* to seek input from others but is only making a gesture. Likewise, if employees believe they are to decide an issue, but the final decision is *not* what they recommended, the entire decision-making process may be undermined.

Before looking at specific methods of decision making and problem solving, you should understand the thinking process and how it functions. Managers are expected to use their heads—their brains. Most managers have attained their present positions because of this ability, which is equated with **intelligence** or mental ability. They have also traditionally relied upon logic and reason to solve problems, but whole-brain research suggests that this may not always be the most appropriate approach.

Whole-Brain Research

The world was amazed 2,500 years ago when Hippocrates suggested that our emotions come from the head, not the heart. Twenty-five years ago another physician, Roger Sperry, reported on significant brain research that established that the right and the left side of the brain each had its own thoughts and memories and *processed information differently.*

Left-brain thinking processes *language* and is primarily *logical.*
Right-brain thinking processes *images* and is primarily *emotional.*

According to Dr. Sperry's research, the two sides of the brain are connected by the *corpus callosum.* In brief, his research identified the division of labor between the two sides of the brain and the critical role of the corpus callosum. He received the Nobel Prize in medicine in 1981 for these remarkable findings.

Current brain research also indicates differences in the way each side of the brain processes information. The left side usually processes information sequentially, logically and rationally in linear fashion. The right side usually processes information spatially, intuitively, holistically and emotionally. The left side uses reasoning; the right side, imagination and creativity.

According to some researchers, people can tell which side of their brain is dominant by which hand they use. Those who use their right hand are left-brained; those who use their left hand are right-brained. According to others, however, the division is not so clear-cut. Researchers have discovered that:

- Right-hemisphere processes add emotional and humorous overtones important for understanding the full meaning of oral and written communication.
- Both hemispheres are involved in thinking, logic and reasoning.
- The right hemisphere seems to play a special role in emotion. If students are emotionally engaged, both sides of the brain will participate in the educational process, regardless of subject matter.

A person's dominant mode of thinking may shift from left to right hemisphere and back again about 10 times every 24 hours. Some research even suggests that you can control which side of your brain will be dominant by switching your breathing. If you want to be more creative, you can activate the right side of your brain by forcing air through the left nostril.

Whether this is true and how distinct the functions of both sides of the brain are may be debatable. What is relatively clear, however, is that when dealing with problem-solving/decision-making situations, our educational system and our culture tend to place more value on those factors associated with the left brain: logical, rational, objective, sequential and so forth.

Our organizations, public and private, also rely heavily on a rational, logical, analytical approach to problems. Further, most effective law enforcement managers are precise, methodical and conservative. They seek to preserve the status quo—to keep things on an even keel.

The logical approach was perhaps more appropriate when organizations were less complex and change was less frequent. Our complex, rapidly changing modern society, however, requires the ability to use *both* logic and creativity in problem solving and decision making, that is, **whole-brain thinking.** The issue is not which is better. As Spring and Deutsch (1981, p. 192) note:

> There is no way to tell whether the patterns extracted by the right hemisphere are real or imagined without subjecting them to the left hemisphere scrutiny. On the other hand, mere critical thinking, without creative and intuitive insights, without the search for new patterns, is sterile and doomed. To solve complex problems in changing circumstances requires the activity of both cerebral hemispheres: the path to the future lies through the corpus callosum.

Modes of Thinking

Closely related to whole brain research is research into modes of thinking. Malone (1994, pp. 29–30) describes a study undertaken by the FBI Academy on the effects of the following common styles of thinking on organizational planning and management:

Pragmatist—Has a short-term orientation. Concerned with the immediate. Good tactician but lacks perseverance.

Analyst—Solves problems systematically and relies heavily on logic and deductive reasoning. Depends on what is historically proven and structured. Tends to lose sight of the department's mission and values. Avoids risks. Tends to try to apply old solutions to new problems.

Realist—Must personally seek, touch, hear and smell before believing. Usually solves problems quickly but tends to deal with symptoms rather than causes. Often operates in a vacuum.

Synthesist—Has an "integrative viewpoint" and seeks change and conflict. Seeks out contradictions and goes beyond what is real. Questions underlying assumptions and tries to identify the cause of problems.

Idealist—Welcomes a broad range of views. Concerned with long-range and strategic plans and the impact of decisions on employees, the law enforcement community, the public and society. Understands the big picture. Tends to be a good listener and nonjudgmental.

Malone (p. 29) reports: "Most of those surveyed [543 first-line supervisors, managers and senior law enforcement executives] had high pragmatic, analytical, and realistic tendencies. . . . While essential for many operational and most day-to-day decisions, these styles are short on the innovative thinking and long-term planning typical of synthesists and idealists." The best managers, like the best drivers, keep their eyes on the horizon while staying attuned to the road directly ahead.

The importance of this research is that most managers and supervisors are probably not functioning in the most effective way for future problem solving and should recognize and address this fact. Obvious options are to develop alternative styles and seek out those in the department who use these styles when they need to.

Effective problem solving and decision making rely on both creativity and logic. Because most managers are more familiar with and reliant on logic, first consider the creative aspect of problem solving.

Creativity and Innovation

Creativity involves originality, uniqueness and innovation. It involves breaking with old ways of thinking.

> **Creativity** is a process of breaking old connections and making useful new ones. It often is synonymous with **innovation.**

One strategy for law enforcement managers to develop more creativity is to increase interaction with corporate leaders and other administrators outside criminal justice. Police management has been evolving for decades and has been described as conservative and traditional. Techniques such as total quality management, team approaches and quality circles are foreign to many police managers, who need to be alert to management changes in the corporate world. Some corporate techniques cannot be adapted to the police environment, but others can. Exposure to new ideas and thoughts stimulates the mind.

Some police administrators reject new programs or ideas because they did not originate with them or because the idea came from the rank-and-file. Many newspapers have excellent articles by management experts, and much of this information is adaptable to police management. In fact, many of the concepts presented in this text came from corporate America.

Our society tends to stifle innovation and creativity. Think about school and what you were taught: Dogs cannot be colored purple; give the "right" answer; do not make a mess; do not be different; stay in line; be quiet; raise your hand if you want to talk and so on. In other words, conform. Our own habits can also stifle creativity.

Thinking Traps and Mental Locks

Thinking traps are habits people fall into without recognizing what they are doing.

> Common thinking traps include:
>
> - Being stuck in black/white, either/or thinking.
> - Being too quick in deciding.
> - Making decisions based on your personal feelings about the proposer of an idea.
> - Being a victim of personal habits and prejudices.
> - Not using imagination.

Being stuck in black/white, either/or thinking. People caught in this trap think that if one answer is bad, the other must be good. This kind of thinking causes people to miss intermediate solutions. Brainstorming many alternatives will help overcome this trap.

Being too quick in deciding. People in this trap jump to conclusions before they hear all the facts or have all the evidence. You can avoid this trap by listing all possibilities and delaying decisions until each has been discussed.

Making decisions based on your personal feelings about the proposer of an idea. Some people tend to favor only what their friends propose. To overcome this, decide that you will listen for the facts and keep your feelings out of your decision.

Being a victim of personal habits and prejudices. "We've always done it that way" thinking can keep programs from moving forward. You can avoid this trap by asking questions such as: Who else can we serve? How can we do it differently? What more might we do?

Not using imagination. People who fall into this trap are too tied to data and statistics. They do not take the risk of using their intuition. To bypass this trap, practice brainstorming and creative thinking—think laterally, horizontally and vertically. Take the risk of going with your hunches.

To illustrate the ease and tendency of getting stuck in a thinking rut, try the "Scottish Names" game on a colleague. (Note: It is more effective if done orally because the solution is obvious when written like this.) Ask a colleague to pronounce M-A-C-T-A-V-I-S-H; then M-A-C-D-O-U-G-A-L; then M-A-C-C-A-R-T-H-Y. Finally, ask them to pronounce M-A-C-H-I-N-E-S. If they respond "MacHines," they have become a victim of preconditioned thinking and have fallen into a common thinking trap.

The mind easily gets stuck in patterns. Creativity consultant von Oech calls such thinking traps *mental locks*. He suggests that sometimes we need a "whack on the side of the head" to jar ourselves out of ways of thinking that keep us from being innovative.

Mental locks that prevent innovative thinking include:

- The right answer.
- That's not logical.
- Follow the rules.
- Be practical.
- Avoid ambiguity.
- To err is wrong.
- Play is frivolous.
- That's not my area.
- Don't be foolish.
- I'm not creative.

The right answer. Most people will have taken in excess of 26,000 tests before they complete their education. Such tests usually focus on "right" answers. According to von Oech (1983, p. 22): "Children enter elementary school as question marks and leave as periods."

That's not logical. People need to learn to dream, create and fantasize. Both "soft" and "hard" thinking are needed. It is like making a clay pot. Clay that is not soft enough is difficult to work with. Once the pot is shaped, however, it must be fired and made hard before it will hold water. Metaphors such as this can help in problem solving as well.

Follow the rules. Parents teach their children to stay inside the lines when they color. People do rely on patterns to analyze problems, but this can be a hindrance.

Be practical. As von Oech (p. 54) notes:

Because we have the ability to symbolize our experience, our thinking is not limited to the real and the present. This capability empowers our thinking in two major ways. First, it enables us to anticipate the future. . . .

Second, since our thinking is not bound by real world constraints, we can generate ideas which have no correlate in the world of experience. . . .

I call the realm of the possible our "germinal seedbed." . . . Asking "what-if" is an easy way to get your imagination going.

Avoid ambiguity. A story told by von Oech involves former FBI director J. Edgar Hoover. Hoover wrote a letter to his agents and as he was proofreading it, he decided he did not like the way it was laid out. He wrote a note on the bottom to his secretary, "Watch the borders," and asked her to retype it. She did and then sent it to all the agents. For the next few weeks, FBI agents were put on special alert along our Canadian and Mexican borders. Ambiguity is usually to be avoided. When thinking creatively, however, ambiguity can help. Ask, how else might this be interpreted?

To err is wrong. This is similar to the first mental lock—that there is a "right" answer. View mistakes as learning opportunities and as a part of risk taking. If you are made of the right material, a hard fall will result in a high bounce. Mistakes or failures can be positive. Henry Ford viewed failure positively: "Failure is the opportunity to begin again more intelligently."

Play is frivolous. According to von Oech (p. 97): "Necessity may be the mother of invention, but play is certainly the father." He urges that people not take themselves too seriously, especially when engaged in innovative thinking.

That's not my area. In our complex society, specialization is a fact of life. Sometimes, however, a person outside the area in which a problem exists is better able to generate possible solutions. It is not always the "experts" who come up with the best ideas.

Don't be foolish. In the Middle Ages, kings often had "fools" as part of their court. A major role these fools played was to ridicule the advice the king's counselors gave him, a forerunner of the "devil's advocate" role in today's society.

I'm not creative. This can become a self-fulfilling prophecy. If you think you cannot do something, you probably will not be able to. Conversely, the power of positive thinking has been proven time after time.

Killer Phrases

Closely related to thinking traps and mental locks are certain "killer phrases" people tend to use that limit the creative participation of *others* in the group.

Killer phrases are judgmental and critical and serve as put-downs. They stifle others' creativity.

Among the more common killer phrases are the following: It's not our policy. It's not our area. We don't have the time. We'll never get help. It's too much hassle. That's too radical. It won't work. Be practical. It costs too much. We've never done it that way before. Be realistic. Where did you come up with *that* idea? This isn't the time to try something like that. It's okay in theory, but

I don't think we're ready for it yet. You don't really think that would work, do you? Get serious.

To handle killer phrases, recognize them, describe to the group what is happening and then challenge them to discuss whether the killer phrases are true. Encourage the group to remain open to all ideas.

Organizations that promote creativity and innovation provide more freedom to think and act, recognize ideas and provide ample opportunities for communication as well as for private creative thinking. They also invest in research and experimentation and permit ideas from outside the organization.

To enhance creative thinking, McDonald (1999, p. 26) suggests freeing your mind by abandoning old, ingrained ways of thinking and allowing your mind to change: "It's okay to change your mind—in fact, it's essential for growth. . . . Change is the only constant we know."

Changing Your Environment

Arnot (2000, p. 7) suggests some steps you can take to create "sizzling mental energy":

- Turn up the lights. Normal room light rarely exceeds 500–600 lux, but we need at least 1,000 lux to reap the biological benefits of light.
- Arrange your space. Black and blue are good office colors. Have at least one window.
- Use aromatherapy. Rosemary, peppermint and eucalyptus can boost mental energy and improve concentration.
- Turn on the tunes. Music is a good stress buster and muscle relaxer.
- Cut the noise. Noise demands a series of cognitive decisions. Neutralize it by turning on a fan or air conditioner.
- Pay attention to air quality. Cool, dry air helps keep you alert.

Methods for Making Decisions or Solving Problems

An important management tool is a **decision-making process,** that is, a systematic approach to solving a problem. This chapter describes several decision-making processes that you may tailor to fit specific law enforcement department problems.

> Methods for making decisions range from using intuition and snap decisions to using a computer, with a systematic individual or group approach in between.

Intuition

Intuition is insight. It is knowing without using any rational thought process. The subconscious makes decisions based on intuition. Dr. Weston Agor, professor of public management at the University of Texas, El Paso, says: "Intuition is what you know for sure without knowing for certain. . . . It is a brain skill that crosses the left and right hemispheres, integrates facts and feelings, and draws on both experience and inherited capabilities" (Johnson, 1993, p. 148).

I (author Bennett, then chief of police) recall a time when there was a series of automobile thefts from a large shopping center parking lot. Surveillance of the lot by binoculars from the shopping center rooftop, unmarked cars, special patrol in the perimeter area and other methods failed to turn up suspects. A sergeant came into my office to talk about the problem. We decided to "go take a look" and headed for a gravel pit near the shopping center. When we arrived, three people were crowded around a car in a far area of the pit. On closer examination, we saw they were spray painting the car red. We arrested the three, and that arrest cleared almost a dozen car theft cases.

It was merely a hunch to go to that location. No one had reported activity in that area. It was purely intuition. Yet, behind the decision to go to the gravel pit was the knowledge that the pit existed and that it just might be a hiding place. Some would call it "sheer luck." Effective managers listen to their hunches, their "gut feelings."

Snap Decisions

Closely related to using intuition are **snap decisions.** Neither takes much of a manager's time. Be decisive. It is not always possible to obtain all the available information. Do not expect every decision to be perfect. Perfectionists find it difficult to make decisions because they never have sufficient information.

Learning to make snap decisions prudently can be extremely beneficial. Many decisions should be made on the spot, whereas some need to mature, and some need not be made at all. A not-so-great snap decision may have better results than a good decision made slowly. This is because any kind of movement often brings a new perspective that makes the right decision more obvious.

Being decisive often inspires support from subordinates and superiors. It also lets you feel in control. Having a list of 10 unsolved problems sitting on your desk can cause anxiety and stress. Many problems and decisions should be made quickly and decisively. Others can be delegated or not even made. Know when to slow down and proceed with caution, and also remember that you can change your mind.

Delegating

Delegation sends the decision-making process to a subordinate. The manager is removed from the process at this point until it is time to report the results. Delegation is an excellent motivating technique and gets the job done at the level of those with firsthand knowledge of the problem. When you delegate, establish a time line also. Delegated tasks should be concise and clear. You must also give authority along with a level of responsibility. Effective managers make sure decisions are made at the lowest level possible. They offer assistance but encourage independence.

Not Deciding

Not to decide *is* to decide. In some instances, any decision is better than none, but in other instances, such as a life-threatening situation, a wrong decision may have disastrous results. Effective managers know when they do not have to make a decision. They use **creative procrastination**—providing time for a minor difficulty to work itself out. In other instances, the thinking trap "if it isn't broken, don't fix it" works to keep managers from getting bogged down in trivia.

Using Computers for Decision Making

A few decades ago law enforcement had limited technological assistance. Managers were truly independent decision makers with little support. The advent of computers has greatly changed this situation. A vast array of software programs is available to assist decision making at all levels.

At the operational or line level, squad cars now have computers that give patrol officers instant access to information. Tracing a license number directly from the patrol car, officers may know the history of the vehicle they are stopping before they approach it. The driver's identification and past record can also be instantly checked. This is important to personal safety and decisions about whether to arrest.

At the management level, administrative programs help with allocating personnel, budgeting, processing reports and many other functions. Computers also provide statistical information as well as analysis of this information and may even suggest implications and alternatives. Called **management information systems (MIS),** these software programs organize data to assist in decision making. They often use "what-if" analysis to project the effects of various solutions. Pilant (1998, pp. 64–65) offers the following suggestions for implementing an MIS:

- *Do your homework.* You cannot find your way into the future of information management if you have no idea where you've been, where you are or where you want to go. . . . Don't skip the needs analysis, the feasibility studies, . . . the surveys. Spend the money on a consultant, or make use of the experts at nearby universities and colleges.
- *Plan for the future.* Look at information management as a way of doing business, not as a project that will automate just one function. . . . Think beyond running tags and warrants. . . . Think about officers doing crime mapping and crime analysis in their cars, about how these systems are going to support what [you] do on the street. Also, plan for maintenance and upgrades. . . . Make system maintenance a budget item.
- *Think of policing as a business.* Most experts also advocate paying for consultants as the need arises.
- *Share and share alike.* Regional information systems, or those that give more than one agency or entity access, are becoming more common.

Pilant (p. 65) concludes: "Records management systems can be integral to managing an entire incident, from the time a 911 call is received. They are becoming much more dynamic systems, and a more cost-effective and efficient way of doing business."

Even with these supports, however, managers must adapt the information to current circumstances and arrive at independent decisions. Computers cannot replace experience and expertise, but they can enhance them. Anyone who works with management information systems must remember the watchword of computer users: "garbage in/garbage out," or **GIGO.**

Computer programs can also help you review goals and objectives. Based on the experience of other organizations, they can project alternatives, one or more of which may apply to a situation. From these alternatives, managers can make more informed choices.

Systematic Approaches to Problem Solving

At times decisions cannot be avoided, delegated, made rapidly or fed into a computer. They must be approached in a systematic, rational way by individuals or groups. Before looking at some of the more common systematic approaches to problem solving, consider the advantages and disadvantages of using a group to solve problems.

Participatory Decision Making (PDM)

A participatory management environment often leads to increased and better decision making. In **participatory decision making,** employees of the organization have a say in the decision-making process. Employees prefer PDM largely because decisions often directly affect them. They also bring a diversity of backgrounds and experiences to the decision making.

PDM provides more input on the number and content of alternatives because of the varied experience and background of the participants. Opportunity for innovative ideas also increases. Shared input fosters better acceptance of and commitment to the final decision. Upward and downward organizational communication also increases, as does teamwork.

The participative manager outlines the problems and leaves the development of alternatives to subordinates. This encourages the creativity of the participants and improves the quality and quantity of the decisions they send to the manager. The group may obtain synergistic results when the process of working together enhances sharing and functional competition. With PDM, conflict is considered an asset, and individuals who do not "go along" are viewed as catalysts for innovative ideas and solutions.

Although obtaining consensus may be more difficult with PDM, it can be achieved if participants avoid arguing in order to win as individuals and keep their focus on reaching the best judgment of the whole group. Group members must also accept responsibility for both hearing and being heard, so that everyone's input receives a hearing. Finally group members should remember that the best results stem from a combination of information, logic and emotion— including participants' feelings about the information and decision-making process will positively affect value judgments as well as the final decision.

An entirely participative decision-making process, however, may be difficult to establish because of lack of training on how to work together. It is difficult for officers to include themselves in the process if it has not been past practice to do so. It is even more difficult for autocratic managers to give up their decision-making authority.

If people are used to being told what to do, they may feel awkward when given a chance to participate. A certain amount of confusion and hesitancy may exist initially.

In addition, discussion and agreement are time consuming. Further, not all decisions *should* be democratic or participatory. Some decisions must be immediate, and others cannot be resolved by agreement. A final decision can be made only after top management considers the alternatives.

Nonetheless, if possible, decisions should involve those who will be affected by them. The synergism of the group can often produce results that a single person or even many people working independently would be unable to produce.

Participatory decision making (PDM) is a process used for making better decisions. Group input is important. Officers from all ranks and divisions are called to assist in discussions leading to major recommendations and decisions.

Further, implementing the selected alternative will be easier because it is more likely to be accepted. *People tend to support what they help create.* Morale is improved, and participants feel commitment and loyalty.

> All levels of the organization benefit from group participation in the decision-making process.

In any law enforcement organization, newer officers can bring fresh approaches and ideas, but these must be balanced by experience.

Although full department meetings are difficult to hold because of multiple shifts, input from all officers can be obtained through shift discussions and a joint meeting of first-line supervisors with middle and executive management. Full department meetings should be called only for critical matters or to communicate a decision.

Although participatory leadership styles support group decision making, disadvantages might also arise, such as time being wasted, responsibility shirked or a tendency for indecisiveness and costly delays.

One of the greatest hazards of participatory decision making is *groupthink*.

> **Groupthink** is the negative tendency for members of a group to submit to peer pressure and endorse the majority opinion even if it is unacceptable to individuals.

Groupthink is more concerned with team play and unanimity than with reaching the best solution. Group members suppress their individual concerns to avoid rocking the group's boat. Strentz (1997, p. 86) notes: "Most people do not like arguments, disagreements, or fights. They want to get along with others. . . . Such groups make poor decision-making teams because their priority tends to be the maintenance of their harmony, not the success of their decision." Dr. I. L. Janis (1972) identified eight major factors that guarantee poor decisions due to groupthink:

1. Illusion of invulnerability that creates excessive optimism leading to extreme risks. This leads to:

2. A collective effort to rationalize in order to discount intelligence or warnings of failure.

3. Unquestioned belief in the group's inherent morality.

4. Stereotyped views of a weak or ignorant adversary.

5. Direct pressure on members who express strong arguments against group stereotypes.

6. Self-censorship of members who go along to get along.

7. A shared sense of unanimity. (Given the enthusiasm generated by 1 through 4, the decision-making process begins to generate so much enthusiasm that those who consider objecting are neutralized. Items 5 and 6 provide a false sense of unanimity.)

8. Self-appointed members who protect the group from adverse information that might shatter their shared complacency about the effectiveness and morality of their decision.

Strentz contends that such faulty decision-making processes have occurred during various historical events and have led to disaster, including the incident involving the ATF at the Branch Davidian compound in Waco, Texas, in 1993. He claims (p. 87): "Not all of the eight symptoms identified by Janis were present among the ATF. However, enough were there to insure failure of the decision-making process." For example (pp. 87–88):

- The illusion of invulnerability based on the recent history of successful ATF raids against gun dealers around the south.
- The command staff's rejection of intelligence from their undercover agents—information that, if heeded, would have led to abortion of the operation instead of a speed up in actions.
- Rejection of a basic tenet of military operations that states the attacking force should outnumber the defenders by three to one. ATF had 75 people on their team, about equal the number of adults in the compound. Yet, ATF believed the women would not shoot back.
- Evident self-censorship by the commander's rejection of intelligence from the lookout across the road from the compound who reported no men were working outside—a clear indication that compound members knew "something was up."
- The isolation of commanders from intelligence that contraindicated the success of their plan—they were so committed to the operation that they refused to consider the possibility of failure.

Groupthink is especially hazardous to law enforcement organizations because of the feeling of "family" that exists. Officers support one another, and sometimes a feeling of "them versus us" exists between law enforcement organizations and those they are hired to "serve and protect."

Even life and death decisions can be affected by groupthink. As noted by Field (1995, p. 90): "It can be very difficult to exercise the courage to speak up and say that the safety conditions are such that a tactical operation should be delayed until additional personnel arrive or conditions are such that the risk to personnel is significantly diminished. . . . It is very hard to be the first one to refuse to go into a barricaded suspect incident with insufficient personnel or wait for a back-up unit on a domestic call."

Whether decisions are made by a group or an individual, often a systematic process is used. Among the most common systematic approaches to problem solving are the seven-step problem-solving approach, force-field analysis, the nominal group technique, the Delphi technique or a modified form of the Delphi technique. These approaches often include brainstorming, which is described following the discussions of systematic problem solving.

The Seven-Step Decision-Making Process

Many problems can be effectively solved through a seven-step decision-making process.

Decision making often follows these seven steps:

1. Define the specific problem.
2. Gather all facts concerning the problem.
3. Generate alternatives.
4. Analyze the alternatives.
5. Select the best alternative.
6. Implement the alternative.
7. Evaluate the decision.

Define the Problem

The logical first step is to identify the problem. It must be located, defined and limited before you can seek solutions. The right answers to the wrong problem will do little to further the department's goals. The successful manager does the right things rather than simply doing things right. It makes little sense to spend valuable time solving problems that do not really matter. The problem needs to be identified *in writing*. Those involved need to agree that it is a priority problem that needs to be solved.

Take care not to confuse a problem with its *symptoms*. For example, patrol officers may be coming to work late or calling in sick more often than in the past. These could be symptoms of a deeper problem—low morale. The problem, not the symptoms, must be addressed.

Another important determination is whether the decision to be made is a large, organizational decision or a small, departmental one. If it is only a small problem, perhaps a command decision is most appropriate. Why waste the energies of top management dealing with a relatively insignificant decision? All too often a myriad of small decisions rob time that should be spent on more major problems.

Gather the Facts

The facts and all relevant data must be obtained and reviewed. Determine existing standards, policies and rules that may affect the problem. If possible, consult everyone involved. At this stage of the decision-making process, be objective. Gather *all* facts related to the problem, not only those supporting your biases. Convert data into information. Data consists of facts and figures. Information is an analysis of these facts and figures.

Experience in dealing with identical or similar problems helps greatly. Sometimes you need to consult experts. Other times a problem may fall within department guidelines and require very little research. Rely on established department policies and practices wherever possible.

Take the time you need to be thorough. Avoid snap decisions for critical or recurring problems. Avoid crisis decisions. Usually time is available to thoroughly investigate. Seek help if needed. For example, if a problem involves your patrol vehicles' performance, seek the advice of a qualified mechanic.

Generate Alternatives

Put the alternatives on a flipchart or blackboard. The following questions can generate alternatives:

- Is there a new way to do it?
- Can you borrow or adapt?
- Can you give it a new twist?
- Do you need more of the same?
- Do you need less of the same?
- Is there a substitute?
- Can you rearrange the parts?
- What if you do just the opposite?
- Can you combine the ideas?

Motivation also has an important role in problem solving. Unless you are motivated to find a solution, you probably will not generate adequate alternatives. Some problems take time to resolve. Ideas may need to incubate, which may take a day or longer. Some of the great scientific discoveries resulted from years of study and work.

Analyze the Alternatives

What are the likely consequences of each alternative? Among the many factors to consider in analyzing the alternatives are fit with the agency mission statement and goals, cost, personnel required, resources available, staff reaction, long-range consequences, union contract provisions, ethical considerations and problems that may arise as a result of the decision.

Time and resources may limit the alternatives. Measure present decisions with past standards.

Select the Most Appropriate Alternative

Choosing the right alternative is the heart of decision making. In normal problem-solving situations, one alternative eventually appears as the best solution. In situations in which all look equal, the choice is more difficult. Most alternatives have advantages and disadvantages. Make a chart with two columns. List each alternative and its advantages and disadvantages. They may be equal in number, but assign a weight to each point. Use the total points as part of your final decision.

Determining alternatives and evaluating them is often difficult. It may require experience, knowledge, training, creativity, intuition, advice from others and even computer assistance. The more input available, the better the decision.

Implement the Alternative

It does little good to decide how to solve a problem and then not implement the alternative selected. Implementation is usually the most time-consuming phase of the decision-making process. It involves several steps and should be carefully planned. Who will do the implementing? What resources will they need? When will the implementation occur?

A critical first step is communicating the decision to everyone involved. Ideally, those involved will have taken part in the decision-making process itself and will already be quite familiar with the options and the reasons a particular option was selected.

If a decision is a command or a consultative decision, such communication is vital. Effective managers keep their people "in on" what is happening and enlist their support from the earliest possible minute. Support those who are implementing the solution. Follow up to see that needed support is continually provided. Seek feedback at all stages of the implementation.

Evaluate the Decision

How effective is the alternative selected? Did it accomplish the expected result? Solve the problem? Evaluation provides information for future decisions. If the solution does not prove effective, learn from the experience. It does little good to brood over solutions that do not work. It does even less good to attempt to place blame.

The primary purpose of evaluation is to improve—to learn what alternatives work and maintain and strengthen them and to learn what alternatives do not work and to change them.

The Steps Applied

Assume that an organizational goal is to reduce accidents by 10 percent. The *problem* is increased traffic accidents. The *cause* of the problem is driving behavior of the motorists. How can police action resolve the problem of reducing accidents by 10 percent?

Once the problem is clearly stated, the next step is to use accident records to obtain data concerning frequency, location, day of week, time of day and causes of accidents. Computer software programs can provide data analysis and instantaneous information.

After information is compiled, alternatives are identified. Alternative A might be to increase radar enforcement to reduce the speed of vehicles because accidents are increasing not only in frequency but also in severity. Increased speed of vehicles involved in accidents results in increased severity. Alternative B might be to station a squad car at high-accident intersections as a deterrent during the day of the week and time of day that accident occurrence is highest. Alternative C might be to add road signs to warn drivers of the accident problem. Alternative D might be to provide additional traffic patrol officers to increase enforcement of traffic violations and increase deterrent visibility. Alternative E might be to station officers in high-accident locations and have them hand out cards to motorists stopping at stop signs. The cards inform the drivers of the accident problem, locations and things they can do to help. Alternative F might be to do nothing.

Next, the alternatives must be analyzed so the best ones can be selected and implemented. Alternative A is accepted, and radar enforcement is increased in selected areas of high accident frequency. Alternative B is eliminated because of time consumption and lack of sufficient vehicles. Alternative C is accepted, and engineering is directed to install signs at the proper locations. Alternative D is eliminated because it requires funds that are not available. Alternative E is eliminated because it would take time to develop and print the card, and the officers do not feel this is good use of their time. Alternative F is ruled out because additional measures are needed to reduce accidents.

The final step is evaluation, which is done six months later. It was determined that accidents were reduced by 5 percent, half the original goal. The results were disseminated to all police department members and the engineering department.

In some instances data and accurate information are not available. In such cases experience, patterns, rules, policies, regulations and personal judgment would be used.

Force-Field Analysis (FFA)

Force-field analysis (FFA) is a problem-solving technique that identifies forces that impede and others that foster goal achievement. Forces that impede goal achievement are called **restraining forces;** those that foster it are called **driving forces.** The problem itself is called **equilibrium.** In a problem situation, the equilibrium is not where you want it to be.

> Force-field analysis identifies factors that impede and enhance goal attainment. A problem exists when the equilibrium is upset because more factors are impeding goal attainment than enhancing it.

Covey (1989, p. 279) explains: "Driving forces generally are positive, reasonable, logical, conscious, and economic. In juxtaposition, restraining forces are often negative, emotional, illogical, unconscious, and social/psychological. Both sets of forces are very real and must be taken into account in dealing with change."

**Table 4.1
Sample Force-Field
Analysis**

Problem: Increasing Drug Abuse in Our Community	
Restraining Forces	Driving Forces
Lack of finances	Increase in drug arrests
Lack of organization/coordination	Church groups
Lack of school cooperation	Parental concerns
Lack of church cooperation	Suicide rate
Lack of available personnel	Increase in drug use
Public apathy	Teen pregnancies
Parental drug use	Fatal accidents
Drug sales profits	

Recommended Action Plan

Create a specialized narcotics unit.

Initiate a 24 hour "hotline."

Pass an ordinance creating a drug-free zone of 1,000 feet around any school.

Conduct educational programs such as DARE in the schools.

Conduct parenting classes.

Conduct drug-free workplace programs.

Start a newsletter to be sent to all residents in the community.

Confiscate all property involved in drug arrests.

Create an Anti-Drug Abuse Council.

Hire a drug counselor for those who cannot afford one.

Source: Stan Kossen. *Supervision*, West Publishing Company, 1991. Reprinted by permission. All rights reserved.

In force-field analysis, you can state the problem as an undesirable situation, then list and label each force as high, medium or low (H-M-L) to indicate the strength. The final step is to devise a plan to change the equilibrium. Select specific ways to reduce the restraining forces and other ways to increase the driving forces. The entire analysis can be put into a chart, as shown in Table 4.1.

The Nominal Group Technique

Researchers Andre Delbecq and Andrew Van de Ven found that some people work better by themselves than in a group. To take advantage of this, yet still capture the synergism of a team approach, they developed the nominal group technique to produce more and better ideas.

> The **nominal group technique** is an objective way to achieve consensus on the most effective alternatives by ranking them.

It works like this:

- Divide the staff or people involved into groups of six to nine.
- Have each person write down as many ideas for solving the problem at hand as they can—without talking to anyone. Allow five to fifteen minutes for this step.

- Go around the group and have each person, including the leader, read one item from his or her list while the leader writes the ideas on a flipchart. No evaluation of the ideas is allowed.
- Continue going around the room until all ideas are posted. If the same idea is given by more than one person, place a tally mark behind it.
- After all the ideas are posted, allow questions to clarify the ideas but no evaluation.
- Hand out notecards and have everyone rank the five best ideas, with "1" being the best.
- Collect the cards and take a break. Total the rankings for each idea and divide by the number of people in the meeting. Then write on the flipchart the five ideas with the highest scores.
- Reconvene the group and have them discuss the five ideas. Usually one best idea will emerge from this discussion.

This technique works well to obtain input from everyone, but it is also very time consuming. It should be reserved for important problems that truly require a consensus decision.

The Delphi Technique   The **Delphi technique** was developed in the 1960s at the Rand Corporation. Like the nominal group process, the Delphi technique is a way to have individual input result in a group effort. Rather than calling a meeting, management sends questionnaires to those who are to be involved in the decision making. Figure 4.1 illustrates a typical Delphi questionnaire.

Survey on Options for Combatting the Drug Problem

As an officer on the street, you are closest to the drug problem our agency is battling. We would appreciate your suggestions on possible approaches to this problem. Please take a few minutes of your time to answer the questions that follow. Your answers will be confidential, but all answers will be shared with all other members of the patrol division.

1. How can we increase community drug education?

   _____
   _____
   _____
   _____

2. What are the three main drug abuse problem areas?

   _____
   _____
   _____
   _____

3. What should we do to reduce the drug problem in our community?

   _____
   _____
   _____
   _____

Figure 4.1
Typical Delphi Questionnaire

Management then circulates the answers to all participants, who are asked to complete the questionnaire again considering the various answers. This continues until a consensus is reached. Usually, three or four cycles is enough.

The Delphi technique uses questionnaires that are completed by individuals. Answers are shared, and the questionnaires are again completed until consensus is reached.

Delphi is actually a really thoughtful conversation in which everyone gets a chance to *listen*. Groups often debate rather than problem-solve. The Delphi technique removes the need for winning points or besting the opposition.

A Modified Delphi Technique

Hartman (1981) has modified the Delphi technique by taking away the open-endedness. This **modified Delphi technique** presents a questionnaire that contains policy statements representing key issues to be decided and a response column with three choices: Agree with, not certain but willing to try and disagree with. Those who do not agree are asked to indicate the changes they would recommend that would make the statement acceptable. This is Phase 1. Figure 4.2 shows an example of how this might look.

Phase 2 shows the number replying with each option for each statement and the choice each respondent circled. Respondents are then asked to reconsider their original responses and make any changes they want based on the responses of others. Figure 4.3 shows how this might look.

1. For each statement below, check the column that best reflects your position:
  A Agree with.
  B Not certain but willing to try for a year and evaluate.
  C Disagree with.
2. For each column where you check C, indicate in the space below the statement how you would like it amended. You may also comment if you checked A or B.			

Suggested Action	A	B	C

To increase community drug education we should:
1. Start a school DARE program.
   Comment:
2. Publish in local papers a series of articles by community leaders.
   Comment:
3. Highlight drug abuse literature at the library.
   Comment:
 	
To reduce the drug problem in our community we should:
4. Increase the number of police.
   Comment:
5. Begin a community-wide Anti-Drug Abuse Council.
   Comment:
6. Provide stiffer penalties to drug dealers and users.
   Comment:			

Figure 4.2
Phase 1 of the Modified Delphi Technique

Following is a tally of responses to the drug questionnaire and suggested changes that we would like you to respond to. As before, for each statement and change, check the column that best reflects your position:

A Agree with.
B Not certain, but willing to try for a year and evaluate.
C Disagree with.

Suggested Action	A	B	C
To increase community drug education we should:			
1. Start a school DARE program.	5	3	3
Change: Also have parenting classes.			
2. Publish in local papers a series of articles by community leaders.	4	4	3
Change: Also articles by victims and cops.			
3. Highlight drug abuse literature at the library.	3	3	5
Change: Distribute literature through civic groups and the schools as well.			
To reduce the drug problem in our community we should:			
4. Increase the number of police.	6	5	0
Change: Increase in areas known to have high rates of drug dealing.			
5. Begin a community Anti-Drug Abuse Council.	4	4	3
Change: Members appointed by chief of police.			
6. Provide stiffer penalties to drug dealers and users.	5	1	5
Change: For dealers only. Counseling for users.			

Figure 4.3
Phase 2 of the Modified Delphi Technique

Phase 3 is a tally of the responses in Phase 2 and a summary of the actions to be taken for each item, based on those responses.

Brainstorming

Most people are familiar with the concept of brainstorming, but often it is not as effective as it might be. Alex Osborn, the originator of the **brainstorming** technique, established four rules:

1. No one is permitted to criticize an idea.

2. The wilder the idea, the better.

3. The group should concentrate on the quantity of ideas and not concern itself with the quality.

4. Participants should combine suggested ideas or build on others whenever possible.

Hurt (1999a, p. 93) suggests another way to generate ideas:

Get together six people you believe to have good insight into the day-to-day operation of your organization. In the meeting, have each of them list three problems they think exist within your organization. Now you have a total of 18 potential opportunities.

Next, have each person show his or her list to another member of the group. The two of them work together to narrow their six problems down to three. Next, have each pair arrange their three problems in descending order of importance.

You now have a total of nine problem statements (three sets of three). The most important problem/opportunity should be at the top of each list.

If you want, you can either discuss each problem/opportunity or collect all the lists and analyze them yourself. This technique will provide you with a great place to start if you are charged with searching out problems/opportunities.

Hurt suggests (1999a, pp. 94–95) that, once basic problems/opportunities are identified and clarified, the team use several techniques to gain the direction needed to solve the problem:

- Ask "What then?" questions—this gets to the heart of the matter and makes sure you're focused on the correct problem.
- Attack and Defend—one or two members of the group stand up and defend the problem as stated. The rest of the group attacks (in a productive way) the problem as stated, to be sure it is as clear and concise as possible. If a change is presented and accepted, the person(s) presenting the change must defend the new objective. This process continues until a statement is reached that is clear and acceptable to everyone. This technique kick-starts the group into problem-solving mode.
- Redefine and Review—have everyone in the group write down two ways of presenting the problem and then report these new statements/objectives to the group to prompt new thinking or changes. It is not critical that the statement/objective be redefined, just that you are sure you have the problem well in hand.

Hurt (1999b, p. 128) also recommends, when you are handling a dilemma, that you hold a "problem briefing" and give participants a pad and pencil: "Urge them to write down any and all ideas that pop into their heads. This is called 'notion noting.'"

Although brainstorming must be unfettered, it is not unstructured as many think. Participants should be prepared. They should know in advance the problem they will address. A leader should keep the ideas flowing and make sure no criticism or evaluation of ideas occurs. Group size should be limited to no more than 15 participants, and they should sit at a round or U-shaped table.

One key to an effective brainstorming session is to write all ideas on a flipchart. As pages become filled, tape them to the walls so that the group will see the flow of ideas and be motivated to continue. All brainstorming sessions should have a definite ending time so a sense of urgency prevails. Time is *not* unlimited.

During brainstorming it is critical that **divergent thinking** (right brain) occur before **convergent thinking** (left brain). Divergent thinking is free-flowing, creative, imaginative and uninhibited. Convergent thinking, in contrast, is evaluative, rational and objective.

To make brainstorming sessions effective:

- Ensure that participants are prepared.
- Write down *all* ideas.
- Allow *no* criticizing of ideas.
- Have a definite ending time.

Brainstorming can be a powerful problem-solving tool.

Other Important Factors

A decision may be logical and legal, but is it ethical—morally right? Many problems facing law enforcement decision makers involve ethical issues. For example, what level of protection is reasonable? Cost effective? Morally responsible? In addition, managers must weigh the risks involved against the possible benefits.

> Ethical considerations and the willingness to take risks are also important considerations in decision making.

Managers must consider not only the logical but also the ethical components of decision. Are issues of fairness or morality involved? Who is affected? Will there be victims? What are the alternatives? Is there a law against some behavior, or does it clearly violate a moral rule? Does the decision accurately reflect the kind of person/department you are or want to be? How does it make you and your department look to the public? To other law enforcement agencies?

Finally, what are the risks involved in deciding? In not deciding? In selecting a different alternative? In being wrong? Edison was quoted as saying he did not fail to make a storage battery 25,000 times 2. He simply knew 25,000 ways *not* to make one. Managers must make decisions and take risks. It comes with the job.

Common Mistakes

Common mistakes in problem solving and decision making include spending too much energy on unimportant details, failing to resolve important issues, being secretive about true feelings, having a closed mind, making decisions while angry or excited, and not expressing ideas. Managers who reject information, suggestions and alternatives that do not fit into their comfortable past patterns can severely limit their decision-making capabilities. Inability to decide, putting decisions off to the last minute, failing to set deadlines, making decisions under pressure and using unreliable sources of information are other common errors in problem solving and decision making. Without the willingness to change, to reach out or to go farther, you cannot be creative or innovative.

Each of these common errors has an alternative, positive approach. For example, rather than making multiple decisions about the same problem, that is, reinventing the wheel, managers should establish standard operating procedures for recurring problems.

Criteria for Decisions

When decisions have been made, they can be evaluated against the following checklist. Is the decision:

- Consistent with the agency's mission? Goals? Objectives?
- A long-term solution?
- Cost-effective?
- Legal?
- Ethical?
- Practical?
- Acceptable to those responsible for implementing it?

Problem-Oriented Policing

Problem-oriented policing (POP) has become extremely popular in many departments and goes hand-in-hand with community-oriented policing. The originator of problem-oriented policing, Herman Goldstein (1990, p. 33), says of the approach:

> Focusing on the substantive, community problems that the police must handle is a much more radical step than it initially appears to be, for it requires the police to go beyond taking satisfaction in the smooth operation of their organization; it requires that they extend their concern to dealing effectively with the problems that justify creating a police agency in the first instance.

The approach used in problem-oriented policing is typically the SARA process.

The SARA problem-solving process involves four steps (Eck and Spelman, 1987, p. xx):

- Scanning (identifying the problem)
- Analysis (looking at alternatives)
- Response (implementing an alternative)
- Assessment (evaluating the results)

Rather than responding to isolated incidents, police focus energies on grouping incidents into problem categories. Once specific problems have been identified, alternatives must be examined. Goldstein's range of possible alternatives (p. ix) includes:

- Concentrating attention on those who account for a disproportionate share of a problem.
- Connecting with other government and private services.
- Using mediation and negotiation skills.
- Conveying information.
- Mobilizing the community.
- Using existing forms of social control in addition to the community.
- Altering the physical environment to reduce opportunities for problems to recur.
- Increasing regulation, through statutes or ordinances, of conditions that contribute to problems.
- Developing new forms of limited authority to intervene and detain.
- Using the criminal justice system more discriminately.
- Using civil law to control public nuisances, offensive behavior and conditions contributing to crime.

Wolfer, Baker and Zezza (1999, p. 11) contend: "The SARA model helps police reduce the crime rate, as well as the fear of crime among citizens." An example of problem-oriented policing in action and the implementation of the SARA process is seen in the way the issue of homeless alcoholics was handled in Madison, Wisconsin. After a homeless alcoholic woman passed out in a snowbank and froze to death near the campus of the University of Wisconsin-Madison during the

In Cleveland, police must move along panhandlers and people sleeping on sidewalks and arrest those who don't cooperate. Here a homeless man protests during a city council meeting against the effects this policy has on homeless people. How could problem-oriented policing be applied to this issue?

winter of 1994–1995, representatives from the university, city and community convened to study and address safety issues in the area. Darden (1998, p. 5) notes how the scanning step of the SARA process was used:

> Scanning—People who are homeless and who suffer from alcoholism were responsible for several problems in the area: sleeping inside and outside buildings, which blocked entry and exit; defecating and urinating in public—often in public view; public consumption of alcohol; panhandling, which was sometimes aggressive; disruptive and disorderly conduct; thefts; drug use; and littering. These individuals also caused problems for themselves: exposure to inclement weather; exposure to diseases; incapacitation due to alcohol abuse; improper nutrition; and victimization due to a reduced ability to care for themselves.

During the analysis step (pp. 5–6), calls for service were examined and linked to certain people. Patterns and trends in call times were also analyzed to obtain a clearer picture of the problem. The response phase (p. 6) included more vigilant handling of calls, seeking permanent solutions to problems, using enforcement whenever people violated the laws and enlisting help from community groups. The assessment phase (p. 6) revealed: "From June 1997 until October 1998, calls for police service by employees and the general public in the lower campus area were down 70 percent from the same time period in 1995 and 1996. The lower campus has also experienced less theft and criminal damage and fewer burglaries."

Sometimes the issue addressed is not a chronic problem but a single critical incident. Problem-solving policing is also applicable in these situations. Ijames (1997, p. 29) states: "The Pre-Incident Planning Model was created to assist police agencies in preparing for high-risk incidents." He also notes (p. 32): "This process is the foundation for effective leadership and decisiveness at the crisis site. The most difficult decisions for management in the tactical environment—and the most productive—are those made before the event takes place."

To ensure appropriate decisions are made, offering the greatest potential for successful resolution of the dilemma, Ijames (p. 29) maintains the preincident planning must address "the critical elements of threat assessment, incident command, operational philosophy and safety prioritization." For example, what are the risks facing the department and the community it serves? Does the community have hardened locations such as fortified crack houses, outlaw motorcycle clubs or correctional facilities? Who in the agency/community is best equipped to respond to these problems?

Another example of problem-solving policing highlights the proactive nature of the effort. A program in Richmond, California, implemented various strategies aimed at suppressing and reducing homicides, a problem previously assumed to be "a product of forces over which the police had little control" ("Problem-Solving Policing Applied . . . ," 1998, p. 2):

> The trend toward problem-solving and community policing has challenged those assumptions. Instead of measuring good policing by officers' success in solving crimes and coping with disorder, the new approach counts success in the *absence* of police business . . . in other words, in the prevention of crimes.

Although the program is still being implemented and evaluated, some have noted (p. 3): "Its early success shows that an effective strategy can be led by an effective police department, but not by the police working in isolation. The involvement of other agencies and an active community are key ingredients."

COPPS and Focus Groups

According to Borrello (1998, p. 24): "COPPS [Community-Oriented Policing and Problem Solving] can generally be described as the reunification of the police and the community they serve. COPPS is meant to be a partnership, a shared responsibility based on trust, to reduce crime, violence and fear in our neighborhoods. To many, it is the changing of policing in America."

The police/community collaboration emphasized in COPPS can be facilitated by using **focus groups** to help identify the most pressing problems of a given area in a jurisdiction. Such groups might consist of members of the educational community, the religious community, Neighborhood Watch groups, business groups, professional groups and the like.

Solmo (1993, p. 78) states: "The focus group format is a beautifully simple one: eight to ten people sit around a table and express their opinions about certain products, concepts, or companies. . . . They're an excellent tool for checking in with your customers [citizens in the community], validating their needs, and determining what directions you should go in." According to Tate (1999, p. 53): "Focus groups are meant to collect broad information on a focused topic in an open, personal environment. . . . Focus groups usually include no more than 10 people and are directed by one moderator." She also recommends that focus groups be used to examine one narrow subject and to understand the community's perceptions of your product or service. They should not, however, be used to make a decision or as a public relations or sales tool.

Summary

Decisions may be strategic—executive level; administrative—middle-management level; or operational—first-line level. Decisions may also be classified as command, consultative or consensual.

Decision making and problem solving involve thinking. Whole-brain research suggests that left-brain thinking processes *language* and is primarily *logical.* Right-brain thinking processes *images* and is primarily *emotional.* Both processes (that is, whole-brain thinking) are needed, especially for creative solutions. Creativity is a process of breaking old connections and making useful new ones. Often synonymous with innovation, creativity can be hindered by thinking traps, mind locks and killer phrases.

Common thinking traps include being stuck in black/white, either/or thinking; being too quick in deciding; making decisions based on personal feelings about the proposer of an idea; being a victim of personal habits and prejudices and not using imagination. Mental locks that prevent innovative thinking include insisting on the "right" answer and the following opinions/statements: that's not logical; follow the rules; be practical; avoid ambiguity; to err is wrong; play is frivolous; that's not my area; don't be foolish; and I'm not creative.

Killer phrases are judgmental and critical and serve as put-downs. They stifle creativity. To handle killer phrases, recognize them, describe to the group what is happening and then challenge them.

Methods for making decisions range from using intuition and snap decisions to using a computer, with a systematic individual or group approach in between.

Participatory decision making has been growing in popularity. All levels of the police department benefit from group participation in the decision-making process. Such an approach, however, poses the potential problem of groupthink, the negative tendency for members of a group to submit to peer pressure and endorse the majority opinion, even if it is unacceptable to individuals.

Whether decisions are made by a group or an individual, often a systematic process is used. Among the most common systematic approaches are the seven-step approach, force-field analysis, the nominal group technique, the Delphi technique and a modified form of the Delphi technique.

The seven-step approach involves defining the problem, gathering the facts, generating alternatives, analyzing the alternatives, selecting the best alternative, implementing the alternative and evaluating the decision. Force-field analysis identifies forces that impede and enhance goal attainment. A problem exists when the equilibrium is upset because more forces are impeding goal attainment than enhancing it. The nominal group technique is an objective way to achieve consensus on the most effective alternatives by ranking them. The Delphi technique uses questionnaires that are completed individually. Answers are shared, and the questionnaires are again completed until consensus is reached.

Many of these logical approaches to problem solving seek creative solutions through brainstorming. To make brainstorming sessions effective, ensure that participants are prepared, write down *all* ideas, allow *no* criticizing of ideas and have a definite ending time.

In addition to seeking logical yet creative solutions, managers must also be concerned with ethical considerations and the risks involved. They may also encourage officers to approach community problems using the SARA approach: scan, analyze, respond and assess.

Discussion Questions

1. Compare and contrast command, consultative and consensual decisions. Which do you prefer?
2. Do you support the findings of whole-brain research? If not, what problems do you see?
3. Can you give an example of when intuition has been important in a decision you have made?
4. Are you comfortable making snap decisions? If so, about what kinds of things? If not, why not?
5. What would your model of decision making look like?
6. Who would you involve in the decision-making process?
7. How important do you feel creativity and innovation are in dealing with typical problems facing law enforcement?
8. How might you engage in "creative procrastination"?
9. Of the systematic approaches to problem solving, which seems the most practical to you?
10. What is the greatest problem you feel law enforcement is facing today? What approaches would you use to attack it?

InfoTrac College Edition Assignment

Find a recent journal article that describes in depth how *problem solving* has been applied by a law enforcement agency. Outline the article. Then decide whether the agency used the SARA approach to problem solving. If not, what approach did they use? Be prepared to share your findings with the class.

References

Arnot, Bob. "Alter Your Biology to Create Sizzling Mental Energy." *USA Weekend,* Jan. 14–16, 2000, pp. 6–7.

Blanchard, Ken; Carlos, John P.; and Randolph, Alan. "Boosting Collective Brain Power." *Security Management,* Vol. 43, No. 9, September 1999, pp. 35–39.

Borrello, Andrew J. "Community-Oriented Policing: Is It Nonsense or Success?" *Police,* Vol. 22, No. 10, October 1998, pp. 24–32.

Covey, Stephen R. *The 7 Habits of Highly Effective People.* New York: Simon and Schuster, 1989.

Darden, Theodore. "University of Wisconsin-Madison Police Response to People Who Are Homeless and Suffer from Alcoholism." *Problem Solving Quarterly,* Vol. 11, No. 4, Fall 1998, pp. 5–6.

Eck, John E. and Spelman, William. *Problem-Solving: Problem-Oriented Policing in Newport News.* Washington, DC: Police Executive Research Forum, 1987.

Field, Mark W. "The Abiliene Paradox." *Law and Order,* March 1995, pp. 89–92.

Goldstein, Herman. *Problem-Oriented Policing.* New York: McGraw-Hill Publishing Company, 1990.

Hartman, Arlene. "Reaching Consensus Using the Delphi Technique." *Educational Leadership,* March 1981, pp. 495–497.

Hurt, Floyd. "Brain Chain Reaction." *Successful Meetings,* August 1999a, pp. 93–95.

Hurt, Floyd. "A Problem Briefing." *Successful Meetings,* February 1999b, p. 128.

Ijames, Steve. "Critical Incident Problem Solving: The Pre-Incident Planning Model." *The Police Chief,* Vol. LXIV, No. 3, March 1997, pp. 29–32.

Janis, I. L. *Victims of Group Think.* Boston: Houghton Mifflin Co., 1972.

Johnson, Virginia. "Intuition in Decision-Making." *Successful Meetings,* February 1993, pp. 148, 152–153.

Malone, Marita V. "Key Thinking Strategies for Future Problem Solving." *The Police Chief,* Vol. LXI, No. 4, April 1994, pp. 29–35.

Martinez, Michael E. "What Is Problem Solving?" *Phi Delta Kappan,* April 1998, pp. 605–609.

McDonald, Tom. "Free Your Mind." *Successful Meetings,* October 1999, p. 26.

Pilant, Lois. "Information Management." *The Police Chief,* Vol. LXV, No. 7, July 1998, pp. 61–65.

"Problem-Solving Policing Applied to Homicides in Model Program." *Criminal Justice Newsletter,* Vol. 29, No. 5, March 3, 1998, pp. 2–3.

Solmo, Regan. "A Matter of Opinion." *Successful Meetings,* March 1993, pp. 78–91.

Spring, Sally and Deutsch, George. *Left Brain/Right Brain.* San Francisco: W. H. Freeman, 1981.

Strentz, Thomas. "Understanding Waco and Other Disasters." *Law and Order,* Vol. 45, No. 4, April 1997, pp. 86–92.

Tate, Julia. "Listen Up." *Minnesota Business and Opportunities,* March 1999, p. 53.

von Oech, Roger. *A Whack on the Side of the Head: How to Unlock Your Mind for Innovation.* New York: Warner Books, 1983.

Wolfer, Loreen; Baker, Thomas E.; and Zezza, Ralph. "Problem-Solving Policing: Eliminating Hot Spots." *FBI Law Enforcement Bulletin,* Vol. 68, No. 11, November 1999, pp. 9–14.

5 Time Management: Minute by Minute

Time management is a question not of managing the clock but of managing ourselves with respect to the clock.

—Alec Mackenzie, time management expert

Do You Know?

- What time management is?
- What the greatest management resource is?
- What is at the heart of time management?
- How the Pareto principle applies to time management?
- How to learn where your time is actually going?
- What helps you manage time minute by minute?
- What the most common external timewasters are?
- What the learning curve principle is and how it relates to time management?
- What three words can prompt you and others to use time effectively?
- What the most common internal timewasters are?
- What creative procrastination is?
- What an effective time manager concentrates on?
- What priorities and posteriorities are?
- How important planning is in time management?
- How to control the paper flood?
- What the results of overdoing it might be?
- How to physically make time more productive?

Can You Define?

creative procrastination	Parkinson's law	skimming
face time	posteriorities	subvocalization
highlighting	priorities	tickler file system
learning curve	procrastination	time abusers
principle	regression	time log
narrow eye span	scanning	time management
Pareto principle	single handling	

INTRODUCTION

Voltaire, an eighteenth-century French philosopher, posed the following riddle *(Zadig: A Mystery of Fate):*

What of all things in the world is the longest and the shortest, the swiftest and the slowest, the most divisible and the most extended, the most neglected and the most regretted, without which nothing can be done, which devours all that is little and enlivens all that is great? *The answer—time.*

Nothing is longer, since it is the measure of eternity.

Nothing is shorter, since it is insufficient for the accomplishment of our projects.

Nothing is more slow to him that expects; nothing more rapid to him that enjoys.

In greatness, it extends to infinity; in smallness, it is infinitely divisible.

All men neglect it; all regret the loss of it; nothing can be done without it.

It consigns to oblivion whatever is unworthy of being transmitted to posterity, and it immortalizes such actions as are truly great.

As Fulton (1997, p. 4) notes: "With every promotion you receive comes an increase in the amount of duties and responsibilities you have to handle. Unfortunately, you don't get a corresponding increase in the number of hours in a day, nor extra days in the week, to handle that increased workload." This chapter discusses the importance of goals in effective time management and ways to organize your time to meet these goals. To identify how you might use time more efficiently, you should know how you are currently spending your time, so the function of time logs is described in detail. Next, the chapter discusses the importance of a "to do" list to make certain that priorities are set and met. This is followed by a look at common time abusers or unproductive time and how you might control this. One important step in managing time is controlling the paper flood and information load so common in law enforcement management. Also important is retaining what you need to remember. The chapter concludes with a discussion of how you can be most productive—the ultimate goal of effective time management.

Time Defined

Time is nature's way of keeping everything from happening all at once. On a more serious note, dictionaries define *time* as "the period between two events or during which something exists, happens, or acts; measured and measurable intervals." Time is most often used in the legal sense to identify specific events. For example, "The accident occurred on January 26, 2000, at 1304 hours."

In the everyday, practical sense we measure time in years, months, weeks, days, hours, minutes and seconds. We also use many devices to measure time, the most popular of which are clocks, watches and calendars.

In spite of much conversation about time, it remains elusive, mysterious and difficult to define. Einstein determined that time is one dimension of the universe and that it is relative. (Two weeks on vacation is not the same as two weeks on a diet.) It is finite, instant, constant and in a sense an illusion. Your time belongs to you and no one else. How you spend your time is your decision. Once used, it can never be regained. Once you have read this paragraph, the time you took to read it is lost forever.

Imagine for a moment that you have a special bank account and that every morning it is credited with $1,440. Whatever amount you do not use each day, however, is taken out of the account. No balance can be carried over. Naturally you would try to use every bit of that $1,440 each day and to get the most out of it. You *do* have such a bank—a time bank. Every morning when you get up you have a 1,440-minute deposit that you can either invest wisely or squander. You cannot save it for tomorrow. Sleep does count as a wise investment.

The following anonymous bit of wisdom is a key point of time management: Yesterday is a cancelled check; tomorrow is a promissory note; today is the only cash you have, so spend it wisely.

Time Management: Planning and Organizing Time

According to Price (1996, p. 19): "Time management is . . . self-management. . . . It's about making time your ally rather than letting it be your master." Time is important to law enforcement managers at all levels and to the people they manage. It is a primary responsibility of law enforcement managers to use both personal time and employees' time productively, and you can accomplish this best through organization, planning and review.

Most law enforcement managers and their subordinates work 40-hour weeks. Some departments schedule five eight-hour days, others four ten-hour days. Each officer has approximately 2,000 working hours annually (allowing for two weeks of vacation). A 20-year law enforcement career has 40,000 assigned working hours, without overtime. Organizing and planning these assigned work hours determines both personal and public benefit: "Do not count time, but make time count." Although this chapter focuses on "work time," the suggestions apply to time away from the job as well.

Successful law enforcement managers at all levels get more done in less time when they develop and follow efficient techniques for using assigned time. They have a sense of time importance and a sense of timing. As noted by management consultant Peter Drucker: "Everything requires time. It is the one truly universal condition. All work takes place in time and uses up time. Yet most people take for granted this unique, irreplaceable, and necessary resource. Nothing else, perhaps, distinguishes effective executives as much as their tender loving care of time."

Managing time involves managing yourself and your daily life. It does not necessarily mean working longer or faster. In fact, as McDonald (1998, p. 22) notes: "There is a big difference between working hard and working smart. One gets you fatigue, the other success." Trying to do everything is not managing. Time management is committing yourself to making quality use of your time to accomplish what is important.

Time management is planning and organizing time to accomplish your most important goals in the shortest time possible.

Time management is a tool to move people from where they are to where they want to be.

This means planning ahead. Jasper (2000, p. 13) observes: "Most people do not plan at all. Those who do often plan from the wrong end. They list the tasks to get them through the day, then do the same thing every day of the week until the year has gone by." Jasper suggests:

> Effective planning works the opposite way. What you want to accomplish by the end of the year determines what you need to do each month.
>
> What must be done this month determines what you should do today and tomorrow. Schedule these tasks into your calendar working backward from your goals.

Value of Time

What is your time worth to you? Have you ever determined in dollars how much your time is worth? Divide your annual salary by the number of annual work hours, usually 2,080 hours. For example, if your annual salary was $50,000, your hourly rate would be $24. If you add in your fringe benefits, your total annual compensation would be much more than that. Your time is valuable and should not be squandered.

When law enforcement managers were asked if they felt they had enough time to do what their jobs demanded, the majority said they could use more hours in the workday. This is *not* a viable solution to time problems.

It is ironic that managers who exercise good time management and complete their duties are often given extra responsibilities. In this situation managers who fail to use time wisely are, in effect, rewarded.

Time is the greatest management resource.

All other resources can be increased, but time is fixed. If a person could gain two more productive hours a day, times five days per week, times fifty working weeks, that would be 500 hours or three extra *months* for each person in the department.

Returning to the definition of time management as "planning and organizing time to accomplish your most important goals in the shortest time possible," the logical place to begin with time management is with *goals*.

Goals and Time Management

The importance of goals has already been stressed. Goals are at the heart of efficiency and time management. It is a waste of time to do very well what you do not need to do at all.

At the heart of time management are *goals*.

Ask yourself: "What is the most valuable use of my time right now?" You can answer this only by looking at the department's goals and objectives and what you must do to accomplish them. Time management needs to be both short and long range. Think in terms of the year, the month, the week, the day and the precise moment.

Segmenting Tasks

Some time management consultants advocate setting up a **tickler file system** consisting of the following 45 files:

- 2 files, one each for the next two years beyond the current year.
- 12 files, one for each month of the current year.
- 31 files, one for each day of the current month.

One reason time management is so difficult is the human tendency to want to accomplish everything at once. Time management requires that time be managed, that is, organized and divided. As the saying goes: "By the yard it's hard. By the inch it's a cinch."

Some important activities may be best set aside until the following year. Simply knowing they are in the upcoming year's file clears your mind of worrying about them for the present. You may put off many activities one or more months. Put them into the appropriate monthly file.

At the end of the month, take the next month's file and divide the activities into the days available. At the end of each day—and this is a key to time management—take the next day's file and plan how to accomplish the activities slated for that day. This brings you to the other half of the time management process—organizing time (to accomplish goals and objectives).

Goals, Objectives and the Pareto Principle

As you consider goals and objectives, the **Pareto principle** comes into play. Alfredo Pareto was an Italian economist who observed that 20 percent of the Italian population owned 80 percent of the wealth. This and similar observations led Pareto to the conclusion that results and their causes are unequally distributed. The percentage is not always 20/80, but it is usually close. Consider the following:

- Twenty percent of your activities may produce 80 percent of your accomplishments.
- Twenty percent of your problem officers may account for 80 percent of the department's problems.
- Twenty percent of your outstanding officers may account for 80 percent of your department's successes.
- Effective leaders pay attention to the 20 percent and concentrate on improvement in those areas.

Effective time management uses the Pareto principle to identify the 20 percent *(few)* *vital tasks* that will account for 80 percent of the desired results. It also identifies and places as low priority the 80 percent *(many)* *trivial tasks* clamoring for attention.

Figure 5.1 illustrates the Pareto principle.

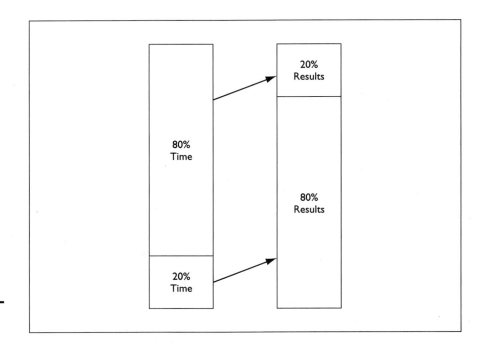

Figure 5.1
The Pareto Principle

Setting Priorities

Time is very important to police departments. In fact, response time presents an interesting time management situation. Although research shows that response time has no effect on arrest rates, it is important for citizen satisfaction and citizens' perceptions of police performance. *Most* departments have to prioritize calls. In some cities, during certain days of the week or times of the day, there may be a backlog of five to ten calls. Field officers have to prioritize calls for service according to severity and importance. Investigators set priorities for cases to investigate, based on the information furnished on the original information record. Field officers' and investigators' responses are reactive. They have little or no control over the types of services required on any specific shift; they have only data based on experience. As departments become more proactive, time management will become more relevant.

Lyndon Johnson once noted: "The trouble with our country is that we constantly put second things first." This, unfortunately, is often true of managers as well.

Urgent vs. Important

According to time management consultant Roger Merrill: "We spend too much time on things that are urgent and not enough time on the things that are important" ("Q & A," 1996, p. 7). Pollar (1996a, p. 78) asserts:

> Achieving and managing success . . . is based on knowing the difference between "urgent" and "important." . . .
>
> A good way to start in differentiating between "urgent" and "important" is understanding the way our responsibilities have changed—how we have more to do, less time to do it, and a critical need to keep balance in our lives. In short, our new predicament can be simplified as a new set of ABCs:

- Accountability—Saying "it's not my job" used to be acceptable, but focusing on customers' needs and hopefully exceeding expectations is everyone's job now.
- Balance—There is more to living than work. If you have career success at the expense of all else, what happens? Career disenchantment.
- Control.

Pollar (1996a, p. 79) concludes:

> Gresham's Law of Time Management says: "The urgent drives out the important." It is the little stuff, the phones, the meetings, a problem, a quick suggestion, interruptions, the mail, etc. . . . These "trivial few" actually hinder you from getting what you need done on a longer-term basis.

The importance of prioritizing is well illustrated by the story of the time management expert who was speaking to a group of high-powered overachievers. He set a one-gallon mason jar on a table along with a dozen fist-sized rocks and carefully began placing the rocks into the jar one at a time until it was filled to the top. At this point he asked, "Is the jar full?"

Everyone in the group shouted, "Yes."

The time management expert replied, "Really?" and reached under the table. He pulled out a bucket of gravel and dumped it in, shaking the jar to cause the pieces of gravel to work themselves down into the spaces between the big rocks. He asked the group once more, "Is the jar full?"

"Probably not," one of the group answered.

"Good," the expert replied, reaching under the table for a bucket of sand. He dumped the sand into the jar, and it went into all the spaces left between the rocks and gravel. Once more he asked, "Is the jar full?"

"No," the group shouted.

Again he said, "Good." Then he took a pitcher of water and began to pour it in until the jar was filled to the brim. Then he asked the group, "What is the point?"

One eager young man raised his hand and said, "No matter how full your schedule is, if you try really hard, you can always fit some more things in it."

"Sorry," the speaker replied. "That's not the point. This illustration teaches us that if you don't put the 'big rocks' in first, you'll never get them all in."

So tonight, or in the morning, when you are reflecting on this short story, ask yourself, "What are the 'big rocks' in my life?" Then put those in your jar first.

Organizing Time

Law enforcement officers can easily visualize the time available for each workday and may also plan for the week, but few officers at any level plan beyond a month. Seldom do people think of their law enforcement careers as 40,000 hours. After a career is over, it is a rare law enforcement officer who would not look back and say: "I could have accomplished a lot more."

This chapter presents several ways to organize and plan time. Select the method you like best or devise your own. The system you use does not matter, only that you do something to make your time more productive. The first step is to know how you are actually spending your time.

Time Logs and Lists

A **time log** is a detailed list of how you spend your time each day. Keeping time logs and lists will show you how you actually use your time. Maintain such logs and lists only until you see which activities actually fill your work time.

> Keeping a daily log or time list tells you how you really spend your time, as opposed to how you perceive you spend it.

Until goals are established and can be adjusted to the actual daily use of time, a great disparity often exists between what people *think* they do and what they *actually* do. Some time experts suggest that a time log be made once a year for several days to a week. When your job changes, make a new time log.

Four Sample Time-Use Logs

The chart in Figure 5.2 asks you to list your starting time for the workday and the ending time of each task you perform. For example, if you start at 0800 hours and your first task is to make a to-do list, which takes 10 minutes, your task ends at 0810, and you are ready for the next task, which may be returning telephone calls. The difference between the times is the total task time.

DAILY USE OF TIME

DATE _____ RANK OR POSITION _____

ARRIVAL TIME AT WORK _____

END TIME	TASK PERFORMED	EVALUATION
_____	_____	_____
_____	_____	_____
_____	_____	_____
_____	_____	_____
_____	_____	_____
_____	_____	_____
_____	_____	_____
_____	_____	_____
_____	_____	_____
_____	_____	_____
_____	_____	_____
_____	_____	_____
_____	_____	_____
_____	_____	_____
_____	_____	_____

This is a task chart, not a goals chart.
List each task in detail.
Mark down time task ended.
Continue listing tasks and end time for entire day.
At end of day, review and evaluate each task as either acceptable or to be delegated, lengthened, shortened or eliminated. Notice that the end of the day you evaluated the time spent on each task as acceptable or to be delegated.

Figure 5.2
Sample Log for Daily Use of Time

Figure 5.3 lists goals and objectives without regard to actual time use. Approximately 50 percent of your time should be spent on priority 1 goals, 40 percent on priority 2 goals and 10 percent on priority 3 goals. Variations of these percentages will occur with levels of manager responsibility. The executive manager may spend 60 to 65 percent of time on priority 1 goals; command or middle-level managers, 40 percent and first-line supervisors, 30 percent.

Determine actual time use for a designated period (perhaps a week). Then review the list and make decisions regarding delegating, shortening time devoted to certain tasks or eliminating a task. If the manager position should change, keep a new time log.

Later compare the actual time logs with the lists of goals and objectives for the position, and make adjustments to bring both lists into one actual time plan. You will need to make adjustments, but once you have learned to make a time-use plan, making changes will be easy.

Figure 5.4 lists time in 15-minute periods. Otherwise, it is the same as Figure 5.2. Figure 5.5 lists only what is considered *unproductive* time, focusing on bad habits. Most people have at least one bad work habit. Many have several. Analyze time logs to identify timewasters.

Law enforcement managers should list their five to ten top timewasters and then make a plan to overcome them. In fact, timewasters could be a training focus or the topic of a staff meeting. Changing bad time habits requires a desire to change. You must put the new habits into daily practice until they are firmly a part of your work routine and continue to practice them until the old habits disappear.

DAILY PRIORITIES AND GOAL LIST

A. Most Important—Priority 1

1_____   2_____
3_____   4_____
5_____   6_____
7_____   8_____

B. Necessary, but Less Important—Priority 2

1_____   2_____
3_____   4_____
5_____   6_____
7_____   8_____

C. Least Important—Priority 3

1_____   2_____
3_____   4_____
5_____   6_____
7_____   8_____

At the end of the day, compare this list with the time-use log. Think about what you are actually doing and what your priorities were. Eventually bring the two into one daily work plan.

Figure 5.3
Sample Daily Priority and Goal List

DAILY USE OF TIME

Time	Activity	Yes	No	Del	Elim
0800–0815	_____	____	____	____	____
0815–0830	_____	____	____	____	____
0830–0845	_____	____	____	____	____
0845–0900	_____	____	____	____	____
0900–0915	_____	____	____	____	____
0915–0930	_____	____	____	____	____
0930–0945	_____	____	____	____	____
0945–1000	_____	____	____	____	____
1000–1015	_____	____	____	____	____
1015–1030	_____	____	____	____	____
1030–1045	_____	____	____	____	____
1045–1100	_____	____	____	____	____

Continue to chart times for your entire workday schedule. Make a chart for your workday using whatever time intervals you desire: five minutes, fifteen minutes, one-half hour or one hour. At the end of the day, decide what tasks were necessary or could be delegated or eliminated. Check the applicable column on the right side of the page for the action you took.

Figure 5.4
Sample Log for Daily Use of Time

UNPRODUCTIVE TIME LOG
Date _____

Task	Approximate time spent on task
_____	_____
_____	_____
_____	_____
_____	_____
_____	_____
_____	_____
_____	_____
_____	_____
_____	_____
_____	_____
_____	_____
_____	_____
_____	_____

At the end of the day, determine whether a task should be: (1) eliminated from the schedule or (2) retained even though unproductive because your position requires it to meet public demand.

After several weeks review this chart with other charts for the two-week period and determine how often the same task occurs. Is it daily, weekly, monthly or seasonal, or is there some other reason the task falls to your position when perhaps it could be performed at another level? Make the necessary adjustments.

Figure 5.5
Sample Log for Unproductive Time

Using the Time Logs

A time log gives you an idea of what you do at work, but you do not always know if you make the most productive use of your time. This is especially true of management positions.

Patrol officers promoted to sergeant do not continue to perform the same duties; in departments where sergeants have eight or more patrol officers to manage, sergeants will find that managing the office is a full-time occupation. In some larger departments sergeants may have up to 25 officers to manage, a severe test for the first-line supervisor. Sergeants need to know how time is actually being used.

Moving up the ladder of command, lieutenants and captains will not perform the same functions they performed as sergeants. Likewise, police executives (chiefs, superintendents or sheriffs) will not perform the same duties as the command level. Each level will find the time log a valuable tool for providing an accurate picture of time use.

Without a time log you do not know where time goes, how much time is spent on what items and how frequently activities occur. Usually only a small portion of the day is uncommitted, but how is it used? A time log shows where it actually goes. After you make revisions, the time log should match the desired time allotted for specific goals and objectives. You have then achieved effective time management.

After logging your time, ask the following questions:

- What am I doing that I don't really have to do?
- What am I doing that someone else could do?
- What am I doing that I could do more efficiently?
- What am I doing that wastes others' time?

Zbar (1999, p. 27) suggests you should also note your productivity peaks and valleys throughout each day.

Objections to Time Logs

The most common objection to keeping time logs is: "I don't have time." It does take time, but the payoff is worth it. Others claim that time use varies from day to day. Again true, yet patterns do exist. Some say their days are already full. Some object to putting what they do on paper. In some instances these objections are only excuses to continue with timewasting habits.

The time log is a tool to help you determine whether a workday is full of the right tasks. If the tasks are wrong for the position, you can delegate, eliminate or otherwise change them. If all the tasks are right and the assigned work schedule is full, you have achieved good time management.

Every manager's time is broken up by diversions, unexpected distractions and interruptions of all types. It is realistic to allocate time for these. Knowing when and how frequently interruptions occur helps you reduce the time you spend on them. Also plan some time during the day for creative thinking about your job.

Controlling Time

The first step in controlling time is to ensure that you are accomplishing the tasks that must get done.

The Daily To-Do List

Although it is not necessary to continuously keep a daily log, it *is* critical to plan each day's time. This is best done the night before. Simply write down everything that you should accomplish the following day. Then prioritize the items as follows:

A   Acute or critical—must be done.

B   Big or important—should do when A is finished.

C   Can wait—nice to do if time allows.

D   Delegate.

E   Eliminate.

The daily to-do list may be the single most important time management tool. It helps you manage minute by minute.

If you make a to-do list the night before, you have a jump on the next day. Sleep will come easier, and this in itself can reduce stress and tension. Do not make the list too full. Leave some time for planning and for those unexpected things that inevitably arise in a manager's life.

Mackenzie (1972) also describes five categories for activities:

- Important and urgent (for example, budget due next week).

- Important but not urgent (getting physically fit).

- Urgent but not important (a meeting you are expected to attend—politically important, but not task related).

- Busy work (cleaning files, rather than starting on a project).

- Wasted time (sitting in traffic with no audiocassettes or cellular phone).

Of these five categories, the biggest problem is usually the important but not urgent task. Such tasks tend to be put off indefinitely. Pollar (1996a, pp. 79–80) offers the following advice on how to integrate long-term tasks into your daily schedule without adding overtime:

1. Put the project in writing.

2. Break it down into small, manageable steps.

3. Set interim deadlines on your calendar.

4. Set aside quiet time.

5. Involve others.

Regarding quiet time, Fulton (p. 4) adds:

Quiet times are those times when everyone else has gone home, or has not arrived at work yet. These times allow you to work on projects without the usual interruptions.

To-do lists and time logs should be used until routine replaces them. Changes in duties or position require new logs and lists.

Don't add quiet times to your work day! Schedule them as a part of your regular work day. You may want to start early, work late or schedule a Sunday shift. Whatever your choice, these times are great for difficult projects.

Other Methods

The Franklin Day Planner is a time-management notebook used by people all over the world and an option for busy law enforcement managers. Another option is to turn your car into a training center. If you live to be 77, and if you drive 10,000 miles a year, you'll spend *three* years of your life in your vehicle. Yet another option is to do the least-liked tasks first. It is natural to avoid things you do not want to do. The trouble is, when you waste energy avoiding the bad things, you may lose your ability to get anything else done. One suggestion for predominantly right-brained managers is to jot each task to be accomplished on color-coded notes and stick them around the desk.

After you have identified the necessary tasks, the next step is to find the time to do them by identifying unproductive time.

Time Abusers: Combatting Unproductive Time

Managers in law enforcement experience the same unproductive time problems found in other professions. Time abusers tend to develop into time-use monsters if not controlled.

Develop an image of time respect. Managers often contribute to their own demise by trying to solve too many problems for others when they should be solving their own. Some of this time abuse is normal and must be accepted as part of a manager's job.

Generally **time abusers** can be divided into external—generated from outside—and self-generated, or internal.

External Timewasters

Among the most common outside or external timewasters are *interruptions*. Managers are interrupted approximately every eight to ten minutes. Controlling and reducing these interruptions is important not only to save time but also to maintain continuity of thought.

> Among the most common external time abusers are the telephone, people who "drop in," nonessential meetings, socializing and "firefighting," or handling crises.

The Telephone

The telephone offers several advantages. You save time when you make a call instead of traveling. You also have more control over the timing of a telephone conversation than you do over a personal visit.

However, the telephone also heads the list of timewasters. Allowing too many calls, permitting conversations to last too long, failing to screen incoming calls, failing to keep conversations purposeful and allowing calls to interrupt quality creative time can be devastating to productivity. Keep a telephone time log if you find the telephone a problem.

Avoid getting caught playing telephone tag. Leave a time to receive calls and find out when individuals you are trying to call will be available.

When making calls, plan what you are going to talk about and stick to the subject. Eliminate as much small talk as possible. Fulton (p. 4) advises: "Learn to keep calls as short as possible, using a timer if necessary. Be cordial and polite, but get off the phone as soon as possible with people who don't seem to be as busy as you are."

Screen your calls through a secretary, a receptionist or an answering machine that can be monitored. Always answer the phone with paper and pencil in hand. Write down the name of the person who is calling and take careful notes. This will save time later.

Always have calls held during your most productive, creative times and during important meetings, whether they are one-on-one or in a larger group. One effective timesaver is to "batch" your calls. This relates directly to what we know of the learning curve principle.

> The **learning curve principle** states that grouping similar tasks can reduce the amount of time each takes, sometimes by as much as 80 percent.

According to the learning curve, each time you repeat the same task, you become more efficient. Telephone calls are one responsibility for which the learning curve can help manage time.

Voice mail can compound the problem, however. Some managers arrive in the morning, check their voice mail, and are greeted with: "You have 37 messages." Not a good way to start the day but a reality in many departments.

The secret is to reduce the disadvantages of telephones and multiply the advantages. Telephone companies have films you can use or trainers who can meet with your staff and point out the most efficient use of telephones. Zbar (pp. 28–30) offers other suggestions to make your phone a power tool:

- When on the phone, type notes directly into the computer.
- Use caller ID to screen incoming calls.
- Dedicate a data line for faxes and online use.

Drop-In Visitors

Put limits on the visits of people who just stop in without an appointment. Be polite but firm. At times you may need to simply close your door when priorities demand that you have time alone.

Hang a "Privacy, Please" sign on your door during periods when you need uninterrupted time. Arrange specific times when others know your door is "open." Communication is, after all, critical to good management, but it also needs to be managed. Be available to others outside your own office. Then you have greater control over ending a conversation. Fulton (p. 4) suggests:

> Once someone is in your office, it can sometimes be difficult to get them to leave, even when their business is completed. . . .
>
> The best way to handle the situation is to keep them out of your office in the first place. Whenever appropriate to do so, meet them at the front desk, in the squad room, or somewhere else where you have better control of when the meeting ends.

Stand up when someone enters your office, and conduct the conversation with both of you standing. Such conversations tend to be brief. Keep socializing to a minimum. Get to the topic that brought the drop-in visitor to your office and stick with that topic.

If a drop-in visitor stays on, you might try saying, "One more thing before you go . . . ." Or you might take the person out in the hall to show him or her something—anything. Of course, you may arrange for a co-worker to interrupt you with an "emergency" if a drop-in visitor stays longer than a specified time.

Be honest. You might simply say, "I've enjoyed our talk, but I really must get *back to work.*" That simple phrase will not only be a clue to the visitor to leave but also serve as a prompt to you.

The three words *back to work* will prompt you and others to keep on task.

Meetings

As much as 50 percent of managers' time may be spent in meetings, and of this, 50 percent of the time is often wasted. Think about the hourly rate of each person attending and be sure the department is getting its money's worth. Wasted time includes not only the time in the meeting but also the time spent winding up a particular task before the meeting, traveling to and from the meeting and then getting back on task.

Organizations might consider designating someone to be a "meeting attender," to go to meetings and make brief written reports. This would create more paperwork but take less time than your attending the meeting and could be useful for informational meetings that do not require the manager's personal participation. Avoid nonessential meetings, and do not call them yourself.

If your sole purpose for attending a meeting is to make a presentation, find out what time the presentation is expected, arrive a few minutes before that time, make the presentation and then excuse yourself. If you find yourself at a nonproductive meeting, it can be most efficient to simply excuse yourself and leave. Use common sense, however, especially if the meeting was called by and is being chaired by your superior.

Socializing

Socializing is a factor in inefficient phone calls, encounters with drop-in visitors and meetings. Relationships are very important, and socializing is an important part of relationships. However, socializing should be confined to coffee breaks, lunch or before or after work. The phrase mentioned earlier, "I've got to get *back to work,*" reminds co-workers that you are not getting paid to socialize.

Political Game Playing

Although most managers seek to avoid politics, you cannot avoid a certain amount of political game playing. If the chief wants to talk about the grandchildren, subordinates would be wise to listen. Seek ways, however, to keep such time to a minimum.

"Firefighting"—Dealing with Crises

Law enforcement managers can expect to confront the unexpected daily. It comes with the job. Allow time in each day for these crises so you can deal with them calmly and rationally. Anticipate what might occur and have policies developed. Is the department likely to receive a bomb threat? To undergo a natural disaster? To be overrun by gang members?

If a crisis occurs for which no policy exists, get the facts, remain objective and think before acting. Then, when time permits, develop a policy for the situation should it arise again.

Internal Timewasters

Not all timewasters come from the outside. Many are self-imposed or the fault of colleagues.

Among the most common internal timewasters are procrastination, failure to set goals and objectives and to prioritize, failure to delegate, personal errands, indecision, failure to plan and lack of organization.

Procrastination

Procrastination is putting off until tomorrow what has already been put off until today. For some people the greatest labor-saving device is tomorrow. Do not delay things. Get them done. Get right to work on priorities.

One reason for procrastination is fear that if you do it, it will be wrong. Set a goal and think only of the goal. So what if you make a mistake? The person who makes no mistakes usually makes nothing at all! Think, "I can do it, and do it now." Motivational speaker Zig Ziglar, author of *See You at the Top,* gives members of his audiences a round piece of wood bearing the word *tuit.* He chides them that they can no longer say they will do something when they get "around to it" because they already have one. Davidson (1999, pp. 62–63) presents six ideas to help you get going on a project:

- Face procrastination head-on—Ask yourself what is blocking you, what the real reason is you don't want to get started. Write it down.

- Choose to easily begin.

- Employ the three-to-five method—Ask yourself, "What are three to five things I could do to just dabble a bit and not tackle the project straight on?"

- Start 'er up—Simply turn the PC on.

- Jump-start the project—Suppose it's Friday afternoon and you have a project to start Monday. To get ready for Monday, use jump-starting: Preview any supporting items, jot down some notes, begin a rough outline, or undertake other supporting activities now—while it doesn't count. Your ideas and thoughts flow freely, and this 10-minute period can be valuable in how your Monday goes—when it does count.

- Tackle big projects one day at a time—For tasks stretching several months or even years, using the day unit is a convenience measure for charting your progress. A day unit is six hours of concentrated labor within a calendar day. Calculate how many day units you'll need to reach a long-term goal. Factor in the weekends, holidays, and other downtime. Now mark your calendar accordingly: "580 days until . . ."; "400 days until . . . ."

Pollar (1996b, p. 67) suggests:

One of the best ways to break the procrastination habit is to reward yourself for good behavior. Reward yourself at milestones in the project process, not only when you finish the job.

When you find yourself blocked and unable to start, ask yourself, "Is there anything, no matter how small, that I am willing to do to get this done?" When you find that one small thing, you are no longer procrastinating.

The following techniques also might help combat procrastination:

- Start with your most unpleasant task to get it out of the way.

- Set aside half an hour a day to work on a given project—schedule the time to do it.

- Do not worry about doing a task perfectly the first time through.

- Work briskly. Speed up your actions.

Another effective way to avoid procrastination is to set deadlines and let others know about them. If others are counting on you to have a task completed by a specific date, chances are you will do it. Accept 100 percent responsibility for completing tasks on time. Help others to do likewise. Finish tasks. Procrastination is one of your worst enemies.

Although you want to overcome the human tendency to procrastinate, you should learn to practice *creative procrastination.*

Creative procrastination is putting off those things that do not really matter.

If you can put tasks off long enough, they probably will not have to be done. A simple example of this is sending holiday greeting cards. If you really do not feel an urgent need to send them and if you can procrastinate long enough, the holiday will pass and so will the need to send them—at least this year.

Failure to Set Goals and Objectives and to Prioritize

Too much of each day is spent by people, managers included, doing very well things that they do not need to do at all.

Effective time managers concentrate on doing the right thing, rather than on doing things right.

The temptation is to clear up all the small things first so the mind is clear for the "big stuff." What often happens is that the whole day is taken up with the small stuff. Or doing the small stuff saps so much energy that little is left for the big stuff. Too many managers become bogged down in routine activities.

How do you differentiate between the trivial many and the significant few—those 20 percent described in the Pareto principle? Consider how combat triage officers divide the wounded into three groups:

- Those who will die no matter what—make comfortable.
- Those who will live no matter what—give minimal medical attention.
- Those who will survive only with medical attention—focus attention here.

The same can be done within law enforcement agencies. Think of the consequences of what you do. Will accomplishing a given task have a positive payoff? Avoid a negative consequence? What will happen if you *do not* get a specific task done? Clearing away the trivial tasks to leave room for single-minded concentration simply does not work. It has no payoff. You never get to the bottom of the stack.

Effective managers set **priorities**—tasks that they must do, have a big payoff and avoid negative consequences. They also set **posteriorities**—tasks that they do *not* have to do, have a minimal payoff and very limited negative consequences.

Many managers excel at setting priorities but have no grasp of setting posteriorities. A day has only so many hours. For each new task a manager takes on, one task should be cut out. To continue to take on new responsibilities without delegating or eliminating others is courting disaster—often in the form of burnout.

Effective managers know how to say no. In fact, one of the most potent time management tools is the simple word no. Pollar (1996a, p. 80) advises: "Remember, the little, urgent tasks tend to multiply. Do not get caught in the activity trap. . . . Saying 'no' may be the magic word. . . . Say 'no' to the extraneous that distract you from the high-value activities." When they cannot say no, effective managers know how to ask for help and to delegate.

Failure to Delegate

Many managers feel that the only way something will get done right is to do it themselves. Such managers need to ask who did it before me and who will do it after me? The effective manager is one who can be gone for a few days or even weeks and everything continues smoothly during the absence. If you do not learn to delegate, there will never be another person trained to perform the work in times of crisis.

Delegate whenever possible. Train subordinates, trust them, set limited and clear expectations, provide the necessary authority for delegated tasks and give credit when they have completed the task. Delegation gives strength to the delegator and the person delegated to. It is not an abdication of responsibility.

Delegation moves organizational communication downward. Delegation must be based on mutual trust, acceptance and a spirit of cooperation between all parties. In addition, subordinates must be empowered to do the delegated tasks.

Put the delegated tasks in writing with set time limits. Keep records and follow through. Do not over-delegate to the same few workers. Delegation helps people develop and spreads responsibility throughout the organization so goals and objectives are more easily attained.

Personal Errands

Only in emergencies should personal errands be attended to during on-duty time. It does not leave a good impression to see law enforcement managers on personal errands during working hours.

Indecision

Subordinates have a reasonable expectation that managers will make final decisions, especially on high-priority issues. Indecisiveness indicates a lack of self-confidence and is most frequently caused by fear of making a mistake. Approach mistakes as learning experiences; the biggest mistake may be never making a mistake. Understanding the decision-making processes described in Chapter 4 can make this managerial responsibility less threatening.

Failure to Plan

The saying goes: "Most people don't plan to fail; they simply fail to plan." Managers must learn to recognize problems and determine their causes, or time will be lost. Working the hardest or doing the most work is not necessarily the best answer if the work you choose is not of value. The average person will spend more time planning a vacation than planning a career.

Planning the use of time may save time threefold, perhaps more.

If you do not take time to plan to do it right, you may have to find time to do it over. Fulton (p. 4) states:

> If you know you have to plan a security detail for the 4th of July Parade, don't try to start it on the 3rd of July. If you do, you'll end up working all day, all night, and end up with poor performance at the parade.
>
> Avoid those stress-filled, all night sessions by starting your planning early. That way, when little stumbling blocks fall in your way, you will have plenty of time to work them out, before your deadline arrives.

Lack of Organization

Desk signs may proclaim: "A cluttered desk is the sign of genius." The truth, however, usually is: "Cluttered desk, cluttered mind." If you cannot see the top of your desk, it is cluttered. One expert suggested getting rid of the desk if you do not need it in your office.

Do not get rid of the clutter by putting it in the drawer. Take some action to get rid of it. Out of sight does *not* necessarily mean out of mind. Set aside time once a week to eliminate clutter. Of course, the right-brained reader might be thinking: "If a cluttered desk reflects a cluttered mind, what is an empty desk a sign of?" The following suggestions may help your office organization:

- Keep on your desk only the project you are currently working on.
- Keep reference books organized and in easy reach, but off your desk.
- Keep office supplies such as paper clips in your desk.
- Set aside a certain time each day for reading.

In addition to keeping your desk and office organized and neat, keep your projects organized. Use organization charts and flowcharts to graphically portray your goals and objectives, work plans and schedules. Use tickler files to find information faster. Know where and how to find needed information.

Timewasters— The Big Picture

Mackenzie's classic *The Time Trap* (1972 pp. 173–176) identified possible causes and solutions to the most common timewasters, which he considered "universal in nature" (Reprinted with permission of the publisher, from *The Time Trap* by Alec Mackenzie, © 1972 AMACOM, a division of the American Management Association. All rights reserved.):

Timewaster	Possible Causes	Solutions
Lack of planning	Failure to see the benefit	Recognize that planning takes time but saves time in the end.
	Action orientation	Emphasize results, not activity.
	Success without it	Recognize that success is often in spite of, not because of, methods.
Lack of priorities	Lack of goals and objectives	Write down goals and objectives. Discuss priorities with subordinates.
Overcommitment	Broad interests	Say no.
	Confusion in priorities	Put first things first.
	Failure to set priorities	Develop a personal philosophy of time.
		Relate priorities to a schedule of events.
Management by crises	Lack of planning	Apply the same solutions as for lack of planning.
	Unrealistic time estimates	Allow more time.
		Allow for interruptions.
	Problem orientation	Be opportunity oriented.
	Reluctance of subordinates to break bad news	Encourage fast transmission of information as essential for timely corrective action.
Haste	Impatience with detail	Take time to get it right. Save the time of doing it over.
	Responding to the urgent	Distinguish between the urgent and the important.
	Lack of planning ahead	Take time to plan. It repays itself many times over.
	Attempting too much in too little time	Attempt less. Delegate more.
Paperwork and reading	Knowledge explosion	Read selectively. Learn speed reading.
	Computeritis	Manage computer data by exception.
	Failure to screen	Remember the Pareto principle. Delegate reading to subordinates.

continued

Timewaster	Possible Causes	Solutions
Routine and trivia	Lack of priorities	Set and concentrate on goals. Delegate nonessentials.
	Oversurveillance of subordinates	Delegate; then give subordinates their head. Look to results, not details or methods.
	Refusal to delegate; feeling of greater security dealing with operating detail	Recognize that without delegation it is impossible to get anything done through others.
Visitors	Enjoyment of socializing	Do it elsewhere. Meet visitors outside. Suggest lunch if necessary. Hold stand-up conferences.
	Inability to say no	Screen. Say no. Be unavailable. Modify the open-door policy.
Telephone	Lack of self-discipline	Screen and group calls. Be brief.
	Desire to be informed and involved	Stay uninvolved with all but essentials. Manage by exception.
Meetings	Fear of responsibility for decisions	Make decisions without meetings.
	Indecision	Make decisions even when some facts are missing.
	Overcommunication	Discourage unnecessary meetings. Convene only those needed.
	Poor leadership	Use agendas. Stick to the subject. Prepare concise minutes as soon as possible.
Indecision	Lack of confidence in the facts	Improve fact-finding and validating procedures.
	Insistence on all the facts —paralysis of analysis	Accept risks as inevitable. Decide without all facts.
	Fear of the consequences of a mistake	Delegate the right to be wrong. Use mistakes as a learning process.

Timewaster	Possible Causes	Solutions
Indecision	Lack of a rational decision-making process	Get facts, set goals, investigate alternatives and negative consequences, make the decision and implement it.
Lack of delegation	Fear of subordinates' inadequacy	Train. Allow mistakes. Replace if necessary.
	Fear of subordinates' competence	Delegate fully. Give credit. Insure corporate growth to maintain challenge.
	Work overload on subordinates	Balance the work load. Staff up. Reorder priorities.

Figure 5.6 summarizes Mackenzie's 35 categories of timewasters according to their management functions.

A Caution

According to Merrill ("Q & A," p. 8):

> Almost all time management books focus on managing to-do lists, learning time-saving techniques, that sort of thing. The problem is that those books treat people as the problem—like, if you can only get people out of your office, or off the phone, or out of meetings, then everything will be okay. But if you want to be an effective person, you have to understand that people are more important than schedules and plans. . . . So you put a priority on them, not on going through that pile on your desk and checking things off a to-do list.

Controlling the Paper Flood and Information Load

Knowledge is doubling every two and one-half years. One issue of the *New York Times* conveys as much information as a person living in the sixteenth century would obtain in a lifetime. The information age places tremendous demands on everyone, especially managers. Managers cannot ignore the paper flood because much of it is information vital to doing an effective job.

> Control the paper flood by using single handling for most items, improving reading skills, delegating or sharing some reading tasks and adding less to the paper flood yourself.

Managers must control paperwork or it will control them. Law enforcement tasks generate extensive paperwork because of the legal requirement to document information. Reports are a large time problem. The sheer volume of reports makes them not only time consuming to read but also difficult to absorb. Goldstein (1999, p. 28) notes:

> The personal computer was supposed to bring the paperless office, but high-speed copiers, laser printers, and fax machines have made that idea laughable. If you've got to have paper around, organize it into vertical files, not horizontal piles.

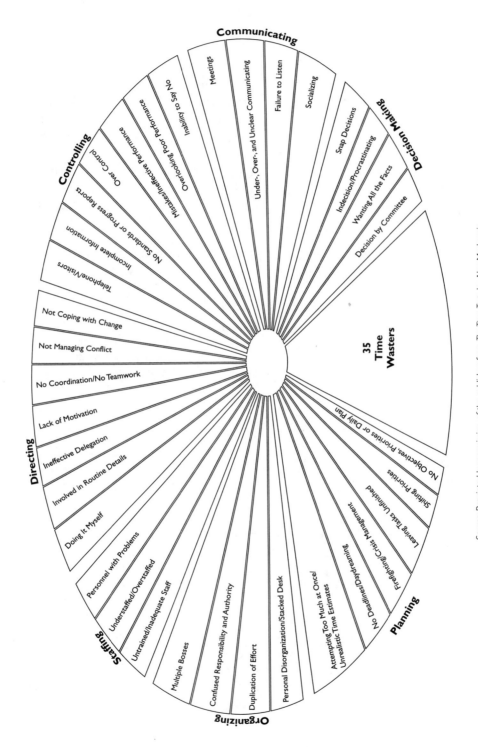

Figure 5.6
**Mackenzie's Timewasters
Related to Management
Functions**

Police administrators must control paperwork, or it will control them. Here a Norfolk police chief has his paperwork neatly organized but must also control interruptions such as phone calls during productive planning time.

In addition to service and offense-related reports, managers deal with mountains of other printed information. Effective managers have a system for handling everything that lands in their "in" baskets, whether it is from an internal or external source. One system that works for many includes four categories:

1. Throw it away—opened or unopened depending on the return address.
2. Route it to someone else (delegate).
3. Take action on it.
4. File it for later action or reference.

This system incorporates **single handling,** that is, not picking up a piece of paper until you are ready to *do* something with it.

Handle paperwork only once—single handling increases efficiency tremendously.

Once printed information is picked up, take action: toss it, pass it on, file it or act on it. The system works best when a specific time is allotted to handle paperwork. Remember the learning curve and the efficiency in "batching" tasks, that is, doing similar tasks at the same time.

Organize the printed information you refer to often. Information that you use every day can be condensed on file cards; put into a Rolodex; added to personal directories, address books and calendars; written on to-do lists; or placed in action files or reference files.

Use microfilm to retain information for long periods in an easily accessible, retrievable form. Prepare master indexes to locate such stored information.

Controlling the paper flood increases your decision-making capabilities, permits planning and lessens the sense of guilt when you do not complete all tasks on schedule. Have a specific place to put everything that comes into your office. Have a working file for frequently used files where they can be reached without leaving the chair.

Another way to control the paper flood is to improve reading efficiency. Learn the difference between **scanning**—reading material rapidly for specific information; **skimming**—reading information rapidly for the main ideas—and actually reading. Scan or skim most reports and publications; read only those of interest and importance.

It has been said that a manager is a person "who wears out two pairs of pants to one pair of shoes." Surveys indicate that managers, indeed, spend a disproportionate number of work hours on paperwork, in the range of 60 to 75 percent.

Mackay (1992, p. 28) suggests reading like a SHARK, which stands for Skim, Highlight, Assess, Reread, Keep:

> Here's how it works: Go through your business reading pile at a quick, even pace. Skim for what you can take in quickly, what you don't need to know and what you need to read in more detail. Assess what you just read. (Do you need to reread it? Save it? To route it?) Reread in greater detail the items that are truly worth your attention. Keep and label just the clippings you want filed.

Three behaviors that slow down the reading process are subvocalization, regression and narrow eye span. **Subvocalization** is moving the lips and/or the tongue to form the words being read. Talking speed is 120–180 words per minute, which is also the speed of readers who subvocalize. Such reading needs to be speeded up. Normal reading is about 250 words per minute. Managers need to read 300–500 words per minute. Subvocalization can be stopped by keeping the lips together and placing the tongue against the back of the teeth when reading. This trains the brain to read and understand words without physically forming them.

Regression is looking back over previously read material, which slows normal reading. To eliminate regression, use the hand or finger sweep. As you read left-to-right, use the finger as a target to follow.

Narrow eye span occurs when a person focuses on one word at a time rather than taking in groups of words and phrases in one look. Adult eye span is between two and three words. To eliminate narrow eye span, search for your name in a magazine or a newspaper. Practice taking two lines at a time as fast as you can and searching back and forth. This is what you do when you look for a name in the phone book. It is necessary to increase not only reading speed but also reading comprehension. This comes only with practice.

Time spent taking a speed-reading course pays huge dividends because it will enhance your ability to scan information with greater comprehension. As you improve your reading skills, also improve your writing and speaking skills. Use fewer, more precise words. According to Oriente (1998, p. 64): "A speed-reading course can triple your reading velocity and improve your learning comprehension. . . . Learning to speed read will also help you become a daily learner. . . . If you learn at least one new idea every day, you will own a treasury of 365 new ideas one year from today."

Delegate reading or divide it among those who are good readers and interested in participating. It is inefficient for several people in the organization to be reading the same outside sources of information. Try having people volunteer to be responsible for a given source, such as *The Police Chief, Law and Order, Law Enforcement News, Police,* national news sources such as *Time* and *Newsweek* and local publications. The person who does the reading can highlight specific items of interest and route them to others within the department. Another way to share the information is to give brief updates at roll call or during regularly scheduled meetings.

Increase your computer skills, also. Many books and training sessions on using computers are available. Computers tremendously increase the ability to retrieve and coordinate information. Oriente (p. 64) notes: "Database management software stores important information and can be quickly installed on your desktop computer, laptop computer, or palm-sized organizer. . . . A database can easily store a person's name, phone number, address, type of business, and will even remind you when a variety of projects/tasks are due." However, McDonald (p. 22) cautions: "One of our great modern myths is that computers increase productivity. What they actually do is save you time. But time saved is not necessarily productivity increased."

Use a cassette recorder, and carry it with you at all times so you can record your thoughts. This is an advantage at meetings, when talking to others (including the media) and in other impromptu situations. It saves time as well as ideas. Oriente (p. 61) states: "Use a recorder to 'dump' all your thoughts and ideas and then return to the task or project you are working on with a clear head."

Finally, do not add to the problem yourself. Some managers like to create paperwork because it gives a sense of personal power and fulfills a desire to influence others. Resist that impulse. Before you add to the paper flood, consider the following:

- Might a phone call work as well as a letter or memo?
- If you must write, is it as brief as possible?
- Who *really* needs copies? Can it be routed instead?
- Do you need copies of reports you are receiving? If not, ask to be taken off the distribution list.
- When you receive written material, if you foresee no further use for it or it will be available somewhere else, do not file it.
- Have a good reason for every contribution to the paper flood created, circulated or filed.

Retaining What You Need to Remember

Some information can be filed and retrieved when needed. Other information, however, should be in your mind. Forgetting has been called the relentless foe. Forgetting takes its greatest toll during the first day after learning something. To slow forgetting you must transfer the information from your short-term memory to long-term memory by *doing* something with it. This might include mentally asking yourself a question about something you have read and answering it, verbally summarizing an important concept to a colleague, highlighting the concept or taking notes on an article.

Highlighting important words or sentences assists retention. It is an active form of reading.

Highlighting is the memory method of choice for most college students, and it is an effective way to transfer information from short-term to long-term memory *if* it is done correctly. Unfortunately, most people simply highlight what they want to remember as they read. This is very ineffective and often results in almost the entire article being highlighted. To highlight effectively, read the entire article (or chapter) first. Then ask: "What is most important about what I have just read?" Then go back and highlight *after* you have finished thinking about what you have read. This is a highly effective way to improve retention.

Productivity— The Bottom Line

What affects productivity? Kelley (1999, p. D4) studied the traits of star performers and isolated 45 qualities he believed to be associated with "stars." He then subjected 200 star and average performers to a two-day battery of tests and found that none of the 45 traits separated the stars from the average performers. What he did find was:

> Average performers think of self-management as techniques to help them better manage their time and projects. But star producers view self-management as creating new opportunities for themselves. They're continually asking how to make themselves more valuable and looking for ways to get the experience and skills they need to get ahead.

In other words, they use their time wisely to boost their productivity. Time management and productivity are integrally related. "Work smarter, not harder" is a truism. Simply "putting in your time" will not make you productive. In fact, the term **face time** has come into vogue in describing the time a person spends coming in early or staying late to impress their superiors. It is the classroom equivalent of "seat time." Sometimes the longer people work, the more tired and unproductive they become.

Overdoing it is not only harmful to your health but often hazardous to the quality of your work.

The most frequent complaint of law enforcement managers is that there are too many interruptions and too many duties and tasks to be performed to accomplish the higher-priority goals of the position. They are unable to control their time to the extent necessary and are constantly operating in a crisis management environment. It is mandatory, however, to establish control not only to accomplish priority tasks but also to make time for creativity, long-term planning and short-term goal innovation; to try new ideas, accept increased responsibilities and make better decisions.

Time is the most important and the scarcest resource managers possess. The organized use of your and all your personnel's time creates a productive department. Control time as you would budget dollars. How you spend time relates to how you can provide more or better law enforcement service. A capable time manager is easily recognized. Time management is one factor that moves employees up the organizational ladder.

With the future probability of fewer rather than more budget dollars, time will become even more important. Because each member of the law enforcement department is interrelated with total department time, the possibility of decreased personnel in ratio to work load will make time an even scarcer resource. This increased demand can be met only by efficient use of available time.

Time is now. You cannot "make time," but you *can* use available time better. Cyril Northcote Parkinson, a British humorist, summed it up neatly in his famous **Parkinson's law**: "Work expands so as to fill the time available for its completion." Consider posting Parkinson's law on the bulletin board for a week.

Time Management in a Service Organization

Many times effective time management is evaluated based on the amount of tangible product produced—this much time spent produced these results. However, service organizations such as law enforcement departments have inherent responsibilities that are time consuming yet not explicitly action-oriented and that yield few tangible results. Nonetheless, these responsibilities are vital to effective customer service, citizen satisfaction and community protection. Such tasks include consoling victims, talking with citizens, having a physical presence in high traffic accident locations, following leads in a criminal investigation in which the actual monetary loss was low and so forth.

The Physiology of Productivity

Although this chapter has focused on working smarter, not harder, that does not preclude the option to work *faster*. Pacing is a matter of habit. Many people walk slowly, talk slowly, think slowly and write slowly. You can physically take control of time and accomplish tasks within the time you have.

Speed yourself up. Walk briskly. Talk crisply. Write rapidly.

You can actually save several minutes each day by simply walking, talking, reading and writing faster. Break out of old habits. Show that time is important by making the most of it. High performance has much more to do with perspiration than with inspiration. Speeding up physically will carry over to your mental state. You will be constantly reminded that you have a finite amount of time to accomplish your goals and objectives.

Summary

Time management means planning and organizing time to accomplish your most important goals in the shortest time possible. In fact, time is the greatest management resource available. At the heart of time management are goals— what you want to accomplish. Effective time management uses the Pareto principle to identify the 20 percent (few) vital tasks that will account for 80 percent of the desired results. It also identifies and places as low priority the 80 percent (many) trivial tasks clamoring for attention.

Keeping a daily schedule tells you what you really do, as opposed to how you perceive that you spend your time. The daily to-do list may be the single most important time-management tool. It helps you manage minute by minute and to control time abusers.

Among the most common external time abusers are the telephone, people who "drop in," nonessential meetings, socializing and "firefighting" or handling crises. When possible, *batch* tasks that are similar, such as making phone calls, because the learning curve principle states that if you do a group of similar tasks together, you can reduce the time they take, sometimes by as much as 80 percent. In addition, the three words *back to work* can prompt you and others to keep on task.

Among the most common internal timewasters are procrastination, failure to set goals and objectives and to prioritize, failure to delegate, personal errands, indecision, failure to plan and lack of organization. One type of procrastination, however, may be effective, that is, creative procrastination—putting off those things that do not really matter. Effective time managers concentrate on doing the right thing rather than on doing things right.

Effective managers set priorities—tasks that they must do, have a big payoff and avoid negative consequences. They also set posteriorities—tasks that they do *not* have to do, have a minimal payoff and have very limited negative consequences. Planning the use of time may save time threefold, perhaps more. An important part of planning is devising a system to control the paper flood. Practices that you might include are using single handling for most items, improving reading skills, delegating or sharing some reading tasks and adding less to the paper flood yourself. Handle paperwork only once—single handling increases efficiency tremendously.

Failure to manage time and ending up overdoing is not only harmful to your health but often is hazardous to the quality of your work. Ways to accomplish more without overdoing include speeding yourself up, walking briskly, talking crisply, reading and writing rapidly. Minute by minute, you *can* manage your time.

Discussion Questions	1. Do you personally use some type of time list or log? A to-do list? Compare yours with others in the class.

Discussion Questions

1. Do you personally use some type of time list or log? A to-do list? Compare yours with others in the class.
2. What is the most unproductive time of your workday?
3. What are your greatest timewasters? Compare yours with those of others in the class.
4. What time management ideas presented in this chapter seem most workable to you? Least workable? Why?
5. How do you determine whether a meeting is necessary? Plan the agenda of a meeting? Control a meeting?
6. What examples of Parkinson's law can you cite in your life or experience?
7. How much of your time is used for paperwork, including correspondence, planning, analysis, reading in-house publications and improving yourself?
8. How would you prioritize your work time?
9. A question to ponder: "Is forgetting caused by time?" Iron rusts with time, but rust is not caused by time. What about forgetting?
10. What are examples of the Pareto principle in your life or experience?

InfoTrac College Edition Assignment

Search for the topic of *time management*. Record how many entries you found. Then select one entry to read carefully and summarize. Be sure to include the full citation for your summary. Be prepared to share your summary with the class.

References

Davidson, Jeff. "Tomorrow Is Another Day." *Successful Meetings,* July 1999, pp. 62–63.

Fulton, Roger. "Managing in the 90s: Getting a Handle on Your Time." *The Police Supervisor,* October–December 1997, p. 4.

Goldstein, Michael. "Getting Out from Under." *Successful Meetings,* October 1999, p. 28.

Jasper, Jan. "Take Back Your Time: Time Wasters . . . Time Savers—Planning Pays." *Bottom Line,* Vol. 21, No. 4, February 15, 2000, pp. 13–14.

Kelley, Robert. "Workplace Stars Are Not Born—They Work at It." (Minneapolis/St. Paul) *Star Tribune,* August 8, 1999, p. D4.

Mackay, Harvey. "Beat the Clock." *Successful Meetings,* October 1992, p. 28.

Mackenzie, R. Alec. *The Time Trap.* New York: AMACOM, 1972.

McDonald, Tom. "Working Smarter." *Successful Meetings,* April 1998, p. 22.

Oriente, Ernest F. "Buying Time." *Successful Meetings,* July 1998, pp. 61–64.

Pollar, Odette. "Get a Grip." *Successful Meetings,* May 1996a, pp. 77–80.

Pollar, Odette. "Just Do It." *Successful Meetings,* August 1996b, pp. 65–67.

Price, Dave. "Getting Time on Your Side." *CityBusiness,* October 4, 1996, pp. 18–19.

"Q & A." *Performance Strategies,* June 1996, pp. 7–10.

Zbar, Jeffrey D. "20 Tips to Better Time Management." *Writer's Digest,* August 1999, pp. 27–30.

6 Budgeting and Managing Costs Creatively

Budget—a mathematical confirmation of your suspicions.
—A. Latimer

Do You Know?

- What a budget is?
- What purposes a budget serves?
- Who is responsible for preparing the budget?
- How most budgets are developed?
- Whose input is vital to any budget?
- What categories are typically included in a budget?
- What is usually the greatest cost in a law enforcement budget?
- What variance analysis is?
- What cutback budgeting involves?
- What common cost choices most organizations face?
- What the first step in managing costs is?
- Who is responsible for reducing costs?
- How subordinates might be involved in managing costs creatively?
- What are some ways a department might reduce costs? Increase revenues?
- How asset forfeiture and the Eighth Amendment are related?

Can You Define?

accounting
accounting period
activity-based costing (ABC)
all-levels budgeting
assets
audit trail
balance sheet
block grant
bottom-line philosophy
budget
capital budget
certified public accountant (CPA)
common costs
contingency funds
cutback budgeting

depreciation
direct expenses
discretionary budget
discretionary grant
expenses
financial accounting
financial budget
financial statements
fiscal year
fixed costs
flexible budget
formula grant
generally accepted accounting principles (GAAPs)
indirect expenses
line items

line-item budgeting
managerial accounting
master budget
operating budget
operating expenses
other expenses
overhead
performance budgeting
petty cash fund
program budgeting
responsibility accounting
semivariable costs
sunk cost
variable costs
variance analysis
zero-based budgeting (ZBB)

INTRODUCTION

Pilant (1997, p. 21) states:

> They are viewed by some police managers as inhumanely boring—eyes glaze over at the mere whisper of the word "budget." The process fills them with dread: citizens clamoring for more services while complaining that taxes are already too high; city officials poking around, looking for a few extra dollars, while police officers lobby for new body armor, radios, vehicles and better benefits.

Nonetheless, the budget is a critical instrument in law enforcement planning, administration and operations. Preparing budgets is difficult because most law enforcement services are intangible. Despite these difficulties, budgets must be prepared for law enforcement agencies. Budgets are synonymous with monetary resources, which in turn are synonymous with personnel, equipment, supplies and, ultimately, the ability to provide comprehensive, continuous law enforcement services.

Each agency has developed guidelines, budget forms and formats. In addition, many computer software programs are in use by law enforcement agencies at all governmental levels.

This chapter focuses on the underlying purposes that budgets serve, what goes into budgets, the planning process, cost estimating and creative ways to manage budgets, including how to involve subordinates in such management. The chapter concludes with a discussion of cutback budgeting, managing costs creatively and increasing income, including resources from asset forfeiture.

Budget Defined

A **financial budget** is a plan or schedule adjusting expenses during a certain period to the estimated income for that period. Brock, Palmer and Price (1990, p. G-1) define budgeting as: "The process of planning and controlling the future operations of a business by developing a set of financial goals and evaluating performance in terms of these goals." Budgets are tools. They do the following:

- Provide a blueprint—It is a framework that can help ensure performance.
- Measure performance—It provides a view of how well you are progressing and serves as a check on performance.
- Control spending—It allows control over expenditures and directs spending to the most profitable areas.
- Provide better coordination—It prevents communication problems, timing problems and staffing problems.
- Are a test of success—It tells whether goals have been reached within the constraints of the available money.

A budget is a working document to be used, not to be cast in stone or held in reverence. A budget, in effect, is a planning and control document, including stated financial expenditure amounts in accordance with a predetermined revenue or income. It is subject to approval by a higher authority than the person or department presenting the budget proposal.

A **budget** is a list of probable expenses and income during a given period, most often one year.

Budget can also be a verb as in, "Let's budget money for this particular project." Usually, however, it is a noun that refers to an estimate of money to be spent during a year.

Types of Budgets

Most departments have two types of budgets. The **operating budget** deals with all expenses needed to run the department. The **capital budget** deals with "big ticket" items and is usually the responsibility of the agency's fiscal unit. Some departments also have a **discretionary budget,** which sets aside funds to be used as needed. This chapter deals with the operating budget.

Budgets are familiar tools to most people. They are used not only by law enforcement agencies, businesses and other organizations but also in personal lives. They are often viewed as negative, restrictive, something to be tolerated. But they also serve some extremely important purposes.

Purposes of Budgets

Budgets control and guide how resources are used and make those in charge of them responsible for their wise use.

Budgets serve as a plan for and a means to control resources.

Budgets establish financial parameters for department needs. The vast majority of plans and projects of the department depend on finances.

Budgets permit decision making at lower levels to work upward through the law enforcement hierarchy. First-line supervisors can present budget ideas that may ultimately be transformed into street operations. For example, the supervisor who develops an accident-prevention program and receives funding to put the program into action must be mindful of budget controls during the entire program.

Budgets also help reduce the tendency for divisions of a department to "build their own little empires" by establishing a maximum line item for each division. The detective division, the patrol division and the juvenile division may each have an allotted amount of funds. Any one division can spend only the funds approved for that division. Without budgeting, serious competition for "total funds" could be detrimental to the departments' overall objectives.

Budgets provide an opportunity to compare expenditures with services provided. For example, the investigative division can compare personnel and other operational costs with the number of cases investigated, cases successfully closed, arrests made and property recovered.

Budgeting is a continuous process and a written commitment. Budgets are a law enforcement agency's work plan transformed into dollars, which translate into salaries, fringe benefits, equipment and special projects. Pilant (1997, p. 21) states: "Budgeting is not an end in itself, but an integral part of the management process, enabling the department to provide the services required by the community."

Budgets are formally approved statements of future expenses throughout the fiscal year. Expenses are constantly balanced against the approved budget allocations. Budgets control available resources and assist in their efficient use. In essence, budgets are a monetary Bible whose First Commandment is: "Thou shalt not spend more than is herein allocated."

Not less than monthly, executive managers receive itemized expenses and a statement of the balance remaining in each budget category. Some communities operate on a **bottom-line philosophy,** which permits departments to shift funds from one category to another as long as the total budget bottom line is not exceeded. Other communities consider each category as separate line items. Any shifting of funds from one category to another must be approved.

Budgets also reflect the political realities of law enforcement agencies and the jurisdictions they operate within. More effective managers are more likely to obtain approval for their programs and projects than less effective managers or those with less political clout. Before looking at who is responsible for preparing the budget and the process involved, take time to familiarize yourself with some budgeting terminology.

Budgeting and Accounting Terminology*

Managers must have a working knowledge of the elements of fiscal management. The following definitions are adapted from Brock, Palmer and Price (pp. G-1 to G-8), with the term *agency* substituted for *business* in many instances. (*Reprinted by permission of Glencoe, a division of McGraw-Hill.)

Accounting is the process by which financial information about an agency is recorded, classified, summarized, interpreted and then communicated to managers and other interested parties.

Accounting period is the time covered by the income statement and other financial statements that report operating results.

Assets are items of value owned by an agency.

Audit trail is the chain of references that makes it possible to trace information about transactions through an accounting system.

Balance sheet is the financial statement that shows the financial position of an agency at a specific date by summarizing the agency's assets and liabilities.

Certified public accountant (CPA) is an accountant licensed by a state to do public accounting work.

Common costs are costs not directly traceable to a segment of an agency such as a department or division. They might include a municipality's insurance costs.

Depreciation is the process of allocating the cost of a long-term asset to operations during its expected useful life. For example, squad cars will decrease in value as they are used.

Direct expenses are operating expenses that can be identified specifically with individual departments. This would include such things as salaries and benefits.

Expenses are the cost of providing services.

Financial accounting is the accumulation of data about an agency's financial transactions, and reporting this data to managers and other interested parties.

Financial statements are periodic reports that summarize the financial affairs of an agency.

Fiscal year is the 12-month accounting period used by an agency. A calendar year, from January 1 through December 31, may or may not be the same as an agency's fiscal year.

Fixed costs are costs that do not vary in total during a period even though the amount of service provided may be more or less than anticipated, for example, rent and insurance.

Flexible budget is a protection that contains budgeted amounts at various levels of service.

Generally accepted accounting principles (GAAPs) are the rules of accounting used by agencies in reporting their financial activities.

Indirect expenses are operating expenses that cannot be easily assigned to a particular department when transactions occur and are recorded. Some indirect expenses, such as depreciation, have a meaningful relationship to individual departments and can be allocated based on this relationship. Other indirect expenses must be allocated on the most logical basis possible.

Managerial accounting is an internal reporting system that gives management financial information for use in decision making and long-range planning.

Master budget is a projection that includes both a detailed operating budget and a detailed financial budget.

Operating expenses are those expenses that arise from the normal activities of the agency.

Other expenses are expenses not directly connected with providing services.

Petty cash fund is a cash fund of a limited amount used to make small expenditures for which it is not practical to write checks.

Responsibility accounting is an accounting system designed to evaluate the performance of the various segments of a business, such as departments, and to assign responsibility for financial results.

Semivariable costs are costs that have characteristics of both fixed costs and variable costs. For example, utility expense is a semivariable cost.

Sunk cost is a historical cost that has already been incurred and is thus irrelevant for decision-making purposes, for example, the purchase of a K-9. Other costs associated with the dog, however, will continue.

Variable costs are costs that vary in total directly with the amount of service provided, for example, personnel costs including overtime.

Responsibility for Preparing the Budget

Budget preparation may be the responsibility of the records department, a financial officer assigned to planning or, in large departments, a separate division.

In smaller law enforcement agencies, executive managers prepare the budget. In larger departments, a person of next lower rank, a staff person, or a special fiscal division is assigned to prepare the details of the budget and present it to the executive manager, who then holds staff meetings or budget workshops to complete the budget. Further workshops determine the final budget.

Executive law enforcement managers should encourage managers in all divisions and at all levels to monitor budget expenditures and justify expenses within their assigned responsibilities. Such a policy encourages budget preparation participation because managers can visualize the total process.

Executive managers or assigned staff need input from all employees. Requested budget information at the various levels should be in a form and language understandable to people not directly connected to preparing the final budget.

The "all-levels" process of budgeting preparation is becoming common in many departments. First-line supervisors know the needs of street-level law enforcement services and will include potentially overlooked items.

> Managers at each level should be responsible for the budget they need, based on input from their subordinates. This results in **all-levels budgeting.**

According to Pilant (1997, p. 22):

> Participative budgeting provides several benefits to the chief executive officer: It reminds employees of the department's policing philosophy, values and mission, as well as upcoming goals and objectives; gives them the opportunity to contribute their ideas in a receptive environment; avoids budgetary oversights, since the people doing the work know what they need and have the opportunity to communicate their budget requirements; opens or enhances lines of communication in a cooperative atmosphere; and provides employees with a greater understanding of the process. Indeed, the whole department becomes part of the process.

If all levels of employees and managers have input into the budget, they will understand it and be more aware of revenue and expenditure balancing. They also become part of not only the process of budget preparation but also the goal development on which the budget is based and the subsequent budget review and possible revisions.

What people help to create, they are likely to support. The budget is one area in which support is critical. Normally the employees' most active interests will be in the areas of salaries and fringe benefits. In reality, some other budget items more severely affect their day-to-day work activities. Effective managers are able to demonstrate this to employees and ensure that subordinates do not focus solely on budget areas that directly affect them but rather on the whole picture.

Budgets prepared using a logical process beginning with the lowest levels of the department and working upward will be more accurate and complete. If the total budget exceeds the amount approved for the agency, the budget must be reviewed line item by line item, and items must be eliminated that will have the least effect on total services provided. Support of all involved is needed to make such cuts without negative effects.

Typical Levels in Developing a Budget

Budget development usually starts at the level of area commands where budget requests originate. Such requests are either (1) funded within the department's base budget, (2) disapproved or (3) carried forward for review by management. At the division level, managers review the area requests, make needed adjustments and submit a consolidated request to the budget section at headquarters. Within two to three months, the budget section identifies proposals for new funding that have department-wide impact and passes them on to the executive level. The commissioner and aides review the figures along with those from other city departments and agree on a budget to submit to the city manager.

The Budgeting Process

Law enforcement budget preparation is a series of events involving hearings, city council workshops, input meetings, cost estimating and a host of other technical details. Realistically, budget preparation should be a year-'round project.

The process generally involves presentation by the finance department at a governmental entity department staff meeting or by written instructions sent to the department head. Sample forms for preparing budgets are included. Dates are set for various levels of preparations, discussions and workshops.

Law enforcement agencies repeat the process with their own personnel. Any changes in procedure from previous budgets are discussed. Dates and times for different levels of completion must be established or procrastinators will be submitting at the last minute, resulting in lower-quality preparation and consideration. This may lead to omission of items important to continued effective operations.

Goals, Objectives and Work Plans

The budgeting process begins with the department's goals, objectives and work plans and the resources needed to carry them out. As Pilant (1997, p. 22) notes: "Because the purpose of any budget is to facilitate the accomplishment of the agency's goals, the development process must begin with a clear understanding of its philosophy, values and mission statement."

Drucker (1982, p. 119) states: "Every police department in the United States knows that crime on the street is a first priority, which requires concentrating uniformed officers on patrol duty. But few police departments dare say 'no' to the [citizen] who phones in to complain that a cat is caught in a tree in her front yard. Instead, it sends a patrol car. Yet police departments probably have the clearest objectives and the keenest sense of priorities of all our public agencies." Such organizational objectives are the basis of financial planning and budgeting.

Past Budgets

Accurate figures of total costs related to successful accomplishment of past goals provide a foundation for future predictions. These figures are then adjusted to allow for increased costs for like items due to inflation and reduced costs due to wider use, wider availability of the product or competition.

Law enforcement managers, even newly appointed, have past budgets as examples. Budget preparation often begins with a review of the previous year's budget. These expenditures were approved and probably apply to the new budget. Hart (1997, p. 34) suggests: "Take full advantage of the department's computer capabilities. [Today], there is no excuse not to commit the budget to

Records help police officers identify areas where expenditures are needed. Using facts, officers can present their budget requests to their superiors. Input from all levels results in the best budget, and it helps make the budget acceptable to officers at all levels.

an electronic spreadsheet. . . . A spreadsheet's biggest advantage is not that it computes the numbers; rather, it allows for easy and frequent revisions without starting all over again."

Assumptions

The next task is to compare cost increases, line item by line item, and adjust, eliminate or add items. These changes should be based on carefully thought-out assumptions. Each year new items and programs appear, and the total amount of available funds varies, but the main budget format remains.

> Most law enforcement budgets are developed by revising the previous year's budget based on logical assumptions.

Most budget items are short term, that is, applicable to current year activities. Because estimated costs are more stable over short periods, short-term expenditures are easier to plan for than long-term expenses. Carryover, or continued items or programs from previous budgets, must include inflationary costs, including cost-of-living increases in salaries, additional fringe-benefit costs and spin-off costs from increased vacation or sick-leave programs.

Law enforcement agencies operate for extended periods with tasks and functions varying from day to day, month to month and year to year. It is therefore a formidable task to foresee all situations that eventually must be converted into cost factors. For example, who can predict whether a squad car will be involved in an accident and "totalled"; or whether 20 inches of sleet and snow will fall, creating numerous accidents; or whether a tornado or flood will occur, requiring hundreds of hours of overtime? **Contingency funds** are set aside for such unforeseen emergencies, but the precise total of allowable expenditures is difficult to ascertain.

Priorities must be weighed. Rarely are revenues sufficient to support all requests, and rarely are all requests justifiable. Justification includes the reasons the item is needed and the effect it would have on the department's operations if eliminated. Items that can be accurately cost-determined should include the source of the cost estimate. The more specific the cost and the justification, the less likely the expense is to be criticized.

Even if all requests are justifiable, final priority decisions must be based on available revenues. Tough decisions are often mandatory. Moreover, not all factors can be measured in dollars. Budgets involve intangibles, such as cost in morale and performance. In some budget preparations, the manager closest to the origin of the financial request is given the total list of requests, the estimated costs and the maximum funding available. Managers are asked to decide what to eliminate.

This prioritization often involves consultation with all employees for whom the manager is responsible. If priorities are set with employees' input, they are more acceptable. Further, employees understand the total budgeting process, which ultimately translates into their everyday operational capabilities for the budget year. Input may be given at one or several stages of the budget process.

Budget preparation should be an annual process of planning, setting goals and objectives, itemizing, obtaining input on needs and comparing the data with past budgets. Information to be used in developing the budget should be collected continuously.

All law enforcement employees should contribute ideas related to budget items as specific needs arise.

Subordinates should submit their ideas to their most immediate manager. At the proper time, managers submit summaries of these suggestions to the next level manager, and so on up to the executive manager. If such ideas are submitted during times of actual need, they will more accurately represent reality when the final budget is developed. Waiting until the last few months before budget presentation time and then rushing to obtain all the necessary information is not good budgeting procedure.

Even with this base, managers may approach budgets with reluctance and apprehension. This is partly because various internal divisions compete, and the agency's total budget competes with all other government departments for available tax revenue dollars. One way to ease the mental anguish of budgeting is to not expect perfection. Having a specific step-by-step procedure for looking at specific areas within the budget can also help lessen anxiety. In the end, as Fuller (1999, p. 49) notes: "The main idea is to effect a viable compromise between the numbers and the people affected."

Budgeting Systems

Law enforcement budgets may take several forms. One of the most common is **line-item budgeting,** initiated in the 1900s and still popular. In this system, specific categories **(line items)** of expenses are identified and dollars allocated for each. Line-item budgets are usually based on the preceding year's budget and a comparison between it and actual expenses. Solar (1998, p. 126) cautions: "Public safety services do not lend themselves well to private sector bottom line analysis."

Performance budgeting, popular in the 1950s, allocates dollars based on productivity. Those divisions who perform most effectively are provided a greater share of the budget.

Program budgeting, popular in the 1960s, identifies the various programs an agency provides and allocates monies for each. A percentage of administrative costs, support costs and **overhead** (operating expenses exclusive of personnel) are assigned to each program. This budgeting approach requires much paperwork, and many managers feel that it is unproductive. However, it can help preserve programs in the face of budget cut pressure, as Solar (p. 126) explains: "If officials insist on budget cutting, the executive can ask them to suggest what specific services or programs should go. . . . Forming linkages to popular programs or necessary functions makes budget cutting more difficult."

Zero-based budgeting (ZBB), popular in the 1970s, requires justification of all expenditures, not only those that exceed the prior year's allocations. All budget lines begin at zero and are funded according to merit rather than according to the level approved for the preceding year. Zero-based budgeting requires management to articulate objectives and then identify alternative methods of accomplishing those objectives, systematically analyzing the effects of various funding levels. Such an approach to budgeting makes comparison of competing programs easier.

Activity-based costing (ABC) is a modern version of the program budgeting system, except that rather than breaking costs down by program, the approach breaks costs down by activity. ABM refers to activity-based management, a logical outgrowth of this approach to analyzing costs. ABC breaks up overhead into neat little cost drivers, the factors that determine the final cost of an operation.

Budget Categories

Regardless of the budgeting system, the budget is usually divided into two classes of expenses: *variable,* which will change depending on the level of service provided, and *fixed,* or overhead, which is relatively constant. Within these two categories, subcategories of expenses can be identified.

> Common budget categories include salaries and wages, services and supplies, training and travel, contractual services and other or miscellaneous.

The miscellaneous category should not be treated as a catchall but should be used for small items such as journal subscriptions or books. Budgets also often contain special one-time requests for capital equipment, such as new police vehicles or investigative equipment.

Typical Allocations
to Various Categories

In most budgets, salaries and wages account for the largest expenditures, typically from 80 to 85 percent. Of this amount, fringe benefits usually amount to 25 percent of the allocation.

Personnel costs usually account for at least three-fourths of the operating budget.

Salaries and wages predominate primarily because of the personnel needed to provide extended-time law enforcement services.

Equipment is also used for the same extended time and consequently must be replaced more frequently. For example, a simple item such as a dispatcher's chair used seven days a week, 24 hours a day is going to need replacement much faster than one used during a five-day, one-shift week. Figure 6.1 shows a typical public safety department's expenditures.

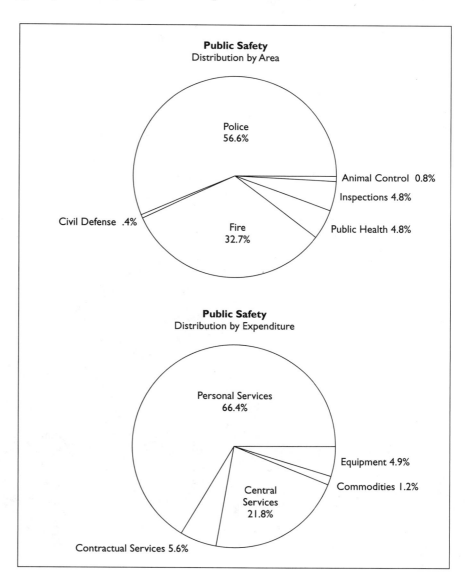

Figure 6.1
**A Typical Public Safety
Department's Allocation
of Resources**

Presenting the Budget for Approval

The law enforcement budget process generally culminates in presentation to the city council or the city manager. Here it competes for revenues with all other departments. Many factors come into play at this point—some factual, some political.

Budget preparations should be made realistically and honestly because the law enforcement budget must be "sold" to a higher body for final approval. Political decision makers need accurate information. "Padding the budget" is often discussed, but in reality city managers, city councils and finance departments are well aware of this tactic. Managers must request funds based on needs, provide a spirit of cooperation and candor and try to avoid serious conflicts. Without factual, accurate information, decisions will likely be made based on personal contacts, innuendo, rumor and community pressure groups. Solar (p. 126) advises: "A wise executive never assumes the budget hearing is just a formality." Hart (p. 35) adds: "Whether before a finance committee or an open town meeting, the approach is the same. The presenter must show a dignified enthusiasm for the budget and convince the overseers that the budget has been prepared with care and with the best interests of the community in mind." Solar (p. 124) explains:

> The fact is, policing does take place in the political environment. The manager who functions without concern for political realities is like a fish that tries to breathe out of water. Some can do it for a short time but they will all die eventually.

To increase the likelihood of budget approval, Solar (p. 124) suggests: "A number of proactive strategies can be undertaken before a crisis emerges which

One important responsibility of the police chief is presenting the budget to the governing body of the jurisdiction. The chief must convince the group that the budget was created responsibly and with the welfare of the jurisdiction in mind.

will increase the influence of the police agency in local government fiscal policy." Two such proactive measures are:

- Forming an advisory committee—such a committee should be representative of the community and the local governing body to ensure a diversity of viewpoints and information.
- Surveying the community—a community survey can be the police executive's back up and can provide information to counter the claims of hostile officials.

After the budget is approved, it must be implemented by converting "dollars and cents" into law enforcement services rendered. It is the manager's responsibility to make sure these dollars are wisely used as budgeted.

Monitoring

The budget is a *tool,* not a document to be approved and then filed. As Hart (p. 35) states: "The budgeting process does not end for the administrator when the budget is finally passed. It is a never-ending process—only the tasks change. The most important task following budget approval is to monitor spending activity."

Variance analysis consists of comparing actual costs against what was budgeted and analyzing differences.

These differences should be contained in a variance report and made known to everyone who directly or indirectly influences the costs. A variance is not necessarily a sign the budget is wrong. Rather, it signals a need for control over income or expenses. Reporting budget variances is an opportunity to provide guidance to management. Variance reports should be made monthly. Problems or deviations should be identified and recommendations made for corrective action. Forms such as those in Figure 6.2 might be used to report variances and requests for budget revisions.

Budgeting is a guideline, not an infallible indicator of the future. No one can do better than an estimate, and variances *will* arise.

Cutback Budgeting

Many departments are being asked to provide more services with fewer funds. Whether called budget reduction, cutback budgeting or reduced expenditure spending, it means added frustration and anxiety for police managers.

Cutback budgeting means providing the same or more services with less funding.

"Doing more with less" is the mandate of the future for most law enforcement agencies. Even successful programs have been discontinued because of lack of funding. To a large extent, budgets control the potential and capabilities of organizations.

Variance Report

Date _____

			YEAR-TO-DATE		
ACCOUNT	REF.	ACTUAL	BUDGET	VARIANCE	%

Variance Analysis

Date _____

	ACTUAL RESULTS	BUDGET ASSUMPTIONS	VARIANCE	%
I: Prior year-to-date				
Total				
II: Current month				
Total				

Figure 6.2
Forms for Reporting and Analyzing Variances

Source: Reprinted by permission of the Publisher from *The Little Black Book of Budgets and Forecasts*, pp. 75, 79, 83. © 1988 Michael Thomsett. Published by AMACOM, a division of American Management Association, New York. All rights reserved.

Causes of Cutback Budgeting

Cutbacks are caused by several factors, the most familiar being "problem depletion," that is, the problem is considered solved. A second cause is "erosion of the economic base," seen especially in our older cities and the Northeast, in the growth of dependent populations and shifts from the Frostbelt to the Sunbelt. Other causes include inflation, taxpayer revolts and actual limits to growth. Whatever the cause, cutback management poses special challenges.

Request for Budget Revision

Account _____   Date _____
YEAR-TO-DATE ACTUAL $ _____
YEAR-TO-DATE BUDGET $ _____
VARIANCE $ _____ % _____

The cause of this variance is: _____

_____

_____

_____

_____

_____

_____

The budget should be changed to: _____

_____

_____

_____

_____ Effective date _____

(Attach revised assumptions)

Approved _____

Title _____ Date _____

Figure 6.2
continued

Doing More with Less   Levine has no pat answers for the challenges and problems he presents, but he does suggest that managers need some new strategies and that these strategies involve making the following choices (pp. 8–9):

Common cost choices management must decide whether to:

- Resist or smooth cuts.
- Make a deep gouge or small decrements.
- Share the pain or target the cuts.
- Budget for efficiency or equity.

In each case, the best choice from a management viewpoint may not make sense politically or from a team-building viewpoint. Levine presents possible solutions (p. 10), such as reassigning functions to county or state governments and the following:

Some services can be "privatized" by installing fees, user charges, and contracting arrangements for special skills, and some services can be consolidated to achieve economies of scale. Services can be "civilized" through the use of volunteers and nonsworn personnel. Some services can be reduced or eliminated by careful monitoring of the differences between citizen "needs" and citizen "wants." And expenses can be trimmed through overtime control, "downtime management," self-insurance, and new pension arrangements.

"The enemies of responsible management in these difficult times," says Levine (p. 10), "are complacency, convenience, and wishful thinking." Compounding the problem are the "political dynamics" with "entrenched interests and neighborhood groups fight[ing] to maintain services at prevailing levels against emerging groups with new demands."

Three steps suggested by Levine might be considered by managers facing cutback budgeting (pp. 11–12):

1. Assume a positive attitude toward innovation; be willing to experiment.
2. Become convinced that fiscal stress can be managed; prioritize services and projects.
3. Develop a marketing strategy to sell taxpayers on the importance and quality of public services.

Each government agency has its sources of revenues and its requirements for services. When sources of revenues do not meet the cost of requirements for services, a cutback budgeting situation develops. New revenues must be designated or services cut. Cost reductions might include cutting overtime, reducing capital outlay purchases, reducing travel, initiating hiring freezes or, in extreme instances, laying off personnel or promoting early retirement.

Seeking new revenues is another solution. A combination of cutback budgeting procedures and new revenues may be necessary.

Managers might look at how budgeting is done in the private sector, with requests for proposals and bidding an integral part of major purchases. Many businesses also use cooperative purchasing, joining together for better pricing. The same can be done in law enforcement. For example, several agencies could go together in purchasing police vehicles, thereby getting a better price.

Managing Costs Creatively

Perhaps without even realizing it, you have already learned about one of the most creative ways to manage costs—managing time. People and their time are a manager's greatest resource. The following discussion assumes that the manager is already paying careful attention to this aspect of "budgeting."

Identifying Common Cost Problems

The first step in solving cost problems is to identify waste areas.

Absenteeism and turnover are major cost problems in most organizations. Managers concerned with controlling costs should have a very clear idea of just how much each subordinate is worth in dollars per day. This figure, coupled with absenteeism, is very important to managers as they look at their budgets.

Other costs managers should target are maintenance of equipment, mail, duplicating, computer and telephone. Are employees using these facilities for personal business? If so, might it make sense to establish a mechanism so they could pay for the convenience? This works well in many organizations.

Meetings are another area, already mentioned, where much waste occurs. Many resource management experts suggest that at least one-fourth of all time (and dollars) spent on meetings is wasted.

Paperwork is another obvious, yet frequently overlooked, area of waste. Americans create over 30 billion documents a year at a cost of $100 billion—an extremely fertile area for cost reduction.

Reducing costs is all employees' responsibility.

Employees should understand where waste is occurring and how they might help reduce it. In addition to this reactive approach to cost containment, a more proactive approach might also be used.

Employee Cost Improvement Suggestion Programs

The idea of a suggestion system is certainly not new, for such systems have been successfully operating for decades in business and industry. A typical system includes guidelines for acceptable suggestions, a mechanism for making the suggestions and rewards for those suggestions selected as feasible.

Employees can suggest ways to cut costs through an employee cost improvement suggestion program.

Successful employee suggestion programs share several common features including clearly informing all employees of the program's details and procedures, provision of fair and meaningful rewards, and continuous publicity regarding the program and its objectives.

Such programs are in keeping with the team concept introduced in the first section of this text and emphasized throughout. Costs must be managed if law enforcement agencies are to provide the services citizens expect and require.

Reducing Costs

Pilant (1998, p. 42) asserts:

> Administrators have to use all the creativity they can muster if they are going to stay ahead of the technology curve and keep their officers supplied with the tools they need to operate efficiently and effectively. . . . It is especially difficult when budgets appear to be shrinking while the public's need for services grows.

Reduce costs by using a regional approach, consolidating service, considering a Quartermaster system, using volunteers and establishing community resource centers.

The Regional Approach

According to Cope and McFaul (1998, p. 46): "One increasingly popular idea for stretching funds is to apply regional approaches to common problems." This allows multiple jurisdictions to pool their resources to form and share teams that are not needed on a full-time basis. Clede (1997, p. 92) notes such specialized regional teams may include SWAT, scuba, accident reconstruction and crime scene units. In one such regional effort, Cope and McFaul (p. 49) observe: "The participating agencies are working to establish a regional jail booking with shared arrest data, enhanced reporting processes and digitized photos and fingerprinting."

Consolidating Service

Similar to the goals of the regional approach, consolidation allows jurisdictions to share staff and services. According to Clede (p. 91): "Two ways cities and towns with medium to small police departments are pursuing these economies are by consolidating emergency services, and by joining with neighboring towns in a region to share specialty teams and service." Clede further notes (p. 91): "There are obvious economies in sharing common facilities, the physical plant, communications, training rooms, parking lot." As an example, many communities have a single "public safety complex," where police, fire and emergency medical service (EMS) personnel are located. In other communities, firefighting and EMS functions are performed by one team.

The Quartermaster System

When examining the best way to equip a department and outfit their officers, many law enforcement administrators face a choice: "Either through the allowance system, where [officers] buy their uniforms, leather, weapons and so forth through outside vendors with checks issued regularly by their employing agencies; or through the Quartermaster system, where the agency keeps a storehouse of these items which are dispensed by someone" (Schmitt, 1998, p. 38). Although stocking such inventory may have some drawbacks, such as limited flexibility for special needs, the Quartermaster system has important advantages. Schmitt (p. 40) notes: "With a Quartermaster, you make a single order in quantity, providing you with a solid supply of identical stock from the same dye lot. . . . You usually get higher quality for a lower price." Furthermore (p. 41):

> A study done by one of the largest departments in the country, which gives its officers about $1,000 annually for their uniform allowance, showed that less than 15% of the officers' checks was being spent on uniforms. . . . Some [officers] wore their shirts until they were ragged . . . because they were reluctant to spend the allowance.

Schmitt (p. 41) suggests:

> If a department prefers the economy, quality and uniformity a Quartermaster system provides, they should have enough leeway in the specs to give officers the chance to utilize brands and styles that work for them. . . . If a department gives its officers allowances, . . . officers shouldn't be pressured to shop at one certain store; . . . they should be allowed to find a supplier who suits them best.

Volunteers

Use of volunteers is increasing in law enforcement departments across the country. According to Pilant (1998, p. 42): "Although many departments have volunteer programs, most of them relegate their workers to enforcing parking violations or watching over handicapped parking spots." However, the volunteer coordinator for the Tempe, Arizona, Police Department (TPD) believes volunteers are capable of much more: "The department's youngest [volunteer] is a

Volunteers can be an invaluable asset to police departments both in terms of cost savings and increased community involvement. Here two volunteers with the Kitsap County Sheriff's Office write a ticket to a person parked without a permit in a handicapped parking place.

12-year-old boy who works with the rangemaster giving demonstrations on the computer and cleaning up the firing range; its oldest—in their late 70s—do crime analysis statistics and fingerprint prisoners" (Pilant, 1998, p. 42). The TPD's volunteer program contributes over 20,000 hours to the agency each year, time valued at more than $250,000.

Using volunteers does more than just save money—it adds value to department services and enhances community policing efforts. As the TPD volunteer coordinator puts it (Pilant, 1998, p. 42): "The more opportunities we open up for the community, the more we are putting the 'community' in community policing, and the more advocates we have in the community."

Community Resource Centers

Another approach to reducing costs is to establish a community resource center (or more than one for large jurisdictions). Combining police services with social services can provide on-site counseling, educational tutoring, legal services, health care and after-school programs. Community-based organizations (CBOs) are provided free space to operate their programs. Stephan (2000, p. 41) cites the following cost savings:

- CBO volunteers are trained in the centers' operations, minimizing the need for city personnel.
- Resource centers located in neighborhoods plagued by extremely high calls for service will reduce the cost of such calls.
- Reduction in policing costs as a result of community mobilization and improved service delivery.
- An immediate reduction in costs associated with vandalism and graffiti.

Increasing Income

Callahan, Gutkin and Rudolph (1997, p. 49) state: "Creativity is the lifeblood of successful funding. A department's ability to combine city budget, grant and other funds to achieve its goals is key, as are diligence, persistence and cooperation."

Departments might increase revenue by fund raising, charging for some services, using asset forfeiture statutes to their advantage and seeking grants.

Fund Raising

The primary source of income for law enforcement agencies is provided by the jurisdiction served by the agency. Local police departments, for example, are supported primarily by tax dollars of that locality. Many police departments find that they are able to increase the dollars available to them by raising funds themselves. Among the methods agencies have used to raise funds are the following:

- Dues to a crime prevention organization.
- Seeking support from civic groups for specific projects, such as K-9 units.

Pilant (1998, p. 44) notes: "The very idea of fundraising generally horrifies most administrators." Nonetheless, for those police administrators who decide to take the plunge, success has been the rule, not the exception. For example, consider one effort by the Crown Point, Indiana, Police Department (CPPD) called the Adopt-A-Car Program (Pilant, 1998, p. 44):

> Although the program initially caused enormous controversy, it since has been hugely successful.
>
> The Adopt-A-Car Program started in 1995 when this small department needed to purchase 10 new cars, but found itself $125,000 short. [A lieutenant] came up with the idea of asking local businesses to donate $1,500 each (tax deductible) to equip the vehicles. In return, the department would paint 'This vehicle is equipped by (business name)' in letters 1 1/2-inches high on the back of the car. . . .
>
> In less than two days, the department had enough financial sponsorship to outfit its new cars and refurbish the old ones.

Contributions made by organizations or citizens are usually tax deductible. In one midwestern community, a citizen crime prevention association has an annual used book sale. Collection boxes are placed in businesses, schools and churches throughout the community, and citizens donate their used books. Each spring, space is donated by a local business, and volunteers conduct a week-long book sale. Profits are in the thousands of dollars. One purchase made with the funds was a K-9 for the police department. The officers named the dog "Books."

Charging for Services

Some agencies have begun charging for traditional services such as DUI arrests. Other departments are billing the hosts of loud parties if the police are called back to the party within 12 hours. In addition to raising revenues, some departments have noticed a 75 percent reduction in second calls about loud parties. Other departments are recouping their costs for extraordinary police services, that is, police services rendered in natural disasters, criminally caused catastrophic events such as bombings or hostage incidents, parades, athletic or timed events.

Other options for creative managers to increase revenues include charging sentenced prisoners an incarceration fee; selling department products, assets, or services, for example, auction surplus equipment or unclaimed items from the

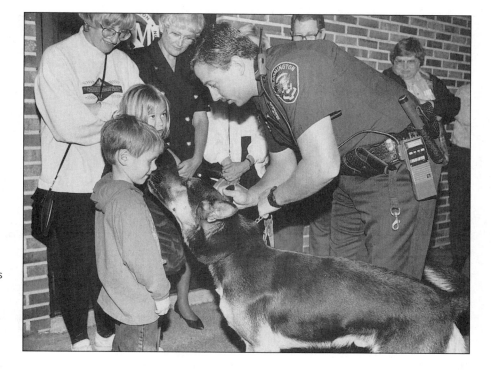

This canine officer and his partner "Books" have just completed a demonstration at the Bloomington, Minnesota, Crime Prevention Association. Books was purchased with funds raised by the association. Such contacts can do much to build good relationships between the police and the citizens they serve.

property room, or providing security at sporting and entertainment events; and selling advertising rights—providing manufacturers with endorsements in exchange for compensation, products, and/or services.

Additional income may be obtained from a variety of sources, such as federal and state grants, foundation funds, direct corporate giving funds, company-sponsored foundations, individual gifts of equipment or money and individual operating foundations. Departments might also charge fees for services such as reports, photographs, fingerprinting, license checks and responding to alarms.

Some agencies have found that accepting credit cards rather than insisting on cash bail has increased revenues collected. Other departments have formed special police assessment districts.

Besides collecting fees as just described, departments may also economize by taking advantage of the rapidly expanding electronic commerce (e-commerce) technologies available over the Internet or via networked kiosks similar to ATMs. Such transactions might include ordering reports, issuing licenses and so on.

Asset Forfeiture

One source of additional income is the asset forfeiture laws, which allow federal agents and local police to seize property owned by those involved in drug trafficking. The Comprehensive Crime Control Act of 1984 authorized the U.S. attorney general to transfer or share forfeited property with participating state or local law enforcement agencies.

The practice of attaching guilt to objects used in committing a crime may have originated with Greek and Roman law. If, for example, a sword was used to kill a man, then it was believed to possess an evil quality independent of the killer. The sword would be confiscated and sold, with the proceeds used for good deeds. Copeland, the director and chief counsel for the Executive Office for Asset Forfeiture, U.S. Department of Justice (1993, p. 86), explains:

> Asset forfeiture takes the profit out of crime and immobilizes crime syndicates by removing the instrumentalities of crime. Forfeiture is also a means of recovering some of the enormous cost of crime to society.

Domash (1997, p. 69) adds: "Used correctly, this legal tool can be a potential windfall for law enforcement agencies while knocking the wind out of criminal pursuits."

One defense of asset seizure is the Innocent Owner Defense—the assets of an owner who had no knowledge of the prohibited activity, either by act or omission, are not subject to forfeiture.

Asset forfeiture is being closely watched by the public and by the Department of Justice. It has also been considered in the U.S. Supreme Court. The Supreme Court has ruled that asset forfeiture is governed by the Eighth Amendment and, as such, must not be so severe as to constitute cruel and unusual punishment.

The Supreme Court considers asset forfeiture to be governed by the Eighth Amendment, which forbids cruel and unusual punishment. It is up to the states to make this determination.

Other Ways to Increase Income

According to Pilant (1998, p. 44): "There are many other avenues to raise department revenues." She lists several successful approaches (pp. 44–45):

> The state of Virginia has a "check-off" donation program built into its state income taxes that brings in about $40,000 each year. The state also has the HEAT (Help Eliminate Auto Theft) program, which has insurance companies returning to the criminal justice system a percentage of every $100,000 in liability insurance they sell. That money is used to address auto thefts, which have dropped 35 percent since the program started. . . .
>
> Criminal restitution can be another revenue producer if the criminal repays the cost of his conviction. . . .
>
> In 1995, the city of Fort Worth, Texas, created a citywide crime control district that lets it levy a half-cent sales tax, with the money going specifically for law enforcement. . . .
>
> The state of California is saving millions with its new CAL-Card, a Visa card program that lets state and local government users make walk-in purchases or place telephone orders of up to $15,000 per transaction. . . .
>
> The 1033 Program . . . makes state and local police departments the recipients of everything from railroad cars to backpacks, all free of charge. It is the ultimate recycling program. The equipment belongs to the Department of Defense (DoD), which either doesn't need it anymore or has replaced it with newer equipment. . . .
>
> The Missouri State Highway Patrol (MSP) built its Aircraft Division out of excess military equipment. Its fleet contains six helicopters and three twin-engine aircraft. . . .

Grants

Numerous grant opportunities exist for law enforcement agencies at both the federal and state level. However, to improve the chances of receiving a grant, it is important to understand the types of grants available and which federal, state and local agencies fund such grants. Reboussin and Schwimer (1997, p. 19) note the distinction between two basic types of grants: "A **formula** or **block grant** [is] awarded by the federal government to the states. In turn, the states make sub-awards to state and local government entities. . . . A **discretionary grant,** by contrast, [is] awarded [based on the judgment] of the awarding agency."

Federal Grant Money   According to Reboussin and Schwimer (p. 19): "The lead federal funding agency for law enforcement programs is DOJ's Office of Justice Programs (OJP). Eight offices within OJP make grants available to law enforcement agencies." They suggest that to win grants from these offices, law enforcement agencies tailor their proposals to meet the specific program area of each office. The eight OJP offices to contact for grant funding are:

- The Bureau of Justice Assistance (BJA)—the primary grant funding arm for law enforcement agencies.
- The Office of Juvenile Justice and Delinquency Prevention (OJJDP)—focuses on operational programs and research designed to prevent and control juvenile crime.
- The Bureau of Justice Statistics (BJS)—collects, analyzes and disseminates statistics. This office can be an invaluable resource for departments needing specific data to include in a grant proposal. BJS also makes discretionary grants to states to encourage development of their own data collection systems.
- The Office for Victims of Crime—supports victim compensation and assistance programs.
- The National Institute of Justice (NIJ)—focuses on research-oriented, rather than operational, projects devoted to new approaches and technologies for combatting crime.
- Drug Courts—support efforts that offer specialized services, treatment and continuing judicial supervision for nonviolent offenders with the potential for rehabilitation.
- Violence against Women—supports efforts to develop and strengthen effective law enforcement and prosecution strategies that address violent crimes against women.
- Corrections Program Office—administers state grants for traditional and alternative correctional facilities, including boot camps.
- COPS Office—makes grants primarily to help agencies hire and deploy new officers.

Regarding COPS (Community Oriented Policing Services) grants, Hoffman (1998, p. 71) notes: "A basic goal of COPS was for departments to use the grant money as they saw fit, as long as the money and additional officers were used in the new Problem Solving styles of policing." According to Hall (1999, p. 28): "The COPS office is credited with funding more than 100,000 officers since 1994 when the agency was created. More than 53,000 of these have already been hired or re-deployed by local law enforcement agencies." Voegtlin and Wilding (1999, p. 8) add:

> President Clinton has announced that his FY 2000 budget will include nearly $1.3 billion—and a total of nearly $6.4 billion over the next five years—for a new "21st Century Policing Initiative" . . . referred to as COPS II. . . .

The COPS II initiative would build on the original COPS program by helping communities continue to hire, redeploy and retain police officers; giving law enforcement access to the latest crime-fighting technologies; and providing funds to allow the involvement of the entire community in preventing and fighting crime.

The COPS program funds grants in several areas, the popularities of which vary significantly. In a random poll of police administrators throughout the country, Sharp (1999, p. 76) found:

> Of the departments polled, 83% had taken advantage of some facet of the program. Most of them, 46%, applied for the Universal Hiring Program (UHP) grants. The second most popular part of the program was COPS MORE (Making Officers Redeployment Effective), which accounted for 32% of the grants. There was a sharp drop-off after that, e.g., Training and Technical Assistance (2%), Community Policing to Combat Domestic Violence (5%), COPS FAST (2%), and COPS Technology Grant for Computer Reporting (2%).

State Grant Money

Funding may also be sought at the state level. Reboussin and Schwimer (p. 20) state:

> At the state level, the office of the governor generally houses contact points for law enforcement-related grants. At a minimum, each state has a contact point for the Byrne formula grants. Byrne grants represent the single largest source of law enforcement-related funding Congress makes available to states by a set formula.

Dunworth, Haynes and Saiger (1997, p. 2) further explain:

> The Edward Byrne Memorial State and Local Law Enforcement Assistance Program makes Federal aid available to State and local criminal justice agencies. Established by the 1988 Anti-Drug Abuse Act (ADAA-88), the Byrne Program is designed to help these agencies control violent and drug-related crime, improve operations, and build coordination and cooperation among the components of the criminal justice system.

Other Sources of Funding

Other sources of funding for law enforcement include direct corporate giving programs, usually foundations, and community-service groups such as the Rotary, Kiwanis and Elks that focus on crime prevention programs, child abuse, drug abuse, senior citizen safety and the like. Perotti and Eisenberg (1998, p. 19) note the Hillsborough County, Florida, Sheriff's Office obtained a $1 million community development block grant from the U.S. Department of Housing and Urban Development (HUD). Another federal funding source is the Weed and Seed program, which promotes the "comprehensive objective of weeding out crime from designated neighborhoods, moving in with a wide range of crime and drug prevention programs, and then seeding these neighborhoods with a comprehensive range of human service programs that stimulate revitalization" (Perotti and Eisenberg, p. 18).

The availability of grants is advertised in the *Federal Register*. This source, published Monday through Friday, also provides the application criteria and details about the grants. Most major libraries subscribe to this publication, and it can be ordered from the Superintendent of Documents, U.S. Government Printing Office, Washington, DC 20402. Other helpful sources of grant information include the following:

- *Foundation Directory*—contains information on the largest U.S. foundations. Available from Columbia University Press, 136 S. Broadway,

Irvington, NY 10533. State foundation directories—many states also have foundation directories. Information on the availability of such a directory for your state can be obtained from the Foundation Center, 888 Seventh Ave., New York, NY 10019. *Corporate Foundation Profiles*—lists over 200 large corporate foundations. Also available from the Foundation Center.

- *Forbes Market 500*—lists the top 500 corporations in the United States. Most of these corporations fund civic projects.

Reboussin and Schwimer (p. 22) advise:

The National Criminal Justice Reference Service (NCJRS) is another valuable source of information for funding available at the federal level. Specifically, an agency can request that NCJRS put it on the mailing list for proposal solicitations and other information, and the agency will thereafter receive all solicitations disseminated by OJP and the COPS office. Administrators can access the NCJRS Website at http://www.ncjrs.org or contact NCJRS via electronic mail at askncjrs@ncjrs.org. They also can direct-dial the NCJRS electronic bulletin board at 301-738-8895.

Grimm (1996, p. 7) suggests other ways to find out about grant programs available to law enforcement agencies:

- Call the U.S. Department of Justice Response Center at (800) 421-6770 and ask to be put on its mailing list.
- Call your state criminal justice program office and asked to be placed on the state programs' mailing list.
- Call your state department of transportation for information on programs involving highway safety issues such as speed and alcohol use.
- Call federal organizations such as the U.S. Department of Health and Human Services (202) 619-0257, the Office of Juvenile Justice and Delinquency Prevention (202) 307-5914 and talk to them about your needs and interests.
- A quick and easy way to find grant information is via the Internet. If you have access, check out your state criminal justice department's home page. . . . Another good address to check is the Bureau of Justice Assistance at http://www.ojp.usdoj.gov/BJA/.

Writing the Proposal

Reboussin and Schwimer (p. 21) note:

The first step for administrators pursuing a specific funding grant is to read the solicitation carefully and follow the instructions exactly. . . .

Administrators should complete all of the forms, fill in all of the blanks, and allow enough time to get all of the required departmental signatures. (Using blue ink for the signatures will more readily identify the original application.) If at all possible, administrators should plan to submit their proposals before the due date to reduce the risks that a minor bureaucratic delay will scuttle the entire grant request. . . .

Where applicable, graphs and charts should be included to help communicate ideas and present data.

Walker (1999, pp. 132–133) suggests how to get a justice block grant proposal approved, stating the four core factors as program concept, local support, written presentation and oral presentation:

Show as clearly as possible that the program you propose would never be funded unless there is outside help. . . . A single most important theme regarding problem concept is: *how is your program idea going to make the state granting agency look good and how can it make it look foolish?* . . .

Local support is important not just for political reasons, but because the better you appear to be at convincing others that you have a good idea, and the more other people have already reviewed your ideas seriously, the more likely that the program will succeed. Keep in mind the question: *is the granting agency risking offending other officials or agencies in your area by giving you funds?*

[The written application] is the point of greatest danger, and greatest opportunity. . . . There is software and equipment available for making slick written presentations; use these tools. But if there is an official form, this will be the document against which your proposal will be compared with others. . . . *Write simply, well, and without boring and obvious statements.* . . .

There may be an opportunity to make an oral presentation. . . . Speak clearly and use proper syntax, correct pronunciation, and modest voice modulation. If you are not able to do this, find someone in your department who can. Do not feel awkward in admitting you aren't a good public speaker. Simply state, "I've asked Robin here to make the presentation. I will be here to field any questions that she can't." . . . Your oral presentation should be pleasant, clear, brief and informative.

Valdez (1998, p. 62) asserts: "Attention to detail is critical in applying for funding through grants." He recommends (pp. 62–63) grant writers pay attention to several vital elements:

- Appearance—The packet should look professional. All comments should be typed.

- Project Strategy and Design—State the purpose of the grant, what the grant will do (project goals) and how it will get done (describe project phases and activities). Clearly define the final product and the project usefulness.

- Organizational Capability—Prove your organization has the experience and ability to manage the grant funds and to complete the stated objectives within the grant's life. Describe previous experience with grants or similar projects. Include appropriation and assignment of professional staff to the project.

- Budget/Plan—Demonstrate cost-effective planning and give a breakdown of costs to give an accurate representation of the total anticipated project cost. Make sure all phases and tasks are clearly defined and timely and that sufficient staff are listed.

- Project Evaluation/Assessment—Provide a clear explanation of how you plan to measure program outcome and list your expected outcome. Describe mechanisms for feedback from users or providers and define your criteria for assessment.

In summary, the six specific components of an effective proposal are:

- A statement of need
- How this need can be met
- Who will accomplish the tasks
- What time line will be followed

- What the cost will be
- When you may look for approval to proceed

Reboussin and Schwimer (p. 21) offer a final piece of advice: "Forward the completed proposal to two or three readers for suggestions and comments before sending it in."

Do not be discouraged if your proposal is turned down. The key to successful grant writing is to learn from your past mistakes. Many very worthwhile and successful programs were rejected repeatedly before eventually being funded. Grant seeking takes knowledge, preparation, patience and endurance. It is not easy, and the competition is keen, but the effort can be rewarding.

Summary

A budget is a list of probable expenses and income during a given period, most often one year. Budgets serve as a plan for and a means to control resources. Managers at each level should be responsible for the budget they need, based on input from their subordinates. This results in "all-levels" budgeting.

Most law enforcement budgets are developed by revising the previous year's budget based on logical assumptions. All law enforcement employees should contribute ideas related to budget items as specific needs arise.

Three kinds of resources must be identified: human, direct and indirect. Common budget categories include salaries and wages, services and supplies, training and travel, contractual services, and other or miscellaneous. Personnel costs usually account for at least three-fourths of the operating budget. Once the budget is developed, it should be used to monitor costs. Variance analysis consists of comparing actual costs against what was budgeted and analyzing differences.

Cutback budgeting means providing the same or more services with less funding. Managers need new strategies that involve making choices as to whether to resist or smoothe cuts; to cut deeply or in small decrements; to share the pain or target the cuts and to budget for efficiency or equity.

The first step in solving cost problems is to identify waste areas. All employees' are responsibile for reducing costs. Employees can suggest ways to cut costs through an employee cost improvement suggestion program. Costs can also be reduced by using a regional approach, consolidating services, using a Quartermaster system, using volunteers and establishing community resource centers.

Many departments are looking for ways to increase revenues, including conducting fund raisers, charging for some services, using asset forfeiture statutes to their advantage and seeking grants. The Supreme Court considers asset forfeiture to be governed by the Eighth Amendment, which forbids cruel and unusual punishment. It is up to the states to make this determination.

Discussion Questions

1. Do you have a personal budget? If so, what are your main categories?
2. Do you belong to any organizations that have a budget? If so, what are their main categories?
3. How do budgets restrict? Provide freedom?

4. What things in addition to money might a law enforcement agency budget (e.g., space)?
5. Is your law enforcement department functioning under cutback budgeting?
6. What percentage of the city's total budget goes to the law enforcement department?
7. What department gets the largest share of the city's budget?
8. What methods might be used to raise funds for your local law enforcement agency?
9. What suggestions do you have for cutting the cost of providing law enforcement services?
10. Why must the budget be updated annually?

InfoTrac College Edition Assignment

Find a recent article on *cutback budgeting in law enforcement.* Outline the suggestions. Star any that were not mentioned in the chapter. Record the full citation for the source. Be prepared to share your findings with the class.

References

Brock, Horace R.; Palmer, Charles E.; and Price, John Ellis. *Accounting Principles and Applications.* 6th ed. New York: Gregg Division, McGraw-Hill Publishing Company, 1990.

Callahan, Tom; Gutkin, Steven; and Rudolph, Mark. "Funding Tomorrow's High-Tech Tools Today." *The Police Chief,* Vol. LXIV, No. 5, May 1997, pp. 47–52.

Clede, Bill. "Consolidating Can Save Money." *Law and Order,* Vol. 45, No. 11, November 1997, pp. 91–93.

Cope, Jeff and McFaul, Nancy. "Five-Step Method to Regional Crime Analysis." *The Police Chief,* Vol. LXV, No. 5, May 1998, pp. 46–49.

Copeland, Cary H. "National Code of Professional Conduct for Asset Forfeiture." *The Police Chief,* October 1993, pp. 86–88.

Domash, Shelly Feuer. "The Assets of Asset Forfeiture." *Police,* Vol. 21, No. 10, October 1997, pp. 69–72.

Drucker, Peter F. *The Changing World of the Executive.* New York: Times Books, 1982.

Dunworth, Terence; Haynes, Peter; and Saiger, Aaron J. *National Assessment of the Byrne Formula Grant Program.* Washington, DC: National Institute of Justice, Research in Brief, June 1997.

Fuller, John. "The Budget Process and the Police Training Administrator." *The Law Enforcement Trainer,* Vol. 14, No. 5, September/October 1999, pp. 48–49.

Grimm, Louise. "Taking the Mystery Out of the Grant Process." *Sheriff Times,* Vol. 1, No. 3, Fall 1996, p. 7.

Hall, Dennis. "COPS Office Achieves President's Goal of Funding 100,000 Officers." *Police,* Vol. 23, No. 7, July 1999, pp. 28–29.

Hart, Fran. "Preparing and Presenting a Budget: An Eight-Step Approach." *The Police Chief,* Vol. LXIV, No. 4, April 1997, pp. 34–35.

Hoffman, John. "COPS Grants." *Law and Order,* Vol. 46, No. 11, November 1998, pp. 71–75.

Levine, Charles H. "Cutback Management in an Era of Scarcity: Hard Questions for Hard Times." *Executive Police Development.* Washington, DC: Department of Justice, National Institute of Justice and the FBI.

Levine, Charles H. "Cutting Back the Public Sector: Hidden Hazards of Retrenchment." *Executive Police Development.* Washington, DC: Department of Justice, National Institute of Justice, and the FBI.

Perotti, Albert, Jr. and Eisenberg, C. B. "Drawing on Federal Resources to Restore Communities." *FBI Law Enforcement Bulletin,* Vol. 67, No. 9, September 1998, pp. 17–20.

Pilant, Lois. "Police Budget Preparation." *The Police Chief,* Vol. LXIV, No. 4, April 1997, pp. 21–32.

Pilant, Lois. "Creative Funding." *The Police Chief,* Vol. LXV, No. 3, March 1998, pp. 42–46.

Reboussin, Roland and Schwimer, Cynthia J. "Grant Writing." *FBI Law Enforcement Bulletin,* Vol. 66, No. 9, September 1997, pp. 18–24.

Schmitt, Sheila. "Write a Check or Keep a Stockroom: What's the Best Way to Equip a Department?" *Law and Order,* Vol. 46, No. 5, May 1998, pp. 38–41.

Sharp, Arthur G. "A Report Card on COPS." *Law and Order,* Vol. 47, No. 2, February 1999, pp. 76–80.

Solar, Patrick J. "The Justification of Training and Other Budget Strategies." *Law and Order,* Vol. 46, No. 10, October 1998, pp. 121–127.

Stephan, Michael, "Union City Community Resource Centers." *The Police Chief,* Vol. LXVII, No. 2, February 2000, pp. 35–44.

Valdez, Al. "Grant Write Your Way to Success." *Police,* Vol. 22, No. 11, November 1998, pp. 62–63.

Voegtlin, Gene R. and Wilding, Marci. "President Clinton Launches COPS II Initiative." *The Police Chief,* Vol. LXVI, No. 3, March 1999, pp. 8–10.

Walker, Bruce. "Persuasive Grant Proposals." *Law and Order,* Vol. 47, No. 6, June 1999, pp. 132–134.

7 Hiring Personnel and Dealing with Unions

Nobody's perfect except when filling out a job application.

—Anonymous

Do You Know?

- What steps are involved in the selection process?
- What the most common screening methods used in the hiring process are?
- What a bona fide occupational qualification (BFOQ) is?
- What major employment legislation affects hiring for law enforcement agencies?
- What the EEOC is, and how it affects hiring practices?
- What goal the Americans with Disabilities Act (ADA) seeks to guarantee?
- What kinds of inquiries or evaluations are prohibited by the ADA?
- What an affirmative action program is?
- In what areas of management EEO and affirmative action policies are important?
- What the National Labor Relations Act requires of management?
- What the National Labor Relations Board is?
- What the basic purpose of unions is?
- Why people join unions?
- What levels of negotiation are usually involved in collective bargaining?

Can You Define?

affirmative action
program (AAP)
arbitration
background check
bona fide occupational
qualification
(BFOQ)
Civil Rights Act
of 1964
closed shop
collective bargaining
delaying tactics
Equal Employment
Opportunity
Commission
(EEOC)

Fair Labor Standards
Act of 1938
halo effect
Landrum-Griffin Act
of 1959
mediation
National Labor
Relations Act of 1935
(Wagner Act)
National Labor
Relations Board
(NLRB)
negligent hiring
Norris-LaGuardia Act
open discussion
rapport

reverse discrimination
right-to-work laws
special employment
groups
Taft-Hartley Act
of 1947
union
union shop
vicarious liability
yellow-dog contract

INTRODUCTION

Today's law enforcement agencies seek a "new breed" of officer—a balance of brawn and brains—one who possesses not only the physical qualities traditionally associated with policing, such as strength and endurance, but also the emotional and intellectual characteristics needed to effect public order in an ever-changing and increasingly diverse society. "People skills" have become a critical tool for law enforcement officers. Nelson (1999, p. 42) notes:

> Law enforcement is not just another job to be filled by placing a want ad in the local paper. Today's professionals face a complex society that demands competence in problem solving, diplomacy, consensus building as well as traditional qualities of courage and the ability to make sound decisions affecting its citizens.

So who do agencies want as police officers, and how do they go about finding such people? According to Nowicki (1999, p. 45): "Unfortunately, there is no scientific formula that can be used to create a highly effective police officer, or determine who will be one. Realistically, being a highly effective police officer is more of an art than it is a science. But certain qualities are imperative for entry-level police officers, such as honesty, ethics and moral character." Nowicki (p. 45) further notes:

> Once our basic police officer foundation is set, there are certain traits that most highly effective police officers have. In the real world most officers will not have all 12, or some will have stronger traits than others. . . .
>
>   The traits listed here were determined after interviews with seasoned rank and file police officers, trainers, supervisors and administrators. There is no exact percentage for each trait, nor are they listed in any particular order of importance.

According to Nowicki (pp. 45–46), highly effective police officers possess enthusiasm, good communication skills, good judgment, a sense of humor, creativity, self-motivation, knowledge of the job and the system, ego, courage, an understanding of discretion, tenacity and a thirst for knowledge. These are the traits law enforcement employers should seek in their officer candidates.

This chapter begins with a discussion of the critical importance of hiring well to avoid litigation from vicarious liability or negligent hiring and many other problems. The chapter then suggests steps departments can take to hire well, beginning with recruiting and continuing through the selection process: the application, testing, background checks and interviews. After looking at the selection process, you will learn about laws that affect the process, including affirmative action and the Americans with Disabilities Act (ADA). Next, the employment criteria that departments might consider in light of these laws are discussed. The chapter concludes with a look at how labor laws and unions affect both the selection process and the functioning of the department, including how management and unions might work together to accomplish mutual goals.

The Importance of Hiring Well

The hiring process is so critical in law enforcement in part because of **vicarious liability,** which refers to the legal responsibility one person has for the acts of another. Managers, the entire agency and even the jurisdiction served may be legally responsible for the actions of a single officer.

Vicarious means "taking the place of another thing or person, substituting for." Law enforcement officers have always been responsible for their individual wrongdoings, criminally or civilly. Civil liability most frequently involves violation of the Civil Rights Act, specifically Statute 42 of the United States Code, Section 1983, which states:

> Every person who, under color of any statute, ordinance, regulation, custom, or usage, of any State or Territory, subjects, or causes to be subjected, any citizen of the United States or other person within the jurisdiction thereof to the deprivation of any rights, privileges, or immunities secured by the Constitution and laws, shall be liable to the party injured in an action at law, suit in equity, or other proper proceeding for redress.

In other words, anyone acting under the authority of law who violates another person's constitutional rights can be sued. In 1978 in *Monell v New York City Department of Social Services,* the court ruled that local municipalities were also liable under Section 1983 (Title 42, U.S.C.).

It is now accepted that local government may be responsible for the wrong-doing of a subordinate enforcing a local ordinance, regulation or policy. In cases in which law enforcement managers directed, ordered or participated in the acts, they are equally liable. Additionally, if upper-level managers are negligent in hiring, assigning, training, retaining, directing or entrusting, they may be liable even if they were not present.

Negligent hiring litigation is becoming more common. Law enforcement managers and supervisors have been held liable for negligence in hiring personnel unqualified or unsuited for law enforcement work. The majority of these cases involve failure to use an adequate selection process or to check for prior offenses or misconduct.

In cases in which the facts indicate the officer should not have been hired, and the officer commits a first offense, the hiring authority may be held liable. In the case of subsequent offenses by the same officer, if no disciplinary action was taken, other supervisors may also be held liable.

In one case an officer was hired on a probationary basis. During the course of patrol, the officer stopped an individual for speeding and driving while intoxicated. In making the arrest, the officer hit the driver with a blackjack with such force that the driver lost one eye. The court concluded that the city equipped the officer with a gun, a gunbelt and a blackjack but had failed to check his background or provide any training.

Negligent hiring and retention have become major problems because of numerous court cases that have resulted in high judgments. Law enforcement agencies are being held to a higher standard than industry for wrongful hiring and retention. It is not only a serious concern but a two-way problem of hiring good candidates and firing incompetent ones. Conducting background investigations, hiring qualified personnel and then developing them into permanent employees can help reduce such lawsuits. Negligent supervision, negligent training and negligent retention will be discussed later in the text.

The initial application is an important document to check in determining a candidate's competence for the job. The consent statement provides the right to verify any information on the application. The application should also have an employment-at-will provision indicating that no contract guarantees permanent employment. Final responsibility for screening out unfit candidates rests with whoever controls the hiring. The basic premise of negligence is whether the hiring agency or person knew or should have known about the employee's conduct or was negligent in checking all information on the application. In some instances information may have been known but was ignored, and the person was hired anyway.

Recruiting and selecting are closely allied. Law enforcement agencies throughout the United States, at all levels of government, have developed varied systems to recruit and select as well as to promote personnel. The following discussion focuses on the initial recruiting; entries into positions above that level are usually from existing personnel.

Recruiting

Recruiting qualified officer candidates is a key element in building an effective and successful law enforcement agency. West (1997, p. 3) notes that many departments now have "aggressive recruitment policies to attract and hire a diverse group of officers who meet the highest standards both personally and educationally, and are representative of the community they serve." According to a study by the Justice Department: "Local police and sheriffs' departments have been hiring new officers at an increasing rate in recent years, and the composition of the forces is changing, with larger numbers of women and minority officers, and more departments that require recruits to have at least some college education" ("Local Law Enforcement . . . ," 1999, p. 4).

Yet the increasing need for qualified recruits does not necessarily translate into rising numbers of qualified applicants. As Nislow (1999, p. 1) states:

> Whether one blames the nation's roaring economy, higher educational requirements or noncompetitive wages and benefits, police and sheriff's departments in virtually every region of the country agree that the generous pool of applicants from which they once sought qualified candidates is becoming increasingly shallow.
>
> An apparently pervasive problem, it has become especially acute for agencies that require college credits.

Departments take a variety of approaches in recruiting suitable candidates. Strandberg (1996, p. 39) states: "Most departments do the same type of recruiting activities: handouts, military recruiting, advertisements (TV, radio, newspapers), job fairs, and visits to colleges—all very traditional recruiting techniques." National recruiting newsletters may also be of assistance, including the National Employment Listing Service and Knights.

Recruiting graduates of college criminal justice programs is one major source of candidates, and the implementation of college internships can be a valuable aid to recruitment. For example, in Idaho, collaboration between several colleges, the law enforcement community at large and the Idaho Peace Officers Standards and Training (POST) Council has led to a successful internship program. Leach (1998, p. 59) cites the benefits to all involved: "The Internship portion of the North Idaho College Law Enforcement Program is mutually advantageous to the student and agency alike. Interns get the opportunity to view an agency from the inside and the agency gets to see a prospective employee in a law enforcement setting."

Another way to reach potential recruits is to go online. Strandberg (p. 39) states: "Some forward thinking departments are also recruiting in cyberspace, with home pages on the Internet. . . . Prospective candidates can find out more about the department, get information on the standards and testing requirements, and find out when the next applications will be taken." Narramore and Stephen (1998, p. 54) add:

> It is estimated one out of every four people currently uses the Internet. Do not overlook this resource. In the near future, almost every law enforcement agency will have its own Internet home page. This is an ideal place to locate potential talent. Via the Internet, entire applications can be completed and the candidate can provide a description of him/herself without any time restraints.

Another avenue in recruiting police candidates is to seek out second-career officers. For example, the Appleton, Wisconsin, Police Department actively recruits new officers from other professions, not necessarily because of their knowledge of police work but because of the maturity and stability they bring. According to the Appleton police chief (Byrne, 1998, p. 183), the most important skills a contemporary police officer can have are not expert marksmanship, report writing proficiency or driving ability but rather people skills—how well the person relates with people: "How does he relate to a diverse group of people? Can he manage conflict? And what's most important—is he a problem solver?" Byrne (p. 183) reports: "Among the recent rookie class, those that joined the Appleton department were a former school teacher, a nurse, a dental technician, an assistant district attorney, a juvenile counselor, a paramedic, a car salesman and a businessman."

The impending retirement of veteran officers presents yet another recruiting opportunity for departments. Weinblatt (1999, p. 127) explains that some departments are holding onto a knowledgeable resource by recruiting reserve officers from their full-time ranks:

> In an age requiring more sophisticated personnel, agencies are increasingly looking to benefit from the wealth of police experience residing in their communities. Retaining full-time expertise in the guise of a reserve officer is a cost-effective way of meeting law enforcement challenges.

Recruiting Women

Recruiting, hiring and retaining female officers is vital to a balanced and effective department. However, the increase in the number of women in policing has been alarmingly slow. Neubauer (1998, p. 53) notes:

> Women are not new to policing. They have been "in the ranks" for decades, but their representation has traditionally been small. Since the early 1970s, however, more women have been applying for police positions. A recent study by the National Center for Women in Policing (NCWP) of 100 of the largest law enforcement agencies in the country revealed that in 1972, women represented 2 percent of all police officers in the agencies surveyed. By 1997, they represented almost 12 percent.

The IACP's 1998 National Police Survey ("Women in Policing," 1998, p. 36) found: "The percentage of female officers in a department is correlated

Many departments use advertising like this poster to specifically target female recruits. The amount of female representation in law enforcement is still low.

with its size. All of the large departments had at least one female sworn officer, and 8 percent had 51 or more female sworn officers. However, 17 percent of all respondents reported that their departments had no female sworn officers."

Despite the modest increase over 25 years, many contend that female representation is still too low, perhaps dangerously so. According to one article ("Rank Objections," 1998, p. 1): "The low proportion of women in policing can have dire ramifications for law enforcement, . . . including more police brutality, ineffective responses to domestic violence, strained police-community relations and costly sexual harassment and sexual discrimination lawsuits."

One major challenge is that women do not apply for police officer positions in the same numbers that men do. Harris (1999, p. 18) observes: "Many departments where women were previously unheard of in sworn positions are aggressively seeking female applicants. Despite their newfound commitment to hiring women, police departments are discovering competition for the small pool of qualified female candidates is fierce." Furthermore (pp. 18–19): "Job fairs and other traditional techniques have been unsuccessful in attracting large numbers of females. According to [one expert], 'A general recruiting effort will not appreciably increase the pool of female applicants.' Instead, women-specific strategies must be used." Such strategies include revising recruiting brochures to include photos of female officers, organizing career fairs specifically for women and displaying recruiting posters in gyms, grocery stores and other places where women are likely to see them.

Basic gender differences must also be taken into account. According to Keller (1999, p. D1), researchers have identified four primary areas in which male and female approaches to workplace issues appear to differ: Men tend to be competitive whereas women tend to be collaborative; men tend to use direct language whereas women use indirect language; men's creativity tends to focus on the scientific compared to women's systems-oriented approach; and men tend to be more company oriented whereas women are more entrepreneurial. Such findings have implications for recruiting women police officers. Advertisement efforts geared to the crime fighting, law enforcing aspects of the profession may be ineffective. In contrast, an emphasis on the helping aspects of the job might be very appealing. Departments must take care, however, not to "turn off" highly qualified male applicants.

One gender difference that has consistently plagued female applicants is the physical agility and strength aspect. Polisar and Milgram (1998, p. 44) report: "Historically, women have been screened out disproportionately in the physical agility phase of the police selection process. . . . [However,] studies by the military have shown that, with training, most women's strength can be greatly increased, permitting them to perform the heaviest tasks required." In their 1998 National Police Survey ("Women in Policing," pp. 36–37), the IACP found: "Twenty-eight percent of respondents had concerns regarding female officers' abilities to handle physical confrontations or situations requiring size or strength, while 44 percent had no concerns regarding women's skills."

If recruiting efforts are successful, the law enforcement agency will receive numerous applications from which to select those best suited for their particular agency.

The Selection Process

Nelson (p. 42) asserts: "Agencies have not only a legal requirement to seek the most qualified applicants, but an even higher moral responsibility to employ only the most fit mentally, morally and physically to serve society. The key to this is in selection."

The selection process may be conducted by an individual or by a committee. It usually is initiated by posting or advertising the need for officers and seeking applicants for the position.

The selection process is based on carefully specified criteria and usually includes completing an application form, undergoing a series of tests and examinations, passing a background check and passing an interview.

A typical sequence of events in the employment process is illustrated in Figure 7.1.

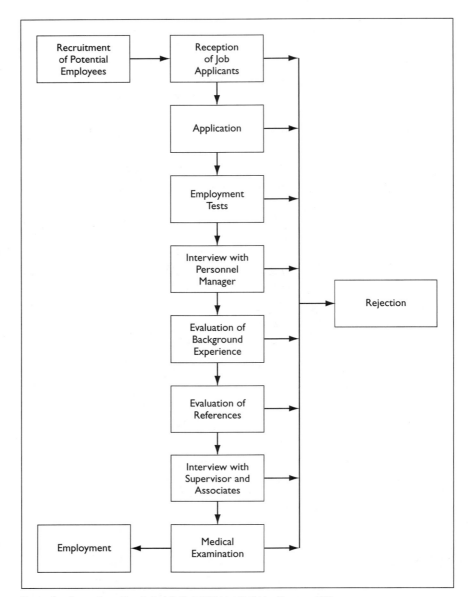

Figure 7.1
**Typical Employment
Process**

Source: Stan Kossen. *Supervision,* 2nd ed. St. Paul, MN: West Publishing Company, 1991, p.
205. Reprinted by permission. All rights reserved.

The Application

Many law enforcement departments use a civil service-type application and selection process. Typically the application includes the person's name, address and length of time the person has lived there, educational background, employment record and personal experiences. It may ask whether the applicant is a citizen of the United States and, if not, whether the person has the legal right to remain permanently in the country. It may also ask whether the person has ever been convicted of a crime and, if so, when and where it took place. It may not ask whether the person has ever been arrested. A sample application is contained in Appendix A.

Other information may be asked for on a voluntary basis, including race, age, disabilities, handicapping conditions and military status. Often a statement such as the following is given: "The Anytown Police Department has an equal employment opportunity/affirmative action policy. Knowledge of your race, sex, age, handicap and medical status is necessary for monitoring the effectiveness of the program. Although you are not required to provide the information requested below, your cooperation is appreciated."

The application usually requires a date and the person's signature verifying that all the information provided is accurate. References are also usually requested.

Restricted Subjects

The following subjects are not allowed for either an application form or an employment interview: race, religion, national origin, gender, age (you may ask whether the applicant is between the ages of 18 and 70), marital status and physical capabilities. Administrators should be able to show that all questions are relevant to the position they are seeking applicants for.

Testing/Screening

Testing usually progresses from the least expensive method, the written examination, to the most expensive, the background investigation, with the number of qualified recruits being narrowed at each step. Because several trips are needed to complete the process, the selection process is difficult for anyone living any distance from the hiring agency. Some agencies, such as the one in Las Vegas, have revised their process so that it can be completed in one trip.

Nelson (p. 43) reports that a nationwide survey of police agencies revealed the five most common screening methods: written test (98% of respondents reported using this method), medical examination (96%), background investigation (96%), psychological examination (94%) and physical fitness test (90%). Other methods used with less frequency included oral boards/oral interviews (80%), polygraphs (63%), chief's and/or command interviews (34%), writing tests (27%) and other tests (12%).

The most common screening methods for selection are basic skills/written tests, medical examinations, background investigations, psychological examinations and physical fitness tests.

Written Tests

Basic skills in math and reading can be assessed using standardized tests. Writing skills can be tested by having candidates write an autobiography or an essay explaining why they want to become a law enforcement officer. Although many conventional written test formats are available, some departments are using innovative written exam alternatives to assess not only applicants' basic skills but also their compatibility with the profession. As Rafilson (1999, p. 84) states:

> The National Criminal Justice Officer Selection Inventory (NCJOSI) is an alternative to conventional law enforcement and correctional officer written entrance examinations. It was designed specifically to predict success for criminal justice officer positions.
>
> While traditional criminal justice entrance examinations only test for cognitive abilities, the NCJOSI includes both a cognitive (i.e., problem solving) component and an attitude/personality (i.e., criminal justice officer orientation) component. Including a personality/attitude component on entry-level exams is a unique approach that increases predictive validity while reducing adverse impact.

The problem-solving component of the NCJOSI includes questions that measure the job-related abilities of reading comprehension, writing and mathematics (p. 85). The criminal justice officer orientation component of the NCJOSI includes questions that assess the job-related personality characteristics of interpersonal ability, assertiveness, stress tolerance, team orientation and ethics/integrity (pp. 85–86).

The Medical Examination

The medical examination assesses overall applicant health and includes more specific tests for vision, hearing and cardiovascular fitness. Departments do allow applicants to have corrected vision with glasses or contact lenses; however, an emerging issue that many agencies are wrestling with has been whether to permit vision correction by laser surgery. The debate centers on the as yet unknown long-term effects of laser correction surgery.

Background Investigations

Candidates should undergo a thorough **background check,** usually conducted by an assigned member of the law enforcement agency. Background checks can prevent many potential problems and save the cost of training an unsuitable employee. Fuss, McSheehy and Snowden (1998, p. 170) assert:

> Background investigations are a critical area of concern among law enforcement agencies when hiring new officers. A thorough background investigation can make the difference between putting a qualified individual on the streets to protect and serve society or sending an unqualified individual who [harms] himself, society and the department that hires him.

Employees are the most important and expensive resource of the police department, and the hiring of an officer could affect department administration and operation for many years. Consequently, preemployment background investigation is essential because it might prevent a negligent hiring or retention lawsuit, departmental disciplinary hearings or, at the least, a less than satisfactory employee. Fuss, McSheehy and Snowden (p. 169) note: "The landmark study on the relationship between background investigations and police officer performance . . . conducted by the Rand Institute in 1973 . . . found that the background investigation was a good predictor of on-the-job behavior." According to Harvey and Ward (1996, p. 51): "The background investigation is the key component of the selection process because it not only verifies past behavior but also confirms the applicant's veracity."

The background check includes past employers and references. The person who conducts the background check should contact every reference, employer and instructor. No final candidates should be selected until reference checks are made, yet many law enforcement agencies fail to do this, depriving themselves of what could be vital information. Reference checks should be done from not only those who provided letters of recommendation but others as well. The same inquiries should be made for each candidate, and the questions must be job related.

The background check might also include queries regarding credit, driving record, criminal conviction, academic background and any professional license required. Candidates might be asked to sign a release and authorization statement such as that illustrated in Figure 7.2. A request should also be made for documents such as diplomas, birth certificates, marriage licenses and drivers licenses. Applicants should be photographed and fingerprinted. Military duty should be confirmed, along with a copy of discharge papers.

Psychological Examinations

Nearly all departments recognize a need for psychological screening of final candidates for a police position, but because of cost or lack of suitable psychologists, it may not be done. Only the leading candidates are evaluated psychologically, which keeps costs down. According to Curran (1998, p. 88):

> The selection of law enforcement personnel who exhibit stable emotional and behavioral functioning has become critical to law enforcement agencies. Excessive-force complaints, community policing initiatives and allegations of negligent hiring have demonstrated to personnel managers that hiring decisions must take into account the psychological characteristics of an applicant.

The psychological tests often include cognitive ability, quantitative and language reasoning and the Minnesota Multiphasic Personality Inventory (MMPI), the most widely used psychological assessment test in the country. Trompetter (1998, p. 104) notes:

> In general, the psychological domains necessary for effective peace officer functioning are as follows:
>
> - Emotional control/anger management
> - Stress and threat tolerance

Figure 7.2
Sample Release and Authorization Statement

Sample Release and Authorization Statement

In connection with this request, I authorize all corporations, companies, former employers, credit agencies, educational institutions, law enforcement agencies, city, state, county and federal courts, military services, and persons to release information they may have about me to the person or company with which this form has been filed and release all parties involved from any liability and responsibility for doing so.

I also authorize the procurement of an investigative consumer report and understand that it may contain information about my background, mode of living, character, and personal reputation. This authorization, in original or copy form, shall be valid for this and any future reports or updates that may be requested. Further information may be available on written request within a reasonable period of time.

_____   _____
Applicant's signature   Date

Source: © 1991 American Society for Industrial Security, 1655 North Fort Myer Dr., Suite 1200, Arlington, VA 22209. Reprinted by permission from the April 1991 issue of *Security Management*.

- Acceptance of criticism
- Impulse/risk control
- Positive attitude
- Assertiveness/tenacity
- Command presence/persuasiveness
- Integrity
- Dependability/reliability
- Initiative/achievement motivation
- Conformance to rules and regulations
- Adaptability/flexibility
- Vigilance/attention to detail
- Interpersonal sensitivity
- Social concern
- Teamwork
- Practical intelligence/decision-making ability
- Objectivity/tolerance

The psychological report should be only one component of the total selection process. When a candidate's psychological tests indicate abnormalities, a department must consider these seriously before hiring. When testing indicates unsuitability or lack of stability, it is best not to hire. Accepting such an applicant leaves an agency open to charges of negligent hiring.

Some psychological testing or assessment agencies provide written tests that are sent to a central location in the United States and evaluated. A written report is then sent to the police department. No in-person evaluation is made although such an interview is desirable.

Psychologists who work with police departments must be familiar with validity and reliability measures of tests, the legal requirements imposed by affirmative action and the ADA, as well as pertinent case law and guidelines. In fact, preemployment psychological evaluation services guidelines adopted by the IACP in 1998 specifically state: "Only licensed or certified psychologists trained and experienced in psychological test interpretation and law enforcement psychological assessment techniques should conduct psychological screening for public safety agencies" ("Pre-Employment Psychological . . . ," 1998, p. 95).

Physical Fitness Tests

Kenny (1999, p. 56) asserts: "The importance of fitness in law enforcement should not be underestimated." Physical-agility tests are most often of the military type and frequently include an obstacle course. The Broward Community College Criminal Justice Institute's testing center, for example, uses the physical-agility course shown in Figure 7.3. In addition, Broward uses the following strength and endurance tests:

- Trigger pull—strong hand 18, weak hand 12
- Ten push-ups
- A standing jump based on the person's height
- Three pull-ups (from dead hang, palms facing away)
- Vehicle push—20 feet (push from rear of vehicle)
- Mile run (5 minutes maximum time)

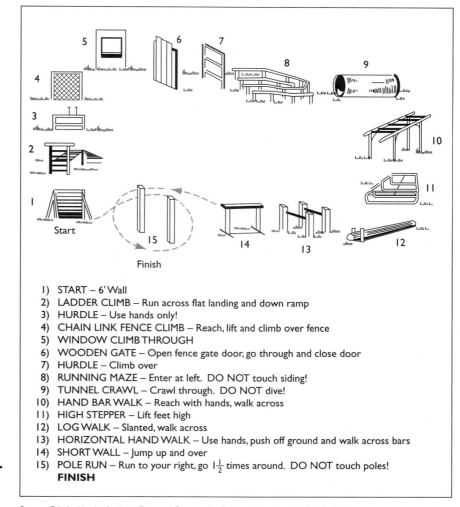

1) START – 6' Wall
2) LADDER CLIMB – Run across flat landing and down ramp
3) HURDLE – Use hands only!
4) CHAIN LINK FENCE CLIMB – Reach, lift and climb over fence
5) WINDOW CLIMB THROUGH
6) WOODEN GATE – Open fence gate door, go through and close door
7) HURDLE – Climb over
8) RUNNING MAZE – Enter at left. DO NOT touch siding!
9) TUNNEL CRAWL – Crawl through. DO NOT dive!
10) HAND BAR WALK – Reach with hands, walk across
11) HIGH STEPPER – Lift feet high
12) LOG WALK – Slanted, walk across
13) HORIZONTAL HAND WALK – Use hands, push off ground and walk across bars
14) SHORT WALL – Jump up and over
15) POLE RUN – Run to your right, go $1\frac{1}{2}$ times around. DO NOT touch poles!
FINISH

Figure 7.3
Physical-Agility Course

Source: Criminal Justice Institute, Broward Community College, Ft. Lauderdale, FL, July 1989.
Reprinted by permission.

The Interview

In-person interviews should be held with each applicant, during which the department can explain the nature and benefits of the position to be filled. In return, the applicant can explain his or her interest in law enforcement and, specifically, your department. Provide an opportunity for the applicant to ask questions. Most applicants have questions about salary, benefits, overtime, promotions, uniform allowances and the like.

The final interview is usually conducted by Civil Service Commission representatives or other selection board personnel. Whether the interview is conducted by an individual or a panel, those responsible should be familiar with what they can and cannot ask and should also take certain steps before, during and after the interview to make it most effective.

The same questions that were prohibited on the application are also prohibited during the interview.

Before the Interview

Those who will be doing the interviewing should review the application forms, letters of recommendation, references, notes and all other application materials. They might be asked to do a preliminary ranking of specific factors. Such materials and information should not be discussed with others in the organization and should be kept secured. Copies should not be made of the material, which ordinarily should not leave the office of the person using the files.

Decide the questions to ask or general areas to cover as well as who will ask each question or cover each area. Design the questions to determine the "fit" between the candidate and the position. Consider asking the following questions:

- Why do you want to become a law enforcement officer?
- What do you feel you will contribute to the department?
- What do you think are the most significant trends in law enforcement?
- How have your education and experiences prepared you for this position?
- What plans do you have for self-development in the next 12 months?
- Why did you select this department/agency?

As you frame the questions, consider the following general guidelines:

- Avoid asking questions that call for a yes/no answer (closed questions). Ask open-ended questions. Interviewers want to hear how candidates think and to see their ability to do so under stress.
- Avoid asking leading questions. Instead ask questions that use "why," "how," "what" and "describe" or "tell me about."
- Avoid asking about any of the prohibited information protected by the Equal Employment Opportunity Act (to be discussed shortly).
- Keep questions job related.

During the Interview

The first step is to establish **rapport,** that is, a feeling of mutual understanding and trust. A warm greeting, friendly handshake, sincere smile and some small talk are all appropriate to establish a relaxed atmosphere.

The next step is usually to explain how the interview will proceed or to set the agenda, including a general time frame. Next you can describe the job and the organization and then ask the predetermined questions. Vernon (1999, p. 24) states:

> Asking the right types of questions [is] pivotal to a successful selection process and help[s] ensure legally compliant interviews. Interview questions should be created carefully, studying the job specifications and matching questions to each particular task, result, or skill sought. The best questions are deep, probing, open-ended questions that require the candidate to explain the who, what, where, when, and how of their skills and experience.

During the question/answer portion of the interview, your listening skills are critical. Some suggest that those who are doing the interviewing should talk no more than 25 percent of the time. Candidates should do most of the talking.

Silences should not be sources of anxiety because candidates often need time to formulate their responses. Wait patiently.

Consider tape recording the interview if you are to conduct several. This can help refresh your memory later. Candidates whose interviews you are recording should be notified of this before the interview begins. Recording all applicants and then listening to them in one sitting allows for better comparisons.

To ensure that interviews are nondiscriminatory:

- Ask the same general questions and require the same standards for all applicants.
- Treat all applicants fairly, equally and consistently.
- Follow a structured interview plan and use predetermined questions that will achieve fairness.
- Be professional and consistent in addressing men and women. If using first names, do so for all candidates.
- Never indicate that you are interested in hiring a woman or minority person to improve your Affirmative Action/Equal Employment Opportunity profile. It is unlawful and insulting to apply different standards based on a candidate's gender or minority status.

Maintaining eye contact, listening carefully and taking notes are ways to show candidates that you are paying attention to their responses. It is often best to take notes on a clipboard held in your lap so candidates do not see what you are writing.

Do not form an opinion early in the interview. Stay neutral throughout. Do not let your opinion of an applicant be unduly influenced by your opinion of applicants you interviewed previously. Avoid the "**halo effect**"—the tendency to assume that candidates strong (or weak) in one area will also be strong (or weak) in other areas.

Allow time at the end of the interview for candidates to ask questions. Conclude the interview with a thank you and an indication of when you might make a decision.

Figure 7.4 summarizes obstacles to effective interviewing. Some agencies use interview rating forms such as that in Appendix B.

After the Interview

After the successful candidates are selected and notified and they accept the position, all other candidates should be notified of the decision. All selection process materials such as ratings, reference check notes and the actual application files should be returned immediately to the personnel office or other appropriate location. Successful candidates are usually required to pass a stringent medical examination prior to finalization of the job offer.

Selection is an expensive, time-consuming process, considering that on the average only two or three candidates out of every 100 are selected. Many agencies have a ratio of 100 to 130 or more applicants per position available. In a state such as New York, an announcement that applications are being accepted for the trooper position draws some 32,000 candidates.

OBSTACLES TO EFFECTIVE INTERVIEWING

Unfortunately, it is easy for an interviewer to make a mistake in an employment interview. Some of the common mistakes that have been detected in poorly conducted interviews are as follows:

Mistakes	Comments
Failing to establish rapport with the applicant.	As a result, the interview never gets off the ground.
Not knowing what information is needed.	Consequently, the interviewer does not know what questions to ask the applicant.
Concentrating exclusively on the applicant as a person.	The perceptive interviewer specifically attempts to compare an applicant's demonstrated abilities and experience with the actual job requirements.
Not remaining silent, or listening, long enough.	The interviewer does too much talking and fails to obtain meaningful information from the applicant.
Not allowing sufficient time to observe the applicant's responses and behavior.	The interview should not be too short and superficial. The longer the interview, the better the chances of gaining meaningful information from the applicant.
Incorrectly interpreting information obtained from the applicant.	The interviewer draws the wrong conclusion about the applicant's ability to perform.
Being unaware of or not dealing directly with biases for or against certain types of applicants (stereotyping).	This includes how you feel about hair styles, clothing, educational background, etc. ("I have never hired a good secretary from that business college.")
Being overly influenced (either favorably or unfavorably) by one characteristic or trait of that particular applicant.	This includes physical appearances, style of dress, personality, etc. ("I can't stand men who have mustaches," or "I'd hire her for this job no matter what her previous experience.")
Making a decision based only on intuition or "first impression," rather than careful insight and analytical judgment.	
Using stress techniques designed to trap or fluster the applicant.	
Conducting a poorly structured or an unstructured interview.	
Looking to see how an applicant's past life compares with the interviewer's.	This results in substantial loss of time, because more effort is spent on the "halo effect" comparison than on obtaining information relevant to the job.
Failing to control or direct the interview.	Whether out of a desire to be courteous or because the applicant is particularly dominant, the interviewer can lose control of an interview. When this happens, the interviewer must regain control skillfully—not abruptly.
Asking questions answerable by a simple "yes" or "no."	People are used to doing this because their daily business conversations are often short and to the point, but in interviewing, the interviewer must endeavor to do just the opposite—to draw the candidate out. This requires minimizing "yes" and "no" answers.
Making judgmental or leading statements.	These telegraph to the candidate desired responses. Most applicants are good enough at reading the interviewer's mind without being provided direct guidance.

Figure 7.4
Obstacles to Effective Interviewing

Source: "Interview Guide for Supervisors." Reprinted with permission of the College and University Personnel Association, Washington, DC.

Selection is also a time-consuming and frustrating process for candidates. Often eligibility lists are obtained even though no actual position may be open. Elapsed time between taking an examination and obtaining a position may vary from two weeks to two years or more.

The hiring process is fraught with the possibility of hiring someone who will turn into a problem employee, and no selection process is absolutely guaranteed to be successful. However, if a candidate is recommended and after employment goes wrong or grossly fails to meet expectations, review the original application for false statements. Add any information you learn to the next selection process.

Some states have considered giving statewide examinations, permitting any participating law enforcement agency within the state to draw candidates from this list. This would eliminate much individual recruiting and selecting and also reduce costs. However, a strong desire for local testing based on local needs remains. A future consideration could be metropolitan, regional or statewide examinations, with each community making its own final selections from this list.

Employment Criteria

To comply with Equal Employment Opportunity requirements and avoid legal problems, law enforcement agencies must hire personnel to meet very specific standards directly related to the job.

A **bona fide occupational qualification (BFOQ)** is one that is reasonably necessary to perform a job.

An example of a bona fide occupational qualification in law enforcement might be that the applicant has normal or correctable-to-normal hearing and vision.

Other employment criteria might include skills that are important, if not essential, to the successful performance of a particular job. According to Wolf (1999, p. 74): "Organizations often make the selection process more difficult by not defining the behaviors they seek in an employee." He further notes (p. 77): "The process of clarifying the behaviors it believes to be productive and non-productive is really helpful to the whole organization. There is a strong team-building aspect to the whole process."

Slahor (1998, p. 60) reports on how the San Bernadino County Sheriff's Department seeks to attract the best-qualified candidates:

> [While] POST standards set the requirements for much of the selection process, . . . the department goes further in making sure it finds people who are problem-solvers and who can make judgments under pressure. Willingness to confront problems, devise solutions and work not only with colleagues, but with the community are also key to the selection process.
>
> Successful candidates must have an interest in people and be sensitive to the best steps to take in a situation. Integrity and dependability are essential, . . . not only for the daily work and for testifying in court, but also in the wider scope of the officer's role in the neighborhood and community.

Schrink, Roy and Ransberg (1999, p. 78) present 18 knowledge-based skills that may be important for a successful criminal justice career. These include the ability to:

- Write reports and communicate in writing.
- Speak a language other than English.
- Speak to groups and communicate verbally.
- Understand the dynamics of human relations.
- Deal with problems of minority group citizens.
- Understand contemporary social issues.
- Remain physically fit.
- Deal with career-related stress.
- Understand and abide by ethical practices.
- Understand the basic precepts of criminal law.
- Understand formal courtroom procedures.
- Understand the functions of the criminal justice system.
- Deal with media relations.
- Deal with domestic conflict situations.
- Deal with dangerous situations.
- Deal with continually changing circumstances and conditions.
- Use computers.
- Understand and use basic research analytical skills.

Keep in mind that these criteria are not necessarily requirements for employment but rather abilities that will likely increase a police officer candidate's chances for success and personal career satisfaction in law enforcement. For this reason, administrators may include such criteria in their candidate selection process. Some of the criteria may also be useful in selecting officers to work on specific task forces or teams.

Educational Requirements

One requirement that may pose difficulties is requiring a certain level of education. "The first emphasis on professional training and education for officers came in 1916 from August Vollmer, father of modern policing" (Stevens, 1999, p. 37). As early as 1931, the National Commission on Law Observance and Enforcement (also known as the Wickersham Commission) insisted that all police officers should have college degrees (Baro and Burlingame, 1999, p. 57). The need for officer candidates to seek higher education even after being hired is stressed by Brand (1999, p. 54), who asserts: "The law enforcement role [in the future] will require personnel who are highly professionalized and are prepared to continually upgrade their knowledge and skill level." Varricchio (1998, pp. 10–11) states:

As officers move to interact with citizens in new ways and address a wide range of issues that impact crime problems in a community, continuing education helps enhance the problem-solving skills necessary for officers to operate successfully in this environment. . . .

A firm educational foundation not only enhances officers' general knowledge, but it also helps strengthen the problem-solving skills that have become integral to contemporary policing.

Yet many law enforcement departments require only a high-school diploma or its equivalent. According to Baro and Burlingame (p. 57): "Only 1 percent of local law enforcement agencies require a four-year degree; and 75 percent have no formal policy linking education with promotion." Nonetheless, higher education may be a deciding factor in determining who gets promoted (Morris, 1997, p. 44). Furthermore, many police chiefs have recognized the benefits to themselves of higher education: "As the demands of running a modern police agency continue to grow in complexity, many chiefs are finding that advanced college degrees can provide them with a crucial managerial edge" ("More Specialization for . . . ," 1998, p. 7). In fact, Fulton (1999, p. 76) notes: "When more than 500 active police sergeants, lieutenants and captains were asked if they should be required to have college degrees, most said, 'yes.' " The four main reasons to have college-educated police supervisors were (Fulton, p. 77):

1. The public expects it as the general population [becomes] more educated.
2. More line officers have degrees. They have little respect for supervisors who do not.
3. The term *professionalism* requires some standard to begin with. Education is usually one of the building points.
4. Better employees.

The most common reason for not requiring higher education was the fear the requirement would be challenged in court or through labor arbitration. A landmark case was *Griggs v Duke Power Company* (1971) in which Griggs, an African-American employee, claimed that the requirement of having a high-school diploma and passing two aptitude tests discriminated against him. The court ruled that any requirements or tests used in selecting or promoting must be job related.

A similar case occurred in *Davis v City of Dallas* (1978). The Dallas Police Department at the time required applicants to have completed 45 semester hours of college credit with a "C" average. In this case the court ruled in favor of the police department:

> The City introduced evidence that supports the educational requirement. Numerous nationwide studies have examined the problem of setting the education requirement for police departments with favorable conclusions. A college education as a condition of hiring as a police officer has been recommended by the National Commission on Law Observance in 1931; by the President's Commission on Law Enforcement and Commission on Intergovernmental Relations in 1971; by the American Bar Association in 1972 and by the National Advisory Commission on Criminal Justice Standards and Goals in 1973.
>
> Defendant's experts established the relationship between college education and performance of police officers. A study by one expert relied upon factual data from

two large metropolitan areas that took two years to complete, showing significantly higher performance rates by college-educated officers. A persuasive point was made that a high school diploma today does not represent the same level of achievement which it represented 10 years ago.

Law Enforcement News ("College Degrees and . . . ," 1999, p. 1) reports:

> The latest challenge has arisen in New Jersey, where the state chapter of the NAACP claims that a four-year college degree requirement for all State Police candidates is not job-related and disproportionately excludes black and Hispanic applicants. . . .
>
> According to a lawsuit filed in 1996 . . . , African American and Latino representation in the State Police Academy classes has plummeted as a result of both the college requirement and new written examination, which NAACP attorneys claim cuts a pool of applicants that is 20 percent minority to less than 8 percent.

Clearly, not everyone agrees that college education enhances patrol officer performance. Molden (1999a, p. 21) maintains: "Education, per se, does not a good cop make. First find a good cop, then educate him and you will probably have a better cop." The biggest objections are that there are not enough promotions to satisfy a college-educated employee, the college-educated employee would be less likely to accept authority, such a requirement would lower the pool of applicants for police positions and would be detrimental to potential minority applicants.

Still, the advantages of advanced education appear to outweigh the disadvantages. The Police Executive Research Forum (PERF) has recommended that, by 2003, all entry-level law enforcement officers have completed a four-year degree. Molden (1999b, p. 18) contends, however, that realization of this recommendation by 2003 is "unrealistic and will exclude many otherwise capable applicants who could become educated while in service." He (1999b, p. 18) further states: "Should a degree requirement be imposed for entry-level officers, the degree should in no way compromise or overshadow other standard entry level requirements. That is the educational requirement will be an addition, not a substitute for good selection procedures."

Various recruitment and scholarship programs have been developed throughout the country to attract and educate those who are interested in criminal justice professions. One national scholarship program called Police Corps recruits and trains college graduates to serve as community police officers. As Wexler (1998, p. 52) explains: "[These] police training programs . . . are similar to the military's Reserve Officer Training Corps (ROTC). College graduates who agree to serve four years in a participating police department will be reimbursed up to $30,000 in education costs."

One concern of those seeking higher education while employed as officers is how to pursue a course of study without taking time off from work or quitting altogether. A solution to this dilemma has become available through the Internet. According to Richard (1999, p. 41):

> Colleges and universities across the United States are beginning to offer educational opportunities through distance learning. Most of these are Internet- or Web-based classes that let the student read lectures and submit homework online, and communicate with instructors and other students in real time. Other classes

are offered via cable television or public television stations, or as part of a video conference broadcast via satellite.

Although Richard acknowledges that distance learning is not a standard that is currently in place in most law enforcement agencies, she (p. 42) does predict: "Within two years, there will be many more online options for law enforcement training. . . . The Federal Law Enforcement Training Center (FLETC) is also just starting its distance training component, having conducted its first telecast training in September 1999."

One question facing applicants and administrators alike is, if a degree is sought, what *type* of degree is most beneficial to the profession? According to Hawley (1998, p. 51):

> Law enforcement administrators . . . have not reached a consensus about the most preferable degree for officers. Although favoring a degree in criminal justice because it introduces the student to the policing profession, most administrators surveyed . . . preferred a liberal arts education because of its emphasis on social issues.

Another item of contention is *how much* advanced education is recommended for officers of varying ranks. In examining whether a master's degree for criminal justice professionals is a wise investment, Carlan (1999, p. 39) found that holders of a master's degree not only earn significantly more than bachelor's degree holders but also demonstrate higher job satisfaction than those holding only bachelor's degrees. However, no difference was observed in self-reported performance levels.

Some experts feel that experience in other law enforcement agencies should substitute for education. What this ratio of experience to education should be is not clear. An officer who has both education and experience is obviously the most desirable. Lateral entry availability applies in many of these cases.

Whatever the decision, a clear policy documenting that a specific level of education is a bona fide occupational qualification (BFOQ) should be established. In addition, it is becoming more common for promotion to be contingent upon a higher level of education. Fulton (2000, p. 102) suggests: "Getting your degrees, going to all kinds of training classes and getting diversified experience is the way to a successful career."

Assessment Centers

Assessment centers are nothing new. As Garner (1998, p. 77) notes: "Assessment Center Testing has been around for the last 60 or 70 years. Both the Allies and the Axis used it during World War II to train their spies. The technique involves putting the candidates in a situation where they must role-play the position they are seeking." Narramore and Stephen (1997, p. 79) add: "An Assessment Center is an approach where candidates participate in several preplanned and structured events designed to evaluate an individual's ability to perform. . . . Each of these events is meticulously observed by evaluators who rate the candidates."

Oliver (1998, p. 8) states: "Law enforcement has used the assessment center method for approximately 15 years, starting in the mid-1980s." Booth (1997a,

p. 96) explains their continued use and growing acceptance: "Assessment centers are popular for the selection and promotion of law enforcement personnel. This technique effectively measures the knowledge, skills, abilities, and traits that are related to success in policing, including leadership, decision making and interpersonal skills." According to Oliver (p. 9):

> The real potential for growth in use of the assessment center method in law enforcement's current environment lies in our search for the prototype police officer. He or she is customer-service-oriented, is a team player, has high moral and ethical standards, has good written and oral communication skills, appreciates human diversity, has a positive attitude, and is a problem solver possessing good decision-making skills. The entry-level assessment center can evaluate these skills, knowledge and abilities.

In defending assessment centers to their critics, Hutton and Sampson (1999, p. 83) state: "It is often said of assessment centres that candidates are 'just a bunch of people putting on a performance.' This may be true. However, if a candidate displays those skills at an acceptable level, at least they have shown that they can do it."

Just as important as hiring excellent officers is the way in which promotions are made. Some police executives also rely upon an assessment center to assist in this process. Booth (1997b, p. 87) notes: "Assessment centers are better predictors of supervisory and managerial success, as well as leadership, decision making, interpersonal skills, and common sense than written tests or interviews."

Whether you use an assessment center or an internal panel, carefully evaluate personal dimensions such as the preceding in the promotional process. Conducting promotional examinations is discussed in detail in Chapter 10. Because managers hire and promote, they must be thoroughly familiar with laws related to employment.

Laws Affecting Employment

Several laws affect employment, including the following:

- *The Equal Pay Act of 1963 (EPA)* prohibits discrimination in wages on the basis of gender for all employers and labor organizations.
- *Civil Rights Acts of 1964 and 1970* prohibit race discrimination in hiring, placement and continuation of employment for all private employers, unions and employment agencies.

Title VII of the **Civil Rights Act of 1964,** as amended by the *Equal Employment Opportunity Act (EEOA) of 1972,* prohibits discrimination based on race, color, religion, gender or national origin for private employers with 15 or more employees, governments, unions and employment agencies.

- *The Age Discrimination in Employment Act (ADEA) of 1967,* amended in 1978, prohibits discrimination based on age for people between the ages of 40 and 70. The public safety officer exemption to this law expired in 1993.
- *Title IX of 1972 Education Amendments* prohibits discrimination in education benefits based on race, color, religion, gender and national origin.

- *The Rehabilitation Act of 1973,* amended in 1980, prohibits discrimination against handicapped individuals for federal contractors and the federal government.

- *The Pregnancy Discrimination Act of 1978,* an amendment to Title VII, prohibits discrimination in employment on the basis of pregnancy, childbirth and related conditions for all private employers with 15 or more employees, governments, unions and employment agencies.

- *The Civil Service Reform Act of 1978* requires a federal government "workforce reflective of the nation's diversity."

- *The Immigration Reform and Control Act of 1986* prohibits discrimination against qualified aliens or on the basis of national origin.

- *The Americans with Disabilities Act of 1990 (ADA)* prohibits discrimination based on physical or intellectual handicap for employers with 15 or more employees.

The legislation guaranteeing rights for people with disabilities provides only for fair and equal treatment in the workplace based on ability. Candidates for employment who are not qualified to perform essential job functions are not required to be hired by private employers or government agencies. The ADA is discussed in detail following this overview.

These laws are enforced by the Equal Employment Opportunity Commission.

The **Equal Employment Opportunity Commission (EEOC)** enforces laws prohibiting job discrimination based on race, color, religion, gender, national origin, handicapping condition or age between 40 and 70.

In an exercise excerpted from an EEOC questionnaire, Kossen (1991, p. 469) presents the following 10-item test to assess an individual's knowledge of antidiscrimination laws related to hiring, firing, promoting and paying. Answer each question true or false.

An employer. . .

1. Can refuse to hire women who have small children at home.

2. Can generally obtain and use an applicant's arrest record as the basis for nonemployment.

3. Can prohibit employees from conversing in their native language on the job.

4. Whose employees are mostly white or male can rely solely on word of mouth to recruit new employees.

5. Can refuse to hire women to work at night because it wishes to protect them.

6. May require all pregnant employees to take a leave of absence at a specified time before delivery.

7. May establish different benefits—pension, retirement, insurance and health plans—for male employees than for female employees.

8. May hire only males for a job if state law forbids employment of women for that capacity.

9. Need not attempt to adjust work schedules to permit an employee time off for a religious observance.

10. Disobeys the Equal Employment laws only when it is acting intentionally or with ill motive.

Each of the preceding statements is false.

Family and Medical Leave Act of 1993

This law requires companies of 50 or more employees to allow employees 12 weeks of unpaid leave of absence for parenting or medical reasons. The law affects public agencies under the Fair Labor Standards Act. Those covered under bargaining agreements were covered as of 1994. Other provisions are explained in the act.

The Americans with Disabilities Act of 1990 (ADA)

The Americans with Disabilities Act, or ADA, is a civil rights law that guarantees equal opportunity to jobs for qualified individuals with disabilities ("The ADA and. . . ," 1997, p. 24).

The Americans with Disabilities Act (ADA) of 1990, Title I, became effective in 1992. Title II, which involves discrimination in employment practices, went into effect in 1994 and applies to all agencies with 15 or more employees.

Law enforcement is directly affected by the ADA's goal of guaranteeing individuals with disabilities access to employment and to governmental programs, services and activities.

The ADA prohibits employers from discriminating against a *qualified individual with a disability* (QID) in all areas of employment, including hiring, training, promoting, terminating and compensation. It also prohibits discrimination in nonemployment areas and requires accessibility to all services and facilities of public entities. The following questions and answers address several concerns that police departments commonly raise when confronting ADA issues ("The ADA and . . . ," pp. 24–26):

Q: Recently, a job applicant for a police officer's job came into the police department with fingers that were visibly impaired. The police department required that he demonstrate that he could pull the trigger on the police-issue firearm and reload it before a conditional job offer was made. Did this violate the ADA?

A: No. If an individual has a known disability that would reasonably appear to interfere with or prevent performance of job functions, that person may be asked to demonstrate how these functions will be performed, even if other applicants are not asked to do so. . . .

Q: May an applicant be asked prior to a conditional job offer whether he has ever used illegal drugs or been arrested for any reason?

A: Yes. It does not violate the ADA to ask whether the applicant has ever used illegal drugs or been arrested for such use. . . .

Q: Are alcoholics covered by the ADA?

A: Yes. . . . An alcoholic is a person with a disability and is protected by the ADA if he is qualified to perform the essential functions of the job. . . . However, an employer can discipline, discharge or deny employment to an alcoholic whose use of alcohol adversely affects job performance or conduct.

Table 7.1 contains a brief explanation of key terms commonly used in the ADA. Notice especially the definitions for *disability* and *otherwise qualified* or QID.

The ADA also establishes the following excluded disorders that are not caused by a physical impairment and thus are not considered disabilities: bisexuality, compulsive gambling, exhibitionism, gender-identity disorders, homosexuality, kleptomania, pedophilia, pyromania, sexual behavior disorder, transsexualism, transvestism and voyeurism.

Table 7.1
Terms Associated with ADA

The ADA uses numerous terms to describe its requirements and the obligations of those covered by the law. Here is a brief index and short explanation of some of the key words and phrases commonly used in the ADA.

Disability	(1) A mental or physical impairment that substantially limits a major life activity; (2) a record of having such an impairment; (3) being regarded as having such an impairment.
Impairment	A physiological or mental disorder.
Substantial limitation	When compared to the average person: (1) an inability to perform a major life activity; (2) a significant restriction on how or how long the activity can be performed; or (3) a significant restriction on the ability to perform a class or broad range of jobs.
Major life activity	Basic functions that the average person in the general population can do with little or no difficulty such as walking, seeing, hearing, breathing, speaking, procreating, learning, sitting, standing, performing manual tasks, working or having intimate sexual relations.
Otherwise qualified	A person with a disability who satisfies all of the requirements of the job such as education, experience, or skill and who can perform the essential functions of the job with or without reasonable accommodation.
Essential functions	The fundamental, not marginal, duties of a job.
Reasonable accommodation	A change in the application process, work environment, or job descriptions involving marginal functions of the job, or the use of modified or auxiliary devices that enable a person with a disability to perform the essential functions of the job without causing an undue hardship or direct threat to the health and safety of herself or himself or of others.
Undue hardship	Significant difficulty or expense relative to the size and overall financial resources of the employer.
Direct threat	A significant risk of substantial harm based on valid, objective evidence and not mere speculation.

Source: Paula N. Rubin. *The Americans with Disabilities Act and Criminal Justice: An Overview.* Washington, DC: National Institute of Justice, Research in Action, September 1993, p. 4.

Employment Issues

This act has had a significant impact on the recruiting process. Most agencies have had to reorganize some of their recruiting procedures. To be in compliance, administrators should identify "essential functions" in job descriptions. Based on these, they should next develop selection criteria—ways to measure an applicant's ability to perform each essential job function.

> The ADA prohibits medical inquiries or evaluations, including some psychiatric evaluations, until after a job offer has been made.

The medical examination remains an important part of the application process, however. Serious consequences could arise as a result of a police officers not having the ability to perform essential job functions. If an applicant's disability would cause a direct threat to the applicant or public safety, the risk must be identified and documented by objective medical evidence as well.

Not all psychological examinations are disallowed under the ADA. Only those tests or scales specifically designed to disclose an impairment are disallowed.

The ADA does not address polygraph tests and does not consider physical agility tests or drug tests to be medical examinations; therefore, such tests are not governed by the ADA. Employees and applicants may be subjected to drug testing. Further, employers may hold illegal drug users and alcoholics to the same performance standards as other employees.

Reasonable Accommodations

Employers must make "reasonable accommodations" for any physical or mental limitations of a QID unless the employer can show that such accommodation would create an "undue hardship" or could threaten the health and safety of the QID or other employees. Reasonable accommodations might include modifying existing facilities to make them accessible, job restructuring, part-time or modified work schedules, or acquiring or modifying equipment. However, reasonable accommodations are not required when providing them causes an undue hardship for the agency, meaning significant expense or difficulty.

It is unlikely that police agencies will be required to make substantial accommodations in the hiring process because the nature of police work requires some degree of fitness that can be substantiated through a job analysis. However, reasonable accommodations goes beyond modifying job descriptions. It also means making buildings accessible to the physically disabled. Accessibility applies not only to employees but to nonemployees as well and involves parking lots, the building itself, the front desk, elevator and staff. Appendix C contains an accessibility checklist. Two government publications that provide assistance in this area are the *ADA Accessibility Guidelines* and the *Uniform Federal Accessibility Standards*.

Nonemployment Issues

The ADA regulates all services and programs provided by public entities, which includes law enforcement agencies. Police agencies report that the greatest difficulties they face when responding to people with disabilities are citizens' misunderstanding the police role in dealing with persons with disabilities; difficulty reaching help on weekends and evenings; and mistaking disabilities for antisocial behavior.

Enforcement of the ADA

The regulating agencies for the ADA are the Department of Justice (DOJ), the Architectural Transportation Compliance Board (ATCB), the Equal Employment Opportunity Commission (EEOC) and the Federal Communications Commission (FCC).

Agencies that are out of compliance may face civil penalties up to $50,000 for the first violation and $100,000 for subsequent violations, in addition to being ordered to modify their facilities to be in compliance.

Affirmative Action

Not only must employers avoid discrimination in the hiring process, in some instances they must actively seek out certain groups of people and make certain they have equal opportunities to obtain jobs.

> An **affirmative action program (AAP)** is a written plan to ensure fair recruitment, hiring and promotion practices.

Affirmative action programs are mandated by several of the employment laws. Their intent is to undo the damage caused by past discrimination in employment. The affirmative action policy of one agency states:

> The Anytown Police Department realizes that discrimination and the prejudice from which it results are deeply ingrained within our culture. Concentration on the mere prevention of discrimination can result in the implementation of practices that provide only superficial equality. Such practices, while possibly within the letter of the law, do not enact the full intent of the federal and state legislation, presidential and gubernatorial executive orders or the courts' interpretation of these mandates. It is, therefore, the intent of the Anytown Police Department to organize and implement policies, procedures, practices and programs that aid in overcoming the effects of past discrimination in regard to all of the protected groups.

Among the **special employment groups** included in affirmative action programs are African-Americans, Asians, the elderly, Eskimos, Hispanics, homosexuals, immigrants, individuals with AIDS, individuals with disabilities, Middle-Easterners, Native Americans, religious group members, substance abusers, war veterans, women and youth.

From this listing, one conclusion is obvious: anyone can fit into a "special employment group." Those responsible for hiring must take precautions to be fair and unbiased. They should recognize existing biases and ensure that biases do not enter into the process—a difficult task. If, for example, an affirmative action plan requires that all members of certain groups, such as minority group members, be given a personal interview, this may cause members not within this group to claim reverse discrimination. **Reverse discrimination** refers to giving women and minorities preferential treatment in hiring and promoting to the detriment of white males.

Several court decisions have struck down affirmative action initiatives as discriminatory. For example, one case considered the use of affirmative action policies at the University of Texas ("Nation's Colleges Shaken . . . ," 1996, p. A18):

> The unanimous ruling by a three-judge panel of the Fifth U.S. Circuit Court of Appeals in New Orleans rejected using race or ethnicity as a factor in admissions, even for what the appeals court called "the wholesome practice of correcting perceived racial imbalance in the student body."

Citizens in other communities have also expressed a desire to ban affirmative action practices. In California, a controversial ballot measure prohibiting state and local government bodies from "granting preferential treatment to any individual or group on the basis of race, sex, color, ethnicity or national origin in the areas of public hiring, contracting or education" was supported by nearly two-thirds of the voters ("California Voters Ban . . . ," 1996, p. A19).

Some departments use a form such as that contained in Appendix D to gather needed affirmative action data.

Equal employment opportunity and affirmative action policies begin with recruiting and selecting but are also important in assigning, training, promoting, disciplining and firing personnel.

Because these EEO and AA policies are important in so many areas of management, it is critical that managers understand their own policies as well as the policies and ordinances or statutes of their municipality, their state and the country. Such knowledge is critical during the selection process. Possible resources are the director of personnel, the city attorney, law enforcement advisory boards, other law enforcement agencies and the International Association of Chiefs of Police.

In addition to laws related to hiring, many managers also must take into consideration restrictions imposed by unions.

Labor Laws and Unions

A **union,** in the broadest context, is any group authorized to represent the members of the law enforcement agency in negotiating matters such as wages, fringe benefits and other conditions of employment. Most states require by statute that certain conditions be met to be recognized as a union or bargaining unit. A **union shop** refers to a situation in which people must belong to or join the union to be hired.

Several laws ensure fair compensation standards, as well as employees' rights to bargain collectively with management. Unions have existed in the United States for more than 200 years, beginning in 1792 when a local union was formed in Philadelphia by shoemakers. In 1932, the **Norris-LaGuardia Act** was passed to regulate employers' use of court injunctions against unions in preventing work stoppages. The Act also made yellow-dog contracts illegal. A **yellow-dog contract** forbids new employees to join a union. To do so would be grounds for discharge.

Another major law, sometimes called the "Magna Carta of organized labor," was enacted in 1935.

The **National Labor Relations Act of 1935 (Wagner Act)** legalized collective bargaining and required employers to bargain with the elected representatives of their employees.

This act sets forth rules and procedures for both employers and employees to follow. Its intent was to define and protect the rights of employees and employers and to encourage collective bargaining.

The **Fair Labor Standards Act of 1938** established the 40-hour week as the basis of compensation and set a minimum wage. The **Taft-Hartley Act of 1947** was passed to balance the power of unions and management by banning several unfair labor practices, including closed shops. A **closed shop** prohibits management from hiring nonunion workers. In effect, this act allowed states to pass their own **right-to-work laws,** making it illegal to require employees to join a union. In addition, the **Landrum-Griffin Act of 1959** required regularly scheduled elections of union officers by secret ballot and regulated the handling of union funds.

The **National Labor Relations Board (NLRB)** is the principal enforcement agency for laws regulating relations between management and unions.

Strong feelings for and against unions are common in the general public and among those in law enforcement. For many law enforcement agencies, unions are a positive force; for others, they create problems and dissension; and in yet others, they are nonexistent. Even in agencies without unions, however, the possibility of employees becoming unionized is always there. Consequently, managers need to understand the current nature of unions and how they can benefit the mission of a law enforcement agency.

The primary purpose of unions is to improve employment conditions through collective bargaining.

Collective bargaining is the process whereby representatives of employees meet with representatives of management to establish a written contract that sets forth working conditions for a specific time, usually one to three years. The contract deals not only with wages and benefits but also with hours of work and overtime, grievance procedures, disciplinary procedures, health and safety, employees' rights, seniority and contract duration. Most states have laws restricting officers from going on strike.

Law enforcement managers must recognize that officers have a right to join a union and to negotiate with management. Unions have caused administrators to reexamine their roles in negotiations, roles that have varied from remoteness to direct involvement at the bargaining table. In more recent years, both sides have engaged outside experts to represent their positions and organizations in negotiations, both at the bargaining table and during arbitration proceedings.

An estimated 66 percent of law enforcement departments in the United States work with some type of union, ranging from officially recognized discussion to representation of employees at grievance hearings, conciliation proceedings, collective bargaining or arbitration hearings. As in all other official proceedings, careful records must be retained by all individuals and at all levels of the agency.

The union is obligated to protect the interests of the union employee. Management is obligated to manage and control the agency. The ultimate goal of both should be excellent law enforcement services. At times the relationship develops into a struggle for power, with each assuming an adversarial position not in the best interests of the community. By working together, management and unions can achieve the agency's mission to provide effective service to the community.

Types of Law Enforcement Unions

Law enforcement labor representation groups or organizations include local department benevolent associations that act on behalf of personnel, independent unions with a regional or state affiliation and nationally supported and organized labor unions such as the AFL/CIO.

Many law enforcement labor organizations simply evolved. A social group would be formed to discuss the interrelationships of the department and plan social events for the year, often including family members. Over the years these groups started discussions concerning perceived department problems and eventually grew into benevolent associations.

In the early 1960s law enforcement unions were largely local and independent. Current estimates show that 30 to 40 percent belong to local unions, 40 to 45 percent to regional or state unions, and 15 to 20 percent to national labor groups. The latter has been steadily increasing. In fact, law enforcement membership in unions is one of the fastest growing labor groups in the nation. It is estimated that in excess of 100,000 officers belong to organized labor unions in the United States. Stone (1998, p. 11) notes: "[1998] marked the 20th anniversary of the International Union of Police Associations, AFL-CIO. . . . The I.U.P.A. began to take shape as the only union exclusively designed for law enforcement personnel back in 1978." Membership in the I.U.P.A. has been increasing in the United States, as well as in Canada and the Virgin Islands. With the recent addition of the Boston Police Patrolman's Association to the union, I.U.P.A. membership numbers now exceed 13,000 officers (p. 11).

One highly debated issue concerning union membership has been who should belong. What ranks should be included? Should managers and supervisors belong to the same union as line officers because their interests in wages and benefits are largely the same? Is there a conflict of interest?

Some studies indicate that 85 percent of law enforcement unions include both patrol officers and sergeant levels or above, which means that only 15 percent consist solely of patrol level. As long as issues are mainly concerned with wages and benefits, this is not a problem. But when issues involve taking more control of what management considers its rights, such as one-officer versus two-officer patrol cars, transfers and promotions, working hour assignments and the like, conflict can occur. Some agencies have formed separate management-level units within the same umbrella as the rank-and-file union to overcome the objections to a single unit.

Police unions are one of the fastest growing unions in the United States. This photo shows the union meeting of a large police department.

Some managers would rather not have unions. If unions are to exist, most managers would rather they be local and independent. Local union membership provides opportunity for personal, face-to-face discussions about local department problems; lower dues; more control over who is to represent the department and control overall expenditures.

On the other hand, national union representation allows national research on wages, benefits and other issues; outside representation at discussions and greater political influence. Legal assistance is often available. Outside representation avoids union conflict issues spilling over into everyday performance and personal relationships. The main national union groups are:

- *International Union of Police Associations*—affiliated with the AFL-CIO.
- *Fraternal Order of Police*—the oldest police organization in the United States. This professional organization emphasizes collective bargaining in some areas and socializing in other areas.
- *National Association of Police Officers*—consists of police unions opposed to affiliation with the AFL-CIO.
- *International Brotherhood of Police Officers*—founded in Rhode Island in 1969; emphasizes collective bargaining.
- *International Brotherhood of Teamsters*—a private union.
- *American Federation of State, County, and Municipal Employees*—a union for public employees founded in 1936, affiliated with the American Federation of Labor.

Each organization decides what kind of union to have and often bases its selection on past local management/rank-and-file relationships. Attitudes toward management have often been as much a reason for union membership as other conditions of employment.

Reasons for Joining Law Enforcement Unions

A common reason for joining a union is a perceived lack of communication, inaction or deliberate disregard for the feelings and reasonable desires of the majority of employees. Other frequently mentioned reasons are lack of concern for the employees' general needs, lower wages and fewer benefits than comparable departments, peer pressure, general frustration, a desire to infringe on management's rights or management infringing on employees' rights, conditions of equipment or employment, imagined wrongs, lack of concern for legitimate grievances, bad attitude of management, badly handled personnel problems, inadequate technical and personal communications, favoritism, constant threats to fire or take disciplinary action, lack of formal grievance procedures, a general feeling of distrust between management and the rank and file, lack of motivational opportunities, disregard of job stress factors, past bad-faith bargaining and negotiating, lack of recognition for a job well done, lack of meeting job satisfaction needs and a general lack of leadership by management.

Another common reason for joining a union is to feel protected from layoffs and from overzealous and unfair supervision and/or political corruption up to and including "raiding" of union pension funds.

> People join unions to ensure fair treatment, to improve their economic situation and to satisfy social needs.

Management vs. Employee Rights

Controversy between management and unions revolves largely around what is perceived as reasonable management and employee rights or demands. Managers must have specific functions reserved. On the other hand, management depends on employees to do the job. The better law enforcement tasks are performed, the better the managers and employees are perceived by the community they both serve. The better the community perception and rating of the agency, the greater the acceptance of law enforcement needs in terms of wages, benefits and general support. The best arrangement is for management and employees to work together, build mutual trust and act in good faith and support of each other.

The most frequently reserved management rights are determining staffing and staffing levels; determining work schedules, patrol areas, and work assignments; controlling police operations; establishing standards of conduct on and off duty; establishing hiring, promoting, transferring, firing and disciplinary procedures; setting work performance standards; establishing department goals, objectives, policies and procedures; and establishing training programs and who should attend. In effect, management decides what, when, where and how work is to be accomplished. Each of the preceding affects the position and tasks of the chief executive law enforcement officer. In effect, the union sometimes becomes a "second chief."

Management should not have these rights unreasonably infringed upon at the bargaining table. Contracts are long-term instruments that affect not only the present regime but future managers as well. Management must possess sufficient rights to fulfill the agency's mission to the community.

The most desirable way to avoid management-employee conflict is to resolve issues at the lowest level possible. Primarily, this means between first-line supervisors and patrol officers (or equal rank). The vast majority of issues should be resolved at this level, and the first-line supervisor must have the responsibility and authority to do so.

Others perceive a more basic conflict—a distinct difference between the professional law enforcement stance and that advocated by unions. The *professional* model would be: we look to lateral entry and professional skills rather than time on the job in our selections. We want to expand the entire profession. The *union* model would be: We protect our people no matter what happens. If we have to pick between the young, educated professional and the old, established worker, we go with the old one every time.

Management, Unions and Politics

Management would like to believe that they can administer a law enforcement agency without being involved in politics. Many administrators say, "I try to stay out of politics." If this means actively supporting candidates during political campaigns, it is possible. But to remove oneself from all "politics" is virtually impossible. Law enforcement budgets are approved by locally elected government officials. Passage of desirable ordinances and statutes depends on elected officials, who may receive complaints about the law enforcement agency and bring them directly to the chief. Gaining the respect and support of these officials, once they are elected, is a necessity to law enforcement administration. In some cities, unions are also very active in elections and in supporting specific candidates.

Law enforcement management involvement in politics is less likely in communities with a council/manager form of government because the chief executive officer reports directly to the city manager. The city manager is a buffer between law enforcement managers and the city's elected officials.

City management has many departments and varied personnel concerns. Even though city government may sympathize with law enforcement demands, it must balance the demands of all departments. City administration may resist binding arbitration for this reason. Final decisions are made by people not associated with the local government, which has no personal stake in how the decision may be implemented financially or managerially.

Levels of Bargaining

Bargaining may take place at various levels ranging from discussion to court settlements. At the most cooperative level, **open discussion** resolves issues and results in a win-win situation, with a contract that both sides consider fair. If discussion does not resolve all the issues, the next level may be **mediation,** bringing in a neutral third party to assist in the discussion. A mediator helps the two sides reach an agreement.

If the negotiation process stalls, the matter may be referred to **arbitration,** with the consent of all parties. Usually three arbitrators are appointed, and a majority makes the decision. Either a statute or agreement of all parties determines the method of selection. Arbitration should be a last resort. Beyond arbitration, the matter can sometimes be appealed to the courts.

Negotiations usually proceed through these levels: discussion, mediation, arbitration and the courts.

Management and Unions Working Together

Law enforcement management/union decision making may involve mayors, councils, city managers and often outside negotiators, arbitrators, grievance committees and even the courts.

Although law enforcement officers usually do not have the right to strike, they may accomplish similar results through actions such as "blue flu" or slowdowns. Bargaining units of some type are a fact of administrators' lives. It is better to form good relationships that lead to positive results for both sides than to begin with adversarial attitudes. Past skirmishes may cloud issues, and supervisors and workers have long memories. Working within the confines of the written contract is important at all levels of supervision and management, from sergeant to chief.

Open communication, reasonable expectations, honest cooperation, upfront presentations, a sincere desire to negotiate, no preconception that negotiations will automatically go to arbitration and common objectives—all are evidence of good-faith reconciliation and bargaining.

Avoid **delaying tactics** such as failing to disclose important demands until the end; deliberately withholding information; deliberately providing misinformation, untruths or distortions; providing only information that weakens the others' position or deliberately exhibiting unwillingness to resolve the issues so as to throw the process into binding arbitration, where one side or the other feels an advantage.

Successful management/union negotiations begin with a positive atmosphere within the agency during everyday activities and normal routine, for here the tone for mutual respect is established. Everyday problems have a way of developing into grievances, which may then become issues in management/union negotiations. When first-line supervisors have open dialogue and communication on problems and this continues up the hierarchy, an avenue is established for later openness in labor relations as well.

Negotiation guidelines for both sides include the following:

- Negotiations should be entered into far ahead of budget deadlines.
- Timing of negotiations should also avoid both city and union elections.
- Both sides should agree on rules for negotiation procedures.
- Both sides should maintain open channels of communication.
- Both sides should present logical, reasonable justification for their positions.
- Both sides should prepare areas of agreement as well as disagreement.
- Areas of agreement should be disposed of as soon as possible to focus energies on differences.
- Both sides should recognize the emotions involved and resist overreaction, which may be detrimental to both sides. Neither side should make rash, emotional statements that may deter honest negotiation settlements.

- Officials on both sides should be aware that off-the-cuff, unsupportable statements can stop negotiations.
- Items for negotiation should not be discussed outside negotiation proceedings.
- Both sides should make every attempt to resolve differences before going to binding arbitration.
- No individual department head should have the authority or responsibility for final settlement.
- Lay the past contract and the proposed contract side by side and compare wording, additions and deletions, word for word, page by page.

The most equitable negotiations take place in an atmosphere of openness, cooperation, faith and trust. Seek fairness and a focus on the main goals of both sides.

Collective Bargaining, Arbitration and the CEO

CEOs (chiefs of police, sheriffs, superintendents, directors of public safety or any other title denoting head of an agency) might take several positions in collective bargaining negotiations. At the very least, CEOs should be available to describe how a prior contract has affected the agency or how changes in the community or the agency require changes in the new contract. During negotiation stages, the CEO or the management representatives should be informed about how matters under discussion might affect their operations.

In some instances CEOs may be facilitators or advisors. In this role they can tell negotiators how specific actions would affect management's ability to administer the agency. In other instances CEOs may actively participate in the prenegotiation stages but become interested bystanders during actual negotiations, or they may actively participate in the negotiations.

In all discussions, mediations and arbitrations, retain careful records. What occurs at one level of negotiations is likely to be reviewed at the next level. In addition, what is stated at any time in the process is usually subject to appeal. Once the negotiation process is completed, a contract is written containing the specific terms of the agreement. Everyone affected by the contract should receive a copy and understand its terms.

Summary

Selection of law enforcement personnel is a critical management function. The selection process is based on carefully specified criteria and usually includes completing an application form, undergoing a series of tests and examinations, passing a background check and passing an interview. The most common screening methods for selection are basic skills/written tests, medical examinations, background investigations, psychological examinations and physical fitness tests.

Selection is often affected by laws related to equal employment, affirmative action and labor (unions). Title VII of the Civil Rights Act of 1964, as amended by the Equal Employment Opportunity Act (EEOA) of 1972, prohibits discrimination based on race, color, religion, gender or national origin for private employers with 15 or more employees, governments, unions and employment agencies. The Equal Employment Opportunity Commission enforces laws prohibiting job discrimination based on race, color, religion, gender, national origin, handicapping condition or age between 40 and 70. Law enforcement is directly affected by the ADA's goal of guaranteeing individuals with disabilities access to employment and to government programs, services and activities. The ADA prohibits medical inquiries or evaluations, including some psychiatric evaluations, until after a job offer has been made.

A bona fide occupational qualification (BFOQ) is one that is reasonably necessary to perform a job. An affirmative action program (AAP) is a written plan to ensure fair recruiting, hiring and promoting practices. Equal employment opportunity and affirmative action policies begin with recruiting and selecting but are also important in assigning, training, promoting, disciplining and firing personnel.

The National Labor Relations Act of 1935 (Wagner Act) legalized collective bargaining and required employers to bargain with the elected representatives of their employees. The National Labor Relations Board (NLRB) is the principal enforcement agency for laws regulating relations between management and unions.

The primary purpose of unions is to improve employment conditions through collective bargaining. People join unions to ensure fair treatment, to improve their economic situation and to satisfy social needs. Negotiations usually proceed through discussion, mediation, arbitration and the courts.

Discussion Questions

1. During which stages of the selection process is discrimination most likely to occur?
2. Compare and contrast the Equal Employment Opportunity Act and an affirmative action plan.
3. Have there been any civil suits related to law enforcement employment in your area in the past few years? In your state?
4. What is the most difficult part of the selection process?
5. What questions would you ask during an employment interview?
6. How much education should an entry-level position in law enforcement require? A management position?
7. What are other bona fide occupational requirements for an entry-level position in law enforcement? For a management position?
8. Have you ever belonged to a union? If so, what were your reactions to it?
9. Do you favor unions for law enforcement employees? What are the advantages and disadvantages for management?
10. Is the law enforcement agency in your jurisdiction unionized? How does management feel about it?

InfoTrac College Edition Assignment

Research one of the following topics and take a position, using specific journal references to support your view.

- Entry-level officers should/should not be required to have a college degree.
- Officers without a college degree should/should not be considered for promotion.
- Assessment centers are/are not an effective and fair way to select recruits.
- Assessment centers are/are not an effective way to determine promotions.

- Affirmative action programs are/are not fair to white males.
- Unions are/are not usually beneficial to law enforcement agencies.

Your support may be in the form of a summary or an outline, but it should be very specific. Be prepared to discuss your views in class.

References

"The ADA and Police Hiring Practices." *The Police Chief,* Vol. LXIV, No. 6, June 1997, pp. 24–29.

Baro, Agnes L. and Burlingame, David. "Law Enforcement and Higher Education: Is There an Impasse?" *Journal of Criminal Justice Education,* Vol. 10, No.1, Spring 1999, pp. 57–73.

Booth, Walter S. "Personnel Assessment Centers." *Law and Order,* Vol. 45, No. 9, September 1997a, pp. 96–99.

Booth, Walter S. "Ten Complaints about Assessment Centers." *Law and Order,* Vol. 45, No. 10, October 1997b, pp. 87–93.

Brand, David. "The Future of Law Enforcement Recruiting: The Impact of Generation X." *The Police Chief,* Vol. LXVI, No. 8, August 1999, pp. 53–63.

Byrne, Edward C. "Recruiting Second-Career Officers." *Law and Order,* Vol. 46, No. 10, October 1998, pp. 183–186.

"California Voters Ban Affirmative Action." (Minneapolis/St. Paul) *Star Tribune,* November 6, 1996, p. A19.

Carlan, Philip E. "Occupational Outcomes of Criminal Justice Graduates: Is the Master's Degree a Wise Investment?" *Journal of Criminal Justice Education,* Vol. 10, No. 1, Spring 1999, pp. 39–55.

"College Degrees and Race Bias." *Law Enforcement News,* Vol. XXV, Nos. 511, 512, May 15/31, 1999, pp. 1, 12.

Curran, Stephen F. "Pre-Employment Psychological Evaluation of Law Enforcement Applicants." *The Police Chief,* Vol. LXV, No. 10, October 1998, pp. 88–94.

Fulton, Roger. "Do Supervisors Need Degrees?" *Law Enforcement Technology,* Vol. 26, No. 3, March 1999, pp. 76–77.

Fulton, Roger. "Building Your Career." *Law Enforcement Technology,* Vol. 27, No. 1, January 2000, p. 102.

Fuss, Timothy L.; McSheehy, Brendan; and Snowden, Lynne. "Under Investigation: The Importance of Background Investigations in North Carolina." *The Police Chief,* Vol. LXV, No. 4, April 1998, pp. 169–172.

Garner, Kenneth. "Assessment Center Testing." *Law and Order,* Vol. 46, No. 11, November 1998, pp. 77–82.

Harris, Wesley. "Recruiting Women: Are We Doing Enough?" *Police,* Vol. 23, No. 8, August 1999, pp. 18–23.

Harvey, Brian and Ward, Thomas. "Starting Off on the Right Foot: The Importance of Proper Background Investigations." *The Police Chief,* Vol. LXIII, No. 4, April 1996, pp. 51–54.

Hawley, Thomas J., III. "The Collegiate Shield: Was the Movement Purely Academic?" *Police Quarterly,* Vol. 1, No. 3, 1998, pp. 35–59.

Hutton, Glenn and Sampson, Fraser. "The Assessment of Potential and the Potential of Assessment." *The Police Chief,* Vol. LXVI, No. 8, August 1999, pp. 79–83.

Keller, Julia. "Great Debate Over Gender, Leadership." (Minneapolis/St. Paul) *Star Tribune,* June 6, 1999, p. D1.

Kenny, Sean M. "Becoming Truly Fit for Duty." *Police,* Vol. 23, No. 6, June 1999, pp. 56–59.

Kossen, Stan. *Supervision,* 2nd ed. St. Paul, MN: West Publishing Company, 1991.

Leach, Tad. "College Internship: An Aid to Recruitment." *Law and Order,* Vol. 46, No. 5, May 1998, pp. 57–59.

"Local Law Enforcement Agencies Hiring at an Increasing Pace." *Criminal Justice Newsletter,* Vol. 30, No. 12, June 15, 1999, p. 4.

Molden, Jack. "College Degrees for Police Applicants." *Law and Order,* Vol. 47, No. 1, January 1999a, pp. 21–22.

Molden, Jack. "College Education for Police Officers: Part II." *Law and Order,* Vol. 47, No. 3, March 1999b, pp. 17–18.

"More Specialization for CJ Grad Programs." *Law Enforcement News,* April 30, 1998, p. 7.

Morris, Cole. "Cop College." *Police,* Vol. 21, No. 1, January 1997, pp. 44–47, 68–70.

Narramore, Randy E. and Stephen, Etienne. "Introduction to Assessment Centers." *Law and Order,* Vol. 45, No. 11, November 1997, pp. 79–80.

Narramore, Randy E. and Stephen, Etienne. "Hire Smart: Develop a Hiring Strategy." *Law and Order,* Vol. 46, No. 5, May 1998, pp. 53–54.

"Nation's Colleges Shaken after Texas Race-Based Admissions Struck Down." (Minneapolis/ St. Paul) *Star Tribune,* March 21, 1996, p. A18.

Nelson, Kurt R. "To Select the Best: A Survey of Selecting Police Officer Applicants." *Law and Order,* Vol. 47, No. 10, October 1999, pp. 42–45.

Neubauer, Ronald S. "The Future of Women in Policing." *The Police Chief,* Vol. LXV, No. 12, December 1998, p. 6.

Nislow, Jennifer. "Is Anyone Out There? Competition for New Recruits Keeps Getting Fiercer." *Law Enforcement News,* Vol. XXV, No. 520, October 31, 1999, pp. 1, 18.

Nowicki, Ed. "12 Traits of Highly Effective Police Officers." *Law and Order,* Vol. 47, No. 10, October 1999, pp. 45–46.

Oliver, Patrick. "The Assessment Center Method: Not Just for Promotions Anymore." *Subject to Debate,* Vol. 12, Nos. 3/4, March/April 1998, pp. 8–10.

Polisar, Joseph and Milgram, Donna. "Recruiting, Integrating and Retaining Women Police Officers: Strategies That Work." *The Police Chief,* Vol. LXV, No. 10, October 1998, pp. 42–52.

"Pre-Employment Psychological Evaluation Services Guidelines." *The Police Chief,* Vol. LXV, No. 10, October 1998, p. 95.

Rafilson, Kimberly. "An Alternative to Conventional Law Enforcement Written Entrance Exams." *Law and Order,* Vol. 47, No. 6, June 1999, pp. 83–88.

"Rank Objections." *Law Enforcement News,* Vol. XXIV, No. 489, May 15, 1998, pp. 1, 10.

Richard, Nancy. "Distance Learning." *The Police Chief,* Vol. LXVI, No. 11, November 1999, pp. 41–45.

Schrink, Jeffrey L.; Roy, Sudipto; and Ransburg, John. "Perceptions of Alumni Concerning Their Level of Preparation for Criminal Justice Careers: A Pilot Study." *Journal of Criminal Justice Education,* Vol. 10, No. 1, Spring 1999, pp. 77–85.

Slahor, Stephenie. "How One Department Gets the Best." *Law and Order,* Vol. 46, No. 5, May 1998, p. 60.

Stevens, Dennis J. "College Educated Officers: Do They Provide Better Police Service?" *Law and Order,* Vol. 47, No. 12, December 1999, pp. 37–41.

Stone, Rebecca. "Police Union Marks 20 Years, Adds Members." *Police,* Vol. 22, No. 6, June 1998, p. 11.

Strandberg, Keith W. "Police Recruiting: Hiring Strategies." *Law Enforcement Technology,* Vol. 23, No. 10, October 1996, pp. 38–42, 128.

Trompetter, Philip S. "Fitness-for-Duty Evaluations." *The Police Chief,* Vol. LXV, No. 10, October 1998, pp. 97–105.

Varricchio, Domenick. "Continuing Education: Expanding Opportunities for Officers." *FBI Law Enforcement Bulletin,* Vol. 67, No. 4, April 1998, pp. 10–14.

Vernon, Arlene. "The Science of Screening." *Minnesota Business and Opportunities,* June 1999, pp. 23–25, 55.

Weinblatt, Richard B. "Holding Onto a Knowledgeable Resource." *Law and Order,* Vol. 47, No. 6, June 1999, pp. 127–130.

West, Duane L. "Officer Looks Back at Recruitment Process—Things Have Changed." *Community Policing Exchange,* Phase IV, No. 13, March/April 1997, p. 3.

Wexler, Sanford. "College Graduates Committed to Community." *Law Enforcement Technology,* Vol. 25, No. 10, October 1998, pp. 52–53.

Wolf, Gordon. "Developing Performance Criteria for Pre-employment Screenings." *The Police Chief,* Vol. LXVI, No. 8, August 1999, pp. 74–77.

"Women in Policing." *The Police Chief,* Vol. LXV, No. 10, October 1998, pp. 36–40.

Chapter 8   Training and Beyond

The mediocre teacher tells. The good teacher
explains. The superior teacher demonstrates.
The great teacher inspires.
—William Arthur Ward

INTRODUCTION

A fundamental responsibility of law enforcement managers is training subordinates. Personnel must be trained as soon as is reasonable after starting employment. Waggoner and Christenberry (1997, p. 3) assert: "The cornerstone of any law enforcement organization is its ability to educate and train its personnel." Huntington (1998, p. 40) adds: "Good training may be the best investment a police officer will ever make." According to Cannon (1996, p. 40):

> It is obvious to anyone in law enforcement that we live and work in a litigious society. The abundance of litigation is mostly viewed in a negative light. There is, however, a positive side. Litigation dictates improved officer training. Improved officer training means better law enforcement as a whole.

Hennen (1996, p. 87) asserts:

> No police professional must ever be guilty of that most inexcusable lapse of professional responsibility—sending ill-trained officers into the streets. Unlike 19th century policemen who were sent on patrol with no training and few instructions beyond those contained in cumbersome and largely irrelevant rule books, today's law enforcement professional must be skilled to the maximum extent possible.

Law enforcement service cannot be of high quality without training and education. The days of "handing officers a badge and a gun and putting them on the street" are long gone. Duties have become extremely variable and can range from handling a "kids playing in the street" call to a hostage situation, all within one shift. Clede (1997, p. 38) notes: "Because law enforcement is such a fluid field, officers face virtually annual update training in many subjects." Pilant (1998, p. 36) adds:

> The challenges of training, particularly when one looks toward the future, are to provide better, faster, less costly training that makes use of new and emerging technologies; to offer realistic training that captures lessons learned in the field and incorporates them into training programs; and to find ways to successfully mix training and education.

This chapter stresses the need for continuous improvement in police professionalism. It begins with a discussion of training as a management function and liability issue and the differences between training and educating. Next the chapter presents the goals of training. A description of the learning process follows, including variables that affect learning, principles of learning and characteristics of effective trainers.

Next the chapter explores instructional methods and materials and looks at levels of training standards. On-the-job training can produce knowledgeable, skilled on-line officers, as well as supervisors and managers. The chapter then examines training at the various levels: new recruits, new sergeants, middle management and executive officers, including how external training is used. In addition to basic certification instruction, a manager must determine ongoing training needs and prioritize subjects to be included. The next discussion emphasizes the importance of ongoing training, the ideal training cycle, evaluation and the benefits of effective training programs. The chapter concludes with a brief look at the Crime Bill and its effects on law enforcement education, community-oriented policing and problem-solving (COPPS).

Training as a Management Function

Training is a major management function. A department's efficiency and effectiveness are directly related to the amount and quality of training it provides. Training not only improves productivity but also reduces liability. Training ensures that subordinates have the necessary skills to perform well, making the manager's job that much easier. For new recruits, training reduces the time they need to reach an acceptable performance level. Training also tells subordinates that the agency and the manager are interested in their welfare and development.

In addition, *legal liability* has risen substantially for actions taken by on-duty officers without proper training. Good training is the key to avoiding costly lawsuits. In *City of Canton, Ohio v Harris* (1989), Geraldine Harris was arrested by the Canton police and taken to the station. When they arrived, the officers found her on the floor of the patrol wagon and asked if she needed medical attention. Her reply was incoherent. While inside the station, she fell to the floor twice, so the officers left her there to avoid her falling again. No medical assistance was provided. She was released to her family, who called an ambulance. She was hospitalized for a week with severe emotional illness and received treatment for a year. She sued the city for failure to provide adequate medical attention while she was in custody. She won, with the court ruling that the city should have trained its officers to handle such situations.

Law enforcement officers need to recognize when they are not adequately trained for a situation and to say, "No, I cannot handle this," and to also know who can help and how to contact them. In addition, all law enforcement training should be logged and permanently recorded.

Peer v Newark (1961) involved a case of negligence. While at home, a police officer was removing his gun from its holster. In the process the gun discharged, and a bullet went through the apartment wall and struck a girl in the next apartment, seriously injuring her. The officer had received no training in handling weapons off duty. The jury found negligence and awarded the girl and her family damages that were upheld by an appellate court.

Undoubtedly, police departments should review high-risk liability incidents and provide adequate training to avoid liability claims being upheld. Such incidents might be high-speed pursuits, detaining individuals, use of deadly force, use of nonlethal weapons, civil rights violations, firearms training and constitutional law training. Special requirements should be instituted so that no officer who has not met qualification standards may carry a weapon while on duty.

A written statement of training *philosophy* should be part of the training policy. The philosophy should state management's attitude toward training, the extent of resources that will be devoted to it and the training's purpose and expectations. The training philosophy should reflect that managers are essentially assigned to develop personnel, who are the most expensive portion of the law enforcement budget.

Developing human resources should be managers' single most important objective.

Unfortunately, it is rarely the highest priority.

The role of law enforcement managers in training depends on the level of the manager. Executive-level managers make the final decisions as to the kind of

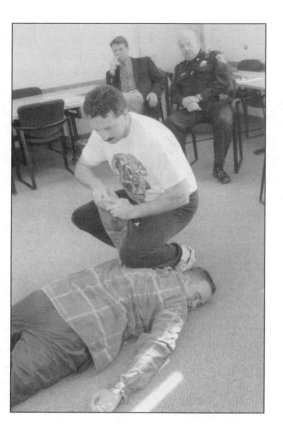

New police recruits receive training from police instructors. Ongoing training extends throughout an officer's career.

training program needed and the groups to be involved. Middle-level management usually prepares the training program and helps determine training needs. First-line supervisors determine the needs of their officers and specialized personnel because they are closest to everyday operations.

Managers must be involved in training from determining needs through evaluation of the program. Management needs to do more than give token support; it must be directly involved. When managers become teachers, they develop jointly with officers. It is often said that people learn best by teaching others. In addition, a bond may develop among personnel, regardless of level within the organization, as they learn together.

When a supervisor sees an officer who is not performing a function, training should be provided to correct the deficiency. Fully trained officers increase productivity and reduce the need for discipline. Major problems in a police organization can often be traced to lack of training. Trained officers are safer officers, and training reflects management's philosophy of concern for employees.

Law enforcement managers need to establish an environment and climate for training, including proper attitudes. Most officers want to be trained. They want to learn as much about their jobs as possible and to do their jobs well. Some officers, however, see training as punishment for not measuring up to management's expectations. Others fear training, feeling they cannot meet the manager's expectations. If training programs are to be effective, managers must allay such fears and negative feelings by peer instruction, line-level selection of training subjects and shared goal setting with managers.

Training vs. Educating

Learning theorists often make a distinction between training and educating. Some go so far as to say, "We *train* animals; we *educate* people." Training is often viewed as a "lower form" of learning, dealing with physical skills, the type of instruction that takes place in vocational schools and on the job in law enforcement agencies. After completing a training session, participants may be awarded a certificate or a license. For example, after receiving training in CPR, participants may be awarded a certificate by the American Red Cross.

Education, in contrast, concerns knowledge and *understanding,* the kind of instruction that takes place in colleges and universities. After completing a specific educational program, participants may be awarded a degree. Some law enforcement agencies pay employees higher salaries if they have attained specific levels of education. Some require a two-year degree, and some states, such as Minnesota and Texas, are considering legislation that would require officers to have a four-year degree before being hired.

> **Training** generally refers to vocational instruction that takes place on the job and deals with physical skills. **Educating** generally refers to academic instruction that takes place in a college, university or seminar-type setting and deals with knowledge and understanding.

Using this distinction, a law enforcement agency might train its personnel to shoot firearms and educate them on the laws of deadly force. It might train personnel in high-speed pursuit techniques and educate them on when high-speed pursuit is to be conducted.

Usually both training and education are needed, and they often overlap. Further, in law enforcement the training may be more important, that is, the *doing* rather than *knowing*. Officers can read extensively about proper shooting techniques, but what matters is receiving expert coaching and practicing on the firing range.

Some have suggested that officers should first receive a comprehensive law enforcement education and then be trained in police work, often under the watchful guidance of a field training officer (FTO). This text does not concern itself further with the distinction between training and education. Because the term *training* is most commonly used in law enforcement—for example, organizations have training departments and a budget line item for training—this term is used throughout this text to refer to both training and education. Both are forms of instruction and involve learning.

Goals of Training

For training to be effective, its goals must be clearly identified. Fisher (1999, p. 9) has developed a tool—a training vision called "The Pyramid of Success"— to help training coordinators focus on what is important:

> The image, the recruit training vision, is a triangle of three equal sides. The core, the center of the triangle, is the [department's] mission statement. Everything emanates from, is related to, and is dependent upon the core. . . . The sides of the triangle consist of three focus topics. These topics are dependent upon each other. They provide the structural support, the stability, for the "Pyramid of Success." . . .
>
> The three focus topics are customer service, individual achievement, and teamwork.

Customer service training entails in-service training that emphasizes citizen needs and the need to be problem solvers and preventers, not just responders (p. 14). The *individual achievement* aspect of training focuses on the reality that "Throughout their careers, [officers] will be expected to generally work alone, make appropriate decisions, and take individual action. Their individual ability to excel will determine their selection into specialized units, promotions, awards, and many other desired results" (p. 10). The *teamwork* focus topic is based on the following:

> As career officers, they will not work in a vacuum. Teamwork with many groups is necessary for them to have a successful career. They are expected to work closely with peers in answering calls for service, to work with supervisors and administration in accomplishing the goals of the department, and to exhibit teamwork with citizens in making the city a safer place.

Variables Affecting Learning

Research on how people learn most effectively suggests that three variables are critical.

Three variables affect learning:

- Individual variables
- Task or information variables
- Environmental/instructional variables

Individual Variables

The first consideration is: *Who* is the learner? Among the important **individual variables** are the learner's age, sex, maturation, readiness, innate ability, level of motivation, personality and personal objectives. The astute supervisor will be knowledgeable about each factor in each subordinate. Questions to ask regarding individual learners include:

- What is the officer's current skill level?
- What has the officer already learned?
- How far, realistically, can one expect this officer to progress in a given time?
- How motivated is this officer?
- Will the officer respond better to praise or criticism? To threats or rewards?
- What are this officer's objectives?

Supervisors have limited control over the individual variables but they must be sensitive to their importance. Of particular importance are the officer's individual training objectives.

Learning Styles

Burg (1996, p. 128) asserts: "Knowing the differences in [learning] style makes the field training process easier." He contends: "There are, for our purposes, four types of learners: auditory, visual, kinesthetic and combination." In other words, some people learn more effectively by *hearing* an explanation of a concept, some learn best by *seeing* things illustrated or performed and others learn best by *touching* or having *hands-on experience* with a new idea.

Another way to look at learning style is to consider personality style. Sample (1999, pp. 56–62) observes that the 16 personality types revealed by the Myers-Briggs Type Indicator (MBTI) are correlated to four learning style preferences: extrovert or introvert, sensing or intuition, thinking or feeling, and judgment or perception. Table 8.1 summarizes the basic content of each and suggests how trainers can meet the needs of officers with different learning styles.

Table 8.1
The Four Learning Style Preferences

Learning Style Preference		Training Suggestions
Extrovert (E) Action is the name of the game for this officer. Extroverts "think" with their mouths open, which is by thinking out loud. They will give immediate answers off the top of their heads.	*Introvert (I)* This person is most at home in the inner world of ideas and concepts. They often detach from class activities and prefer to work completely alone or in very small groups. They will likely take a while to formulate an answer.	This preference concerns from where we get our energy. Plan enough activities to keep extroverts from getting bored, yet give introverts enough time to process information internally. One way to do this is to provide optional exercises. Providing an agenda before class allows introverts to process what will be covered ahead of time, thus allowing them to participate more fully.
Sensing (S) Officers perceive their world in terms of facts, data and details. They are realistic, down to earth and practical. They live in the here and now and learn by experience. Repetition does not bother sensors. Sensors work from the bottom up—gathering details before creating the big picture. Most police officers are typed as sensors.	*Intuition (N)* Officers perceive their world in terms of possibilities, theories, ideas and relationships. They are future-oriented, imaginative and sometimes live with their heads in the clouds. Variety stimulates intuitors, who work from the top down—needing to know how everything fits together before they can learn the details.	This preference concerns how an officer will absorb information or perceive their world. Without explaining how all the pieces of subject matter fit together, you will lose the intuitors. However, if you spend too much time on the big picture, you will lose the sensors (likely most of the class). The best approach is to briefly set the stage by painting the big picture and follow with an in-depth look at each piece. When developing class exercises, give officers the option of similar exercises (repetition for sensors) or several very different exercises (variety for intuitors).
Thinking (T) Officers use a logic based on cause and effect. They prefer to do objective critiques and analyses. Problem-solving is done in terms of right versus wrong principles. These are the trainees who will ask for the reason something is done a certain way. Most police officers are typed as "thinkers."	*Feeling (F)* Officers use a logic that is subjective and personal. Decisions are made based on what is valued and not valued; problems are solved according to what is most important to the people involved—"feelers" will ask how decisions will affect people.	This preference deals with how officers evaluate the information they perceive and how they make decisions. Present class material in a systematic way (for thinkers), making sure the reasoning is logically sound. Also present material in a personal way (for feelers), and make sure you give value or meaning along with the logic. Thinkers need to have a sense of mastery and achievement during and after the class, whereas feelers need a sense of personal support and approval.
Judging (J) Officers like to come to closure. They plan ahead. Time is a resource to be managed. Judgers want structure and predictability, are more decisive than curious and do not want to waste class time with endless discussions. Their goal is to get things done, preferably early. Most police officers are typed as judgers.	*Perceiving (P)* Officers tend to be more spontaneous. They need flexibility and leave themselves open for more data and possibilities. They view time as something to be enjoyed. Their goal is the adventure of discovery; getting things done is not a priority.	This preference determines which style officers prefer to use when dealing with the outside world. Develop an agenda with time frames you can stick with so the class will begin and end on time (for judgers). However, build in some flexibility so the perceivers don't feel railroaded. You may also schedule optional time after class for perceivers to further explore the material being covered. In preparing class exercises, have one right answer for each problem so judgers will know they have reached the goal. Also be prepared to respond to perceivers who will expect to explore different angles and will always want more information.

Source: Adapted from John Sample. "Personality Type, Learning Styles and Police Training." *The Law Enforcement Trainer,* Vol. 14, July/August 1999, pp. 56–63. Reprinted by permission of John Sample.

Adult Learners

The principles of adult learning should also be considered in training programs. Research and common sense suggest that adults learn differently from children. In fact, according to Molden's article (1993, p. 15) referring to a concept in Malcolm C. Knowles's book *The Modern Practice of Adult Education:* "The tongue twisting term **andragogy** [the process of teaching adults, as opposed to pedagogy, the process of teaching children] posits that adults are not grown up children; they learn differently." Because of this, Molden (pp. 15–16) suggests 10 characteristics and principles of adult learning:

1. Adults have more life experiences than do children.
2. Adults are highly motivated to learn.
3. There is strong competition for an adult's time.
4. Adults may lack confidence in their ability to learn.
5. There are greater differences between adults than between children.
6. Adults want to participate in their learning experience.
7. The training environment should be adult related. . . . Adults learn better in a casual, relaxed atmosphere.
8. Adults come to training with problems to solve.
9. Adults prefer to set their own learning pace.
10. Adults need regular feedback.

Because of more advanced cognitive abilities, adults should not be "spoon fed" the "right" answer to a given problem but rather encouraged to think through a problem and to develop an appropriate response. Weinblatt (1999a, p. 84) discusses a new police training philosophy based on this concept:

> The Adult Learning Model is believed by its proponents to be the radical new look of police training in the 21st century. . . .
>
> Under the new wave, referred to by some as Problem-based Police Training (PPT), problems and scenarios become the conduit through which an understanding and ability to problem solve develops. Instructors serve as guides and facilitators, forcing students to find answers on their own much as they would have to on the street. . . .
>
> [As one trainer put it], "We want our people to learn *through* problem solving, not about problem solving."

Task or Information Variables

Task or **information variables** relate to *what* is to be learned. This might involve knowledge, skills or attitudes.

The basic curriculum for recruits must be valid and job related. The first step in validation is to conduct a job analysis defining both the tasks that constitute the job and the knowledge, skills and abilities an individual must possess to perform the job effectively. To establish **content validity,** the direct relationship between tasks performed on the job, the curriculum and the test must be established. In *Kirkland v Department of Correctional Services* (1974), the court held that "the cornerstone in the construction of a content valid examination is the job analysis."

Job analysis is the key to determining the content to teach and test. When content relates directly to the tasks to be performed, it is considered valid. Tests that measure competence in these tasks are then also valid.

According to Krieble (1996, p. 54): "The importance of job task analysis cannot be overstated—particularly in a community policing environment, where job tasks and behaviors must be assessed in order to develop complementary personnel systems."

The next step is translating worker requirements into training/learning objectives. The results of these efforts is that police recruits are exposed to a curriculum that truly prepares them for a law enforcement career.

Training can focus on knowledge, skills or attitudes.

Knowledge is often equated with "book learning," theory and education and includes facts, ideas and information. The steps involved in loading and firing a gun or in obtaining information and then writing a report are usually first presented as facts—information. Often other information, such as that related to safety or legal concerns, is included. Officers are expected to apply most of the knowledge presented to them.

Skills generally involve applying knowledge. These may be technical or motor skills, such as firing a gun, or conceptual skills, such as writing a good report. Law enforcement officers are eager to be proficient in using their equipment and in dealing face-to-face with citizens.

Attitudes are the most difficult to deal with through formal training. They are influenced primarily by the positive and negative examples set by managers, supervisors and others in the department. Officers may learn in training sessions that stress is a hazard of law enforcement work and that pessimism and cynicism are other occupational hazards. They may feel they are immune to stress, just as they may feel they are immune to getting shot. This "it can never happen to me" syndrome so frequently attributed to law enforcement officers is not effectively dealt with through knowledge-centered training sessions.

Relevant questions about task or information variables include:

- How meaningful is the task or information?
- How difficult is it?
- How similar is it to tasks and information already mastered?
- How pleasant or unpleasant is the task?
- How is the instruction organized or presented?

Supervisors have great influence over this variable because they can try to ensure that the task or information being taught is seen as relevant, practical and indeed essential. They can facilitate the learning by breaking the information into small, easily mastered steps. They can relate the material to similar material that officers have already mastered. Probably the most important variable here is the last one: how the instruction is organized or presented.

Environmental/ Instructional Variables

Environmental/instructional variables refer to the *context* in which the training is provided. Important factors include the following:

- Physical setting
- Active learning
- Amount of practice
- Knowledge of results
- Incentives

Common sense suggests that officers will learn better in a comfortable setting where they can see and hear what is happening and distractions are limited.

Involving students in training is more difficult and time consuming and requires more teaching skill, creativity and a greater depth of instructor knowledge. However, it is widely accepted that application is an integral part of the training process. People learn by doing. Practical applications might include case studies and role playing, small-group activities, field trips and individual student performances (discussed shortly).

Common sense also suggests that the more practice officers get with a given task, the more proficient they will become. A critical factor here is that they are practicing correctly. All too often practice does *not* make perfect; it makes an incorrectly practiced procedure *permanent* and therefore counterproductive.

Knowledge of results, or feedback, also greatly enhances learning. Feedback motivates and helps ensure that the correct learning has occurred. Incentives may be related to staying alive, becoming an exemplary officer, promotions, pay raises, threats or any number of factors. Chapter 10 deals with incentives and motivation.

Implications

Given the variables affecting learning, the bottom line is: *There is no one best way to instruct.* The most effective instruction is adapted to:

- The individual officers.
- The specific knowledge, skill or attitude being taught.
- The setting in which the training occurs.

Principles of Learning

Familiarity with the basic principles of learning may help trainers express key concepts more effectively and enable trainees to absorb such concepts more fully. First, learning is not a spectator sport. Use active learning techniques with trainees. Second, give feedback promptly—knowing what you know and do not know sharpens learning. Third, emphasize time on task. Fourth, communicate high expectations. The more you expect, the more you will get. Finally, respect diverse talents and ways of learning. As discussed, trainees will exhibit a variety of learning styles. Several principles of learning have been stated or implied in the preceding discussion. They are summarized as follows:

Principles of Learning:

- Base training on an identified need.
- Tell officers what the learning objective is.
- Tell officers why they need to learn the material.
- Make sure officers have the necessary background to master the skill (the **prerequisites**). Provide a way to acquire the prerequisites.
- Present the material using the most appropriate materials and methods available. When possible, use variety.
- Adapt the materials and methods to individual officers' needs.
- Allow officers to be as active and involved as possible during training.
- Engage as many of the senses as possible during training.
- Break complex tasks into simple, easy-to-understand steps.
- Use repetition and practice to enhance remembering.
- Give officers periodic feedback on how they are performing.
- Whenever possible, present the "big picture." Teach an understandable concept rather than relying on simple memorization or **rote learning.**

Some managers and supervisors feel they should tell their officers as little as possible, not wanting to confuse them with "details." They often make little effort to organize the material they expect officers to learn into "meaningful wholes." To appreciate the value of giving officers the big picture and of organizing material into a meaningful whole, consider the following exercise.

Concept vs. Rote Learning

A group of officers is told that they are about to learn a symbol system for counting to replace the traditional 1 through 10 system. The group is divided into two subgroups. Group A is given Instructions A; Group B is given Instructions B. They have two minutes to learn the new system. After the two minutes they are given a test. Look at the two sets of instructions in Figure 8.1. You should easily see which group will do better.

A key learning principle is that of interval reinforcement. **Interval reinforcement** means presenting information several times, perhaps as follows:

First time—In the introduction of a lecture.

Second time—In the middle of the lecture.

Third time—At the end of the lecture in a summary.

Fourth time—In a quiz a few days later.

Fifth time—In a review session a week later.

Sixth time—In an application of the information.

Notice that the information is repeated with intervals between the repetitions. Studies have shown that if learners are presented information once, they remember only 10 percent of it after 30 days. If, on the other hand, they are exposed to the same information six times, they remember 90 percent of it after 30 days (Figure 8.2).

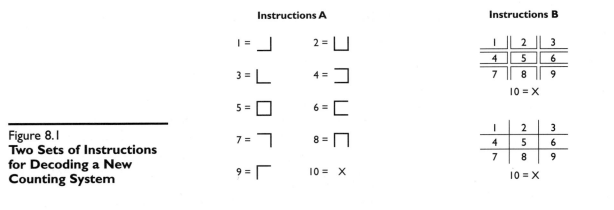

Figure 8.1
Two Sets of Instructions for Decoding a New Counting System

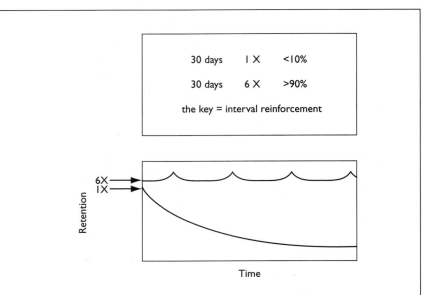

Figure 8.2
Interval Reinforcement

Source: Robert W. Pike. *Creative Training Techniques Handbook.* Minneapolis, MN: Lakewood Books, 1989, p. 15. Used with permission of Robert W. Pike, President, Creative Training Techniques International, Inc., Eden Prairie, MN.

Kolb Model of Learning

Bozarth (1999, p. 32) states:

> David Kolb's ground breaking *Experiential Learning: Experience and the Source of Learning and Development* has . . . become one of the training industry's standard references. . . .
>
> Kolb proposed that all learners move through fairly well-defined stages of acquiring information, a process he describes as "learning around the cycle." According to Kolb, trainees must first find a compelling reason for learning material before they will be receptive to the content.

Kolb's cycle of learning involves four phases. Phase I involves creating a reason for learning. In this phase the instructor acts as a motivator and provides concrete reasons for learners to become involved. Phase II is content presentation and often involves lecturing. Bozarth (p. 33) notes: "A crucial facet of this phase, though one that many trainers overlook, is the learner's need for time to digest the information. Giving opportunities for reflection heightens the learning experience."

Phase III is the practice phase, where, according to Bozarth (p. 33): "The instructor changes from expert to coach, providing a safe environment for trial and error in practicing a new skill." Kolb suggests that peers evaluate each others' performance during this phase. In Phase IV the trainee is encouraged to explore applications. At this stage Bozarth (p. 34) suggests: "Interactive group activities might include games and competitions or one of the most powerful confidence-builders of all: let learners teach the new material to someone else."

As a final word of caution, Bozarth (p. 34) notes: "Not all learners move through the cycle at the same speed, so it's important that the instructor keep an eye on the pace of the class.

Training Tips

- Work one on one.
- Show more than you tell.
- Review often, but give time to practice as soon as possible.
- Reinforce your training with practice, positive feedback and praise.
- Always recognize improvement.

Having looked at basic principles of effective training, next consider some common mistakes trainers make.

Training Pitfalls

Following are the most common training mistakes.

Training Pitfalls

- Ignoring individual differences, expecting everyone to learn at the same pace
- Going too fast
- Giving too much at one time
- Using tricks and gimmicks that serve no instructional purpose
- Getting too fancy
- Lecturing without showing
- Being impatient
- Not setting expectations or setting them too high
- Creating stress, often through competition
- Delegating training responsibilities without making sure the person assigned the task is qualified
- Assuming that because something was assigned or presented, it was learned
- Fearing subordinates' progress and success
- Embarrassing trainees in front of others
- Relying too heavily on "war stories"

Effective Trainers

Trainers are usually taken for granted, but good teachers are hard to locate. Molden (1994, p. 10) suggests that: "Exceptional teachers are truly exceptional—they are stage performers, entertaining, highly verbal, quick witted, knowledgeable and charismatic." Molden (pp. 10, 105) says that to be highly effective, trainers must possess a passion for excellence and a respect for and an interest in students. They must not take themselves too seriously but must be fully prepared. They should be enthusiastic and present with animated mannerisms and gestures. They must have excellent communication skills and a moral and ethical commitment to instructing.

Tate (1999, p. 37) asserts: "Realizing that repetition, frequency, timely fault correction and reward coupled with a positive environment will ensure proper skills performance is paramount to the professional trainer."

Instructional Methods

Many training methods are available. Which to select depends on how much time is available, the kind and amount of training needed, how many officers need to be trained and the cost.

Instructional methods include lecture, question/answer sessions, discussion, videoconferencing, demonstration, hands-on learning and role playing.

Lecture

Lecture, direct oral presentation, is the traditional way to instruct. It is efficient, can be used with large numbers of people and is cost effective. It is well suited to conveying large amounts of information.

A lecture can successfully introduce a new subject to a group of students as well as provide supplemental information on a topic particularly to students who have little experience in that area. Because one instructor can reach a large number of students, lectures can also reduce the cost of instruction—a relevant consideration for budget-conscious training departments. Lectures are flexible and can be personalized.

Unfortunately, lecture is sometimes overused and sometimes abused. It can be boring and completely ineffective if skills are to be taught. In fact, 40 years ago Staton (1960) defined a lecture as "a process by which facts are transmitted from the notebook of the instructor to the notebook of the student without passing through the mind of either."

Among the disadvantages of lecture are that they are a passive means of communication and they cannot meet the needs of both fast and slow learners. A primary disadvantage of lecture is that it does not allow for learner participation. A second disadvantage is that it does not provide the lecturer/trainer with feedback on how thoroughly learners are acquiring the desired information. Given these shortcomings, lectures should be limited to short periods and supplemented with as many visual aids as possible, including diagrams on chalkboards, flip charts, overheads, slides and videos.

Guided lectures enable students to assimilate more of the lecture material while enhancing their note taking. Provide the lecture objectives before the lecture; then encourage students to put their pens down. Use the first half of the class time to deliver the lecture, and then ask students to briefly jot down as much material as they can recall. Next, place students into small groups and have them reconstruct the lecture based on their own notes. The cooperative interaction not only generates enjoyable discussion but provides students with notes that are superior to those produced individually.

Question/Answer Sessions

Question/answer sessions, or **Q & A** sessions, are of two basic types:

- Learners ask the instructor questions.
- The instructor asks the learners questions.

Some lecturers will invite listeners to interrupt with questions that come to mind during the lecture itself. This is usually an effective way to break the monotony of a lecture, and it is usually the most appropriate place for the information.

Other lecturers ask that listeners hold their questions until the end to make certain they cover all the information. The disadvantages of this approach are that people often forget their questions, the questions seem irrelevant later in the lecture or people are in a hurry to leave.

A third approach, if time is limited, is to provide listeners with cards on which to write their questions. If another session is planned, the questions can be answered then. If the present session is the only one to be conducted, participants can put their name and phone number on the card and the lecturer can get the answer to them.

Instructors can encourage students to ask questions by praising good questions, repeating them and never embarrassing a student. There is no such thing as a "dumb" question—except perhaps the one not asked.

Another approach to using questions is for the instructor to ask the students questions. Questioning helps keep the students awake and alert and provides feedback to both instructor and students.

Trainers may call on individuals to answer or wait for volunteers. Asking for volunteers creates a more "comfortable" atmosphere but allows some students to dominate and others to sit back and let them. It may, however, be threatening to call on individuals for answers, especially if the material is relatively difficult. Some trainers use a combination. Trainers have three basic types of questions: factual, rhetorical or opinion based.

Factual questions test students' grasp of the concepts presented, reinforcing learning through repetition. A factual question would be: "What are the elements of first-degree murder?"

Rhetorical questions are those to which an answer is not expected, asked to get the listener thinking about a topic. For example, "What are we doing here?" The questioner does not expect an answer because it would be only speculation until more information is provided.

Opinion-based questions get students to share their personal feelings about a topic. There are no right or wrong answers, but some are more plausible than others. For example, "What type of weapon is most effective for law enforcement officers to carry?" The resulting interchange of opinions, perhaps even arguments, could lead to another instructional method—discussion.

Discussion

Discussion involves an interchange of ideas. It allows learners to be active participants and is usually motivating. Effective discussions do not just happen. They require a skilled leader, usually the supervisor or trainer, to do the following:

- Guide the discussion.
- Keep it on track.
- Control the amount of time devoted to each topic.
- Ensure balanced participation by learners.
- Summarize the key points at the end.

Law enforcement incident reviews of how specific cases were handled make excellent topics for discussion. The strengths and weaknesses of the cases can be identified and discussed, as can other approaches that might have been equally or more effective.

Videoconferencing

Videoconferencing is simultaneous, interactive audio and video communication. Although videoconferencing has advantages, the cost of purchasing the equipment is substantial, and lengthy booking dates may be required for a multipoint hook-up. Other ways training can take place from a distance include computer-based training (CBT), satellite training and teleconferencing, simulators, electronic bulletin boards (EBBs), on-line computer forums, "train-the-trainer" programs and correspondence courses.

Demonstration

Many skills can be taught most effectively through *modeling* or *demonstrating* how to do something, such as how to give CPR, handcuff a suspect or frisk someone. An effective **demonstration** has the following characteristics:

- Everyone can see the demonstration.
- Each step is explained as it is slowly done.
- The purpose of the step is also explained.
- Questions are allowed along the way.

The demonstration is repeated at normal speed as many times as needed until everyone understands.

Hands-On Learning

Often, after a demonstration, learners are asked to do the procedure that was demonstrated. **Hands-on learning,** or actually doing what is required on the job, is an ideal form of training. It is motivating to learners and needs no "transfer" to the real world. Whenever possible, theoretical information should be followed by some kind of actual performance. In 451 B.C. Confucius said, "What I hear, I forget; what I see, I remember; what I do, I understand." Centuries later Aristotle said: "What we have to learn to do, we learn by doing." Some things do not change.

The effect of hands-on learning on retention is clear from the curve shown in Figure 8.3. We retain 10 percent of what we read compared to 90 percent of what we say and do. Sometimes, however, the real thing is not possible. In such instances role playing can be very useful.

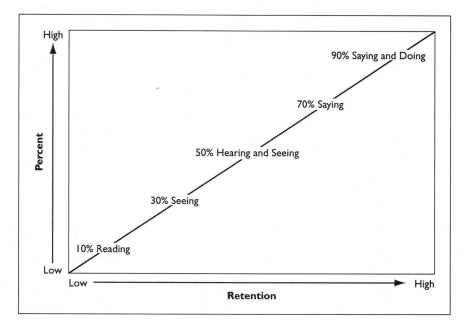

High

90% Saying and Doing

70% Saying

Percent

50% Hearing and Seeing

30% Seeing

10% Reading

Low

Low ——————————————————→ High

Retention

Figure 8.3
The Retention Curve

Role Playing

As the name implies, **role playing** casts people into specific parts to act out. For example, one student might take the role of an arresting officer and another the role of the person being arrested. Sometimes specific scripts are provided. Other times, just the general situation is described. Role playing is an excellent way to practice on-the-job skills "safely."

In role playing the actors learn from doing and from class criticism. The watchers learn from what they see and from finding strengths and weaknesses in the performance. Role playing is especially useful in making officers more sensitive to how others feel and how their behavior affects others. Maxwell (1998, p. 60) notes that the Federal Law Enforcement Training Center (FLETC) in Georgia routinely uses role playing to train law enforcement personnel from over 70 federal agencies nationwide: "Over 200 role players aid in the training, portraying criminals, police, witnesses to crimes and crime victims, in approximately 2,200 roles each month."

Simulations

A **simulation** or imitation of a process is yet another effective means of training. As Strandberg (1999, p. 32) notes: "The idea behind using simulators in training is to make the scenarios as real as possible so the instructor can see, grade and correct how the officers react. If training scenarios can approximate the stress of the street, they are a good litmus test to predict how an officer responds under pressure."

Simulators for firearms training and driving are popular. According to Houston (1998, p. 3) , the police department in West Covina, California, has realized several benefits from such programs:

> The administration felt strongly that realistic training programs in [enforcement-related driving and firearms use] would reduce liability and accidents while improving the department's performance. . . .

The value of a program that covers both driving and shooting comes from the high teaching potential that a realistic training course offers. It maintains the feel of a real-life situation as it takes the officer from hot pursuit into a use-of-force scenario.

Campbell (1998, p. 30) notes that training simulators test more than just shooting skills:

> Several new training systems have come onto the market. Utilizing combinations of laser, video and computer technologies, these products provide a higher degree of realism for officers, confronting them with real-life scenarios that test both their shooting and judgment skills.

The "virtual environments" created by computer technology are also helping officers hone their driving skills. As Paynter (1999, p. 84) states: "The software . . . presents visual and auditory information to the user and measures his ability to react to it. The software gives the driver feedback as to what he saw, what he missed and where he looked; then makes suggestions on how to improve."

Combination

Usually a combination of instructional methods works best. The methods selected will depend on what is being taught.

Individual, Group or Whole-Department/Agency

Instructional method also includes whether the training should be individual, group or entire agency. Such decisions are based on similarities of office behavior and individual differences.

The individual, mentor or field training officer (FTO) approach is a tradition within most local agencies and has been considered effective. Clearly, individual training is important and can be highly motivating. It is also very costly.

Group training has the advantage of giving everyone in the group the same basic knowledge and approach. Law enforcement officers must often rely on each other, sometimes without time or opportunity to discuss what action to take. Group training is more likely to produce the expected unspoken reaction. If each group member is trained to perform a specific way in a specific set of circumstances, officer safety is greatly enhanced. Group training is also more cost effective than individual training.

Some topics are important for everyone within the agency. In such instances training must be arranged to cover all shifts.

In addition to being familiar with instructional methods, trainers also need to know what instructional materials they might use.

Instructional Materials

Instructional materials include printed information, visuals, bulletin boards, audio- and videocassettes, television programs, other training options and computer programs.

Printed Information

Printed materials are by far the most common and most widely used. New recruits may receive a department policy and procedure manual to memorize. New policies and procedures are distributed in print, department-wide, for all employees to "learn." When new equipment is purchased, instruction books frequently accompany it. When employees enroll in more formal training programs, they may have texts to read.

In addition, professional organizations such as the International Association of Chiefs of Police (IACP) have training materials on a wide variety of topics, as do other professional law enforcement institutions throughout the country. Self-study, correspondence courses or tutorial courses are also available to help officers learn information at their own rate and convenience.

Training bulletins are ideal for low-cost training on many subjects. One authoritative source of such bulletins is the IACP, whose bulletins cover all aspects of law enforcement work at all levels. They are inexpensive and can be tailored to local department needs.

Printed materials are uniform, flexible and inexpensive. They also have disadvantages, however. They tend to be impersonal, require expertise and can be boring.

Visuals

Appropriate visuals can enhance learning and help reduce barriers of time, space and language. Visuals are usually divided into two types: projected and nonprojected. Projected visuals include computer graphics, films, filmstrips, overheads, slides and videotapes. Nonprojected visuals include chalkboards, charts, diagrams, flipcharts, graphs, maps and models.

A picture is much more effective than words alone, and words and pictures together are even more effective. One reason visuals are so powerful is the gap between the rate of speaking and listening. Visuals can help bridge this gap, as Figure 8.4 illustrates.

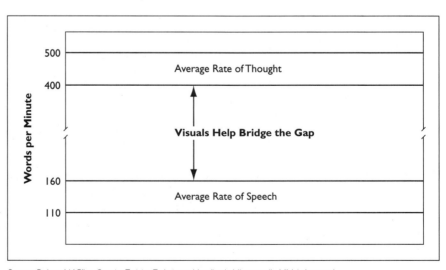

Figure 8.4
The Power of Visuals

Source: Robert W. Pike. *Creative Training Techniques Handbook*, Minneapolis, MN: Lakewood Books, 1989, p. 34. Used with permission of Robert W. Pike, President, Creative Training Techniques International, Inc., Eden Prairie, MN.

Bulletin Boards

Bulletin boards can be effectively used for instruction. The key is to have someone responsible for maintaining the bulletin board and to have a long-range plan for what is to be "taught" each week or month. The bulletin board should be attractively arranged, not cluttered, and contain only up-to-date material. Each item posted on the board should have a removal date clearly marked in a uniform position.

Borrello (2000, p. 27) suggests the bulletin board should be in a well-traveled area of the department and that it continually contain training bulletins that update and refresh the training that officers have received as well as inform them of available training courses. A separate bulletin board should be used for noneducational purposes, for example, for department members trying to sell used guns, cars or furniture, as well as for jokes, cartoons and announcements.

Audio- and Videocassettes

These instructional media are becoming increasingly popular and affordable. They have the same advantages of printed material, that is, individual pacing and convenience of timing. They have a further advantage in that many officers learn more easily from this method than from the more passive activity of reading. In addition, they can listen to instructional tapes while on routine patrol or during quiet shifts.

Departments might want to build a library of audio- and videocassettes on relevant topics. They might even include simulations and games that provide practice in problem solving and decision making as well as in manual dexterity.

Television Programs

Educational television has much to offer on general topics such as communication skills, dealing with people and cultural awareness. It is often also "educational" to watch popular "cop shows" to see what image of policing the public is watching.

The development of the Law Enforcement Television Network (LETN) offers departments across the country up-to-date programming on a variety of topics, covering patrol, drug enforcement, legal issues and professional development ("Training via Television. . . ," 1999, p. 57). LETN, a private satellite television system, is available on a subscription basis. Currently more than 2,000 city, county and state law enforcement agencies subscribe to it. The programs are encrypted for authorized law enforcement viewing only.

Because of the extended work period of law enforcement agencies, LETN programming is planned to reach each shift with identical information, providing uniformity of training. It is difficult if not impossible for local departments to provide training on each shift unless the training is done by the shift managers or supervisors. This usually means that it is not presented the same way to each shift.

The Law Enforcement Television Network (LETN) is a private satellite television system that provides current programs on a variety of law enforcement subjects, available through subscription.

Law Enforcement Television Network (LETN) is a major opportunity for officers today to obtain expert training at the police station, on or off duty. Training videos are also more readily available.

LETN works closely with the International Association of Chiefs of Police. Clede (1998, p. 89) states: "Today, LETN is recognized in 26 states to fulfill some or all of mandated in-service training requirements. Five more states accept LETN for credit, even though there is no in-service training mandate."

Another televised training option is the Law Enforcement Satellite Training Network (LESTN), cosponsored by the Kansas City, Missouri, Police Department and the FBI. LESTN broadcasts teleconferences on current topics. Viewers can call in their questions and talk with experts on the panels at no charge. The seminars are broadcast to all 50 states, Canada, Puerto Rico and parts of Mexico.

Computer Programs

"Computer-based training (CBT)," says Dees (1999, p. 13), "is a popular and cost-effective way to provide certain types of training to employees. . . . CBT also insures that each training session will be identical." Learners are more active than when simply reading, listening to or viewing materials. The programs allow learners to proceed at their own pace, and most provide immediate feedback on the accuracy of responses. Many programs allow learners to skip material they can show they already know. According to Pilant (p. 33):

> Computer technology has probably been one of the stronger influences in training—not only in how it's delivered but in the cost of delivery. Many trainers understand that the unadorned classroom lecture is slowly becoming a thing of the past.

Distance Learning

Levin (1999, p. 12) notes: "Distance learning and training (DLT) in one form or another has been around for a long time," beginning with the correspondence schools popular in the 1950s and 1960s. Distance learning has come a long way since then. According to Nelson (1998, p. 333): "Interest in distance education to deliver college courses in general and criminal justice courses in particular has been growing at an increasing rate." In fact, as Garson (1999, p. 105) suggests: "Virtual universities, online learning, distance education—the new world of higher education virtual reality is misty and elusive to the grasp."

Smith, Bradley and Benscoter (1999, p. 298) caution: "Although distance learning can increase access, opportunity, and convenience for persons who otherwise might not be served as students, the successful development and delivery of distance education involves complex issues and requires comprehensive planning."

Morrison (2000, p. 98) reports: "The distance-learning products on the market today cover a variety of topics and methods of instruction. Everything from CPR, first responder and EMT training to hostage negotiations and emergency vehicle operations is available outside the classroom."

Peterson's *Guide to Distance Learning for 2000* lists 878 institutions that offer distance learning. According to Clede (1999, p. 33), 90 percent of the nation's 2,267 four-year colleges and universities will offer distance learning by the end of 2000. Waggoner and Christenberry (pp. 3–4) state:

> In today's complex policing environment, administrators may find it difficult to meet the training needs of their officers with only a limited number of qualified instructors. The Online Police Academy (OPA) of the Millersville University of Pennsylvania was born of the frustration some police trainers felt over this dilemma. With its World Wide Web-based delivery system, OPA links students and instructors from all over the world.

Another state-of-the-art training and education network is Law Enforcement Online (LEO):

> This new computer network, sponsored jointly by the FBI and Louisiana State University, provides a cost-free means for law enforcement officers to conduct research, communicate with peers, and ultimately take courses online (Waggoner and Christenberry, p. 4).

Other Training Options

Other organizations available to assist with training include the American Society of Law Enforcement Trainers (ASLET), the National Association of Field Training Officers (NAFTO), the Federal Law Enforcement Training Center (FLETC), the National Center for State and Local Training, the FBI National Police Academy and the FBI itself.

The American Society of Law Enforcement Trainers (ASLET) was founded in 1987 and now has approximately 2,500 members. The National Association of

Field Training Officers (NAFTO) was chartered in 1991 to advance the interests of field training officers in all areas of criminal justice.

The Federal Law Enforcement Training Center (FLETC) seeks to provide high-quality, state-of-the-art law enforcement training for a broad spectrum of participating agencies in a cooperative, interagency manner. The National Center for State and Local Training is a component of the Federal Law Enforcement Training Center established in 1982 by then-President Reagan to provide training in advanced topic areas and develop specialized law enforcement skills.

A major training program is the FBI National Police Academy. The FBI sustains all costs for sessions. The Academy started in 1935 and is located on the U.S. Marine Base at Quantico, Virginia, about 40 miles south of Washington, DC. The Academy lasts 11 weeks and is held four times a year. Each session includes 250 selected personnel. In addition, the FBI holds schools ranging from one hour to three weeks for local and state law enforcement officers.

Training Standards

Standards for police training, how much and what it should consist of, have been controversial since the early 1800s when Peel set forth his principles of reform. Compared to other professions, law enforcement does not require extensive formal training. Attorneys receive over 9,000 hours of instruction and doctors over 11,000 hours. Officers receive between 400 and 800 hours of instruction.

In 1967 the President's Commission on Law Enforcement and the Administration of Justice recommended that Peace Officer Standards and Training (POST) commissions be established in every state. These boards were to set mandatory minimum requirements and provide financial aid to governmental units to implement the standards.

Peace Officer Standards and Training (POST) commissions exist in every state to set requirements for becoming licensed as a law enforcement officer.

Among the specific charges of the POST commissions were the following:

- Establishing mandatory minimum training standards (at both the recruit and in-service levels), with the authority to determine and approve curricula, identify required preparation for instructors and approve facilities acceptable for police training
- Certifying police officers who have acquired various levels of education, training and experience necessary to adequately perform the duties of the police service

Table 8.2 provides a recommended basic training curriculum, as well as the specific subjects included in each topic.

Table 8.2
Recommended Basic Training Curriculum

Topic*	Number of Hours	Percent of Total Course
Introduction to the Criminal Justice System	32	8
Law	40	10
Human Values and Problems	88	22
Patrol and Investigation Procedures	132	33
Police Proficiency	72	18
Administration	36	9
TOTAL	400	100

*The specific subjects included in each topic were as follows:
Introduction to the Criminal Justice System: An examination of the foundation and functions of the criminal justice system with specific attention to the role of the police in the system and government;
Law: An introduction to the development, philosophy, and types of law; criminal law; criminal procedure and rules of evidence; discretionary justice; application of the U.S. Constitution; court systems and procedures; and related civil law;
Human Values and Problems: Public service and noncriminal policing; cultural awareness; changing role of the police; human behavior and conflict management; psychology as it relates to the police function; causes of crime and delinquency; and police-public relations;
Patrol and Investigation Procedures: The fundamentals of the patrol function including traffic, juvenile, and preliminary investigation; reporting and communication; arrest and detention procedures; interviewing; criminal investigation and case preparation; equipment and facility use; and other day-to-day responsibilities;
Patrol Proficiency: The philosophy of when to use force and the appropriate determination of the degree necessary; armed and unarmed defense; crowd, riot, and prisoner control; physical conditioning; emergency medical services; and driver training;
Administration: Evaluation, examination, and counseling processes; department policies, rules, regulations, organization, and personnel procedures.

Source: *Report on Police* (1973), Standard 16.3, p. 394.

Source: Terry D. Edwards. "State Police Basic Training Programs: An Assessment of Course Content and Instructional Methodology." *American Journal of Police,* Vol. 12, No. 4, 1993, p. 27.

Basic Certification Instruction

Some agencies require a certificate or license before they will hire an individual. Others prefer to do the training themselves. In some instances state statutes specify a certain level of education and training before a person can become a law enforcement officer. One such state is Minnesota, whose Peace Officer Standards and Training (POST) Board accredits colleges to provide the academic subjects (education) and a skills program.

The *academic* learning objectives cover these subjects:

- Administration of justice
- Minnesota statutes
- Criminal procedure
- Human behavior
- Juvenile justice
- Operations and procedures
- Cultural awareness

The *clinical skills* learning objectives cover these areas:

- Techniques of criminal investigation and testifying
- Patrol functions
- Traffic law enforcement
- Firearms
- Defensive tactics

In addition to the basic core information and skills, officers should be provided with ongoing training throughout their careers.

Academy Training for New Recruits

The quality of people who are becoming officers has changed. Fewer have military backgrounds—more have college educations. The boot-camp approach using stress in academy training may make officers question their self-worth and willingness to follow orders blindly. When modern adult learning principles and self-image psychology are examined, it is revealed that the application of pressure to create a stressful response prior to training is *counterproductive*. Applying extreme pressure prior to training is as ineffective as giving new recruits handguns and expecting them to qualify prior to firearms training.

The traditional high-stress boot-camp model flies in the face of what is known about how adults learn. The academic model, in contrast, trains recruits in the necessary knowledge and skill areas. They have little or no staff contact outside the formal training. A weakness of this model is that it fails to indoctrinate recruits into the law enforcement culture, an important part of their overall training.

Another approach, the individual development or academic model, maximizes adult learning principles (discussed earlier in the chapter), avoids personally derogatory or discriminatory practices and reflects the values of the agency.

In discussing paramilitary versus academic training, Weinblatt (1999b, p. 28) notes:

> The seemingly laid back, academic model of basic training has been ridiculed by many traditionalists. But an increasing number of agencies look to that method to fill their ranks with a more well-rounded officer that they say more accurately reflects the diversity of our society. Backers of the paramilitary approach claim the "softer" approach comes at the expense of discipline, an ability to withstand stress in the streets and a marked increase in physical cowardice.
>
> In interviews with various experts in law enforcement training and management, a preferred method emerged that involved a blending of the two paths.

Of the training models typically used for law enforcement recruits, experts recommend a blending of the paramilitary and the academic.

On-the-Job Training

The most common and frequent training in law enforcement agencies is on-the-job training.

On-the-job training (OJT) may occur during field training, in-house training sessions or roll call.

Field Training

Field training may take several forms. It might consist of *rotation,* which provides opportunity for additional knowledge and possible increased competence in a specialized area. Rotating through various specialities provides opportunity for more of the total-person approach to learning.

Coaching or **counseling,** both forms of one-on-one field training, can also take place on the job as the need arises. Coaching is excellent for practical task development. Counseling is usually presented by staff or the personnel department on a wide variety of job and personal problems.

First-line supervisors have many opportunities for individual training. Usually the supervisors' primary responsibility is to listen and to encourage conversation.

Subbing, another form of field training, takes place when individuals must be absent from their jobs for some reason. A law enforcement supervisor might be ill, and a senior patrol officer might take charge. Or the supervisor may be gone to a conference for a week, and a subordinate may be left in charge.

Supervisors should train their subordinates to the point that one could assume their job. This *does not* constitute a shirking of duties by the supervisor but is simply another step in developing better officers.

Instruction by a **field training officer (FTO)** is perhaps the best known on-the-job training. Rookie officers are assigned to a field training officer who teaches them "the ropes." This is an excellent opportunity for job task development. Not all law enforcement officers make good FTOs, however. All FTOs should be carefully selected and then thoroughly trained before undertaking the instruction of others.

The most common type of on-the-job training for new recruits is done by the field training officer, or FTO.

FTO programs help compensate for selection errors. They provide role models for recruits and allow for application of knowledge and skills that cannot occur in a classroom. Henderson (1998, p. 44) maintains that self-motivation, reflection and evaluation are critical components when considering assignment as an FTO:

> Training officers are, for the most part, the brightest, most knowledgeable and professional members of their agencies. They must be; their departments' futures depend on it. If you were to look at a cross section of trainers throughout criminal justice, some common attributes will surface. Probably the foremost is the willingness to go beyond the minimum of what it takes to get the job done.
>
> You will find that a good FTO will often be "the source" of information for the squad or team for general criminal justice topics. A good FTO is a prepared FTO. Sensitivity, understanding and strong communication abilities are also present. We must not forget a sense of humor and adventure. A good trainer strives to maintain a professional level that results in them being highly respected. Patience is not only a virtue, it is something that a successful FTO must have in abundance.

FTOs must also be well organized and able to handle copious amounts of paperwork. Fortunately, software is now available for FTO program management. As Dees (1998, p. 179) notes:

More experienced officers have often been through the same situations as new officers and can share information that will help them avoid mistakes. They can also provide solid police instructions and constructive criticism for the new recruits.

A big headache in administering a field training officer (FTO) program is the amount of paperwork necessary.

. . . Daily Observation Reports (DORs) are mislaid, misfiled or not turned in at all. The consequence is that the all-important training files get out of whack.

A software solution for this situation is ADORE: Automated Daily Observation Report and Evaluation software.

In-House Training Sessions	In-house training sessions, also called **in-service training,** are frequently used in local law enforcement departments. Specific portions of a shift may be set aside for training and repeated for each shift. Instruction may be by the supervisor, by someone else within the department or by an instructor brought in from another department or from outside the law enforcement field itself. In-house training sessions should be based on the department's needs. Their length will depend on the instructor, the material to cover and the time available.

Consultants are not used more often primarily because of the extra expense. Consultants are used mainly for their expertise and ability to look at problems without local bias or obligations.

In areas where several law enforcement departments exist in proximity, it is sometimes cost effective to share training. One department, for example, might be known for its outstanding work on community relations. Another might be known for its expertise in investigating cult-related criminal activity. Yet another might be known for its work with juveniles. These three departments might share their expertise during in-service training sessions.

Relationships might also be established with local, state and federal agencies to exchange instructors and perhaps materials on special problem areas such as drug investigations. They might also include prosecutors and courts, the coroner's office, private security consultants and social services personnel.

Roll Call	Training given during **roll call** is popular and economical. With the advent of brief videos and restricted training budgets, it is a viable training option for most departments. The time must be used wisely because roll call generally lasts only 10 to 15 minutes. Nonetheless, training in short bursts is much more effective than long sessions for some subjects. Roll call is well suited to short topics of specific, immediate interest to the on-line officer, and that interest increases training success. Swope (1999, pp. 165–166) stresses:

> Roll call . . . can be the most valuable period of time in the day for managers and supervisors of a police agency. . . .
>   It is an opportunity to significantly enhance a department's operation through training, information exchange, team building and inspections. . . .
>   All departments have some policies that are so important that they demand constant reinforcement. The guidelines on the use of service firearms, or the use of force in general, may require continual review. It may be vehicular pursuit, or proper conduct and behavior that needs regular attention.
>   Ethics and integrity may be on the top of the list for training during roll call. By taking the time in roll call, five or ten minutes on a continual basis, the policy is not only communicated, but the message has been emphasized that it is important to the agency. Clear expectations have been conveyed.
>   Roll call is an opportunity to present new laws, directives and policies. While such items are likely distributed in writing to all members, roll call training affords the opportunity to ask questions and clarify possible misinterpretations and misunderstandings by using two-way communication.

Remedial Training	One of the most unpleasant tasks a manager faces is dealing with unsatisfactory performance. But, as Phelan (2000, p. 48) suggests: "Practical and procedural support when managing unsatisfactory behavior is likely to promote proper

skills development as well as an effective training environment." Phelan (p. 50) describes four essential components of the remedial process:

1. Performance review: Explain precisely what error/omission occurred.
2. Demonstration/explanation: Tell/show the proper procedure.
3. Resource acquisition: Inform the member what resources are required to correct/modify the behavior.
4. Compliance time line: Give a defined period of time in which to correct the problem.

Becoming a Sergeant

Of particular importance is effective training for newly promoted sergeants. This promotion is a critical and challenging adjustment for the officer who for the first time must supervise others.

Fulton (1999b, p. 102) observes: "All too often, police administrators with 20-plus years of experience forget how difficult the transition from patrolman to sergeant can be." He (1999a, p. 74) also notes:

> Perhaps the gravest error some administrators commit is promoting new supervisors and thrusting them into their new assignments without training. Even when states mandate training for police supervisors, the language of the law often is couched in terms such as, "must attend X hours of supervisory training within one year of promotion."
> Too often this phrase is interpreted as "within one year AFTER promotion."

Fulton (1999b, p. 102) asserts: "Since training programs are available to teach basic supervisory skills at most regional academies, there is little excuse for not sending new supervisors to the training they so desperately need to be successful in their new position."

Training at the Management Level

According to Austen-Kern (1999, p. 24): "Currently, there are only a few states that require a police department manager to attend any form of management training program." However (p. 64): "Departments should not underestimate the long-term value of providing a comprehensive and continuing management development program for their managers. The proper training of managers is critical to building and maintaining a strong and professional police department."

Manager training should be initiated only after determining both individual and organizational training goals. Usually the goal of manager training is to develop better individual performance, improve the necessary skills required of managers and improve overall knowledge beyond the job.

Management on-the-job training can consist of using actual past department problems and requesting managers to offer solutions. The advantage of this is that the problems are related to the department in which the manager operates and are not simulated, fictional or abstract.

Technical skill development can take place through reviewing the total law enforcement experience, then evaluating what was done and deciding how it could be done better through identifying the basic problem, developing alternative solutions and choosing the best one.

Managers can improve their human-relations skills by attending seminars, workshops, conferences or courses at colleges and universities.

A number of approaches to management training are available. Some departments rotate the manager from patrol to administrative, investigative, juvenile or narcotics divisions. Job rotation, although sometimes painful, gives the police manager a total department experience. Other departments do not like rotation, and once managers are appointed, they remain in that position until their next promotion or retirement. As a result, stagnation often reigns in such agencies. New managers may be assigned to experienced managers who act as mentors.

Large city departments provide their own management training, tailored to their own special problems and needs. Smaller agencies use a combination of methods: lecturers from federal, state and local law enforcement agencies or special management seminars. Smaller departments may band together in training groups to share resources.

Management and supervisory training is available externally at the federal, state and local levels. The FBI, Northwestern Traffic Institute and Southern Police Institute are among the agencies providing training for qualified officers nationally.

External law enforcement management courses are available through the International City Managers Association, the International Association of Chiefs of Police and the American Management Association. They are also available through local universities and colleges. External management training offers interaction with people from identical positions from other agencies. This sometimes establishes a long-term relationship for future exchange of information. These seminars also expose local managers to new ideas and programs.

Opportunities for self-development are also available through correspondence courses, as well as individual management courses offered by universities, colleges and other agencies. Such courses are valuable for their content as well as for the self-discipline required to complete them independently.

External Training

Attendance at training sessions and seminars held outside the law enforcement department is costly, but it introduces officers to new ideas and subjects not available locally. External training provides the opportunity to meet officers from other departments, to share problems and to appreciate the universal nature of some law enforcement problems. Possibilities for external training include local college courses; the Federal Bureau of Investigation; the Northwestern Traffic Institute; the International Association of Chiefs of Police; the Bureau of Alcohol, Tobacco and Firearms, the Drug Enforcement Agency and the U.S. military branches of service.

Officers should document in writing their participation in such external training.

External training may take the form of college classes, seminars, conferences, workshops and independent study.

College Classes

Colleges and universities offer a wide variety of courses on subjects not taught by law enforcement departments. The department may pay for the tuition, fees, books and other costs, or officers may pay for them. In either case, such training usually takes place during officers' off-duty hours.

Some departments have incentive programs that permit officers who attend college courses for credit to receive extra pay. The increase in availability of college-level courses has had a tremendous impact on raising the level of police education. During the years of LEAA funding, thousands of police officers attended college courses, and many of them obtained degrees. College-level or academic courses are still considered the epitome of training, although in-service police training programs are also vital. According to Molden (1999, p. 21): "Both the Police Executive Research Forum and the International Association of Directors of Law Enforcement Standards and Training passed resolutions supporting college graduated police."

Ironically, some college-educated officers find varying degrees of acceptance by older officers of the police department. This resentment is beginning to be minimized by the many candidates today with degrees in criminal justice and the number obtaining degrees while working. The debate surrounding the educational requirements for officers was discussed in Chapter 7.

Seminars, Conferences and Workshops

Pick up any law enforcement journal and the opportunities available for training through seminars, conferences and workshops become immediately apparent. In a single month, for example, the IACP offers the following training programs:

- Administering a Small Law Enforcement Agency
- Police Records Management
- Innovative Approaches to the Public Information Process
- Progressive Patrol Administration
- Police Planning, Research and Implementation
- Criminal Investigations Management Symposium

Costs for seminars, workshops and conferences vary greatly, ranging from free (not very common anymore) to hundreds of dollars per participant. Travel costs are also often involved. Nevertheless, this is sometimes the most effective alternative for obtaining needed expertise in a given topic. Many service clubs, such as Rotary, Kiwanis and Optimist, will financially assist law enforcement agencies for such educational opportunities.

Conferences for professional law enforcement organizations also offer sessions on a wide variety of topics and have the added advantage of allowing for the interchange of ideas among professionals from around the country. Indeed, as one chief (Sharp, 1999, p. 150) summarized: "A primary benefit of any conference is the networking and exchange of information with other attendees." If budget allows, attendance at state-level and even national conferences should be a part of the training program.

Who to send is often a key question for management. One way to decide is to consider who would make the best in-service instructor to share what was learned. Officers who attend conferences, workshops or seminars should be expected to share the information gained. Usually the officer who attended puts on a training session. This sharing improves the instructor officer's self-esteem and professional reputation, which is valuable in establishing credibility in court as an expert witness. Most of all it enhances the agency's reputation as an outfit that employs quality people and trains them well.

Even if the budget will not allow for officers to attend conferences and conventions, the information from them is often available through publications of professional organizations.

Independent Study

Some departments have limited opportunity for external training. Most officers in such departments, however, will have access to a public library. At the library, officers can set their own pace for education that supplements their formal training. Many law enforcement texts have been written in the past few years. In addition, local libraries have statewide access, a rich resource to be tapped.

Another avenue of independent study is the variety of distance learning and training (DLT) courses now available online, as already discussed. Replacing the "correspondence courses" popular in previous decades, Levin (p. 12) notes: "More modern approaches use e-mail, listservs, Internet-based compressed video, Web-supported courses and Web-only courses. . . . DLT courses are the wave of the future. They require students with initiative and maturity, but they provide significant potential benefit to the agency and its employees."

Ongoing Training

Before getting the job, as a rookie, upon promotion to sergeant and beyond—throughout a law enforcement career—training should be ongoing. Regardless of the methods used, law enforcement training must be continuous because people fail to remember a high percentage of what they learned. New subjects continually arise that must be learned, including new laws and court decisions.

Officers' training should be ongoing—lifelong learning.

In addition, opportunities for self-development training are unlimited through videos, closed-circuit television and printed materials. Such independent learning is well suited to the extended service hours of law enforcement work and to the preferred learning styles and paces of individual officers.

Determining Ongoing Training Needs

Training needs of officers at various levels of experience can be determined in a number of ways. Among the most common are these:

- Reviewing new statutes that relate to law enforcement and that affect police operations and investigations
- Taking department surveys
- Reviewing reports and noting deficiencies
- Reviewing internal and external complaints
- Reviewing lawsuits against the agency
- Analyzing specific law enforcement functions
- Interviewing line officers and detectives

- Interviewing managers and supervisors
- Getting input from other agencies and the community

In determining subjects to include in the training program, managers can consult their most recent performance evaluations, consider their current observations and consult with their officers. They might also review disciplinary actions and records that may reveal training needs. Exit interviews of officers who leave the department are an important information source. In addition, complaints received about officers or the agency may identify problems that training might correct.

These various methods of identifying training needs are likely to indicate what subjects are considered priorities, as well as various types and levels of training needed in any given department.

Police officers in the field are an excellent information source for training needs. They see the practical application and value of training, and they bear the initial responsibility when a liability suit is filed against the department. Police management bears the overall responsibility for failure to train.

The Training Cycle

Jones (1999, p. 243) stresses: "Training is a never ending process meant to keep law enforcement officers updated on legal issues, bring new trends to the forefront, and sharpen a variety of perishable skills." Jones further notes: "To avoid the waste of precious training resources, police training managers may adopt five steps designed to generate successful training implementation." Because effective training is ongoing, it can be viewed as a cycle, as Figure 8.5 illustrates.

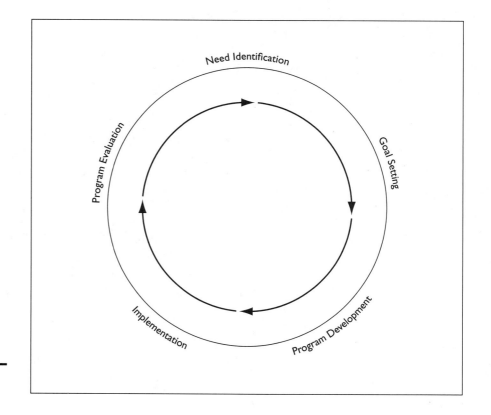

Figure 8.5
The Training Cycle

The training cycle consists of need identification, goal setting, program development, program implementation, program evaluation and back, full circle, to assessment of need based on the evaluation.

Need Identification

Training programs must emphasize actual individual and department goals and needs that come to light from conversations with officers, supervisors' and managers' observations, complaints, officers' suggestions and other sources.

Goal Setting

As with any type of goal setting, training goals should reflect specific training objectives that meet the following criteria:

- Specific and observable
- Measurable, with a set criteria
- A clear time line for achievement

In identifying training goals, Jones (p. 243) asks:

What does the training manager hope to accomplish with the time and money invested? Do specific issues need to be addressed? e.g., liability reduction, citizen complaints, officer safety, morale, union grievances, employee turnover, absenteeism, etc. Is there an improvement initiative that has been launched or is being planned, such as accreditation?

Program Development

After the needs have been identified and goals and objectives specified, the actual training program must be developed or, for existing programs, revised based on the needs assessment.

Because time and opportunity for training are limited, excellent instructional materials and good lesson plans are important. Because law enforcement departments are in operation seven days a week, 24 hours a day, it is extremely difficult to pull together all employees at one time for a department training program. Most training has to be presented by shift or individually, with only the most serious and important matters reserved for full department training. Law enforcement training is well suited to the normal procedures of learning and training:

- Determine subject matter and objectives based on identified needs.
- Prepare the training.
- Select the most appropriate method(s).
- Select/write materials, including tests, and select/develop audiovisual aids.
- Select the instructor.
- Schedule the training.
- Reserve the facility.
- Present the training.

- Evaluate.
- Learners apply new knowledge on the job.
- Evaluate.

Who should provide the training? Managers, by their position, should be constantly providing on-the-job training, helping subordinates to grow and develop on the job. Managers may also schedule more formal training sessions and present information themselves. They may seek assistance from someone else in the department who has expertise in a specific area. Or they may bring in someone from outside the department—perhaps even from outside law enforcement. Whether managers do the actual training or not, they are responsible for ensuring that it is effective and meets their subordinates' needs. The ultimate responsibility is theirs.

Cost The amount of money budgeted for training varies greatly from department to department. In addition to the costs for instructors and materials, the cost of officers' salaries during training should also be factored in. Training costs can be cut by sharing resources with other departments, cohosting training, using FBI programs, seeking scholarships for officers to attend training and seeking sponsors for officers.

Facilities The type of training, method of instruction and audiovisuals will affect the physical facilities needed. The facility should be conducive to learning and to two-way communication. It should be well lit and well ventilated, contain adequate seating and writing surfaces and have good acoustics. Depending on the size of the training group, a microphone may be necessary. If so, the most effective type is a small, wireless microphone—which should not pose a problem for most law enforcement departments.

Program Evaluation

Like training, evaluation should be continuous. The officers' grasp of the material should be tested in both the classroom and on the job. Such evaluation will help determine whether further training is needed in a specific area.

One effective nontest way to evaluate training effectiveness is to compare officers' work performance before and after training. Other before-and-after information that might reflect the effectiveness of training can be obtained from records of complaints, grievances, absenteeism, turnover and the like. Jones (p. 244) suggests: "Measuring performance change can be done through pre-test/post-test comparisons to control groups not trained, and complete a 360 degree survey of subordinates, managers, and peers." However, some aspects of training are not easily measured, including attitudes that managers/supervisors seek to instill in their officers.

Trainers should consider having the trainees complete an evaluation of the training session, including responding to such questions as these:

- How effective was the instructor?
- How interesting was the session?
- How relevant was the material?

Evaluation Form Skill Development Workshop

Items below evaluated on a 1 to 10 scale. Please circle number that indicates your evaluation. (10 represents the most positive reaction; 1 the least positive)

1. How well did the training program hold your interest?	10 9 8 7 6 5 4 3 2 1
2. How would you evaluate the leader's knowledge of the topics?	10 9 8 7 6 5 4 3 2 1
3. How effective was the leader's presentation?	10 9 8 7 6 5 4 3 2 1
4. How useful were the notebook/handouts?	10 9 8 7 6 5 4 3 2 1
5. How useful was the group participation?	10 9 8 7 6 5 4 3 2 1
6. How useful were the audio/visuals?	10 9 8 7 6 5 4 3 2 1
7. What overall rating would you give the program?	10 9 8 7 6 5 4 3 2 1

8. How would you evaluate your participation in the program? (check one)

Overall workload	Too heavy _____	Just right _____
	Too light _____	
Classroom demands	Too heavy _____	Just right _____
	Too light _____	
Homework assignments	Too heavy _____	Just right _____
	Too light _____	

9. If asked by a co-worker to describe the workshop and its value to you, what would you say?

10. In what specific ways could this program be improved?

Figure 8.6
Sample Evaluation Form

Source: Stan Kossen. *Supervision*, 2nd ed. St. Paul, MN: West Publishing Company, 1991, p. 285. Reprinted by permission. All rights reserved.

- How was the pacing of the session?
- What did you like most about the training?
- What could be improved?

These questions could be posed during interviews or through more formal questionnaires such as that illustrated in Figure 8.6.

Benefits of Effective Training Programs

Businesses spend over $2 billion yearly to train employees and feel the money is well spent. The same is true of the $200 million spent yearly by law enforcement.

Training programs can benefit individual officers, supervisors, managers, the entire department and the community.

Benefits for Individual Officers

Benefits for individual officers include improved chances for career success, increased motivation to work, improved morale, increased productivity, greater feelings of self-worth, reduced chances of injury on the job, greater confidence, pride, improved work attitudes and increased job satisfaction.

*Benefits
for Supervisors
and Managers*

Among the many benefits supervisors of those trained might enjoy are getting to know officers better, furthering their own advancement and career, gaining more time, establishing better human relations, increased confidence in officers' abilities, increased flexibility, increased creativity, fewer discipline problems and improved discipline and fewer mistakes.

*Benefits for the Entire
Department
and Community*

Many benefits enjoyed by individual managers also benefit the entire agency. In addition, the organization and ultimately the community benefit from training in more efficient, effective officers; increased quantity and quality of work; reduced turnover, absenteeism, waste, complaints and grievances; greater public support and increased departmental pride.

Clearly, training is an important function of the effective manager/supervisor at all levels of the department.

The Violent Crime Control and Law Enforcement Act of 1994

In 1994, President Clinton signed the "Violent Crime Control and Law Enforcement Act of 1994" containing appropriations for the "Ounce of Prevention" program and the "Cops on the Beat."

> The Violent Crime Control and Law Enforcement Act of 1994 authorizes major funding for law enforcement training.

The federal crime bill's Police Corps and in-service scholarship programs represent the largest federal investment in education for law enforcement personnel since the Law Enforcement Education Program in the late 1960s and 1970s. The Act also puts hundreds more officers on the street in an effort to bolster community policing.

Training and COPPS

As more agencies nationwide adopt a community-oriented policing and problem solving (COPPS) philosophy, training of recruits must incorporate these shifts in principles and practices. Harvey (1999, pp. 38–39) asserts: "The recruits' first introduction to COP should be within the academy training phase. . . . Once the recruit begins the field training phase, the FTO should present COP and POP (Problem Oriented Policing) applications in a positive light." Birzer (1999, pp. 17–18) adds:

> If police agencies require officers to become proactive problem solvers, resource catalysts, and communicators, they must foster and support this philosophy at the recruit and in-service training level.
>
> Because of the increased contact that the police have with citizens, officers must receive training in such areas as interpersonal interaction, ethnic diversity, drug and alcohol awareness, and domestic violence. . . . Academy instructors should train officers in de-escalation skills and "verbal judo" techniques.

Birzer (p. 18) further asserts: "Training conducted in the police academy should highlight self-directed learning, which goes hand in hand with community policing. For community policing to succeed, police officers must be self-directed; when they discover a problem, they must solve it."

Summary

Developing human resources should be managers' single most important objective. This objective requires providing both training and education. Training generally refers to vocational instruction that takes place on the job and deals with physical skills. Education generally refers to academic instruction that takes place in a college, university or seminar-type setting and deals with knowledge and understanding. Training and education are both needed for effective learning.

Three variables that affect learning are individual variables, task/information variables and environmental/instructional variables. Training can focus on knowledge, skills or attitudes.

Job analysis is the key to determining the content to teach and test. When content relates directly to the tasks to be performed, it is considered valid. Tests that measure competence in these tasks are then also valid.

Important learning principles include the following: base training on an identified need; tell officers what the learning objective is; tell officers why they need to learn the material; make sure officers have the necessary background to master the skill (the prerequisites); present the material using the most appropriate materials and methods available; when possible use variety; adapt the materials and methods to individual officers' needs; allow officers to be as active and involved as possible during training; engage as many of the senses as possible during training; break complex tasks into simple, easy-to-understand steps; use repetition and practice to enhance remembering and give officers periodic feedback on how they are performing. Whenever possible, present the "big picture"—teach an understandable concept rather than relying on simple memorization.

Training pitfalls to avoid include ignoring individual differences; expecting everyone to learn at the same pace; going too fast; giving too much at one time; using gimmicks that serve no instructional purpose; getting too fancy; lecturing without showing; being impatient; not setting expectations or setting them too high; creating stress, often through competition; delegating training responsibilities without making sure the assigned person is qualified; assuming that because something was assigned or presented that it was learned; fearing subordinates' progress and success; embarrassing trainees in front of others and relying too heavily on "war stories."

Effective learning depends on intelligent selection of methods and materials. Instructional methods include lecture, question/answer sessions, discussion, demonstration, hands-on learning and role playing. Instructional materials include printed information, visuals, bulletin boards, audio- and videocassettes, television programs and computer programs. The Law Enforcement Television Network (LETN) is a private satellite television system that provides current programs on a variety of law enforcement subjects, available through subscription.

Other organizations available to assist with training include the American Society of Law Enforcement Trainers (ASLET), the National Association of Field Training Officers (NAFTO), the Federal Law Enforcement Training Center (FLETC), the National Center for State and Local Training, the FBI National Police Academy and the FBI itself.

Peace Officer Standards and Training (POST) commissions exist in every state to set requirements for becoming licensed as a law enforcement officer.

Of the models of training typically used for law enforcement recruits, experts recommend a blending of the paramilitary and the academic. The most common training is on-the-job training. It may occur during field training, in-house training sessions or roll call. The most common type for new recruits is that done by the field training officer, or FTO. External training may take the form of college classes, seminars, conferences, workshops and independent study.

Officers' training should be ongoing. This results in a training cycle consisting of needs identification, goal setting, program development, program implementation, program evaluation and back, full circle, to assessment of needs based on the evaluation. Training programs can benefit individual officers, supervisors, managers and the entire department and community.

The Violent Crime Control and Law Enforcement Act of 1994 authorizes major funding for law enforcement training.

Discussion Questions

1. How would you compare and contrast training and education?
2. Which instructional methods do you feel are most effective? Least effective?
3. Which instructional materials do you feel are most effective? Least effective?
4. What is the role of the employee in self-development?
5. When would you use a group or conference method of training?
6. When would you use external training programs?
7. What are the major considerations in developing a law enforcement training program?
8. What would you include in a law enforcement training philosophy statement?
9. What five subjects do you consider most essential for a management development training program?
10. What training could be conducted during a cutback budgeting period and still provide reasonable training?

InfoTrac College Edition Assignment

Research the topic of *distance learning in law enforcement* in at least two journals. List the advantages and disadvantages according to your sources. Be sure to give the full references for each source. Be prepared to share your findings with the class.

References

Austen-Kern, Laurie. "Management Training Programs." *The Law Enforcement Trainer,* Vol. 14, July/August 1999, pp. 24–26, 64.

Birzer, Michael L. "Police Training in the 21st Century." *FBI Law Enforcement Bulletin,* Vol. 68, No. 7, July 1999, pp. 16–19.

Borrello, Andrew. "Tips to Enhance and Reinforce Police Training." *Police,* Vol. 24, No. 1, January 2000, p. 27.

Bozarth, Jane. "Teaching around the Cycle: Creative Training Techniques and the Kolb Model of Learning." *The Law Enforcement Trainer,* Vol. 14, No. 5, September/October 1999, pp. 32–35.

Burg, Mike. "Learning Styles." *Law and Order,* Vol. 44, No. 5, May 1996, p. 128.

Campbell, Frank. "Tailor-Made Training." *Police,* Vol. 22, No. 6, June 1998, pp. 30–33.

Cannon, Jerry L. "Fighting Crime . . . and Litigation." *Law Enforcement Technology,* Vol. 23, No. 1, January 1996, pp. 40–41.

Clede, Bill. "New Ways to Train Police." *Law and Order,* Vol. 45, No. 12, December 1997, pp. 37–42.

Clede, Bill. "Innovations in Police Training." *Law and Order,* Vol. 46, No. 6, June 1998, pp. 85–92.

Clede, Bill. "Distance Learning a Necessity Today." *Law and Order,* Vol. 47, No. 12, December 1999, pp. 33–35.

Dees, Tim. "Software for FTO Program Management." *Law and Order,* Vol. 46, No. 10, October 1998, pp. 179–181.

Dees, Tim. "The Ever-Shrinking Data Terminal and Computer-Based Training." *Law and Order,* Vol. 47, No. 11, November 1999, pp. 13–16.

Fisher, Dell. "In Search of a Training Vision." *The Law Enforcement Trainer,* Vol. 14, No. 5, September/October 1999, pp. 8–14, 21.

Fulton, Roger. "Helping New Supervisors Succeed." *Law Enforcement Technology,* Vol. 26, No. 1, January 1999a, p. 74.

Fulton, Roger. "Training a Newly Promoted Supervisor." *Law Enforcement Technology,* Vol. 26, No. 7, July 1999b, p. 102.

Garson, David. "Distance Education: Assessing Costs and Benefits." *The NEA Higher Education Journal,* Vol. XV, No. 2, Fall 1999, pp. 105–117.

Harvey, William L. "Build Support for Community Policing through FTO Programs." *Police,* Vol. 23, No. 10, October 1999, pp. 38–40.

Henderson, Joseph C. "Becoming a Field Training Officer." *Police,* Vol. 22, No. 1, January 1998, pp. 44–45.

Hennen, Christopher G. "Staying Prepared: Nine Fundamental Principles for Ongoing Police Training." *Law and Order,* Vol. 44, No. 9, September 1996, pp. 85–87.

Houston, Alex B. "Simulator Training Improves Performance, Reduces Accidents." *Community Policing Exchange,* July/August 1998, p. 3.

Huntington, Roy. "Thunder Ranch: Training for Life." *Police,* Vol. 22, No. 1, January 1998, pp. 40–43.

Jones, Tony L. "Successful Program Implementation." *Law and Order,* Vol. 47, No. 10, October 1999, pp. 243–245.

Krieble, James. "Job Task Analysis." *The Police Chief,* Vol. LXIII, No. 8, August 1996, pp. 49–54.

Levin, Bernard. "Training and Learning at a Distance." *The Police Chief,* Vol. LXVI, No. 1, January 1999, p. 12.

Maxwell, Helen. "Playing for Keeps at the 'Center.' " *Police,* Vol. 22, No. 11, November 1998, pp. 60–61.

Molden, Jack B. "Adult Learning: Ten Characteristics and Principles of Adult Learning." *Law and Order,* Vol. 41, No. 11, November 1993, pp. 15–16.

Molden, Jack B. "Characteristics of an Effective Trainer: Eight Practices for Excellence." *Law and Order,* Vol. 42, No. 3, March 1994, pp. 10, 105.

Molden, Jack. "College Degrees for Police Applicants." *Law and Order,* Vol. 47, No. 1, January 1999, pp. 21–22.

Morrison, Richard D. "Interactive Training." *Law Enforcement Technology,* Vol. 27, No. 1, January 2000, pp. 97–98.

Nelson, Steven D. "Distance Learning and Criminal Justice Education: Exploring the Possibilities." *Journal of Criminal Justice Education,* Vol. 9, No. 2, Fall 1998, pp. 333–342.

Paynter, Ronnie L. "Software Hones Driving Skills." *Law Enforcement Technology,* Vol. 26, No. 8, August 1999, pp. 84–86.

Phelan, Regis Leo. "Use a Systematic Approach in Remedial Training to Modify, Improve Job Performance." *Police,* Vol. 24, No. 1, January 2000, pp. 48–50.

Pilant, Lois. "Training Delivery Methods." *The Police Chief,* Vol. LXV, No. 1, January 1998, pp. 31–36.

Sample, John. "Personality Type, Learning Styles and Police Training." *The Law Enforcement Trainer,* Vol. 14, July/August 1999, pp. 56–63.

Sharp, Arthur G. "Conferences Expand Horizons." *Law and Order,* Vol. 47, No. 10, October 1999, pp. 148–153.

Smith, Sherri; Bradley, Peggy; and Benscoter, Andrea. "Providing Distance Education in a Criminal Justice Degree Program: A Team Approach." *Journal of Criminal Justice Education,* Vol. 10, No. 2, Fall 1999, pp. 297–312.

Staton, Thomas F. *How to Instruct Successfully: Modern Teaching Methods in Adult Education.* New York: McGraw Hill Book Company, 1960.

Strandberg, Keith W. "To Shoot or Not to Shoot." *Law Enforcement Technology,* Vol. 26, No. 8, August 1999, pp. 32–36.

Swope, Ross E. "Conducting Effective Roll Calls." *Law and Order,* Vol. 47, No. 10, October 1999, pp. 165–168.

Tate, Hugh. "Critical Skills Are Perishable Skills." *The Law Enforcement Trainer,* Vol. 14, No. 6, December 1999, pp. 36–39.

"Training via Television: Making Life Safer in the Field." *Law and Order,* Vol. 47, No. 12, December 1999, pp. 57–58.

Waggoner, Kim and Christenberry, Tom. "Virtual Learning: Distance Education for Law Enforcement." *FBI Law Enforcement Bulletin,* Vol. 66, No. 10, October 1997, pp. 1–8.

Weinblatt, Richard B. "New Police Training Philosophy: Adult Learning Model on Verge of Nationwide Rollout." *Law and Order,* Vol. 47, No. 8, August 1999a, pp. 84–90.

Weinblatt, Richard B. "The Paramilitary vs. Academic Training." *Law and Order,* Vol. 47, No. 12, December 1999b, pp. 28–31.

Chapter 9

Promoting Growth and Development

None of us is as good as all of us.

—Ray Kroc, founder of McDonalds

Do You Know?

- What the workplace culture is?
- What norms are and why they are important?
- How managers can shape the workplace culture?
- What the Johari Window describes?
- What a necessary first step for growth and development is?
- What personal goals specify and what areas they should include?
- What touchstone values and daily values are and how they are related?
- What a "balanced performer" manager is?
- What stages of growth people typically go through?
- What mentoring is?
- How someone might develop a positive image?
- In what areas of cultural awareness law enforcement officers need development?
- What ethics entail and how to develop ethical behavior?
- What "Four I's" team members may contribute?
- Why it is important to help officers grow and develop?

Can You Define?

"balanced performer" managers	independent	open self
blind self	integrity	police culture
cultural awareness	interdependent	racial profiling
daily values	job description	shared responsibility
dependent	Johari Window	subconscious self
ethical behavior	key result areas	supernorms
ethics	majority world view	touchstone values
hidden self	mentor	undiscovered self
holistic personal goals	minority world view	workplace culture
	norms	

INTRODUCTION

Law enforcement managers have two obligations as developers: developing themselves and developing their subordinates. Both are normally accomplished simultaneously.

Because managing is getting work done through others, you will get the best from subordinates by developing their abilities. This is not always accomplished by being the "good guy." It is pleasant to have good interpersonal relationships with all workers, but it is not always possible. There are times for praise and times for discipline.

Growth and improvement are part of the job, but not all subordinates will improve at the same rate because abilities are varied. One managerial responsibility is to recognize ability and develop it by whatever method works best. Managers must understand how many law enforcement tasks are routine and how many are open to improvement through creativity. A job description helps officers understand what is expected of them.

This chapter begins by discussing job descriptions and the workplace culture. Next it describes the importance of developing positive interpersonal relationships and of goal setting. This is followed by a look at "balanced performer" managers and how they might empower those who report to them. Next you will learn the stages of growth employees go through, the important managerial role of mentors, and approaches to developing positive attitudes, a positive image, cultural awareness and a sense of ethics. A logical, hoped-for outgrowth of the preceding is an efficient, effective law enforcement team. The chapter concludes with a discussion of the long-range importance of developing personnel, how managers can be motivators for change and how they might evaluate the workplace climate for growth, development and change within their department.

Job Descriptions

A **job description** is a detailed, formally stated summary of duties and responsibilities for a position. It usually contains the position title, supervisor, education and experience required, salary, duties, responsibilities and job task details.

Job task details make a specific position different from all others in an organization. Patrol officers' duties are different from those of detectives, dispatchers, narcotics officers or juvenile officers. Likewise, the duties of sergeants, lieutenants and chiefs differ.

Job descriptions are not limiting or restrictive. They are simply minimum requirements, and the job description should make this clear. Employees who can expand these tasks or do them differently and better should be encouraged to do so. Job descriptions provide the basis not only for getting work done but also for setting expectations and standards for evaluation.

Tasks must be broadly stated and leave room for growth, change and expansion. They should also be reviewed at least annually, when some tasks may be eliminated and others added. For example, in recent years the major concern of U.S. citizens is not crime in general but more specifically drug-related crime. Law enforcement managers must respond to that national interest.

All law enforcement personnel have opportunities to expand their tasks and perform them better. Public service is virtually unlimited. Any law enforcement task can be done better, with greater total effect. Managers need to use every available resource to develop the best in each individual and the team. A supervisor is responsible for improving the performance of subordinates individually and as a team. One key is a positive work culture.

The Workplace Culture

The workplace culture is evident in many organizations. Visit an engineering firm, and you are likely to encounter a well-dressed staff who greet you quite formally. Visit the local newspaper, and you are likely to encounter a casually dressed staff who greet you quite informally. Further, within many workplace cultures, subcultures exist. Within an advertising agency, for example, the sales force may dress up, whereas the creative staff may favor T-shirts and blue jeans. Each workplace develops its own culture.

> The **workplace culture** is the sum of the beliefs and values shared by those within the organization, serving to formally and informally communicate its expectations.

These beliefs and values are a sort of "collective conscience" by which those within the group judge each other.

The Socialization Process

Sherman (1999, p. 301) explains:

> Every occupation has a learning process (usually called "socialization") to which its new members are subjected. The socialization process functions to make most "rookies" in the occupation adopt the prevailing rules, values, and attitudes of their senior colleagues in the occupation. Very often, some of the existing informal rules and attitudes are at odds with the formal rules and attitudes society as a whole expects members of the occupation to follow. This puts rookies in a moral dilemma: should the rookies follow the formal rules of society, or the informal rules of their senior colleagues?

He (p. 302) also states:

> There are four major stages in the career of anyone joining a new occupation:
> - The *choice* of the occupation
> - The *introduction* to the occupation
> - The first *encounter* with doing the occupation's work
> - The *metamorphosis* into a full-fledged member of the occupation

Police officers go through these stages just as doctors and bankers do. But the transformation of the police officer's identity and self-image may be more radical than in many other fields.

Sherman (p. 304) further explains:

> In the encounter stage, the rookie gets the major reality shock in the entire process of becoming a police officer. The rookie discovers that police work is more social work than crime fighting, more arbitration of minor disputes than investigations of major crimes, more patching of holes in the social fabric than weaving of webs to catch the big time crooks. . . .
>   The result of those encounters is usually a complete change, a total adaptation of the new role and self-concept as a "cop." And with that transformation comes a stark awareness of the interdependence cops share with all other cops. . . . They

are totally and utterly dependent on other police to save their lives, to respond to a call of an officer in trouble or need of assistance.

This perspective is a defining element of the police culture.

The Police Culture

The **police culture** has been extensively written about and is often described as isolationist, elitist and authoritarian. Some departments have even been characterized as brutal and racist. Indeed, most law enforcement organizations do have a distinct culture. Haught (1998, p. 7) states: "An agency's true culture is its default setting. In other words, the behavior that occurs when important people are visiting is not the department's 'culture,' but rather it's what takes place while conducting 'normal' business." According to Worden (1995, pp. 49–50):

> Conventional wisdom—both academic and popular—once held that police officers have distinctive belief systems, quite different from those of the people they serve. Police officers were depicted as a homogeneous occupational group, isolated from their clientele and intensely loyal to one another, and having in common particular psychological attributes that distinguish them from the rest of the population. They were said to be preoccupied with order, suspicious, secretive, cynical, conservative, and—more generally—authoritarian. Together these traits comprised what became known as the "police personality." . . . But more recent research has revealed attitudinal heterogeneity among police officers that either did not exist a decade earlier or, if it did exist, was not detected by social scientists. This research shows that police officers differ both about ends—the functions that police are properly expected to perform—and about means—how those functions should be performed.

Haught (p. 7) found officers split among two general views: "They either saw their jobs as 'macho police work' where officers 'had to be so tough they would give their own mother a ticket,' or a service profession that went beyond just being tough with lawbreakers."

According to Skolnick: "One underpinning of the police subculture is the belief among police officers that no one—i.e., management or the public—understands them" (Gaffigan and McDonald, 1997, p. 30). Skolnick's *Beyond 911* suggests the police culture is based on several fundamental beliefs, including (p. 30):

- The police are the only real crimefighters.
- No one else understands the work of a police officer.
- Loyalty counts more than anything.
- It is impossible to win the war on crime without bending the rules.
- The public is demanding and nonsupportive.
- Working in patrol is the least desirable job in the police department.

Sherman (p. 305) adds four other beliefs officers hold about the nature of their world, which can be seen as variations of those listed by Skolnick:

- Loyalty to colleagues is essential for survival.

- The public, or most of it, is the enemy.

- Police administrators are also the enemy.

- Any discrepancy between these views and the views of family and friends is due simply to the ignorance of those who have not actually done police work themselves.

Managers must be aware of the culture of their group as well as of the entire organization. Solar (1998, pp. 22–23) states: "Understanding cultural influences means understanding the history of an organization; the context in which events took place; the values and tendencies of the people involved, both current and former members; and other factors." The first step in this awareness is to identify the *norms* that are operating.

Norms are the attitudes and beliefs held by the members of a group.

Norms are, in effect, what is "normal." Most people do not want to be considered "abnormal," so they do and say what others expect of them, for example:

- Do the job the way you're told.
- It's okay to be late.
- Always read the newspaper on the department's time.
- Never give so many citations you make your colleagues look bad.

Sherman (pp. 305–306) lists some other norms commonly found in the police culture:

- Discretion A: Decisions about whether to enforce the law, in any but the most serious cases, should be guided by both what the law says and who the suspect is.
- Discretion B: Disrespect for police authority is a serious offense that should always be punished with an arrest or the use of force.
- Force: Police officers should never hesitate to use physical or deadly force against people who "deserve it" or where it can be an effective way of solving crime.
- Due Process: Due process is only a means of protecting criminals at the expense of law-abiding citizens and should be ignored whenever it is safe to do so.
- Truth: Lying and deception are an essential part of the police job, and even perjury should be used if it is necessary to protect yourself or get a conviction on a "bad guy."
- Time: You cannot go fast enough to catch a car thief or traffic violator or slow enough to get to a "garbage" call, and when there are no calls for service, your time is your own.
- Rewards: Police do very dangerous work for low wages, so it is proper to take any extra rewards the public wants to give them, like free meals, Christmas gifts, or even regular monthly payments (in some cities) for special treatment.
- Loyalty: The paramount duty is to protect your fellow officers at all costs, as they would protect you, even though you may have to risk your own career or your own life to do it.

These norms are enforced by putting pressure on those who do not conform. Norms can hurt or help managers. Negative work norms can destroy morale and decrease performance; positive norms can heighten morale and improve performance.

Managers can shape the workplace culture by doing the following:

1. Identify existing norms.
2. Evaluate the norms—do they work for or against the department's mission?
3. Encourage positive norms and try to eliminate negative ones.

Shaping the workplace culture requires the type of participatory management discussed earlier. Recognize at this point, however, that when shaping the workplace culture, you can expect to encounter a kind of "Catch-22" in the form of **supernorms**, that is, overriding expectations of a given work group, for example, never volunteer information or do not criticize. Many of the communication skills discussed in Chapter 4 will help you deal with these supernorms and change those that are counterproductive.

You might also find the best subculture in your organization and hold it up as an example from which others can learn. Do not expect change overnight—it may take several years. Perhaps most important, live the culture you want. Walk the talk.

Within the workplace culture you and your people can grow and develop personally and professionally. The culture must expect, encourage and reward growth. Establishing a nurturing workplace culture depends on developing positive interpersonal relationships.

Developing Positive Interpersonal Relationships

Developing good manager–subordinate relations requires fairness, trust and confidence on everyone's part. It is not always the formal relationships, important as they are, that establish a rapport between manager and subordinate. It is a two-way feeling of respect, regard and trust.

Consider the employee who says, "I would do anything for the boss I have now. He demands a lot, but he is fair, and I trust that he will do what he says." More than likely this employee's manager has emotional maturity, displays confidence without being overbearing, knows his and the subordinate's job, would not ask the subordinate to do anything he would not do, expresses confidence in the subordinate and deals with the subordinate with compassion. Mutual respect develops when both manager and subordinate deal with each other in the same way.

Effective managers are not preoccupied with their own problems and therefore have time to see other people's problems. They have sufficient self-confidence to project this image to their employees. They can develop the same feelings in their subordinates. They can accept subordinates as they are and work from there.

To respect and admire a subordinate is no more difficult than to respect and admire a superior. It is not the position or the rank, but the individual who fills the position. Position and rank have authority and power, but they do not automatically create personal respect. Managers who place themselves above their subordinates will never command respect and admiration. "What is given is returned in kind" is as true in the work environment as in life. Effective managers regard the word subordinate as describing a position in the organizational chart, not as suggestive of personal worth or value.

Self-Disclosure and Feedback

An important part of developing relationships is for managers to get to know each member of the work unit better and, in the process, get to know themselves better. A model termed the Johari Window (named after the authors Joe and Harry) illustrates how people can learn more about others and themselves. The model is based on the premise that everyone has four parts to their identity, as Figure 9.1 illustrates.

Your **open self** is what you know about yourself and what you show to others. Your **hidden self** is the secret part that you do not share with others. Your **blind self** is the part of you that others can see but you do not know about yourself. Your **undiscovered** or **subconscious self** is the part of you that neither you nor others have yet discovered.

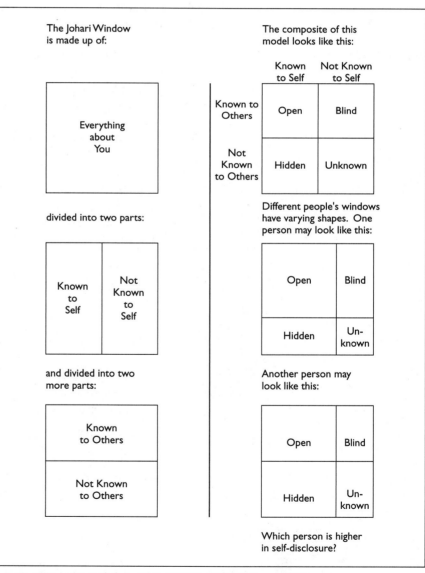

Figure 9.1
The Johari Window

The **Johari Window** describes four parts of identity:

- The open self
- The hidden self
- The blind self
- The subconscious self

According to this model, through the process of self-disclosure and feedback—that is, honest interaction with others—you can widen the area of openness, reduce the hidden and blind parts and learn something about your undiscovered self.

Honest, open interaction with subordinates can help *everyone* within the workplace culture grow and develop. The direction this growth and development takes depends on the goals that are set.

Goal Setting

The importance of organizational goals has been discussed, especially as they relate to time management and budgeting. Within organizational goals, managers should include growth and development, both individual and organizational. Remember that goals are targets: specific, measurable outcomes with a time line.

Personal and organizational goals are a necessary first step for growth and development.

Goals are not fantasies or attempts to escape reality but are the first step in taking positive action toward a desired outcome. They represent your desire to be better tomorrow than you are today. Goals should be:

1. Stated positively.
2. Realistic and attainable.
3. Personally important.

A personal goal states what, when and how much.

The *what* is the specific result to achieve. The *when* is the target date by which the goal will be reached. The *how much* is, whenever possible, a quantifiable measure. Effective goals meet several of the following criteria. They:

1. Are specific and realistic.
2. Are action oriented.
3. Are consistent with ability and authority.
4. Are measurable.
5. Include "stretch."
6. Have a set deadline.

Law enforcement managers may set a goal of "talking to their subordinates about organizational and personal problems." They may help subordinates set their goals, which should be discussed and then written down. A specific time period should be established to accomplish the goals, and progress should be reviewed at the end of that period.

Goals should be specific. Vague, general goals are rarely accomplished. Saying you are going to "reduce accidents by 10 percent" is not necessarily a goal that you can achieve, desirable as it might be. You have no control over many variables associated with the goal, so select a realistic goal. Law enforcement officers in the field may set a goal of "increasing contacts with traffic violators by 10 contacts per day." This *would* be both realistic and achievable.

In the same vein, goals should not be excessively difficult. Excessively high goals destroy the chance for personal achievement. Goals must be attainable. If employees can help determine goals, they are more likely to achieve them. These goals may be higher than if managers establish them. An example of an unrealistic goal would be that all officers become expert sharpshooters. Varied levels of shooting ability do exist. A more realistic goal would be that all officers take range practice and qualify.

Goal setting, goal achievement and ultimate performance are directly related. It is exciting to realize that few people use more than 20 to 30 percent of their potential. Neurosurgeons have discovered from examining human brains that millions of cells have been totally untapped. People have few limits except those they impose on themselves. The four-minute mile was considered impossible—until Roger Bannister ran it. The seven-foot high jump, the 17-foot pole vault . . . the impossible achieved.

Untapped potential exists in you and your people. The task is to create an exciting workplace in which people want to grow and develop and are helped to do so.

Holistic Goal Setting

Although managers are not technically responsible for their subordinate's off-the-job activities and aspirations, people have much more to them than their job. Indeed, a common problem of law enforcement officers is that their jobs become all-encompassing, overshadowing other important aspects of life. Effective managers consider themselves and those they manage as "total" people.

Holistic personal goals should include:

1. Career/job.
2. Financial.
3. Personal.
4. Family/relationships.
5. Spiritual/service.

Managers will naturally be most concerned with the career/job-related goals such as learning new skills, but the other areas are also important. Managers should take care not to foster a lopsided workplace culture, focused entirely on career/job goals. Figure 9.2 illustrates the various aspects of each individual that need to be part of any growth and development program.

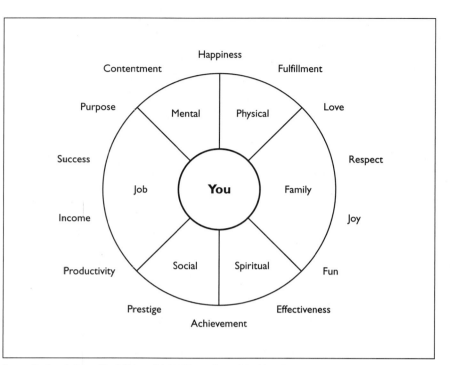

Figure 9.2
Life's Circle

Source: Stephen R. Covey. *The 7 Habits of Highly Effective People* (New York: Simon and Schuster, 1989), p. 270. Copyright © 1989 by Stephen R. Covey. Reprinted by permission of Simon and Schuster, Inc.

Goals and Values

Closely related to goals are the values you hold—what is important to you. What are your **key result areas**—broad categories people often talk about as important? Table 9.1 lists 20 key result areas commonly identified. Rank from 1 to 10 (1 being the most important) what you want. These are your **touchstone values.** Then rank how you actually spend the majority of your time, energy and money day-to-day. These are your **daily values.** How do the rankings compare?

> *Touchstone values,* what people say is important to them, and *daily values,* how people actually spend their time and energy, need to correlate.

Often what people value and what they spend the majority of their time on conflict. For example, a person may have family as his or her number-one touchstone value, yet have work as the number-one daily value. Managers and those they manage need to examine their touchstone and daily values and seek a closer correlation between them.

"Balanced Performer" Managers and Empowerment

It cannot be repeated often enough: The most effective managers are those who accomplish priority tasks through their people. Managers who do everything themselves, no matter how well the tasks are done, are *not* effective managers, as Figure 9.3 illustrates.

Table 9.1 **Touchstone and Daily Values in Key Result Areas**	Touchstone Values	Daily Values	Key Result Areas
	_____	_____	Achievement (sense of accomplishment)
	_____	_____	Work (paying own way)
	_____	_____	Adventure (exploration, risks, excitement)
	_____	_____	Personal freedom (independence, choices)
	_____	_____	Authenticity (being frank and genuinely myself)
	_____	_____	Expertness (being excellent at something)
	_____	_____	Service (contribute to satisfaction of others)
	_____	_____	Leadership (having influence and authority)
	_____	_____	Money (plenty of money for things I want)
	_____	_____	Spirituality (my religious beliefs/experiences)
	_____	_____	Physical health (attractiveness and vitality)
	_____	_____	Emotional health (handle inner conflicts)
	_____	_____	Meaningful work (relevant/purposeful job)
	_____	_____	Affection (warmth, giving/receiving love)
	_____	_____	Pleasure (enjoyment, satisfaction, fun)
	_____	_____	Wisdom (mature understanding, insight)
	_____	_____	Family (happy/contented living situation)
	_____	_____	Recognition (being well known; prestige)
	_____	_____	Security (having a secure, stable future)
	_____	_____	Self-growth (continuing development)

Source: David G. Lee, Senior Consultant with Personal Decisions, Inc., of Minneapolis, MN. Reprinted with permission.

Figure 9.3 **Balanced Performer**

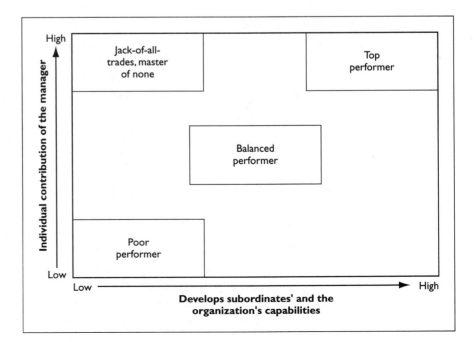

Managers who concentrate on excelling themselves, on climbing up through the ranks, rather than on helping their subordinates to excel are not "balanced performers." Nor are the managers who do little or nothing themselves, relying on subordinates to carry the load but without providing an example for them to follow.

Managers who contribute their efforts to accomplishing department goals while simultaneously developing their subordinates into top performers are superior **"balanced performer" managers** who empower others.

Managers who empower allow subordinates to grow to their fullest potential.

Stages of Growth

The stages of growth in a manager–employee relationship can be compared to that of a parent and child.

The three stages of growth are dependent, independent and interdependent.

The first stage is the **dependent** stage. Rookies are initially just learning the job and are very dependent on others. They watch, follow and need direction. The manager's role at this stage is usually to *tell* them what to do.

As officers grow, develop and gain confidence, they become more **independent,** just as adolescents learn to be less dependent on their parents. The manager's role at this point is to allow more freedom and give more responsibility. Traditionally, managers who brought their people to this level felt they had done their job—moving their subordinates from dependence to independence.

More progressive managers, those who use participative leadership approaches, take their subordinates one step further, moving them to being **interdependent.** The role of the manager shifts to that of a collaborator—similar to the relationship of a parent to an adult son or daughter. Covey (1989, p. 279) suggests: "In an interdependent situation, synergy is particularly powerful in dealing with negative forces that work against growth and change." He illustrates how synergy is a function of cooperation, trust and open communication (Figure 9.4).

One major problem for supervisors is adjusting techniques for handling personnel on the same shift who have diverse experience. Supervising an officer with 10 years' experience demands different approaches than would be used with a new recruit. Veteran officers have knowledge, experience and self-confidence lacking in rookies. Supervisors should seek input on decisions from these veteran officers, giving credit where merited, praising good work and mentoring rather than managing. Supervisors should not unknowingly punish veteran officers by overloading them because of their experience.

Education is one important way to take employees from dependence to independence and finally to interdependence. All members of the police department should be encouraged to continue their education through special seminars, undergraduate and graduate courses, inservice training, research, writing and teaching.

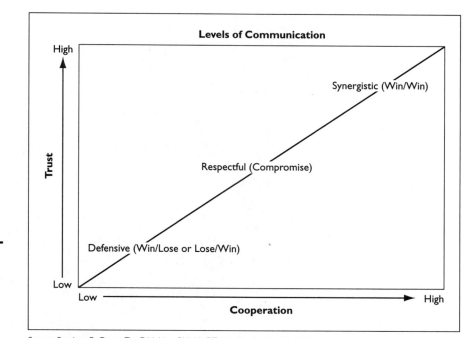

Figure 9.4
The Interaction of Cooperation, Trust and Open Communication to Produce Synergism

Source: Stephen R. Covey. *The 7 Habits of Highly Effective People.* New York: Simon and Schuster, 1989, p. 270. Copyright © 1989 by Stephen R. Covey. Reprinted by permission of Franklin Covey Co., www.FranklinCovey.com.

Managers as Mentors

Kranda (1997, p. 52) asserts: "Confronted by budgetary constraints and diminished staffing levels, we must explore new and innovative strategies for recruitment, selection and retention of our officers. New-hire mentoring is a critical tool in meeting this challenge." Edmundson (1999, p. 17) states:

> In a mentoring program, a veteran officer shares knowledge, skills, and expertise with a recruit. This mutual relationship benefits the participants and the organization, as well. The mentor can fill a void in the officer's first days on a new job, sometimes in an unfamiliar city, and also help give the employee a positive perception of the agency.
>
> A mentoring program not only integrates recruits into the department and institution, but it also can foster self-esteem, affirm potential, provide access to information and resources, and enhance empowerment. . . .
>
> Employees who act as mentors represent the single most important part of a successful program. Because mentors can serve various roles—teachers, guides, counselors, sponsors, and role models—for recruits, agencies must select them carefully.

Mentoring involves teaching, coaching, counseling and guiding. Every law enforcement organization has employees who need help to be better people and better employees. Managers can make that difference through the role of mentor.

A **mentor** is a wise, trusted teacher or counselor. Law enforcement managers are in an ideal position to be mentors.

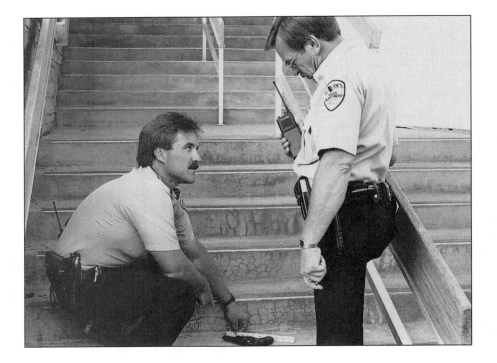

Mentors can play a vital role in developing employees, offering them their knowledge and skills, and giving them encouragement and support.

Usually a mentor is a person of senior status who counsels a younger person, but sometimes mentors are of equal seniority. In fact, two people may be mentors to each other in different areas of work.

Mentors help further the right type of education, express confidence in the other person, correct actions that, if continued, could be detrimental to advancement and foster the right attitudes. Edmundson (p. 18) identifies the responsibilities and qualities of mentors: "[Mentors] welcome recruits and take a personal interest in their development; share their knowledge, skills, and experience with their recruits; recognize and encourage excellence in others; and listen well, remain sensitive to the needs of others, and recognize when they require support, assistance, or independence."

Realize that the purpose of mentoring is to help mentees reach their full potential. Townsend (1998, p. 70) cautions: "We become greedy as supervisors—we want to keep our good people. So when chances for a special assignment, or a promotion for them comes along, it is tempting to hold them back. But don't punish your hardest workers by holding them back. Push them forward instead. The best compliment you will ever receive will be that of someone you helped reach their potential." Most law enforcement officers who have worked their way to the top of the organization have had mentors along the way.

Developing Positive Attitudes

Effective managers are upbeat and positive. They see an overcast day as partly sunny rather than partly cloudy. They see opportunities in setbacks. They encourage risk taking and are supportive when mistakes happen. And they encourage these attitudes in their subordinates.

Personality problems can be more devastating to employees than poor work performance. Managers must help certain employees to develop—those who are loners, who are sarcastic, who talk incessantly about themselves, who constantly complain or who have other personality problems. Directing them to outside counseling may be necessary. Managers have a responsibility to deal with problems in employee attitudes.

Attitudes are not something managers can take away from someone. They are intangible. What people say and do and how they behave determine how others perceive them. Working with employees on specific negative attitudes can be an important part of their growth and development. British psychiatrist J. A. Hadfield illustrates the power of a person's mental attitude in his book, *The Psychology of Power*. He describes having three people test the effect of mental suggestion on their strength, as measured by gripping a dynamometer. Hadfield first tested them for a baseline, giving no suggestions. The average grip was 101 pounds. He then hypnotized them and suggested they were very weak. Their average grip dropped to 29 pounds. He next suggested they were very strong, and the average grip jumped to 142 pounds.

Officers' attitudes are important personally, but they are also critical to the public's perception of officers in general and the department they represent.

Developing a Positive Image

How people see themselves is their self-image. How others see them is their public image. The two often differ, as the Johari Window illustrated earlier.

A critical part of a subordinate's development is creating a positive public image. As Will Rogers noted: "You never get a second chance to make a good first impression." This is particularly true for law enforcement officers, who often have only one contact with individual citizens. Officers in a large city who make a traffic stop, for example, are unlikely to ever see that particular driver again. How they approach the driver, what they say and do, is the image the driver will retain of the officer. It may also become the image that person has of the entire law enforcement organization. Mader (1997, p. 8) states:

> Public perception of the police fundamentally affects every facet of our work. Strong community support can assist us in meeting the overall police mission and contribute toward generating voluntary compliance. This, in itself, can help to reduce crime.

Managers must help subordinates learn to make favorable impressions whenever and wherever possible. Because law enforcement officers are so visible, they leave an impression even when they make no contact, merely by the way they patrol, their appearance, their manner and their attitude.

Their uniforms, their badges, their guns—all smack of authority. Add mirrored sunglasses, handcuff tie tacks and a swaggering walk, and a negative image is likely to be conveyed. Law enforcement officers should be encouraged to consider how they look, how they walk and how they talk to the public, especially when in uniform. They should consider the public as their "customers" or "clients" and treat them with respect.

> Law enforcement officers who have a good appearance and act with competence and courtesy will leave a favorable impression with the majority of the public.

A positive image will be greatly enhanced by treating all citizens fairly and equally. This often requires officers to recognize their own personal biases and to deal with them.

A study released by the Bureau of Justice Statistics reveals: "Overall, some 85 percent of residents queried in a 12-city survey reported they were well served by the men and women who police their neighborhoods" ("Study Finds Police . . . ," 1999, p. 1). Other national surveys support this positive image of the police. According to a 1998 nationwide Gallup poll, 58 percent of those polled reported a "great deal" or "quite a lot" of confidence in the police; 30 percent reported "some" confidence; 10 percent reported "very little" confidence; and 1 percent reported "no" confidence in the police (*Sourcebook*, 1998, p. 107). When asked to rate the honesty and ethical standards of 26 various occupations, the police ranked sixth, behind pharmacists, clergy, medical doctors, college teachers and dentists (Gallup, 1997, p. 23). However, although such surveys may indicate a generally positive public image of the police, some note the poll rankings for law enforcement professionals are not as high as they used to be. According to Vicchio (1997, p. 9), when comparisons were made of Americans' confidence ratings of 12 professions during a 15-year interval: "Trust in police officers recorded the largest drop from 1980 to 1995."

To achieve a positive image, pay attention to how you speak as much as to what you say. We all recognize certain voices on the telephone. In fact, we form an image of how strangers might look from their telephone voices. Few of us know how we sound to others, on the phone or in person, and few of us have even thought about it. But your voice may cause people to think of you negatively. Your voice should come across as positive and strong.

To understand how you sound, tape your voice. Practice what you are going to say before making an important call. Ask friends for constructive criticism. An officer often needs to use different tones of voice for different situations; for example, handling a drunk, assisting a lost child or speaking with the city manager. It is possible to train your voice so that you leave a better image.

Developing Cultural Awareness

Cultural awareness is another critical area of development for law enforcement personnel.

> **Cultural awareness** means understanding the diversity of the United States, the dynamics of minority–majority relationships, the dynamics of sexism and racism and the issues of nationalism and separatism.

Ramirez (1999, p. 13) asserts: "Ethical behavior, compassion and sensitivity to diverse cultures cannot be mandated via a training session. These behaviors are the result of core values, which must be willingly held by the organization and its members." Most people understand and accept that our society is multicultural.

Although the United States is a "melting pot" of people from all parts of the world, some enjoy majority status, whereas others are viewed as minorities.

Members of the majority often view things quite differently from those in the minority. Elements of majority and minority world views have been outlined by the Minnesota Peace Officer Standards and Training (POST) Board.

The **majority world view** includes the following:

- The majority views its philosophy and ideas as being the most legitimate and valid.
- Minority viewpoints, although their expression may be tolerated, lack the force and power of the majority and therefore are less valid than and secondary to the majority viewpoint.
- Minority members have the option of leaving society if they cannot abide by majority rule.
- Alternative viewpoints are often disruptive or disloyal.
- Power, status and wealth are the result of hard work and/or genetics.

The **minority world view** includes the following:

- Minorities must perform better to be accepted as average.
- Majority groups have power and control major institutions.
- Minority groups lack the power to control their own destiny.
- The minority views fairness as more valid than power, status and wealth.
- The minority views success as achievable only by working through the rules set by the majority.
- The minority world views the criminal justice system as biased against minorities.

In addition to members of minority groups who are U.S. citizens, the United States is faced with thousands of illegal immigrants of different races, ethnic groups, religions and cultures. As Hawley (1999, p. 28) notes: "Thousands of people—many from south of the border—stream into the country every day in defiance of federal law. For law enforcement, this circumstance poses unique challenges and occasional dilemmas." She (p. 29) continues:

> Police officers making a routine stop or arrest generally won't know if a person is a citizen or alien. . . . In our multi-racial, multi-ethnic society a person can be raised speaking Spanish and be a born citizen. The way a person looks or speaks doesn't matter.

Citizenship is an important issue for arresting officers because, under Vienna Convention rights, officers must notify noncitizens of their right to contact their consulate before making any postarrest statements.

Another challenge regarding immigrants is that they often settle in poor neighborhoods that have high crime rates and may therefore be associated with crime. Law enforcement personnel must guard against stereotyping such immigrants as criminals simply because they live in crime-infested neighborhoods. Such stereotyping is an element of **racial profiling,** the practice of using certain

When a member of a minority group is arrested, the arresting officer must make certain the arrest was not made based on the suspect's race. Such racial profiling is illegal throughout the country.

racial characteristics as indicators of criminal activity. It is acting on personal bias. Strandberg (1999, p. 62) asks:

> If a bulletin states a suspect in a robbery is an Arab, 5-foot 10-inches tall and driving a late-model tan car, and the officer stops people fitting this description, is it racial profiling?
>
> If you know that statistics say the majority of drug arrests in one particular neighborhood have been Jamaican males, ages 18 to 24, and you spot a Jamaican male acting strangely, and decide to stop him and ask some questions, is that racial profiling?
>
> If you're searching for a gunman, who has been described as a white male, 6-foot 2-inches tall, and you stop the first white man you see that's about that height, is it racial profiling?
>
> The [preceding] examples . . . from a law enforcement perspective are considered standard police work. That's what the general public doesn't understand.

Kennedy (1998, p. 28) states: "The great majority of police officers, lawyers, and judges would agree that acting *solely* on the basis of race would be wrong and is illegal. The controversial issue is whether police ought to be allowed to use race *at all* in determining suspicion." However, Strandberg (p. 66) notes: "The 'catch-22' of it all is that race is part of the general description." Indeed, Kennedy (p. 30) echoes: "Police . . . use race as part of an array of factors threaded together to create a net with which to go trawling for criminals." And the courts are generally supportive of such police action, as Kennedy (pp. 30–31) explains:

> Most courts have broadly affirmed the constitutional legitimacy of this practice. Consider the case of *United States v Weaver*. A DEA officer stopped and questioned Arthur Weaver, who had just exited an airplane at the Kansas City, Kansas, airport . . . because he was "roughly dressed," young, black, and on a direct flight from Los Angeles, a source city for drugs. In addition, the DEA

officer said he suspected Weaver because he walked rapidly from the airplane toward a cab, had two carry-on bags and no checked luggage, and appeared nervous. Although the young man, as it turned out, was carrying illegal drugs, he challenged the legality of the officer's intervention. The Eighth Circuit Court of Appeals upheld the officer's conduct . . . and explained its position in this way:

> Facts are not to be ignored simply because they may be unpleasant—and the unpleasant fact in this case is that he [DEA agent] had knowledge, based upon his own experience and upon the intelligence reports he had received from Los Angeles authorities, that young male members of the African-American Los Angeles gangs were flooding the Kansas City area with cocaine. To that extent then, race, when coupled with the other factors [the agent] relied upon, was a factor in the decision to approach and ultimately detain [the suspect]. We wish it were otherwise, but we take the facts as they are presented to us, not as we would wish them to be.

Despite such court support, officers must be educated on how to avoid unintentional racial profiling based on personal bias. Strandberg (p. 65) observes: "Almost any case can be perceived as racially motivated if there is a person of color involved, so it makes sense for law enforcement to go out of its way to explain the reasoning and procedures behind every stop, every detainment, every arrest." To help officers overcome the problem of racial profiling, Matthews (1999, pp. 38–39) suggests:

> First, remember that profiling is simply a tool that may enable you to decide if you want to continue your observation of the individual or investigate further.
>
> Second, remember that profiling looks at the minute details of evidence or helps to provide the profiler with a comprehensive list of characteristics. Profiling must be evaluated in a systematic fashion that provides an overview and not an isolated environment where a few dominating factors (young, black, male) may outweigh others.
>
> Third, officers must have a legitimate and legal reason, *that they can properly articulate,* to stop and search a vehicle and its occupants.

Many immigrants may become victims, but because they come from cultures in which law enforcement officers are feared rather than seen as "protectors," they are unlikely to cooperate with officers. According to Davis and Erez (1998, p. 1): "The consensus among officials who responded to [a] national survey . . . is that many recent immigrants do indeed fail to report crimes. Many of the study participants saw this failure to report crimes as a serious problem, allowing criminals to go free and eroding the ability of the criminal justice system to function effectively." Even those who might be willing to cooperate will likely be hindered by a language barrier.

In a sense, law enforcement officers are in a better position than many to understand minority status because they often view *themselves* as being in the minority, isolated from the mainstream of society.

As law enforcement officers become aware of their own culture and as community-oriented policing gains ground, officers may seek to reduce this view of themselves as a minority, to interact more with the public and to see themselves as part of the mainstream.

Another aspect of cultural awareness is understanding and respecting differences in sex as well as differences in sexual preference. Cultural awareness also means identifying and respecting the rights of specific separatist/nationalist groups currently active in American society, including the Ku Klux Klan, the American Nazi Party, neo-Nazi skinheads, the Aryan Brotherhood/White Supremacists, Posse Commitatus, the National Socialist Party, the Black Muslim Movement, the American Indian Movement (AIM) and the Jewish Defense League (JDL). When such groups engage in terrorist activity, such as the bombing of Oklahoma City's Murrah Federal Building in 1995, it may be difficult to remain objective. When hate groups' words translate into criminal actions, they have gone well beyond exercising their civil rights.

In addition to helping subordinates develop a positive attitude, a positive image and cultural awareness, managers should foster a strong sense of ethical behavior.

Developing a Sense of Ethics and Integrity

Ruby Ridge, Waco, O. J. Simpson, Rodney King . . . names and places that arguably have the law enforcement community reeling from attacks on its integrity and ethical standards. . . . These attacks . . . suggest a public distrust of U.S. law enforcement agencies as corrupt, unethical and, at times, out of control (Santos, 1997, p. 8).

Ethics refers to the rules or standards of fair, honest conduct. Ethics has become a primary focus in almost every profession and is the topic of countless articles, seminars and workshops.

Integrity refers to steadfast adherence to an ethical code.

Ethical behavior is that which is "moral" and "right." Law enforcement personnel must develop high ethical standards both on and off duty.

According to Klockars (1983, p. 427): "Some areas of human conduct or enterprise develop their own distinct ethics while others do not." He suggests that special codes of ethics are developed if the area:

- Has some special features making it difficult to bring under the domain of general, conventional ethics. Police, for example, can use force, even deadly force, and may lie and deceive people in their work.
- Involves issues of concern not just to those who practice them, but to others. They involve moral controversy.
- Involves certain types of misconduct that cannot or perhaps should not be controlled by other means.

Law enforcement fits all three conditions, partly because of its great discretionary power.

A multitude of personal, departmental and external forces shape the dynamics of police integrity that ultimately affect each police officer's career (Gaffigan and McDonald, p. 92). Personal forces that affect police personnel include economy/personal finances, diversity issues in the department, family values/moral literacy, experience with aggressive police tactics, the police subculture, community response to police activities and presence, frustration with the criminal justice system, peer influence and alcohol/drug abuse. Departmental forces that affect police personnel include the promotion system, leadership, reward structures, departmental values/policies, the accountability system, the quality of supervision, the disciplinary system, inservice training, entry-level training and the selection/hiring process. These departmental forces are influenced in part by external forces that affect the entire agency, such as civilian complaint boards, news media, political influences, community demands and other sectors of the criminal justice system (courts and corrections). (See Figure 9.5.)

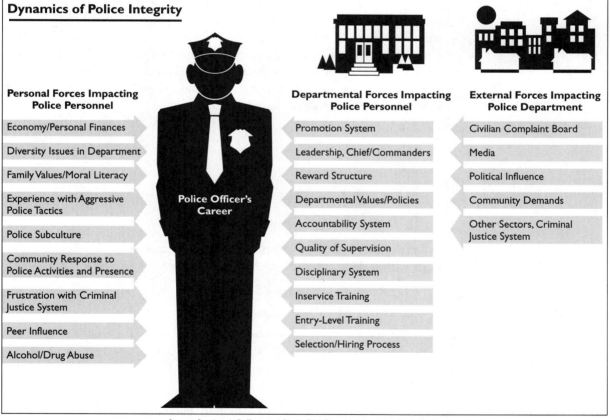

Dynamics of Police Integrity

Personal Forces Impacting Police Personnel

Economy/Personal Finances

Diversity Issues in Department

Family Values/Moral Literacy

Experience with Aggressive Police Tactics

Police Subculture

Community Response to Police Activities and Presence

Frustration with Criminal Justice System

Peer Influence

Alcohol/Drug Abuse

Police Officer's Career

Departmental Forces Impacting Police Personnel

Promotion System

Leadership, Chief/Commanders

Reward Structure

Departmental Values/Policies

Accountability System

Quality of Supervision

Disciplinary System

Inservice Training

Entry-Level Training

Selection/Hiring Process

External Forces Impacting Police Department

Civilian Complaint Board

Media

Political Influence

Community Demands

Other Sectors, Criminal Justice System

Source: Stephen J. Gaffigan and Phyllis P. McDonald. *Police Intergrity: Public Service with Honor.* U. S. Department of Justice, January 1997, p. 92. (NCJ-163811)

Figure 9.5
Dynamics of Police Integrity

To clarify the expectations regarding officer ethics and integrity, most law enforcement departments have a formal code of ethics, often framed and hanging on the wall. Such codes usually have at least three important themes:

- Justice or fairness is the dominant theme. Officers are not to take advantage of people or accept gratuities.
- Because of the importance of the law and the officer as tools of the Constitution, law enforcement behavior must be totally within the bounds set by the law.
- At all times, law enforcement officers must uphold a standard of behavior consistent with their public position.

The "Law Enforcement Code of Ethics" of the International Association of Chiefs of Police (IACP) (Figure 9.6) is an example of such a standard. A code of ethics helps officers make decisions lawfully, humanely and fairly.

Slahor (1999, p. 123) states: "Ethical behavior and leadership require speaking out even when doing so is not popular. . . . Ethics is about character and courage, and how we meet the challenge when doing the right thing will cost more than we are willing to pay." According to Smotzer (1999, p. 32): "Ethics isn't a written code, it's about what we do." He (p. 32) cites the Six Pillars of Character as trustworthiness (honesty, integrity, promise keeping and loyalty), respect, responsibility (accountability, pursuit of excellence and self-restraint), justice and fairness, caring, and civil virtue and citizenship. He also stresses the principles of ethical policing (p. 32):

- Fair Access
- Public Trust
- Safety and Security
- Teamwork
- Objectivity

Campion (1998, p. 3) provides a six-step process to follow when you are faced with making an ethical decision:

1. Determine whether the potential action or decision is legal.
2. Decide on the best solution for the greatest number of people.
3. Consider what would happen if the action you are about to engage in becomes a universal standard.
4. Think about how you would feel if your actions were made public. Would you be proud?
5. Follow the Golden Rule: "Do unto others as you would have them do unto you." Would you be happy with the decision if its outcomes were directed toward you?
6. Obtain a second opinion from a friend who is not vested in the outcome.

Law Enforcement Code of Ethics*

All law enforcement officers must be fully aware of the ethical responsibilities of their position and must strive constantly to live up to the highest possible standards of professional policing.

The International Association of Chiefs of Police believes it is important that police officers have clear advice and counsel available to assist them in performing their duties consistent with these standards and has adopted the following ethical mandates as guidelines to meet these ends.**

Primary Responsibilities of a Police Officer

A police officer acts as an official representative of government who is required and trusted to work within the law. The officer's powers and duties are conferred by statute. The fundamental duties of a police officer include serving the community; safeguarding lives and property; protecting the innocent; keeping the peace; and ensuring the rights of all to liberty, equality and justice.

Performance of the Duties of a Police Officer

A police officer shall perform all duties impartially, without favor or affection or ill will and without regard to status, sex, race, religion, political belief or aspiration. All citizens will be treated equally with courtesy, consideration and dignity.

Officers will never allow personal feelings, animosities or friendships to influence official conduct. Laws will be enforced appropriately and courteously and, in carrying out their responsibilities, officers will strive to obtain maximum cooperation from the public. They will conduct themselves in appearance and deportment in such a manner as to inspire confidence and respect for the position of public trust they hold.

Discretion

A police officer will use responsibly the discretion vested in the position and exercise it within the law. The principle of reasonableness will guide the officer's determinations and the officer will consider all surrounding circumstances in determining whether any legal action shall be taken.

Consistent and wise use of discretion, based on professional policing competence, will do much to preserve good relationships and retain the confidence of the public. There can be difficulty in choosing between conflicting courses of action. It is important to remember that a timely word of advice rather than arrest—which may be correct in appropriate circumstances—can be a more effective means of achieving a desired end.

Use of Force

A police officer will never employ unnecessary force or violence and will use only such force in the discharge of duty as is reasonable in all circumstances.

Force should be used only with the greatest restraint and only after discussion, negotiation and persuasion have been found to be inappropriate or ineffective. While the use of force is occasionally unavoidable, every police officer will refrain from applying the unnecessary infliction of pain or suffering and will never engage in cruel, degrading or inhuman treatment of any person.

Confidentiality

Whatever a police officer sees, hears or learns of, which is of a confidential nature, will be kept secret unless the performance of duty or legal provision requires otherwise.

Members of the public have a right to security and privacy, and information obtained about them must not be improperly divulged.

Integrity

A police officer will not engage in acts of corruption or bribery, nor will an officer condone such acts by other police officers.

The public demands that the integrity of police officers be above reproach. Police officers must, therefore, avoid any conduct that might compromise integrity and thus undercut the public confidence in a law enforcement agency. Officers will refuse to accept any gifts, presents, subscriptions, favors, gratuities or promises that could be interpreted as seeking to cause the officer to refrain from performing official responsibilities honestly and within the law. Police officers must not receive private or special advantage from their official status. Respect from the public cannot be bought; it can only be earned and cultivated.

*Adopted by the Executive Committee of the International Association of Chiefs of Police on October 17, 1989, during its 96th Annual Conference in Louisville, Kentucky, to replace the 1957 code of ethics adopted at the 64th Annual IACP Conference. **The IACP gratefully acknowledges the assistance of Sir John C. Hermon, former chief constable of the Royal Ulster*

Constabulary, who gave full license to the association to freely use the language and concepts presented in the RUC's "Professional Policing Ethics," Appendix I of the Chief Constable's Annual Report, 1988, presented to the Police Authority for Northern Ireland, for the preparation of this code.

Continued

Figure 9.6
Law Enforcement Code of Ethics

Law Enforcement Code of Ethics

Cooperation with Other Officers and Agencies

Police officers will cooperate with all legally authorized agencies and their representatives in the pursuit of justice.

An officer or agency may be one among many organizations that may provide law enforcement services to a jurisdiction. It is imperative that a police officer assist colleagues fully and completely with respect and consideration at all times.

Personal/Professional Capabilities

Police officers will be responsible for their own standard of professional performance and will take every reasonable opportunity to enhance and improve their level of knowledge and competence.

Through study and experience, a police officer can acquire the high level of knowledge and competence that is essential for the efficient and effective performance of duty. The acquisition of knowledge is a never-ending process of personal and professional development that should be pursued constantly.

Private Life

Police officers will behave in a manner that does not bring discredit to their agencies or themselves.

A police officer's character and conduct while off duty must always be exemplary, thus maintaining a position of respect in the community in which he or she lives and serves. The officer's personal behavior must be beyond reproach.

Figure 9.6
continued

Fulton (1999, p. 94) offers some guidelines regarding supervisory ethics and advises police supervisors to ask themselves a few simple questions to help make correct, ethical decisions throughout their careers:

Is my decision legal? . . . Is my decision based on emotion rather than facts? . . . Is it worth my job and/or my career? . . . Is my decision fair to all? Is it the right thing to do? . . .

In your daily activities, as well as in those difficult dilemmas, rely on your years of police education, training and experience. In difficult situations stop and ask yourself the five preceding questions. Then make your decision. Chances are you will be doing the right thing.

Unethical Behavior

Unethical behavior, in contrast, includes discourtesy, brutality, false testimony, divulging confidential information, drinking on duty, concealing or failing to report criminal conduct of fellow officers and misuse of authority for personal gain. Other behaviors may also be viewed as unethical, including excessive off-duty drinking, extramarital affairs, gambling and excessive indebtedness.

Addressing unethical behavior has become a top priority and major challenge for police administrators. O'Malley (1997, p. 20) states: "In the last few years, ethical issues in law enforcement have been affected by three critical factors—the growing level of temptation stemming from the illicit drug trade, the challenges posed by decentralization, and the potentially compromising nature of the police organizational culture." Carter (1999, pp. 311–312) adds:

The cause of corruption is not a simple issue. There is always the proverbial "bad apple" who somehow slipped through the department's selection process. However, more disturbing are the cases of officers who have good work records and appear dedicated yet they slip into a mode of corrupt behavior. Administrators are frequently at a loss to explain how this occurred to a "good officer." Many factors could contribute to this, including:

- Greed
- Personal motivators such as ego, sex, or the exercise of power

- Tolerance of the behavior by the community
- Socialization from peers and/or the organization
- Inadequate supervision and monitoring of behavior
- Lack of clear accountability of employees' behavior
- No real threat of discipline or sanctions

Carter (pp. 316–318) further discusses several factors that, if left uncontrolled, can contribute to an environment wherein corruption will flourish, including rationalization ("It was just drug money. Taking it didn't hurt anyone."), a sense of invulnerability ("Whose word will they believe? A criminal's or a cop's?") and a code of secrecy (where honest officers disassociate themselves but do not report the corruption for fear of being labeled a "rat").

According to Bergner (1998, p. 88): "No matter what else is going right, a department cannot be truly successful if it operates with serious unethical behavior." She lists several varieties of common ethical violations in law enforcement agencies (p. 88):

> Unethical work habits, such as overly long breaks, abusing sick time, arriving late for work, unnecessary or false overtime is one area of ethical violations.
>
> Accepting free coffee or food is common. While not necessarily unethical in itself, it sets up the potential for being unethical. Most chiefs believe it should be eliminated or at least limited.
>
> Conduct unbecoming an officer, such as getting into bar fights off-duty, is problematic.
>
> Lying to superiors, compromising an investigation by tipping off the criminal object of the investigation, or tampering with evidence are, of course, entirely unacceptable.

Terestre (1999, p. 50) notes: "One of the most widely discussed ethical problems today is the law enforcement officer's perception of right and wrong and this relationship to the duty entrusted to [the officer] by the public." Sherman's "Slippery Slope of Corruption" posits that police corruption begins with a lowering of ethical expectations and values to attain a gratuity of minor value, for example, accepting a free cup of coffee. Although this action in itself is most likely harmless and inconsequential as a corrupting force, it may over time produce a snowball effect, leading an officer to accept gratuities of larger magnitude. Furthermore, such practices often lead those providing the "freebies" to expect preferential treatment by recipient officers. "In fact," notes Terestre (p. 50), "the most insignificant gratuities may produce an obligation, especially if awarded on a routine basis." As one officer explained: "Hey, I wouldn't mind a free coffee, but they begin to think they own you for it. I'd rather pay for it myself than deal with the notion that I can be bought out for a dollar cup of coffee" (Terestre, p. 50).

Another facet of unethical behavior concerns the noble cause corruption dilemma, in which officers believe unlawful means are justified when the result is the protection of human life or some other "noble cause." Unquestionably, law enforcement officers face difficult decisions daily. Yet, as Harrison (1999, p. 7) states: "Sometimes situations arise that require [officers] to weigh the laws they are sworn to uphold against the life of an innocent victim. Such incidents force officers to confront the noble cause corruption dilemma of violating fundamental laws to serve a greater moral good." However: "When officers use unlawful means to gain a desired end, they damage the system they represent. . . . The eventual result to society is a loss of confidence in those charged with the protection of others" (p. 5).

Adcox (2000, p. 19) notes: "The tendency of police officers to place ends over means is not new. There is ample historical evidence to suggest that similar police values, beliefs and practices have existed since the inauguration of modern policing in the United States."

Schofield (1998, p. 28) asserts: "Public trust is undermined whenever officers lie or remain silent when questioned about law enforcement matters." According to Delattre (1996, p. 68):

> Those who serve the public must hold to a higher standard of honesty and care for the public good than the general citizenry does. . . .
>
> A higher standard is not a double standard. Persons accepting positions of public trust take on new obligations and are free not to accept them if they do not want to live up to the higher standard. A higher standard as such is not unfair; granting authority to an official without it would be unfair to the public.

Fair or not, the conduct of law enforcement personnel is expected to be above reproach. As role models, managers must exemplify such behavior and reward it in subordinates.

Promoting Ethical Behavior and Integrity

The IACP's AdHoc Committee on Police Image and Ethics (1998, p. 14) asserts: "Ethics is our greatest training and leadership need today and into the next century." As a symbolic statement of commitment to ethical behavior, the IACP has recommended a Law Enforcement Oath of Honor (p. 19):

On my honor,
I will never betray my badge,
my integrity, my character,
or the public trust.
I will always have
the courage to hold myself
and others accountable for our actions.
I will always uphold the constitution
and community I serve.

Bennett et al. (1999, p. 29) contend: "Ethics can be a perishable commodity that will suffer erosion if not continually reinforced. The Oath of Honor provides a continuous and powerful reinforcement for our employees and our organizations."

In addition to the Oath, numerous departmental policies and procedures have been identified as helping foster an environment of ethical behavior and officer integrity. Hunter (1999) discusses a questionnaire administered to officers to assess their opinions of police misconduct. Of officers surveyed, 87.7 percent reported police misconduct as a real problem (p. 164). Officers also expressed strong support for some prevention strategies regarding police misconduct, with the highest level of support given to strict and fair discipline as a means of regulating police conduct (98.5 percent strongly agreed or agreed). Other supported means of regulating police conduct included (p. 164):

- Developing clear policies and procedures (95.4 percent)
- Developing professional (ethical) standards (95.4 percent)
- Hiring capable police supervisors (95.4 percent)
- Expecting supervisors and administrators to serve as moral examples (95.3 percent)
- Terminating officers who engage in illegal behavior while on duty (90.7 percent)
- Hiring capable administrators (89.2 percent)
- Considering the attitudes of fellow officers (87.7 percent)
- Providing better training (86.2 percent)
- Restrictive selection (86.1 percent)
- Officer involvement in decision making (83.1 percent)

As discussed in previous chapters, this final item—encouraging officers to make decisions—is a vital element in promoting community-oriented policing and problem solving.

Ethical Considerations in Community-Oriented Policing and Problem Solving

Ethical behavior and integrity are critical to the successful implementation of community-oriented policing and problem solving (COPPS). Peak, Stitt and Glensor (1998, p. 20) observe:

> With the shift to COPPS, some concerns have been raised about the increased potential for ethical dilemmas confronting the police as they have a greater degree of discretion, decentralization and interaction with the public in implementing solutions to neighborhood crime and disorder problems.

They (p. 33) conclude: "While it is always critical for police officers to anticipate the nature and consequences of their actions, this discernment is greatly magnified in a COPPS environment. . . . A variety of ethical problems can confront the police under COPPS. But with proper leadership, there is a greater chance that officers will choose right over wrong."

Swope (1998, p. 37) suggests that departments moving toward, or already involved in, community policing must be vigilant in maintaining a high level of ethical officer conduct and departmental integrity: "The combination of added discretion, reduced supervision, creative problem solving, increased community involvement, the need for self-initiative and a host of other changes means that a police department cannot afford to permit a decline. It has a responsibility to its citizens, and ineffective service will not be accepted."

> Public trust, not weapons or force, is the most important tool the police possess to carry out their job. That trust is based largely on the integrity of the police agency and its reputation for fairness and respect—toward the community it serves, and toward its own people ("Police, Prejudice and Respect. . . ," 1997, p. 3).

In addition to encouraging individual ethical behavior and personal growth and development, managers must also shape subordinates into an effective team.

Team Building Revisited

To build an effective team, managers need to recognize these different ways of looking at reality and of thinking and to capitalize on the strengths of each. The individual differences of one person, plus the differences of a second, plus all the differences of team members produce a whole that is much greater than the sum of the individual differences, that is, synergism.

In an effective team, members recognize and complement each other's strengths and weaknesses and share the responsibility to achieve their common goals.

Identifying Strengths and Weaknesses

One way to identify the strengths and weaknesses of the team is to have individual team members think about and list three or four past work accomplishments. Next, have them identify four to six abilities they used. For example, one officer set up a traffic accident reduction program. In doing so he needed to analyze the problem, gather and analyze data, make recommendations and report the findings. He also needed to persuade his sergeant that the plan was workable and then to train the traffic officers who would implement it.

Next, have team members identify four or five subjects they feel proficient in. These might include accident investigation/reconstruction, communications, community relations, crime prevention, criminal procedure, defensive tactics, emergency response, ethics, firearms, first aid, interviewing/interrogating techniques, investigation, juveniles, patrol functions, searching or traffic.

Then ask team members to identify the role they feel most comfortable in when interacting with other team members. They might select from the following: coach, coordinator, counselor, director, doer, follower, leader, manager, mentor or team player.

Finally, ask team members to determine what motivates them to accomplish things. They might select from motivators such as to promote advancement, to be in command, to develop self, to gain recognition, to fulfill expectations, to shape or influence the organization, to discover and learn, to excel or be the best, to master or perfect a skill and to serve or help.

Having team members identify individual abilities, subject expertise, preferred ways of interacting and motivators will help identify strengths and weaknesses within the team.

Sharing Responsibility

One key characteristic of an effective team is **shared responsibility,** that is, establishing a work culture in which all team members feel as responsible as the manager for accomplishing the team's goals and objectives.

Recall that the third stage of growth is interdependence, which is a way of relating that recognizes and uses each member's strengths and minimizes the effect of each member's weaknesses.

The Four I's

In addition to sharing responsibility, an effective team releases untapped resources that Cohen and Bradford (1984) refer to as the "Four I's."

> Team members can contribute information, initiative, innovation and implementation.

Information

In this information age, it is impossible for one person, including managers, to know everything. Subordinates may have technical knowledge and skills managers do not have. They are closer "to the streets" and to the needs of citizens. They may be aware of problems managers know nothing about.

Initiative

Often subordinates *must* act on their own in certain circumstances; they cannot wait to be told what to do. Effective team members will be able to act independently when necessary, taking the initiative in a professional way.

Innovation

As suggested by Rosabeth Kanter in *The Change Masters,* some innovations can and must come from within. Much innovation must come from the middle of organizations and below because people at these levels are in a better position to see opportunities and identify potential problems.

Implementation

In most instances the subordinates will actually carry out the activities necessary to accomplish the team's goals. The manager becomes the coach.

Team Building in Action

Team building is one of the most recognized ways to cause change, make decisions and move off the status quo in an organization. Joining a team does not mean giving up individuality. You assume more responsibility when you are a team member.

Many organizations empower teams to reach conclusions and take action based on their decisions. For example, a drug raid team meets to discuss all the intelligence they have on a specific drug bust to be conducted. Each team member contributes expertise, and the team agrees on a strategy that combines this expertise. Each member is expected to contribute, and each member gains confidence from each new experience as a team member.

No one has a corner on ideas. In team building you have to speak up before fellow employees and superiors alike. The team-building approach should be a permanent part of problem solving and decision making within the department. Teams can also be created to make specific decisions—for example, what type of new squad cars to purchase—and then be dissolved.

The Long-Range Importance of Developing Personnel

Developing individuals and team players is important because most future law enforcement managers will come from the lower levels of the organization.

If officers are not self-developed or developed by managers at all levels, where are future executives to come from?

Fulton (1994, p. 82) observes: "You can control your own destiny by consciously developing qualified subordinates so that they can eventually take over the running of critical segments of your organization." He suggests five steps to develop subordinates:

Identify winners. With an open mind, it's really quite easy to identify those individuals in your organization who have the potential to be successful in the long term.

Train them. . . . Knowledge is power, and your subordinates need to receive all of the knowledge you can give them if they are to effectively serve your department and the community.

Groom them. . . . Without that informal knowledge imparted to them by those who "know the ropes," total success can be a difficult battle.

Encourage them. In many departments, promotions can be few and far between. It is your duty to keep your subordinates motivated during the time they are awaiting an opening for a promotion.

Promote them. . . . Your future success depends on placing the most competent people in your most critical positions.

Managers as Motivators for Change

Law enforcement organizations are similar to all other organizations. They constantly change. If they are to flourish, they must embrace change and make it work for them.

Sometimes change occurs in a revolutionary manner, but most often it is evolutionary. Law enforcement managers at all levels play a significant role in this process, which may involve change in the organizational structure, its goals and objectives; its members or in the community it serves. Change involves alteration of attitudes and work behavior as individuals, as team members and as members of the department.

The major impetus for change rests with the executive manager but should be accomplished only after consulting with staff and, in some cases, all members of the department. In the end, change may involve the entire community, for example, changing speed limits in a school zone, permitting or prohibiting street parking of recreational vehicles and adjusting curfew hours.

Other changes involve internal administration and operations, for example; new shift assignments, creation of an investigative or juvenile bureau and changes in medical insurance coverage or fringe benefits. Regardless of the changes being recommended, law enforcement managers are the liaison for change.

Change and conflict are often closely related. Change can precipitate conflict. Many members of an organization like to retain the status quo because they are comfortable with what they have been doing and the way they have been doing it.

With the advent of participative rather than authoritarian management, law enforcement managers are a vital part of this development and introduction to change, the feedback process and the ultimate evaluation of the changes implemented. Although providing stimulation for change is much more difficult than simply ordering it, in the end it is much more rewarding.

Middle managers are in a difficult position between top-management ideas and the line personnel who are directly affected by and must implement change. If a change is made in a speed zone, management will discuss and decide to initiate the change, but the patrol officers must enforce it and take the "heat" from drivers who violate the new speed limit. The patrol officers may want a "window" or grace period during which "warning tickets" can be issued to make the transition more acceptable to the community.

Change is rarely immediate or easy. Middle managers can work for change with both their superiors and their subordinates and, as such, are critical in the change process. If a recommendation for change arises from subordinates, it is the middle manager's responsibility to bring this to the attention of superiors, with credit for the idea given to the proper source. Middle managers should never take credit for a recommended change unless they personally originated the idea.

The Sergeant as a Key Change Agent

Glensor (1994, p. 3) stresses the importance of the sergeant as a "change agent": "First-line supervisors must play a key role in modifying their agencies' culture. However, convincing sergeants of the need for change is no easy task." It is much easier for them to maintain the authoritarian style of supervision and simply give orders. To allow those they supervise to make decisions on-line can be extremely threatening to sergeants' feelings of authority. In switching to a problem-oriented approach to policing, Glensor (p. 8) suggests that a sergeant should have the following attributes (reprinted with permission from *Problem Solving Quarterly,* Winter/Spring 1994, Police Executive Research Forum, © 1994):

- Allows officers freedom to experiment with new approaches.
- Insists on good, accurate analysis of problems; coaches officers through the problem-solving process; gives advice.
- Grants flexibility in work schedules when requests are proper; helps officers manage their time and develop work plans.
- Allows officers to make most contacts directly and paves the way when they are having trouble getting cooperation.
- Protects officers from pressures within the department to revert to traditional methods, as well as from undue criticism.
- Runs interference for officers to secure resources; identifies new resources and contacts for officers and makes them check them out.
- Knows the problems officers are working on and whether the problems are real.
- Knows officers' beats and important citizens in them and expects officers to know the beats and citizens even better.
- Supports officers even if their strategies fail, as long as they learned something useful in the process and completely thought out the strategies.

- Manages problem-solving efforts over a long period of time; doesn't allow efforts to die just because officers get sidetracked by competing demands for time and attention.

- Gives credit to officers and lets others know about their work; provides more positive reinforcement for good work than negative reinforcement for bad work.

- Allows officers to talk about their work with visitors and at conferences.

- Coordinates efforts across shifts, beats and outside units and agencies.

- Identifies emerging problems by monitoring calls for service, crime patterns and community concerns.

- Assesses the activities and performance of officers in relation to identified problems, rather than with boilerplate measures.

- Expects officers to account for their time and activities, giving them a greater range of freedom.

- Provides officers with examples of good problem solving so they know what generally is expected.

- Realizes that this style of police work cannot simply be ordered; officers and detectives must come to believe in it.

Evaluating the Climate for Growth, Development and Change

Law enforcement managers who want to evaluate their workplace culture and its conduciveness to growth, development and change can use the brief survey in Figure 9.7.

Evaluate Your Organization

1. Inflexible: discourages the new and unusual	1 2 3 4 5 6 7	Open to new ideas; receptive	_____
2. Focused on present or past	1 2 3 4 5 6 7	Future oriented; anticipates future	_____
3. No way to train further or develop new skills	1 2 3 4 5 6 7	Many opportunities to learn new skills	_____
4. Individual effort more important than group effort	1 2 3 4 5 6 7	Cooperative efforts, participation in group is important	_____
5. Little planning and communication	1 2 3 4 5 6 7	Active planning, with involvement of others	_____
TOTAL			_____

If your organization scored between 5 and 19, it is *not* conducive to growth and development. If your organization scored between 20 and 29, the growth and development environment is positive but needs improvement. A score of 30 and above indicates that your organization values growth and development.

Figure 9.7
Evaluate Your Organization

Summary

The workplace culture is the sum of the beliefs and values shared by those within the organization, serving to formally and informally communicate its expectations. These group attitudes and beliefs are called norms.

To shape the workplace culture, managers should identify existing norms, evaluate them and then encourage positive norms and try to eliminate negative ones. A positive workplace culture promotes good interpersonal relationships. Such relationships must be built on self-understanding. A model, the Johari Window, shows how people can learn more about themselves and others. The Johari Window describes four parts of a person's identity: the open self, the hidden self, the blind self and the subconscious self.

Personal and organizational goals are a necessary first step for growth and development. A personal goal states what, when and how much. Holistic goal setting should include career/job, financial, personal, family/relationships and spiritual/service. Goals should also consider values. Touchstone values, what people say is important to them, and daily values, how people actually spend their time and energy, need to correlate.

Managers who contribute their efforts to accomplishing department goals while simultaneously developing their subordinates into top performers are superior "balanced performer" managers who empower others. As managers help their people grow and develop, they should be aware of the three stages of growth. Employees initially are dependent. As they grow and develop they become independent and finally interdependent. Managers can often help their people through these stages by mentoring. A mentor is a wise, trusted teacher or counselor. Law enforcement managers are in an ideal position to be mentors. As mentors, managers should help their subordinates develop positive attitudes, a positive image, cultural awareness and a strong sense of ethics.

Law enforcement officers who have a good appearance and act with competence and courtesy will leave a favorable impression with the majority of the public. To create such positive impressions, law enforcement personnel must develop cultural awareness and sensitivity. They must understand the diversity of the United States, the dynamics of minority–majority relationships, the dynamics of sexism and racism and the issues of nationalism and separatism.

Another important area for growth and development is in ethics. Ethical behavior is that which is "moral" and "right." Law enforcement personnel must develop high ethical standards both on and off duty.

In addition to helping people grow and develop, managers are also responsible for building a team. Team members can contribute information, initiative, innovation and implementation. Developing individuals and team players is important because most future law enforcement managers will come from the lower levels of the organization.

Discussion Questions

1. How can participating in sports develop a sense of teamwork?
2. What would you include in a job description for a law enforcement officer? A sergeant? A chief or sheriff?
3. What norms would you like to see in the law enforcement agency you work for?
4. What do you consider the five most important touchstone values listed in Table 9.1?

5. What ethical problems have you faced in your life?
6. What are your three most important touchstone values? Your three most important daily values? Do they correlate? If not, what should you do?
7. Have you had any mentors in your life? Been a mentor to someone else? If so, what seemed to enhance the experience?
8. Have you been a member of a team or an organization? If so, what role did you play? Was this satisfactory to you?
9. What do you consider your greatest strengths? Weaknesses?
10. What skills would you like to further develop? How important would this be to your law enforcement career?

InfoTrac College Edition Assignment

Select one of the topics introduced in this chapter to study in more depth. Find a recent article related to it and either summarize or outline the article. You may use more than one article if you want. Be sure to give the full reference citation. Be prepared to discuss your findings with the class.

References

Adcox, Ken. "Doing Bad Things for Good Reasons." *The Police Chief,* Vol. LXVII, No. 1, January 2000, pp. 16–28.

Bennett, Charles; Bushey, Keith; Cummings, Patrick; Doherty, Ann Marie; Hesser, Larry; Jahn, Mike; and Melton, Richard. "The Law Enforcement Oath of Honor." *The Police Chief,* Vol. LXVI, No. 10, October 1999, pp. 24–29.

Bergner, Laurie L. "Changing Departmental Ethics: Tips from Chiefs for Chiefs." *Law and Order,* Vol. 46, No. 9, September 1998, pp. 87–89.

Campion, Michael A. "Good Character, Good Policing–Then and Now." *Community Policing Exchange,* March/April 1998, p. 3.

Carter, David L. "Drug Use and Drug-Related Corruption of Police Officers." In *Policing Perspectives,* edited by Larry Gaines and Gary Cordner. Los Angeles: Roxbury Publishing Company, 1999, pp. 311–323.

Cohen, Allan and Bradford, David. *Managing for Excellence.* New York: John Wiley and Sons, 1984.

Covey, Stephen R. *The 7 Habits of Highly Effective People.* New York: Simon and Schuster, 1989.

Davis, Robert C. and Erez, Edna. *Immigrant Populations as Victims: Toward a Multicultural Criminal Justice System.* Washington, DC: National Institute of Justice, Research in Brief, May 1998. (NCJ-167571)

Delattre, Edwin J. *Character and Cops,* 3rd ed. 1996.

Edmundson, James E. "Mentoring Programs Help New Employees." *FBI Law Enforcement Bulletin,* Vol. 68, No. 10, October 1999, pp. 16–18.

Fulton, Roger. "Surround Yourself with Competence." *Law Enforcement Technology,* Vol. 21, No. 10, October 1994, p. 82.

Fulton, Roger. "Do the Right Thing: Supervisory Ethics." *Law Enforcement Technology,* Vol. 26, No. 4, April 1999, p. 94.

Gaffigan, Stephen J. and McDonald, Phyllis P. *Police Integrity: Public Service with Honor.* Washington, DC: National Institute of Justice and the Office of Community Oriented Police Services, January 1997. (NCJ-163811)

Gallup, George, Jr. *The Gallup Poll Monthly,* No. 387. Princeton, NJ: The Gallup Poll, December 1997.

Glensor, Ron. "The Sergeant's Role as a Change Agent." *Problem Solving Quarterly,* Winter/Spring 1994, pp. 3, 8.

Harrison, Bob. "Noble Cause Corruption and the Police Ethic." *FBI Law Enforcement Bulletin,* Vol. 68, No. 8, August 1999, pp. 1–7.

Haught, Lunell. "Meaning, Resistance and Sabotage—Elements of a Police Culture." *Community Policing Exchange,* May/June 1998, p. 7.

Hawley, Donna Lea. "Police Action against Illegal Immigration: Where Does It Stand?" *Police,* Vol. 23, No. 6, June 1999, pp. 28–34.

Hunter, Ronald D. "Officer Opinions on Police Misconduct." *Journal of Contemporary Criminal Justice,* Vol. 15, No. 2, May 1999, pp. 155–170.

IACP AdHoc Committee on Police Image and Ethics. "Ethics Training in Law Enforcement." *The Police Chief,* Vol. LXV, No. 1, January 1998, pp. 14–24.

Kennedy, Randall. "Race, the Police, and 'Reasonable Suspicion.' " *In Perspectives on Crime and Justice: 1997–1998 Lecture Series.* Washington, DC: National Institute of Justice, November 1998, pp. 29–50. (NCJ-172851)

Klockars, Carl B. *Thinking about Police, Contemporary Readings.* New York: McGraw-Hill, 1983.

Kranda, April H. "A Mentoring Program to Help Reduce Employee Turnover." *The Police Chief,* Vol. LXIV, No. 6, June 1997, pp. 51–52.

Mader, Charles J. "The Police Image: What's Wrong?" *Police,* Vol. 21, No. 10, October 1997, pp. 8–10.

Matthews, John. "Racial Profiling: A Law Enforcement Nemesis." *Police,* Vol. 23, No. 11, November 1999, pp. 38–39.

O'Malley, Timothy J. "Managing for Ethics: A Mandate for Administrators." *FBI Law Enforcement Bulletin,* Vol. 66, No. 4, April 1997, pp. 20–26.

Peak, Kenneth J.; Stitt, B. Grant; and Glensor, Ronald W. "Ethical Considerations in Community Policing and Problem Solving." *Police Quarterly,* Vol. 1, No. 3, 1998, pp. 19–34.

"Police, Prejudice and Respect for Diversity: Principles for Decision Makers." *Subject to Debate,* May 1997, pp. 3, 8.

Ramirez, Steve. "The Tribe That Wouldn't Fish." *The Law Enforcement Trainer,* Vol. 14, No. 5, September/October 1999, pp. 12–13.

Santos, Michael R. "Establishing a Foundation for Ethical Conduct." *The Police Chief,* Vol. LXIV, No. 3, March 1997, pp. 8–10.

Schofield, Daniel L. "Ensuring Officer Integrity and Accountability: Recent Court Decisions." *FBI Law Enforcement Bulletin,* Vol. 67, No. 8, August 1998, pp. 28–32.

Sherman, Lawrence. "Learning Police Ethics." In *Policing Perspectives,* edited by Larry Gaines and Gary Cordner. Los Angeles: Roxbury Publishing Company, 1999, pp. 301–310.

Slahor, Stephenie. "Ethical Leadership." *Law and Order,* Vol. 47, No. 7, July 1999, pp. 123–124.

Smotzer, Andrew A. "Ethics Training for Law Enforcement." *Law and Order,* Vol. 47, No. 2, February 1999, p. 32.

Solar, Patrick J. "Changing Organizational Culture." *Law and Order,* Vol. 46, No. 5, May 1998, pp. 22–27.

Sourcebook of Criminal Justice Statistics—1997. Washington, DC: Bureau of Justice Statistics, 1998. (NCJ-171147)

Strandberg, Keith W. "Racial Profiling." *Law Enforcement Technology,* Vol. 26, No. 6, June 1999, pp. 62–66.

"Study Finds Police Keeping Their Customers Satisfied." *Law Enforcement News,* Vol. XXV, Nos. 515/516, July/August 1999, pp. 1, 9.

Swope, Ross E. "The Core-Virtue Bell Curve." *The Police Chief,* Vol. LXV, No. 1, January 1998, pp. 37–38.

Terestre, David J. "The Doughnut Shop Dilemma: Cops, Coffee and Ethics." *Police,* Vol. 23, No. 8, August 1999, pp. 50–53.

Townsend, Josephine C. "Mentors in the Art of Leadership." *Law and Order,* Vol. 46, No. 5, May 1998, pp. 70–71.

Vicchio, Stephen J. "Ethics and Police Integrity." *FBI Law Enforcement Bulletin,* Vol. 66, No. 7, July 1997, pp. 8–12.

Worden, Robert E. "Police Officers' Belief Systems: A Framework for Analysis." *American Journal of Police,* Vol. XIV, No. 1, 1995, pp. 49–81.

Chapter 10 Motivation and Morale

The convict's stroke of the pick is not the
same as the prospector's.
—Antoine de Saint-Exupéry

You can buy a man's time; you can buy his
physical presence at a given place; you can
even buy a measured number of his skilled
muscular motions per hour. But you cannot
buy enthusiasm . . . you cannot buy
loyalty . . . you cannot buy the devotion of
hearts, minds, or souls. You must earn these.
—Clarence Francis

Do You Know?

- What motivation is?
- What theories of motivation have been proposed by Maslow? Herzberg? Skinner? Vroom? Morse and Lorsch?
- Which kind of reinforcement is more effective?
- When reinforcement should occur?
- What the most common external motivators are?
- What internal motivators include?
- How you can make the law enforcement job more interesting?
- What morale is?
- What factors might indicate a morale problem?
- What factors might be responsible for morale problems?
- Who is most able to raise or lower individual and department morale?
- How you might increase morale?
- What you should base promotions on?
- What three phases an assessment center typically uses for law enforcement personnel?
- Whether promotions should be from without or within?
- What existing incentives you might publicize to improve morale?

Can You Define?

assessment center	hygiene factors	job enrichment
contingency theory	incentive programs	job rotation
expectancy theory	intangible rewards	morale
external motivators	internal motivators	motivation
hierarchy of needs	job enlargement	motivator factors

negative reinforcement   Pygmalian effect   self-motivation
perception   reinforcement theory   tangible rewards
perks   self-actualization   two-factor theory
positive reinforcement   self-fulfilling prophecy

INTRODUCTION

Why do some law enforcement officers arrive at work ahead of time, eager to perform? Why do others arrive just in the nick of time? Why do some perform at a high level without direction and others need constant direction? Why are some upbeat and others chronic complainers? What motivates such behavior?

Consider the following conversation between two officers, one who had just completed an especially frustrating shift. This officer asked the other, "Why do we come here day after day and put up with this crap?" The other officer thought for a moment and then answered, "I don't know. I think it has something to do with house payments." Most people do need to work to survive. What will make them also enjoy their work and do their best? What will motivate them? Brown (1999, p. 114) cautions: "Law enforcement is one profession where society cannot afford to have complacent and non-motivated employees."

This chapter looks first at definitions of motivation and self-motivation. Next the motivational theories of Maslow, Herzberg, Skinner, Vroom, and Morse and Lorsch are discussed. This theoretical discussion leads into a more practical examination of external, tangible motivators and then internal, intangible motivators. Next is the critical question that managers at all levels ask: "What is really motivational?" The chapter then looks at the law enforcement career as a motivator.

The discussion then turns to morale and its definitions, both individual and organizational. Next indicators of morale problems are presented, along with a discussion of some reasons for such problems. Specific suggestions for building morale are then outlined, followed by a discussion of the relationship between promotions and morale and descriptions of two successful programs for combatting morale problems. The chapter concludes with a discussion of the role of incentive programs in building morale and an example of one innovative program geared to improve morale inexpensively.

Motivation Defined

Motivation is an inner or outer drive to meet a need or goal.

Self-motivation is derived from within an individual. Outer motivation is provided from external sources to influence an individual or to furnish a reason for another person to do a desired act in a desired way. A *motive* is an impetus, an impulse, an intention that causes a person to act, individually or collectively, in a directed manner.

Motivation and *morale* are terms often used in management but not easily defined or understood. Lack of motivation is often the reason for low morale.

Research psychologists have outlined factors that affect motivation and morale. Incentives must be worthwhile to employees; they must be reasonably attainable, and employees must feel a sense of responsibility to achieve them. In modern police terms, employees must be empowered. Motivation requires a sense of well-being, self-confidence and accomplishment. To keep levels of motivation and morale high, managers must give recognition.

Can managers motivate their subordinates? According to some, motivation can come only from within. A story from business helps illustrate the point. A young salesperson was disappointed because he had lost an important sale. Discussing it with the sales manager, the man lamented, "I guess it just proves you can lead a horse to water, but you can't make him drink." To which the sales manager replied, "Let me give you a little advice. Your job isn't to make him drink. It's to make him thirsty."

Managers can, however, create an environment that will motivate people by creating opportunities for success and recognizing accomplishments.

Self-Motivation

When employees know an agency's goals and choose to help meet them, this is **self-motivation.** Fortunately for management, most employees want to do a good job. It is management's job to help and to provide additional motivation when needed. For example, an officer who works long after the shift is over to make certain a victim is adequately taken care of may be "rewarded" by being given time off during the next shift. Many incentives other than monetary ones encourage employees and cost nothing. They take little time, yet are seldom used. Most employees have pride in their work. They want to satisfy themselves and their employers.

Self-motivated law enforcement officers work for personal job satisfaction. Law enforcement work gives them a sense of accomplishment and personal value. Self-motivated officers are dedicated to their work and make every hour on the job count.

Job satisfaction remains a basic reward of working, even though not many employees would mention it as a benefit. Recreation and time for home life, children and rest are equally important. Self-motivated employees are more apt to work toward organizational as well as personal goals because the melding of both provides even more job satisfaction.

Not all jobs provide an enjoyable environment. Many people work only to make a living, to provide security for their families and to supply the funds to enjoy the other things in life.

Many work at jobs they do not like. Not all law enforcement officers like their work. In these situations managers need to be motivators.

Many theories of motivation have been developed based on extensive research of employees in the work environment. These studies reveal that although monetary rewards are a necessary part of jobs, money is *not* the major consideration as long as it is basically adequate for living.

Motivational Theories

Each individual has needs even though that person may not have a list of needs or even have consciously thought about them. These needs make each of us what we are and cause us to do what we do. Each individual takes action to meet these needs.

The 1960s saw the development of many theories about motivation. Knowledge of these theories helps us understand what people can do for themselves and what managers can do for employees. The results of studies by human-behavior researchers apply as much to law enforcement as to any other profession.

The Hierarchy of Needs— Abraham Maslow

One of the best known studies of human needs was conducted by Abraham Maslow in 1962. He concluded that every human has five basic needs, which he assembled into a hierarchy, as Figure 10.1 illustrates.

Maslow's **hierarchy of needs** is, in the order they need to be met, physiological, safety and security, social, esteem and self-actualization.

At the base of the hierarchy are *physiological needs:* air, food, water, sleep, shelter and sex. It is mandatory that at least air, food, water and sleep be satisfied, or a person could not function or proceed to the next level. Some segments

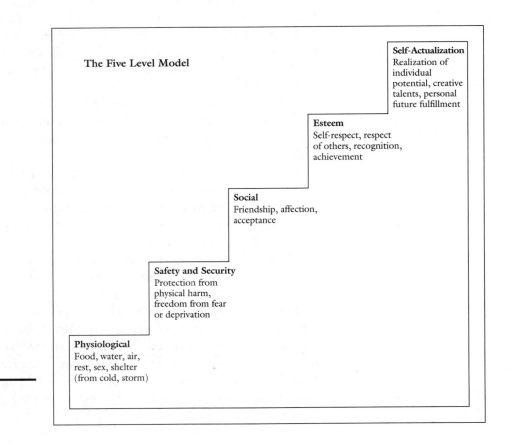

The Five Level Model

Self-Actualization
Realization of individual potential, creative talents, personal future fulfillment

Esteem
Self-respect, respect of others, recognition, achievement

Social
Friendship, affection, acceptance

Safety and Security
Protection from physical harm, freedom from fear or deprivation

Physiological
Food, water, air, rest, sex, shelter (from cold, storm)

Figure 10.1
Maslow's Hierarchy of Needs

of the world's population live their entire lives just trying to satisfy this level of need. Shelter could be added to the list because it is more than merely a place to sleep; it is protection from the elements.

The second level, *safety and security,* includes protection from serious injury and death, freedom from fear and a clear authority structure. Humans function better in an environment free from fear. Fear is a negative, an interference with normal life. It has long been known that children need a set of standards even though they tend to rebel against them. Adults also need a set of standards, an authority structure, even though they, too, sometimes rebel. People want a level of certainty, to know "where they stand." This translates at work to safety from accidents, a reasonable promise of job security and an opportunity for increases in pay and promotions.

The third level, *social,* includes friendship, love, affection and group and team belonging. These are important needs for everyone. Workers want peer acceptance, approval, sharing and friendship.

The fourth level, *esteem,* includes self-respect, respect and recognition from others, status, a title, added responsibility, independence and recognition for job performance.

The fifth level, *self-actualization,* refers to achievement, to meeting individual goals and fulfilling one's potential. **Self-actualization** is what you do when all the other needs are satisfied. It is fostered by the chance to be creative and innovative and by having the opportunity to maximize skills and knowledge.

According to Maslow's theory, people's wants are always increasing and changing. Once an individual's basic (primary) needs have been satisfied, other needs take their place. The satisfied need no longer acts as a motivating force. If a number of needs are unsatisfied at any given time, an individual will try to satisfy the most pressing one first. Maslow believed that all levels of needs probably exist to some degree for individuals most of the time. Rarely is any one need completely satisfied, at least for long. Hunger, for example, may be satisfied after eating, but it emerges again later.

Maslow's theory of needs is popular because it makes sense. People can identify these needs in their own lives. In addition, they can be seen operating on the job. In many jobs, including law enforcement jobs, the first two levels of needs are automatically provided. Safety, for example, is extremely important in law enforcement. The law enforcement organization must do everything possible to ensure its officers' safety—and the officers should know what steps have been taken.

Satisfied needs do not necessarily become inactive needs. If law enforcement officers receive salary increases, they may raise their standard of living and then another salary increase is as welcome as the first.

Law enforcement organizations may meet the needs of the group but not of individuals. For example, with a minimal number of promotions, other means of satisfying the need for recognition must be found. Managers can play an important role in providing on-the-job authority structure. They can provide respect through praise and recognition for tasks well done.

Managers can help subordinates meet even the highest goals, fulfilling individual potential through training and on-the-job educational opportunities. Officers seek challenging opportunities to provide service to the community. If their performance is good, they expect fair compensation and rewards. The agency should provide clear goals that have been mutually agreed upon, and officers should expect to meet those goals, both individually and as a group. Maslow's five levels of needs and their translation into specific job-related factors are illustrated in Figure 10.2.

Two-Factor Hygiene/Motivator Theory—Herzberg

Another behavioral psychologist, Frederick Herzberg, developed the **two-factor theory,** or the hygiene/motivator theory. Herzberg's theory divides needs that require satisfaction through work into two classes: hygiene factors and motivator factors.

> Herzberg's **hygiene factors** are **tangible rewards** that can cause *dissatisfaction* if lacking. **Motivator factors** are **intangible rewards** that can create *satisfaction.*

Dissatisfaction and satisfaction are not two ends of a continuum, for people can experience lack of dissatisfaction without necessarily being satisfied.

Tangible rewards pertaining basically to the hygiene factors do *not* provide satisfaction. They simply prevent dissatisfaction. Having officers who perform

Complex	Self-actualization	Challenging job
		Creativity
		Achievement in work
		Advancement
		Involvement in planning
		Chances for growth and development
	Esteem	Merit pay raises
		Titles
		Status symbols/awards
		Recognition (peer/boss)
		Job itself
		Responsibility
		Sharing in decisions
	Social	Quality supervision
		Compatible co-workers
		Professional friendships
		Department pride/spirit
	Safety/Security	Safe working conditions
		Fringe benefits
		Seniority
		Proper supervision
		Sound department policies
		Protective equipment
		General salary increases
		Job security
		Feeling of competence
Basic	Physiological	Heat/air conditioning
		Base salary
		Cafeteria/vending machine
		Working conditions
		Rest periods
		Efficient work methods
		Labor-saving devices
		Comfortable uniform

Figure 10.2
Maslow's Levels of Needs and Job Factors

only because they are not dissatisfied is seldom conducive to high performance. Providing more tangible rewards is highly unlikely to accomplish better results.

The hygiene factors are similar to Maslow's lower-level needs. People assume they will be met. If they are not, people will be dissatisfied. Company policies, job security, supervision, a basic salary and safe working conditions are extrinsic factors that do not necessarily motivate people to do better work. They are expected.

Herzberg's hygiene factors help to explain why many people stick with jobs they do not like. They stay because they are not dissatisfied with the tangible rewards such as the pay and the retirement plan even though they are definitely not satisfied with the work itself.

Industry found that when many of the wage increases, fringe benefits, seniority and security programs were initiated, they did not substantially reduce the basic problems of low productivity, high turnover, absenteeism and grievances. Herzberg claimed that approach was wrong. Instead, jobs should provide greater control over outcomes of work, have clearly established goals and have more to do rather than less. Figure 10.3 shows the relationship between Maslow's hierarchy of needs theory and Herzberg's two-factor theory.

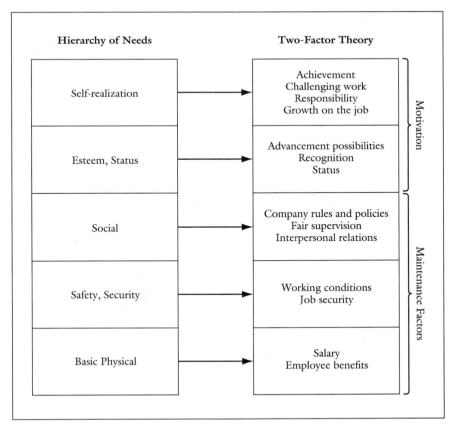

Figure 10.3
Comparison of Maslow and Herzberg

As Herzberg (1978, p. 49) pointed out: "A man whose work possesses no contentment in terms of self-fulfillment, but exists exclusively to fulfill the purposes of the enterprise or a social organization, is a man doomed to a life of human frustration, despite a return of animal contentment. You do not inspire employees by giving them higher wages, more benefits, or new status symbols. It is the successful achievement of a challenging task which fulfills the urge to create. . . . The employer's task is not to motivate his people to get them to achieve; he should provide opportunities for people to achieve, so they will become motivated."

Herzberg's theory, like Maslow's, does not consider differences in people, for the same motivators will not motivate everyone. Law enforcement managers, for example, will find that not all patrol officers are motivated by the same needs. Managers have to adjust motivational approaches to the individual.

Most employees still believe that satisfying work is more important than increased salary and advancement, *if* the basic salary is adequate. The job itself—law enforcement work—is a good example: The work is satisfying because what officers do is meaningful to them and to the community they serve. Most law enforcement officers are *not* in it for the money.

Reinforcement Theory—Skinner

Extremely influential writings by B. F. Skinner suggest that behavior can be shaped and modified using positive and negative reinforcement. Skinner's pioneering work in behavior modification was first described in his book *The Behavior of Organisms,* published in 1938 and expanded in *Walden Two,* published in 1948. A key conclusion of Skinner's research is that behavior is a function of its consequences. The ethics behind "modifying" behavior became highly controversial in the 1960s. Nonetheless, Skinner's theories *are* still relevant to managers, are implicit in the motivational theories just discussed and seem to be simple common sense.

In reinforcement theory employees are rewarded for "good" behavior. They repeat the behavior to achieve the reward, and it becomes a learned behavior. Employees are punished for "bad" behavior. They stop the punished behavior to avoid future punishment. Rewards are called **positive reinforcement;** punishments, **negative reinforcement.**

> Skinner's **reinforcement theory** suggests that positive reinforcement increases a given behavior and negative reinforcement decreases a given behavior.

Use of both positive and negative reinforcement is readily seen on the job. Often both are used, and both make sense. Other principles of reinforcement theory also have relevance for managers.

> Positive reinforcement is more effective than negative reinforcement. The closer in time to the behavior, the more effective the reinforcement will be.

What is the problem with punishment? With a history as old as the human race, it is the belief that the harsher the punishment, the greater its effectiveness in changing behavior. Many managers, including those in penology, still adhere to this belief.

The means to inflict punishment have changed, with the whip, the rack and the stock falling into disfavor. Today's punishments are more subtle but have the same effect. Punishment-oriented managers might use techniques such as criticizing or ridiculing someone in public, ignoring a job well done, withholding needed information or avoiding discussion on an expected promotion or raise.

Although the punishments have changed, the problems associated with using a punishment-oriented management style have not. First, and perhaps most important, punishment can cause a "get even" attitude. This can take the form of "fight"—where the employees cause problems by what they say or do. Or it can take the form of "flight," where the workers "quit but stay." They simply put in the required time and do as little as possible.

A second problem is that managers have to be constantly watching over employees. If vigilance is relaxed, the negative behavior is likely to recur.

A third problem is that subordinates may come to associate punishment with the manager's presence and may dread seeing the manager coming around. They may become defensive every time the manager appears.

Yet another problem with punishment is that sometimes any kind of attention, even punishment, is considered more positive than being ignored. Teachers are well aware of this phenomenon with "problem" students who act up merely for the attention they get when they do. Law enforcement officers who crave acknowledgment of their existence by their superiors may feel that criticism is preferable to being totally ignored.

The other principle of the reinforcement theory that managers need to consider is the time factor. Many incentives once thought to be powerful motivators are delayed—and scheduled. A good example is the paycheck. A law enforcement officer may conduct an excellent investigation on the first of the month but not be paid until the fifteenth of that month. In such cases, the paycheck is not seen as related to the investigation.

That is why incentives such as praise and recognition, given *immediately,* can be powerful motivators. Positive reinforcement can be highly motivating, but the theory also has some disadvantages. It does not consider human needs and tends to simplify behavior and rewards. It does not consider that employees may be motivated by the job itself, may be self-motivated or may consider rewards as manipulation, which they will eventually reject. Failing to reward can lead to less production, and failing to punish poor performance can reinforce that behavior.

The Expectancy Theory—Vroom

Victor H. Vroom's expectancy theory looks at options employees have on the job. It combines some features of the preceding theories and advances the ideas that employees believe good work on the job will lead to high job performance and that high job performance will lead to job rewards.

Regardless of the chief individual motivating factors, if employees feel that performance will lead to satisfying motivational needs, they will work hard.

Naturally, employees must be able to perform. According to Vroom's theory of motivation, employees become motivated to take action when the following three-step process takes place:

1. A motivating factor—a need to satisfy or goal to achieve—exists that is important to the employee.
2. The employee believes that by putting in the required or requested effort, the job can be performed.
3. The employee believes that by successfully performing the job as requested, the need will be satisfied or the goal will be achieved.

Employees have an effort expectancy and a performance expectancy. If managers clearly define the tasks and help employees with direction and skill training to perform the job, effort expectancy will rise. Managers can help achieve performance expectancy by providing means of satisfying individual needs.

Managers must know what opportunities specific jobs offer before they can use them as motivational opportunities for employees. These may be money, opportunity for educational or job growth, praise or peer recognition. Expectancies vary even with individuals doing the same job. Expectancy theory integrates ideas about employee motivation.

_____

Vroom's **expectancy theory** suggests that employees will choose the level of effort that matches the performance opportunity for reward.

For example, if a law enforcement officer investigating an accident that happened one-half hour before shift change realizes that completing the investigation will take an hour, he or she can complete it, ask another officer to take over the investigation or do a poor job by leaving the investigation before obtaining the needed information.

The officer knows doing the complete job will receive recognition by the sergeant. He or she knows asking someone else to complete the investigation will lead to complications in obtaining facts and completing reports. He or she knows that leaving the scene without information for proper reporting will be reason for reprimand. The officer will probably choose to put in the extra time and complete the report because the rewards are a better expectancy than a reprimand. It will also look better on his or her record. The officer should also understand that making repeated comments to those involved in the accident that "this is on my own time" are negative and may result in a complaint. On the other hand, the satisfaction of a job well done and the good inner feeling that results may be motivating in themselves.

Contingency Theory— Morse and Lorsch

Closely related to the expectancy theory is the contingency theory developed by John J. Morse and Jay W. Lorsch. They built on McGregor's Theory X and Y (Chapter 2) and Herzberg's motivation and maintenance factors in their research on how an organizational task *fit* affects and is affected by task performance and employees' feelings of *competence.* The four key components of the contingency theory are the following:

- People have a basic need to feel competent.
- How people fill this need varies and will depend on how the need interacts with other needs and the strengths of those needs.
- Competence motivation is most likely to exist when task and organization "fit."
- Feeling competent continues to be motivating even after competence is achieved.

Morse and Lorsch's **contingency theory** suggests fitting tasks, officers and the agency's goals so that officers can feel competent.

Contingency theory further suggests that highly structured tasks might be performed better in highly structured organizations that have a management structure that resembles McGregor's Theory X approach. Conversely, highly unstructured tasks might be performed better in more flexible organizations whose management structure resembles the Theory Y approach. In law enforcement work, both kinds of tasks occur. Consequently, flexibility in management style becomes very important.

Motivational theory has important implications for law enforcement managers and supervisors. No matter what theories they believe have the most credence, managers must understand that certain external, tangible motivators and certain internal, intangible motivators are important in accomplishing goals through others.

Causes and Symptoms of an Unmotivated Work Force

Causes of an unmotivated work force might include overwork, downsizing, endless restructuring, boredom, frustration and promotions—who gets them and why—work conditions and the court system.

Symptoms of an unmotivated officer include absenteeism, constant complaining, lack of care for equipment, lack of respect for other officers, lack of respect for rules and regulations, low morale, sleeping or loafing on duty, slovenly appearance and tardiness. Dealing with these symptoms is the focus of the next section. In addition to recognizing the causes and symptoms of lack of motivation, managers must also understand and know how to use the knowledge that certain external, tangible motivators and certain internal, intangible motivators are important in accomplishing goals through others.

External, Tangible Motivators

Although external motivators no longer have the power they once had, they are expected. As Herzberg's theory states, basic needs must be met or dissatisfaction will result. This is not to say that lack of dissatisfaction will be motivating. It is likely, however, to keep people on the job and to keep them from counterproductive behavior.

Among the most common **external motivators,** or tangible rewards, are salary, bonuses, insurance, retirement plans, favorable working conditions, paid vacation and holidays, titles and adequate equipment.

The Compensation Package

The law enforcement profession is not known for its great salaries. Nonetheless, money is important to most employees. They want and need enough salary to be comfortable and to meet their basic financial responsibilities. Some officers work two jobs until they have the amount of money they consider necessary. It is true that money talks. What managers must remember, however, is that it says different things to different people.

Although pay in the law enforcement profession is not at the top of the scale, the entire compensation package is usually competitive. One important factor is an equitable procedure for raises. In a well-managed department, employees would not have to ask for raises. They would know what to expect—and when—in return for their performance and dedication. Given the hazardous nature of law enforcement work, the compensation package should include health, disability and life insurance.

Perks

Perks, or tangible rewards, can be as large as a luxury cruise for the "training suggestion of the year" or as small as a reserved parking spot. Little extras can contribute much to making jobs more attractive. Some perks cost nothing, and others are relatively inexpensive. Consider the following:

- Cards or small gifts for special occasions such as birthdays or service anniversaries
- Tickets to sporting events and shows for outstanding performance
- Free coffee and snacks
- Facilities for heating meals, such as microwave ovens
- Daily newspaper and magazines, including professional journals
- Personal notes for achievements—on the job and off
- Support for league teams such as softball and bowling
- SMILES

Working Conditions

Employees expect adequate heat, light, ventilation and working hours. They also expect a well-maintained squad car and up-to-date equipment. Having a desk or a private office can also be rewarding. Inadequacies in working conditions can cause great dissatisfaction.

Security

Although this may seem like an internal reward—or motivator—many aspects of security are indeed external, tangible and expected. Among them are fair work rules, adequate grievance procedures, reasonable department policies and discipline and seniority privileges. Some aspects of the compensation package such as insurance and retirement plans also meet basic security needs.

Social

Like the need for security, employees' social needs can fall within the external, tangible category when such things as parties, picnics, breaks and social gatherings are considered. Opportunities to mix with one's peers and superiors, sometimes including spouses, may be very rewarding.

Status

The need for status can also be partially met by external, tangible rewards such as privileges, titles, private offices, awards and other symbols of rank and position.

These external, tangible factors are sometimes called *maintenance* factors. Provided in adequate quantity and quality, they merely prevent dissatisfaction. The best managers can hope for is a "fair day's work for a fair day's pay." To get subordinates to truly perform, managers usually need to provide internal, intangible motivators as well.

Internal, Intangible Motivators

Internal, intangible motivators can spark employees to give their best effort to accomplishing individual and department goals.

> **Internal motivators** or intangible rewards include goals, achievement, recognition, self-respect, opportunity for advancement, opportunity to make a contribution and belief in individual and departmental goals.

Goals and Expectations

Goals need to be set and met. Specific goal setting results in higher accomplishment. Goals should make officers reach to their levels of competence. Different goals are often needed for individual officers. The reason some students fail in school is because goals are too easy and they become bored. On the other hand, the same goals may be too high for other students to achieve and they become frustrated. Students who achieve to their level of competence will be motivated.

The highly touted management by objectives, or MBO, relies on clear, meaningful goals, both for individual officers and for the organization. Goals establish future direction of effort. Accomplishing goals provides room for creativity, innovation, diversity and a sense of accomplishment.

Operational goals should be set by first-line and middle managers, with the participation of patrol officers. Goals should be consistent and communicated. Realistic goals, proper resources to do the job, employee communication and a personal and organizational sense of accomplishment all play a major role in law enforcement motivation.

Closely related to goals are expectations. As Swope (1998, p. 32) notes:

> An elementary tenet of superior leadership is conveying expectations. . . . Clearly defined and communicated expectations are vital to police officers and law enforcement agencies, since they help set goals and markers by which officers can measure their progress.

To illustrate the importance of expectations, Swope describes the **Pygmalion effect** (p. 32): "What managers expect of their subordinates and how they treat them largely determine their performance and career progress." It is a type of self-fulfilling prophecy.

Achievement, Recognition, Growth and Advancement

Achievement is a motivator. It can be a series of small accomplishments or one accomplishment that ultimately grows to a larger one. It can be a task done well for the first time, something done better than before, a higher score or committing fewer errors.

Recognition is also a motivator, whether it comes from peers or managers. Recognition is most effective if it can be related to a person's personal qualities rather than to the performance itself. For example, rather than saying "Good job on solving the XYZ case," emphasize the personal qualities involved, such as, "I admire your determination to keep working on the XYZ case until you got it solved."

Recognize accomplishment. Too often managers fail to use this reward that costs nothing. Recognition of something well done, offered at the time of accomplishment, is a powerful motivator: "Thank you for working overtime to get that report to me." "I have just reviewed your case report. It is excellent and reflects a lot of thought." Some employees report that their managers have never complimented or praised them in an entire year. Some managers cannot bring themselves to praise subordinates either because it is not their nature or they are too busy. Take time. Do it the next valid opportunity. See how much better it makes them and you feel. Rachlin (1996, p. 85) asserts:

> Awards and ceremonies honoring officers generate positive publicity and are a good public relations tool for the agency. Such publicity alerts the community to the heroic acts and everyday public service deeds of local officers. It can do wonders toward gaining or restoring public confidence in police officers as a professional group.
>
> An honored officer may be inspired to work with greater purpose, energy and efficiency, feeling the sense of a mission. He or she is, in the eyes of others, a respected and honorable worker, and this impacts psychologically, giving greater pride in career, agency, and self.

In addition to recognition, employees want growth and advancement in their jobs. It does not have to be promotions or pay raises. It can be little things: being given personal responsibility for a task, a title, concern for employees' health and welfare, a little risk taking for excitement or deserved praise for a not-so-important task done well. All can contribute to a critical motivator: self-esteem.

Self-Esteem

Self-esteem involves self-confidence, a feeling of self-worth. As individual tasks are successfully accomplished, self-esteem builds. A sincere compliment by another person on your ability to perform a task also builds self-esteem. It is law enforcement managers' responsibility to build self-esteem in their team. The more self-esteem individuals in the agency have, the higher the organizational esteem will be. Leonard (1997, p. 15) asserts: "An employee's job satisfaction is directly linked to individual recognition and positive reinforcement for work done well. Continued lack of recognition can have deteriorating effects on personnel and, in turn, on the department."

Recall Maslow's hierarchy of needs and, specifically, the fourth level labeled "Esteem." Leonard (p. 15) notes: "At this level, individuals need to be seen as people of worth by others; they search for recognition, status, prestige, and praise." Unfortunately, many supervisors fail to sufficiently praise their subordinates, and, according to Leonard (pp. 15–17), the reasons for the lack of praise are numerous:

- The perceived paperwork nightmare
- Commitment to favorable annual performance
- Spectacular acts belief
- Fear of competition
- Jealousy
- Lack of interpersonal communication skills

Officers with low self-esteem will perform low-level work. If they have been told they are incompetent, they probably will not perform well. This has been referred to as **self-fulfilling prophecy.** People tend to behave and eventually become what they think others expect of them. Law enforcement managers need to apply the implications of the self-fulfilling prophecy to everyday employee/law enforcement task performance. As Leonard (p. 18) states: "If supervisors praise deserving employees, they will reap the benefits of highly motivated individuals performing their duties as best they can." Coates (1998) notes: "Your self-concept depends on what you do and what you're called. . . . Many people would rather have a prestigious title than money, probably because a title boosts job satisfaction." As one poster reads: "Every job is a self-portrait of the person who did it. Autograph your work with excellence."

Officers' perceptions of themselves and other people will directly influence how the officers conduct themselves in public. This is important because law enforcement is a "people" profession. Officers' attitudes directly influence how they handle other people. Officers with low self-esteem are overly concerned with themselves because they fear failure and know they are not functioning as well as they should.

Managers can build individual self-esteem in the following ways:

- Do not embarrass subordinates, especially in front of others.
- Recognize and build on individual accomplishments.
- Give praise for things done well at the same time as you give criticism for things not well done.
- Give personal attention.
- Ask employees' opinions on problems.
- If an employee gives an opinion or suggestion, act on it in some way. Do not ignore it.
- Help individuals to develop to their potential.
- Give employees breathing room for ideas, creativity and innovation.
- Give special task assignments.
- Get to know them as individuals.

- Give certificates of appreciation when deserved.
- Truly listen.
- If employees express an idea, write it down in their presence.
- If someone has complimented an officer, pass it on.
- Assign part of the next departmental meeting to different officers.
- Share important information. Let everyone be "in the know."
- Acquire a new piece of equipment that will help officers do a better job.

A Feeling of Importance

Managers must let their subordinates know they count. One manager used the following memo to let his employees know how valuable they were:

"You Arx A Kxy Pxrson" Xvxn though my typxwritxr is an old modxl, it works vxry wxll—xxcxpt for onx kxy. You would think that with all thx othxr kxys functioning propxrly, onx kxy not working would hardly bx noticxd; but just onx kxy out of whack sxxms to ruin thx wholx xffort.

You may say to yoursxlf—"Wxll I'm only onx pxrson. No onx will noticx if I don't do my bxst." But it doxs makx a diffxrxncx bxcausx to bx xffxctivx an organization nxxds activx participation by xvxry onx to thx bxst of his or hxr ability.

So thx nxxt timx you think you arx not important, rxmxmbxr my old typxwritxr. You arx a kxy pxrson.

(*Pasadena Weekly Journal of Business,* 155 S. El Molino Ave., Suite 101, Pasadena, CA 91101. Reprinted by permission.)

One of the best ways managers and supervisors can let their people know they are important is to *listen* to them. Chapter 3 emphasized the role listening plays in communication. Law enforcement managers who truly listen to their subordinates will learn a great deal about their needs and feelings. The more managers know about their officers and their needs, the more they can help them meet those needs.

The more managers concentrate on the person talking to them, the more they show how much they value that person. Psychiatrists usually spend most of a patient's time listening. They understand this primary need of the patient to unburden, to let it all out. At the same time they learn a tremendous amount of information about the patient.

Effective listening is an *active* form of communication. You must work at it. Physically show your attentiveness. Ask questions. Clarify. Take notes. Keep eye contact. If you do not believe that listening is active, the next time someone tries to tell you something, do not pay attention, excuse yourself and start to make a phone call, or simply look away from the person, in no way encouraging them to continue the conversation. The person will immediately be able to tell that you are not interested.

Being Involved, Included and "in" on Things

The importance of participative management has been discussed. The more employees feel a part of a department the harder—and better—they will work. To establish and maintain involvement, use a team approach and encourage suggestions.

Effective supervisors listen to their subordinates, letting them express their opinions and making them feel their input is of value.

What Is Really Motivational?

Citing a Gallup Poll survey conducted over a 25-year period of a million employees as to what motivates people at work, McDonald (1999, p. 31) states: "What really makes the difference to people is an *immediate* boss who interacts well with them on a daily basis." To become a great boss and inspire your employees, McDonald suggests:

- Build on their strengths.
- Give them direction and tools.
- Catch them doing the right things.

McDonald also quotes a motivational revelation from *First, Break All the Rules: What the World's Greatest Managers Do Differently,* by Buckingham and Coffman (Simon and Schuster, 1999): "It's better to work for a great manager in an old-fashioned company than for a terrible manager in a company offering an enlightened, employee-focused culture."

Recognizing the uniqueness of individuals, Fulton (1999, p. 94) states: "Each individual is motivated by individual special needs," including:

- The need for affiliation.
- The need for power—these individuals are a competent commander's dream and an incompetent commander's nightmare. Successful commanders recognize that these individuals are future commanders or informal leaders.
- The need for autonomy.
- The need for equity.
- The need to achieve—these are generally your best and most dedicated individuals who are upwardly mobile and seek promotions. It is up to you to cultivate these individuals and help them grow.

Study after study highlights the importance of the job, of doing things of value, of accomplishing worthwhile tasks and of growing and developing. Research by Zhao, Thurman and He (1999, pp. 167–168) revealed:

> Work environment is an essential feature of police officers' job satisfaction. . . .
>
> Police officers' satisfaction with work is associated positively with their perceptions about the importance and significance of their work, the recognition they receive, their autonomy, and the capability to do their work. . . .
>
> Police officers like to work in an environment where they enjoy considerable freedom to decide what they will do.

Dr. Douglas Heath, professor at Haverford College, looked at motivators beyond those provided by the job in what he called "Whole Person" motivation. Dr. Heath has surveyed thousands of people across the country about the most commonly held hopes, goals and achievements. He has his audiences rate from 1 to 12 the following hopes and goals adults have for their lives:

- Leadership/power
- Happy marital relationship
- High income
- Being a competent parent
- Psychological maturity
- Self-fulfillment/happiness
- Ethical sensitivity/idealism
- Fulfilling sexual mate
- Competence in a vocation
- Contributing citizen to community/nation
- A close, same-sexed friend
- Good physical health

You may want to rate them yourself before reading the results of Heath's research.

According to Heath, the seven highest goals were, going from most to least important: self-fulfillment/happiness, good physical health, psychological maturity, happy marital relationship, ethical sensitivity/idealism, competence in a satisfying vocation and satisfaction in being a competent parent. Clearly, managers should be concerned with more than strictly job-related factors when considering what will motivate their subordinates.

Managers need to know what might be motivational for their employees or "what makes a person tick."

The Law Enforcement Career as a Motivator

Law enforcement work itself can be a motivator. Many officers find that law enforcement tasks, in and of themselves, are a basis for self-motivation. When a law enforcement applicant appears before an interviewing board and is asked, "Why do you want to be a law enforcement officer?" the answer is invariably a variation of "Because I like to work with people," or "I want to provide a service, and I think law enforcement work is an opportunity to do that."

Law enforcement entails a great variety of skills: handling an automobile, using weapons, conversing with all types of people, interviewing and interrogating, using computers and computerized information, setting up case investigations and so on. Everything law enforcement officers do provides task significance. They have a high degree of autonomy in their decisions and actions. Decisions are often instantaneous and permanent. In addition, their actions are highly visible because of their uniforms. This visibility should provide motivation to do the best possible job at all times.

Personal growth can be achieved by providing opportunities for departmental training, seminars, college classes or public talks to civic organizations and youth groups. These types of job enrichment opportunities can also provide a higher degree of self-motivation and self-control in performing law enforcement tasks in emergencies, without close manager control.

The law enforcement job is generally not perceived as boring and routine. If it becomes that way, it is generally the officer's fault because ample opportunities exist to make it more exciting. Even routine foot and vehicle patrol should not be boring. Many exciting things happen on a shift or at least have the potential for happening.

The importance of interesting work is illustrated by the story of a man visiting Mexico who found in a little shop a very comfortable, attractive, reasonably priced handcrafted chair. Extremely pleased, the tourist asked the shop manager if he could make him a dozen chairs just like it. The Mexican nodded and, obviously displeased, said, "But the señor knows that I must charge much more for each such chair."

The tourist, astonished, exclaimed, "More? In the United States if you buy in quantity, you pay less. Why do you want to charge me more?"

The reply, "Because it is so dull to make twelve chairs all the same."

Managers should make the law enforcement job itself more interesting and challenging for officers, provide goals, make challenges out of routine work and make contests among employees. Law enforcement tasks can be studied and made more interesting. Assignments can be made more efficiently and with greater variety to make the total job more satisfying. COPPS certainly offers the opportunity to make a difference.

Giving more responsibility, providing opportunity for employees to perform the job without being directly told what to do, treating each employee according to his or her own needs—these actions are motivating.

Law enforcement work can be made more interesting and motivating in three important ways:

- Job rotation
- Job enlargement
- Job enrichment

Job Rotation

Job rotation can make the job more challenging. Job rotation also serves as a training opportunity and provides variety—an opportunity to understand the total law enforcement job. Different things happen on the day shift than on the night shift or middle shift. Job tasks are different in the patrol, detective, juvenile, narcotics and administrative divisions.

Job rotation is often done on a temporary basis. Such cross-training not only provides a better understanding of the total law enforcement effort but also gives supervisors more flexibility to deal with absences and requests for vacations. Job rotation also prepares officers for promotions and can serve as a motivator as such officers begin to feel competent doing new and different tasks.

Job Enlargement

Giving additional responsibilities, such as making a survey of vehicle licenses to determine the number of outsiders in the community, can add to routine patrol and provide helpful information for the department, other departments or the community. Increasing the number of tasks to do may be perceived as a threat. Given the right training and tools, officers should perceive **job enlargement** as motivating, giving them renewed interest in and enthusiasm for law enforcement work.

Job Enrichment

Job enrichment is similar to job enlargement, except that in job enrichment the focus is the quality of the new jobs assigned rather than the quantity. Job enrichment emphasizes adding variety, deeper personal interest and involvement, increased responsibility and greater autonomy. Job enrichment is appropriate for any highly routine job.

For some officers, however, job enrichment might also be perceived as threatening. Some officers do not want enrichment. They do not need more challenges because they may already be working to capacity. They may be comfortable in their routine, or they may be burned out.

Not all officers will want to do all law enforcement tasks. Maybe they are satisfied with routine tasks. The lower level of tasks may satisfy their needs of security, money and group belonging. Even if given the opportunity, they may decide they like one division more than another. Not all officers want promotions. They would rather be responsible for only what they do, not for getting results from other people.

Benefits of Motivated Personnel

The benefits of having highly motivated personnel are numerous—less sick leave, better coverage, more arrests and better investigations. In fact, most of the numerous benefits listed in Chapter 9 as resulting from an effective training program would also result from effective motivation. With both effective training and motivational programs, these benefits are highly probable. The key, according to McDonald (1998, p. 28) is to motivate employees to manage themselves: "Smart managers . . . don't try to motivate their employees. Instead they create environments where people choose to motivate themselves." McDonald (p. 28) lists four ways to become this "new breed of environmental manager:"

- Lay out the big picture.
- Encourage your people to be leaders.
- Be tolerant of mistakes.
- Give personal feedback.

McDonald (p. 28) concludes by noting: "American Express recently asked American workers how they wanted to be rewarded for doing a good job: 46 percent said the reward they most wanted is personal feedback; 32 percent chose financial rewards and only 3 percent selected small gifts. Personal feedback is the least expensive, most effective way to reward today's employees."

The price of not paying attention to motivation is often low morale and a generally negative environment.

Morale: An Overview

An office poster designed to inspire employees to greater efforts read: "You can—if you will!" Beneath it, someone had scrawled, "And you're canned if you won't!" Both sayings relate directly to morale and employees' attitudes toward their jobs.

Morale can make or break an individual or an organization. As Napoleon observed, referring to his army: "An army's effectiveness depends on its size, training, experience and morale . . . and morale is worth more than all the other factors combined."

Morale is *always* present. It might be high, low or on an even keel, but it exists perpetually. Management's responsibility is to keep morale as high as possible and to be alert to signs that it may be dropping. The morale of individuals, work units and an entire agency concerns managers and supervisors.

Achieving high morale is a complex challenge, with different problems depending on the size of the department and the leadership style. Even within the same agency, morale, as it relates to job satisfaction, can differ from one position to another.

Morale is somewhat elusive and difficult to define. Individuals and organizations differ greatly, and what would induce high or low morale in one might be the opposite in another. Good or poor morale is generally attributed to individuals, whereas high or low morale characterizes the entire organization.

> **Morale** is a person's or group's state of mind, level of enthusiasm and amount of involvement with work and with life.

Good or high morale is a *can-do* attitude. As Admiral Ben Morrell says: "Morale is when your hands and feet keep on working when your head says it can't be done." The right kind of persistence *does* pay. Coaches stress the importance of that "second effort" in winning games. The willingness to make another try when the first one fails distinguishes the average player and employee from the star. A Chinese proverb proclaims: "The person who says it cannot be done should not interrupt the person doing it."

Douglas MacArthur, the general so instrumental in helping win World War II, might never have gained his status without persistence. When he applied for admission to West Point, he was turned down, not once but twice. He persisted, however, applied a third time, was accepted and marched into history.

Morale can be measured by observing the actions and statements of employees. Are they positive and upbeat? Do people take pride in their work? Are they supportive? Or are they negative? The quality of officers' work will be affected as much by their morale as by their skill. Effective managers know that people's job performance is directly related to how they feel about the job, themselves, their peers, their manager and their agency.

Although an increase in morale will not always increase employees' effectiveness and productivity, it puts employees in the frame of mind to be productive. Given good supervision and good working conditions, employees with high morale will be extremely effective. As Andy Granatelli noted: "When you are making a success of something, it's not work. It's a way of life. You enjoy yourself because you are making your contribution to the world."

Indicators of Morale Problems

Good managers are always alert for changes in work attitudes that may indicate trouble. They might notice sullenness, irritability, indifference, tardiness or increased absenteeism. Among the most common indicators of morale problems are the following:

- Noticeably less positive attitude
- Loss of interest and enthusiasm
- Negativism
- Excessive absenteeism
- Excessive sick leaves
- Longer lunch hours and/or breaks
- Coming in late and leaving early
- Failure to volunteer
- Excessive turnover
- Lack of respect
- Low productivity

- Less attention to personal appearance
- Many grievances and complaints
- Many accidents
- General lack of cooperation

Indicators of low morale include lack of productivity, enthusiasm and cooperation; absenteeism; tardiness; grievances; complaints and excessive turnover.

Managers may recognize these "red flags" in individual officers, or they may be pervasive throughout the department. In the latter case, the manager faces a much greater challenge. A first step is to identify *why* morale might be low. Seldom is the answer simple or singular.

To identify causes of morale problems, some managers distribute a survey that includes questions such as the following (to which respondents answer: strongly disagree, disagree, uncertain, agree or strongly agree):

1. This is a good department to work for.
2. My supervisor understands me.
3. My supervisor listens to my concerns.
4. I have the training I need to do a good job.
5. I have the equipment I need to do a good job.
6. I am proud to be a member of this department.

Such a survey not only helps identify areas that might be causing morale problems but also lets employees communicate their feelings and know that these feelings are important to the department. However, the results of the survey must be *used.* Employees who feel the department is insensitive might use a lack of follow-through to support their contention.

Surveys are not the only way to identify factors contributing to a morale problem. Managers who communicate well with their subordinates can often discover problems simply by having an open-door policy and listening to what people say. The closer managers are to their employees, the easier it will be for them to recognize changes in morale before they become disruptive.

Reasons for Morale Problems

The underlying causes of morale problems are not always easy to determine. Individual morale can be low and the organizational morale high, or the reverse can be true. Some point out that morale is related to happiness and well-being. Others say it is more related to work benefits. Still others believe it is a philosophical problem of self-fulfillment. In general, employees who work toward organizational goals are deemed to have high morale, and those who do not are deemed to have low morale.

If a law enforcement agency has inadequate, nonequitable salaries and fringe benefits, lacks modern equipment and does not provide adequate resources, morale is likely to be low. Measures must be taken to correct these inadequacies. If all these factors *are* met and morale is still low, the problem is probably centered in individual needs.

Causes for low morale include job dissatisfaction and failure to meet important individual needs.

One important cause of low morale is job dissatisfaction. Among the job-related factors contributing to low morale are lack of administrative support; ineffective supervision; lack of necessary equipment or training to perform effectively; lack of promotion opportunities; political interference; corruption within the department; the criminal justice system itself, which may appear to be a "revolving door" for criminals; and the image of the police frequently portrayed by the media.

In addition, police wages and salaries have never been high, although the total benefit package and sense of job security have always made the job desirable. Given that police endure a high level of stress, most certainly face an abnormal risk of injury or death on the job and have a higher rate of burnout than most workers, police positions are underpaid.

When individual morale is low, employees should first examine themselves. Mental attitudes toward superiors, fellow workers and the public have a great deal to do with job satisfaction.

Perception, the angle from which people view things, makes a tremendous difference in what they see. For example, the difference between a cute little mischief-maker and a juvenile delinquent is whether the child is yours or someone else's.

A story about a young couple who opened their own salmon cannery in Alaska also illustrates this point. They were having a hard time selling their salmon, despite an extensive advertising campaign. The problem was that their salmon was grey, not the pink salmon customers were used to. They pondered the problem for several days and then had a brainstorm. They changed the can's label, putting in bold letters right under the brand name "The only salmon guaranteed not to turn pink in the can." It worked.

A similar situation exists in how subordinates rate certain job factors and how managers rate the same factors. Consider the survey results summarized in Table 10.1. Full appreciation of work done and feeling "in" on things led the workers' list. These same factors were at the bottom of the supervisors' ratings. Similarly, good wages were at the top of the supervisors' list and in the middle of the workers' list. Such information is critical for managers to know.

For those who firmly believe in Abraham Maslow's "hierarchy of needs," it may be time to check the employees' needs for affiliation, achievement and self-actualization.

Table 10.1
Worker and Supervisor Ratings Compared

Job Conditions	Worker Rating	Supervisor Rating
Full appreciation of work done	1	8
Feeling "in" on things	2	10
Sympathetic help on personal problems	3	9
Job security	4	2
Good wages	5	1
"Work that keeps you interested"	6	5
Promotion and growth in company	7	3
Personal loyalty to workers	8	6
Good working conditions	9	4
Tactful disciplining	10	7

Source: William B. Melincoe and John P. Peper. *Supervisory Personnel Development*. California State Police Officers Training Series, #76, Sacramento, CA, p. 87.

Building Morale

The individual most able to raise or lower individual and department morale is the manager/supervisor.

Improving morale requires certain attitudes on the manager's part. First, managers must believe that subordinates *can* grow and change—they can improve their attitudes/morale given the right circumstances. Managers must be like the tailor, who, according to George Bernard Shaw, is the "only person who behaves sensibly because he takes new measurements every time he sees me."

Second, managers must be open and honest with their subordinates, treat them with respect and seek to understand them. Managers cannot expect to see eye to eye with someone they are looking down on.

Finally, managers must understand themselves. They must recognize their own prejudices, their own strengths and weaknesses, their own obstacles to high morale and their critical role as a model for others.

The story is told of the Reverend Billy Graham visiting a small town and asking a young boy how to get to the post office. After receiving directions, Dr. Graham invited the young lad to come to the church and hear him explain to the townsfolk how to get to heaven. The boy declined, saying, "I don't think so. You don't even know how to get to the post office."

Credibility is critical. Managers who seek to build morale must exhibit high morale themselves. Only then can they hope to raise the work unit's morale. Several options for morale building are available to managers and supervisors.

Options for building morale include:

- Being positive and upbeat.
- Setting clear, meaningful goals and objectives.
- Setting appropriate standards.

- Being fair.
- Making no promises that cannot be kept.
- Providing the necessary resources.
- Developing organizational and personal pride.
- Providing a sense of participation—teamwork.
- Treating each person as an individual.
- Giving deserved recognition.
- Criticizing tactfully.
- Avoiding the "boss" attitude.
- Communicating effectively.
- Accepting what cannot be changed.

Be Positive and Upbeat

People enjoy working with a boss who is cheerful and optimistic. Like magnets, people are drawn to the positive and repelled by the negative. An upbeat attitude is contagious—as is a negative attitude. A shoe manufacturer recently ran an ad on slippers that read: "Keeps your feet from getting cold." The ad was a total flop. When the copy was changed to read "Keeps your feet warm and comfortable," sales doubled.

Set Clear, Meaningful Goals and Objectives

You have heard it before, but goals and objectives are at the heart of most management areas, and this certainly includes morale.

Companies with the least employee turnover and the highest morale are those that have successfully communicated the company's mission and goals. Law enforcement executive managers should set department goals and objectives with the input of their subordinates—and this includes the line officers.

The moment officers get the feeling they are not sharing in the department's goals, in what is going on, morale will drop, productivity will decrease and serious problems will arise. A dangerous morale problem can develop when one or more law enforcement employees are united in a goal not aligned with stated department goals.

Set Appropriate Standards

Reasonable, clear, fair employee standards for conduct and behavior should be established, published and made known. Employees expect this, and the law enforcement organization cannot function without these standards.

Be Fair

As obvious as it may sound, it is critical that managers be fair in all aspects of the job. Most employees do not mind reasonably strict rules and procedures if they make sense and apply equally to everyone. Fairness is a common denominator for increased employee morale.

Make No Promises That Cannot Be Kept

Promises are like money—easier made than kept. Managers should never promise things they cannot deliver. They should not be overly optimistic, trying to please their subordinates or telling them what they want to hear simply to keep them happy. It is very tempting to do so and to hope that things will work out for the best, but this can lead to problems.

Provide the Necessary Resources

Law enforcement employees need resources to do a good job and to feel good about themselves and what they do. Training is critical. All employees need to feel competent in the tasks for which they are responsible. Training also needs to be ongoing so officers are up to date. Their equipment should also be current and in good working condition.

The appearance of the station, the squad cars, the insignia on the squad car door, identification or name signs on each room in the station, desk name signs, uniforms that leave a favorable impression—all reflect morale. Many of these do not cost lots of money but can make a significant difference in how officers feel about themselves and their organization.

Develop Organizational and Personal Pride

Organizational and personal pride are closely related. Employees like to work for an organization they can be proud of. All law enforcement organizations have individual identities based largely on management goals and objectives. Bring up the subject of department and personal pride at staff and department meetings. Do not just think you are the best; really work at being the best. Often, competing in intradepartmental competitions, such as sharpshooting or physical fitness, or intradepartmental sports can contribute to a feeling of pride. These can also foster a sense of participation, another factor contributing to high morale.

Provide a Sense of Participation— Teamwork

Employees like to be in on things. They like to feel that what they do counts. They want to be part of the action. Participation does not mean a brainstorming session or a debate every time change is needed, but there should be opportunity for employee input.

If employees express good ideas, praise them. If an idea is not workable, explain why. Do not ask for input and then be negative about the ideas expressed.

Get everyone pulling together. The philosophy of Coach Bear Bryant is typically included in texts and speeches on morale building. According to Coach Bryant:

> I'm just a plowhand from Arkansas, but I have learned how to hold a team together. How to lift some men up, how to calm down others, until finally they've got one heartbeat together, a team. There's just three things I'd ever say:
>
> If anything goes bad, I did it.
> If anything goes semi-good, then we did it.
> If anything goes real good, then you did it.
>
> That's all it takes to get people to win football games for you.

A much less publicized story about teamwork involves the former president of United Air Lines, W. A. "Pat" Patterson. When Patterson became president of United, he made a point of getting to know all his people, calling them by first name, listening to their concerns, hopes and dreams. He made the employees feel the company was theirs, and he maintained a strict open-door policy.

One winter during the recession two pilots came to Patterson and said they wanted to discuss wages. Expecting the pilots to ask for a raise, Patterson was deeply touched when, instead, the pilots said that the entire staff wanted to take a voluntary 10 percent pay cut to see the company through the hard times.

Patterson thanked them but said that would be the last thing he would consider. Noting that a 10 percent pay cut would save United about $300,000 a year, he suggested they might save that much by eliminating waste. The two pilots quickly passed the word that Patterson refused to cut wages but suggested they organize a drive against waste in effort and materials. It worked. United made it through the recession without laying off a single employee or cutting wages.

Treat Each Person as an Individual

Despite an emphasis on teamwork, every employee is an individual and must be recognized as such. Call them by the name they prefer to be called, including nicknames in appropriate situations.

Take an interest in their problems. Employees who have problems at home cannot function at full efficiency on the job. Although managers cannot usually *do* anything about such problems, they can lend a sympathetic ear.

Give Deserved Recognition

Too many law enforcement managers criticize when things go wrong but fail to praise when things go right. This is illustrated in the story about the first month of World War I, when generals were handling huge armies under unprecedented circumstances. On the Western front, the Battle of the Marne ended the German advance, stabilized the front and saved France. Leading the French armies was Marshal Joffre, a soldier viewed by most as unimaginative. Years later when the battle was analyzed, military commentators tried to decide who should receive credit for this decisive victory. The commentators could come to no agreement other than that surely some general had made a crucial move at the correct moment. They decided to ask Marshal Joffre who was responsible.

Joffre's reply was: "I really don't know who ought to get credit for the victory at the Marne. I know only one thing. If we had been defeated, everyone would have agreed at once that the fault was mine."

Show judgment in giving credit and praise. It can be carried to extremes so that subordinates come to rely on it for every task they complete. Such people are like the little boy who said to his dad, "Let's play darts. I'll throw and you say 'Wonderful.' "

Criticize Tactfully

Tact has several definitions, including the following:

- The knack of making a point without making an enemy
- Telling someone he or she has an open mind when you really mean he or she has a hole in the head
- The ability to hammer home a point without hitting the person over the head
- The art of building a fire under people without making their blood boil

A wise manager once said, "That criticism is best which sounds like an explanation." It is easy to be critical. The real management challenge is to come up with constructive alternatives. Several other considerations are important when criticism is necessary.

- Be certain of the facts. Do not "make mountains out of molehills."
- Correct in private (praise in public). Former hockey goalie Jacques Plante was quoted as saying: "How would you like a job where, if you made a mistake, a big red light goes on and 18,000 people boo?"
- Be objective and impersonal. Do not compare one officer unfavorably to another.
- Ask questions; do not accuse. Allow those you are correcting to explain themselves.
- Focus on the action that needs correcting, not on the individual officer. Emphasize what is to be done, not what is wrong.

The legitimate purpose of criticism is *not* to humiliate but to help subordinates do better next time. Remember that criticism is seldom as effective as praise in changing behavior. Before managers give a person a "kick in the pants," no matter how much it is deserved, they should raise their sights and *try* to give a pat on the back instead.

Avoid the "Boss" Attitude

Managers should strive to be friendly, yet businesslike, to think of "We" instead of "I." They should encourage expression of opinion while avoiding ridicule or sarcasm. When appropriate, smile and be enthusiastic.

Communicate Effectively

Communication builds morale. Employees want to know what is going on and how they are doing. Employees cannot act or react in a vacuum. Department newsletters, letters of commendation, constructive criticism, news releases, department bulletin boards, personal conversations, department or staff meetings—all are forms of communication.

It is demoralizing for officers to hear "inside information" from news media rather than from their superiors. It is essential that police administrators keep their officers informed. Among the ways to do this are newsletters, attending roll call, going on ride-alongs and simply walking around the department (sometimes referred to as Management by Walking Around [MBWA]). Administrators who take this approach should be prepared to hear negative comments, especially at first.

Individual department members have a responsibility to bring morale problems to the attention of management, and management in turn has an obligation to respond. The fastest way to kill rumors or innuendos is to tell the truth. Employees should like their work, their fellow employees and themselves. Problems should be discussed openly, not whispered behind management's back.

Accept What Cannot Be Changed

Much of job satisfaction comes from accepting what cannot be changed. Such acceptance makes life easier for all and greatly lessens personal stress and tension.

A law enforcement department is not like Cape Canaveral. It cannot anticipate a time when all systems will be "GO." Alcoholics Anonymous' Serenity Prayer says: "Change what is possible; live with what cannot be changed." Managers must help subordinates to know their limitations and to realize that no two situations will be identical.

Promotions and Morale

Management positions within the law enforcement profession are more limited than in almost any other profession. This can cause severe morale problems. The promotion process must be fair, and those who want promotions must be helped in their quest. According to McCormack (1999, p. D2):

> If a manager doesn't handle a promotion with equal sensitivity to all the parties involved—the rewarded as well as the passed over—the promotion could end up backfiring. People could leave the organization in anger, or take sides against the newly promoted. The fallout could be disruptive. . . .
>
>   Having some clear criteria for who gets the promotion can minimize this . . . :
>
> - Which of the candidates can you least afford to lose? The fallacy here is that the promotion doesn't always go to the best person for the job but rather to the one who is most willing to jump ship if not promoted. . . .
> - Who has the best track record? This is the most objective criterion. . . . The fallacy here is that the skills that help someone excel at Job A are not always transferable to Job B. . . .
> - Who will offend the fewest people? This turns the promotion into a popularity contest. . . .The big problem here, of course, is that you are turning your responsibility into a group decision. . . .
> - Who do you think can do the job? . . . This is inherently arbitrary, but you can make the contest a little more fair by letting the candidates make their case to you.

Not everyone is management material. Those who are not should be guided into seeking satisfaction on the job in other ways, perhaps in developing a specialty the agency needs. The future of law enforcement agencies rests in making the best use of personnel. Those who are best suited for management— who have leadership qualities and communication skills—are those who should be promoted.

Promotions must be fair and based on management qualities, not on technical skills or seniority.

Written examinations have been the most frequently used technique to make promotional selections of mid- to lower-level police positions. Any examination should be validated for the type and size of the agency using it. Written examinations, oral examinations and on-the-job performance ratings can be used for promotional positions.

Most law enforcement agencies use a civil service examination, both written and oral. It is common to require minimum or maximum ages, terms of service, specific types of experience and other criteria for eligibility to take the examination. Most merit systems provide similar examinations. Final selection of the top three candidates (or any preestablished number) is made from the written and oral examination. The Civil Service Commission, the city manager, the mayor with the city council's approval or the law enforcement chief executive officer then makes the choice.

A trend is to use an **assessment center** to select those eligible for promotion, especially at the upper levels. Examples of the methods used in assessment

This officers beams as he is greeted by a fellow Kentucky State Police officer after their promotions in Frankfort, Kentucky. He was promoted to the rank of Major, becoming the first black Major on the force.

centers are contained in Table 10.2. The total assessment typically is organized into three phases.

Assessment centers use three phases:

1. Testing: written examination, verbal screening and psychological testing
2. Oral board interview, situational testing, leaderless group discussion and individual psychological interview
3. Polygraph examination, background check, physical examination and officer/staff interviews

During the second phase, candidates confront hypothetical problems that managers typically encounter. At the end of the second phase, candidates are ranked using the information from the first two phases. A predetermined number are selected in rank order to complete the third phase. As Hutton and Sampson (1999, p. 79) note:

> When assessment centres are used to select personnel, the content (syllabus) and context (scenarios) can be very effective at changing behaviour. Candidates about to undergo an assessment centre will demand knowledge about the areas on which they are to be assessed, training in those areas and the opportunity to develop the relevant skills in their workplace before the assessment process. . . . If you tell 100 candidates for a management assessment centre that they will encounter an exercise on racism in the workplace, then—irrespective of the individual outcomes of the assessment—you end up with 100 managers who know much more about racism in the workplace that they did before!

Whether an assessment center is used or the promotions are done in house, whenever possible it is usually best to promote from within the agency. This is

Table 10.2 **Typical Management Assessment Center Methods**	Method	Description	Example Traits Analyzed
	Management game or simulation	Participants perform in a simulated setting, sometimes with a computer simulation, make necessary decisions and analyze the results.	Organizing ability, financial aptitude, decision making, efficiency under stress, adaptability and leadership capacity
	Leaderless group discussions	Participants in a group with no formally appointed leader are asked to solve a business problem.	Aggressiveness, persuasiveness, verbal skills, flexibility and self-confidence
	In-basket exercise	A mail in-basket for an ill executive is given to the participants to analyze, to set priorities and to take action on.	Organizing ability, decision making under stress, conceptual skills, ability to delegate and concern for others
	Role playing	Participants are asked to take the roles of hypothetical employees, as in a performance evaluation interview.	Insight, empathy to others, human and technical skills and sensitivity to others
	Psychological testing	A series of pencil-and-paper instruments is completed by the participants.	Reasoning, interests, aptitudes, communication tendencies, leadership and group styles, motivation profile and the like
	Case analysis	Participants are given a case to analyze individually and present to a group of evaluators.	Verbal ability, diagnostic skills, conceptual skills, technical skills and so on
	In-depth interviews	Participants are interviewed by raters—usually after some of the above exercises have been completed—regarding a variety of personal interests, skills and aptitudes.	Verbal ability, self-confidence, managerial skills, commitment to career and so on

Source: International City Managers Association, 1120 G Street, NW, Washington, DC, p. 253. Reprinted by permission.

not always easy. Sometimes this decision is not up to the immediate supervisor or manager. But studies and common sense show that passing over qualified personnel to bring in an outsider almost invariably erodes morale.

When possible, promote from within.

Seeing colleagues receive a promotion can be highly motivating for those who also want to be promoted.

Incentive Programs

How do incentive programs fit into efforts to keep morale high? Most do *not*. Surprising as this may sound, most **incentive programs** should be used to *motivate*, not to build morale.

In the late 1980s the Anne Arundel County Police Department undertook a study to determine whether monetary incentives in a field training program built morale. Here is what they learned (Johnson and Cheatwood, 1992, p. 36): "The financial incentive used . . . produced as many unforeseen problems as benefits. By itself, money is not enough to ensure long-term commitment or even short-term reliability." Johnson and Cheatwood (p. 36) offer the following suggestions for avoiding the problems the Arundel County Police Department encountered with their field training program:

1. Tap into the esprit de corps of your subordinates and peers.
2. Interview each potential candidate and clearly identify what is expected of them and what they can expect from you. Secure a commitment.
3. Be honest with FTOs about their removal from the program should substandard work be detected.
4. Attach a special significance to the FTO position by using them as a control group to test new procedures and equipment.
5. Use the program to identify quality personnel in the field.

Sometimes, however, particularly if pay is not especially competitive, non-monetary incentives can help raise morale. Managers can rebuild pride by emphasizing the nonmonetary incentives the department offers. *Accentuate the positive,* offer what you provide, not what you cannot provide.

> Incentives that might be publicized include benefits, vacation and sick-time policies, workstation review, performance appraisals, job classification and education.

Benefits

Often employees have no idea what their benefit package contains—or its monetary value. To make employees aware of their benefits, newsletter articles might cover one specific area each issue.

Sometimes a comparison with the past makes personnel more appreciative of their job. In the 1940s and early 1950s, it was common for law enforcement officers to work ten-hour days, six days a week, at a monthly salary of $150 to $200. Police chiefs of communities up to 35,000 were being paid $300 monthly. A one-week vacation was standard. Medical insurance benefits, sick leave, workers' compensation and early retirement plans were nonexistent. The situation has certainly improved since then.

Gradually fringe benefits and extrinsic rewards have begun to accrue. Early retirement and pension plans are now universal. Many law enforcement officers take early retirement and have a second part-time or full-time career. Government payment of medical insurance programs (medical, disability, eyeglasses and dental) is the norm, although cutback budgeting is beginning to threaten some of these benefits. Overtime pay, life insurance, paid vacations and sick leave, increased opportunity for promotion, paid educational seminars and other perks are also common. In the 1950s the benefit package was equal to 25 percent of the total payroll cost, whereas in the 1990s it had risen to 38 percent and more.

Vacation and Sick-Time Policies	These policies can be reviewed and compared with what is offered by comparable professions. An additional personal leave day might be added, or additional vacation time could be provided after a given number of years of service.
Workstation Review	The work environment can have a great impact on morale. People appreciate working in a clean, attractive and healthy environment. A local florist might be approached to donate some plants to brighten up the offices. Seasonal decorations can help add to appropriate holiday spirit. Attractive artwork can liven up otherwise drab hallways. Interested employees might want to form a committee, organize a garage sale to raise money and decorate certain areas of the department according to a planned schedule. The options are limitless.
Performance Appraisal	Performance appraisals serve two functions. They let employees know how they are doing so they can continue doing what is effective and make improvements on what is not so effective. They also provide management a tool for meaningful praise and recognition. One way to make performance appraisal more systematic is to develop an appraisal form. Managers might want to have employees complete the form themselves and then compare their answers with how the manager responds. Performance appraisals are discussed in depth in Chapter 16.
Job Classification	Job classifications are built into most law enforcement departments. Officers know who is above and who is below them. Seniority often plays a role also. If salary structure is coordinated with job classification and seniority and combined with performance appraisals, salaries can be equitably raised.
Education	The importance of training has already been stressed. Law enforcement agencies might go further than job-related training, however, and provide opportunities (and perhaps pay) for employees to obtain college or university degrees or specialist certificates in various areas.
Police/Family Programs	The police career is difficult to keep separate from officers' personal lives. Tasks and experiences are often intermixed with family well-being. Job stress is often family stress. Traumatic experiences do not end with the termination of the shift or on arrival home. Incidents that result in shooting a suspect or end with an officer being injured or killed on duty are endured by the family as well as by the officer. Police family members often have no more understanding of the police job than the average layperson. To compound the problem, police spouses often have careers in addition to family responsibilities. The officers' daily interactions with the seamy side of life and with problem people may cause a distorted, unbalanced view of society. In severe cases this can lead to alcoholism, drug abuse, separation, divorce or even suicide.

To cope with these problems, a number of police departments have experimented with police-spouse seminars to explain work shifts, police jargon, salaries, fringe benefits, types of police incidents, types of people police come in contact with, police equipment, police training and panel discussions on selected subjects, with the panel consisting of officers, spouses and experts on the subject. Expectations and fears of officers and their spouses are discussed freely. Spouses often form support groups that meet regularly or when a crisis arises.

An Innovative Program for Maintaining Veteran Officers' Morale

Promotions are extremely hard to come by in law enforcement, and many officers do not want them, preferring to drive a squad car rather than sit behind a desk. Administrators are often faced with the difficult task of keeping morale high for patrol officers who have been on the job for several years. One innovative approach to this challenge was developed by the Pierce County Sheriff's Department in Tacoma, Washington—the Master Patrol Officer Program (MPO). This program has three distinct phases: the Entry level, the Advanced Patrol Officer level and the Master Patrol Officer level. Table 10.3 describes the requirements for each. The Master Patrol Officer point system gives credit for education, experience and involvement in law enforcement service or in the community. Table 10.4 gives the highlights of the Master Patrol Officer point system. Physical recognition of Master Patrol Officer status is provided by double chevrons or corporal stripes worn by MPOs.

Morale and Integrity

Brown (1998, p. 3) notes: "An independent study conducted by the National Institute of Ethics found that the average time when an officer becomes involved in unethical activities is 7.2 years." He (pp. 63–64) continues:

> Morale and integrity share a common space. Many of the reasons why departments suffer from low morale are the same that cause unethical activity, i.e., low compensation, lack of appreciation, apathy, inadequate leadership, etc. . . .
>
> If a system is in place to develop officers to be better individuals, they would be less inclined to suffer low morale and less likely to engage in unethical activities. . . .
>
> Police agencies with high morale make for a win-win situation. Management benefits by having its goals realized, which enhances public confidence in its police department. Individual officers do not fall prey to the evils of domestic violence, drug and alcohol abuse, stress and suicide. Society benefits by being protected by officers who feel good about the job and [are] not merely earning a paycheck.

Morale, Motivation and COPPS

One benefit often attributed to community-oriented policing and problem solving is that officers are more motivated and morale is heightened. This is a result of officers feeling they are indeed making a significant difference in the community. Officers in departments embracing COPPS report greater job satisfaction. Some officers, however, find this approach to policing to be "soft on

Table 10.3
MPO Requirements of the Pierce County Sheriff's Department (Tacoma, Washington)

Phase I

Entry Level Requirements

1. Three years as a Deputy Sheriff with the Pierce County Sheriff's Department.
2. Last two evaluations must have a total score of 70 or better. A current evaluation from within the last 12 months must be provided.
3. Candidates must apply with a typewritten letter which must be endorsed by his/her immediate supervisor.

Phase II

Advance Patrol Officer Requirements

1. A total of six years with the department, 50% of which must have been spent in the field force.
2. Upon completion of the sixth year, a candidate's last two evaluations must be 80 or above with no individual factor below 70.
3. An average shooting score of expert or better while in this phase.
4. At least four points accumulated as an accident-free driver (entry level time included).
5. Three years to complete this phase.

Education:

Sixteen points total required with a minimum of eight points from any approved law enforcement training classes. Points may be accumulated for higher learning achieved prior to coming into the department.

Experience:

Fifteen points total with a minimum of six from specialized support assignments from within the department.

Major involvement:

No points necessary for this segment. However, points may be earned for use in Phase III.

Phase III

Master Patrol Officer Requirements

1. A total of ten years minimum with the department, 70% of which must have been spent in field force patrol (3 years advanced; and 4 years master phase).
2. Accumulate a total of 7 years of accident-free driving points.
3. Shooting scores shall average expert or better during this 4 year phase.
4. Typewritten letter requesting consideration as an MPO and showing that all requirements have been met.
5. Evaluations must be 80% or above with no individual factor below 70%.

Education:

Eight additional points accumulated from law enforcement training classes.

Experience:

Twelve points total with three points required from specialized support assignments within the department.

Major involvement: Six points total.

Paul D. Thrash. "An Incentive Program: Boosting Morale of Veteran Officers." *Law Enforcement Technology,* October 1992, p. 53. © PTN Publishing Co. *Law Enforcement Technology,* October 1992. Reprinted by permission.

**Table 10.4
The MPO Point System**

Education		Major Involvement	
AA degree or 90 quarter hours	4 pts	In House participation or service on:	
BA degree	6 pts	Board of Professional Standards	2 pts per year
MA degree	8 pts	FTO Advisory Board	2 pts per year
PhD degree	10 pts	Accident Review Board	2 pts per year
Approved law enforcement classes	1 pt per 8 hr class	Radio Users Committee	2 pts per year
Mandatory or refresher classes do not receive points. A maximum of four points for a one-week school and eight points for a two-week school.		Special Project Boards or Committee	1 pt per project
		Publish an article in a law enforcement-related magazine or journal	1 pt per article

Experience

Accident-free driving record	1 pt per year
Master shooter (96% and above)	2 pts
No sick leave usage	.5 pt per year
Medal/awards	3 pts per year
Specialized support assignments	3 pts per year (maximum 6 pts)
(K-9, Juvenile, Civil, Traffic, DARE, Warrants, etc.)	
Field Training Officer (FTO)	5 pts per year (maximum of 10)
Assigned responsibilities	2 pts per year (maximum of 6)
(SWAT, Bomb Squad, Dive Team, Search/Rescue)	

Community Involvement

Involvement in any community service project or social service project as a leader or board member.	2 pts per project
a) sports	
b) other civilian non-profit organization	
c) Military Reserve Service	
Involvement as an officer (one year minimum)	2 pts per project
a) union/guild	
b) law enforcement	
c) any statewide or national law enforcement support group approved by the MPO board. Serves as president of any of the above organizations for a minimum of one year	3 pts per office

Source: Paul D. Thrash. "An Incentive Program: Boosting Morale of Veteran Officers." Law Enforcement Technology, October 1992, p. 56. © PTN Publishing Co. Law Enforcement Technology, October 1992. Reprinted by permission.

crime" and see officers committed to COPPS as social workers rather than crime fighters. This can lead to problems within the department and needs to be addressed.

In assessing deputies' views of what constitutes "real police work," Haught (1998, p. 7) found two distinct philosophies: those who saw their jobs as "macho police work," in which officers "had to be so tough they would give their own mother a ticket," and those who saw their jobs as service professions that "went beyond just being tough with law breakers." In applying these observations to how COPPS influences a department's morale, Haught found (p. 7):

> Resistance . . . was a problem commonly faced by departments trying to implement community policing . . . . Many officers who were said to be resistant were actually just trying to figure out what community policing meant in relation to how they were currently doing their jobs. These deputies responded not unlike [anyone] trying to adapt to a new culture. Basically, they were just determining what the differences were and deciding if any of these new strategies really mattered. . . .
>
> Rather than judging staff as resistant, consider that they may be "checking things out." By not assuming that most acts are resistant (read: negative), departments can be more flexible and clear in their implementation.
>
> Sometimes, however, employee resistance is exactly what is stated and more. When it is more, it becomes sabotage. . . . Some supervisors . . . wait until a ranking officer was out of earshot before proceeding to tell their staff "how it's really going to be.". . . It's natural for people to want to maintain their power base. . . .
>
> Many organizations have underestimated community policing's importance to officers and as a result have shortchanged the training and conversations necessary for the philosophy to be fully embraced.

Summary

Motivation is an inner or outer drive to meet a need or goal. Researchers who have studied motivation and proposed theories about it include Maslow, Herzberg, Skinner, Vroom, and Morse and Lorsch.

Maslow's hierarchy of needs is, in the ascending order they need to be met, physiological, safety and security, social, esteem and self-actualization. Herzberg's hygiene factors are tangible rewards that can cause dissatisfaction if lacking. Motivator factors are intangible rewards that can create satisfaction.

Skinner's reinforcement theory suggests that positive reinforcement increases a given behavior and negative reinforcement decreases a given behavior. Positive reinforcement is more effective than negative reinforcement. In addition, the closer in time to the behavior, the more effective the reinforcement will be.

Vroom's expectancy theory suggests that employees will choose the level of effort that matches the performance opportunity for reward. Morse and Lorsch's contingency theory suggests fitting tasks, officers and the agency's goals so that officers can feel competent.

No matter what theory or combination of theories law enforcement managers subscribe to, external and internal rewards are important. Among the most common external motivators or tangible rewards are salary, bonuses, insurance, retirement plans, favorable working conditions, paid vacation and holidays, titles and adequacy of equipment. Internal motivators or intangible rewards include goals, achievement, recognition, self-respect, opportunity for advancement, opportunity to make a contribution and belief in individual and departmental goals. Law enforcement work can be made more interesting and motivating in three important ways: job rotation, job enlargement and job enrichment.

Morale is a person's or group's state of mind, level of enthusiasm and amount of involvement with work and life. Indicators of low morale include lack of productivity, enthusiasm and cooperation; absenteeism; tardiness; grievances; complaints and excessive turnover. Causes of low morale include job dissatisfaction and failure to meet important individual needs.

The individual most able to raise or lower individual and department morale is the manager/supervisor. Options for building morale include being positive and upbeat; setting clear, meaningful goals and objectives; setting appropriate standards; being fair; making no promises that cannot be kept; providing necessary resources; developing organizational and personal pride; providing a sense of participation—teamwork; treating each person as an individual; giving deserved recognition; criticizing tactfully; avoiding the "boss" attitude; communicating effectively and accepting what cannot be changed.

One important factor affecting morale is promotions. Promotions must be fair and based on management qualities, not on technical skills or seniority. Some law enforcement agencies use assessment centers to determine promotions. Such centers typically involve three phases: (1) testing: written examination, verbal screening and psychological testing; (2) oral board interview, situational testing, leaderless group discussion and individual psychological interview and (3) polygraph examination, background check, physical examination and officer/staff interviews. When possible, law enforcement administrators should promote from within to improve overall morale.

Incentives that might be publicized include benefits, vacation and sick-time policies, workstation review, performance appraisals, job classification and education.

Discussion Questions

1. What motivates you?
2. What do you consider your basic needs? Write down the top five.
3. What are five motivators that make you do better work?
4. What would not motivate you?
5. Do you agree or disagree with the following statement: "It is not possible to motivate anyone." Why?
6. What makes *your* on-the-job morale go down? Go up?
7. What are some ways to give personal recognition for a job well done?
8. What job conditions make you feel best?
9. How do morale and motivation interact?
10. If you could make one change in your life that would improve your morale, what would that change be?

InfoTrac College Edition Assignment

Search for a recent article on *what is motivational on the job*—either in the businesss world or in law enforcement. Outline your findings and give the full source. Be prepared to share your findings with the class.

References

Brown, Edward S. "Police Motivational Training: The New Frontier." *Law and Order,* Vol. 46, No. 5, May 1998, pp. 63–65.

Brown, Edward S. "Police Success Development Training 2000." *Law and Order,* Vol. 47, No. 4, April 1999, pp. 112–114.

Coates, Claudia. "What's in a Title? Job Satisfaction, Ego and Self Esteem." (Minneapolis/ St. Paul) *Star Tribune,* July 31, 1998.

Fulton, Roger. "Motivating the Individual." *Law Enforcement Technology,* Vol. 29, No. 9, September 1999, p. 94.

Haught, Lunell. "Meaning, Resistance and Sabotage—Elements of a Police Culture." *Community Policing Exchange,* Phase V, No. 20, May/June 1998, p. 7.

Herzberg, Frederick. "The Human Need for Work." *Industry Week,* July 24, 1978, pp. 49–52.

Hutton, Glenn and Sampson, Fraser. "The Assessment of Potential and the Potential of Assessment." *The Police Chief,* Vol. LXVI, No. 8, August 1999, pp. 79–84.

Johnson, Robert A. and Cheatwood, Derral. "Do Monetary Incentives in a Field Training Program Build Morale?" *The Police Chief,* November 1992, pp. 35–36.

Leonard, Karl S. "In Search of Praise." *FBI Law Enforcement Bulletin,* Vol. 66, No. 4, April 1997, pp. 15–18.

McCormack, Mark. "Promotions Can Create as Much Turmoil as Firings." (Minneapolis/ St. Paul) *Star Tribune,* July 13, 1999, p. D2.

McDonald, Tom. "Beyond Empowerment: How to Motivate People to Manage Themselves." *Successful Meetings,* February 1998, p. 28.

McDonald, Tom. "Peerless Leaders: How to Fire Up the People Who Work for You." *Successful Meetings,* September 1999, p. 31.

Rachlin, Harvey. "Honoring Police Officers." *Law and Order,* Vol. 44, No. 10, October 1996, pp. 83–85.

Swope, Ross E. "Conveying Expectations." *The Police Chief,* Vol. LXV, No. 11, November 1998, pp. 32–34.

Zhao, Jihong; Thurman, Quint; and He, Ni. "Source of Job Satisfaction among Police Officers: A Test of Demographics and Work Environment Models." *Justice Quarterly,* Vol. 16, No. 1, March 1999, pp. 153–173.

Chapter 11 Discipline and Problem Behaviors

I would rather try to persuade a man to go along, because once I have persuaded him, he will stick. If I scare him, he will stay just as long as he is scared, and then he is gone.

—Dwight D. Eisenhower

Do You Know?

- What discipline is?
- How morale and discipline differ?
- What the purpose of discipline is?
- What the foundation for most disciplinary actions is?
- What a fundamental management right is?
- What a primary rule for the timing of discipline is?
- What to consider when assessing penalties?
- What steps are usually involved in progressive discipline?
- What balance of consequences analysis is?
- What consequences are most powerful?
- How managers can use the balance of consequences?
- What the PRICE method consists of?
- How much time effective praise and reprimands require?
- What ratio of praise to blame is usually needed?
- What strokes managers can use?

Can You Define?

appeal
balance of
   consequences
   analysis
comprehensive
   discipline
demotion
disciplinary actions
discipline

dismissal
gunny sack approach
just cause
negative discipline
negligent retention
one-minute managing
positive discipline
PRICE method
progressive discipline

reprimand
self-discipline
stroke approach
summary discipline
summary punishment
suspension
termination

INTRODUCTION

Managers are challenged in the area of discipline as in no other. Values have changed, and court decisions have supported more liberal views of discipline over the past decades. The days of autocratic, despotic discipline are gone.

Imposing some form of discipline is almost sure to be a part of law enforcement managers' responsibilities during their careers. How often and under what circumstances are matters of individual and organizational policy. Managers must be prepared to exercise this responsibility when necessary. Dealing with discipline and problem behaviors is a formidable challenge in an age that emphasizes freedom, rights and victimization.

Workers' jobs are a major portion of their lives. Losing a job because of a disciplinary action is a traumatic experience that seriously affects employees and their families. Yet discipline must be maintained, and few people have not been disciplined at some time. Most people assume that when discipline is discussed, it refers to punishment in its various forms. But discipline is far broader than punishment.

This chapter begins with a definition of discipline, followed by a description of positive, constructive self-discipline and a look at the typical rules and regulations for law enforcement departments. Of importance when considering discipline is the tension between clarity of role and creativity, as well as common problem behaviors you can anticipate.

Next, the need for managers to accept that positive discipline is not always effective and to recognize the need for negative discipline/punishment is examined, including guidelines for administering negative discipline, for using progressive discipline, for using summary punishment and for providing a process to appeal and important legal considerations. This is followed by a discussion of comprehensive discipline, including such systems as the balance of consequences analysis, the PRICE method, one-minute managing and the stroke approach. The chapter concludes with a brief description of an effective disciplinary system.

Discipline Defined

Discipline is training expected to produce a desired behavior—controlled behavior.

Discipline should never be an end in itself. It should be used to develop highly trained, efficient law enforcement officers. Those officers with the highest performance have a high level of determination, pride, confidence and self-discipline. **Self-discipline** is a set of self-imposed rules governing a thinking person's self-control. Leaders throughout the world set degrees of discipline, as do religions. Discipline can be a form of voluntary obedience to instructions, commands or expected demeanor.

Discipline is closely related to morale. As discussed in Chapter 10, morale is a state of mind, an employee's attitude. Discipline, in contrast, is a state of affairs, or how employees act.

Morale is how a person feels; discipline is how a person acts.

Morale and discipline are closely related because the level of morale affects employees' conduct. The higher the morale, the fewer the discipline problems. Conversely, the lower the morale, the more likely discipline problems will erupt.

The purpose of discipline is to promote desired behavior, which may be done by encouraging acceptable behavior or punishing unacceptable behavior.

Although noting that conflict and confrontation are part of the disciplinary process, Field and Meloni (1999, p. 85) also stress: "Discipline, as opposed to punishment, does not hinder an employee's self-esteem. Self-esteem is strengthened when an individual is able to meet appropriate expectations. . . . Discipline supports an officer's integrity and ability to make and keep promises and honor commitments." They also note (p. 85):

> Discipline builds organizational prestige by sustaining effective organizational performance and preserves spirit. Its goal is internal order and individual accountability, with an emphasis upon the discovery of truth and is based upon a solid framework that respects public, agency and employee needs. . . .
>
> A primary focus by a rewards system on good performance has a resultant positive influence on internal discipline. Often, leaders commit disproportionate time and attention to a small group of problematic employees while nominal regard is given to successful employees.

First-line supervisors are the key to law enforcement agencies' discipline. The author (Bennett) was to give a lecture to a class of Chicago Police Department supervisors. Before the lecture, he asked O. W. Wilson, then superintendent of the Chicago Police Department, whether he had anything he would like to pass on to the class. His answer: "Get the first-line manager to accept his responsibility."

Positive, Constructive Self-Discipline

Positive, constructive self-discipline, like self-motivation, is usually most effective. **Positive discipline** uses training to foster compliance with rules and regulations and performance at peak efficiency.

Maintaining Positive Discipline

It is to law enforcement managers' advantage to maintain a high degree of self-discipline within subordinates. They might begin by exercising self-discipline as an example. A second step is training employees and telling them how and why each task is necessary to a specific job. Third, managers should provide a motivating climate in which officers want to perform at top capacity, as discussed in Chapter 10. Fourth, there should be one-on-one discussions of self-discipline and how it benefits both the individual and the organization.

When employees willingly follow the department's rules and regulations and put forth full effort to accomplish their individual and departmental goals, positive discipline prevails. The Navy would call this a "taut ship."

When people feel good about working, discipline problems decrease. Where department esprit de corps exists, discipline is not a major problem. Officers who feel part of a team are not as apt to do things that let other members down. But officers need to know the rules and what is expected of them.

Knowledge of Rules, Regulations and Expected Behaviors

Everybody should understand what they can and cannot do. The more employees know, the more able they are to conduct themselves as expected. As Field and Meloni (p. 85) state: "Discipline helps officers meet expectations and stay within reasonable performance and behavioral limits."

To inform employees, managers might post rules on bulletin boards, distribute Standard Operating Procedure manuals and discuss the rules at meetings. Indeed, as Ellman (1999, p. 146) notes: "Written policies should have two goals: to keep everyone informed about operations and to support the supervisors in enforcing practices and procedures."

> An agency's policy and procedure manual is the foundation on which most discipline must be based.

Ellman adds (p. 147): "Written policies help relieve the feeling of insecurity that many employees sense. Sound policies assure your staff that you run a fair but tight operation. This usually pays off in increased productivity, less turnover and a greater return on your payroll dollars."

Officers should have input on rules. If they have a voice in establishing the rules, they are more likely to support them. Having a few rules that everyone supports is better than having many rules that are violated.

Officers must know the organization and how they fit into it. Officers are interdependent even though they may work different shifts. Failure of an officer to perform on one shift may affect the tasks to be performed on another shift. In serious situations failure to perform may endanger another officer's life. A number of approaches help officers understand the organizational relationships: job descriptions, the organizational chart, training programs, department rules and regulations and procedure manuals. Even after experience, officers need to review these fundamentals from time to time.

Typical Rules and Regulations for Law Enforcement Departments

Rules and regulations are often established by civil service boards and will vary with each department. Officers should be aware of all rules and regulations, and all members of the agency are subject to disciplinary action if they violate these.

General Conduct

Officers are expected to report for duty at the designated time and place. They must not engage in disorderly conduct or accept gifts from suspects, prisoners or defendants. Officers must refrain from using unnecessary force on any person. They shall not act as newspaper, radio or television correspondents or reporters without authorization. Officers must object and refuse to obey an immoral or illegal order.

Performance of Duty

Officers shall preserve the law, protect life and property and enforce those federal statutes, state laws and county and city ordinances that the department is required to enforce. All officers shall perform all other lawful duties as required by competent authority.

Officers are required to discharge their duties calmly and firmly, to act together and to assist and protect each other to maintain law and order. Officers shall act promptly, firmly, fairly and decisively at crime scenes, disorders, accidents, disasters or when dealing with suspects or other situations that require law enforcement action. Any officer who fails to comply, by act or omission, with any order, procedure, rule or regulation of the department, or who fails to perform official duties or who acts in the performance of official duties in a way that could discredit himself or herself, the department or any other member of the department may be considered in neglect of duty.

Officers shall at all times be courteous, patient and respectful in dealing with the public. Officers shall respond promptly to all calls for law enforcement assistance from citizens or other officers.

Prohibited Acts While on Duty

Officers shall not congregate in the dispatch area or engage in horseplay or loud, boisterous conversations in public view or hearing. Officers shall keep their quarters, lockers, vehicles and desks neat, clean and orderly. Officers shall not read newspapers, magazines or similar matter in public view except in the line of duty. Officers shall not smoke while in direct contact with or serving the public. Officers shall not loiter in cafes, drive-ins, service stations or other public places.

Other Restrictions on Behavior

Officers shall not knowingly make a false report, either oral or written. When on duty, officers shall be neat and clean in appearance in public, in or out of uniform. Grooming and appearance are critical, and uniformity of appearance is a constant issue of concern and potential discipline.

In addition to the department's rules and regulations, federal, state and local laws must also be considered. For law enforcement organizations that are unionized, relevant provisions of the labor agreement must be considered as well. In fact, methods for dealing with problem behaviors and discipline in civil service departments are often guided by contractual obligations and guidelines entered into by the union and local government officials.

Some supervisors fear that with a union contract they cannot make discipline stick. This is *not* true. No union contract protects workers from discipline when a valid work rule is violated.

Maintaining discipline is a fundamental management right.

Policy vs. Discretion

Although clear policies and procedures are necessary, they can be overdone. Too often the policy and procedure manual collects dust on the shelf because it is just too big. Effective managers recognize when control is necessary and when discretion should be allowed. Policies should be made to cover high-risk, low-frequency police functions, for example, use of deadly force and high-speed pursuits. Other police functions, such as most domestic dispute calls, require discretion within guidelines. Yet other functions, such as telephone contacts with citizens, may actually be hindered by controlling policies. Figure 11.1 shows a continuum on which control and discretion may be viewed.

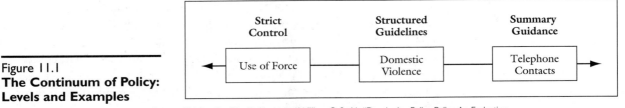

Source: Geoffrey P. Alpert and William C. Smith. "Developing Police Policy: An Evaluation of the Control Principle." *American Journal of Police*, Vol. 13, No. 2, 1994, p. 9. Reprinted by permission.

Figure 11.1
The Continuum of Policy: Levels and Examples

Clarity of Role vs. Creativity

Specific rules and regulations leave little doubt as to what is expected of officers in each area of their job. This emphasis on formal rules is the result of three developments: the need for due process in discipline; protection against civil litigation; and the accreditation movement. Despite this emphasis on rules and regulations, the question arises, do such written directives help officers learn the correct way to do law enforcement work and motivate them to do so, or do they send a message to officers that they are not trusted?

An excessive number of rules may discourage innovation, risk taking, imagination and commitment to the department's mission. The trend in business is just the opposite. Control is achieved not through formal, written rules and regulations but by developing team spirit and a commitment to shared values.

The administrator's challenge is to lead by instilling the desired values and culture within the organization. This might include gearing recruiting, selecting and socializing toward basic departmental values; basing assignments, promotions and other rewards on these basic values; and posting the mission statement and a code of ethics.

Every law enforcement manager would like the idyllic situation in which all officers voluntarily perform as required. Fortunately, most officers are trained in and informed concerning what they are to do. They have the competence to perform and a high degree of individual conscience and do not need external disciplinary measures.

Common Problem Behaviors

In local law enforcement agencies, the most frequent charges are intoxication on the job, insubordination, frequent tardiness, negligence, prohibited moonlighting, incompetence or unsatisfactory performance, improper handling of evidence, willful failure to perform, violation of a municipal ordinance, conduct unbecoming an officer, use of abusive/racial/ethnic language, failure to report for duty or leaving duty without permission, abusive actions against prisoners or people under arrest and careless operation of a vehicle. Among the most challenging problem behaviors are substance abuse, use of excessive force, corruption, sexual harassment and insubordination.

Dealing with Substance Abuse in the Workplace

Telltale signs of substance abuse in the workplace include an increase in absenteeism, employee grievances, employee theft, accidental injuries and workers' compensation claims. Other signs include a decrease in job interest, productivity and quality of work.

Managers should recognize the symptoms of alcohol or drug abuse. If they suspect an employee is abusing alcohol or drugs, they should never accuse the employee of doing so because this could open the manager and the department to a slander or defamation of character lawsuit. Rather, focus on job deficiencies and corrective action. Show a genuine concern for the employee's problem and attempt to refer him or her to a qualified specialist.

Give officers ample opportunity to seek assistance. Follow up if an employee enters a program.

Dealing with Use of Excessive Force

Meyer (1999, p. 26) notes: "Law enforcement officers are unique in society because they are permitted by law to use phyiscal force to compel others to do their bidding." He also notes, however: "When officers use force, they must do so to control a situation, not to punish an offender. "

Neubauer (1999, p. 6) states: "Excessive use of force [is] the application of an amount and/or frequency of force greater than what is required to compel compliance from a willing or unwilling subject." Use of excessive force has always been difficult, resulting in numerous lawsuits. Use of force is sometimes a necessary part of the job, but determining what is reasonable is highly subjective.

The Eighth Amendment explicitly prohibits "cruel and unusual punishment," yet, as Hall (1999, p. 32) notes: "The due process standard [of the Fourteenth Amendment] gives considerable deference to an officer's judgement in high-stress and fast-moving situations." According to Mueck (1999, p. 22): "Officers are allowed to use force to overcome resistance, protect lives and property, and achieve legitimate law enforcement objectives. . . .However, the law also requires an officer to keep their use of force proportionate to the attack." Henriquez (1999, p. 155) puts officer use of force into perspective:

> During 1997, . . . police used force at a rate of 3.41 times per 10,000 calls for service. This translates to a rate of use of force of 0.0341. Expressed another way, police did not use force 99.966 percent of the time.

To deal with use of force issues, Williams (1999, p. 42) recommends: "Use of force policies should be brief, concise and follow state and federal laws governing officers' action. Twenty-page monsters are useless." He further notes:

> Force policies mandating certain techniques, tactics or defensive tactics systems offer officers two poor choices. Violate policy and hopefully survive unhurt through needed improvisation, or risk injury using obligatory methods of control and defense in a situation the officer's policy and directed "techniques" fail to adequately address.

Williams also describes three key concepts involved in making any use of force policy defensible: "Avoiding the use of a 'Force Continuum' in the policy, providing reasonable and ultimately usable deadly force directives, and avoiding the words 'shall' or 'must' in any force policy."

One way to reduce the force needed might be using K-9s as suggested by Smith (2000, p. 36): "In light of several court decisions around the country, consider using law enforcement-trained K-9s as an alternative—and safer—means of applying force."

Dealing
with Corruption

Corruption is another area of concern because those in the field are exposed to numerous opportunities to benefit personally from actions they take against criminals. They may be offered bribes. They may come across huge amounts of drugs or cash. They may feel overworked, underpaid and therefore entitled to take what they consider "just compensation" for the risks they face on the job. Yet, whenever one member of a police department is found to be corrupt, the hundreds of thousands of honest, hardworking officers suffer. As Higgenbottom (1997, p. 12) states: "There is little that is more damaging to a police department than having an officer arrested and charged with a crime. Public trust is vital to the success of a police department, and that trust is damaged whenever an officer breaches his duty to uphold the law."

The problem of police corruption affects agencies of all sizes, in all areas of the country. According to Hall (1998a, p. 20):

> In recent years, the FBI has arrested police officers for corruption in every region of the nation, in large, medium-sized and small cities, towns and villages; from the inner city precincts to rural sheriff's departments.
>
> From 1994 to 1997, a total of 508 persons were convicted in law enforcement corruption cases investigated by the FBI.

Hall (1998b, p. 6) further reports: "As of mid-June [1998], there were 548 local, state and federal law enforcement officers in federal prisons alone—up from 107 in 1994." According to another report ("LAPD Corruption Scandal. . . ," 1999, p. 3): "Hundreds of criminal convictions may be called into question in Los Angeles due to a police corruption scandal that involves allegations of officers framing innocent people, lying in court, and shooting unarmed suspects."

As this text goes to press: "At last count, 32 criminal convictions have been overturned, and so far 20 officers have been fired, suspended or have quit. It is one of the most corrosive police corruption cases ever in Los Angeles and, by all accounts, the investigation has only scratched the surface ("Police Corruption. . . , 2000, p. A20).

Yet another source states: "Corruption [takes] many forms, as a roundup of examples from around the country shows, but none seemed so systemic as that found in police departments in West New York, N.J., and Cicero, Ill. In both cases, the agencies were so riddled with illegal activities that their entire command structures had to be dismantled" ("On the Side of . . . ," 1998, p. 17).

The temptations of law enforcement work and the type of conduct acceptable in each case should be discussed. This could be as simple as reacting appropriately to an offer of a free cup of coffee (coffee-and-doughnut ethics) or as complex as reacting appropriately to a bribe to not make an arrest. In each case,

Law enforcement officers are frequently exposed to tempting situations. These DEA officers are packing money seized in a drug bust in Miami that involved seven arrests and the dismantling of a Haitian smuggling organization operating in South Florida.

officers need to discuss what they should and should not do. This should be reviewed in group training sessions or at shift change. It should be repeated at least annually or when appropriate. Hall (1998b, p. 6) asserts there should be zero tolerance for police corruption: "Because police work is an honorable profession, police officers are supposed to be a serious cut above the citizenry in ethics and integrity not to mention other characteristics."

Dealing with Sexual Harassment

"Police agencies across the nation are paying the piper, in sums that reach millions of dollar for acts of harassment and discrimination against women officers" (Horne, 1999, p. 59).

Sexual harassment has increased in visibility over the past decade and has also resulted in numerous lawsuits. Sexual harassment is a type of sex discrimination prohibited by Title VII in federal law, as well as by most state laws. The federal government defines sexual harassment as "unwelcome sexual advances, requests for sexual favors, and other verbal or physical conduct of a sexual nature" ("Preventing Sexual Harassment," n.d., p. 1). Byrd (1998, p. 147) notes the distinction between two basic types of sexual harassment:

> The quid pro quo type of sexual harassment . . . involves a supervisor's demand for sexual favors from an employee in return for a job benefit. . . . Essentially, the courts usually agreed that depriving an employee of a job benefit because the employee refused to engage in sexual activity with a supervisor was action by the employer that should be treated no differently than any other discrimination claim (such as race- or gender-based termination or demotion). . . .
>
> With hostile-environment harassment, the courts have generally agreed that an employer is liable for hostile environment (whether created by co-employees or by supervisors) only if the offensive conduct was sufficiently severe or pervasive to

alter the terms and conditions of employment, and the employer knew, or should have known, about the offensive conduct. In such cases, the employer could avoid liability by establishing that it had in place an adequate sexual harassment policy that the offended employee failed to use or that it had taken prompt, effective action to remedy the complaint of an offended employee.

The police environment may be more conducive than others to sexual harassment because of the nature of the work, for example, investigating sex crimes and pornography rings. Some evidence also suggests that sexual harassment is significantly higher in male-dominated occupations.

To prevent liability from charges of sexual harassment, departments need a clear policy that identifies conduct that may constitute sexual discrimination or harassment. The policy should also include a statement that such conduct will not be tolerated and that those found guilty of prohibited conduct will be subject to appropriate disciplinary action.

Dealing with Insubordination

Policing has traditionally followed a quasi-military structure, with higher-ranking officers authorized to give lawful orders to lower-ranking officers that must be obeyed, whether they personally agree with them or not. Failure to carry out such lawful orders can expose an officer to discipline for insubordination. As Collins (1999, p. 12) states:

> It is essential to the proper operation of a police agency that officers promptly obey all lawful orders. The usual penalty for insubordination is termination. So long as the order is lawful, any intentional violation would justify dismissal. . . .
>   If the order is reasonable, the general rule traditionally upheld by the courts requires subordinate officers to carry out the orders under protest, and question them later.

Before an officer may be disciplined for insubordination, however, certain factors must be taken into account. According to Collins (p. 14):

> A chief must review not only the wording of the order allegedly disobeyed, but also the circumstances under which it was issued or conveyed. There must be no doubt that the party issuing the order both had the authority to do so and clearly conveyed his intent that it be obeyed.

Negative Discipline/ Punishment

Law enforcement managers at all levels will sometimes find it necessary to use negative discipline. **Negative discipline** uses reprimands and punishments for wrong behavior in an effort to compel expected behavior.

As stated, most law enforcement agencies retain elements of a quasi-military organization and, at least in operational and emergency situations, demand immediate compliance to orders. In less than emergency situations, managers should make reasonable efforts to gain voluntary compliance. If that fails, managers must exercise the disciplinary responsibilities of their position.

Negative discipline should follow positive efforts to gain voluntary compliance only after determining the facts and circumstances and only when enforced objectively. Managers may seek the opinion of superiors. If disciplinary action is taken and later appealed, superiors will have to make the decisions.

The purpose of negative discipline is to help offenders correct behavior and to send a message to others that such behavior is not acceptable. The ultimate decision to bring a disciplinary action may arise because an employee commits a number of minor violations or an obviously serious one. Law enforcement managers must consider the ultimate effect on the individual and the organization.

Those being disciplined must fully understand what they are being disciplined for and why. Managers must have the authority to exercise discipline and be willing to proceed through hearings and appeals if necessary. The discipline recommended should fit the offense and be neither excessively harsh nor lenient.

Law enforcement managers must consider the effects of either taking or failing to take action. If a situation demands disciplinary action, failing to take it will result in losing control. By failing to maintain control, managers contribute to the seriousness of an incident and the ultimate action that will have to be taken.

A primary rule of effective discipline is that it should be carried out as close to the time of the violation as possible.

Delays cause further problems. Witnesses may have left employment, different versions may be manufactured, or facts may be forgotten.

Disciplinary actions, whether verbal reprimands or more serious action, should be carried out in private to avoid embarrassment and defensiveness. One exception to the "privacy rule" is if an employee openly confronts a manager in front of others. In such cases the manager must take immediate, decisive action to maintain respect and control of the department.

Initial disciplinary action should be *corrective*. Only when corrective discipline, training and counseling have little or no effect should disciplinary action be punitive. Punishment has the disadvantage of showing what should not be done, rather than reinforcing what should be done. It is a negative approach to achieve a positive result. If the desired result can be achieved in any other way, it should be.

Supervisors first need to identify which officers, through their actions or lack thereof, deserve punishment or other disciplinary action. They must then determine which action is most appropriate and consider how to administer it.

Identifying the Problem Performer

Although the majority of officers in a department readily cooperate with supervisors and their performance requests, some resist supervisory requests by repeatedly challenging and questioning orders, and still others outright fail to perform. To the question, "Who are problem performers?" Jones (1999, p. 183) states:

> Problem performers are often dedicated, career-long non-performers. These officers can sometimes survive for over 30 years in departments without performing to standards because they either have not been held accountable by supervisors, or when confronted, they know how to manipulate supervisors.

Supervisors must recognize that problem performers are master manipulators who use a variety of strategies, including (p. 183):

> (1) distracting or diverting a supervisor's attention, (2) criticizing supervisors, (3) blaming others, (4) accusing supervisors, (5) using guilt, (6) verbal abuse or

static, (7) humor, joking or wit, (8) seeking pity, (9) apologies, (10) agreeing with the supervisor, (11) placating the supervisor with no resulting behavior changes, (12) debate, (13) arguing with the supervisor, (14) expressing a bad attitude through body language, (15) not taking responsibility for their actions, (16) defiance, (17) withdrawal, and (18) denial.

Jones (p. 183) also warns: "Counseling the problem officer can be a stressful task, requiring a great deal of supervisory preparation. The manipulative officer will certainly test a supervisor's best communication skills."

Determining Penalties

No matter how positive or constructive management may be, people will violate rules and regulations; therefore, some form of corrective action is necessary for organizational control and continued provision of services. In many cases, a penalty is the appropriate corrective action.

Many variables enter into penalty determination; for example, is it a first offense or a repeated offense? Are there extenuating circumstances? Each case must be tried on its own set of facts, and penalties must be assessed in the same way. No single penalty will do justice to every individual or set of circumstances. Each disciplinary action should observe the employee's rights as well as the organization's interests. The action should have a legal and moral basis and should include an appeal process. Penalties should also be reasonable for the severity of the action—if they are viewed as too lenient, they probably will not be enforced because it is not worth the effort. If they are too harsh, they may not be enforced because they are too severe.

The offense and offender, how the offense was committed and the offender's attitude and past performance are important considerations in assessing penalties.

A manager's job would be easier if all rules and regulations had a specific set of penalties for violation. Most law enforcement departments have either departmental or civil service rules and regulations that define what behaviors are violations and the penalty for each. Punishments vary from warnings to discharge or to actual termination of employment. Some departments use a table of offenses, penalties and application of appropriate disciplinary actions. Appendix E contains a sample of such a table. Such tables are not to be used automatically. Supervisors must consider the specific circumstances carefully when evaluating offenses and penalties, including the employee's work history, contribution to the agency and probability of rehabilitation. *Each case must be considered individually.*

The most frequent **disciplinary actions** in municipal law enforcement employment are oral or written reprimands, efficiency rating demerits, summary punishment for minor offenses, withholding part or all of an officer's salary for a specified time, decrease of seniority rights, a fine or financial penalty, suspension, demotion in rank or dismissal.

Progressive Discipline

Many departments operate under the concept of progressive discipline. Employees are usually given a light penalty for the first infraction of a rule, a more severe penalty for the next infraction and so on. The primary objective of pro-

Sometimes unfortunate circumstances compel a manager to resign. Here, Mayor Paul Schell, left, listens to former Seattle Police Chief Norm Stamper talk about his resignation in December 1999. Stamper's resignation came a week after violence at the World Trade Organization meeting in Seattle.

gressive discipline is to give employees a chance to voluntarily improve their behavior or work performance and to clearly inform employees that stronger disciplinary actions will be taken in the event that they do not correct the behavior or work performance.

Progressive discipline uses disciplinary steps based on the severity of the offense. The steps usually are:

- Oral reprimand.
- Written reprimand.
- Suspension/demotion.
- Discharge.

The most frequent type of penalty is an oral or a written *warning*. Sometimes this is called a **reprimand.** An *oral reprimand* is a conversation between a supervisor and an employee about a specific aspect of the employee's performance. It informs employees that continued behavior or level of performance will result in more serious action. The supervisor must provide specifics. Employees should know what to correct and how and must have sufficient time to make the correction before other action is taken. Normally employees cooperate and problem behavior is eliminated.

If the warning is important, the supervisor should make a written record and place it in the personnel file. A *written reprimand* is a formal written notice to the employee regarding significant misconduct, specific inadequate performance or repeated offenses for which the employee has received an oral reprimand. The same conditions apply as for a warning. The violation should be stated in detail, along with what actions will correct the behavior, a time limit, whether there have been previous oral warnings for the same conduct and what will occur if the employee does not correct the violation. A written reprimand is usually recommended for a violation that must be corrected immediately. It should be given by at least a first-line supervisor and perhaps a middle-line manager, with the supervisor as a witness. The employee should receive a copy of the written reprimand.

A warning or a reprimand sends a signal to employees that management has disapproved. It is best to handle all employee penalty matters person to person. The procedure may permit the employee to state his or her position before management takes final action. In some departments warnings and reprimands are not subject to appeal.

A **suspension,** being barred from a position, is the next most serious punishment. Suspensions may be with or without pay. Normally, suspensions are given after consultation with the middle manager and the executive manager. Seniority will probably continue during a suspension. Suspensions with pay normally are given to provide time for management to investigate the situation. It is not in any way a finding of wrongdoing. For example, an officer who shoots and kills a suspect may be suspended with pay while the matter is investigated. A coroner's jury will probably be held, and management will consider their findings in making a final decision. If the officer's action was justified, the officer is returned to duty as though no action had been taken.

Suspensions may usually be appealed to the executive manager, city manager, civil service board or a special board. They may also be a matter for union support or denial.

The most serious forms of punishment are *demotion* and *dismissal* or *termination.* These actions are taken by the head of the law enforcement department or the government jurisdiction and are also subject to appeal. These actions are end-of-the-road punishments, administered in very serious first offenses or in situations in which the employees have disregarded other warnings, reprimands and suspensions.

A **demotion** places an employee in a position of lower responsibility and pay and can seriously impede the remainder of the employee's career.

Dismissal or **termination** is the most serious form of penalty. It is used when management decides strong action must be taken in the best interests of the organization and its other employees. Termination is necessary when employees do not respond to attempts to correct behavior that violates written rules and regulations and of which the employees were provided proper notice. Incompetence and inability to get along with other employees are two major reasons for termination. Other major reasons are dishonesty or lying and insubordination.

Technically, dismissal and termination are slightly different. *Dismissal* is an action taken by a hiring and firing authority. It is not voluntary on the part of the employee. It is, in effect, a discharge or firing. *Termination* is also an end to employment, but it may be voluntary or involuntary. Employees may terminate employment due to reasons such as illness or accepting a different job. The differences are basically a matter of semantics, as Solomon (1999, p. 40) observes:

> As far back as 1825, . . . people were getting *sacked.* By 1868, they were getting *laid off;* by 1887, *bounced;* by 1905, *canned;* and by the mid 50s, *given the gate, a pink slip,* or *the old heave-ho.* . . .

At the other end of the semantic spectrum are euphemisms, ideal for obfuscation by those who do the dirty deed . . . *derecruiting* . . . *downsizing* . . . *rightsizing* . . . *outplacement.*

Whatever term is used, the result is the same—the employee is gone.

Terminations are costly to the organization. Replacement selection costs are high, and training is a long-term commitment. Unfortunately, in some situations termination is the only recourse. Most managers will say that firing an officer is one of their most distasteful tasks. As Branch (1999, p. 36) states: "Firing people . . . remains a curious taboo, one that's lately been obscured by topics like employee loyalty, recruitment, and retention, the byproducts of a job market gone berserk." She continues:

> In the fine art of firing, inertia can be a dangerous thing. Not only does it prevent managers from facing conflict, but it also makes them anxious to the point of distraction: Will I be seen as the bad guy? Will I get sued? It can also numb them to the big-picture hazards of keeping drudges around.

Although firing someone is seldom easy, it is almost always easier than keeping them. Normally termination occurs only after a serious offense, after repeated offenses by the same employee or after a series of the same type of offense where warnings, oral and written reprimands, suspension or similar previous dispositions of a disciplinary action went unheeded.

Wrongful termination lawsuits have been rising in the past decade. These actions arise from the due process clause of the Fourteenth Amendment of the U. S. Constitution, which prohibits persons acting as agents or employees of the state or its political subdivisions from depriving a person of property or liberty without due process of law. A person has the right not to be terminated from employment except for good or just cause. Title 42, U.S.C., Section 1983, provides a procedure by which a person employed by a state, county or municipal government can bring suit against a department or supervisor for violating the person's constitutional rights in the termination process. Additionally, the discharge of a person for an act not committed by that person may be deprivation of the person's liberty interests. Managers and supervisors must be careful in conducting termination investigations, differentiating gossip and hearsay from personal knowledge and facts. Management should gather all the evidence and make the decision to terminate only on the evidence. Due process requires a valid reason for termination, procedural action notification of the person to be terminated and an opportunity for a hearing.

Difficult as termination is for police managers, it remains their responsibility. Failure to exercise it when justified results in the ultimate failure of manager effectiveness. Should a manager fail to terminate an officer when justified, and the officer does anything "wrong" in the public's eyes, the manager and the entire department could be sued for **negligent retention.** The manager most familiar with the details of the termination and who has authority to terminate should perform the task. If the executive manager is the only person with authority, a lower-level manager familiar with the details should be present. Employees should be told why the department is terminating them.

Discharge should be presented so employees can retain self-esteem, if possible. They should be told whether they can expect references for what they did well while on the job, when the termination takes effect, how the announcement will be made and whether they can resign voluntarily for the record. Any actions taken should center on the behavior or offense rather than on the individual.

Discharge should follow proper procedures. Properly document prior disciplinary actions and all evidence leading to the firing. It may be best to discuss the matter with the city attorney before taking action because the attorney may be the one handling the case for the jurisdiction before a civil service or other hearing board.

Summary Punishment

Not all disciplinary actions fall within the realm of progressive discipline. Managers must have the authority to exercise *summary* discipline when certain infractions occur. **Summary discipline,** or **summary punishment,** is discretionary authority used when a supervisor feels an officer is not fit for duty or when, for any reason, the supervisor feels immediate action is needed.

Summary punishment may require officers to work a day or two without pay or excuse them from duty for a day without pay. Officers who receive summary punishment have a right to a hearing.

Guidelines for Administering Negative Discipline

When you use negative discipline, what you do not do is often more important than what you do. Officers may become defensive and less concerned with listening than defending themselves. Communication skills and tact are essential in these situations.

The following guidelines apply when you must use negative discipline:

- Get the facts first. Consider the circumstances. Was the misbehavior accidental? Did the person know the rules? Was this the first offense? Keep adequate records.
- Be calm. Allow tempers to settle. Avoid sarcasm. Do not threaten, argue or show anger.
- Know your powers as outlined in your job description.
- Check on precedents for similar offenses.
- Suit the disciplinary action to the individual and the situation. Know each subordinate and his or her record. The severity of the discipline should match the seriousness of the offense.
- Focus on the behavior and not on the person. Be sure the behavior is something the person has control over or can change.
- Do not ascribe intent to the behavior or imply it was done on purpose. Focus only on the behavior.
- Be sure the person is attentive and emotionally ready to listen.
- Be clear, specific and objective. Use actual examples of problem behavior.
- Be decisive.

- Check for understanding by asking questions. How is the person taking the criticism?
- Respect the employee's dignity.
- End with expectations for changed behavior.
- Follow up.

Effective discipline is more easily maintained with a written set of guidelines such as the preceding. Managers should coordinate their disciplinary efforts. Every manager should enforce every rule, regulation and policy equally. Rules that are unenforced or unenforceable should be changed or cancelled. Further, managers should set the example, letting their subordinates know they mean what they say.

Supervisors should avoid the **gunny sack approach** to discipline. This occurs when managers or supervisors accumulate negative behaviors of a subordinate and then dump them all on the officer at the same time rather than correcting them as they occur. Accumulated, they may be serious enough to warrant dismissal. However, handled one at a time, the officer might have had a chance to change.

Steps in Administering Negative Discipline

To apply discipline, write down your main goal in taking disciplinary action—to change the employee's behavior and reduce the chances of it happening another time. Write down the violation and what conduct was involved, much the same procedure used in making a charge against a citizen. State the reason for the action, specifically, what has been violated and how. Show how the behavior creates a problem. State how you feel about it.

Listen to the employee's explanation. Remember that to err is human. To blame somebody else is even more human. Anticipate this and help employees sort out their responsibilities. Also recognize that if an excuse is good enough, it becomes a reason. Managers and supervisors cannot know everything. They, too, can make mistakes. If this happens, managers must openly admit their mistake and offer a sincere apology for the *misunderstanding*.

Suggest corrective action and, if possible, involve the person in the suggestion. Be firm but fair. Fairness does not mean treating everyone equally. A rookie will make mistakes that might not be tolerated if made by a veteran officer. State exactly what action you are going to take and explain that further violations will bring more severe results. Offer assistance in resolving the present problem, as long as the ultimate responsibility for doing so rests with the employee. Describe how you value the person as an individual and as an important part of the work group and the entire law enforcement department. Secure a commitment to future positive behavior.

McGregor (Theory X, Theory Y) says the lessons learned from a hot stove should be present in effective discipline. When a person touches a hot stove (violates a rule or regulation), the burn (punishment) is immediate, consistent (it happens every time) and impartial (it is the same for everyone). Further, the severity of the burn depends on the length of time the stove and victim remain in contact and the heat of the stove. The burned individual may initially feel anger at the stove, but in reality, the anger is an indictment of oneself and the carelessness causing the burn. The anger will lessen, and the victim will have a healthy respect for the stove in the future.

The final step is to tell the individual how to appeal the decision. The right to appeal should be inherent in any disciplinary action.

Appeal

An **appeal** is a request for a decision to be reviewed by someone higher in command. The most frequent appeals are to a review board or department disciplinary board. Appeals can also be made to a civil service board review, a district or high court and, in some cases, a management-labor board. Many departments use an internal review procedure, including the following steps.

Step One

The employee requests a face-to-face meeting with the immediate supervisor within five working days. The supervisor and employee meet, and the supervisor decides to withdraw or stand by the disciplinary action.

Step Two

An employee who is not satisfied with the results of step one presents the written reasons for dissatisfaction to the department head within five days. The department head sustains or rescinds the disciplinary action within three working days.

Step Three

An employee who is not satisfied with the results of step two presents the written reasons for dissatisfaction with the department head's response to the top-level manager of the jurisdiction. Within five days the manager or representative either sustains or rescinds the disciplinary action. This is the final step.

Departments may also have a process for employees to appeal disciplinary actions to a civil service commission. This process usually involves the employee appearing for a hearing before a board that rules in the matter. Such hearings may be closed to the public. The decision and findings of the commission are in writing and are considered final.

Legal Considerations

The terms *just, good* or *sufficient cause* appear in many discipline cases. Black's Law Dictionary refers to **just cause** as "a reasonable cause which must be based on reasonable grounds, and there must be a fair and honest cause or reason, regulated by good faith."

Just cause requires a statement of the charge or charges, a procedure for answering the charges and a process of review. Due process also applies, which means every employee is entitled to certain rights. Federal laws prohibit firing employees on the basis of race, religion, sex, age, national origin, union memberships or activities or because of work missed due to jury service.

Disciplinary actions are subject to specific procedures as established by the civil service or department rules and regulations. If an officer is charged with a criminal offense, the legal procedure is the same as for any citizen. In these cases, violation of civil service rules and regulations of the law enforcement department would in all probability await the outcome of the criminal action even though they are completely separate actions.

If the situation involves the arrest of an officer, the input of the local district attorney's office should be obtained as early in the investigation as possible.

The criminal violation is more than likely a joint violation of department rules and regulations but must be charged and tried separately. Each case may proceed differently, depending on the local court process. Criminal charges are involved in very few of the total violations of rules and regulations cases. The officer may be suspended, with or without pay, pending the outcome.

In general, violations of department rules and regulations are investigated using the same basic procedures as those accorded criminal violations. All facts must be carefully documented. Search warrants should be obtained where legally required to secure evidence. Gathering evidence, taking statements, seeking witnesses and adhering to legal procedures of handling evidence are all important.

Civil service hearings are similar to criminal hearings. Legal procedures vary, but the charges are read in an open hearing, witnesses are called and the employee is present. Employees may or may not testify because they are not required to give incriminating evidence against themselves.

Past personnel records may be introduced into evidence if relevant. Proper, detailed documentation of the facts supporting any violation of department rules and regulations is the key to justice. Most disciplinary action cases overturned by the courts have involved situations in which proper documentation was lacking, prejudice was involved, the violation was based on an action deemed a discretionary matter on the officer's part, violations of sick leave rules were not administered consistently, evidence was based on polygraph examinations or violations of due process procedures were involved.

Comprehensive Discipline

Comprehensive discipline uses both positive and negative discipline to achieve individual and organizational goals. Several specific approaches to comprehensive discipline have been developed, including the balance of consequences analysis, the PRICE method, the one-minute management approach and the stroke approach.

The Balance of Consequences Analysis—Wilson Learning Corporation

Building on Skinner's reinforcement theory and Vroom's expectancy theory, Wilson Learning Corporation developed the **balance of consequences analysis.** This process uses a grid such as that shown in Figure 11.2 to analyze problem behavior.

For example, Officer Jones is a popular foot patrol officer. He spends lots of time chatting with citizens on his beat, having made friends with shopkeepers and owners of business establishments as well as residents in the area. The problem is that he is always late with his incident reports. Investigators complain that they do not have the reports when they need them. Further, Jones often has to put in overtime to get his paperwork done (with no pay).

His sergeant does not want to lose him because he is a skilled officer, and his friendliness and popularity are an asset to the department. But the lateness

Behavior	
Undesired (current)	Desired
Positive Consequences	Positive Consequences
Negative Consequences	Negative Consequences

Figure 11.2
Balance of Consequences Analysis

Source: Steve Buchholz, *The Positive Manager*, p. 125. Copyright © 1985 by John Wiley and Sons, Inc., New York. Reprinted by permission.

of his reports is causing problems. The sergeant analyzes the consequences operating in this situation.

First, what are the rewards Jones receives from socializing?

- Pleasant visits with citizens
- Satisfaction from knowing people like him
- Praise from peers and superiors for being "people oriented"

Against this list, the negative consequences of the behavior must be looked at. These include:

- Complaints from the investigators.
- Overtime (unpaid).
- Reduced chances for promotion.

Next consider what positive results would occur if Jones stopped socializing and got his reports done on time:

- Investigators would stop complaining.
- Unpaid overtime would stop.
- Chances for promotion will increase.

On the other hand, what negative consequences might result?

- Miss the good times socializing
- Miss the praise for being "people oriented"
- More actual work to do

BEHAVIOR	
Undesired (current)	**Desired**
Late reports	Reports on time
Positive Consequences	**Positive Consequences**
Pleasant visits	Less criticism
Satisfaction	Less overtime
Praise	Promotion more likely
Negative Consequences	**Negative Consequences**
Criticism	No pleasant visits
Overtime	Less praise
Promotion less likely	More work

Figure 11.3
**Officer Jones' Balance
of Consequences Analysis**

The balance of consequences grid would look like Figure 11.3.

> The balance of consequences analysis considers behavior in terms of what positive and negative results the behavior produces and then focuses on those results.

A final piece of information is needed to complete the analysis, that is, the strength of the consequences. Consequences fall into one of three either/or categories. Every consequence is either:

- Personal or organizational (P or O).
- Immediate or delayed (I or D).
- Certain or uncertain (C or U).

> Personal, immediate and certain (PIC) consequences are stronger than organizational, delayed or uncertain (ODU) consequences.

Look at Jones' positive consequences for the undesirable behavior:

- Pleasant visits with citizens—personal, immediate, certain (PIC)
- Satisfaction from knowing people like him—personal, immediate, certain (PIC)
- Praise from peers and superiors for being "people oriented"—personal, delayed, certain (PDC)

Compare this with the positive consequences if he should do less socializing and get his paperwork done on time:

- Investigators would stop complaining—personal, delayed, certain (PDC).
- Overtime (unpaid) would stop—personal, delayed, certain (PDC).
- Chances for promotion will increase—personal, delayed, uncertain (PDU).

Clearly, the positive consequences for the *undesirable behavior* are stronger than those for the desirable behavior. The same is true for the negative consequences. The negative consequences associated with the undesirable behavior are delayed and uncertain. The negative consequences for less socializing are immediate and certain. The message for management:

Change the balance of consequences so that employees are rewarded for desired behavior and punished for undesired behavior—not vice versa.

Managers can change the balance of consequences by:

- Adding positive consequences for desired behaviors.
- Adding negative consequences for undesired behaviors.
- Removing negative consequences for desired behaviors.
- Removing positive consequences for undesired behaviors.
- Changing the strength of the consequences, that is, changing an organizational consequence to a personal one, a delayed consequence to an immediate one or an uncertain consequence to a certain one.

Consider the following situation: A law enforcement department is doing an analysis of its efficiency and has asked all officers to complete time sheets at the end of their shifts. One shift sergeant is having difficulty getting her officers to turn in their sheets. The officers see the sheets as busywork, interfering with efficiency rather than helping to improve it, so they often leave work without completing them. The sergeant then has to track them down the next day to get them to fill them in. As a solution to the problem, the sergeant gets on the P.A. system at the beginning of the shift, reads the names of those who did not complete their time study and asks them to report to the front desk to fill them in. Examine the following list of consequences of the described behavior.

- Filling out the sheets takes a few minutes past quitting time.
- This results in getting caught in a traffic jam.
- Officers may get chewed out by the sergeant if they do not fill in the sheet.
- Officers are given time at the beginning of their next shift to fill in the sheets.
- Officers get their names read over the P.A. system.
- Colleagues clap and cheer when the names are read.
- The efficiency study will not be reliable if all officers do not complete the time sheets.
- The sergeant has to spend time getting officers to comply with the request.

BEHAVIOR	
Undesired (current) Not filling in time sheets	**Desired** Filling in time sheets
Positive Consequences Get time next shift (PIC) Get name announced (PIC) Colleagues cheer (PIC)	**Positive Consequences** NONE
Negative Consequences Make supervisor unhappy (ODC) Unreliable survey results (ODU)	**Negative Consequences** Caught in traffic (PIC) Name will not be read (PIC)

Figure 11.4
Balance of Consequences Analysis—Time Sheet Problem

This problem can be looked at using the balance of consequences analysis. A key to using this tool is to look at the behavior through the eyes of the beholder—in this instance, the problem officers. The analysis will look like the chart in Figure 11.4.

> The manager's challenge is to change the balance of consequences so that officers are rewarded for desired behavior and punished for undesired behavior—not vice versa.

In this case it is obvious that reading the names over the PA system is positively reinforcing the undesired behavior, not punishing it. Peer pressure might be brought to bear on those who do not participate. Or those who turn their sheets in as desired could be rewarded in some way.

The Price Method

The PRICE method, developed by Blanchard (1989, p. 18), is a five-step approach to employee performance problems such as attendance. According to Blanchard, such problems cost American employers a "staggering 40 million workdays a year. That represents $26 billion in lost production."

> The **PRICE method** consists of five steps:
>
> - **P**inpoint
> - **R**ecord
> - **I**nvolve
> - **C**oach
> - **E**valuate

The five steps are applicable to most problem behaviors. The first step is to *pinpoint* the problem behavior and make certain the employee knows about it. Say, for example, an officer frequently uses profanity in public. This unacceptable behavior needs to be changed. Exactly what constitutes "profanity" must be specified.

The second step is to *record* how often and when the problem behavior occurs. Under what circumstances does the officer use the profanity? Who else is usually present? What triggers it? How often does it happen? At any certain time of day? This record establishes the behavior as problematic and also provides a baseline from which to work.

Third, *involve* the officer in setting a goal to eliminate the problem behavior and deciding on specific strategies to meet this goal. The strategies should include a specific time line as well as incentives for specific accomplishments toward goal achievement.

Fourth, *coach* the officer regularly and consistently. According to Blanchard: "This is the most critical part of the plan. It is also the step where managers most frequently stumble." Provide positive reinforcement whenever the officer substitutes an acceptable word for what would normally elicit a profanity. Enlist the aid of other officers to help provide positive reinforcement. Make certain others do not use profanity without being criticized. Double standards will undermine the PRICE method.

Finally, *evaluate* the performance according to a predetermined schedule to monitor progress.

One Minute Managing

The One Minute Manager, for which Blanchard is perhaps best known, suggests that managers can use **one minute managing,** including both praise and reprimands, to get their subordinates to perform at peak efficiency with high morale.

Both praise and reprimands can be effectively accomplished in one minute.

Blanchard and Johnson (1981, p. 44) suggest that *one minute praising* works well when managers:

1. Tell people *up front* that you are going to let them know how they are doing.
2. Praise people immediately.
3. Tell people what they did right—be specific.
4. Tell people how good you feel about what they did right and how it helps the organization and the other people who work there.
5. Stop for a moment of silence to let them "feel" how good you feel.
6. Encourage them to do more of the same.
7. Shake hands or touch people in a way that makes it clear that you support their success in the organization. (Any such physical contact should be done in a way that could never be construed as sexual harassment.)

Blanchard and Johnson (p. 59) suggest that *one minute reprimands* work well when managers:

1. Tell people *beforehand* that you are going to let them know how they are doing and in no uncertain terms.

The first half of the reprimand:

2. Reprimand people immediately.
3. Tell people what they did wrong—be specific.
4. Tell people how you feel about what they did wrong—and in no uncertain terms.
5. Stop for a few seconds of uncomfortable silence to let them *feel* how you feel.

The second half of the reprimand:

6. Shake hands, or touch them in a way that lets them know you are honestly on their side. (Again, with any physical contact, avoid any appearance of sexual harassment.)
7. Remind them how much you value them.
8. Reaffirm that you think well of them but not of their performance in this situation.
9. Realize that when the reprimand is over, it's over.

Figure 11.5 illustrates how one minute praisings and reprimands constitute a comprehensive disciplinary approach. Blanchard (1987, p. 14) cautions that simply knowing the "secrets" of one minute praising and reprimanding is not enough:

> To use these tools well, you must understand some specific management techniques. . . .
> Giving an equal amount of praise and criticism may not be enough to save you from being thought of as a bad boss. In most groups, there's a need for four times as many positive interactions—that is, praising—as negative interactions. . . .
> A reprimand has such a powerful effect that it takes four positive words to balance one negative word.

An effective manager usually gives four times more praise than blame.

Blanchard describes a corporation he worked with where criticism and praise were approximately equal. The employees thought their relationship with their boss was "totally negative." Even when the ratio was changed to two praisings for every one reprimand, people still thought their boss was "all over them." Only when the ratio became four praisings to one criticism did the employees feel they had a "good relationship" with their boss.

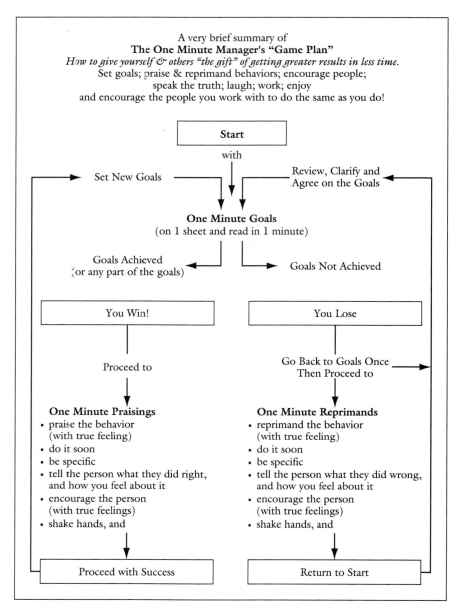

A very brief summary of
The One Minute Manager's "Game Plan"
How to give yourself & others "the gift" of getting greater results in less time.
Set goals; praise & reprimand behaviors; encourage people;
speak the truth; laugh; work; enjoy
and encourage the people you work with to do the same as you do!

Start

with

Set New Goals — Review, Clarify and Agree on the Goals

One Minute Goals
(on 1 sheet and read in 1 minute)

Goals Achieved
(or any part of the goals) — Goals Not Achieved

| You Win! | You Lose |

Proceed to — Go Back to Goals Once Then Proceed to

One Minute Praisings
- praise the behavior
  (with true feeling)
- do it soon
- be specific
- tell the person what they did right,
  and how you feel about it
- encourage the person
  (with true feelings)
- shake hands, and

One Minute Reprimands
- reprimand the behavior
  (with true feeling)
- do it soon
- be specific
- tell the person what they did wrong,
  and how you feel about it
- encourage the person
  (with true feelings)
- shake hands, and

| Proceed with Success | Return to Start |

**Figure 11.5
The One Minute
Manager's "Game Plan"**

Source: Kenneth Blanchard and Spencer Johnson. *The One Minute Manager*, p. 101.
Copyright © 1981 by William Morrow and Co. Used by permission of William Morrow
and Company, Inc., Publishers, New York.

The Stroke Approach

The Better Than Money Corporation is founded on the principle that management has available to it several options that are "better than money" to motivate employees. This principle carries over into the corporation's main business, consulting on excellence in customer service. Its **stroke approach** includes five kinds of strokes:

- Positive—any sincere, positive comment or expression. Clearly a warm fuzzy.

- Negative—any negative action or word that is clearly a cold prickly.

- Absent—lack of any word or recognition.

- Crooked—a positive stroke followed by a negative one, for example, "That's a beautiful dress you have on. I wonder when it will be in style."

- Plastic—a comment given as a ritual, for example, "How are things going?"

Managers can give strokes that are positive, negative, absent, crooked or plastic. They should focus on positive strokes.

To use strokes effectively, managers should concentrate on the positive strokes as much as possible. Figure 11.6 shows how a manager might set "stroking objectives" each day.

A Disciplinary System   A fair, equitable disciplinary system has the following characteristics:

- Reasonable, necessary policies, procedures and rules to govern employees' conduct at work and promote both individual and organizational goals. Regular review of these standards.

- Effective communication of these policies, procedures and rules as well as the consequences for noncompliance.

- Immediate, impartial and consistent enforcement of the policies, procedures and rules.

- An appeals procedure.

STROKING OBJECTIVE FOR:

Date: _____

1. Give out two Positive Strokes per day.
      Genuine
      Sincere
      Specific
      Timely

2. Identify one top performer in your work group.
   Name _____
   Give two Positive Strokes per week. (Do not combine with #1).

3. Identify one marginal performer in your work group.
   Name _____
   Give two Positive Strokes per week. (Do not combine with #1).

Figure 11.6
**Using Strokes
to Discipline Positively**

Source: Copyright © 1980 by John Tschohl, Better Than Money Corporation. Courtesy of Service Quality Institute, Minneapolis, MN. Reprinted by permission.

Summary

Discipline is training expected to produce a desired behavior—controlled behavior. Discipline and morale are closely related. Morale is how a person feels; discipline is how a person acts. The purpose of discipline is to promote desired behavior. This may be done by encouraging acceptable behavior or punishing unacceptable behavior. An agency's policy and procedure manual is the foundation upon which most discipline must be based.

A primary rule of effective discipline is that it should be carried out as close to the time of the violation as possible. Progressive discipline uses disciplinary steps based on the severity of the offense. The steps are usually (1) oral reprimand, (2) written reprimand, (3) suspension/demotion and (4) discharge. The offense and offender, how the offense was committed and the offender's attitude and past performance are important considerations in assigning penalties.

Discipline, either positive or negative, depends on the use of consequences. The balance of consequences analysis considers behavior in terms of what positive and negative results the behavior produces and then focuses on those results. Personal, immediate and certain (PIC) consequences are stronger than organizational, delayed or uncertain (ODU) consequences. Managers should change the balance of consequences so that employees are rewarded for desired behavior and punished for undesired behavior—not vice versa.

The PRICE method consists of five steps: (1) pinpoint, (2) record, (3) involve, (4) coach and (5) evaluate. Both praise and reprimands can be effectively accomplished in one minute. An effective manager usually gives four times more praise than blame. Managers can also give strokes. These strokes might be positive, negative, absent, crooked or plastic. The focus should be on positive strokes.

Discussion Questions

1. Why is discipline a broader term than punishment?
2. What level of law enforcement manager should investigate the majority of discipline problems?
3. What is constructive discipline?
4. Do you feel written departmental rules and regulations are necessary? For what areas?
5. What behaviors would be severe enough violations to warrant termination?
6. What would be a constructive law enforcement department philosophy for discipline?
7. Are there too many departmental rules and regulations? Not enough? What are the most important ones?
8. Why is discipline necessary for individual functioning? For organizational functioning?
9. Pick a problem behavior you would like to change and do a balance of consequences analysis. Are there changes you can make to help change the problem behavior?
10. As a manager, what types of positive and negative discipline would you be inclined to use?

InfoTrac College Edition Assignment

Select one of the following topics and find a recent article about it:

- Progressive discipline
- Excessive use of force

- Sexual harrassment on the job
- Police corruption

Summarize the main points of the article and give the full reference. Be prepared to share your findings with the class.

References

Blanchard, Kenneth. "Praise and Criticism: Finding the Right Ratio." *Today's Office,* April 1987, p. 14.

Blanchard, Kenneth. "A PRICE That Makes Sense." *Today's Office,* September 1989, p. 18.

Blanchard, Kenneth and Johnson, Spencer. *The One Minute Manager.* New York: William Morrow and Company, 1981.

Branch, Shelly. "You're Fired!" *Your Company,* February/March 1999, pp. 34–40.

Byrd, Edwin H., III. "Title VII and Employer Liability." *The Police Chief,* Vol. LXV, No. 10, October 1998, pp. 145–150.

Collins, John M. "Discipline for Insubordination." *The Police Chief,* Vol. LXVI, No. 9, September 1999, pp. 12–14.

Ellman, Edgar S. "Put Your Policies in Writing." *Law and Order,* Vol. 47, No. 6, June 1999, pp. 146–147.

Field, Mark W. and Meloni, Thomas E. "Constructive Police Discipline: Resurrecting the Police Spirit." *Law and Order,* Vol. 47, No. 5, May 1999, pp. 85–91.

Hall, Dennis. "Corruption Report Fails to Raise Ire Among IACP Chiefs." *Police,* Vol. 22, No. 12, December 1998a, pp. 20–22.

Hall, Dennis. "Report on Police Corruption Should Concern Every Officer." *Police,* Vol. 22, No. 8, August 1998b, p. 6.

Hall, John C. "Due Process and Deadly Force: When Police Conduct Shocks the Conscience." *FBI Law Enforcement Bulletin,* Vol. 68, No. 2, February 1999, pp. 27–32.

Henriquez, Mark. "The IACP National Police Use-of-Force Database Project." *The Police Chief,* Vol. LXVI, No. 10, October 1999, pp. 154–159.

Higgenbottom, Jeffrey. "Due Process in Suspensions without Pay." *The Police Chief,* Vol. LXIV, No. 11, November 1997, p. 12.

Horne, Peter. "Special Report: Equality in Policing." *Law and Order,* Vol. 47, No. 11, November 1999, pp. 52–62.

Jones, Tony L. "Confronting the Problem Performer." *Law Enforcement Technology,* Vol. 26, No. 10, October 1999, pp. 183–185.

"LAPD Corruption Scandal Forces Review of Many Convictions." *Criminal Justice Newsletter,* Vol. 30, No. 9, May 3, 1999, pp. 3–4.

Meyer, Greg. "Current Use of Force Issues." *The Law Enforcement Trainer,* Vol. 14, No. 6, November/December 1999, pp. 26–33

Mueck, Robert P. "Probable Signs of Submission." *The Law Enforcement Trainer,* Vol. 14, July/August 1999, pp. 22–23, 67.

Neubauer, Ronald S. "Police Use of Force in America: An IACP Update." *The Police Chief,* Vol. LXVI, No. 8, August 1999, p. 6.

"On the Side of the Law—or Are They?" *Law Enforcement News,* Vol. XXIV, Nos. 501/502, December 15/31, 1998, p. 17.

"Police Corruption Scandal in L. A. Is Growing Bigger by the Week." (Minneapolis/St. Paul) *Star Tribune,* February 13, 2000, p. A20.

"Preventing Sexual Harassment." St. Paul, MN: Equal Opportunity Division, Department of Employee Relations, n.d.

Smith, Brad. "Police Service Dogs: The Unheralded Training Tool." *Police,* Vol. 24, No. 1, January 2000, pp. 36–39.

Solomon, Jolie. "How Do I Put This . . .? Saying 'You're Fired!' " *Your Company,* February/March 1999, p. 40.

Williams, George T. "Re-Thinking 'Force' Policies." *Law and Order,* Vol. 47, No. 12, December 1999, pp. 42–46.

Chapter 12 Complaints and Grievances

> A complaint is an opportunity to prove the kind of stuff you and your department are made of, a chance to cement a relationship so solidly it will last for years. That's much more important than who's right and who's wrong.
>
> —Anonymous

- How a complaint and a grievance differ?
- Who may register a complaint?
- What common categories of law enforcement misconduct are often included in external complaints?
- How complaints might be avoided?
- What the most common causes of internal complaints are?
- How job satisfaction, communication and performance are related?
- What the Pinch Model illustrates?
- When complaints do not need to be taken seriously?
- What two functions are served by a careful complaint investigation?
- What the majority of grievances concern?
- What the outcome of a complaint or grievance might be?
- How officers may protect themselves legally when under investigation?

Can You Define?

arbitration	external complaints	not sustained
civilian review boards	Garrity protection	pinch
complainant	grievance	Pinch Model
complaint	grievant	sustained
crunch	internal complaints	unfounded
exonerated	mediation	

INTRODUCTION

Chapter 11 discussed problem behaviors perceived by managers. This chapter reverses the perspective and looks at problems perceived by subordinates and by those outside the law enforcement organization. These perceived problems may result in complaints or grievances.

It is an organizational fact of life that most law enforcement supervisors must deal with complaints as part of their responsibilities. How supervisors react to complaints will directly affect the organization's ability to function effectively. If complaints are not dealt with promptly, thoroughly and fairly, the result will be serious negative consequences for the entire organization.

This chapter begins with definitions that differentiate between complaints and grievances. It then examines the difference between external and internal complaints, as well as complaint policies and how complaints are handled and investigated, including the role of internal affairs investigations and the civilian review board. Next, grievances are discussed, including their causes and resolution, followed by an examination of the disposition of complaints and grievances. The chapter concludes with discussions of how to handle the chronic complainer, complaints, COPPS, legal rights and procedures for officers named in disciplinary actions.

Definitions

By definition, a complaint and a grievance are basically synonymous. Either can be described as a criticism, charge, accusation, offense or finding of fault. Complaints and grievances may also be described as circumstances or conditions thought to be unjust, whether real or imagined.

> A **complaint** is a statement of a problem. A **grievance** is a formally registered complaint.

A complaint or grievance is an initial action taken by someone against a person or an organization for a perceived wrong. Whether real or imagined, the wrong is sufficient in the mind of the person complaining that the matter must be brought to the attention of the proper authority. The action taken may be an oral criticism, a written statement, a listing of wrongs, a civil service procedure, a meeting demand, a hearing demand or a formal legal action.

Complaints

Complaints are an unavoidable part of being a manager. Even the most efficient managers get their share of complaints—justified or unjustified.

> A complaint may be made by the general public, by people arrested or by employees of the law enforcement department, including peers or managers. The person or group filing the complaint is called the **complainant.**

Complaints may be external or internal.

External Complaints

Law enforcement departments exist to serve their communities. With this basic premise, citizens can be thought of as consumers of law enforcement services and, like any business, departments should "aim to please." Research suggests

External complaints from citizens should be taken seriously and investigated thoroughly.

that customers who have bad experiences tell approximately 11 people about it; those with good experiences tell just 6. Managers should recognize that it is impossible to please everyone all the time. Some citizens, rightly or wrongly, will perceive a problem and register a complaint.

External complaints are those made by citizens against a law enforcement officer or officers, a supervisor, support staff and/or the entire department. The complaint may be made by an individual or a group. It may be as "trivial" as a citizen receiving what he or she perceives to be an unjustified parking ticket or as serious as a charge of brutality or racism.

The St. Louis Police Department had postcards printed and gave them to any citizen "on request" to indicate how well a law enforcement officer responded to a call. The outcome was nine to one pro-officer conduct, an effective public relations move.

External complaints may come from victims or from those responding on behalf of others. A person who reports being a victim of police brutality would be a complainant with firsthand knowledge. A neighbor acting on behalf of a friend who was the alleged victim of police brutality would be a secondhand information complainant.

People who call in complaints without leaving a name are generally not as credible as those who identify themselves. This does not mean, however, that anonymous complaints should be ignored. Today, with the drug problem as serious as it has become, with intimidation, injuries and in some cases death threatening people who provide information, it is understandable that people may not want to give their names.

An employee who receives a complaint should obtain all possible information about the incident, whether the complainant is known or not. Sometimes the complainant may be under the influence of alcohol or other drugs and, if interviewed later, may give a considerably different story. Many departments have dispatcher complaint forms readily available. Many others automatically record all calls into and out of the department.

The motive for the complaint should be determined. The author recalls a series of complaints from one person concerning a local judge's driving. It developed that the complainant had been before the judge on a D. U. I. , charged and sentenced. Since then he had been following the judge when the judge was driving and reporting every minute infraction of traffic laws, even one mile over the speed limit. He never wanted to sign a complaint or appear as a witness, just to make nuisance reports that took up law enforcement time. After a personal interview, the calls ceased.

The Police Executive Research Forum has published a "model policy statement" for handling citizen complaints. The intent of the policy statement is to provide precise guidelines to ensure fairness to officers and civilians alike. It seeks to improve the quality of services in three ways: (1) by increasing citizen confidence in the integrity of law enforcement actions, thereby engendering community support for and confidence in the department; (2) by permitting law enforcement officials to monitor officers' compliance with department procedures and (3) by clarifying rights and ensuring due process protection to both citizens and officers.

Causes

Specific categories of misconduct subject to disciplinary action need to be clearly defined.

> Common categories of officer misconduct often included in external complaints are crime, excessive force, false arrest, improper entry, unlawful search, harassment, offensive demeanor and rule infractions.

The annual report of a large urban police department included information about complaints, including the types of complaints processed and their disposition, as summarized in Table 12.1. The most common complaint in this department, and also the most frequently sustained complaint, was conduct unbecoming an officer. The most common disciplinary action taken was written reprimand. Interestingly, the second most frequent allegation, and the most frequently exonerated, was excessive force. Suspension and counseling were other frequently used disciplinary actions. Such reports tell the public that police agencies do not take officer wrongdoings lightly and support the fact that police departments do have in-house procedures to investigate public and individual complaints about officer conduct and actions.

Reducing External Complaints

The policy of the Police Executive Research Forum (1985) emphasizes preventing misconduct as a primary way to reduce complaints, stressing that agencies should make every effort to eliminate organizational conditions that may foster, permit or encourage improper behavior by officers.

> Complaints can be reduced through effective recruitment and selection, training, written directives manuals, supervisory responsibility, community outreach and data collection and analysis.

Table 12.1
Disposition of Allegations against the Police

	Exonerated	Unfounded	Not Sustained	Sustained	Totals
Excessive force	55	1	14	3	73
Attitude/Language	8	6	31	11	56
Conduct unbecoming a police officer	13	5	22	38	78
Attn. to duty	1	0	0	0	1
(Substandard performance)					
Lack of police service					
Violations regarding reports	1	1	0	0	2
Other	17	1	36	65	119
Totals*	95	14	103	117	329

Summary of Disciplinary Actions Taken in Response to Sustained Allegations

Dismissed from the department	
Sworn	1
Suspended	25
Written reprimand	32
Oral reprimand	2
Referred to training	10
Counseling	23
Psychological evaluation	5
Off-duty employment ban	1
Officers resigned	3
Total	102

*There are 25 cases pending disposition.

Data collection and analysis might reveal problem behavior before complaints are registered. In one department, for example, an officer had a fine record on traffic enforcement, but analysis revealed that he was giving tickets to men and warnings to women, with seven women warned for each man given a ticket.

Internal Complaints

Complaints by officers are generally brought to the attention of the next highest manager. If the complaint is against a manager, it is brought before the next highest manager. If the complaint is against the head of the department, it is brought before the city manager or other head of local government, following the chain of command.

When investigating internal complaints against specific employees, the primary purpose should be to correct the behavior and make the employee a contributing member of the department. Employees are a tremendous investment. Everything reasonable should be done to reach a conclusion satisfactory to management and the employee.

The following guidelines might assist in handling internal complaints:

- Always be available to your employees.
- Listen carefully.

Officers may file grievances if they feel they have been wronged. Such grievances flow up the chain of command and may end in mediation or arbitration.

- Gather all the facts.
- Address the problem.
- If an apology is called for, do so immediately.
- Explain why. Always tell an employee why you made the decision you did.
- Explain to your employees how they can appeal your decision.

A manager's attitude toward complaints can mean the difference between a temporarily rocky road and a permanent dead end. Recall that many complaints may be symptomatic of low morale or of problems with employees' feelings of self-worth.

Causes

Law enforcement officers are not known to be "cry babies." They usually pride themselves on being tough, disciplined and able to take whatever they need to. They may, however, be harboring feelings of dissatisfaction that manifest themselves in observable behaviors management should be alert to. A number of conditions can cause officers to complain.

> Most **internal complaints** are related to working conditions or management style.

Officers may be dissatisfied with safety conditions, condition of vehicles, failure to provide the equipment necessary to do the job or other conditions of the work environment. They may also feel their managers are too strict or too lenient, have too high standards or too low standards, oversupervise or undersupervise, give too little credit and too much criticism, will not accept suggestions, will not communicate freely, show favoritism or make unfair job assignments. The discussion of motivation and morale in Chapter 10 included signs that officers were unmotivated and/or experiencing low morale—instances in which complaints and grievances are likely to appear.

Reducing Internal Complaints

When signs of employee dissatisfaction appear, preventive action is needed. When managers sense that "things are not going right," it may be time to set up a personal talk or a shift or department meeting. Determine the type of discontent and the cause. Pay special attention to what employees are saying in small groups. Talk with individual officers about "things in general." Make it known that you are available to discuss matters formally or informally. As noted by Buchholz and Roth (1987, pp. 70–71):

> For many years researchers have looked for a correlation between satisfaction and performance. They have researched satisfaction about self, job, peers, management, and organizations. They found that a person could be satisfied with all of these and still not perform well.
>
> The breakthrough came when satisfaction was correlated to *communication*. The results of this research can be summarized as follows:

Satisfaction	Communication	Performance
high	high	highest
low	high	high
high	low	low
low	low	lowest

From this research you can conclude that employees who were satisfied and talked about it performed the best; employees who were dissatisfied and did not talk about it performed the worst. They probably used their energy to remain hidden. These are findings you might expect. Surprisingly, however, those who were satisfied but did not talk about it were ranked lower in overall performance than those who were dissatisfied but talked about it. What does this mean? Even people who may not be fully satisfied but have an environment where they can *communicate* about their dissatisfaction perform better than those who may be satisfied but are in a climate that lacks open communication.

Communication is directly related to job performance. Those who are dissatisfied on the job and communicate perform better than those who are satisfied and do not communicate.

Let subordinates be "in the know." Communicate and encourage two-way conversations, with *listening* to employees the most important part. Such communication will not only help employees be more satisfied but also help identify problems before they become major. This is illustrated in the **Pinch Model,** Figure 12.1, which illustrates the importance of open communication and the likely consequences of its absence.

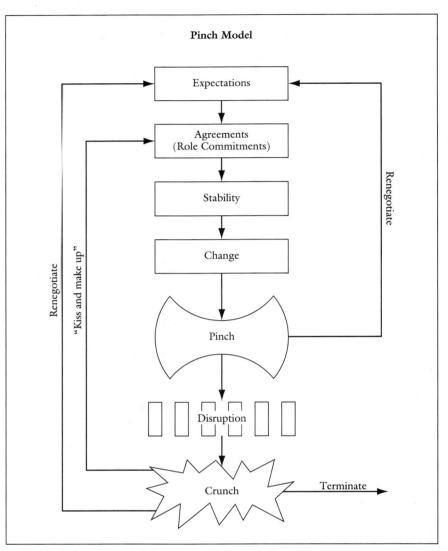

Figure 12.1
The Pinch Model

Source: Steve Buchholz and Thomas Roth. *Creating the High-Performance Team*, p. 73.
Copyright 1987 by John Wiley and Sons, Inc. Reprinted by permission.

Buchholz and Roth (p. 72) define a **pinch** as "a small problem or interpersonal disturbance between individuals. A pinch is a situation in which an individual or individuals feel something is wrong. It's not a full-blown problem or crisis—*yet*." Pinches result from such things as the supervisor changing the rules, changing the schedule, failing to provide expected support or feedback or failing to keep a promise. They can also result from misunderstandings and failure to clarify expectations on the job. If small problems are handled effectively, major problems can be avoided. If they are *not* dealt with, they may accumulate and disrupt performance and relationships, usually leading to a major confrontation, or **crunch.**

Buchholz and Roth (p. 74) maintain: "A crunch occurs when the problem becomes serious. It is marked by strong emotional reactions from both sides.

This may mean a heated discussion or total avoidance." At this point two alternatives often occur. First, those involved in the crunch may "kiss and make up" but without dealing with the root problem. This results in a vicious cycle, with pinches leading to crunches and more confrontation. Or it may result in transfer or termination. The Pinch Model suggests that when pinches or crunches occur, manager and subordinate need to renegotiate, starting with an open discussion of expectations.

> The Pinch Model illustrates the importance of communication in dealing with complaints and the consequences of not communicating effectively.

In addition to keeping lines of communication open and encouraging subordinates to express their concerns, managers can help reduce complaints in other ways. They can help employees improve their education and their work conditions; inspect and improve equipment and determine what additional equipment can be requested in the next budget; give praise when it is deserved and when criticism is deserved, make it constructive criticism delivered in private.

Managers should not feel differently about an employee because the employee has a complaint or grievance. It is much better to be aware of a problem situation, even if it is negative, and be able to resolve things from the subordinate's viewpoint. Sometimes the person complaining begins to see the problem in a new light just by having the chance to say something about it and to listen to the other side.

Often people with complaints have tunnel vision and have not considered points on the other side. A complaint is usually nothing personal. Regard it as a chance for successful change. Be positive rather than negative. Surprisingly, most complaints can be worked out if they are not allowed to proceed too far. Complaints handled inappropriately often become grievances.

Complaint Policies

Any manager and any department that wants to operate efficiently and maintain high morale must take every complaint seriously. No matter how trivial or unreasonable a complaint may seem to managers, it does not appear that way to the person making it.

> A basic rule: *Never* take a complaint lightly.

Every police department should have a written complaint review policy containing the following sections:

- Purpose
- Types of complaints investigated
- Definitions of terms used in the policy
- Procedures used to investigate complaints
- Supervisors' roles
- Supervisors' investigation
- Responsibilities of internal affairs authority

- Officers' rights and duties during the investigation
- Counsel at interview
- Special examinations conducted
- Supervisory and command actions
- Chief's actions
- Disposition without charges
- Disposition with charges
- Departmental hearings
- Appeal procedures

Citizen support of and confidence in the police department are essential. A complaint policy not only establishes a plan but also states the department's philosophy regarding public complaints. Police administrators know that police-civilian encounters will inevitably cause problems. Police have unique authority in the community, as well as considerable discretionary power. The agency, community, employee and complainant all benefit from a fair, open investigation policy of complaints against the police.

Regardless of its origination, whether external or internal, the complaint must be investigated and resolved.

Handling and Investigating Complaints

Complaints can be received from any source, in person, by mail or by phone. Even complaints from juveniles, anonymous sources and arrestees should be accepted if the facts warrant.

Making a complaint should be easily accomplished. A clearly marked, easily accessible office should be open from early morning until evening. Often this is the office of internal affairs. Phone complaints should be accepted any time.

Whenever possible, complaints should be in writing. If this is not possible, the department should complete a complaint description form and send it to the complainant to be reviewed, signed and returned to the agency.

Having a complainant sign a statement can also protect the officer and department from false allegations. Scoville (1999, p. 28) notes that, although citizen complaints are part of the police business, new laws are being implemented to protect officers from rising numbers of false complaints. Some states now require all citizens who file complaints against law enforcement officers to sign a statement similar to the following:

> If you make a complaint against an officer knowing that it is false, you can be prosecuted on a misdemeanor charge.
> I have read and understand the above statement.

Unfortunately, as Scoville (p. 29) notes: "Once filed, false complaints may become a permanent record in an officer's complaint history. He or she may be subject to professional and personal embarrassment, delayed or denied promotions, or suffer punitive demotions or transfers."

A complaint against an officer, support staff or the entire department must be investigated thoroughly, following the same principles as in a criminal investigation. This is true whether the complaint is from someone outside or within the department. The investigation and adjudication of complaints will depend on the specific charge and on the past record of the officer involved. The investigation process should have a definite time limit, such as 120 days, with a one-time, 30-day extension possible.

, A careful investigation of a complaint instills confidence in management's fairness and protects those accused of a wrongdoing.

Complaints require mandatory action. In some cases the basis for the complaint is readily discernible and easily verified. In other cases, however, the facts are not as clear or even in dispute. These matters are considerably more difficult to resolve. In yet other situations the complaint is completely irrational, but it still has to be dealt with rationally.

Most complaints about minor infractions such as discourtesy or sarcasm can be investigated by the accused officer's first-line supervisor. More serious allegations should be assigned to the department's Internal Affairs (IA) department, as discussed shortly.

In dealing with complaints, determine the exact nature of the complaint. What specifically occurred that caused the complainant to take action? An investigation must support the specifics and must involve the person complained against.

If a police officer is charged with a violation of rules and regulations and feels the charge is unjust, the officer can request a hearing. If the charge is upheld at the hearing, the appeal procedure will vary from department to department. The hearing may be with the city manager, city council, police complaint board or civil service commission. If upheld by one of these hearing authorities, it may be possible to appeal to the District Court. Officers' rights regarding complaints and grievances are discussed later in the chapter.

The person assigned to the investigation must be able to draw a conclusion from the specifics of the complaint. All complaints against law enforcement employees must be investigated within the constraints of the legal process. Inquiries must be objective. Conclusions and final decisions should be avoided until all facts are available. In spite of their seemingly minor nature, complaints may have a major impact on department morale if not investigated properly. It is necessary to investigate complaints to clear the person complained against as well as to serve the interests of justice. Considerations in the investigation should include:

- Investigating immediately.
- Collecting both positive and negative facts.
- Interviewing those complained against as well as the complainant.
- Taking written statements, if necessary.
- Checking prior personnel records of those accused.
- Checking on prior complaints of the person accusing.
- Conducting a fair hearing.

Good complaint investigations not only protect the reputation of the department and any accused employee but also provide an opportunity for the complainant to be heard and the public to be notified of the results. Immediate disposition of such incidents builds public confidence, law enforcement morale and a general sense of justice.

Actions to be taken, offenses deemed to be wrongs, the status of the employee until the case is decided and other matters are often defined in the department rules and regulations on grievance procedures established by union contracts.

Internal Affairs Investigations

Arnold (1999, p. 43) states that internal affairs investigations are an integral part of a law enforcement agency and a vital step in policing its own:

> Internal affairs investigations, also known as personnel complaint investigations, are a significant part of any police executive's job. Whether only occasionally investigating minor complaints in a small department, or conducting internal affairs investigations full time for a large agency, executives have an important obligation. . . .
>
> Simply stated, the job is to determine the facts. Supervisors must view each case just as they would any other investigation, even though the "crime" may be a violation of department rules and the "suspect" is an employee.

Arnold (pp. 43–44) offers several guidelines for supervisors involved in internal affairs investigations:

> The first step is to review all pieces of evidence. Carefully examine all documents, statements, and photographs submitted by the complainant.
>
> Next, obtain copies of all associated elements of the case. These can include a copy of the crime or arrest report, a computer printout of the call-for-service, a copy of the radio transmissions, and any other retrievable items.

A fundamental component of most investigations is interviewing all involved parties. According to Arnold (p. 44): "There is an advantage in conducting interviews in a specific order. . . . By interviewing witnesses first, questions can be developed for the complainant and the subject officer when they are interviewed later." He (pp. 44–45) suggests the following interview order:

Independent witnesses

Witnesses identified by the complaint

Employees who witnessed the incident

The complainant

Subject officer(s)

Once interviews are completed, an investigative report must be written. Arnold (p. 46) stresses:

> Investigative reports will be reviewed by others up the chain of command and may resurface in a later grievance hearing or a possible civil suit. Therefore, investigators must make every effort to conduct detailed, thorough, and unbiased investigations and submit professional reports reflecting their diligence.

Civilian Review Boards

In some communities, **civilian review boards** have been designated to investigate and dispose of complaints against law enforcement officers. Law enforcement agencies have usually opposed such civilian review boards on the grounds that they erode the authority of the responsible law enforcement manager. Walker and Kreisel (1996, p. 65) note:

> The review of citizen complaints about police behavior has been a controversy in American law enforcement for many years. In response to public dissatisfaction with internal police complaint review procedures, many cities and counties have established external (or citizen) complaint review procedures.

Despite the controversy, many larger cities have civilian review boards. According to one account, approximately 100 municipalities throughout the country use civilian panels to investigate complaints ("NYPD Watchdog . . . ," 1999, p. 4).

At the heart of the debate regarding the civilian review boards is the question of whether police possess the ability, the structure and the will to police themselves. Those in favor of review boards feel they take pressure off the police to investigate their own and help reduce public feelings that the police will whitewash wrongdoing within the agency. Further, because the review board is an external agency, it can be more independent in its investigation. As Walker and Kreisel (pp. 68–69) explain:

> Citizen review developed as a strategy for enhancing the accountability of the police to the public. The core assumption is that the involvement of citizens will provide a more independent and therefore more effective review of citizen complaints than internal review. . . .
>
> The idea that citizen review is more independent and effective than internal review involves four closely linked propositions, which may be summarized as follows:
>
> 1. Citizens will be more objective than sworn police officers, and will therefore conduct more thorough investigations.
> 2. Greater objectivity and thoroughness will result in more complaints being sustained and more disciplinary actions being taken against officers.
> 3. A higher rate of sustained complaints and disciplinary actions will deter police misconduct more effectively than internal review (through both general and specific deterrence).
> 4. The actual and perceived independence of citizen review will produce higher levels of satisfaction on the part of both individual complainants and the general public.

In addition, membership of the review board can represent more elements of a diverse community.

Police, on the other hand, feel that the department can police its own, that it has its own complaint-handling procedures through existing department policies and that the police have governed themselves and will continue to do so. Many police executives feel that civilian review boards substantially reduce the effectiveness of the police agency administration. Accountability is the essence of the issue. Police feel they have accountability through the existing structure of first-line supervisor, middle manager, upper-level manager and, finally, chief of police.

A case can be made for either side. However, the agency assumption is that the organization should investigate and dispose of its own matters. If there is a serious fault in the final disposition of a complaint, the appointing authority can take action against the responsible manager, but managers should have authority to deal with matters within their own departments. Other remedies such as civil or criminal actions or hearings before civil service boards are also usually available.

Civilian review boards typically have the power only to make recommendations to the police chief executive, not to impose discipline, following consideration of a complaint. Some, however, are advocating a modification in the nature of such boards, from a strictly reactive body to one more involved in prevention of incidents leading to complaints. As Walker asserts ("Civilian Review Needs . . . ," 1998, p. 1): "Citizen review procedures need to define their role in proactive terms, and stop limiting themselves to the receiving, investigating and disposing of individual citizen complaints."

Interestingly, the presence of a citizen review board does not necessary correlate with increased citizen confidence in the handling of complaints against the police. As Johnson (1998, p. 4) notes:

> Citizens in communities with a civilian review system do not appear to have more confidence in the manner in which departments handle citizen complaints. Studies analyzing several different civilian review systems revealed that citizens felt just as unsatisfied when a civilian review board handled their complaints as when the police handled their complaints.

It is conceivable that citizens might expect more sympathy from a panel of other civilians, yet such findings support the notion that civilian review boards are capable of making fair, objective, unbiased decisions regarding complaints, not automatically and disproportionately siding with the citizen complainant to the detriment of the officer or the department.

Grievances

Grievances are as much a part of law enforcement managers' responsibilities as complaints. Grievances can come only from law enforcement employees, not from the public. A grievance is a claim by an employee that a rule or policy has been misapplied or misinterpreted to the employee's detriment. The person filing the grievance is known as the **grievant.**

Grievances are a right of employees. Formal grievance procedures are not provided to cause problems but rather to promote a more harmonious, cooperative relationship between employees and management.

Managers' decisions are not always correct. Different interpretations can be put on rules, regulations, policies and procedures. The grievance procedure provides a means of arriving at decisions concerning these varied interpretations. In most instances the final decision may be more satisfactory to all parties involved because it involves input from a number of sources and is not the opinion of just one person. Law enforcement managers should not treat employees who file grievances any differently from any other employee.

Causes

Dissatisfaction with physical working conditions and equipment causes the majority of grievances. Almost a third are caused by dissatisfaction with management's actions.

Vehicle condition, quality and timeliness of repair, equipment used in emergencies, lighting conditions, office space, excessive reports, type of acceptable firearm, protective equipment such as armored vests and tear gas and other physical items are the subject of much debate and dissatisfaction. Law enforcement supervisors need to discuss these matters at staff meetings because they are generally budget items that depend on decisions made by higher-level managers.

Roughly 30 percent of grievances result in management taking some behavior or action. This includes plural standards of conduct, failure to recognize good work, obstinate dealing with subordinates, failure to use procedures uniformly and fairly, use of obscene language, discrimination and other types of objectionable manager behavior.

Grievances concerning rules, regulations, policies and procedures center primarily on violations of civil rights. In the early years of policing, requirements were harsh concerning hair style, facial hair and off-duty employment. Employees realize some rules and regulations are necessary for the common good of management, employees and the community. They object, however, to what they consider over-regulation. Many also object to off-duty conduct regulations. They feel that stricter regulations should not apply to officers simply because of their profession.

Law enforcement organizations generally have standard policies for vehicle operation, physical use of force and when to use firearms. Even so, some objections arise on grounds that officers should be able to use individual discretion. Civil and criminal actions against law enforcement officers have tended to force standardized procedures in these areas. In general, objections are low if the rules and regulations are communicated to the entire department and a two-way discussion is held concerning limitations and reasons.

The failure of management to do what employees expect also causes employee dissatisfaction. Employees, in general, want to do a good job and resent too many impediments. Among perceived impediments are the following:

- Failing to communicate and to train employees to do the job effectively
- Failing to explain procedures and then blaming employees for not doing it right
- Failing to praise when it is deserved
- Managers' failing to set a good example for subordinates

Managers should not penalize employees for things not directly related to performance of duty or to the best interest or safety of other department employees and not specifically in the rules, regulations, policies or procedures.

Law enforcement officers cannot charge citizens with offenses that are not made wrongful acts by municipal, county, state or federal legislative bodies. Like-wise, officers should not be charged with conduct not addressed by the official regulations. If an action is objectionable but is not spelled out in the regulations, the regulations should be changed. Officers object to inconsistency in enforcing rules and regulations and to penalties they consider too harsh for the specific situation.

Resolving Grievances

Most noncontractual grievances are resolved at the first-line supervisor level. These are matters not associated with salaries, fringe benefits or conditions negotiated by the labor union or an employee group representative. The first-line manager talks to the grievant or the group filing the grievance. Through two-way communication, an objective approach by both sides, common sense, fair play and discussion of all issues and alternatives, the matter may be resolved at this level.

If the matter is not resolved at the first level, a formal grievance is filed and forwarded to the next level manager. If not resolved at this level, it proceeds to the head of the department. If it fails to be resolved at this level, the matter proceeds to voluntary arbitration, civil service board proceedings or other assigned hearing boards. Figure 12.2 illustrates the chain of command a grievance may go through. Many law enforcement departments have ordinances, statutes or formal procedures for handling grievances. Following is an example of a grievance ordinance.

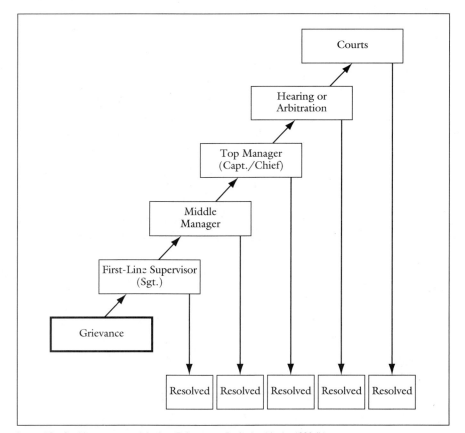

Figure 12.2
Grievance Chain
of Command

Source: "Conflict Management and the Law Enforcement Professional in the 1990s," *Law and Order*, May 1994. Reprinted by permission of the publisher.

Informal Grievance Procedure. Any employee or group of employees having a grievance shall first discuss the grievance with their immediate supervisor within five working days of the occurrence which caused the grievance. Within five working days, the supervisor shall reply. If the supervisor's answer does not satisfactorily adjust the grievance, the employee shall follow, within five working days, the formal grievance procedure outlined in the next section.

Formal Grievance Procedure. The following steps are used in the formal grievance procedure.

Step 1. The grievance shall be submitted in writing to the employee's immediate supervisor. The supervisor shall meet and discuss the grievance with the employee and/or their representative, if any, and reply in writing to the employee within five working days.

Step 2. If a settlement is not reached, the written grievance will be presented within five working days to the next level of supervision. The second level supervisor or their representative shall have five working days to investigate and render a written decision.

The procedure continues in this fashion, going up the hierarchy to the department head, the city manager and finally the civil service commission.

The ordinance provides employees an opportunity and right to bring dissatisfactions to management. It does not necessarily mean that the grievance is justified, but it provides a procedure for having the matter heard and decided. It is an orderly procedure that applies to all employees equally and is "free from interference, restraint, coercion or reprisal." The intent is to make grievances a free, above-board matter for discussion rather than a "behind the back" approach to problems.

The ordinance's wording makes it clear that employees have a chance to be heard. Grievance procedures are provided to avoid having problems fester, grow and become unmanageable. The results of such a procedure are most often positive for employees, management and the organization.

Mediation and Arbitration

Sometimes mediation or arbitration is used to settle grievances. **Mediation** brings in a neutral outside third party who tries to reconcile the two sides after hearing both and recommending a solution, which is not binding on either party.

Arbitration also brings in a neutral outside third party who, like the mediator, listens to both sides. The arbitration hearings may be informal or formal. After hearing both sides, the arbitrator recommends a solution. Unlike the mediator's recommendation, however, the recommendation of the arbitration *is* often binding.

Disposition of Complaints and Grievances

A complaint or grievance investigation usually results in one of four findings: sustained, not sustained, exonerated or unfounded.

A **sustained** complaint or grievance is one in which the investigative facts support the charge. If the investigative facts are insufficient, that is, the evidence does not support the accusations, the complaint or grievance is **not sustained.** An **exonerated** complaint or grievance is one in which the investigation determines that the matter did occur but was proper and legal. An **unfounded** complaint or grievance is one in which either the act did not occur or the complaint was false.

Whatever the outcome, the officers and department are "marked." The complainant or grievant, the person against whom the accusation was made, superiors and the press (if the matter had been previously publicized) should be notified of the findings and outcome.

Most cases are disposed of in a relatively short time, either as sustained or not sustained. A surprisingly small number have little basis for further action. If a complaint or grievance is sustained against an individual, progressive discipline such as that discussed in Chapter 11 is recommended. If corrective measures are necessary, they must be executed as soon as possible. At a set future time, the matter must be rechecked to determine whether further action is needed.

The Chronic Complainer

There is a story about a hound sitting in a country store in the Ozarks, howling. A stranger comes into the store and asks the storekeeper, "What's the matter with the dog?"

"He's sitting on a cocklebur."

"Why doesn't he get off?"

"He'd rather holler."

Some people are basically negative about everything. Griping has become a habit—a chronically dismal way of looking at one's department, supervisor and fellow officers. Some people just are not happy unless they are complaining about something. Managers who have such individuals as subordinates should recognize the problem and make a concerted effort to at least not let the negative attitude affect other subordinates. Among the tactics managers might attempt are the following:

- Do not overreact to the negativism. When possible, ignore it.
- Relax tension. Negative people often make those around them feel stressed. Do not let that happen. Break the tension with a little humor.
- Promptly undo any damage. Negative workers often stir up their peers and disrupt the department or work group. If this happens, send the negative person out of the common work area and get everyone else back on track.
- Make your expectations clear. Have a heart-to-heart talk with the negative person. Try to find out why he or she is so negative. Let the person know you expect the negativism to be kept out of the department.
- Set an example. Be as optimistic and upbeat as possible. Encourage your subordinates to act positively, too.

Complaints and COPPS

Johnson (p. 1) notes:

Citizen complaints against police officers act as a barometer measuring the community's satisfaction with the police service they receive. . . . Citizen complaints can serve as quality control for police services because the citizens represent the customers who purchase police service with their tax dollars.

Studies, however, have found that complaints are not filed evenly by persons across all demographic parameters. A complainant profile generated by such studies shows that nonwhite, unmarried, low-income males under the age of 30 are the citizens most likely to complain about the police. In fact, nearly 75 percent of all complaints against officers come from this segment of society. According to Johnson (p. 2): "This fact underscores the importance of community policing efforts targeted at improving relations with youth, racial minorities, and those individuals in lower socioeconomic groups."

The studies also revealed that the officers most likely to receive complaints against them were those assigned to uniformed patrol duties and those under age 30, with fewer than 5 years of police experience and only a high school education (p. 2). Circumstances leading citizens to file a complaint were, naturally, quite varied, but several patterns were observed (p. 3):

> Over one-half of the situations that result in a citizen complaint come from on-site interventions with police officers rather than a call dispatched from a citizen's report. . . .
> A large percentage of complaint-producing incidents involve situations when the police contact complainants in front of their families and friends. . . .
> The majority of complaint-producing incidents occurred within 1 or 2 miles of the complainant's home. Citizens may feel the police disrupt the comfort and security of their homes when confronted in their own house, apartment complex, or neighborhood.

Johnson (p. 5) summarizes the way in which such research demonstrates the importance of interpersonal communications in police work, a vital implication for community-oriented policing and problem solving efforts: "The community should view the police as their partners in the neighborhood, not as outsiders who are indifferent to their concerns."

Before concluding the discussion of complaints and grievances, consider the rights of officers named as subjects in such charges.

Officers' Rights and Legal Procedures

The nature of police work makes officers vulnerable to a variety of legal actions. In October 1990 the National Law Enforcement Rights Center was formed. This center, an offshoot of the National Association of Police Organizations (NAPO), provides legal resources to police defendants and their attorneys. According to *Law Enforcement News* ("Capital Idea," 1994, p. 3) and the executive director of NAPO, Robert Scully, the center was established to protect officers' legal and constitutional rights that "are being infringed upon by a wave of anti-police litigation." Says Scully: "Basically, we're trying to put police officers in this country on a level playing field with everybody else."

A variety of legislation has also been proposed throughout the past decade to protect due process rights of officers involved in disciplinary hearings and other court actions. Hoffmann (1997, p. 73) notes: "Bills titled Law Enforcement Officers' Bill of Rights Act (H. R. 350/S. 348) were introduced in Congress on January 7, 1997 with bi-partisan sponsors." In fact, several states have enacted Law Enforcement Officers' Bills of Rights (LEOBR). The Violent Crime Control and Law Enforcement Act of 1991 contains proposed federal legislation concerning mandated due process rights afforded to peace officers who are the subject of internal investigations that could lead to disciplinary action. In other jurisdictions, contracts resulting from collective bargaining provisions may affect the investigative process where police officers are involved.

In general, a Police Officers' Bill of Rights gives law enforcement officers, sheriffs and correctional officers the right to be notified of any pending disciplinary action within a reasonable time prior to the action taking effect, to be treated with a specific minimum standard of fairness while under investigation, to request a hearing if an investigation results in a recommendation of disciplinary action, and to advanced review and comment on any adverse material being placed in the officer's personnel file. According to Hoffmann (p. 74):

> For police administrators in states with LEOBR there are mixed reviews. Some, especially those with large departments who deal with disciplinary issues daily, find that the LEOBR is helpful by telling the department exactly what it has to do to suspend or fire an officer, and creates a level playing field for the department and the accused officer. It also reduces post termination lawsuits.
>
> Chiefs of small departments, however, find that a statewide LEOBR can create a situation where a department is forced to spend large amounts of money to discipline or fire an officer.

Another right of law enforcement officers involved in disciplinary proceedings concerns statements made by an officer during an investigation, known as the Garrity procedure. As McGuinness (1999, p. 42) explains:

> The **Garrity protection** applies whenever an employee is required by the employing agency to answer questions in an investigation. Under Garrity, the employer should provide an affirmative guarantee that the information sought will not be used against the officer in a criminal proceeding and warn the employee that the failure to respond to questioning could lead to disciplinary action. . . .
>
> For Garrity to apply, the officer must believe that his statement is being compelled under threat of substantial discipline. [emphasis added]

McGuinness (p. 42) advises: "Officers must be trained to protect themselves by incorporating a protective Garrity assertion before giving any statements in connection with an investigation into his or her conduct. Wherever possible, officers should 'Garrity-ize' themselves." He (p. 43) suggests a constitutional protection statement for officers to use when preparing statements or reports in response to departmental requests, including use-of-force, accident and injury reports:

> On _____ (date), at _____ (time), at _____ (place), I was ordered to submit this report (or give this statement) by (name and rank). Consequently, I submit this report (give the statement) involuntarily and only because of that order as a condition of continued employment. . . .
>
> It is my belief and understanding that the department requires this report (statement) solely and exclusively for internal purposes and will not release it to any other agency or authority . . . [nor will it be] provided to any subsequent proceeding other than disciplinary proceedings within my employing department itself. . . .
>
> I hereby specifically reserve my constitutional rights to remain silent under the Fifth and Fourteenth Amendments. . . . Further, I rely specifically upon the

protection afforded to me under the doctrines set forth in Garrity vs. New Jersey, 385 U.S. 493 (1967).

While under investigation, officers may find legal protection from a Law Enforcement Officer Bill of Rights (LEOBR), if one has been enacted in that state, and under the Garrity protection.

Summary

A *complaint* is a statement of a problem, whereas a *grievance* is a formally registered complaint. A complaint may be made by the general public, by people arrested or by employees of the law enforcement department, including peers or managers. The person or group filing the complaint is called the complainant.

Complaints may originate externally or internally. External complaints are those made by citizens against a law enforcement officer or officers, a supervisor, support staff and/or the entire department. Common categories of officer misconduct included in external complaints are crime, excessive force, false arrest, improper entry, unlawful search, harassment, offensive demeanor and rule infractions. External complaints can be reduced through effective recruitment and selection, training, written directives manuals, supervisory responsibility, community outreach and data collection and analysis.

Most internal complaints are related to working conditions or management style. Many could be avoided if communication were improved. Communication is directly related to job performance. Those who are dissatisfied on the job and communicate their discontent perform better than those who are satisfied and do not communicate. The Pinch Model illustrates the importance of communication in dealing with complaints and the consequences of not communicating effectively.

A basic rule is to *never* take a complaint lightly. A careful investigation of a complaint instills confidence in management's fairness and protects those accused of wrongdoing.

A grievance is a claim by an employee that a rule or policy has been misapplied or misinterpreted to the employee's detriment. The person filing the grievance is known as the grievant. Dissatisfaction with physical working conditions and equipment causes the majority of grievances. Almost a third are caused by dissatisfaction with management's actions.

Mediation and arbitration bring in a neutral outside third party to intervene in grievance proceedings. A complaint or grievance investigation usually results in one of four findings: sustained, not sustained, exonerated or unfounded.

While under investigation, officers may find legal protection from a Law Enforcement Officer Bill of Rights (LEOBR), if one has been enacted in that state, and under the Garrity protection.

Discussion Questions

1. How are complaints and grievances similar? Different?
2. Why is it important to investigate complaints immediately?
3. How would you investigate a complaint from a person who does not want to give a name?
4. What is your position on civilian review boards?

5. Can you think of an example of some "pinches" in your work? Crunches?
6. What changes would you suggest in the grievance procedure?
7. How would you reduce the frequency of grievances within a law enforcement organization?
8. Which would you prefer to settle a grievance: mediation or arbitration? Why?
9. Do you know of any grievances filed in your local law enforcement agency? If so, what was the problem and how was it resolved?
10. Have you ever been involved in a complaint or grievance, either as the one being charged or the one making the charge?

InfoTrac College Edition Assignment

Once you have taken a position on civilian review boards (see Discussion Question #4), find a recent journal article to support that position. Outline the main points supporting your position. Be sure to include the full reference cite. Be prepared to discuss your position and support with the class.

References

Arnold, Jon. "Internal Affairs Investigations Guidelines." *Law and Order,* Vol. 47, No. 5, May 1999, pp. 43–46.

Buchholz, Steve and Roth, Thomas. *Creating the High-Performance Team.* New York: John Wiley and Sons, 1987.

"Capital Idea: Center for Police Rights." *Law Enforcement News,* November 30, 1994, pp. 3, 10.

"Civilian Review Needs a More Proactive Stance." *Law Enforcement News,* November 15, 1998, p. 10.

Hoffmann, John. "Officers Bill of Rights." *Law and Order,* Vol. 45, No. 12, December 1997, pp. 73–76.

Johnson, Richard R. "Citizen Complaints: What the Police Should Know." *FBI Law Enforcement Bulletin,* Vol. 67, No. 12, December 1998, pp. 1–5.

McGuinness, J. Michael. "Point of Law." *Police,* Vol. 23, No. 9, September 1999, pp. 42–43.

"NYPD Watchdog Is Due for a Better Bite, But Critics Take Wait-and-See Attitude." *Law Enforcement News,* Vol. XXV, No. 518, September 30, 1999, p. 4.

Police Executive Research Forum. "Police Agency Handling of Citizen Complaints: A Model Policy Statement." *Police Management Today.* Washington, DC: International City Managers Association, 1985.

Scoville, Dean. "Citizen Complaints Are Part of the 'Business': Has the Situation Gotten Out of Hand?" *Police,* Vol. 23, No. 11, November 1999, pp. 28–32.

Walker, Samuel and Kreisel, Betsy Wright. "Varieties of Citizen Review: The Implications of Organizational Features of Complaint Review Procedures for Accountability of the Police." *American Journal of Police,* Vol. XV, No. 3, 1996, pp. 65–88.

Chapter 13 Conflict—It's Inevitable

> Parties in conflict must be able to disagree
> without being disagreeable.
>
> —Anonymous

Do You Know?

- Whether conflict must be negative?
- What possible benefits conflict might generate?
- What major sources of conflict exist in the law enforcement organization?
- What the 10/80/10 principle is?
- What management's responsibility is as far as conflict is concerned?
- How conflicts that arise during crises should be dealt with?
- How a problem employee is characterized?
- What types of personalities might be likely to result in conflict?
- How managers can deal with problem people?
- What the confrontation technique is and what to expect from it?
- What healthy conflict does?
- What the keys to maintaining healthy conflict are?
- What the intersubjectivity approach to resolving conflict involves?

Can You Define?

approach-approach conflict	confrontation technique	nonactor liability
approach-avoidance conflict	exploders	passives
avoidance-avoidance conflict	healthy conflict	pessimists
avoiders	intersubjectivity	positive conflict
bullies	intersubjectivity approach	principled negotiation
complainers	know-it-alls	problem employee
conflict	marginal performer	snipers
	negative conflict	yes people

INTRODUCTION

Most people agree that death and taxes are inevitable. Add *conflict* to the list of inevitables for managers, especially within a law enforcement organization. One reason is that our society has become increasingly complex. Choices used to be simpler. Coffee, tea or milk? Vanilla, chocolate or strawberry ice cream? Think about the number of choices *within* choices. What kind of Coke? With or without calories? Caffeine? Salt? What kind of weapons? Squad cars? Uniforms? Investigative equipment?

Another reason conflict is inevitable is that managers deal with people, and within the law enforcement agency people have strong egos and are used to speaking their minds and getting their way. But they are also people who depend on each other to get results—sometimes to stay alive.

A third reason conflict is inevitable is that resources are limited, and the law enforcement organization is no exception. Choices must be made as to allocation of human resources (who is assigned to what shift) and monetary resources (salaries, perks).

Indeed, all organizations, including law enforcement, will have conflict. Individual and organizational goals; differences in employee lifestyles and individual needs; varied interpretations of rules and regulations; physical, social and psychological differences and variations in viewpoints all exist and contribute to disagreement and conflict.

This chapter takes a closer look at the conflicts law enforcement managers must deal with, including some conflicting views of conflict, sources of conflict and the responsibility of managers to reduce negative conflict and make positive conflict work for the benefit of the organization. This is followed by a discussion of how to recognize and acknowledge conflict, how to manage crisis conflict and how to deal with problem employees, including problem behaviors and difficult people. Next the probability of role conflict within the organization is examined, followed by a look at external conflicts and "politics," both internal and external. The chapter concludes with a discussion of how to maintain healthy conflict and the importance of conflict resolution skills.

Conflict Defined

Conflict is a struggle, a mental or physical fight, a controversy, a disagreement or a clash. Conflict can range from an internal struggle within a person over whether to have a cigarette or a drink to armed combat between nations over boundaries or religious beliefs.

Conflict can be fleeting or prolonged, conscious or subconscious, destructive or constructive. Conflict may be:

- **Approach-approach conflict**—selecting one of two positive alternatives.
- **Approach-avoidance conflict**—selecting one positive alternative that will also produce a negative consequence.
- **Avoidance-avoidance conflict**—selecting one of two negatives, commonly referred to as "the lesser of two evils."

Because conflict is inevitable for managers and supervisors, they must have the skills to manage it effectively. In fact, one significant test of managers' ability is how well they manage conflict.

Conflicting Views of Conflict

Conflict has always existed between people and organizations. The first reaction to conflict is that it is bad and should not exist. However, considering the tension that exists within individuals and the competition between people and organizations, it is reasonable to expect disagreements created by everyday interactions.

Law enforcement organizations are no different. Officers as individuals have all the personal problems of other employees. Law enforcement organizations consist of a number of divisions and a hierarchy of command. Most requests for law enforcement service and contacts involve conflicts. Citizens call the police when they have problems they cannot resolve.

People believe conflict is always negative because they see the destructive results of conflict in wars, in marriages, in organizations and among individuals. Law enforcement departments also have traditionally regarded conflict as inherently bad. Administrators note its damaging effects. Morale decline, lower productivity, lack of creativity, poor performance and many other ills have been blamed on **negative conflict.** The prevailing attitudes are to avoid or eliminate conflict by adding more and more rules and regulations. Law enforcement agencies where conflict reigns are regarded as poorly administered. In departments in which conflict is poorly handled, it *is* a destructive force. Excessive conflict without resolution *is* negative and can lead to disunity in individual and organizational purpose, decreased morale and lower productivity.

This need *not* be the case, however. Conflict does not have to be destructive. If it is recognized for what it is, conflict can be a positive influence because it can bring attention to problems that need to be resolved. **Positive conflict** can result in personal or organizational growth.

> How managers approach conflict determines whether it is a negative or a positive force within the organization.

Although organizations with badly managed conflict are hamstrung with dissension, those with *no* conflict are in an equally unproductive situation. Organizations with no conflict are dormant, static, unimaginative, unable to change and in danger of becoming obsolete.

> A healthy amount of conflict, properly handled, motivates individuals and organizations. It exposes problems, defines causes, obtains input from those involved toward constructive solutions and may develop new outlooks.

Conflict is constructive if it:

- Encourages change.
- Makes life more interesting.
- Reduces irritation.
- Enriches a relationship.
- Encourages better decisions.
- Increases motivation to deal with problems.
- Is stimulating.

Conflict can be agitating and exciting, indicating organizational vigor. It can keep a groove from turning into a rut.

Conflict that opposes without antagonizing can be extremely beneficial to a law enforcement organization, keeping it innovative and responsive to change.

It is usually not disagreement that creates anger and hostility; rather, it is the manner in which the disagreement is handled. As George Bernard Shaw noted: "The test of breeding is how people behave in a quarrel." The challenge to managers is not to suppress conflict but to minimize its destructiveness and to transform the anger often associated with it into positive, creative forces.

Sources of Conflict

Conflict originates from several sources. In law enforcement organizations the most common forms of conflict are internal, between two or more individuals, between organization and officer, between groups within the organization or between officers and other agencies and the public.

Conflict may come from individual, interpersonal or job-related sources as well as from sources outside the organization. Change is a major source of conflict.

Individual Sources

Individual, internal conflict exists because of uncertainty, lack of knowledge, criticism, pressures of superiors or the organization, differing opinions on organizational goals, policies of enforcement or the fear of doing something wrong.

Many law enforcement personnel hearings involve actions such as conduct off duty, failure to cooperate, insubordination, excessive use of force, violation of duty requirements, excessive use of alcohol, the filing of false reports or other violations of rules and regulations. In most instances, some internal conflict is at the heart of the problem and manifests itself in a conflict with other officers or with management.

Personal problems at home can be brought to the workplace, for example, problems with children, financial matters, one's spouse and the like.

Interpersonal Sources

Interpersonal sources of conflict result because personnel come from different cultures, have different backgrounds and have different dominant needs. Many conflicts arise because of personality differences and may be the result of prejudices or biases or of different perceptions and values. Much conflict results from the various ways people view the world—ways that reflect the individual's upbringing, culture, race, socioeconomic class, experience and education. This conflict is often expressed this way: "He has never done anything to me, but I just can't stand him."

Sometimes a large group is dissatisfied, usually as a result of factors such as low pay, inadequate benefits, poor working conditions or exceptionally strict discipline. Frequently, whole group dissatisfaction arises during contract negotiations, and management must communicate openly during such times.

Small group dissatisfaction illustrates the management theory referred to as the 10/80/10 principle, which divides members of a department into three categories:

- Ten percent who are self-motivated, high achievers
- Eighty percent, the core group, who do average work
- The bottom ten percent who cause management ninety percent of their problems

---

The 10/80/10 principle divides the work force into three categories: 10 percent who are high achievers, 80 percent who are average achievers and 10 percent who are unmotivated troublemakers and cause 90 percent of management's problems.

Job-Related Sources

Job-related conflicts usually involve organizational and administrative objectives, goals, rules and regulations; the hierarchy structure; differences on how to use resources and conflicts between personnel and groups. Conflict may arise from differences over facts, methods or basic philosophies on such matters as use of force.

Groups within the organization may be promoting self-interests ahead of organizational interests. Internally, departments such as administration, dispatch, juvenile, investigation and patrol compete for allocated budget funds.

Competition also adds to conflict. Most officers seek recognition and promotion, which may result in extremely destructive interpersonal conflicts. Conflict may arise when an officer of less seniority is promoted over an officer of more seniority, a patrol officer turns over a case to an investigator and never hears anything more about the case or one officer does the work and the shift manager takes the credit. Conflict may also arise when a senior patrol officer gets a smaller salary than a starting detective, when a senior officer is assigned to patrol in a new squad car or when officers are given preferential shift assignments.

Use of Force: A Major Source of Conflict

Excessive use of force has been a major issue for police and a "hot" political issue in many cities. Several chiefs of police in major cities have lost their positions as a result of wrongful use-of-force incidents under their administration.

Law enforcement officers are empowered with the most serious responsibilities under the U.S. Constitution: possible deprivation of property, liberty and even life. The power of arrest is an awesome responsibility. The Fourteenth Amendment states that: "No state shall deprive any person of life, liberty or property, without due process of law, nor deny any person within its jurisdiction equal protection of the laws." The Fourteenth Amendment was added in 1868, and soon afterward Congress passed Title 42, U.S. Code, Section 1983, to provide a means by which individuals can seek civil remedies in either a state or federal court against a law enforcement officer who deprives them of a constitutionally protected right while acting under the color of the law. The government entity may also be sued if the officer was following an accepted organizational procedure.

The majority of excessive force claims are filed against police officers and agencies under Section 1983. Claims arise in three major areas: arrests and seizures of criminal suspects, postarrest or pretrial detention and postconviction confinement.

Excessive-use-of-force charges are most frequently encountered in arrest situations. Police officers experience incidents in which the degree of force needed to make an arrest ranges from none whatsoever to use of a firearm. Police officers are empowered to use such reasonable force as is necessary to make an arrest. If there is no resistance, no force is necessary. If force is required, when the resistance stops, so should the use of force.

In one use-of-force complaint, a father and son appeared at a police station, the son showing serious cuts and bruises to his face and head. The father claimed police had beaten his son during a traffic stop, one officer holding the boy's arms back while the other struck him repeatedly, all prior to a formal arrest. During the complaint investigation, the supervisor located several photographs taken at the county jail, two hours after the boy's arrest, clearly showing the young man's face and head free of injury. When the supervisor confronted the father and son with the time-and-date-stamped photos, they demanded to speak to their attorney. Apparently the father had beaten the son for getting arrested and then plotted to sue the police department for monetary damages. In this case basic investigatory processes revealed a false use-of-force complaint.

Perhaps the best known use-of-force case is that of *Rodney King v Los Angeles*. Both the city and the officers involved were sued under Section 1983. Additionally, other officers who stood by and did nothing to prevent the alleged wrongful acts were involved under the **nonactor liability** provisions. That is, officers who were present at a scene at which use of force was in question or where force was obviously excessive yet did nothing to prevent it have also been held liable by the courts.

A frequently cited precedent case is *Byrd v Brishke* (1972). In this case the plaintiff was surrounded by a dozen officers and repeatedly struck. Because he could not identify the officers who beat him, he filed on the theory that the officers not involved in the beating should be held liable for negligently or intentionally failing to protect him from others who violated his rights by beating him. The court established a clear duty to act on the part of both supervisors and peer officers who observe other officers committing unconstitutional acts.

Miraglia (1999, p. 30) contends departments must address use-of-force complaints before they happen by teaching excessive-force intervention techniques:

Teaching excessive-force intervention is a delicate and controversial topic. . . . Preventing incidents of excessive force [involves] teaching officers how to recognize when an incident is about to occur and how to intervene appropriately. Another important component addresses how to manage the incident following the use of force in order to prevent an already bad situation from getting worse.

Administrators should ensure that recruits receive instruction on how to handle various levels of force. Miraglia (p. 33) states:

During basic training, evaluating a new officer's ability to use appropriate levels of force must include an evaluation of his ability to recognize when force is inappropriate and excessive. This can best be done with role-playing scenarios and demonstrations. New officers must have the chance to "see and feel" an excessive-force incident in order to become sensitized to and comfortable with appropriate intervention tactics.

When a use-of-force complaint is received, a supervisor must thoroughly investigate. Fulton (1997, pp. 54–55) suggests the following guidelines when conducting use-of-force investigations:

- Investigate early.
- Be objective.
- Document your findings.
- Leave no stone unturned—The findings in a use-of-force investigation have the potential to save or ruin careers, build up or tear down public trust, and enhance or harm the reputation of your department.
- Prepare for court.

Harassment: Another Major Source of Conflict

In recent years the number of cases of alleged harassment has increased substantially. According to the Equal Employment Opportunity Commission (EEOC): "Sexual harassment is unwelcome sexual attention, whether verbal or physical, that affects an employee's job conditions or creates a hostile working environment." Although this seems a simple definition, it has initiated complex, unsettling lawsuits with substantial risks for both plaintiff and defendant. One standard is what a reasonable person would think is out of bounds or would interfere with work.

As noted in Chapter 11, law enforcement agencies must have a clear written policy forbidding harassment of any form, including sexual or racial harassment. The policy should state its purpose, describe the prohibited activities or conduct, outline employees' and supervisors' responsibilities and detail the complaint procedure. Although the majority of sexual harassment complaints are initiated by women, the same conditions apply to men.

Sources of Conflict External to the Law Enforcement Organization

Municipalities have limited resources to operate the total city government. The law enforcement organization is one agency competing for a share of these resources. If law enforcement personnel perceive they are not obtaining sufficient resources for reasonable operation, conflict will arise. If, for example, the fire department receives more dollars than the law enforcement department or vice versa, heated disagreement is likely.

Change—Yet Another Major Source

Change is constant in most people's lives, both at home and at work, and people tend to resist it. Change threatens the status quo and the basic need for security. People like what is familiar to continue, but change means dealing with an unknown.

In law enforcement work, change is constant. Technological advances have introduced a variety of new equipment. Laws and court decisions are constantly in dispute and changing. When change occurs in administration or operations, managers tend to be more involved with the organizational aspects of the change than with human relations. The organization changes, but the organization is people. It is how people react to change that is important.

Change affects individuals in a law enforcement organization because it requires new learning and new approaches and introduces a fear of the unknown. A change of shift, assignment to a new manager, change of patrol partner, placing computers in the squad cars and many other changes affect officers. Change should be made with the employees' complete knowledge and an opportunity to ask questions.

The first reaction to change is usually reluctance to accept it or fear that it will not work. Management must explain changes and provide training so that personnel can make a successful transition. Failure to explain change will bring resistance, thus two-way communications must be established. Managers should explain not only that a change will be made but also that input from employees is desired and that there will be a follow-up and assessment. As Leonard (1997, p. 64) states: "Police departments will change; it is inevitable. But more importantly, they need to develop an atmosphere where change is looked forward to. Change should become a positive occurrence instead of a negative one." Because change accomplished in stages may be more successful, it should be viewed as a process, not a single-stage event.

Responsibility for Conflict Management

Law enforcement agencies have a number of levels at which conflict may be resolved. Supervisors are the front line to resolve conflict at its source and are directly responsible for most personnel. Yet personnel are the most frequent source of conflict, and personnel conflicts should be resolved at this level when possible.

Supervisors are also essential to conflict management because they are usually the first to know that conflict exists in the ranks. It is their responsibility to mediate these conflicts unless they believe the conflicts are deeper and more involved than the shift level of management can handle.

Group conflicts may have to proceed to middle or upper management. Using higher-level authority sometimes resolves a situation temporarily but may not always identify the problem.

If there is conflict in the relationships of manager and subordinates, such as a past problem or personal prejudices, the matter should be sent to the next management level. If conflicts exist between supervisors, responsibility shifts to middle-management level. All conflicts could potentially shift to the executive manager, city manager, civil service proceedings or the courts. Resolution at the lowest level is preferable.

Recognizing and Acknowledging Conflict

Regardless of the level of intervention, the best method to resolve conflict is usually to deal directly with those involved, determine the cause of the conflict and seek a solution. Delaying the inevitable only increases the probability of a worse problem.

Avoiding is a decision to "leave it to someone else." Managers who accept responsibility have choices of actions to minimize or eliminate the conflict and in many cases to rise to new levels of performance and productivity because of it. Often managers wish a problem would simply go away. They would like to have officers who all agree with their opinions. They dislike officers who dis-agree with them and may even consider them insubordinate. Such managers would rather use the power of their position to resolve conflict than to resolve it through input and cooperation.

One reason law enforcement managers tend to avoid or delay personnel problems is lack of training. Training in handling problem employees is seldom provided before promotion. Managers may also not understand the exact responsibilities at each management level.

Traditionally, most managers have thought that expressing anger or opposing the majority opinion is not professional. But simply because a feeling is not expressed does not mean it will go away. It often remains and influences a person, whether it is recognized or not. A statement such as, "My sergeant and I just don't see things the same way" often really means, "I don't like my sergeant."

In addition, even if a feeling or an idea is not spoken, it may still be expressed. Facial expressions and other behaviors can clearly convey a message. For example, McLaughlin and Brilliant (1997, p. 117) note that certain gestures and behaviors, such as finger-pointing, standing too close to someone, eye rolling and "dirty looks," are conflict escalators. The result of such action is that the conflict is still there, but because it has not come out into the open or been put into words, it cannot be resolved.

> A manager's responsibility is to recognize conflict when it occurs, have a system for reporting conflict and take action as soon as possible.

Evading an issue does not resolve the conflict. Transferring or isolating indi-viduals does not identify a conflict either and may interfere with the entire orga-nization's operation. Some managers avoid conflict by seeking out employees who are not apt to "rock the boat," using the authority of their position auto-cratically, increasing feelings of agreement but never actually agreeing or stalling for time, hoping the problem will go away. Willingness to do battle when neces-sary is a form of honesty and is expected of managers and supervisors.

Managing Crisis Conflict

Conflict is a constant concern of management. Usually it is best handled through discussion, exploration of causes and alternatives and participatory leadership. In crises, however, such conflict management is not possible.

> Conflicts that arise during crises must be managed following established procedures and the chain of command.

Such management is usually reactive rather than proactive. Procedures must be established to minimize conflicts and to resolve those that occur during a cri-sis. The following guidelines might assist:

- Anticipate the kinds of conflict and who might be involved. Establish precedents to follow.
- Make certain one person is clearly in charge.

- Make certain all officers know what they are responsible for doing.
- Let no one shirk assigned responsibilities.
- Keep lines of communication open. Keep everyone involved informed, including your superior, but also control the flow of information.
- Make decisions that allow the most options.
- If the crisis is prolonged, be sure personnel get rest and can attend to personal needs.
- If the crisis is prolonged, put someone in charge of routine duties that still must be performed while the crisis continues.
- As the crisis winds down, expect delayed stress reaction (depression, irritability, irrational outbursts, etc.). Hold debriefings.
- Return to normal operations as soon as possible.
- Evaluate performance and identify conflicts that should have been avoided or handled differently.

Dealing with Problem Employees

Employees have many reasons for exhibiting objectionable behavior. A formerly excellent employee may change behavior due to physical illness or emotional or mental breakdown. This may not be exhibited violently or suddenly but subtly and over a long period. A change in behavior may also occur in response to disruptive and objectionable changes in department rules or regulations.

A key question is: Are problem employees too costly to retain, or is it wiser to change their behavior? Changing behavior is usually more cost-effective than replacing employees, so managers must learn more about employee assistance programs (EAP) and their underlying philosophy. Many law enforcement agencies operate their own EAPs. Others contract with outside agencies to provide services such as counseling and peer support, as discussed in the next chapter.

A **problem employee** exhibits abnormal behavior to the extent that the behavior is detrimental to organizational needs and goals as well as the needs and goals of other law enforcement personnel.

Such behavior reduces the department's effectiveness and the desired professional level of law enforcement service to the community and results in numerous conflicts.

A **marginal performer** is an employee who has demonstrated ability to perform but does just enough to get by.

Often employees themselves are responsible for their problems: their mental attitude, physical condition and emotional well-being. The manifestations of such problems are laziness, moodiness, resistance to change, complacency, absence or tardiness and disorganization. These problems could probably be altered with changes in attitude, physical condition or emotional well-being.

Many factors affect employees and determine their behavior. New law enforcement employees enter the field with expectations of becoming professionals already having some college education or a college degree. In addition, new officers expect law enforcement education courses more directly related to their career while on the job. Many of today's officers plan to attend college-level criminal justice courses after employment. With education come higher expectations of special tasks, promotions, specialized assignments and higher salaries.

Dealing with Difficult People

Personality problems such as hostility, excessive sensitivity or bad attitudes can disrupt a law enforcement organization. In severe cases it may be necessary to refer an employee to outside counseling or assistance. With hostile employees it is best to listen and make arrangements to discuss the matter later when emotions have subsided. During later discussion managers should make it clear that the behavior is unacceptable because of its effect on other employees and operations.

Conflict often results from personality clashes. Personality types can be placed on a continuum ranging from those who are always in total agreement to those who are always in total disagreement. In the middle are those who are noncommittal, never taking one side or the other (see Figure 13.1).

> Difficult people include yes people, passives, avoiders, pessimists, complainers, know-it-alls, exploders, bullies and snipers.

Yes people are vocally supportive in your presence but rarely follow through. They smile, nod and do nothing. They always have excuses when a deadline rolls around. Yes people have a high need for acceptance and usually avoid open conflict. They tell you what they think you want to hear.

Tactfully confront the no-action behavior. When you make an initial request, give them time to say no. If they do not, have them put the commitment in writing or say exactly when they will complete the project. Do not allow them to make unrealistic promises. Build incremental steps, deadlines and checkpoints. Follow up and monitor the expected results. Show your approval when the promised action is taken.

Figure 13.1
Personality Types

Passives are silent, unresponsive people who seldom offer their own ideas or opinions, keeping their feelings to themselves. Their responses are usually short and noncommittal. Some will put in writing what they will not say. Working with passives can be frustrating. The major coping strategy is to get them to open up and talk to you. Comment on their quietness. Help reduce their tension. Ask open-ended questions and wait for them to answer, and then thank them for their ideas.

Avoiders put things off; they procrastinate or physically absent themselves to avoid getting involved. To deal with indecisive avoiders, find out why they are stalling. Probe. Question. Listen. Move away from vagueness toward specificity. Express the value of decisiveness. Explore alternatives. Help them make decisions, and then give support after they have made a decision.

Pessimists always say "no," are inflexible and resist change. Structure their work relationships so they have little contact with other workers.

Closely related to pessimists are **complainers**—those who find fault with everything and everyone. These people continually gripe but take no personal responsibility for anything. Confront them, interrupt the complaining and have them detail the problem. Acknowledge and understand the complaint, but do not agree with it, argue about it or accept blame for it. Discuss the realities of the situation and focus on solving it.

Know-it-alls are highly opinionated, speak with great authority, are sure of themselves, have all the right answers (or think they do) and are impatient with others. Know-it-alls have a strong need for order and structure, to be right (or at least to never be wrong), to be seen as competent and to be admired and respected. Use the know-it-alls' expertise and at the same time be sure your ideas are fully considered and used. Acknowledge their expertise, but help them see their effect on others. Show them how their ideas are helpful and yet not necessarily the only way to view an issue. Avoid being a counterexpert, but do your homework and know your facts. Raise questions without confrontation. Let them save face.

Exploders yell and scream. They are overemotional and sometimes even hysterical. Because you cannot talk to people who are yelling and screaming, first disarm the anger. Stand up and face them squarely. Do not let them go on for more than 30 seconds, but do not tell them to calm down. Put your hand out to stop them. Call them by name and keep repeating the name until they stop yelling. Validate their feelings: "I understand you are angry. I want to work with you but not this way." Help them regain self-control. Let them cool off. Ask, "What do you need right now?" As a last resort, simply walk away from them.

Bullies attack verbally or physically, using threats and demands to get their way. They are like steamrollers, using unrelenting, hammering arguments to push people to back down. They have a high need to be correct and are impatient with others. Stand your ground without being aggressive, and avoid a head-on fight. Do not argue or worry about being polite. Use low-key persistence. Do not let them interrupt. Establish eye contact, call them by name and be clear about what you do and do not want.

Snipers are hostile, aggressive people who do not attack openly like the exploder and bully but rather engage in guerrilla warfare, using subtle digs, cheap shots and innuendos. Like exploders and bullies, snipers have a strong judgmental view of how others should think and act, but they choose to stay hidden and attack covertly. Neutralize sniping without escalation into open warfare. Meet in private and avoid countersniping. Bring them out into the open while avoiding a direct confrontation by saying things such as, "Are you trying to make a point?" "What are you trying to say?"

> To deal with problem people, get their attention, identify the problem behavior, point out the consequences, ask questions, listen and explain expectations. Avoid defensiveness.

Handling Personal Attacks

Personal attacks normally arouse anger in the person who is attacked. Do *not* become angry. An angry exchange of words seldom accomplishes anything except damage. Instead, analyze the behavior and the attacker's charges. Take a deep breath and concentrate on remaining calm. The longer you remain calm and in control, the more likely you are to take positive steps toward resolving the conflict. Recognize that no one can make you angry but yourself. You are in sole control of how you react. Do not relinquish this control to others. At the same time, accept the right of others to disagree with your views.

If you find that you are becoming angry, acknowledge it out loud: "This is starting to really irritate me." This gives the other person fair warning that you may blow up and is another way to buy time while you maintain control.

Respond to the person rather than *reacting*. Think with your head, not your feelings. Listen to what the person is asserting. Could it be right? Ask clarifying questions. State your own position clearly.

Defuse the other person's anger. Get on the same level physically, that is, sit if the person is sitting; stand if the person is standing. Be quiet and allow the person to vent. Empathize by saying something such as: "I can see how you might feel that way." But do not patronize.

Focus on the present and the future, on resolving the conflict rather than on placing blame. It takes two people to make a conflict. Open the lines of communication and keep them open, but do not exceed your level of authority. Make only promises that you can keep.

If the person continues to be angry and confrontational, ask, "What do you expect me to do?" or "What do you want?" Such statements may disarm a vindictive troublemaker. They may also help you discover a person's genuine concerns. If the person asks for something you cannot deliver, say so.

If all the preceding fail, accept that this person must want the conflict to continue for some reason. At this point seek intervention from a higher level of authority or suggest that the attacker get help from another source. Distance yourself from people who seem intent on making your job more difficult, and limit their access to you.

It is probably a truism that no one truly "wins" an argument. This is illustrated by the law enforcement lieutenant who was hardworking, conscientious and highly skilled but had not received a promotion in 10 years. Asked to explain his failure to advance, he replied, "Several years ago I had an argument with the chief. I won."

Handling Disagreements between Others in the Department

The first step in handling disagreements between two subordinates is to decide whether intervention is wise. Some conflicts are truly personality clashes rather than problem centered. In such cases it is fruitless to intervene and will only weaken your leadership when conflicts involve true problems rather than simply personalities.

Some managers rely on the confrontation technique to handle such disputes.

> The **confrontation technique,** insisting that two disputing people or groups meet face-to-face to resolve their differences, may effectively resolve conflicts or it may make them worse.

Sometimes those in conflict will resolve their differences themselves. Often, however, the differences intensify, positions harden, people become angry and defensive and logic gives way to personal attacks. Those in conflict refuse to back down on any points. The adversaries bluff, almost as in a poker game, not wanting to show their true feelings.

Managers might intervene in conflicts if employees cannot reach a solution or the solution does not end the conflict. They should intervene if the conflict is disrupting the department. Once you decide it would be beneficial to intervene, meet with each person privately to discuss issues and to confirm the willingness of both parties to resolve the conflict. Then select a neutral meeting location.

If the conflict is truly disruptive, consider using the power of your position and issue an ultimatum to stop the bickering: "Come to an agreement by the end of the shift, or I'll come up with one for you that neither of you will probably like." At other times one subordinate may be clearly in the right on a given issue. In such instances an effective manager will serve as a mediator between the conflicting employees to resolve the conflict as rapidly as possible.

Most often, however, both subordinates are partially right and partially wrong. In such instances, the following guidelines may be helpful:

- Listen to both sides to understand the issues.
- Do not take sides.
- Separate the issue from personalities.
- Do not speak for one to the other.
- Get the parties to talk with each other and to listen.
- Point out areas of misunderstanding, but place no blame.
- Get the parties to reverse roles to see the other's point of view.
- Search for areas of agreement.
- Allow both to save face in any solution reached.
- Stress the importance of resolving the conflict.
- Monitor any solution agreed upon.
- If no solution can be reached, suggest a third-party mediator or negotiator.

The confrontation technique requires two disputing people or groups to meet face-to-face to resolve differences.

Helping Employees Get Along

Although conflict can be healthy, it can also be destructive. You cannot row a boat in two directions at the same time. Law enforcement employees have to pull together to accomplish their goals and objectives. It is management's job to see that they do so most of the time.

Conflicts between groups or divisions generally involve dispatch and patrol, patrol and investigation, line and manager or line and communications. Most law enforcement departments have a regulation that states: "Officers and employees of the department shall conduct themselves in a manner that will foster the greatest harmony and cooperation between each other and organizational units of the department." Violations of this rule generally occur due to lack of cooperation, lack of understanding of the others' duties, lack of two-way communication or personality differences.

Employee conflicts may also arise from the constant internal struggle for recognition and authority, from one division feeling another division is slacking off or from one shift thinking the other shifts are "dumping" on them.

When this type of conflict is not resolved, employees tend to choose sides, leading to more serious group as well as individual confrontations. Organizational goals will take a back seat to individual bickering. Hassles develop in the squad room. Officers meet over coffee or park in out-of-the-way areas of the community, talking to each other from squad car windows, discussing the latest developments. Managers who look the other way let the problem become worse.

Managers should call all parties involved in the conflict to determine the main issues. The earlier this takes place, the better the chances of resolution. As in any conflict, this should be done in private. All parties should have a chance to tell their side of the problem. Until the causes of the problem can be determined, there is no chance for solution. Ask for a frank statement of the problem as each individual sees it.

No one should be allowed to interrupt another person unless the person being interrupted is out of reasonable control. Merely providing an outlet for frank discussion sometimes brings about a better feeling.

Once all sides have been presented, go over the total problem and point out differences. Ask whether anyone has ideas about how the differences can be eliminated. Point out strengths and weaknesses of the varied positions. Be firm that the matter must be resolved, and then find points on which the parties can agree.

Employees can do more than they think about their own problems by just getting together, listening to the other side and calmly discussing the problem. When serious personal conflicts develop that are beyond the manager's training and skills, it may be necessary to call in a specialist or to temporarily transfer employees to another shift or other duties. If necessary, take the matter to a higher level of management. Prepare a written report covering the details, parties to the dispute and actions taken and ask for a date for further discussion.

Role Conflict of Sergeants

Sergeants find themselves in a position filled with potential role conflict. One basic issue is that of loyalty. Do sergeants owe first allegiance to their patrol officers or to their superiors? An IACP survey showed that patrol officers and lieutenants each felt that sergeants owed their first allegiance to them; sergeants were generally uncertain.

Fulton (1999, p. 94) lists some common mistakes committed by supervisors who have not had previous supervisory experience:

- Failure to take charge—New supervisors often fail to make the transition from worker to manager. They continue to be "one of the guys." . . . Help your supervisors avoid these problems by ensuring that they understand their role as a supervisor and leader—before they take over a unit.

- Failure to maintain good morale—A competent supervisor treats subordinates fairly, keeps them informed, encourages dialogue and shares the unit's successes with them. . . . You can help prevent morale problems by ensuring that your new supervisors understand that they are the single greatest influence on morale in their units.

- Failure to make proper decisions—Clearly delineate each supervisor's duties and areas of responsibility, both orally and in writing.

To make the transition from patrol officer to supervisor less stressful, managers should provide sergeants with a clear, concise, written job description and training. Ideally, veteran sergeants might serve as mentors to newly promoted sergeants.

Some departments have implemented a Field Training Sergeant (FTS) program, similar to the popular Field Training Officer programs. Hamilton and Warman (1997, pp. 28–30) describe the three-phase FTS program used at the Louisville, Kentucky, Division of Police:

> The first phase consists of a 120-hour curriculum designed to address topics pertinent to the prospective sergeant's position as a first-line supervisor, including disciplinary and grievance procedures, counseling techniques, media relations, stress management, budget orientation, time management, forms management, employee performance appraisals, payroll, records, etc. Successful completion of the classroom instruction is a prerequisite for entering Phase II.
>
> The second and third phases of the program consist of eight to 10 weeks of supervised practical application in two separate patrol districts and the Traffic Unit. These last two phases are coordinated through the use of field training sergeants.

Dealing with External Conflicts

External conflicts can be with other agencies or with the public.

Conflicts with Other Agencies

External conflict may exist between law enforcement organizations at municipal, county, state and federal levels, as well as with private police and security agencies. Disagreements over jurisdictional authority, powers of arrest, who is in charge at the scene of an incident involving several jurisdictions, specialized and technological duties at the scene of a crime and many other issues cause conflict. Often it is the same basic conflict that exists internally within a law enforcement organization, that is, a lack of understanding and communication that deteriorates into a personality conflict. The goal of providing the best possible public service is lost.

Conflicts with the Public

Law enforcement personnel often come into conflict with angry citizens with complaints, people being arrested or given a citation or citizens angry about a general law enforcement situation they have heard about.

The potential for conflict between officers and the public exists because officers' perception of their duties may differ from the public's. Officers on traffic patrol may enforce speeding laws. Offenders given citations may ask, "Why are you picking on me for going five miles over the speed limit on this open stretch of road? I'm not hurting anyone. Why aren't you over by the school where you could do some good?" Or "Why aren't you picking up criminals?" Officers rarely see traffic accidents happen, but they are expected to determine who is in the wrong—a potential for conflict of opinion.

Dispatchers or desk personnel are often on the receiving end of such complaints. How they handle them may be important to present and future public relations. Over the years a number of approaches for handling angry complainants have been developed.

People involved in these conflicts have learned that the first stages are important to defusing the situation. Except when the complainant is intoxicated or emotionally or mentally disturbed, the defusing phase takes from one to five

Los Angeles police officers confront UNITE (Union of Needletrades, Industrial and Textile Employees) union members celebrating their union victory against Guess to settle charges the company thwarted union organizing efforts. No violence or arrests occurred, but the potential for conflict was present.

minutes. Things have either calmed down by that time or the complainant is not going to be satisfied with anything you try to do.

In the first few seconds of the conflict, look directly at the complainant, maintaining eye contact when possible. Move to a position on the same level as the complainant (standing or sitting), make sure you provide direct attention and show concern for the person's problem. Use an unemotional tone and start a sympathetic approach by giving a corroborative response to the problem. This helps take them off the defensive. If the person is shouting or excessively abusive, take him or her into another room. The person may enjoy a sense of importance by telling you off in front of others. If the abuse continues, tell the person the acceptable limitations and that he or she could be charged with disorderly conduct (if your local judges support such arrests).

When the person has calmed down, get further information about the complaint itself. Take notes. This shows the complainant that you are interested enough to record the information and by itself may calm some people down.

Follow the monologue and, if necessary, interrupt with questions to stop a prepared harangue by causing the complainant to think about something less emotional. Determine what, if any, action you can take. Consider alternatives mentally. Explain what you can do for the complainant. If you cannot resolve the problem, explain why and refer it to the proper sources. Take action at your level if you can. You are selling a service to the public.

Mediation and Community Policing

McGillis (1998, p. 13) notes: "In . . . community mediation programs across the Nation, the vast majority of cases that proceed to mediation—in schools, businesses, public policy arenas, etc.—result in settlements between disputing parties." He further states:

> As American society becomes increasingly diverse and complex, and as conflicts of all sorts—from interpersonal disputes to conflicts between groups and organizations—grow, the work of [mediation] programs . . . can be of great assistance in helping citizens address and resolve troubling and potentially escalating conflicts.

Cooper (1999, p. 5) contends law enforcement officers may facilitate such mediation among citizens through community policing efforts:

> As a component of community policing, mediation should be used by patrol police officers when responding to calls-for-service. . . .
>   If patrol police officers address interpersonal disputes through mediation, many of the goals of community policing are satisfied. Patrol officers play the role of mediator or third party who assist disputants to fashion their own resolution to conflicts. In these ways, the officer is defined as a "helper," championing a central community policing objective: citizen empowerment.
>   When a patrol officer employs mediation with citizens, he/she empowers them to handle their own interpersonal disputes.

According to McGillis (p. 13):

> Mediation provides disputants with the opportunity to communicate face to face, enables disputants to see each other as human beings rather than abstract opponents, and provides opportunities to identify common ground that can lead to the resolution of conflict.

However, it must also be noted (p. 13):

> Mediation is clearly not an option in all cases, and a variety of types of cases are [commonly] excluded . . . from mediation, such as those involving domestic violence, alcohol and drug abuse, significant mental impairment of one of the parties, and severe power disparities between parties.

Dealing with Internal and External "Politics"

Dealing with conflicts, internal or external, can be hazardous to managers, even if they are not directly involved. Intra- and interagency conflicts inevitably involve "politics." People take sides; battle lines are drawn. Managers who attempt to stay out of conflict may be perceived as wishy-washy or fence sitters. In the midst of the conflict, managers have to keep their employees functioning efficiently.

To do so, managers should first separate their responsibility from the political games going on, focusing on the tasks to be accomplished. They should refrain from discussing any politically sensitive situation with subordinates. This is quite a different matter from keeping your people "in the know." Managers should also respect the chain of command even if they tend to side with the position taken by someone lower in the hierarchy. In addition, managers should say the same thing to everyone involved. They must remain honest and objective and not simply tell people what they want to hear. Finally, when the conflict ends, as it inevitably will, managers must help smooth the return to normalcy. When it's over, it's over.

Police chiefs should become politically active in supporting political issues affecting delivery of law enforcement services.

Maintaining Healthy Conflict

Law enforcement managers seek to control destructive conflict, but at the same time they should maintain healthy conflict to improve performance and productivity.

> **Healthy conflict** challenges the status quo and offers constructive alternatives.

Healthy conflict breeds change and improvement. In fact, bringing conflict into the open is often one of the healthiest things we can do because it clarifies issues, reduces stress, clears the air, stimulates decision making and brings things to a forum where they can be dealt with, enabling relationships to continue to grow.

Managers should also provide a healthy state of conflict in their relations with their superiors because they need challenges as much as subordinates. Healthy conflict induces creative alternatives and innovative approaches to ideas and problems.

Law enforcement managers who ignore or put down subordinates' opinions, who think only their ideas are of value or who constantly remind employees of what they have not accomplished do not foster healthy conflict.

Managers should encourage subordinates to make suggestions. It is healthy to receive input from others because their ideas and creativity can be valuable to the organization. Guidelines for competition must be established to keep it within healthy boundaries. Such opposition is a help. Kites rise against the wind, not with it.

> Keys to maintaining healthy conflict include open, two-way communication, receptivity to new ways of doing things and encouragement of risk taking.

Healthy conflict in law enforcement organizations may include:

- Competition between patrol zones, shifts and patrol and investigative units.
- Brainstorming sessions to develop new techniques for patrol and investigations.
- Contests for creative and innovative ideas on law enforcement projects and programs.
- Idea-developing sessions for improving task performance.

An organization that has too little conflict is no better than one that has too much. One is dormant, the other paralyzed. The secret in organizational conflict is establishing a balance between none and too much. Law enforcement departments with a balance of conflict are active, progressive organizations.

Managers can help create constructive conflict by encouraging subordinates to disagree and to question the status quo and rewarding them when they do. If they suspect subordinates are afraid to voice disagreement, they should assure them that their ideas are needed and welcomed.

Avoiding the Suppression of Conflict

Some managers avoid conflict, preferring instead to always act as peacemakers. This is certainly appropriate in many instances, but sometimes it may result in delaying the resolution of arguments or finding the best solution to problems. To avoid suppressing conflict that may result in beneficial change, consider the following guidelines:

- Allow all sides to be heard. Encourage participation. Explain why the debate must continue.
- Recognize that some people are threatened by conflict and want disputes resolved as quickly as possible. Help them feel less threatened.
- Make it clear that conflicts are to be expected and that they serve a valuable purpose. Encourage those who disagree in a healthy manner, who are innovative and who have suggestions for doing things differently.

Understanding

A key to positive conflict is to pursue agreement with understanding. Those involved should agree to agree or agree to disagree, but understanding is a must. The classic failure in interpersonal communications is the failure to recognize the other person's right to believe in the good sense of his or her point of view. A problem-solving approach to conflict would include the following:

- Understand each party's views.
- Identify underlying needs and concerns.
- Search for potential solutions.
- Enumerate probable consequences.
- Select manageable alternatives that satisfy all parties.
- Develop mechanisms to monitor and adjust.

Learning more about each other and about the task required of those involved in a conflict is helpful. Lack of understanding of each other's jobs increases conflict. Some departments rotate officers between shifts and patrol zones to provide a broader understanding of the total problems of the community. This also applies to divisions. For example, transferring some patrol personnel to investigations may help patrol understand investigating division problems.

Another solution is to have each person or group state what they would do if they were the other person or group in the conflict. In other words, force them to perceive the issue from the other side. It is much the same approach as having others state how they perceive you and comparing this with how you perceive yourself. Such an approach can be very revealing.

Another approach to solving group conflict is **intersubjectivity.** This refers to people's mutually understanding and respecting each others' viewpoints, a kind of reciprocal empathy. In this approach, each person's most important ideas about the problem and its solution are recorded on separate 3" × 5" cards. From the total set of cards, about 40 are chosen to represent all contributions.

The group involved in the conflict meets, and each person is given a set of cards and asked to organize them in a meaningful way. Most people arrange their cards on the table in plain view, and discussion arises as to how each is sorting and arranging. The power of the exercise is not in what each person does with the cards but in the discussion it produces. This provides a basis for deepening mutual understanding and for the eventual merging of different perspectives.

> The **intersubjectivity approach** uses 3″ × 5″ cards as a means to get people in conflict to share their most important ideas about a problem and to come to a mutual understanding of and respect for each other's viewpoints.

The goal of conflict negotiation is not total solution but a manageable level of conflict.

Conflict Resolution Skills

Conflict is inevitable, so managers must learn to deal with it effectively and manage it positively. Conflict resolution skills should be part of every officer's training because it will be invaluable "on the streets" as well as in interactions within the organization. Conflict can result in one of three situations: win-lose, lose-lose and win-win.

In *win-lose situations,* the supervisor uses command/control authority, giving orders and expecting them to be carried out. The subordinate must either obey or face disciplinary action. This is how conflicts have traditionally been managed within law enforcement organizations. Win-lose can produce frustration.

In *lose-lose situations,* a conflict is settled through an ineffective compromise, with neither side feeling they have accomplished their purpose. The underlying philosophy is that "something is better than nothing" and that direct confrontation should be avoided. Such short-term solutions may result in even greater conflict in the future.

In *win-win situations* the focus is on the basic merits of each side rather than on "interpersonal haggling." Billy and Stupak (1994, p. 41) note that research from the Harvard Negotiating Project has resulted in a method known as **principled negotiation,** a higher-level approach to effective mediation:

> Principled negotiation pays attention to basic interests and mutually satisfying options. Positional bargaining is avoided since arguing over position tends to produce rushed agreements which can lead to damaged relationships.

Four specific strategies might be used in win-win mediation (Billy and Stupak, pp. 41–42):

1. Separate the people from the problem. . . . The participants . . . should come to view themselves as working together to solve a particular problem.

2. Focus on interest(s), not positions. [Consider, for example, two individuals who both want a pumpkin. One solution would be to cut the

pumpkin in half. But unless the *interests* of each party are considered, this may not be the best solution. What if one person wanted to make pumpkin seeds and the other wanted to make a pumpkin pie? Here the resolution could result in a win-win situation for both.]

3. Look at the options.

4. Establish that a single opinion without dialogue is unsatisfactory ("the issue of stubborn negotiators").

Principled negotiation proceeds in four basic steps, each involving both theory and practice, as Figure 13.2 illustrates.

First, clearly identify the problem. Is the problem actually the heart of the conflict or merely a symptom of a deeper problem? Once you have identified the problem, analyze it to determine its underlying causes. The third step is to discuss alternative approaches to resolving the conflict. Fourth, reduce these

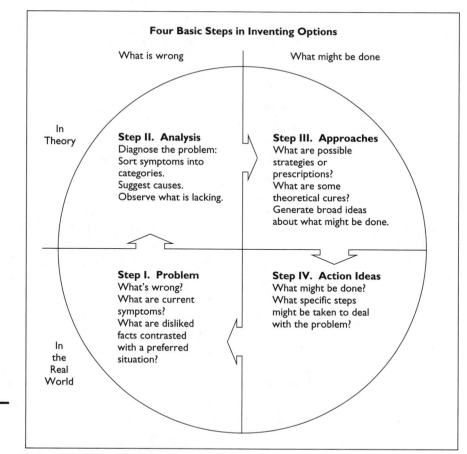

Four Basic Steps in Inventing Options

What is wrong | What might be done

In Theory

Step II. Analysis
Diagnose the problem:
Sort symptoms into categories.
Suggest causes.
Observe what is lacking.

Step III. Approaches
What are possible strategies or prescriptions?
What are some theoretical cures?
Generate broad ideas about what might be done.

Step I. Problem
What's wrong?
What are current symptoms?
What are disliked facts contrasted with a preferred situation?

Step IV. Action Ideas
What might be done?
What specific steps might be taken to deal with the problem?

In the Real World

Figure 13.2
The Steps in Principled Negotiations

Source: Joseph Billy, Jr. and Ronald J. Stupak. "Conflict Management and the Law Enforcement Professional in the 1990s." *Law and Order,* May 1994, p. 39. Reprinted by permission of *Law and Order.*

Table 13.1 **Mediation**	Approach	When to Use
	Ask employees to pinpoint the root of the problem.	To build cooperation To pave the way for yielding to an employee's suggestion To maintain harmony and good will
	Take charge of the situation.	In an emergency where quick action is vital To implement unpopular ideas To enforce rules or discipline (Use sparingly.)
	Work toward a reasonable compromise.	When other methods aren't working To establish a middle ground To get quick group agreement
	Integrate all parties into a creative solution.	To benefit from merging insights of people with different perspectives To get long-term commitment from everyone involved
	Step back from the whole situation.	An issue is trivial Someone else can be more effective The issue is part of a bigger problem that must be solved separately

Source: Adapted from Dorothy Simoneli, "War of the Workers," IB
(*Independent Business*, May–June 1994 pp. 72–73. Reprinted with permission
from *Independent Business*, May/June 1994. Copyright 1994 by Group IV
Communications, Inc., 125 Auburn Court, Suite 100, Thousand Oaks, CA
91362.

alternative approaches to action ideas—steps that you can implement to resolve the conflict.

How to approach mediation often depends on the specific circumstances. Table 13.1 provides basic approaches to mediation and when each might be appropriate.

Summary

How managers approach conflict determines whether it is a negative or a positive force within the organization. A healthy amount of conflict, properly handled, motivates individuals and organizations. It exposes problems and may create a forum in which people can define the problem's causes. Those involved can provide input that leads to constructive solutions and developing new outlooks. Conflict that opposes without antagonizing can be extremely beneficial to law enforcement organizations, keeping them innovative and responsive to change.

Conflict may come from individual, interpersonal or job-related sources as well as from sources outside the organization. The 10/80/10 principle divides the work force into three categories: 10 percent who are high achievers, 80 percent who are average achievers and 10 percent who are unmotivated troublemakers and cause 90 percent of management's problems.

The manager's responsibility is to recognize conflict when it occurs, have a system for reporting conflict and take action as soon as possible. Conflicts that arise during crises must be managed following established procedures and the chain of command.

A problem employee exhibits abnormal behavior to the extent that the behavior is detrimental to organizational needs and goals as well as the needs and goals of other department personnel. In addition to problem employees, law enforcement managers must also be able to deal with people who, although not technically "problem" employees, are extremely difficult to work with. These include yes people, passives, avoiders, pessimists, complainers, know-it-alls, exploders, bullies and snipers. To deal with problem people, get their attention, identify the problem behavior, point out the consequences, ask questions, listen and explain expectations. Avoid defensiveness.

Conflict need not be negative. To bring conflict into the open, some managers use the confrontation technique, which brings two disputing people or groups face-to-face to resolve their differences. It may either effectively resolve conflicts or make them worse. Healthy conflict challenges the status quo and offers constructive alternatives. Keys to maintaining healthy conflict include open, two-way communication, receptivity to new ways of doing things and encouragement of risk taking. One way to foster healthy conflict is the intersubjectivity approach, which uses 3" × 5" cards as a means to get disputing parties to share their most important ideas about a problem and to come to a mutual understanding of and respect for each others' viewpoints.

Managing conflict is a great responsibility.

InfoTrac College Edition Assignment

Conflict is a very broad topic. Search this topic to find a subtopic of interest to you. Read at least one recent article on it and outline the main points. Include the full reference cite. Be prepared to discuss your findings with the class.

Discussion Questions

1. What is the supervisor's role in managing conflict?
2. What are some steps to reduce conflict?
3. What are examples of destructive conflict? Constructive conflict?
4. What are sources of conflict among law enforcement agencies at different levels of government?
5. What are possible sources of conflict between the police and the public?
6. What are signs of conflict between law enforcement employees?
7. How would you recommend reducing, controlling or preventing conflict?
8. Can you identify "difficult people" you know who fit the categories described in this chapter?
9. What are the biggest changes law enforcement has faced in the past decade that might cause problems for personnel?
10. Do you know of instances in which conflict has produced positive results? Would these results have been accomplished without conflict?

References

Billy, Joseph, Jr. and Stupak, Ronald J. "Conflict Management and the Law Enforcement Professional in the 1990s." *Law and Order,* Vol. 42, No. 5, May 1994, pp. 39–43.
Cooper, Christopher. "Mediation by Patrol Police Officers." *Police Forum–Academy of Criminal Justice Sciences Police Section,* Vol. 9, No. 2, April 1999, pp. 1–6.
Fulton, Roger. "Use-of-Force Investigations." *Law Enforcement Technology,* Vol. 24, No. 8, August 1997, pp. 54–55.
Fulton, Roger. "Supervising Your Supervisors." *Law Enforcement Technology,* Vol. 26, No. 11, November 1999, p. 94.

Hamilton, Douglas and Warman, Barbara. "First-Line Supervision: Preparing Officers to Face the Transition to Command." *The Police Chief,* Vol. LXIV, No. 11, November 1997, pp. 28–31.

Leonard, Karl. "Making Change a Positive Experience." *Law and Order,* Vol. 45, No. 5, May 1997, pp. 63–64.

McGillis, Daniel. *Resolving Community Conflict: The Dispute Settlement Center of Durham, North Carolina.* Washington, DC: National Institute of Justice, Program Focus, September 1998. (NCJ-172203)

McLaughlin, Karen A. and Brilliant, Kelly J. *Healing the Hate.* Washington, DC: Office of Juvenile Justice and Delinquency Prevention, 1997.

Miraglia, Greg. "Teaching the Tactics of Intervention." *The Police Chief,* Vol. LXVI, No. 11, November 1999, pp. 30–33.

Chapter 14 Stress

> Your day-by-day—sometimes minute-by-minute—contact with criminals, complainants and citizens alike who are crying, cursing, bleeding, puking, yelling, spitting . . . and just plain crazy subjects your system to repeated onslaughts of disturbance.
>
> —Charles Remsberg, The Tactical Edge

Do You Know?

- Whether stress must always be negative?
- What common sources of stress are?
- What may be a major source of stress?
- What the four categories of stress are?
- What PTSD is? Who is most at risk for PTSD?
- Which law enforcement employees face stress from additional sources?
- How stress can affect people?
- What physical problems stress is related to?
- What percentage of illness is stress related?
- What symptoms of burnout are?
- How managers can help prevent burnout?
- What coping mechanisms may be used?
- How stress can be reduced?
- How alcohol, drugs and smoking relate to stress?
- What programs can reduce stress?
- What departments can provide to help officers?

Can You Define?

acute stress
afterburn
blue flame
burnout
chronic stress
circadian system
critical incident
critical incident stress debriefing (CISD)
cumulative stress

desynchronization
disequilibrium
distress
diurnal
employee assistance program (EAP)
eustress
external stress
homeostasis
operational stress

organizational stress
personal stress
post-traumatic stress disorder (PTSD)
psychological hardiness
stress
traumatic stress
type A personality
type B personality
zeitgebers

INTRODUCTION

Hans Selye, MD (1907–1982), the "father of the stress field," originally defined *stress* as the body's nonspecific response to any demand placed on it. He later said stress was simply the wear and tear caused by living. In fact, Thompson (1999, p. 109) noted: "Stress is the product of an entire lifestyle, not an isolated incident. Someone once said that the only way to rid the body of stress was to die."

Stress, like conflict, has both a positive and a negative aspect. In ancient China the symbol for stress included two written characters—one for opportunity and one for danger.

Stress can be helpful (eustress) or harmful (distress), depending on its intensity and frequency, as well as on how it is mediated.

Eustress is positive stress that enables people to function and accomplish goals. It allows law enforcement officers to react instantaneously in life-threatening situations, to feel the excitement, the energy and the heightening of the senses. **Distress,** in contrast, is negative stress that can lead to a variety of diseases including depression.

Although stress can be positive, most people equate stress with distress. The remainder of this chapter will use the term in this sense because it is the negative stress that managers must try to manage effectively. Lost hours, illness and reduced performance are costly to any organization. Law enforcement workers' compensation claims have increased substantially due to stress-related disorders. They account for approximately 14 percent of occupational medical claims. This rise in stress-related claims may be due to excessive, unremitting stress. In activities at home and at work, too many high-stress incidents are occurring with no chance to "come back to normal" between incidents. Stress becomes overpowering.

This chapter begins by defining stress and identifying some major sources of stress, including general sources, personality factors and job-related sources. This is followed by an in-depth discussion of post-traumatic stress disorder, those most likely to suffer from this condition and the effects of line-of-duty deaths. Next, the chapter examines the additional stressors that women, minorities, field training officers, detectives and managers often encounter. After the various sources of stress have been explored, the discussion turns to reactions to stress or the symptoms likely to be present, including physical, psychological, behavioral and on-the-job functioning. Levels of stress, including the most extreme—burnout—are identified, followed by a discussion of coping with stress. Next, the chapter presents ways managers can reduce their own stress levels and looks at how the organization can help prevent or reduce stress with specific programs. The chapter concludes with an examination of the manager's/supervisor's role in minimizing the negative effects of stress.

Stress Defined

Stress means different things to different people. To a mechanical engineer, it means the point at which objects break or deteriorate from excessive pressures

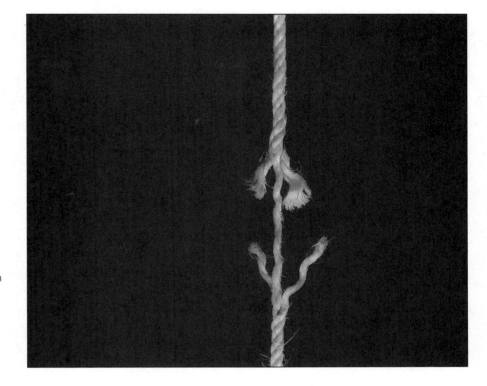

Even a stout rope will break from too much stress. Police are often placed under sudden and excessive stress. Some police departments provide counselors or use outside professionals to promote officers' well-being.

or physical tension. Stress is not that much different in humans. A single high-stress incident or recurring minor stress can cause the mind, emotions or physical body to deteriorate or break down completely.

Stress is generally thought of as tension, anxiety, strain, extreme exertion or pressure. It is sometimes described as nervous strain, mental pressure, depression, conflict or frustration. A person subjected to stress for a period of time is said to be stressed.

The biological concept of homeostasis helps explain how stress works. **Homeostasis** is the process that keeps all bodily functions, such as breathing and blood circulation, in balance. To see homeostasis at work, run in place for a few minutes and then sit down. The running mildly stresses your body, temporarily putting it out of balance. After you rest, however, your body returns to normal.

The same thing happens in acute stress, illustrated in Figure 14.1. **Acute stress** is severe, extremely intense distress that lasts a limited time and then the person returns to normal. It is sometimes called **traumatic stress** and has been compared to a cannon shot. **Chronic stress,** in contrast, is less severe but continues and eventually becomes debilitating. It is sometimes called **cumulative stress** and has been compared to grape shot. A person suffering from chronic stress does not return to normal but remains in a state of **disequilibrium,** as illustrated in Figure 14.2.

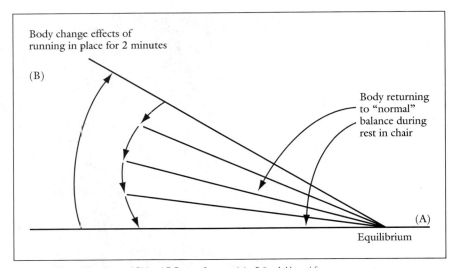

Body change effects of
running in place for 2 minutes

(B)

Body returning
to "normal"
balance during
rest in chair

(A)
Equilibrium

Figure 14.1
**Acute Stress
and Homeostasis**

Source: Lynn Hunt Monahan and Richard E. Farmer. *Stress and the Police: A Manual for
Prevention.* Pacific Palisades, CA: Palisades Publishers, 1980, p. 6. Reprinted by permission.

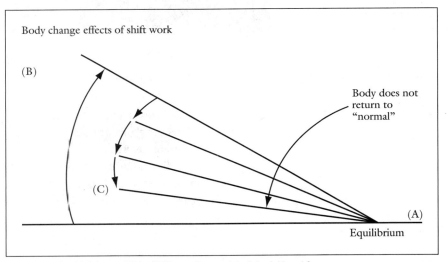

Body change effects of shift work

(B)

Body does not
return to
"normal"

(C)

(A)
Equilibrium

Figure 14.2
**Chronic Stress
and Disequilibrium**

Source: Lynn Hunt Monahan and Richard E. Farmer. *Stress and the Police: A Manual for
Prevention.* Pacific Palisades, CA: Palisades Publishers, 1980, p. 7. Reprinted by permission.

Sources of Stress

Stress comes from several sources, some work related and some not.

Stress commonly arises from uncertainty, lack of control and pressure.

Uncertainty is an unavoidable part of life and of law enforcement. Officers responding to a call often have no idea what awaits them. They may be unsure of who they can trust or believe. Uncertainty is usually associated with change, going from the known to the unknown. Major changes in a person's life such as getting married, having children or having someone close to you die are all stressful.

Lack of control can be seen when law enforcement officers apprehend suspects they believe to be guilty and see these suspects not prosecuted or found not guilty. Officers must work with assigned partners about whom they have little to say. They must be polite to surly citizens.

Pressure is also abundant in law enforcement, with work overloads, paperwork, sometimes unrealistic expectations from the public and the responsibility to protect life and property and to preserve "the peace."

In addition to these three general categories of stressors, sources of stress can also be found by looking at a person's lifestyle, personality and job.

Sources of stress can be found in a person's daily living, personality and job.

Daily Living or General Sources of Stress

Some common stress producers of daily living are changing relationships, a lifestyle inconsistent with values (too committed), money problems (credit-card debt, poor investments), loss of self-esteem (falling behind professionally, accepting others' expectations), and fatigue or illness (poor diet, lack of sleep or lack of exercise).

Personality as a Source of Stress

Psychologists often divide individuals into two types: **type A personality,** an aggressive, hyperactive "driver" who tends to be a workaholic; and **type B personality,** who has the opposite characteristics. The type A person is more likely to experience high stress levels.

Job-Related Sources of Stress

Stress is often caused by the department and the job itself. Among the stressors are mandatory overtime, severe consequences for making a mistake, varied workloads, the need to react quickly and effectively to rapidly changing conditions, personal conflicts, limited opportunities for advancement, a flood of paperwork, inadequate equipment, pay below the going rate, rotating shifts, isolation from other officers, lack of privacy, unpredictable meal breaks and work that alternates between being sedentary and physically exhausting.

Kirschman (1998, p. 127) adds other organizational stressors to this list, including inadequate training, poor supervision, lack of administrative support, politics, unfair shift assignments and workload distribution, unfair disciplinary practices, favoritism, poor leadership and lack of clarity and feedback about roles, expectations and responsibilities. One survey of police officers identified some serious stressors found within their departments, the top five of which were, beginning with the most stressful, inadequate support from the department, understaffing, unrealistic department regulations, lack of recognition and inability to get along with a supervisor ("Studies and Trends . . . ," 1997, p. 3). Kanable (1999, p. 79) notes:

> The Society for Police and Criminal Psychology lists on their Web site (www.heavy.badge.com) the [top] reasons cops are different . . . from others in society [regarding job stressors.] . . . Their work environment is very negative, they have "burst stress" (they go from calm to high activity and pressure in one "burst"), they must constantly control their emotions, they don't work 9 to 5— they work shifts, they wear uniforms to distinguish them from society (this also

can separate them from society), they work in a quasi-military structured institution, and there are laws to follow and no gray areas.

A major source of employee stress may be upper-level management.

Some top police managers must accept responsibility for causing stress among their employees by their management style. Autocratic managers are insensitive to employees' feelings and needs. Managers who seek no input from employees, who do not make them part of the decision-making process, increase stress. Managers who do not keep employees informed also cause stress. All of these are needless stressors. Some managers feel threatened by participative management, but this is unfortunate because employees who feel threatened are less productive.

Law Enforcement-Related Sources of Stress

Law enforcement is a high-stress profession. When officers receive a radio call to proceed to an armed robbery in progress, a domestic disturbance involving shooting, a murder or a serious accident involving death or injuries, it is traumatic. Law enforcement officers *do* have periods of boredom, but they also have periods of high anxiety, similar to those experienced during war. Officers know their lives may be in danger, often at the most unexpected times. They also know the officers they work with experience the same danger.

Doing routine tasks and then suddenly being thrown into a traumatic situation is exceptionally stressful.

Officers are on the alert immediately upon being notified of a call. They go from passivity to frenzy within moments. Their bodies become pumped with energy. The adrenalin flows. The heart and pulse rate jump. Breathing is rapid. When they arrive, they know they have to decide what action to take. Officers cannot leave or avoid the cause of the stress as a normal person might want to do because it is their responsibility to resolve the incident. With excessive stress, performance suffers. A single instance is normally not overwhelming, but continued similar incidents over extended periods accompanied by changes in health, stamina and age eventually take a toll.

Everyday confrontations with crime victims and those who commit crimes are also stressful.

When people request law enforcement services, it generally means problems, conflict and stress. Officers are well aware of these probabilities when they enter law enforcement. What they are really not aware of is the total effect of stress-inducing incidents over time.

Many officers make it a personal responsibility to work on certain special-interest cases and work overtime on their own. Even when not physically working overtime, they are doing so mentally and emotionally. Some officers allow certain types of cases to become obsessions. Some crimes are so hideous that the officers cannot rest until they have apprehended the perpetrator. They virtually put themselves in the victim's place, unable to disassociate themselves from the event mentally or emotionally.

An officer arriving at a bank holdup never knows how life threatening the situation may become. All too frequently officers become involved in "life and death" situations, and some require counseling to reduce internal conflict and emotional damage.

Officers also investigate incidents involving confrontation and violence. These incidents create stress equal to or higher than that in most occupations. Many participants in these incidents have been involved in violence before the officers arrive, and often the violence continues after they arrive. Domestic disputes, disorderly conduct, rape and gang activities are examples of such confrontations.

Officers seldom have a chance to discuss events during emergencies. They receive orders and act on them. The quasi-military nature of law enforcement structure prevents them from questioning orders. Although officers have legal authority and responsibility to carry out their duties, they often have to repress how they feel when dealing with the public. For example, drunks often verbally abuse officers, and although the officers may make an arrest, they normally accept such verbal abuse as part of the job. Repressed feelings remain when this occurs several times during a shift.

Officers have an opportunity to take control in various situations, and this does release stress. Officers can also make independent decisions, which normally increases confidence, self-assurance and self-esteem. Because most of these situational feelings can be discussed only with other officers, police officers tend to become isolated from society in varying degrees, and this can produce anxiety.

Another source of stress officers have is fear of legal action taken against them and their agency. Lawsuits may be brought for many reasons. Every arrest is a possible basis for a lawsuit. Once publicized, a lawsuit suggests that the officer was wrong in many people's opinion even though the suit has no legal basis.

It is difficult to preassess the total effect of going from boredom to high stress, dealing with conflict and confrontation, coping with the criminal element, facing the adversity of courtroom tactics, enduring some degree of public ridicule, dealing with the spin-off effects on family members, writing tedious reports, handling criticism by managers and many other everyday pressures of the job.

Four categories of law enforcement stress are external, organizational, personal and operational.

---

(1) **External stress** is produced by real threats and dangers, for example entering a dark and unfamiliar building, responding to a "man with a gun" alarm, and high-speed pursuit. (2) **Organizational stress** is produced by elements inherent in paramilitary organization such as changing schedules, odd hours, and detailed rules, policies and procedures. (3) **Personal stress** may be generated by an officer's race or gender or in adjusting to the police culture's values. (4) **Operational stress** is daily confrontation with tragedy, deceit, immorality, brutality and danger.

These many sources of stress have a cumulative effect on officers. Dumont (1999, p. 98) notes: "Unfortunately, on average, police officers die five years after retirement. These tragic figures can be attributed to the stress endured by officers during their careers."

One very stressful responsibility for law enforcement officers is notifying family members of a death, either accidental or caused by a criminal action.

Death Notification

Delivering death notifications can be an extremely stressful duty for officers. As Bateman (1998, p. 128) observes:

> I liken a death notification to a use-of-force situation. By this I mean that an officer giving a death notification is sure to deliver an incapacitating, heart-wrenching message, guaranteed to drop even the strongest person to his or her knees in tears. . . .
>
> Most officers want to get in and out as quickly as possible during a death notification to minimize the amount of grief they witness.

Scott (1999, p. 11) advises: "Officers can lessen the negative, stressful impact on themselves and the receivers of such painful news by following some simple, yet proven, procedures." Included in the protocol are the following (pp. 11–12):

- Knowing what to expect—Denial, anger, hysteria, fainting, physical violence, shock, indifference, amnesia and hostility represent typical responses.
- Making the notification—First, gather all of the information. Next, decide who takes the lead. Commonly two people, one of whom may be a civilian (e.g., religious representative, family physician, medical examiner or close friend), notify the next of kin. Finally, deliver the news as expeditiously as possible.

As an overview, Scott (p. 13) provides the following death notification guidelines:

- Always make the notification promptly and in person.
- Always try to have a two-person notification team.

- Always make the notification in private and with the receiver seated.
- Always remember that shock is a medical emergency.
- Always refer to the victim by name.
- Always offer to contact a support person and stay with the survivor until that person arrives.
- Always use clear, plain language.
- Always provide the next of kin with the procedures for obtaining the victim's personal effects; never deliver these items at the time of notification.
- Always be compassionate.

Another stressful aspect for many officers is working irregular hours.

Shift Work

Human beings are naturally "day-oriented" (**diurnal**) in their activity patterns. They are equipped with a complex biological timekeeping system (the **circadian system**). This system's major function is to prepare the organism (body) for restful sleep at night and active wakefulness during the day. The circadian system has a resetting (entrainment) mechanism that realigns it, *but* that mechanism is designed to cope with a "fine tuning" of *only* one hour or so per day. It is *not* designed to cope with the gross changes characteristic of moves to and from night work (or moves rotating from shift to shift).

Consequences of poorly scheduled shift work are serious. As Thompson (p. 108) explains: "The brain relies on outside influences or '**zeitgebers,**' German for 'time givers' [to keep time]. The most obvious zeitgeber is daylight. . . . Other zeitgebers are sleep, social contact and even regular meal times" [emphasis added]. When these timekeeping clues are altered through shift work, the body's circadian rhythm is negatively impacted. Thompson (p. 108) asks:

> Are continually changing sleep patterns due to shift work a stressor? You bet! **Desynchronization** (deviation from the night-sleep, day-wake pattern) can cause insomnia, infertility, stomach problems and cardiovascular illness. As a result, performance wanes, accident rates rise, attentiveness decreases. [emphasis added]

Patterson (1997, p. 36) notes other problems associated with shift work:

> Divorce rates are estimated at 30 to 40 percent higher for shift workers. Workers on 12-hour shifts may make more mistakes and become careless. Shift workers develop sleep problems that range from not getting enough sleep to not getting quality sleep. . . .
> Lack of sleep affects mood, health and metabolism. Forty-five percent of all shift workers seek medical attention for digestive disorders compared with only nine percent of day workers. Drug and alcohol abuse is triple for shift workers. Shift workers abuse caffeine, alcohol and sleeping pills in an attempt to stay awake or go to sleep.

Shift work may wear down the body's defenses, thus magnifying the effects of other stressful events. Among the most stressful events encountered in police work are critical incidents.

Critical Incidents

A **critical incident** is any event that elicits an overwhelming emotional response from those witnessing it and whose emotional impact goes beyond the person's coping abilities. Stevens (1999, p. 77) adds:

> Critical incident refers to any high-risk encounter with officer-civilian contacts when officers reasonably believe they might be legally justified in using deadly force, regardless of whether they use such force or avert its use. Examples of such incidents might include apprehending emotionally disturbed offenders, domestic terrorists, hostage-takers, barricaded subjects, riot control, high-risk warrant service, and/or sniper incidents.

In one study ("Studies and Trends," p. 3), the top four stressors identified by officers were of a critical incident nature: (1) killing someone in the line of duty or witnessing a fellow officer being killed, (2) being physically attacked, (3) responding to a battered child call and (4) high-speed chases. Stevens cites another study in which officers were asked to rank-order the stress experienced during critical incidents and general work experiences; he (p. 78) notes an interesting finding: "Some of the general work experiences [regulation conflict, shift work] produce more stress than critical incident expectations. " The rank order of 14 stressor variables from this study is shown in Table 14.1.

Officer-involved shootings have been identified in numerous studies as critical incidents that cause considerable stress in officers. Honig and Roland (1998, pp. 116–119) note that officers involved in shooting incidents experienced a wide range of effects after the events, including perceptual disturbances (tunnel vision, sense of time slowing down, memory loss), a sense of helplessness, fear about future situations and anger/rage. They (p. 118) report: "The top six reactions experienced by officers were legal concerns (55 percent), heightened sense of danger (56 percent), second-guessing of oneself (57 percent), sense of vulnerability (53 percent), flashbacks (48 percent) and sleep disturbance (40 percent)."

Table 14.1
Rank Order of 14 Stressor Variables (N = 415) (5 = highest; 1 = lowest)

Stressor	Mean
Child Beaten/Abused	4.39
Harming/Killing Innocent Person	3.93
Conflict with Regulations	3.90
Harming/Killing Another Police Officer	3.89
Domestic Violence Calls	3.89
Another Officer Killed	3.71
Hate Groups/Terrorists	3.67
Poor Supervisor Support	3.64
Riot Control	3.43
Public Disrespect	3.41
Barricaded Subjects	3.28
Shift Work	3.08
Another Officer Hurt	3.08
Hostage-Takers	2.96

Source: Dennis J. Stevens. "Police Officer Stress." *Law and Order*, Vol. 47, No. 9, September 1999, p. 79. Reprinted by permission.

Rail (1997, pp. 44–45) notes that an awareness of the effects of stress on an officer's body during a confrontational incident may help improve job performance:

> When we experience stress, blood is restricted to our major muscle groups, leaving the brain to function under this new set of circumstances. . . .
>
> "Seeing stars" or black spots in your vision . . . are common changes to your sight when your body experiences stress. . . . Colors lose their vividness. . . . Vision may be blurred, or peripheral vision can be totally lost. . . . Depth perception is also affected. . . .
>
> While experiencing stress . . . many times voices will sound faint or distant. . . . Echo effects are commonly heard . . . [and] high and low frequencies can become lost under stress. . . .
>
> When an increased stress level causes blood to flow to the major muscle groups, you lose a great deal of sensitivity in your extremities. . . . Muscular control is affected. . . . Muscles in the legs can tremble or lock, hands will shake and muscles in the upper back and shoulders can go into spasm. . . .
>
> The perception of the passing of time is greatly affected by all our senses, especially under stress. . . . High-stress situations cause time to appear to pass very slowly, or just the opposite can occur.

Rail (p. 45) concludes: "When you understand why you're behaving a certain way it helps you react more appropriately. What you are experiencing is very normal. Just keep thinking, breathe deeply and stay alert."

The impacts of officer-involved shooting incidents can be long lasting. Parent (1999, p. 158) cites one study of officer-involved shootings that found: "Most of the individuals reported personal upheaval and tragedy that they continue to carry with them, several years after the shooting incident." In addition to long-term effects on the officer, shooting incidents may also have far-reaching impact on those close to the officer, such as family members and close friends. Parent (p. 157) notes: "Several of the officers stated that their spouse, or their children, also suffered as a result of their incident. . . . In addition to changes in personal relationships, several of the officers indicated they became heavy substance abusers shortly after their incident."

Especially traumatic for officers are "suicide by cop" (SBC) incidents. Burke and Rigsby (1999, p. 97) explain: "SBC is defined as 'an incident in which an individual bent on self-destruction engages in life-threatening and criminal behavior in order to force law enforcement officers to kill him/her.' " According to one study ("Ending Your Own Life . . . ," 1999, p. 1): "In 1997. . . suicide-by-cop incidents made up 25 percent of all fatal and non-fatal officer-involved shootings . . . and 27 percent of fatal shootings that year by county sheriff's deputies." The most common methods of attracting police officers, according to Pinizzotto and Davis (1999, p. 95) are a direct call to the local 911 operator or to police dispatch.

Scoville (1998, p. 43) warns: "The taking of another's life can become psychologically debilitating for the involved officers." He (p. 44) further notes: "Incident commanders who have ordered someone to take a shot may have as difficult a time dealing with the trauma as if they were actively involved—perhaps more so." Scoville (p. 43) relates the fate of one officer forced into an SBC situation, who developed an excessive interest in suicide: "Within 18 months of taking the life of another, the officer took his own life as well."

Line-of-Duty Deaths

Line-of-duty deaths are a reality. In 1998, 155 law enforcement officers were killed in the line of duty in the United States, an average of 1 every 56.5 hours, according to the National Law Enforcement Officers Memorial Fund (NLEOMF) ("Officer Death Rate . . . ," 1999, p. 8). Furthermore: "Since the first recorded police death in 1794, there have been more than 14,600 law enforcement officers killed in the line of duty" ("Facts and Figures . . . ," 1999, p. 22). Such deaths place a tremendous strain on any department.

Although any line-of-duty death will affect an agency, the death of a partner can be especially devastating. Any department might experience such a tragedy, and each should be prepared to properly handle the situation. Policies should be put in writing regarding how to notify the family, how to assist with funeral arrangements, how to help the family complete paperwork required to receive benefits and how to provide continuing support to the survivors. Officers should understand the Public Safety Officers' Benefits (PSOB) program, which, Flemmings (1999, p. 40) explains, "awards death, disability and education assistance benefits to the survivors of law enforcement officers who are killed or permanently and totally disabled in the line of duty as the result of a

A hearse carrying the body of fallen Capitol Police Officer John Gibson turns off Memorial Drive and into Arlington National Cemetery in Arlington, Virginia, during his funeral procession in July 1998. Gibson and his partner were gunned down while on duty in the White House.

traumatic injury." In 1998 Congress and the president created the Public Safety Officers' Educational Assistance (PSOEA) Program, which also makes benefits available to spouses and children of public safety officers killed or permanently and totally disabled by catastrophic injuries sustained in the line of duty. The benefits are provided directly to dependents, who attend an educational program at an eligible educational institution ("Officers' Educational Assistance Program," 1999, p. 119). The BJA also funds yearly line-of-duty death training through the Concerns of Police Survivors (COPS), Inc., a national support group founded in 1984 for spouses and children of officers killed in the line of duty. In addition to providing support groups, COPS sends approximately eight mailouts a year to its members. Regular mailing are also sent to the 4,000 agencies in their database.

Peer support and support groups are helpful in many ways. Veteran members may advise new members on available financial benefits and can shepherd them through the complex paperwork and procedures. They can make referrals for local services for everything from a funeral home to a psychological counselor. They provide a shoulder to cry on. Support groups may hold regular meetings for problems and issues to be discussed. They present a unified force to pursue mutual goals and to overcome whatever obstacles they encounter.

The results of critical incidents can be far reaching, including problems within the family, post-traumatic stress disorder and even suicide.

Victimized Families

As mentioned, the aftermath of a stressful incident can greatly affect an officer's family and leave damaging emotional scars, a phenomenon identified as **afterburn.** According to Ryan (1997, p. 68): "Family members, significant others and co-workers are all burned by their vicarious exposure to crime and their direct exposure to the officer." He (p. 64) also explains:

> Exposure to violent crime, others' pain and suffering, and man's inhumanity to man all potentially impose a heavy toll on the police officer as a primary victim and family members as secondary victims. The impact of violent crime can be severe; a significant number of officers involved in a critical incident will show transitory post-traumatic stress symptoms. Significantly, secondary victims will also feel the emotional pain and, without assistance, will become emotionally depleted over time.

Greene (1997, p. 70) identifies several risk factors that make a police family vulnerable to stress, such as limited knowledge of police work among family members, a conflict between job and family priorities and roles for the officer, and isolation felt by the officer and spouse. Protective factors that may help police families increase their resilience and better handle the stress of police work include an awareness of job-related stress factors, a negotiated family structure with clear roles and responsibilities, conflict resolution skills and a social support system.

The AFTERBURN training program for law enforcement addresses the needs of police officers and their families following the officer's involvement in a critical incident. Ryan (p. 68) states: "Programs such as AFTERBURN are attempts to bring deserving recognition to *all* victims of crime today. We have ignored the police family far too long. Moreover, we have failed to realize the valuable resource we have in the police family."

Post-Traumatic Stress Disorder

As they wage "war" on crime and violence, law enforcement personnel may have a problem similar to that experienced by military combat personnel. During World War I, soldiers were *shell-shocked*. In World War II, they suffered from *combat fatigue* and *battle stress*. Psychologists gradually came to realize that civilians involved in major catastrophes such as earthquakes, fires, accidents and rapes experienced similar stress disorders. Symptoms included diminished responsiveness to their environment, apathy, disinterest, pessimism and diminished sex drive.

> Law enforcement officers may experience **post-traumatic stress disorder (PTSD),** a clinical name associated with a debilitating condition suffered by Vietnam War veterans.

Traumatic events (1) are likely to be sudden and unexpected, (2) threaten officers' lives, (3) often include loss (partner, physical ability or position) and (4) may abruptly change officers' values and self-confidence.

The first phase after the incident, the initial impact phase, may last a few minutes or a few days. Attention is on the present, with the officer stunned or bewildered and having difficulty coping with normal situations. According to Dumont (p. 94): "Shock, disorientation, shortness of breath, excitability and fear may follow."

This phase may be followed by the recoil phase of wanting to retell the experience and attempt to overcome it through this retelling. The need is for support from fellow officers. Personal reactions may be withdrawal, anxiety, hopelessness, insomnia and nightmares. Dumont (p. 94) states: "Also common are . . . guardedness, an inability to concentrate, irritability and explosions of anger and aggression. Other reported symptoms commonly experienced are flashbacks, depression, sexual dysfunction, obsessive behavior (particularly with alcohol and drugs) and fear." Brogan (1999, p. 33) adds that survival guilt and memory impairment may also follow a traumatic experience.

Those who can be of greatest assistance are fellow officers, immediate supervisors, unit commanders, peer counselors, chaplains, mental health professionals, the officer's family and, in some cases, the media and citizens, depending on the circumstances. Those who assist should be good listeners, show empathy and concern, offer reassurances and support and provide group grief sharing.

> Officers in larger law enforcement departments and those assigned to more difficult and violent tasks, such as murders, SWAT teams or narcotics teams, are the most likely candidates for PTSD.

Dumont (p. 97) stresses the importance of recognizing symptoms of PTSD and realizing that such symptoms are common and treatable, noting: "Peer support is vital to the recovery process in that it allows the officer an opportunity to vent his/her feelings to someone who has 'been there, done that' and understands what they are experiencing."

In addition, as Heiskell (2000, p. 10) suggests: "Because PTSD is an anxiety disorder in which the victim is left jittery and tense, the practice of exercise and relaxation techniques is extremely valuable. Massage therapy has also proved to be effective in lowering anxiety and stress for some individuals. Acupuncture has been shown also to ease excessive fear reactions and can reduce traumatic dreams."

Suicide

The profound impact of stress on officers cannot be ignored. According to Strandberg (1997, p. 38): "Police officers commit suicide more than any other professional group, and the incidence is increasing." Zamora (1997, p. A9) adds: "Studies indicate police officers . . . are more than twice as likely to kill themselves as the general population. . . . [Furthermore], officers [are] eight times more likely to kill themselves than to be killed by criminals."

Various studies reveal: "Alcohol, family issues and the breakup of a relationship all contribute to the rate of police suicides, but experts point to stress as another major factor" ("PDs Grope for . . . ," 1999, p. 5). Quinnett (1998, p. 20) notes that one of the primary reasons law enforcement officers present an elevated suicide risk is their reluctance to seek help voluntarily or in a timely fashion. He proposes a three-step police suicide prevention technique (p. 19): "Called QPR, the intervention consists of three bold steps: *questioning* the means of possible suicidal communications, *persuading* the person in crisis to accept help, and *referring* the person to the appropriate resource."

Law Enforcement Personnel with Additional Stressors

Some officers are assigned to high-stress assignments such as narcotics, undercover and fugitive squad units. Stress levels vary tremendously depending on the assignment, the area and the shift.

> Additional stress is often experienced by women officers, minority officers, investigators and managers.

Women Officers

In addition to the stress experienced because of the job they have selected, female officers have some stressors not faced by their male counterparts, for example, male chauvinism, lack of respect and support, higher rate of turnover, citizen negativism and sexual harassment.

Women currently constitute about 14 percent of all sworn law enforcement officers nationwide, a relatively small increase over the past 25 years. According to a study by the National Center for Women and Policing ("Women Underrepresented in . . . ," 1999, p. 7), the primary barrier to increasing the number of women in policing has been the attitudes and behaviors of their male counterparts. Public support, or lack thereof, has been another barrier. According to one anonymous Arizona officer (Molinaro, 1997, pp. 65–66): "A woman in law enforcement must not only deal with acceptance from other officers, most of whom are males, but [also] from the public. A female officer should not try to be accepted as 'one of the guys,' but strive to gain acceptance and respect as a police officer."

Other barriers identified in the National Center study included recruitment policies that favor men; widespread discrimination on the job, such as intimidation and harassment, as women are promoted; and sanctioning of an outdated model of policing that rewards "tough," "aggressive" and sometimes violent behavior (p. 7). Similarly, a study by the IACP ("The Future of Women . . .," 1999, p. 53) revealed:

> Female officers still face bias from males; . . . female officers may face gender discrimination and a "glass ceiling" that inhibits promotion; sexual harassment still occurs in many departments; and while the need is great, there are very few mentoring programs for female officers.

Another stressor on female officers, seemingly more so than for males, includes personal issues related to home life and the issue of who is expected to care for family members. According to one article ("Plenty of Talk . . .," 1999, p. 14):

> More than half of female officers—60 percent—who leave law enforcement do so between their second and fifth year on the job. . . .
>
> While the reasons may vary, family pressure is the most frequently cited factor in female officers leaving the job. [One chief] said she had lost a good officer because she had to stay home with her children. Another left to care for elderly parents out of the area.
>
> [One officer] said her first marriage broke up because of an undercover assignment in which she had to spend a lot of time in bars. "It was a super-secret operation," she said. "I couldn't tell him anything. He couldn't handle it." She had to make a choice. "I loved the job too much."

Minority Officers

Minority police officers may have more stress than majority police officers because they are expected to be more tolerant of community problems within their minority population, yet are also expected to enforce the law impartially. They may also be expected to join a minority organization within the department, separating them from the majority of the force. In addition, plainclothes minority officers are at greater risk of being mistaken for criminals by other officers in large departments, where officers in one precinct do not necessarily know officers in another precinct.

Investigators

Several stressors accompany the responsibilities of being a criminal investigator. They may have to investigate several cases at once, often within short time-frames, because suspects can be incarcerated for only a short time without sufficient evidence. Many investigators work long hours, often on their own time, which can lead to fatigue and eventually burnout. They may also become frustrated with the court system and the perception of a "revolving door" criminal justice system. In addition, they may be under constant scrutiny of citizens who expect cases to be solved rapidly. They may not get needed backup or may have less sophisticated equipment than the criminals they are investigating. Finally, they may question society's values as they deal with horrible, inhumane crimes.

Managers/Supervisors

When officers are promoted, they assume the added stress of being managers. Promotion often involves managing officers who formerly were peers. Sometimes these relationships are difficult because of close, even social friendships, or prior antagonistic relationships. Most officers, however, understand what is required of the law enforcement manager position. They know that managers have to discipline and correct.

The amount of stress managers face varies with the position, level and assigned duties. First-line supervisors often work in the field with the officers, performing the same duties, especially in smaller departments. In addition, they have the problems of managing others.

The higher the level of law enforcement manager, the more stress in developing programs, preparing budgets, making speeches, settling personnel grievances and complaints, resolving citizen complaints and many other duties. Top managers have more control over their work and less stress from lack of control. Middle and first-line managers have more stress because of lack of control over their work.

Reactions to Stress/Symptoms

Stress demands a response, which may range from minimal to serious.

> Stress affects people in numerous ways: mental, physical, emotional and psychological.

Law enforcement managers need to recognize signs of stress in their subordinates and in themselves. Symptoms of stress appear differently in different people. Symptoms indicate stress when they appear in excess of what would be considered normal and cause abnormal personal and work behavior.

Physical

Medical researchers have reported a connection between stress and a number of serious diseases. Medical reports have indicated that as many as 60 percent of patients have indications of stress that negatively affect their health.

> Stress is related to heart problems, hypertension, cancer, ulcers, diabetes, chronic headaches, depression, anxiety-related disorders, asthma, excessive eating from nervous tension, decreased sex drive, fatigue, dizziness, muscle aches and tics, backaches and frequent urinating.

Stress can cause these medical conditions, or the conditions can be prolonged, increased in severity or aggravated by stress. Living in our complex, fast-paced society results in many stress-related diseases.

> An estimated 85 percent of all illnesses are stress related.

According to the American Medical Association, approximately 23 million prescriptions are written each year for stress-related illnesses. Physical symptoms of stress include abdominal pains, diarrhea, fatigue, headaches, increased pulse rate/pounding heart, overeating or hunger for something sweet, sleep problems, stomach upsets and weight increase or decrease. If these symptoms persist, the person should have a medical examination.

Psychological

Psychological symptoms of stress include boredom, defensiveness, delusions, depression, apathy, emotional illness, hostility, loneliness, nervousness, paranoia, sudden mood changes and tension.

Behavioral

Behavioral symptoms of stress include accident-proneness, anger, argumentativeness, blaming others, drug and/or alcohol abuse, excessive violence, irritability, inability to concentrate, lack of control, neurotic behavior, nail biting, obsession with work, rage, rapid behavior changes, uncontrollable urges to cry and withdrawal.

One person, after reading about the common symptoms of stress just discussed, commented, "I've had all these symptoms." This is probably true of most people. It is only when the symptoms appear in excess or several appear simultaneously that problems arise.

On the Job

Stress reactions found among police officers include repression of emotion, displacement of anger, isolation and unspoken fears. In addition, police officers may behave inappropriately under stress, for example, becoming verbally or physically abusive, looking for any excuse to call in sick, arguing with other officers, placing themselves in danger or engaging in "choir practice" (heavy drinking with peers). They may argue with supervisors, criticize the actions of fellow officers and supervisors, lose interest in the job or sleep on duty.

Levels of Stress

Comments of people in various stages of stress include the following: "I'm tired all the time," "My stomach feels like it has a thousand butterflies," "I just can't concentrate on anything anymore," "I'm really tense, but I feel better after a couple of beers," and "What's wrong with me?"

Stress can progress through escalating stages such as emotional distancing, denial, isolation, agitation, irritability, depression, anger, blaming others, changing relationships, overreacting or underreacting on the job and taking excessive risks.

Excessive stress usually develops over time. Initially one or more symptoms appear in a mild form. Sleep may be affected, drinking may increase or imagined illnesses may appear. At this level some actions mentioned later in the chapter should be considered.

In the next level the signs of stress are more aggravated but not so much so that the person cannot maintain acceptable work patterns or comparatively normal behavior. The person may experience singular or infrequent occurrences of mild outbursts, crying, withdrawal or impulsiveness.

In the final level of stress, people become nonfunctional. They exhibit easily recognized abnormal behavior at home and on the job. The symptoms in the preceding level become more aggravated and frequent or even constant. Depression or anxiety appears, and a feeling of hopelessness develops. People at this level may feel they will never get better. For them, life has little purpose. Work performance decreases drastically, and the person takes frequent days off due to illness. Employees may not be able to go to work or, if they do, they cannot concentrate and experience great difficulty making decisions.

The following quiz (Table 14.2 "How Much Do You Know about Stress?" *Las Vegas Review Journal,* February 2, 1994) allows you to evaluate your stress level:

Stress at its most advanced stage is often called burnout.

Table 14.2
Stress Level Quiz

Take this simple quiz to evaluate your own stress level. The "Social Readjustment Rating Scale," as it is called, was designed by social scientists Thomas Holmes and Richard H. Rahe on the premise that health and survival are based on the body's ability to maintain a balance of all its physical and mental processes. Too much change in our lives can overtax our adaptive resources, causing illness. The forty-one positive and negative life events listed here are valued according to the amount of adjustment needed to cope with each.

Directions: Add up the indicated points for every life event or change that you have experienced during the past year.

Life Event	Life-Change Units
Death of spouse	100
Divorce	73
Marital separation	65
Imprisonment	63
Death of close family member	63
Personal injury or illness	53
Marriage	50
Dismissal from work	47
Marital reconciliation	45
Retirement	45
Change in health of family member	44
Pregnancy	40
Sexual difficulties	39
Addition of new family member	39
Business readjustment	39
Change in financial state	38
Change in number of spousal arguments	35
Major mortgage	32
Foreclosure of mortgage or loan	30
Change in responsibilities at work	29
Son or daughter leaving home	29
Trouble with in-laws	29
Outstanding personal achievement	28
Spouse begins or stops work	26
Begin or end school	26
Change in living conditions	25
Revision of personal habits	24
Trouble with boss	23
Change in work hours or conditions	20
Change in residence	20
Change in schools	20
Change in recreation	19
Change in church activities	19
Change in social activities	18
Minor mortgage or loan	17
Change in sleeping habits	16
Change in number of family reunions	15
Change in eating habits	15
Vacation	13
Christmas	12
Minor violation of the law	11

YOUR TOTAL ⎯⎯⎯

Scoring: Accumulating more than 300 stress points in one year greatly increases the risk of illness. From 150 to 299 points, the risk is reduced by 30 percent. A total of less than 150 points involves a low risk.

Source: Adapted from *The Book of Stress Survival* by Alix Krista. Copyright © 1986 Gaia Books Limited. Reprinted with permission of Gaia Books Limited. U.S. edition published by Fireside, Simon and Schuster, Inc.

Burnout

Burnout occurs when someone is exhausted or is listless because of overwork or stress. Burnout results from long-term, unmediated stress. A once-motivated, committed employee experiences physical and emotional exhaustion on the job brought about by unrelieved demands.

> Symptoms of burnout include lack of enthusiasm and interest, decreased job performance, temper flare-ups and a loss of will, motivation or commitment.

Those most likely to experience burnout are those who are initially most committed. You cannot burn out if you have never been on fire. In fact, as Kaighin (1999, p. 248) notes, to those in police work: "The **blue flame** [is] the symbol of a law enforcement officer who [wants] to make a difference in the world" [emphasis added]. The enthusiasm shown by rookie officers as they recover their first occupied stolen vehicle or make their first collar is like a torch being lit. The key, according to Kaighin, is in knowing how to keep the flame burning throughout the many stresses of an entire law enforcement career.

Burned out employees can often be helped by a change—something to motivate them. Sometimes changes in the job itself help—adding new tasks or new dimensions to old tasks. Expert assistance is usually needed at this level and counseling or psychological advice may be necessary.

> To avoid burnout, keep the work interesting, give recognition, provide R and R [rest and relaxation], avoid "other duties" and limit the assignment.

Coping with Stress

No one escapes stress. How people *deal with* it determines whether they cope and develop or deteriorate. Stress in its more severe stages can be totally devastating. The severity of stress must be taken into account when considering how best to reduce its effects to a tolerable, manageable level.

> Coping mechanisms commonly used by law enforcement officers include cynicism, secrecy and deviance.

Take definite steps to reduce stress. Most people need to work to earn a living but may need to change their attitudes about their work or about the people they work with. The symptoms of stress are often obvious, but its cause is more difficult to determine and even more difficult to change. Unfortunately, we tend to treat the symptoms rather than reduce the causes of stress. A story told by Saul Alinsky illustrates this point:

> A man jumps into a river to rescue a drowning man. He saves the first victim but has to jump into the river again to save a second and then a third. After a fourth rescue he rushes from the scene. When an onlooker asks where he is going, he responds, "Upstream to stop whoever is pushing these guys into the river!"

Although the rescuer's decision seems reasonable, it is not likely to be appreciated by the fifth and sixth drowning victims. Managers must pay attention not only to the victims of stress but also to the conditions that created it.

In law enforcement the source may be an incident, a citizen, a manager, a fellow officer or other sources. Having identified the source of the stress, study all methods of relieving stress and determine what might work best.

Haarr and Morash (1999) examined gender, race and strategies of coping with occupational stress in policing and found a variety of techniques that officers used, including the following:

- Changing job assignments
- Escape (ignoring/living with the situation, suffering in silence, avoiding superiors and/or co-workers)
- Expressing feelings of anger or hurt to co-workers
- Taking formal action (filing a complaint, taking legal action, seeking professional help)
- Getting co-workers to like oneself
- Co-worker camaraderie (blowing off steam with co-workers, getting help from co-workers/mentors, seeking extra training/education)
- Forming racial bonds
- Keeping written records of action to protect oneself
- Seeking support from superiors, co-workers, or family

In studying ways in which gender and race affect the coping methods used to handle stress, Haarr and Morash (pp. 325–326) discovered:

> Men and women employ a wide array of strategies in dealing with stress, and to a large extent they use similar methods. Significant gender differences come into play only for escape: Women report a significantly higher level of use than men. . . .
>
> Our analysis revealed considerably more variation in coping strategies with respect to race than to gender. African-American officers were significantly more likely than Caucasians to report, as a coping strategy, bonding with officers with whom they share a racial bond. Caucasian officers, on the other hand, reported using escape, expression of feelings, formal action, getting others to like them, and co-worker camaraderie significantly more often than did African-Americans. . . .
>
> We also compared officers with high and low occupational stress, and found that high-stress officers used escape, expressed feelings of anger and hurt to co-workers, got co-workers to like them, kept written records, and relied on support from co-workers, superiors, and families significantly more often than officers with low stress.

Thompson (pp. 109–110) offers the following advice on how to manage stress: "Realize the potential for self direction, assume responsibility for your well being, minimize its detrimental effects, restore a sense of harmony with your particular environment, and achieve and maintain a high level of health."

Especially important is assuming responsibility for your own well-being. Having to continuously work the night shift because he was a sergeant, one officer decided to turn in his stripes, saying: "Sometimes we need to take a step back and decide which is more important, career success or personal happiness. There is a life beyond law enforcement" (Burg, 1999, p. 117). Burg's advice is as follows: "Sometimes the way to maintain personal happiness combined with a long and successful carreer is to climb *down* the ladder of success." Most promoted officers, however, would not consider this an option.

How Managers Can Reduce Their Own Stress Levels

Managers can use any of the strategies just presented and more. Fulton (1999, p. 78) suggests ways to manage stress before it manages you: "The dual demands of police work and management, by their very nature, lead to mental and physical tension. . . . To help you control your stress:

- Be technically proficient.
- Maintain a positive attitude.
- Don't expect too much.
- Take care of yourself.
- Maintain your sense of humor.
- Don't be a source of stress."

Managers can reduce their own stress levels through physical exercise, relaxation techniques, good nutrition, taking time for themselves, making friends, learning to say no, staying within the law, changing their mental attitude, keeping things in perspective and seeking help if it is needed.

Physical exercise is beneficial for two reasons: It improves the body's stamina to deal with stress, and it provides time away from work temporarily, which is also healthy. Exercise at least three times a week.

Relaxation techniques are often helpful. Most consist of removing all distractions, closing your eyes, imagining yourself in a peaceful setting and breathing slowly and deeply for 10 to 20 minutes. Courses on relaxation are often offered through community health programs. The local library has information on these techniques, as do many physicians. Some people meditate as a relaxation technique. Determine when you feel most relaxed and increase this type of relaxation as close to the time of need as possible.

Good nutrition also helps reduce stress. A diet that improves general health will help reduce stress. Information on diets is available from physicians, community health programs or libraries. Select the diet that best meets your needs. Reducing cholesterol levels requires one type of diet, whereas losing weight or dealing with a specific physical condition may require another type of diet.

Take time for yourself. Take vacations. Try to keep your mind off job-related matters when not on duty. Develop hobbies and outside interests; volunteer. Some officers write poetry to relieve stress. Take walks, listen to music, go to the zoo and go window-shopping. You will accomplish more at work if you are mentally and physically recharged by some time off.

Make friends both within and outside the department. Get active in a club or civic group. Problems and worries become smaller if you have others to share them with.

Learn to say no. Do not be taken advantage of. A sweatshirt bears the message: "*Stress*—what happens when your gut says 'no' and your mouth says 'Of course, I'd be glad to.'" Do not volunteer for more than you can reasonably carry.

Stay within the law, no matter what temptations arise. Do not add to daily life stressors by doing something illegal. Yes, law enforcement officers can and do perform illegal acts, and this adds to job tension. Consider what you do not only from a legal but also from an ethical standpoint. Doing "right" things reduces stress; doing "wrong" things increases stress. There is no "right" way to do a "wrong" thing. Be honest with yourself first and also with others.

A *change in mental attitude* can provide release from stress. You can maintain the same job, relate to the same problems that caused the stress and reduce the stress by a change in your mental attitude about your work. As the adage says, "Accept what you cannot change." The power of the mind is strong. Positive attitudes provide a new outlook on life and your cause of stress. Negative attitudes can be self-defeating. Positive attitudes can even change your personality. Adopting a positive attitude does not mean ignoring a problem but merely provides a better alternative to looking at a situation.

Keep things in perspective. If you think something is threatening, it is almost as dangerous as if it were. Do not blow things out of proportion. Be realistic. Your mistakes almost never last in other's minds as long as they do in your own.

Seek help if you need it. Law enforcement officers deal with life-threatening situations as part of their job. Personal attitudes determine the degree of stress this aspect of the job causes. Unless they have latent suicidal tendencies, no one wants to die, even in the performance of duty. If you need help coping with the job's dangers, seek counseling or psychological assistance. Talk about the problem with other officers and see how they deal with it. It is as real to them as to you. Most mental health agencies and private practitioners will run support groups for law enforcement agencies or may train officers to run them themselves. Mental stress is often more difficult to deal with than physical stress.

Finally, *do NOT smoke,* and if you drink, *drink in moderation. AVOID drugs* to control stress unless recommended by a qualified physician, and even then use them only to the extent absolutely necessary to get to a level where you can cope without drugs.

Alcohol, drugs and smoking increase stress over time and can also seriously affect physical health.

Stressful situations are not necessarily permanent. Situations change, as do levels of stress. You have a role to play in determining what happens. Develop a personal strategy for dealing with your stress. Reexamine your personal goals. Maybe you have set them too low or too high or need to change them completely. If necessary, change your lifestyle. Get plenty of rest and eat right. Laugh more often. Smile. And don't take yourself too seriously. Try to reduce uncertainty at work and at home. Confront situations, deal with them and put the unknown behind you. You will be better able to get on with the important things.

One technique to reduce stress is to prepare a list of stressors at work and in your personal life. List as many as you can, and then consider what action you can take to reduce each.

How the Organization Can Help Reduce Stress

Testing and Selection

The law enforcement administration can do much to reduce employee stress.

First, administrators can continue the strong testing already in use to select candidates most likely to cope well with stress by being physically fit, mentally stable and emotionally well balanced. Law enforcement employees who start healthy have a good foundation for remaining healthy during their careers. Physical examinations, physical agility testing, intelligence testing and psychological tests have produced better academy candidates. Administrators need to demand tests designed specifically for the needs of law enforcement personnel selection.

Law enforcement budgets provide training, weapons and vehicles, and they should provide funds for keeping fit. As in the medical profession, those in law enforcement must sometimes cope with emergency situations that demand immediate yet highly analytical responses. In both professions life may depend on the action officers take. These decisions must arise from a combination of intelligence, training and education, experience and sufficient ability to think quickly and logically.

Psychological testing and screening are only part of the selection process, but they are important because they relate to stress. Making logical decisions under stress is difficult. Mentally and emotionally weak or unstable employees can place law enforcement departments in an undesirable legal position if actions they take go wrong.

Psychological testing and interviews can help screen out such applicants. Doing so is not only a good procedure for the department but is also best for the candidates, even though they may not believe so at the time. The department benefits by less sick leave and absenteeism, greater productivity, better employee relationships, fewer resignations, fewer new hirings (with the associated costs), more work hours available due to less new officer training time and many other benefits.

Potential employees are saved from attempting a career likely to fail, loss of time spent in the wrong vocation or possible public humiliation in a critical situation. Psychological testing also helps detect applicants who have psychiatric problems, personality abnormalities, alcohol or drug abuse problems or other associated problems.

In one instance a finalist for an entry-level law enforcement position was at the top of the eligible list. After the interview the board agreed that he was the best selection from approximately 125 applicants. He proceeded to the psychological test, and the resulting report stated that the candidate had bipolar disorder (manic depression), so much so that he might be suicidal. Because the board could not assume the risk, the candidate was turned down. What would have happened without the psychological test, especially when this officer would be carrying a weapon and investigating suicides? Would the stress of law enforcement tasks such as this have been the breaking point? No one will know because he was not put into service, but the case shows the importance of psychological screening for law enforcement employees.

Ongoing
Psychological Support

Periodic psychological fitness-for-duty evaluations are also important. Psychological reviews should be available for employees who have developed mental or emotional problems after employment. They should also have psychological assistance available after a killing or other severely traumatic event while on duty. Continued annual physical examinations should also be mandatory.

Some agencies have full-time police psychologists. Others have regular access to confidential psychological services. Many agencies are now using self-help groups for police who are plagued with problems such as alcoholism and post-traumatic stress disorder. In addition some areas have treatment centers for law enforcement personnel with job-related stress disorders and other types of psychological problems.

Some agencies use a psychologist jointly with the county or state. Smaller departments may obtain the assistance of a retired psychologist in the community as a volunteer or on a small retainer.

Be aware that officers may resist professional help because they view it as a sign of weakness. They may be reluctant to admit they have stress-related problems for fear of losing their co-workers' respect or lessening their chances for promotion. However, as Kirschman (1997, p. 46) reassures: "There are an endless number of reasons to start therapy, but one thing's for sure: you don't have to be 'nuts' to be in therapy. It's enough to count yourself among the 'worried well.' " She (p. 52) lists some of the concerns that lead people to therapy, including emotional pain; poor self-esteem; difficulties coping with everyday life; high stress and/or stress-related medical problems; severe depression or the chronic "blahs"; chronic irritability; anxieties, fears, phobias and panic attacks; marital problems; sexual problems; relationship problems; troubles with kids or parents; job problems and career concerns; grief that will not stop; addiction to drugs, alcohol, gambling, eating or spending; big decisions to make; post-traumatic stress reactions and nightmares; trouble sleeping; and feeling stuck. Kirschman (p. 61) concludes:

> Counseling or psychotherapy is an investment in yourself, your family and your future. It takes guts to face problems and humility to ask for help, especially for law enforcement professionals. Seeking help when you need it is a sign of emotional health, not an indication that you are nuts or broken and need to be fixed.

Programs to Prevent/Reduce Stress

The business world has implemented stress-reduction programs such as athletic club memberships, physical activities, flex time, free time and company gripe sessions. Some of these programs might be options for law enforcement organizations. Other programs include peer support groups, critical incident stress debriefing and chaplain programs.

Peer Support Groups

Peer support groups are a particularly effective type of stress-reduction program.

Cohen, Hirsh and Katz (1996, pp. 88–89) note how police departments of all sizes are implementing peer support programs to help officers deal with stress and emotional difficulties:

> Peers who are trained to recognize (not treat) various symptoms and problems, and to make appropriate referrals, can have a strong impact. . . .
>
> Police officers will be more willing to trust and confide in a fellow officer, and will use a peer support officer as a sounding board to ventilate and explore problems if they feel safe, that they are not being judged, and that what they say will be kept confidential. A peer support team can reduce the daily stress of police work and the emotional impact of critical incidents, preventing the buildup of anger, frustration and despair that often lead to alcohol abuse and suicide.

Finn and Tomz (1998, p. 11) add that peer support groups have the three major responsibilities of listening, assessing and referring and serve two major functions (p. 10):

> First, they provide a source of help for officers who are unwilling to bring their problems to mental health professionals because they mistrust "shrinks," would feel stigmatized for not being able to handle their problems on their own, or are afraid that entering therapy might hurt their careers. . . .
>
> Second, peer supporters can refer receptive officers to professional counselors.

Such a group was started in New York by Detective Richard Pastorella. In 1982 Pastorella was left blind, half deaf and missing a hand from a failed attempt to disarm a terrorist bomb. As he lay recuperating in his hospital bed,

Police departments nationwide have implemented peer support groups to help officers deal with problems. Officers are more willing to confide in their colleagues because they share the same set of stresses.

alone, depressed, feeling utterly worthless, he decided other officers in similar circumstances should not have to suffer alone as he was. Three months after his discharge from the hospital he started the Police Self-Support Group. The group's membership included officers wounded by criminal violence, injured in traffic or other accidents, or traumatized by seeing a fellow officer go down. Almost all suffered from post-traumatic stress disorder.

No amount of police machismo can deflect the cold, hard reality of PTSD. Like a relentlessly corrosive force if left unattended, PTSD can gnaw away at one's psychological bridges until they collapse. A similar type of program aimed at alleviating stress, particularly PTSD, is critical incident stress debriefing.

Critical Incident Stress Debriefing

Critical incident stress debriefing (CISD) is another effective way to prevent or reduce stress. In CISD, officers who experience a critical incident such as a mass disaster, an accident with multiple deaths or a particularly grizzly murder are brought together as a group for a psychological debriefing soon after the event. A trained mental health professional leads the group members as they discuss their emotions and reactions. This allows officers to vent and to realize that they are not going crazy but are responding normally to a very abnormal situation. Goldfarb (1998, p. 121) notes: "The CISD is not intended to be therapy, but rather a cathartic/educational tool that could lessen either how badly or for how long a person is affected by a traumatic incident."

Thompson (p. 107) asserts: "Perhaps the most important aspect of the group debriefing is that it is considered to be the single most powerful therapeutic tool in preventing post-traumatic stress disorder." McNally and Solomon (1999, p. 21) explain various elements of the FBI's Critical Incident Stress Management (CISM) Program:

> The program offers a continuum of interventions and services, which provides both immediate and long-term support. These include defusings, critical incident stress debriefings, family outreach, manager support, referrals and follow-up services, eye movement desensitization and reprocessing treatments, and postcritical incident seminars.

A CISD should take place within 24 to 72 hours after a critical incident. Earlier is usually too early for full emotional impact to have occurred. If only one officer is involved in the critical incident, he should be joined in the CISD by volunteers from the department who have experienced a similar incident or have been trained in PTSD.

To overcome officers' reluctance to participate in a mental health program, attendance at a CISD should be mandatory. A CISD should not become an operational critique. The groups should be kept small and everything said kept confidential.

Law enforcement departments should include an **employee assistance program (EAP)** or provide referrals to outside agencies for psychological and counseling services and to assist officers with stress, marital or chemical dependency problems.

Chaplain Corps

When troubled or stressed out, many people turn to their faith for guidance and solace. Some departments are applying this concept and coping technique by making chaplains available to officers who need a place to turn to in times of stress. Getz (1999, p. 63) describes the volunteer chaplaincy in place at the Largo, Florida, Police Department, aptly dubbed "The God Squad":

> While some departments have a lone chaplain, Largo expanded the concept to a chaplain corps with the goal of having [a] team of clergy representing all faiths and beliefs.
>
> The six pastors so far enrolled in the program minister to the officers and staff of the department, as well as their families and victims of crime. There is always a chaplain on call—24 hours a day, seven days a week—to respond to an emergency. In addition, each chaplain spends at least eight hours a month riding with patrol officers.

Getz (p. 64) notes the increasing popularity of such programs in departments across the country:

> Involvement of religious ministers, priests and rabbis in law enforcement is at an all-time high. It is a growing trend throughout North America as departments focus on community policing and partnering with key constituencies in their communities including spiritual leaders.

Other Stress Management Programs

Health programs and stress management seminars are another means to help law enforcement officers prevent destructive stress or at least reduce it.

Health programs include medical and psychological services and fitness programs. Law enforcement administration can also provide in-service health and fitness training, weight control classes and individual and group training in these areas.

Law enforcement management should also provide an opportunity for employees to attend stress management seminars. All personnel, including dispatchers, should attend. A distinct benefit from attending such seminars is a better understanding of the nature of stress and ways to prevent, cope with or reduce its effects. The FBI has all new agents complete a Stress Management in Law Enforcement (SMILE) course to help them better understand the stress they may encounter on the job. Through such exposure they become more aware of the emotional and psychological dangers of the job, beyond the physical ones most expect to find in law enforcement.

Individuals who can successfully cope with stress have what psychology has termed **psychological hardiness.** Such individuals have usually found meaning in their life. They believe they can influence and control it and accept change as normal and positive.

The Role of the Manager/Supervisor

Law enforcement managers have an important role in minimizing the effects of stress in themselves and their subordinates. First-line supervisors are in daily contact with shift officers, need to work with them to reduce stress and have concern for their problems.

Establishing rapport with all officers is essential to reducing stress. Law enforcement managers can provide both positive reinforcement and constructive criticism if there is a foundation of respect and communication. Because nearly all law enforcement managers have been previously of that rank, they have experienced the events that cause stress in subordinates. They also know what is expected of the supervisor position, including fairness, consistency, constructive criticism, deserved praise, support when needed, coaching and counseling.

Law enforcement managers must keep close personal touch with their subordinates and recognize the symptoms of stress. If an officer shows such symptoms, the manager should be ready to assist and reduce to whatever level possible the degree of stress. Sometimes just having someone to talk to is the most helpful.

If counseling or psychological assistance is needed, it should be provided or information furnished regarding local sources of assistance. Some medical insurance plans provide financial assistance for such treatment. If agency insurance is used, take care to ensure the confidentiality of the treatment. Different officers respond in different ways to similar stress, so law enforcement managers must be aware of these differences.

Managers must also receive the same consideration from their superiors because they are no less vulnerable to stress. For example, author Bennett recalls an incident involving a personal, prolonged negotiation of four hours with an armed person. After the incident the city manager invited the author to his home, where reduction of tension and opportunity for relaxing conversation could take place away from the law enforcement environment and the press. Bennett found this extremely important.

Summary	Stress can be helpful (eustress) or harmful (distress), depending on its intensity and frequency as well as on how it is mediated. Stress often arises from uncertainty, lack of control and pressure. Sources of stress can occur in a person's daily living, personality and job.

A major source of employee stress may be upper-level management. Doing routine tasks and suddenly being thrown into a traumatic situation is exceptionally stressful. Everyday confrontations with crime victims and those who commit crimes are also stressful. Four categories of law enforcement stress are external, organizational, personal and operational.

Law enforcement officers may experience post-traumatic stress disorder (PTSD), a clinical name associated with a debilitating condition suffered by Vietnam War veterans. Officers in larger departments and those assigned to the more difficult and violent tasks, such as murders, SWAT teams or narcotics teams, appear to be the most likely candidates for PTSD.

Additional stress is also often experienced by women officers, minority officers, investigators and managers.

Stress affects people in numerous ways: mental, physical, emotional and psychological. Stress is related to heart problems, hypertension, cancer, ulcers, diabetes, chronic headaches, depression, anxiety-related disorders, asthma, excessive eating from nervous tension, decreased sex drive, fatigue, dizziness, muscle aches and tics, backaches and frequent urinating. An estimated 85 percent of all illnesses are stress related.

Symptoms of burnout include lack of enthusiasm and interest, decreased job performance, temper flare-ups and a loss of will, motivation or commitment. To avoid burnout, keep the work interesting, give recognition, provide R and R (Rest and Relaxation), avoid "other duties" and limit the assignment. Coping mechanisms commonly used by law enforcement officers include cynicism, secrecy and deviance.

Managers can reduce their own stress levels through physical exercise, relaxation techniques, good nutrition, taking time for themselves, making friends, learning to say no, staying within the law, changing their mental attitude, keeping things in perspective and seeking help if needed. Alcohol, drugs and smoking increase stress over time and also can seriously affect physical health.

Support groups are one particularly effective type of stress-reduction program. Critical incident stress debriefing (CISD) is another effective way to prevent or reduce stress. Law enforcement departments should include employee assistance programs (EAP) or provide referrals to outside agencies for psychological and counseling services and assistance for officers with stress, marital or chemical dependency problems. Health programs and stress management seminars are other means to help officers prevent destructive stress or at least reduce it.

Discussion Questions

1. What do you consider the five most stressful aspects of work in law enforcement?
2. What are major stressors in your life right now?
3. How would you reduce your level of on-the-job stress?
4. Has the level of stress changed in your life with job changes? Age changes? Changes due to a singular incident? Changes due to a series of similar incidents?
5. Have you taken any psychological tests? Which ones?
6. Are you a type A or a type B personality? What significance does that have to your work in law enforcement?
7. Have you ever participated in a support group? How effective was the experience?
8. Do you know anyone who has burned out? Can you explain why?
9. How does stress at the management level differ from that at the line level?
10. Does your local law enforcement agency have an EAP or other forms of employee support to reduce stress?

InfoTrac College Edition Assignment

Select a topic related to *stress in law enforcement* and find a recent article dealing with the topic. Summarize the main ideas of the article and include the full reference cite. Be prepared to share your summary with the class.

References

Bateman, Ronald S. "Death Notifications." *Law Enforcement Technology,* Vol. 25, No. 10, October 1998, pp. 128–130.

Brogan, George. "Post-Trauma Bereavement in Long Branch, New Jersey." *The Police Chief,* Vol. LXVI, No. 5, May 1999, pp. 31–38.

Burg, Mike. "Climbing Down the Ladder of Success." *Law and Order,* Vol. 47, No. 12, p. 177.

Burke, Tod and Rigsby, Rhonda. "Suicide by Cop Revisited." *Law and Order,* Vol. 47, No. 6, June 1999, pp. 97–102.

Cohen, Daniel; Hirsh, Ronnie M.; and Katz, Rachelle. "Peer Support Programs." *Law and Order,* Vol. 44, No. 9, September 1996, pp. 88–90.

Dumont, Lloyd F. "Recognizing and Surviving Post Shooting Trauma." *Law and Order,* Vol. 47, No. 4, April 1999, pp. 93–98.

"Ending Your Own Life Just Got Easier—Get a Cop to Do It." *Law Enforcement News,* Vol. XXV, Nos. 503/504, January 15/31, 1999, pp. 1, 14.

"Facts and Figures from NLEOMF." *The Police Chief,* Vol. LXVI, No. 5, May 1999, p. 22.

Finn, Peter and Tomz, Julie Esselman. "Using Peer Supporters to Help Address Law Enforcement Stress." *FBI Law Enforcement Bulletin,* Vol. 67, No. 5, May 1998, pp. 10–18.

Flemmings, Ashton E. "Responding to Line-of-Duty Deaths: Understanding the PSOB." *The Police Chief,* Vol. LXVI, No. 5, May 1999, pp. 40–42.

Fulton, Roger. "Managing Stress before It Manages You." *Law Enforcement Technology,* Vol. 26, No. 5, May 1999, p. 78.

"The Future of Women in Policing: Mandates for Action." *The Police Chief,* Vol. LXVI, No. 3, March 1999, pp. 53–56.

Getz, Ronald. "The God Squad: Chaplain Corps Serves Department and Community." *Law and Order,* Vol. 47, No. 10, October 1999, pp. 63–68.

Goldfarb, Daniel A. "In Search of the Silly Thought: An Addition to the Debriefing Process." *The Police Chief,* Vol. LXV, No. 10, October 1998, pp. 121–123.

Greene, Lorraine Williams. "Uplifting Resilient Police Families." *The Police Chief,* Vol. LXIV, No. 10, October 1997, pp. 70–72.

Haarr, Robin H. and Morash, Merry. "Gender, Race, and Strategies of Coping with Occupational Stress in Policing." *Justice Quarterly,* Vol. 16, No. 2, June 1999, pp. 303–336.

Heiskell, Lawrence. "Post-Traumatic Stress Disorder." *Police,* Vol. 24, No. 3, p. 10.

Honig, Audrey L. and Roland, Jocelyn E. " 'Shots Fired; Officer Involved.' " *The Police Chief,* Vol. LXV, No. 10, October 1998, pp. 116–120.

Kaighin, Barbara. "Keeping the Flame Lit." *Law and Order,* Vol. 47, No. 10, October 1999, p. 248.

Kanable, Rebecca. "Under the Gun." *Law Enforcement Technology,* Vol. 26, No. 7, July 1999, pp. 78–82.

Kirschman, Ellen. "Getting the Help You Need When You Need It." *The Police Chief,* Vol. LXIV, No. 10, October 1997, pp. 45–61.

Kirschman, Ellen. "Organizational Stress: Looking for Love in All the Wrong Places." *The Police Chief,* Vol. LXV, No. 10, October 1998, pp. 127–134.

McNally, Vincent J. and Solomon, Roger M. "The FBI's Critical Incident Stress Management Program." *FBI Law Enforcement Bulletin,* Vol. 68, No. 2, February 1999, pp. 20–26.

Molinaro, L. A. "Advancement of Women in Law Enforcement." *Law and Order,* Vol. 45, No. 8, August 1997, pp. 62–66.

"Officer Death Rate Fails to Pace Crime Decline." *Police,* Vol. 23, No. 3, March 1999, p. 8.

"Officers' Educational Assistance Program." *Law and Order,* Vol. 47, No. 12, December 1999, p. 199.

Parent, Richard B. "Surviving a Lethal Threat: The Aftermath." *Law and Order,* Vol. 47, No. 10, October 1999, pp. 155–158.

Patterson, Mary. "Shift Your Approach to Handle those Varied Work Schedules." *Police,* Vol. 21, No. 12, December 1997, pp. 36–37.

"PDs Grope for Answers to Cop Suicide." *Law Enforcement News,* Vol. XXV, No. 514, June 30, 1999, p. 5.

Pinizzotto, Anthony J. and Davis, Edward F. "Suicide by Cop: Implications for Law Enforcement Management." *Law and Order,* Vol. 47, No. 12, December 1999, pp. 95–98.

"Plenty of Talk, Not Much Action." *Law Enforcement News,* Vol. XXV, Nos. 503/504, January 15/31, 1999, pp. 1, 14.

Quinnett, Paul. "QPR: Police Suicide Prevention." *FBI Law Enforcement Bulletin,* Vol. 67, No. 7, July 1998, pp. 19–24.

Rail, Robert R. "Confrontational Incident Stress Takes Physical Toll." *Police,* Vol. 21, No. 3, March 1997, pp. 44–45.

Ryan, Andrew H. "Afterburn: The Victimization of Police Families." *The Police Chief,* Vol. LXIV, No. 10, October 1997, pp. 63–68.

Scott, Brian J. "Preferred Protocol for Death Notification." *FBI Law Enforcement Bulletin,* Vol. 68, No. 8, August 1999, pp. 11–15.

Scoville, Dean. "Getting You to Pull the Trigger." *Police,* Vol. 22, No. 11, November 1998, pp. 36–44.

Stevens, Dennis J. "Police Officer Stress." *Law and Order,* Vol. 47, No. 9, September 1999, pp. 77–81.

Strandberg, Keith W. "Suicide in Law Enforcement." *Law Enforcement Technology,* Vol. 24, No. 7, July 1997, pp. 38–40, 74–77.

"Studies and Trends: Police Stressors." *Knight News,* July–September 1997, p. 3.

Thompson, Mike. "Avoiding the 'Killer in the Shadows.' " *Law and Order,* Vol. 47, No. 8, August 1999, pp. 107–110.

"Women Underrepresented in Law Enforcement, According to Recent Study." *NCJA Justice Bulletin,* Vol. 19, No. 7, July 1999, pp. 7–8.

Zamora, Jim Herron. "Suicide Prompts Review of Cop Stress." *San Francisco Examiner,* May 12, 1997, pp. A1, A9.

15 Deploying Law Enforcement Resources and Improving Productivity

The deployment of police strength both by time and area is essential.

—Basic Tenet of the Peelian Reform Act of 1829

Do You Know?

- What function police logs serve?
- What the largest law enforcement division is?
- How area assignments are determined?
- How patrol size is determined?
- Why rapid response is important?
- What basic premise underlies random patrol?
- What the Kansas City study of preventive patrol found?
- What methods of patrol might be used?
- Whether one- or two-officer patrol units are more effective?
- What civilianization is and how it affects personnel deployment?
- What predisaster plans should include?
- What the crime triangle is?
- How to most effectively channel resources to fight crime?
- How community policing affects deployment?
- How to measure law enforcement productivity?
- How law enforcement productivity has traditionally been measured?
- How to improve law enforcement productivity?
- What a management information system (MIS) is?
- What key ingredients ensure a successful quality circle?
- What the single most important factor in high productivity and morale is?

Can You Define?

aggressive patrol
civilianization
cone of resolution
crime triangle
dog shift
hot spots
incivilities
lag time

management
information system
(MIS)
police logs
productivity
proportionate
assignment
quality circle

quota
random patrol
shift
technophobia
watch

INTRODUCTION

Law enforcement agencies exist for a purpose—to fulfill a specific mission. Management, in conjunction with line personnel, sets forth this mission and the requirements for accomplishing it. Missions mean little without action, and in most businesses, including law enforcement, that means schedules. The link between mission and schedules is illustrated in Figure 15.1. The characteristic that distinguishes law enforcement personnel allocation from most business and industrial situations is the manner in which tasks are generated. In most nonlaw enforcement situations, the tasks to be performed are known in advance, and the number of people required to complete them is easily determined. For example, if a shoe manufacturing plant needs to produce 10,000 pairs of shoes next week to meet orders, the tasks to perform and the number of people needed to perform them can be determined with some precision.

Some law enforcement tasks are also predictable. For example, escorting distinguished visitors or maintaining order along a parade route are services known ahead of time. Personnel requirements can be determined and allocated well in advance of the event. Most law enforcement tasks, however, can be predicted only in terms of the likelihood of their occurring at a specific time and place. Such tasks make up the bulk of law enforcement work and are the basis of the personnel allocation problem. To understand the problem in this context, it is helpful to view each law enforcement task that occurs as having two coordinates: (1) the time at which the event occurs and (2) where it occurs.

Each time a task is generated, one objective of many law enforcement departments has been to move a patrol unit to the scene as quickly as possible. How quickly the patrol unit arrives depends on its location relative to the location of the task.

Law enforcement executive managers have always been faced with the challenge of providing satisfactory levels of services with a fixed number of personnel and resources. Recently many have been faced with the reality of providing

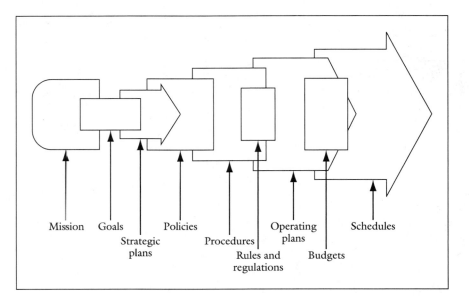

Figure 15.1
How Plans Interlock: From Missions to Schedules

Source: Lester R. Bittel. *The McGraw-Hill 36-Hour Management Course,* New York: McGraw-Hill Publishing Company, 1989, p. 77. Reprinted by permission.

more services with *less* personnel. This requires budget cutbacks and increased emphasis on planned deployment of existing personnel.

Many departments can answer only actual requests for services, with no time available for routine patrol. Some departments must establish priorities criteria for answering service requests. For them, not only is routine patrol time nonexistent, but requests for service are backlogged. A burglary in progress call would be answered, but a barking dog complaint would be deferred or not answered at all.

This chapter examines the key management function of deploying personnel, including how they have traditionally been deployed, factors affecting deployment, assignment rotation, overtime and research findings about deployment and response time. Next is a look at differentiated response and random patrol, including the results of the Kansas City Preventive Patrol Experiment, followed by a presentation of the methods of patrol currently in use. This is followed by a look at other ways the law enforcement personnel pool might be expanded, including involving citizens through citizen police academies, citizen patrols and reserve units; using departmental volunteers and civilianizing departmental positions. Next is a discussion of the deploying of resources during emergencies, the traditional goal of deploying resources to "fight crime" and how community policing affects the deployment of personnel.

The chapter then examines law enforcement productivity and ways that managers and supervisors can improve productivity through those they oversee. A definition of productivity is presented as well as a look at how it has traditionally been measured. This is followed by an examination of some symptoms of productivity problems and how such problems might be addressed. Among the most promising ways to enhance productivity are to use computers and other recently developed technology. The discussion next focuses on specific approaches that have proven successful, including the use of quality circles. This is followed by a look at how to promote productive work teams. The chapter concludes with a return to previous discussions of leadership, discipline, motivation and morale as they relate to productivity.

Traditional Means of Deploying Personnel

Accomplishing law enforcement tasks and goals follows a logical sequence. Law enforcement organizations are a major division of a larger community, whether it is federal, state, county or municipal levels of government. Organizational charts divide and subdivide services within the law enforcement organization.

All levels of law enforcement managers provide direction, and all have authority to act and need training to provide direction. Managers must understand what needs to be accomplished, how, by whom, where, when and why.

Managers must prepare a plan before assigning personnel to perform tasks. Total availability of law enforcement personnel is subject to budget maximums, applicant quantity, the total traffic and crime problem and the level of services the community demands. Once the personnel factor is known, personnel can be deployed and the action plan completed. The plan must include a system to use data to assign personnel to be in the right places at the times needed and in appropriate numbers.

A good operational plan based on facts is the executive's defense against pressure groups, who generally make demands based on political considerations,

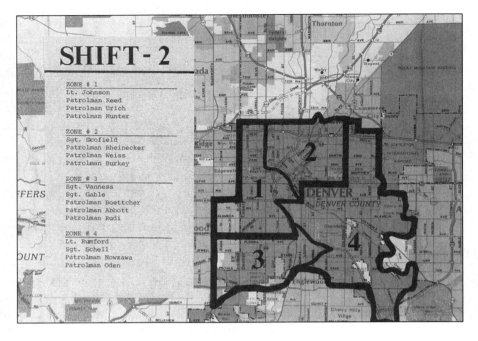

Deploying law enforcement personnel and equipment to the right areas of the jurisdiction, at the right time, is an important management function. Deployment should be flexible, constantly reviewed and based on facts.

June 24, 2000   Officer James Jones
Reported for duty: 1500 hours

1500 report of accident	1545	45 min.
1545 patrol	1555	10 min.
1555 domestic	1620	25 min.

Figure 15.2
Sample Log

emotions or personal opinions. Managers should review, evaluate and revise plans as necessary to meet changing needs and goals. They can do this by measuring productivity and reviewing various reports.

Police Logs

One way to determine needs and time requirements is to have each officer complete time logs and then analyze tasks.

Police logs provide data for better deployment of personnel.

The logs need not be complicated. They can simply list requests for services, time, nature of the request and time the incident was completed, as Figure 15.2 illustrates. Such logs provide information for studying the types of incidents that occur, the best ways to investigate them and ways to assign personnel where they are needed most. They need not be completed every day but over enough time to determine basic information and to revise them to reflect changes in the community.

Figure 15.3 illustrates a simplified, hand-tabulated version of data collected in a community of approximately 12,000. Such data indicate the various breakdowns

Anytown Police Department
Police Incident Analysis
July 2000

INCIDENTS by DAY of WEEK

Day	Count	%
Sunday	114	18.0%
Monday	78	12.3
Tuesday	72	11.4
Wednesday	75	11.8
Thursday	78	12.3
Friday	116	18.3
Saturday	100	15.8

INCIDENTS by SHIFT

Shift	Count	%
Day Shift	191	30.2%
Swing Shift	265	41.9
Grave Shift	177	28.0

INCIDENTS by RESPONSE TIME-ZERO RESPONSE

Zone	Count
Zone 1	4
Zone 2	0
Zone 3	2
Zone 4	1
Zone 5	1
Zone 6	1
Zone 7	0
Zone 8	0
Zone 9	3
Zone 10	1
Zone 11	0
Zone 12	0
Zone 13	0
Zone 14	0

INCIDENTS by RESPONSE TIME

Shift	Time
Day Shift	4.50 minutes
Swing Shift	3.88 minutes
Grave Shift	3.06 minutes

INCIDENTS by ZONE

Zone	Count
Zone 1	61
Zone 2	35
Zone 3	78
Zone 4	26
Zone 5	73
Zone 6	34
Zone 7	28
Zone 8	42
Zone 9	113
Zone 10	44
Zone 11	18
Zone 12	20
Zone 13	10
Zone 14	42

Figure 15.3
Sample Data Derived from Police Logs

Continued

INCIDENTS by TYPE of SERVICE

Suspicion	114
Crimes-Arrests	50
DOC	30
Assault	0
DUI-DWI	15
Assists	77
Emergencies	71
Accidents	21
Traffic	58
Juvenile	34
Animal	20
Vandalism	22
Suicide	0
Domestics	18
Alarms	35
Miscellaneous	67

INCIDENTS by TIME of DAY

0000–0100	26
0100–0200	29
0200–0300	24
0300–0400	12
0400–0500	14
0500–0600	5
0600–0700	16
0700–0800	20
0800–0900	19
0900–1000	28
1000–1100	18
1100–1200	32
1200–1300	31
1300–1400	21
1400–1500	35
1500–1600	28
1600–1700	30
1700–1800	26
1800–1900	35
1900–2000	27
2000–2100	39
2100–2200	40
2200–2300	25
2300–2400	35

Figure 15.3
continued

needed to meet the needs for law enforcement services. Many departments use computers and special software programs to analyze their needs.

Computer Scheduling

DeFranco (2000, p. 80) points out: "Creating a workable schedule is one of the toughest tasks challenging law enforcement managers." She suggests:

> Not only must the department's shifts be taken into account, but individual officers' time-off needs and agency requirements for officer training that leave holes in the schedule have to be factored in. Officer seniority and shift preferences also have to be considered. What often emerges is a chart that makes no one happy. . . .

But if an agency researches the scheduling programs available and chooses the one that best meets its specific needs, the computer can be used to improve the quality of work for everyone from the supervisors charged with designing the schedule to the officers assigned to it. Once the software is in place, creating a suitable work chart can be as simple as clicking a mouse.

Factors Considered in Employee Deployment

A law enforcement agency has a specific number of fixed positions. The only way these can be reduced is to adopt a "flattened" organization, for example, reducing the number of middle-level managers, using joint dispatching with another community or using joint jail services with the county or a neighboring community. With the rising cost of jail services to meet federal standards, it is increasingly popular to use joint jail services.

After the fixed positions are filled, the remaining personnel are assigned to uniformed patrol, investigative, juvenile or other specialized divisions.

The largest division is the uniformed patrol unit, which provides services seven days a week, twenty-four hours a day.

Other specialized divisions have fewer officers and often provide services for only portions of the day. Specialized personnel are assigned by demand based on frequency of incidents and cases requiring a specific service. A typical division of personnel is illustrated in Figure 15.4. If law enforcement managers examine the service call data, they will readily observe variations in all areas. Personnel assignment should match those variations as much as possible.

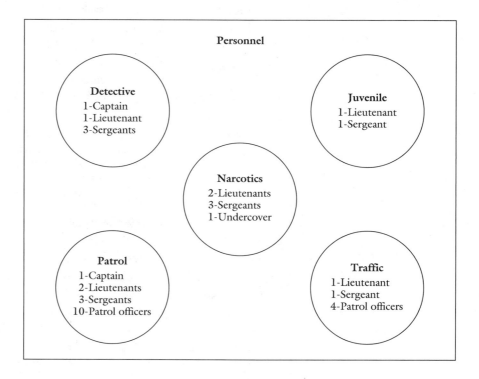

Figure 15.4
Division of Personnel

The teams should usually be under the leadership of a local commander. As Anemone and Spangenberg (2000, p. 23) state: "There is no one more capable of determining the best way to solve local problems than the man or woman who commands the precinct." Although community policing emphasizes the importance of allowing the patrol officer to problem solve and use discretion, Anemone and Spangenberg point out: "Most officers on patrol lack the expertise, authority or network of connections necessary to handle problems on their own." They (p. 24) suggest four requirements for a successful commander: (1) accurate and timely intelligence, (2) rapid deployment, (3) effective tactics and (4) relentless follow-up and assessment.

Shifts

Shift work has increased since the invention of the electric light bulb, and with the increase has come problems (described in Chapter 14) for those working the night shift. Patrol shifts traditionally have three eight-hour shifts, five days a week, with two days off. A **shift** is simply the time span to which personnel are assigned. Some departments call it a **watch.** One common division is 7 A.M. to 3 P.M.; 3 P.M. to 11 P.M.; and 11 P.M. to 7 A.M. (the **dog shift**).

Shift assignments should be based on data. Regular assignments, split shift assignments or overlapping shift assignments can be considered. Some departments simply divide personnel into three equal shifts, but this is seldom effective. Rarely should personnel be equal on all shifts. Assignment of personnel by day of week and determination of days off are also based on data. Maintain a balance between actual needs and the effects of some assignments on morale. Because computers allow rapid statistical data to be developed, personnel shifts can be made at any time from one area to the other.

In recent years 10- and 12-hour shifts have become common and have frequently resulted in higher officer satisfaction and easier scheduling. In a typical 3/12 shift plan, an officer works three 12-hour shifts, three days a week for three weeks. The fourth week generally involves four 12-hour shifts, and then it is back to three days a week for three weeks, and so on. Such shift formats appear popular with officers and citizens alike. According to one advocate ("Yours, Mine and Hours," 1998, p. 5):

> The 3/12 plan [offers] numerous . . . benefits, including fiscal savings to the city, improved officer morale and greater productivity. In all the time the [3/12 plan] was in operation, we never had a grievance, we never had disruptions of police service. People in the community liked it because they knew who their police officers were, and the days and hours they would be working.

Many departments rotate shifts and areas or both. Other departments, especially those using community policing, assign permanent shifts, areas or both, believing this allows officers to become more familiar with their assignment and therefore more effective. Still others have experimented with and implemented alternative scheduling formats.

Allgower and Henry (1998, p. 85) explain an alternate team staffing concept that offers benefits to officers and management:

> In many agencies the opportunity for patrol officers to change duty assignments is infrequent at best. This can lead to feelings of stagnation and boredom.

Additionally, the demands of alternating shift work are cited as the most stressful aspects of police work.

The challenge to management is to offer patrol some choice and variety in their duty schedule, while maintaining safe and acceptable levels of staffing. An approach to staffing that satisfies both of these goals is a new team staffing concept that utilizes two different shift lengths—three 12½-hour shifts, alternated with four 10-hour shifts.

There are some sound benefits to this system:

- Allows for an integrated "team" concept
- Maximizes staffing levels with current manpower
- Creates a flexible work environment
- Allows for a training day every other month
- Reduces overtime requirements
- Enhances officer safety
- Works well for management and line personnel

There are intrinsic benefits to both work schedules. The 12½-hour shift team works three consecutive days, then has four days off. . . .

The 10-hour shift team works four consecutive days, then has three days off. . . .

An overall advantage to both teams is that the days off are consistently the same days of the week—there is no rotation built into this schedule. Line officers and management can plan well in advance for vacations, school events, training, etc.

This plan intensifies the team concept.

Allgower and Henry (p. 87) further explain:

The 12½-hour team is broken up into three shifts; day (0600–1830), swing (1300–0130), and graveyard (1800–0630). This places the maximum number of officers on the street when they are needed most—the overlap between swing and graveyard shifts from 1800 hours until 0130 hours.

Similarly, the 10-hour team is broken up into the same three shifts, with different hours. Day shift is from 0630–1630 hours, swing is from 1500–0100, and graveyard is from 2100–0700. This provides an overlap of officers from 2100–0100.

Allgower and Henry (p. 88) conclude: "Management likes the strategic planning opportunities and reduced overtime that this schedule offers. . . . It is legal, moral, and ethical. It gives officers more control over their careers and their lives. Bottom line is—IT WORKS!" Figure 15.5 shows how the alternate team staffing schedule works.

The Elk Grove, Illinois, Police Department has enhanced its organizational efficiency through an alternative scheduling program based on equal workloads for allocated personnel, that is, based on calls for service (CFS). The program is limited to patrol and is based on voluntary selection of permanent shifts. The program is structured around three shifts:

- 11 P.M. to 7 A.M.—a permanent first shift.

- 7 A.M. to 3 P.M.—the second shift, which rotates with the third shift.

- 3 P.M. to 11 P.M.—the third shift, which rotates with the second shift.
  Some officers are permanently assigned to this shift by their own request.

Careful consideration must be given to shift scheduling. Shift work can be directly related to disasters, creating a vulnerable window from about 1 A.M. to 6 A.M. It was during this time that the Exxon Valdez, Three-Mile Island and

January

Sunday	Monday	Tuesday	Wednesday	Thursday	Friday	Saturday
1 12½ OFF 10 WORK	2 12½ OFF 10 WORK	3 12½ WORK 10 OFF	4 12½ WORK 10 OFF	5 12½ WORK 10 OFF	6 12½ OFF 10 WORK	7 12½ OFF 10 WORK
8 12½ OFF 10 WORK	9 12½ OFF 10 WORK	10 12½ WORK 10 OFF	11 12½ WORK 10 OFF	12 12½ WORK 10 OFF	13 12½ OFF 10 WORK	14 12½ OFF 10 WORK
15 12½ OFF 10 WORK	16 12½ OFF 10 WORK	17 12½ WORK 10 OFF	18 12½ WORK 10 OFF	19 12½ WORK 10 OFF	20 12½ OFF 10 WORK	21 12½ OFF 10 WORK
22 12½ OFF 10 WORK	23 12½ WORK 10 WORK	24 12½ WORK 10 OFF	25 12½ WORK 10 OFF	26 12½ WORK 10 OFF	27 12½ OFF 10 WORK	28 12½ OFF 10 WORK
29 12½ OFF 10 WORK	30 12½ OFF 10 WORK	31 12½ WORK 10 OFF				

*January 23 would be the Training Day for the 10-hour team and "Payback" day for the 12½ hour team.

April

Sunday	Monday	Tuesday	Wednesday	Thursday	Friday	Saturday
1 12½ OFF 10 WORK	2 12½ OFF 10 WORK	3 12½ WORK 10 OFF	4 12½ WORK 10 OFF	5 12½ WORK 10 OFF	6 12½ OFF 10 WORK	7 12½ OFF 10 WORK
8 12½ OFF 10 WORK	9 12½ OFF 10 WORK	10 12½ WORK 10 OFF	11 12½ WORK 10 OFF	12 12½ WORK 10 OFF	13 12½ OFF 10 WORK	14 12½ OFF 10 WORK
15 12½ OFF 10 WORK	16 12½ WORK 10 OFF	17 12½ WORK 10 OFF	18 12½ OFF 10 WORK	19 12½ OFF 10 WORK	20 12½ WORK 10 OFF	21 12½ WORK 10 WORK
22 12½ WORK 10 OFF	23 12½ OFF 10 WORK	24 12½ OFF 10 WORK	25 12½ OFF 10 WORK	26 12½ OFF 10 WORK	27 12½ WORK 10 OFF	28 12½ WORK 10 OFF
29 12½ WORK 10 OFF	30 12½ OFF 10 WORK	31 12½ OFF 10 WORK				

Figure 15.5
The Alternate Team Staffing Concept

*If the changeover occurred in April, this is the way it would look. The actual changeover is the week of the 15th. The 10-hour team had changed to having weekends off. The only concern for scheduling should be requests for time off, as some officers do not like to work during this somewhat confusing period.

Source: Ron Allgower and Michael P. Henry. "Alternate Team Staffing Concept Offers Benefits to Officers and Management." *Law and Order,* Vol. 46, No. 8, August 1998, p. 88. Reprinted by permission.

Chernobyl incidents occurred. Kohl (1994, p. 58) suggests: "Poorly scheduled shift work can reduce cognitive abilities and lead to fatal accidents, or to sleep apnea, a breathing disorder that causes insomnia in 270 million Americans." He (p. 61) reports on studies that show: "There are often 'consequences' to the kind of scheduling many police departments use—impaired performance and increased risk of accident." In one study more than half the officers surveyed had moderate to severe problems with poor-quality sleep. Further, almost 80 percent of those on the night shift fell asleep while on duty.

The Center for Design of Industrial Schedules (CDIS) created a more effective schedule for police work that included the following features (Kohl, p. 62):

> The changes included a clockwise rotation of shifts, as well as an increase in the number of six day cycles on a shift from one to three. Work time was modified so officers spent an average of four days at work with two days off.

After the new shifts had been in effect for six months, the number of on-the-job automobile accidents and near-miss accidents was reduced by 40 percent.

Different shift systems work best in different departments. As Simpson and Richbell (2000, p. 21) suggest: "Managers . . . should experiment with different shift systems to find the one that works best for their departments."

Proportionate Assignment

> Area assignments are determined by requests for services based on available data. This is called **proportionate assignment.** No area should be larger than the time it takes a car to respond to emergency calls in a reasonable time.

Area boundaries should be primary arteries, if possible, to provide faster access. Car assignment plans generally follow size of areas to be patrolled and frequency of request for services in those areas. If personnel is not sufficient to provide the level of services the community needs or demands, additional personnel must be requested. If this cannot be provided, explore using law enforcement reserves or other methods.

A number of factors determine proportionate assignment. A first step is to list those items requiring time and to weight the importance of each. For example, felonies are generally weighted heavier than misdemeanors. In recent years drug offenses and related problems have required specialized personnel and increased training of regular officers. If a high proportion of offenses are committed by gangs, emphasize that area.

> To determine patrol area size, consider square miles, street miles and response time.

Rotation

Assignment rotation is another aspect of deploying law enforcement resources, although it is a somewhat controversial one. Marvin (1998, p. 22) states: "A rotation program represents one way for officers to gain valuable leadership experience and a broad-based view of the organization, better serve the agency and the community, and enhance their own career goals and satisfaction." He (p. 23) also notes:

> Unfortunately, most police agencies provide only two paths for police officers to enhance their status and salary—promotion to a higher rank or a transfer to a

specialized unit. This encourages police officers with ambition and initiative to flee from the largest and most visible facet of the department—patrol operations.

Instead, departments should place the most experienced officers in the patrol position, where 90 percent of the department's work is done. Patrol officers can enhance the image of the department, while affecting the crime rate and criminal activities.

In assignment rotation, patrol officers receive training and gain experience and competence in investigative methods while detectives are rotated back to patrol on a regular basis. According to Geberth (1998, p. 194):

> Detective rotation was originally introduced as a process to augment the capabilities of investigative divisions by providing cross training to all members of the department. The premise was there would be a cadre of potential investigative resources to replace detectives who were promoted or were slated to be retired.
>
> As further justification of this practice it was explained that it would create opportunities for patrol officers to expand their careers.

Marvin (p. 23) cautions, however:

> These tasks must be accomplished without adversely affecting morale. Reassigning to the patrol division an officer who has served as a detective for 3 or 4 years might impact negatively on this individual officer. To prevent this from occurring, the chief must effectively explain how rotating officers will help fulfill the mission of the department at the same time that it benefits individual officers. . . . If handled properly by the department, most officers will view rotation as an opportunity to round out their backgrounds and build their resumes for future advancement.

Opponents of rotation argue that even if personnel understand and support the theory of staff cross training and the generalization and diversification of job responsibilities, criminal investigation remains a highly specialized function requiring ongoing, uninterrupted development and application of skills. Geberth (pp. 194–195) asserts:

> Periodically transferring experienced investigators back to patrol is counterproductive to the professional investigative process. Experience is one of the best resources for the continuing education necessary in developing a proficient investigator. . . .
>
> Rotation impedes career growth and frustrates professional ambition.

Geberth (p. 195) notes other disadvantages to rotation:

> From an administrative perspective, there should be concern about the costs of continually having to train newly assigned officers. It certainly isn't cost effective.
>
> More importantly, the community, which depends upon their police department to solve crime, is done a disservice. Officers transferred out of an investigative assignment leave behind active cases. . . . Investigations are disrupted, and frequently cases remain unsolved when the original investigator leaves.
>
> If there ever was an argument against detective rotation, Boulder, Colorado has made a compelling case in their mishandling of the Jon-Benet Ramsey investigation. The Chief, a staunch proponent of rotation, mandated that every two years personnel assigned to investigations are routinely transferred back to patrol. The department had no experienced investigators to process the crime.

Overtime

According to Bayley and Worden (1998, p. 1): "There is a sense both inside and outside the law enforcement community that overtime is overused, misused, and only halfheartedly controlled." Through their study they discovered that police departments across the country vary considerably in the attention paid to overtime management and the ability to produce data about it. They (p. 2) also found:

> Overtime can be successfully controlled through a combination of analysis, recordkeeping, management, and supervision.
>
> Police managers should analyze overtime in terms of work done on paid overtime and on unpaid, or compensatory, overtime. Paid overtime increases policing activity, while compensatory time represents less policing because it must be repaid by taking time and a half from other activities.

In examining whether overtime is being abused, managers should record the following (Bayley and Worden, p. 4):

- The department's total obligations and payments for overtime
- The obligations and expenditures of overtime by individual officers and commands or budgetary units
- The uses of overtime (holdovers, shift extensions, holidays, court appearances, emergency mobilizations, special events, briefings and roll calls, etc.)
- The circumstances of overtime use
- The sources of overtime payments

Managers must also bear in mind (pp. 5–6): "Overtime is critically affected by labor rules—the 'contract'—that mandate uses and rates. . . . 45 percent of police departments reported that overtime was governed by collective bargaining agreements." In summary, Bayley and Worden (p. 2) note the following implications of police overtime:

> Overtime should be viewed, within limits, as an unavoidable cost of policing. Overtime charges cannot be eliminated altogether, regardless of the number of police officers employed, because of inevitable shift extensions, court appearances, unpredictable events, and contract requirements. Concerns about overtime usage should be addressed through controlling it with improved management techniques.

Kammerer (2000, p. 34) suggests that departments consider reducing court overtime by creating a full-time court liaison sergeant's (CLS) position. The Torrance, California, Police Department did so and saw an immediate increase in savings. The sergeant worked with the district attorney's office to determine which officers were really required to testify. In one case the district attorney's office had subpoenaed 17 officers for a preliminary hearing. When the CLS called and questioned the necessity of so many officers, the district attorney told him the case was being continued and no officers would need to appear. The CLS asked the district attorney to review the case to determine which officers were absolutely necessary before resubpoenaing. The district attorney called back the next day to say only six officers needed to appear. In this case alone the Torrance Police Department saved approximately $2,525 in court overtime.

Response Time

Most statistical breakdowns provide information on patrol areas and response times. A federal study released in the 1960s stated that a response time of one minute or less was needed to increase arrests at a crime scene. Few law enforcement departments can guarantee a response time of less than three minutes on all calls for service. Klockars (1983, p. 130) notes: "Police currently make on-scene arrests in about 3 percent of the serious crimes reported to them. If they traveled faster than a speeding bullet to all reports of serious crimes, this on-scene arrest rate would rise no higher than 5 percent." Reasons other than on-scene arrests, however, also require rapid response.

A response as rapidly yet as safely as possible builds public confidence in law enforcement capabilities and competence. It also places officers at the scene to protect evidence before it is destroyed by people or the elements. It increases the chances of locating witnesses and making arrests. Further, it increases the chances of providing lifesaving emergency first aid to crime victims.

Other considerations in response time are barriers to patrol such as ditches, hills, water, number of officers available, total size of the patrol area, number of subpatrol areas, types of offenses and types and quantity of service requests. Safety is of utmost importance. The response should not pose a more significant threat to society than the incident to be investigated.

An even more important factor than police response time is the time between the occurrence of the incident and the report to the police, commonly referred to as **lag time,** over which police have no control. Another time factor important to total response is the time between when the dispatcher receives the call and dispatches it to a patrol car. Perhaps the most important factor, however, is citizen expectation.

The Kansas City Response Time Analysis study found that a large proportion of Part I crimes were not discovered until some time after they occurred and were therefore unaffected by rapid police response. The Police Executive Research Forum (PERF) replicated the Kansas City study over three years and confirmed the findings (Caplan, 1983, p. 3):

- Eighty-six percent of all calls were placed more than five minutes after the incident occurred—the time period critical for making an on-scene arrest.
- On-scene arrests attributed to fast police response were made in only 2.9 percent of reported serious crimes.
- Fast response may be unnecessary in three out of every four reported serious crimes.

Differentiated Response

It is only logical that the type of call influences the response. Following a literature review and a survey of over 200 police departments serving jurisdictions of more than 100,000, a group of police practitioners and researchers were charged with developing a model for police response to citizen calls for service. The result was the Differential Police Response Strategies Model, which consists of three key components:

- A set of characteristics to define a type of incident
- A time factor to identify the relationship between the time the incident occurred and the time the police received the call
- A full range of response strategies, ranging from an immediate response by a sworn officer to no response, with numerous alternatives in between (Table 15.1)

Table 15.1
General Differential Response Model

Type of Incident/Time of Occurrence

Response Alternatives		Major Personal Injury			Major Property Damage/Loss			Potential Personal Injury			Potential Property Damage/Loss			Minor Personal Injury			Minor Property Damage/Loss			Other Minor Crime			Other Minor Noncrime		
		In-Progress	Proximate	Cold	In-Progress	Proximate	Cold	In-Progress	Proximate	Cold	In-Progress	Proximate	Cold	In-Progress	Proximate	Cold	In-Progress	Proximate	Cold	In-Progress	Proximate	Cold	In-Progress	Proximate	Cold
Sworn	Immediate																								
	Expedite																								
	Routine																								
	Appointment																								
Nonsworn	Immediate																								
	Expedite																								
	Routine																								
	Appointment																								
Nonmobile	Telephone																								
	Walk-In																								
	Mail-In																								
	Referral																								
	No Response																								

Source: Raymond O. Sumrall et al. *Differential Police Response Strategies*. Washington, DC: Police Executive Research Forum, 1981, p. 9. Reprinted by permission.

479

Operation Bullseye

One precinct of the Phoenix Police Department has developed a special form of response called Operation Bullseye, whose basic idea is containment. When an emergency call involving a felony comes in and the felony has occurred within five minutes of the call and a subject and vehicle description is available, two units respond to the scene. All other available units go to major intersections and observe traffic moving away from the scene. The crime scene is the bullseye, with concentric rings representing time and distance from the scene.

Random Patrol

During "routine" patrol, officers frequently establish a pattern, which can become known to criminals and used to their advantage. To overcome this potential problem, many departments use **random patrol,** that is, patrol by random number selection.

One type of random patrol uses a computer to select random numbers. Officers going on duty are provided an envelope with these numbers, which they select at random. Officers then patrol the area designated by that number for no longer than 10 minutes and then select another number. Criminals cannot know where officers will patrol because the officers themselves do not know until they reach in the envelope for the area number.

> The basic premise of random patrol is to place officers closer to any potential incident or request for service before it happens, based on data provided by experience. Goals are to reduce response time and erase set patrol pattern habits.

If patrol areas are assigned to cars on a purely random basis, probability theory predicts that patrol cars will be closer to the point of need when they are requested than under any other system of patrol assignment.

The Kansas City Preventive Patrol Experiment

Although the Kansas City Preventive Patrol Experiment was conducted almost 30 years ago (1972), it remains the most comprehensive study of routine preventive patrol. The experiment divided 15 beats in Kansas City into three groups, each having 5 beats:

Group 1—Reactive beats—no routine patrol, responding only to calls for service

Group 2—Control beats—maintained their normal level of routine preventive patrol

Group 3—Proactive beats—doubled or tripled the level of routine preventive patrol

The results were as follows:

> Given the large amount of data collected and the extremely diverse sources used, the overwhelming evidence is that decreasing or increasing routine preventive patrol within the range tested in this experiment had no effect on crime, citizen fear of crime, community attitudes toward the police on the delivery of police services, police response time or traffic accidents (Klockars, p. 160).

The Kansas City Preventive Patrol Experiment found that increasing or decreasing routine preventive patrol had no effect on crime, citizen fear of crime, community attitudes toward the police on delivery of police services, police response time or traffic accidents.

Klockars (p. 130) commented on the results of the Kansas City experiment: "It makes about as much sense to have police patrol routinely in cars to fight crime as it does to have firemen patrol routinely in fire trucks to fight fire."

Aggressive Patrol

"**Aggressive,** or proactive, **patrol** focuses on the prevention and detection of crime by investigating suspicious actions, events and behaviors" (Swope, 1999, p. 79) [emphasis added]. The premise behind aggressive patrol is that through purposeful contact with individuals, officers will build an intelligence base of information regarding who lives, works, hangs out and who might be involved in what on their beat (p. 79). Swope notes that one such contact is field interrogation: "This personal contact can span a wide range of encounters, but need not be adversarial or confrontational. In fact, it can even be friendly under the right circumstances."

Another application of such patrol is aggressive traffic enforcement of suspicious vehicles (e.g., those driving at night without headlights, speeding or weaving through traffic), which often leads to arrests. Swope (p. 81) gives other examples of situations in which an officer might inquire into an unusual or suspicious circumstance: "Persons wandering an office building on a weekend, people loading a truck at a construction site at 2300, a man in a trench coat when it is sunny and 80 degrees, a clean license tag on a dirty, mud splattered car, etc." He (pp. 81–82) further observes:

Aggressive patrol fits into community policing very well. In most such operations, officers work in only one community. This geographic permanence improves their effectiveness, raising their ability to recognize the unusual, the suspicious and the undesirable and taking the appropriate response.

Operations Security (OPSEC)

It has often been said: "The best way to catch a criminal is to think like a criminal." Glorioso and Ritter (1998, p. 96) state: "One way of employing this adversary perspective is to use a process utilized extensively in operations security (OPSEC). This process is referred to as the 'adversary strategy.' " They (p. 96) further note that the OPSEC process aids in both the planning and execution of police operations by providing an opportunity to view the mission from the criminal's standpoint.

The OPSEC process consists of five steps that can be applied to any law enforcement operation (p. 97):

1. Identifying critical information
2. Conducting a threat analysis
3. Performing a vulnerability analysis
4. Assessing risk
5. Applying countermeasures

Those who have used the OPSEC process describe it as "a flexible and effective procedure that increases the probability of a successful conclusion" (p. 97).

Methods of Patrol

Given the wide range of circumstances encountered during police patrol, a variety of patrol methods have been devised. The most common, however, remains automobile patrol.

Common methods of patrol include automobile, bicycle, motorcycle, foot and air patrol. Other methods use mounted, water and special-terrain patrol.

Table 15.2 provides a summary of patrol methods.

Table 15.2
Summary of Patrol Methods

Method	Uses	Advantages	Disadvantages
Foot	Highly congested areas Burglary, robbery, theft purse snatching, mugging	Close citizen contact High visibility Develop informants	Relatively expensive Limited mobility

Automobile	Respond to service calls
	Provide traffic control
	Transport individuals,
	  documents and
	  equipment
		Most economical
		Greatest mobility and
		  flexibility
		Offers means of
		  communication
		Provides means of
		  transporting people,
		  documents and equipment
			Limited access to certain
			  areas
			Limited citizen contact

Motorcycle	Same as automobile,
	  except that it can't be
	  used for transporting
	  individuals and has
	  limited equipment
		Maneuverability in congested
		  areas and areas restricted
		  to automobiles
			Inability to transport
			  much equipment
			Not used during bad
			  weather
			Hazardous to operator

Bicycle	Stakeouts Parks and beaches Congested areas	Quiet and unobtrusive	Limited speed
Mounted	Parks and bridle paths Crowd control Traffic control	Size and maneuverability of horse	Expensive
Air	Surveillance Traffic control Searches and rescues	Covers large areas easily	Expensive
Water	Deter smuggling Water traffic control Rescues	Access to activities occurring on water	Expensive

Special-terrain	Patrol unique areas
	  inaccessible to other forms
	Rescue operations
		Access to normally
		  inaccessible areas
			Limited use in some
			  instances

Source: Henry M. Wrobleski and Kären M. Hess. *Introduction to Law Enforcement and Criminal Justice*, 6th edition. Belmont, CA: Wadsworth Publishing Company, 2000, p. 219. Reprinted by permission.

Automobile Patrol

Numerous factors make automobile patrol the preferred patrol method for the majority of departments because they can respond rapidly to a scene, carry multiple passengers and types of equipment and work well in a variety of weather situations. There remains some controversy, however, regarding whether one- or two-officer patrol units work better.

One-Officer vs. Two-Officer Patrol Units

Officer safety is at the core of the argument favoring two-officer patrol units, which also make a shift less boring and provide a chance for officers to develop working relationships. However, officer productivity and operational efficiency are increased using one-officer patrol units. If two officers are needed, two squads can be sent on a call.

Using one-officer units with appropriate delay procedures for another car to arrive at a scene is an effective administrative and budgeting procedure. The use of electronic patrol car locators can enhance officer safety in a one-officer unit. Such locators are also of great value in deploying patrol personnel. According to Wrobleski and Hess (2000, pp. 211–212):

> The one-officer unit offers several advantages including cost effectiveness in that the same number of officers can patrol twice the area, with twice the mobility, and with twice the power of observation. In addition, officers working alone are generally more cautious in dangerous situations, recognizing that they have no backup. And officers working alone also are generally more attentive to patrol duties because they do not have a conversational partner. The expense of two cars compared to one, however, is a factor.

According to Johnson (1999, p. 68):

> Proponents of the two-officer patrol tend to cling to the idea that it is safer for the officer, but studies have not found this to be true. Experiments by the Police Foundation using both types of unit staffing in a large city police department revealed that officers in two-officer units were more likely to be assaulted by a citizen, be injured in the line of duty, and have a suspect resist arrest. Studies that have looked at the frequency of assaults and injuries to patrol officers have upheld these findings that single-officer units tend to be safer.
>
> In addition to being more costly and possibly more dangerous for the police, . . . two-officer units are more likely to generate a complaint from a citizen.

Whether a one- or two-officer patrol unit is used should be determined by individual circumstances.

Some districts may require two-officer units and, under specific instances and for short periods, more than two. Sometimes union contracts dictate that two-officer units be used, which can seriously hinder management as it plans for the most effective deployment of its personnel.

Two patrol methods that have become more popular with the adoption of community policing are bicycle patrol and foot patrol.

Bicycle Patrol

Bicycle patrols are reported to be more effective than automobile patrols in certain instances. Officers on bicycles can cover larger sections of the community and are especially effective for night patrol. In addition, bikes can go places

The Petersburg, Virginia, Bureau of Police formed a bicycle unit in 1993 to patrol some of the most crime-ridden areas of the city. Criminal activity decreased with roundups of street-level drug dealers. Why do you think bicycle patrols were effective in this situation?

vehicles cannot go and are very maneuverable. They can go over curbs, down steps and into otherwise inaccessible places. Particularly effective in enforcing drug laws, they are visible, mobile and responsive to citizens and have been excellent public relations tools.

Mountain Bikes

Mountain bikes for patrol are becoming increasingly popular in departments around the country. In Reno, Nevada, for example, Dees (1998, p. 62) notes:

> Pedaling a bike on patrol might have been regarded as an undesirable assignment at one time, but it has become one of the most desired assignments in the department. Bike officers enjoy great police-citizen relationships, are free from some of the more routine and mundane aspects of patrol work and can act immediately and personally on real crime problems as they arise.

Zappile and Schmid (1999, p. 146) state:

> Bicycle patrols have proven to be a valuable asset in promoting the Philadelphia Police Department's community policing philosophy. They are used to combat crime, solve quality-of-life problems, bond with the community, increase the feeling of safety within a community and provide effective crowd control.

As with any other aspect of policing, officers performing bicycle patrols must complete specialized training. Zappile and Schmid (p. 145) note that in Philadelphia, all bicycle officers are required to complete 40 hours of training in the following areas:

- Tactical uses of the bicycle as both an offensive and defensive weapon (including suspect approach and take-down tactics)
- Riding in the urban environment
- Crowd control

- Repair and continued maintenance of the equipment
- The importance of proper diet and health care
- The use of a firearm and high-retention holster while under physical stress
- Long-distance/on-road/off-road response
- Familiarity with gearing and proper use of 21- and 27-speed bikes
- Current state laws governing bicycle use
- The community relations aspects of bike patrol

Electric Bikes

Because bicycle patrol can be a physically challenging duty, many departments are using electric bicycles. In fact, according to Siuru (1999, p. 81): "Over 150 law enforcement agencies now [use] electric bicycles." He explains:

> Electric bikes are really "electrically assisted," you pedal the bike most of the time and switch on an electric motor, or twin motors in the case of ZAP bikes, when you want an assist. This gives a turbocharged-like boost for climbing a hill or a burst of speed. For example, a police officer could use both the motors and his legs when in a hot pursuit. Then just before arriving at the crime scene, the officer could let the motor do the work while resting a moment to catch his breath.

Motorcycles

Another type of popular two-wheeled patrol vehicle is the motorcycle. Strandberg (1999, p. 110) states:

> Motorcycle units, better known as 'motors,' are a staple to many departments because they do so many things so well. . . .
>
> These units are highly visible and more than a little intimidating. . . .
>
> Oddly enough, law enforcement is discovering the public finds motorcycle patrols a little more approachable. Citizens are drawn to the motorcycles and often will strike up a conversation with the cops riding them more readily than an officer in a squad car.
>
> The machines themselves . . . are very effective in tight spaces, very maneuverable and can go places that no squad car can go.

Despite the maneuverability and cost-effectiveness, motorcycle patrol is much more vulnerable to the weather than automobile patrol. Furthermore, as Strandberg (p. 114) notes: "Motorcycling is inherently more dangerous than driving a car—there is more exposure, and thus more risk."

Foot Patrol

Foot patrol, the oldest form of patrol, has many of the same advantages as bike patrol and is making a comeback in many jurisdictions. Foot patrol is an excellent means to develop rapport between the beat officer and citizens. Foot patrol officers can instruct citizens in crime prevention techniques and refer them to available governmental services.

Foot patrol is *proactive* rather than reactive, seeking to handle neighborhood problems before they become crimes. However, foot patrol does have disadvantages. It is relatively expensive and limits officers' ability to respond rapidly to calls for service in another area.

Many studies show that increasing the number of officers on foot patrol may not reduce crime but will increase citizens' feelings of safety. Foot patrol is also an important component of community policing. Community policing, in turn, is part of a trend to bolster personnel available to law enforcement by enlisting the aid of citizens, either as volunteers or as employees.

Air Patrol

The patrol function is further enhanced by the availability of airborne law enforcement units. As one pilot puts it (Paynter, 1999a, p. 132): "To combat crime effectively, we need eyes in the sky." According to Wexler (1998, p. 20):

> The nation's first airborne law enforcement unit took to the skies above New York City in 1929. . . .
>   Today, there are more than 200 airborne law enforcement units throughout the nation. Every day they are up in the sky performing an astonishing number of crime-fighting and life-saving operations. Choppers are supporting officers on the ground, apprehending dangerous fugitives, rescuing, and even assisting in aerial firefighting. Often, they are in the air when weather conditions are far from ideal. Sometimes, they are the only ones in the sky, when most civilian aircraft is grounded.

One disadvantage of air patrol is the high cost. As Paynter (1999a, p. 132) notes: "Helicopters are extraordinarily complex machines comprised of a collection of gears, transmissions, clutches, drivetrains and blades. This complexity is what makes a helicopter expensive to maintain." To combat the often prohibitively high operation and maintenance costs associated with airborne units, some departments have begun using gyroplanes as a more cost-effective alternative aircraft. Paynter (p. 132) reports: "Gyroplanes pack a big advantage over other means of flying, in some instances with operating costs less than half that of a helicopter of comparable performance."

Water Patrol

In many areas water patrol is an important addition to peace keeping. Weiss and Dresser (2000, p. 75) suggest: "Tactical operations in and around water and floating crime targets present a unique set of challenges for law enforcement." They list several issues, including the weight of the equipment, how to perform teammate rescues if submerged, water approaches and tactics for dealing with boats, ships and other floating structures. They (p. 77) conclude:

> Tactical water training for law enforcement officers is increasingly important because more and more departments are looking at the water as a new avenue to help them in their fight against crime.

Expanding the Law Enforcement Personnel Pool

Agencies have expanded their personnel pool through the use of citizen police academies, citizen patrols, reserves and volunteers within the department—frequently, retired individuals, including retired police officers. Another trend is the civilianization of certain law enforcement functions.

Citizen Police Academies

Several police departments seeking to implement community policing have started citizen police academies (CPAs). Since the organization of the first recorded U.S. citizen police academy in Orlando, Florida, in 1985, many communities have developed their own academies, each with its own unique focus. According to Ellis (1997, p. 56), CPAs allow residents to unite with their police departments to fight to keep what is theirs: the community.

Weinblatt (1997, p. 86) asserts that civilian academies permit law enforcement to take community policing to the "next level." One police captain maintains (Weinblatt, p. 86): "The citizens involved essentially become ambassadors for our cause to the community and offer positive support for what we do." Maffe and Burke (1999, p. 77) state:

> Police "academies" for citizens are the latest hot item for law enforcement.
>
> Citizen police academies enable the residents of a community to become more familiar with the day-to-day operations of their police departments. Participants gain a better understanding of the procedures, responsibilities, guidelines, demands of personnel and the policies and laws that guide decision making.

They (p. 77) continue:

> The benefits of a citizen police academy are significant and foremost is the power of proactive policing within the community. The only exposure most citizens have with a police officer is usually when a motor vehicle violation has occurred and a traffic citation is issued. This is usually viewed as a negative experience.
>
> Proactive law enforcement, such as a police citizen academy, places officers in a positive light. Understanding and cooperating with citizens is vital for effective police-community relations. Pro-activity is the critical foundation of understanding, and a citizen police academy bridges the gap between the citizens and the police.

Kanable (1999a, p. 57) notes: "Although the concept of what the citizen police academy is all about is consistent across the nation, the curricula are as different as the departments putting them together." For example, the 12-week academy sponsored by the Fond du Lac County, Wisconsin, Sheriff's Department teaches students about patrol, community services, domestics, drugs, arson, emergency communication, the canine unit, the dive team, the boat patrol, SWAT, crime scene processing, surveillance, investigations/ interrogations, corrections, civil process and the criminal justice system as a whole ("Building the Trust," 1999, p. 60). Many academies also offer ride-along programs.

The success of CPAs is without question. Kanable (1999a, p. 56) claims: "If citizen police academies were graded, there's no doubt they'd receive an A+ from law enforcement officers throughout the nation." To learn more about citizen police academies, contact the National Citizen Police Academy Association at 630-801-6563.

Citizens on Patrol

In other jurisdictions community policing strategies include citizen patrols. One such citizen patrol, operating in Fort Worth, Texas, encouraged community residents to patrol their own neighborhoods and be directly responsible for reducing crime. The program currently has over 2,000 patrollers, representing more than 87 neighborhoods in the city.

The St. Petersburg, Florida, Police Department has implemented a citizen patrol program, and Woodyard (1997, p. 180) reports:

> The main objective is to look for, and report, suspicious and unusual activity whether in the form of persons and/or vehicles. Under no circumstances do volunteers approach suspicious persons or vehicles, or stop a vehicle.
>
> Complaints [that] volunteers are able to investigate [include] abandoned vehicles, assist patrol officer when requested, found property, area check, information, bicycle theft with no suspect, traffic hazards, disabled vehicle, accidents (Blue Form), contact messages (nondeath) and 911 hang-ups (children).

In Delray Beach, Florida, a city with a population of 50,000, the police department's largest volunteer project is the Citizens Observer Patrol (COP), whose three primary goals are to:

- Effectively reduce crime and disorder in selected communities.
- Establish a working relationship between the Delray Beach police and its citizenry.
- Empower people and have them take ownership of their communities to reduce crime.

Overman (1997, p. 3) notes: "Currently, the Delray Beach Citizens Observer Patrol has 850 members in 21 sectors. Crime has markedly diminished in every area. Some sectors report a 75 percent decrease in burglary, auto theft and vandalism."

Reserves

Reserve officers, sometimes called part-timers, auxiliaries, specials or supernumeraries, are valuable assets to police departments in the effort to expand law enforcement resources. Reserve officer programs vary considerably from department to department. Weinblatt (1999a, p. 25) notes:

> Arroyo Grande [California], like many agencies in the western United States, trains and deploys reservists along the lines of the full-time officers. Standards and expectations remain equally high for both groups. At the other end of the spectrum, some agencies, such as many in the New York City metropolitan region, have gravitated towards a separation, which entails reserves patrolling alone or with another reservist.

In some jurisdictions reserve officers have powers of arrest and wear the same uniform as law enforcement officers except for the badge, which says "reserve." They may even purchase their own firearm and ballistics vest and drive their personally owned vehicles during operations.

Some jurisdictions recruit reserves from those retiring from their full-time ranks. Weinblatt (1999c, p. 127) observes:

> A lot of time and money is invested in veteran officers who could continue sharing that knowledge as a reserve officer.
>
> In an age requiring more sophisticated personnel, agencies are increasingly looking to benefit from the wealth of police experience residing in their communities. Retaining full-time expertise in the guise of a reserve officer is a cost-effective way of meeting law enforcement challenges.

Many reserve units function in specialized roles. For example, Weinblatt (1999b, p. 18) notes, numerous departments across the country are using reserves to perform search-and-rescue operations because of the prohibitively high costs of full-time, paid search-and-rescue personnel:

> The Los Angeles County Sheriff's Department has 110 non-compensated reserve deputies and in excess of 40 civilians. Reserve Chief Jack said his group donated 13,000 hours last year in training and 7,600 hours of actual time in 350 search and rescue operations. . . .
>
> San Diego County also has its share of specialty units. Their array of 11 units include tactical search (man tracking), mounted unit, motorized unit (personally owned four wheel drives to move personnel in and out of areas), aero squadron (privately owned fixed wing aircraft), and medical unit.

In summarizing his opinion of the reserve program, the Union County, North Carolina, sheriff states: "They help us . . . to help the citizens. We've gotten tenfold over what we've put into this" (Weinblatt, 1999b, p. 18). He also asserts that volunteers involved in search-and-rescue operations are really "an extension of community policing. Through this partnership with the citizens, we have extended our reach into the community" (p. 20).

Concerns exist regarding the use of reserves, in particular labor and liability concerns. Weinblatt (1999a, p. 26) notes: "The driving force behind some agency's reluctance to deploy reserves on an equal footing is based on resistance from employees and their labor organizations." To allay this concern, some departments have a contract with full-time officers stating that reserves are used only if a regular officer turns down the overtime or wants to take "comp" time off. To address liability issues, most agencies require reserves to complete rigorous training courses. Some, in fact, require reserves to go through the full basic academy, not accepting the reserve academy training as adequate.

As Bair (2000, p. 66), a reserve officer, says: "Reserve officers really want to be the best that they can be, but we can only be as good as the training that we are given."

Volunteers

The three groups of law enforcement personnel just discussed—citizen police academy participants, citizen patrols and reservists—consist primarily, if not solely in many jurisdictions, of volunteers. And, as discussed, their numbers are increasing. According to Jensen (1998, p. 102): "Many a law enforcement agency has discovered one of the best ways to cope with shrinking budgets and the high cost of technology is looking to the community for volunteer help." Sharp (1999, p. 204) adds:

> Volunteers have been used by law enforcement agencies for different jobs for many years. They have done so because they have proved their worth.
>
> A growing number of police agencies are viewing volunteers as integral parts of their community policing programs. Not only do volunteers perform a variety of tasks that might otherwise occupy the time of sworn officers, but they can also save the department money.

Indeed, as Paynter (1999b, p. 32) reports, volunteers in Phoenix, Arizona, donated more than 29,000 hours to the police department in 1998, saving the agency over $500,000. Paynter (1999b, p. 30) notes: "Volunteers can be an untapped resource that can help law enforcement save money and add services. . . . Jobs volunteers can do for law enforcement run the gamut from traditional clerical work and data entry to things like assisting stranded motorists." A jurisdiction in New Jersey that found it needed extra help to investigate animal cruelty cases formed a volunteer SPCA division. Weinblatt (1999d, p. 21) states:

> New Jersey has some 11 independent SPCA enforcement units that have volunteer investigative personnel carrying out the animal protection mandate. . . .
>
> In addition to reacting to reported investigative situations, the uniformed and armed volunteer officers have an active bike patrol that patrols the many sprawling mall parking lots . . . [looking] for jurisdictionally relevant violations such as dogs locked in hot cars during the summer.

In Henderson County, North Carolina, approximately 60 people are part of the Volunteers in Partnership with the Sheriff, or VIP, a group that donates about 1,000 free hours to the department each month performing functions such as answering telephones, greeting the public, doing report follow-ups, conducting research and development for new programs, assisting the Civil Process Division in serving subpoenas, manning the metal detector at the county courthouse, leading courthouse tours, providing security at the county library, fingerprinting, helping with traffic control and assisting DARE officers (Noble, 1997, p. 2).

As with the concern over using reserves, some paid, full-time officers are hesitant to embrace volunteers. To overcome staff resistance to volunteer programs, Jensen (p. 105) advises "talking up" the program beforehand: "Stress that no volunteer is there to take work away from an employee, but only to make it easier on the paid staff." Paynter (1999b, p. 34) adds:

> Increasing services and saving money by using volunteers can be a boon to the financially strapped law enforcement agency. But volunteers win too by helping their community. "My main goal is to put an officer out on the street where they can do their job best," [one volunteer] says. "My main motivation is to free up sworn personnel and put them somewhere doing a job only they can perform."
>
> And keeping officers on the streets, where they belong, is what a volunteer program is all about.

One innovative program uses volunteers to assist in a private/public sector partnership—state safety teams. Weinblatt (2000, p. 19) describes the team established by the North Carolina Transportation Association, which has counterparts nationwide. The association has 50 designated safety officers, of which 19 are active on road safety patrol. Other activities include public and law enforcement training endeavors geared toward drug interdiction, commercial vehicle inspection and accident investigation.

Civilianization

Civilianization refers to hiring citizens to perform certain tasks for the law enforcement department.

Civilianization is a cost-effective way to make use of the numerous and varied capabilities of citizens, while at the same time freeing up law enforcement personnel to concentrate their efforts on tasks they have been specifically trained for. Many routine functions performed by officers do not require their expertise nor their special authority and arrest powers. Animal-control officers, dispatchers, jailers and others might be civilians, rather than sworn peace officers.

Citizens and agencies within a jurisdiction are also of extreme importance when management is faced with deploying resources during an emergency.

Deploying Resources in Emergencies

During normal deployment, law enforcement managers have time to use statistics and studied judgment to determine allocation requirements, but during emergencies, present circumstances and experience largely dictate what personnel are deployed. Results depend on what managers in the field decide in those first minutes at the scene. Furthermore, as Denton (1999, p. 111) notes: "Law enforcement's role and response to handling critical incidents are high-risk in both physical terms and the potential for liability."

Law enforcement managers must be trained in emergency procedures, including medical emergencies, earthquakes, tornados, hurricanes, flooding, radioactive waste accidents, hostage taking, bomb threats, terrorist attacks, aircraft crashes, large fires, gas leaks, riots or other large crowd disturbances and snipers. They must be familiar with Civil Emergency Preparedness plans and the availability of assistance locally and from other agencies. They must be aware of the availability of emergency equipment and the location of area hospitals and rescue squads. This information should be condensed into written predisaster plans.

Predisaster plans should include the following:
- Which emergencies to prepare for
- What must be done in advance (supplies on hand, agreements with other agencies, etc.)
- What specific functions must be performed during the emergency and who is responsible for performing them, including outside organizations and agencies that might help
- What steps need to be taken to restore order after an emergency has ended
- How to evaluate a response

The plan should be made by top management in conjunction with those who would be involved in implementing it, including government officials, fire department personnel, health care personnel and so on.

Many jurisdictions use a three-level approach, with *Level 1* for minor events that can usually be handled by on-duty personnel. *Level 2* is for moderate to severe situations requiring aid from other agencies and perhaps other jurisdictions. *Level 3* is for catastrophes in which a state of emergency is proclaimed and county, state and perhaps federal assistance is requested. In such instances the National Guard may be called. The emergency plan should identify the levels of emergencies that might occur and the level of response required. Increasingly, law enforcement agencies across the country are devising and implementing Incident Command Systems (ICSs) to coordinate their emergency response. According to Connor (1997, p. 14): "As a planning tool, ICS designates in advance the specific duties of all participants. Perhaps more important, it determines who will be in charge at the scene." Ruff (2000, p. 52) suggests: "There must be a firm commitment to the principle that the first responding police officer is the initial incident commander." He contends that: "ICS is designed as a standard system allowing personnel from diverse agencies to meld into a common and unified emergency management structure."

Unfortunately, many managers place emergency planning as a low priority, feeling that such emergencies are unlikely to happen in their jurisdiction. But they could, and when they do, most citizens expect their law enforcement agencies to alert them, deal with it and keep them informed.

Managers should not only have predisaster plans and *practice* them but also be familiar with establishing command posts, furnishing information to the press and obtaining intelligence information on which they can make decisions. Accurate information is needed to know whether to evacuate, provide extra security, treat injured people, prevent looting, put up barricades or redirect traffic. Most law enforcement departments have experienced managers who have been involved in similar incidents. No fixed rules will serve in every situation, but there are guidelines. A great deal of independent decision making occurs in these moments. Law enforcement decision makers must be prepared for short, intense incidents or long-term sieges involving many hours.

The first law enforcement manager at the scene must take control, regardless of rank. Stalling for a manager of higher rank to take over could be fatal to people who need evacuation or rescue or to people being threatened. Normally, time is on the side of law enforcement in criminal or hostage situations. Subterfuge to gain time is important. Direct confrontation should be avoided unless it is the last resort. Each incident of this type has individual elements to consider, and no matter how many incidents an officer has been called on to resolve, a surprise element usually requires a considered, different decision.

Emergencies do not happen only in crowded metropolitan areas with dozens of onlookers and witnesses. For example, Sanow (1999) explains how small towns are developing response strategies to "shots fired" calls:

> Train for this kind of threat. The incidence of rifle assaults on police officers is on the increase. In April [1999], Indiana State Police trooper Cory Elson was shot and killed in Decatur, population 8300. Elson had stopped a vehicle for no taillights, a low-risk vehicle stop. The assailant stepped out of the truck and fired a 7.62×39 mm rifle. Elson returned fire but was shot when going for cover behind his cruiser.
>
> Officers and police managers need to plan how they will respond after a shooting. What should happen in the first five minutes? What should happen in the next 30 minutes? What should happen in the next 60 minutes? In three hours, the scene will almost certainly be taken over by state troopers or SWAT teams. It is the job of local law enforcement to "isolate and contain" until then.

Technological Aids

A variety of technological devices are helping law enforcement better cope with resource deployment during and following emergencies. For example, in the hurricane-vulnerable region of the Florida Keys, rugged PC Mobile laptop computers were used by sheriff's deputies during an evacuation to help with radio time, security sensitive data and prioritizing who needed to be evacuated from the barrier island chain first ("Hurricane Evacuations . . . ," 1999, p. 27).

In Manhattan Beach, California, after several high-profile crimes, solutions were sought to enhance community security and reduce the sense of fear. Hensley (1999, p. 53) notes: "Several options to elevate safety and security were identified with the two most popular being emergency call boxes and video cameras." Emergency call boxes have been used in the United States since the early 1900s, but their use and popularity waned following World War II, when two-way radio communications became available to law enforcement. Recently, however, emergency call boxes have seen a resurgence.

Hensley (p. 54) lists their potential benefits as well as their possible drawbacks. Benefits include citizens being able to report a crime as it occurs; the strategic placement of call boxes allows easy access to police services even in remote locations; the visibility of call boxes may deter potential criminal offenders; they provide a link between the community and the police; and call boxes promote positive community relations. Drawbacks include the possibility of unnecessary calls, prank calls or vandalism (video cameras may help deter this), weathering of the units and the cost to install and maintain the devices.

Another technological aid helping law enforcement handle medical emergencies is the automated external defibrillator (AED). According to Hall (1999, p. 16), the number of agencies now using the devices to help treat the approximately 350,000 annual victims of sudden cardiac arrest (SCA) has risen rapidly. Kanable (1999b, p. 30) reports: "Throughout the country there are 1,900 AEDs standing ready in marked patrol cars, marine units, mounted units, helicopters and bicycles." The AEDs are "small, lightweight, portable, relatively inexpensive (about $3,000), easy-to-use and virtually foolproof, error-free machines." Weimer (1999, p. 41) agrees AEDs are easy to use, noting that in most circumstances, officer training is eight hours or less.

Because medical research has shown that up to half of all SCA deaths could be prevented with early defibrillation and officers commonly arrive on the scene of an SCA before paramedics or other personnel, many departments believe it makes sense to have AEDs and officers trained in their use. One officer states (Kanable, 1999b, p. 28): "Whether they become certified or not, police officers almost always are the first responders. Whether they want to or not, they're going to find themselves in situations where people need help, and it's always so much better to have the tool to do the job rather than just having to do the best you can." Others, however, are concerned about the liability issues of using these devices. Yet, as one medical doctor believes (Kanable, 1999b, p. 30): "Over time, as the public becomes more aware of AED efficacy, the tables will turn from being more liable if you have an AED program to being more liable if you don't."

Deploying Resources to "Fight Crime"

Many individuals in law enforcement and probably the majority of the citizens they serve consider "crime fighting" as one of the primary responsibilities of their agency. It is. Doing so has become more difficult, however, given shrinking resources and the advanced technology many criminals have.

Crime Triangle

One tool to help law enforcement tackle crime through problem solving is the crime triangle, shown in Figure 15.6. The Minneapolis Police Department's Repeat Call Address Policing (RECAP) experiment used the crime triangle as part of its strategy. Buerger (1999, p. 151) explains:

> Theoretically, the basis for the RECAP strategy lies in Cohen and Felson's Routine Activities Theory, which proposes that crime occurs during the intersection, in time and space, of motivated offenders and suitable victims (or targets), under circumstances of absent or inadequate guardianship: a Crime Triangle similar to the fire triangle of fuel, heat, and oxygen. Crime was presumed amenable to suppression if any of the three legs of the triangle was removed, or neutralized.

The **crime triangle** is a model that illustrates how all three elements—motivated suspect, suitable victim and adequate location—are required for a crime to occur.

One side of the crime triangle, the suspect, is most often the focus of crime-fighting efforts.

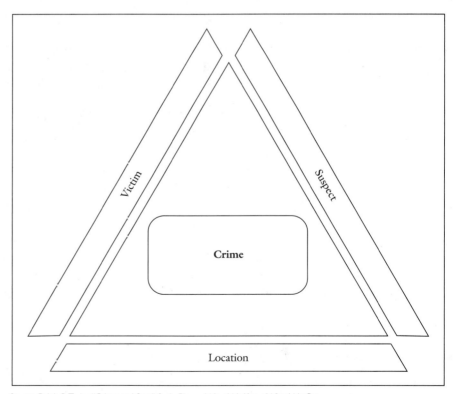

Figure 15.6
Crime Triangle

Source: Ralph B. Taylor. "Crime and Small-Scale Places: What We Know, What We Can Prevent, and What Else We Need to Know." In Taylor et al. *Crime and Place: Plenary Papers of the 1997 Conference on Criminal Justice Research and Evaluation,* July 1998, p. 2.

Focus on Criminals

Just as managers are beginning to tap into the resources of their community, they are also beginning to do more "partnering" with other agencies to apprehend criminals. A prime example of such a partnership is that between the Metro-Dade Police Department, Miami, and the Bureau of Alcohol, Tobacco and Firearms (ATF), Miami District Office. The program is called Project Achilles because they target "career criminals" who are known to possess firearms. This possession of firearms makes them vulnerable, putting them within both the state and the federal criminal justice system. The program grew out of studies that indicate that 6 percent of the criminals arrested commit up to 70 percent of all serious crime.

> Focusing on career criminals is a logical approach to fighting crime. Equally promising in crime-fighting efforts is a focus on high-crime locations.

Focus on Location

In the crime triangle, location is a critical element. Weisburd (1997) notes how criminal justice researchers and practitioners have only recently begun to focus on *places* where offenses occur in addition to *people* who commit crimes. One result of this shift has been the identification of hot spots, a term borrowed from geology to designate a region of potentially volatile geologic, or volcanic, activity. **Hot spots** are specific locations with high crime rates. Taylor (1998, p. 3) explains: "A hot spot may be a single address, a cluster of addresses close to one another, a segment of a streetblock, an entire streetblock or two, or an intersection."

To organize data about crime over time at various levels of analysis, criminologists have applied the concept of the **cone of resolution** (Figure 15.7), this

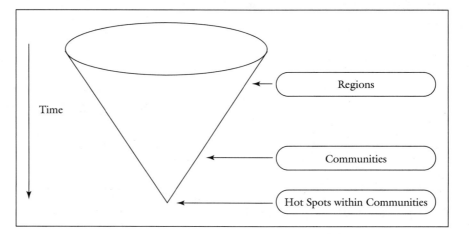

Figure 15.7
Cone of Resolution

Source: Ralph B. Taylor. "Crime and Small-Scale Places: What We Know, What We Can Prevent, and What Else We Need to Know." In Taylor et al. *Crime and Place: Plenary Papers of the 1997 Conference on Criminal Justice Research and Evaluation*, July 1998, p. 2.

time borrowing from geography. Taylor (p. 1) states: "Spacial patterns observed for crime rates vary as you progress down the cone to increasingly smaller scales of analysis. . . . Over the last century and a half, criminological researchers have moved progressively down this cone of resolution. In the past 10 years, criminological researchers and police departments have looked closely at the relationship between crime and specific street addresses."

Borrowing another concept, this time from ecology, Braiden (1998, p. 8) suggests another way to view the significance of location—"the hunt and the habitat":

> I can't think of two special-interest groups more philosophically opposed to each other than hunters and animal rights activists, yet there are two things they totally agree upon: The species will survive the hunt; it will not survive loss of its habitat.
>
> What can policing learn from this basic principle of nature? Well, if the ultimate goal is to eliminate the criminal species forever, surely the best way to do that is to eliminate the habitat that spawns and sustains that species. Structured as it is, the criminal justice system puts 95 percent of its resources into the hunt while the habitat is left almost untouched. We can never win working that way, because the habitat never stops supplying new customers for the hunt.

Another way of viewing the role of habitat or location as an element of crime causation is to consider **incivilities,** or signs of disorder. Piquero (1999, p. 793) states: "Both criminologists and policy makers have argued that abandoned cars, buildings, and apartment units, public drunkenness, graffiti, and other assorted unpleasantries communicate to many persons the absence of both formal and informal social control." Wilson and Kelling's classic "broken windows" theory suggested that such incivilities lead to higher crime rates, victimization rates and residents' perception of the fear of crime.

A focus on the third side of the crime triangle—the victims and reducing their suitability as targets—brings community policing into the scene.

Community Policing and Deployment of Personnel

Community policing assigns officers to specific neighborhoods and actively involves them in helping the neighborhood solve its problems and avoid victimization. This proactive approach usually includes increased emphasis on foot patrol.

Miller and Hess (1998, p. xxii) note:

> Community policing offers one avenue for making neighborhoods safer. Community policing is not a program or a series of programs. It is a philosophy, a belief that working together, the police and the community can accomplish what neither can accomplish alone. The *synergy* that results from community policing can be powerful. It is like the power of a finely tuned athletic team, with each member contributing to the total effort. Occasionally heroes may emerge, but victory depends on a team effort.

Cordner (1999, pp. 138–145) identifies four major dimensions of community policing and the common elements of each:

> *The Philosophical Dimension*—Many . . . advocates emphasize that community policing is a new philosophy of policing, perhaps constituting even a paradigm shift away from professional-model policing. Three of the most important [elements] . . . are citizen input, broad function, and personalized service. . . .

The Strategic Dimension—Includes the key operational concepts that translate philosophy into action. These . . . are the links between the broad ideas and beliefs that underlie community policing and the specific programs and practices by which it is implemented . . . . Three strategic elements of community policing are reoriented operations, geographic focus, and prevention emphasis [being proactive]. . . .

The Tactical Dimension—Translates ideas, philosophies, and strategies into concrete programs, practices, and behaviors. . . . Unless community policing eventually leads to some action, some new or different behavior, it is all rhetoric and no reality. . . . Three of the most important tactical elements of community policing are positive interaction, partnerships, and problem solving. . . .

The Organizational Dimension—It is important to recognize an organizational dimension that surrounds community policing . . . and consider a variety of changes in organization, administration, management, and supervision. . . . Important organizational elements of COP are structure and management.

Regarding the organizational dimension of community policing, Cordner (p. 145) explains that the restructuring of an organization typically includes a decentralization of authority, a flattening of hierarchical layers, the use of teams and the implementation of civilianization. In addition, new management styles require more coaching, mentoring and empowerment of subordinates.

Another element of community policing requires assigning officers permanently to defined beats, allowing them the benefit of "owning" their neighborhood beats. This further enables officers to participate in community-based problem solving and to balance reactive responses to crime incidents and emergencies with a proactive focus on preventing problems before they occur or escalate.

In fact, community policing is an ideal way to increase productivity. As Bauman (2000, p. 32) suggests: "Police productivity is a state of the mind, an approach to the job." He offers some "tried-and-true" suggestions for making good use of down time:

- Concentrate on problem areas—talk to neighbors. One problem solved today might prevent ten calls next month.

- Consider "knock and talks"—knocking on a door, engaging occupants of a problem location in conversation and looking around for any plain-view evidence, perhaps even asking for consent to search.

- Hide and watch—using binoculars in a problem area.

- Working traffic—can be very productive even if you are not inclined to write lots of tickets. Big criminals often commit little crimes.

- Engaging in building and bar checks—you might find an open door before a burglar does, surprise a burglar or encounter someone making a drug deal.

Appendix G contains sample goals, daily routines, methods, responsibilities and duties of a community policing officer.

Citizen Involvement

DiIulio (1993, p. 9) suggests that citizens must become "co-producers of justice":

Citizens in a democracy must begin by holding themselves and their neighbors accountable for public affairs. A democratic vision of the justice system, therefore, is anything but a sop to public frustrations with crime and disorder. Citizens who expect judges, police, and other justice officials to solve society's crime problems are unrealistic; citizens should not expect the officials to succeed without the active cooperation and support of the community.

Alpert and Moore (1993, p. 132) suggest:

> The two fundamental features of a new police strategy must be these: that the role of private citizens in the control of crime and maintenance of public order be established and encouraged, not derided and thwarted, and that the police become more active, accessible participants in community affairs.

One example of a joint activity between police and members of the community was a one-day cleanup campaign of an area in a Florida community, which resulted in collecting over 100 tons of garbage, 10 tons of rusted-out appliances and junk and over 50 abandoned vehicles. The waste management department furnished the hauling equipment. Departments might start a DARE program in a school, an Operation Identification program or a Neighborhood Watch Program. They might also conduct monthly meetings for police, residents and business people to discuss mutual problems, possible causes and viable solutions or begin foot patrol, bicycle patrol or mounted patrol in high-crime areas.

Citizen input on perceived officer effectiveness and efficiency will help managers assess departmental productivity. Police are effective when they produce the perception that crime is under control. Managers need to find out how the public perceives the police department's efforts. This is often very different from what those within the department think.

Law Enforcement Productivity

Productivity from the law enforcement department, one of the most costly municipal services, is expected. Managers' effectiveness is judged by the results they obtain using the available resources, and today's police administrator is pressured to provide more services with fewer resources.

Jokes about productivity are common in the workplace. For example, when one man was asked how long he had been working for his company, he answered, "Ever since they threatened to fire me." Or the supervisor who when asked how many people worked for him replied, "Oh, about half." Lack of productivity is no joke.

Productivity Defined

Productivity measures results gained from a specific amount of effort. The concept of value is implicit in productivity and differentiates it from measures of efficiency or effectiveness. An efficient use of resources alone may not be effective or meet a desired need. An effective use of resources may not be efficient or sufficient in overall impact. Productivity planning helps to strike a balance between efficiency and effectiveness guided by an overall desire for value. **Productivity** is converting resources to achieve results efficiently and effectively.

Measuring Law Enforcement Productivity

Law enforcement services are not as measurable as production-line efforts. Production lines measure productivity in units manufactured; businesses measure it in profits.

Officers provide numerous services to their jurisdictions. However, some departments are finding it necessary to cut back on specific services to increase their overall productivity. For example, response to a property damage accident may involve an officer reporting to the scene and furnishing forms for those involved to complete.

Law enforcement productivity is measured by the quality and quantity of services provided.

Increased productivity is a desirable management goal. A great deal of emphasis has been given to time-and-motion studies and to breaking tasks into their simplest elements. Although every attempt is made to determine the right way to do each task, this also depersonalizes the task and deprives it of much of its meaning.

The scientific approach to accomplishing tasks has to be tempered with regard for human beings. A balance between management and worker expectations has to be achieved without abandoning the concept that work must be productive.

Reasonable standards must be determined. Desired management productivity and employee performance capability must be balanced. Once this balance is determined, employees have a standard against which management can measure them. If accurate records are kept, employees will know where they stand in relation to what is expected and to all other employees who perform the same functions.

In law enforcement, tasks can be determined through job analysis, and time limits can be established for various repetitive tasks. Other areas, however, do not lend themselves to such analysis. Law enforcement services required by the community break into general categories such as crime, accidents, emergencies, juvenile and arrests.

> Law enforcement productivity has traditionally been measured by arrests, stops, traffic citations, value of recovered property and reduction of accidents and crime.

The main concern with these productivity measurements is that law enforcement officers may not have much control over them. Reduction in accidents or crime may be short term, or there may be no reduction at all, but this does not necessarily mean that officers are not productive.

Quotas vs. Performance Standards

Productivity normally involves setting minimum standards, which, in law enforcement, brings up the question of quotas. A **quota** is a specific number or proportional share that each is expected to contribute or receive.

It is difficult not to use arrests, tickets issued, number of service calls answered and number of reports and activities initiated by officers as a basis for productivity because these are what officers do. But also important are how these tasks are executed, the quality of the reports and the public's perception of the officers. Van Meter (1998, p. 12) notes: "When law enforcement administrators attempt to establish productivity standards, they are often accused of setting 'quotas.' " Quota systems are frequently challenged as being arbitrary, capricious, unreasonable and unfair. According to Van Meter (p. 12):

> In practice, most of the systems that are challenged as "quotas" have four distinguishing features:
>
> - Management determines what an expected number of tickets for a specific period of time should be;
> - Quantity (a set number) is the only criterion by which performance is judged;
> - The number of tickets expected is usually set so low that it insults the typical performer;
> - Some form of discipline results if the requisite number of tickets is not met.

Van Meter (p. 14) also asserts: "A system of well defined and job-valid standards is not a quota." To avoid the quota mentality and instead develop a system of reasonable productivity standards that are fairly enforced and related to the agency's legitimate business goals, Van Meter (p. 14) suggests managers "ensure that factors such as work shifts, zones, and time of week or day are used to segregate productivity data so that no unfair comparisons between work units are made." Furthermore:

> Performance theory can show that employees who have been given the opportunity to perform to standards but fail to do so are either insubordinate or incompetent. Arbiters and courts alike have held that either reason is just cause for discipline, including termination.

Productivity Problems   Symptoms of productivity problems are similar to those of motivation/morale problems: high absenteeism and turnover, high levels of waste, high accident rates and unreasonable complaints and grievances.

One of the most serious challenges to productivity is the unproductive executive. According to Bushey (1999, p. 69): "The unproductive traits of a high-level leader present a poor example for subordinates, raise legitimate questions of hypocrisy with respect to prevailing expectations and send the wrong message to other officials and to the public." Bushey (p. 71) further stresses: "The development of subordinate leaders is among the most important and solemn responsibilities facing a law enforcement administrator." He (p. 71) advises:

> Never underestimate the impact of your words and actions on subordinates. Casual comments, unintended slights, unacknowledged greetings—in short, anything that could be misconstrued as criticism—could cause needless worry among subordinates and affect morale. . . .
>
> Don't resign yourself to the marginal performance of a weak subordinate manager. Work with him to find and develop skills.

Improving Productivity

Often the difference between promising ideas and productive results is a good manager. Productivity is directed from the top and accomplished at the bottom of the organizational hierarchy. Such productivity can be improved by the following:

- Clearly explaining organizational goals
- Permitting more decisions to be made at the "doing" level
- Supporting creativity and innovation
- Increasing individual control over the tasks for which officers are responsible

Furthermore, managers and supervisors at all levels must set performance expectations and then insist that those they oversee meet these expectations. Each department level must hold the next level accountable.

Law enforcement productivity can be improved by:

- Training and experience.
- Rewards and incentives.
- Improved equipment.
- Technology.

Training and experience can improve productivity by helping people do tasks more efficiently. Productivity can also be increased through a reward system. Deserved praise, commendation and personal recognition are rewards. Monetary rewards, although effective, may not be as effective as personal rewards that build self-esteem and self-worth. All the concepts in Chapter 10 related to motivating employees are relevant.

In addition, improved law enforcement productivity can be accomplished by introducing improved equipment. An up-to-date communications and computer center can assist officers; however, the equipment should be procured based on a realistic cost assessment in relation to expected benefit. Many smaller, less costly pieces of equipment can increase patrol productivity. For example, cell phones

Computers have made the job of patrol officers more efficient and safer. They can enter license numbers, addresses and the like and find out almost instantly whether they are dealing with a wanted person. Here a police officer is entering data into the computer on the dashboard of his squad car.

for each unit, radar installed in most beat cars, a car desk or lighted clipboard for report writing are small items that can increase productivity.

Implementing mobile computing systems has several benefits including higher crime-solution rate, greatly reduced clerical costs and, most important, increased officer safety. Such systems are excellent examples of ways in which technology can increase productivity.

Technology

Productivity can be increased without adding employees by using technology presently available and soon to become available. Taping reports to be recorded later by clerk typists, using computers, installing improved 911 and CAD systems, superhighway police information systems and a host of other future technologies will vastly enhance police productivity.

Computers can be used in a variety of ways to enhance productivity, for example, record keeping, data analysis, word processing, investigating, inventorying property rooms and maintaining stolen-property files. One way computers are improving departments' productivity is by facilitating the organization of data through a management information system (MIS). Figure 15.8 illustrates the components of a management information system. MIS procedures include collecting, analyzing and reporting past, present and projected information from within and outside the organization.

A **management information system (MIS)** provides data for planning and decision making.

One computerized program in the war on crime is the FBI's *Drugfire.* Siuru (1994, p. 47) explains:

> *Drugfire* is a computerized database that forensic labs can use to maintain and search Open Case Fired Ammunition Files (OCFAF) with greatly increased

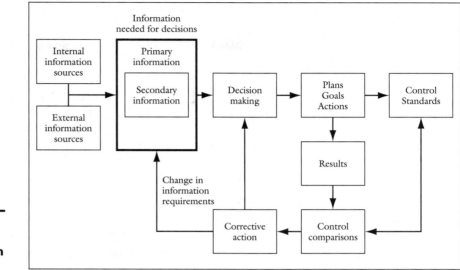

Figure 15.8
Components of a Management Information System (MIS)

Source: Lester R. Bittel. *The McGraw-Hill 36-Hour Management Course*. New York: McGraw-Hill Publishing Company, 1989, p. 234. Reprinted by permission.

effectiveness. *Drugfire* was developed by the FBI and its database stores high-definition digital "snapshots" of the markings on spent bullets or casings as they appear through the microscope. . . .

Drugfire can perform remote side-by-side comparison of fired ammunition specimens in near-real time using the images in the database rather than physically mounting and examining the actual fired rounds under the same microscope.

The same database can be used by several labs, allowing comparisons to be made without having to physically transfer the evidence.

The FBI will offer *Drugfire* to any qualified forensic laboratory that routinely conducts examinations of firearm evidence.

Strandberg (1998a, p. 31) notes that computer capabilities are constantly evolving and improving, further enhancing their ability to increase police productivity:

Palm-sized computers take the downsizing of computer hardware to the next degree. Having a computer that you can hold in one hand means being able to take that computer anywhere—into a crime scene, on a car stop, into position for a hostage negotiation . . . anywhere you can go, it can go.

Computers are also assisting with crime analysis and investigation. Strandberg (1998b, p. 41) states:

Analysis of crime is one of the things computers are very well suited for, crunching numbers and evaluating objective trends, and one of the most effective ways of analyzing crime involves mapping the crime and examining trends. This was once done with a huge map on the wall and with pushpins.

Computers further enhance productivity by conducting vehicle tracking and mapping, as Strandberg (1998b, p. 43) explains: "Vehicle tracking is important to law enforcement departments, in that dispatchers can know where all their vehicles are at any point in time. You can manage your fleet more effectively if you know the location of the closest car to a situation."

Integrated justice systems are improving not only the productivity of law enforcement but also that of the entire criminal justice system. As Strandberg (1998a, p. 31) explains, an integrated justice system takes a computer-aided dispatch message and rolls it right into an automated reporting system, which goes directly into the police records system:

> As someone is charged, it becomes a DA report, then the same electronic file is passed on into the appropriate court system. When the court system discharges that person, the same file would go to the corrections facility. . . .
>   The ultimate goal is to have the original information, collected by the cop on the street, "flow" into every other application used by every other step in the justice system.

Faced with an endless barrage of technical advances and innovations, managers might become overwhelmed and intimidated. They must strive to avoid technical obsolescence by preventing employees and themselves from succumbing to **technophobia,** the fear of using technology because of unfamiliarity or uncertainty as to how it works. Gordon (1998, p. 39) explains: "Consider a fax machine. Many people use one almost every day. How does it work? Who cares! It works! These people are proudly becoming known as TIFA individuals— Technologically Ignorant, Functionally Adequate individuals."

To keep up with technology, managers might use the National Aeronautics and Space Administration's (NASA) Technology Utilization Program, which was established in the early 1960s by congressional mandate to promote the transfer of aerospace technology to other areas. For example, a Pennsylvania police department called upon NASA's ability to enhance ATM films so the images were sufficiently sharpened to identify a car and driver, resulting in the arrest of a kidnapper/murderer.

In addition to capitalizing on technological advances to enhance productivity, some agencies are taking approaches successfully used in business to reorganize the way officers within the agency work together. An example is the quality circles approach to productivity.

Quality Circles Approach

A **quality circle** is a group of five to ten employees with common interests and common work hours who volunteer to meet to solve problems in their workplace. Quality circles began in the early 1960s in Japan, as management sought to improve productivity by raising worker satisfaction. In the 1970s Lockheed and Honeywell used quality circles with great success. During the 1980s quality circles expanded into the private and public service sector.

Recall that such abstract motivational theories as McGregor's "Theory Y" and Maslow's "Hierarchy of Needs" contend that employees, if allowed to influence job-related decisions, tend to take more personal interest and pride in their work. This results in increased productivity and a more effective organization. Participation in a quality circle increases workers' job satisfaction, allowing them to satisfy their needs for personal achievement, recognition and increased self-esteem.

Team members should receive training in brainstorming, problem definition, data collection and analysis.

Key ingredients for successful quality circles include in-depth training, management participation, feedback and publication of circle achievements.

The quality circle *coordinator* is responsible for establishing and monitoring the program. The coordinator also trains the facilitators and provides materials the circles need. The organization of typical quality circles is illustrated in Figure 15.9.

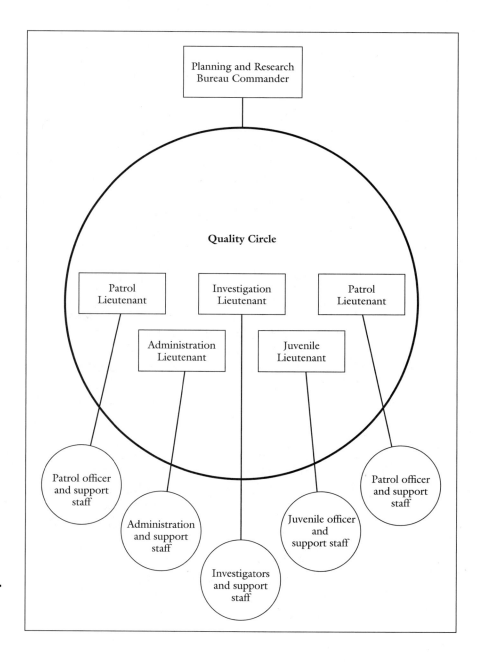

Figure 15.9
Typical Quality Circle Organization

Productive Work Teams

Productive work teams have several characteristics, most of which have already been discussed in other contexts. In a productive team, members work toward common goals that everyone knows, understands and accepts. The goals not only serve the organization but also give team members opportunities to develop professionally. Members know their individual responsibilities and priorities and how they relate to those of other members. Policies that govern team interaction are fair, consistently applied and subject to change. Obsolete policies are replaced with ones appropriate to the team's current circumstances. When team actions are decided, individual assignments are understood and accepted.

The work atmosphere is informal, comfortable and fairly free of tension but still dynamic. Work discussions are numerous and always pertinent to the team's tasks. Communication lines are open. During discussions all members feel free to express their ideas and opinions. Members not only speak their minds and relay information about team assignments and procedures but also listen to each other. Members feel comfortable asking questions if they do not understand. No one pretends to know it all. Criticism is acceptable and is delivered frequently, frankly and constructively, never as a personal attack. The team is comfortable with conflict. Members recognize disagreements and work fairly and intelligently toward resolving them.

Members have a great amount of confidence and trust in one another. They cooperate rather than compete. They are eager to help each other with tasks and with developing to the fullest professional potential. They encourage one another to achieve at high levels but do so without setting unrealistic expectations. Individuals may voice opposition to proposals but respect the team's final decision.

Team morale and productivity are high. Members' enthusiasm prompts them to work hard. They attend to details, follow through on intentions and perform to the best of their ability. Members take pride in their achievements and readily accept feedback on performance.

The team leader takes pride in the team's work record. The leader shows interest in each team member's achievement and regularly provides feedback on performance. The leader consults members before making changes affecting the team. The leader does not dominate the team, nor do members defer unduly to the leader. When work circumstances do not call for participative leadership, members are comfortable with the leader assuming control. The team operates without power struggles; the issue is not who controls but what is the best way to do the job.

Members always know how the team is progressing toward its goals. The team frequently evaluates how well it is operating, openly discussing problems. Members do not feel threatened by change but are eager to try creative approaches.

Leadership, Discipline, Motivation and Morale Revisited

A quote by an anonymous author reads:

> Interest and attention are just as important to people as grease and oil are to a machine. Without it they don't run smoothly, never reach top speed and break down more frequently.

Developing a spirit to perform is one of management's jobs. Law enforcement managers use four motivating techniques: redesigning the law enforcement job; providing productive work and an opportunity for achievement and recognition; stating clear, concise and achievable goals; and providing some form of reward and enticement system for excellent performance. Intrinsic rewards can be used as well as extrinsic rewards.

> The quality of management in the organization is the single most important factor for high productivity and morale. They are integrally related.

Let officers know what is expected of them and follow up to see that they meet expectations. Not every law enforcement task will lead to achievement. However, law enforcement work provides a high potential for individual performance based on individual competence.

All law enforcement employees should know what is regarded as productive work. They should know what is expected on the job. They should know how their performance will be judged and receive feedback on how well they accomplished it. The relationship between job performance and expected results should be clear. Officers should leave each shift with a sense of individual and organizational achievement.

Summary

Police logs provide data for better deployment of personnel. The largest division is the uniformed patrol unit, which provides services seven days a week, twenty-four hours a day.

Area assignments are determined by requests for services based on available data. This is called proportionate assignment. No area should be larger than the time it takes a car to respond to emergency calls in a reasonable time. To determine patrol area size, consider square miles, street miles and response time. Although rapid response may not deter crime or increase the apprehension of criminals, it *is* important because fast response builds public confidence in law enforcement capabilities and competence. It also places officers at a scene to protect evidence before it is destroyed by people or the elements. It increases the chances of locating witnesses and making arrests. Further, it increases the chances of providing lifesaving emergency first aid to victims of crimes.

Most law enforcement departments use some form of random patrol, the basic premise of which is to place officers closer to a potential incident or request for service before it happens, based on data from experience. Goals are to reduce response time and erase set patrol pattern habits. However, the Kansas City Preventive Patrol Experiment found that increasing or decreasing routine preventive patrol had no effect on crime, citizen fear of crime, community attitudes toward the police on delivery of police services, police response time or traffic accidents.

Common methods of patrol include automobile, bicycle, motorcycle, foot and air patrol. Other methods use mounted, water and special-terrain patrol. A consideration related to automobile patrol is whether one- or two-officer units should be used, which should be determined by individual circumstances.

Many managers, in an attempt to expand their employee base, have begun using alternative personnel resources, including citizen patrols, reserves and volunteers, in addition to civilianizing some law enforcement functions. Civilianization refers to hiring citizens to perform certain tasks for the law enforcement department.

Managers also must be prepared to deploy resources during times of emergency and, therefore, should have carefully formulated predisaster plans. These plans should include, at minimum:

- What emergencies to prepare for.
- What needs to be done in advance (supplies on hand, agreements with other agencies, etc.).
- What specific functions must be performed during the emergency and who is responsible for performing them, including outside organizations and agencies who might help.
- What steps need to be taken to restore order after the emergency has ended.
- How the response is to be evaluated.

Managers are also expected to fulfill their responsibility to deploy resources to fight crime. The crime triangle is a model illustrating how all three elements—motivated suspect, suitable victim and adequate location—are required for crime to occur. Focusing on career criminals (suspects) is one logical approach to fighting crime. Focusing on specific locations with high crime rates, areas known as hot spots, is another approach. Focusing on victims brings community policing into the crime fighting scene.

Community policing assigns officers to specific neighborhoods and actively involves them in helping the neighborhood solve its problems and avoid victimization. This proactive approach usually includes increased emphasis on foot patrol. It often incorporates problem-oriented policing, which is also proactive rather than reactive, seeking out problems and their solutions instead of attempting to solve crimes after they have occurred.

Law enforcement productivity is measured by the quality and quantity of services provided. It has traditionally been measured by arrests, traffic citations, value of recovered property and reduction of accidents and crime.

Law enforcement productivity can be improved by training and experience, rewards and incentives, improved equipment and technology. One means to improve productivity is through a management information system (MIS), which provides data for planning and decision making.

Quality circles can help enhance productivity. A quality circle is a group of five to ten employees with common goals and hours who volunteer to meet to solve problems in their workplace. Key ingredients for successful quality circles include in-depth training, management participation, feedback and publication of team achievements.

The quality of management in the organization is the single most important factor for high productivity and morale. They are integrally related.

Discussion Questions

1. What factors should be considered in determining personnel assignment to shifts?

2. What is your opinion of the random patrol method of deploying law enforcement personnel?

3. Do you favor one- or two-officer patrol units? Why?

4. Does your law enforcement agency use civilianization? If so, for what positions? Could this be expanded?

5. What emergencies should be planned for in your jurisdiction?

6. Have you ever been involved in a disaster or emergency that required law enforcement officers? If so, how effectively did they perform?

7. What proportion of resources do you feel should be allocated to "fighting crime"?

8. What innovative ideas can you think of to increase effectiveness and productivity?

9. How does your law enforcement agency use computers?

10. When are you highly productive? What factors are present during those times?

InfoTrac College Edition Assignment

Research two *methods of patrol* that are of interest to you. Outline the main characteristics of each as well as any other information you find interesting. Include the full reference citations. Be prepared to share your findings with the class.

OR

Read and outline the article "British Policing and the Ottawa Shift System" by Simpson and Richbell in the *FBI Law Enforcement Bulletin,* January 2000, pp. 19–26. Be prepared to share your outline with the class.

References

Allgower, Ron and Henry, Michael P. "Alternate Team Staffing Concept Offers Benefits to Officers and Management." *Law and Order,* Vol. 46, No. 8, August 1998, pp. 85–88.

Alpert, Geoffrey and Moore, Mark H. "Measuring Police Performance in the New Paradigm of Policing." In *Performance Measures for the Criminal Justice System.* Bureau of Justice Statistics and Princeton University, October 1993, pp. 109–142.

Anemone, Louis R. and Spangenberg, Francis E. "Building on Success: TrafficStat Takes the NYPD's CompStat Method in a New Direction." *The Police Chief,* Vol. LXVII, No. 2, February 2000, pp. 23–28.

Bair, John M. "Just a Reserve? The Contributions Can Be Many." *Police,* Vol. 24, No. 3, March 2000, p. 66.

Bauman, Michael P. "Police Productivity: A State of Mind, An Approach to the Job." *Police,* Vol. 24, No. 1, January 2000, pp. 32–34.

Bayley, David H. and Worden, Robert E. *Police Overtime: An Examination of Key Issues.* Washington, DC: National Institute of Justice Research in Brief, May 1998. (NCJ-167572)

Braiden, Chris. "Policing—The Hunt and the Habitat." *Law Enforcement News,* October 31, 1998, pp. 8, 10.

Buerger, Michael E. "The Problems of Problem-Solving." In *Policing Perspectives: An Anthology,* edited by Larry K. Gaines and Gary W. Cordner. Los Angeles: Roxbury Publishing Company, 1999, pp. 150–169.

"Building the Trust." *Law Enforcement Technology,* Vol. 26, No. 10, October 1999, p. 60.

Bushey, Keith D. "The Unproductive Executive." *The Police Chief,* Vol. LXVI, No. 3, March 1999, pp. 69–71.

Caplan, Marc H. "Efficient Use of Police Resources." Washington, DC: National Institute of
     Justice, November 1983.
Connor, T. W. "Incident Command Systems for Law Enforcement." *FBI Law Enforcement
     Bulletin,* Vol. 66, No. 9, September 1997, pp. 14–17.
Cordner, Gary W. "Elements of Community Policing." In *Policing Perspectives,* edited by Larry
     K. Gaines and Gary W. Cordner. Los Angeles: Roxbury Publishing Company, 1999,
     pp. 137–149.
Dees, Tim. "The Biggest Little Bike Team in the World." *Law and Order,* Vol. 46, No. 4,
     April 1998, pp. 59–62.
DeFranco, Liz. "Computer Scheduling." *Law Enforcement Technology,* Vol. 27, No. 1, January
     2000, pp. 30–82.
Denton, John E. "Perception: A Core Issue in Crisis Intervention." *Law and Order,* Vol. 47,
     No. 8, August 1999, pp. 111–115.
DiIulio, John J., Jr. "Rethinking the Criminal Justice System: Toward a New Paradigm." In
     Performance Measures for the Criminal Justice System. Bureau of Justice Statistics and
     Princeton University, October 1993, pp. 1–18.
Ellis, Tom. "The Citizen's Police Academy." *Law Enforcement Technology,* Vol. 45, No. 10,
     October 1997, pp. 56–60.
Geberth, Vernon J. "Detective Rotation: An Enigma." *Law and Order,* Vol. 46, No. 10,
     October 1998, pp. 194–196.
Glorioso, John E., Sr. and Ritter, Robert B. "Operational Planning: Taking the Adversary's
     Perspective." *Law and Order,* Vol. 46, No. 7, July 1998, pp. 96–99.
Gordon, Kevin. "World Wide What?" *Law and Order,* Vol. 46, No. 2, February 1998, pp. 39–42.
Hall, Dennis. "Defibrillators Charging Up: America's Law Enforcement First-Response
     Responsibility." *Police,* Vol. 23, No. 1, January 1999, pp. 16–27.
Hensley, John D. "Emergency Call Boxes: An Old Idea Is Reborn." *Law and Order,* Vol. 47,
     No. 1, January 1999, pp. 53–54.
"Hurricane Evacuations Eased with Laptops." *Law and Order,* Vol. 47, No. 1, January 1999,
     pp. 27–29.
Jensen, Marilyn. "Volunteers Can Make a Difference." *Law and Order,* Vol. 46, No. 9,
     September 1998, pp. 102–105.
Johnson, Richard. "The Advantages of Two-Officer Patrol Teams." *Law and Order,* Vol. 47,
     No. 1, January 1999, pp. 68–70.
Kammerer, Robert K. "Become a Master, Not a Slave, to Your Court Overtime." *The Police
     Chief,* Vol. LXVII, No. 1, January 2000, pp. 34–37.
Kanable, Rebecca. "An Apple for the Officer: Citizen Police Academies Keep Officers in Touch
     with the Community." *Law Enforcement Technology,* Vol. 26, No. 10, October 1999a,
     pp. 56–58.
Kanable, Rebecca. "Protect and Save: Easy-to-Use AEDs Help Save Lives in a Heartbeat." *Law
     Enforcement Technology,* Vol. 26, No. 11, November 1999b, pp. 28–30.
Klockars, Carl B. *Thinking about Police: Contemporary Readings.* New York: McGraw-Hill, 1983.
Kohl, Martin. "Modifying Police Shifts Increases Police Efficiency." *Law and Order,* Vol. 42,
     No. 3, March 1994, pp. 58–62.
Maffe, Steven R. and Burke, Tod W. "Citizen Police Academies." *Law and Order,* Vol. 47,
     No. 10, October 1999, pp. 77–80.
Marvin, Douglas R. "Ready, Set, Rotate: A Management Diversification Plan for Small to Midsized
     Agencies." *FBI Law Enforcement Bulletin,* Vol. 67, No. 11, November 1998, pp. 22–25.
Miller, Linda S. and Hess, Kären M. *The Police in the Community: Strategies for the 21st Century,*
     2nd ed. Belmont, CA: West/Wadsworth Publishing Company, 1998.
Noble, Bob. "Volunteers Find Numerous Ways to Help Police Serve Their Community." *Sheriff
     Times,* Spring 1997, p. 2.
Overman, Richard G. "Citizens and Police Form Solid Alliance." *Community Policing Exchange,*
     Phase IV, No. 15, July/August 1997, p. 3.

Paynter, Ronnie L. "Gyroplanes: A Cost-Effective Alternative." *Law Enforcement Technology,* Vol. 26, No. 10, October 1999a, pp. 132–135.

Paynter, Ronnie L. "Helping Hands." *Law Enforcement Technology,* Vol. 26, No. 3, March 1999b, pp. 30–34.

Piquero, Alex. "The Validity of Incivility Measures in Public Housing." *Justice Quarterly,* Vol. 16, No. 4, December 1999, pp. 793–818.

Ruff, Gary W. "Using Routine Incidents to Develop Effective Incident Command System Skill." *The Police Chief,* Vol. LXII, No. 1, January 2000, pp. 52–54.

Sanow, Ed. " 'Shots Fired!' How One Small Town Responded." *Law and Order,* Vol. 47, No. 7, July 1999, pp. 115–120.

Sharp, Arthur G. "The Value of Volunteers." *Law and Order,* Vol. 47, No. 10, October 1999, pp. 204–210.

Simpson, Mike and Richbell, Suzanne. "British Policing and the Ottawa Shift System: Easing the Stress of Rotating Shifts." *FBI Law Enforcement Bulletin,* Vol. 69, No. 1, January 2000, pp. 19–26.

Siuru, Bill. "FBI's Drugfire: Computers Help Solve Gun-Related Crimes." *Law and Order,* Vol. 42, No. 11, November 1994, pp. 47–49.

Siuru, Bill. "Turbocharging Bike Patrols: Electric Bikes for Law Enforcement." *Law and Order,* Vol. 47, No. 4, April 1999, pp. 81–82.

Strandberg, Keith W. "Law Enforcement Computers and Software: Part I." *Law Enforcement Technology,* Vol. 25, No. 4, April 1998a, pp. 30–34.

Strandberg, Keith W. "Law Enforcement Computers and Software: Part II." *Law Enforcement Technology,* Vol. 25, No. 5, May 1998b, pp. 40–45.

Strandberg, Keith W. "Electra Glide in Blue: Motorcycle Patrols Take Community Policing to the Streets." *Law Enforcement Technology,* Vol. 26, No. 10, October 1999, pp. 110–114.

Swope, Ross. "Aggressive Patrol: Forward to the Past." *Law and Order,* Vol. 47, No. 7, July 1999, pp. 79–82.

Taylor, Ralph B. "Crime and Small-Scale Places: What We Know, What We Can Prevent, and What Else We Need to Know." In *Crime and Place: Plenary Papers of the 1997 Conference on Criminal Justice Research and Evaluation.* Cosponsored by the Office of Justice Programs, the National Institute of Justice, the Bureau of Justice Assistance and the Office of Juvenile Justice and Delinquency Prevention, July 1998. (NCJ-168618)

Van Meter, D. J. "Setting Productivity Standards, Not Quotas." *Law Enforcement News,* February 14/28, 1998, pp. 12, 14.

Weimer, Mark. "Automated External Defibrillator Programs." *Law and Order,* Vol. 47, No. 6, June 1999, pp. 40–41.

Weinblatt, Richard B. "Academies Put Civilians in the Shotgun Seat." *Law and Order,* Vol. 45, No. 9, September 1997, pp. 86–88.

Weinblatt, Richard B. "Deploying Reserves: Solo or Partnering Patrol Options." *Law and Order,* Vol. 47, No. 7, July 1999a, pp. 25–26.

Weinblatt, Richard B. "Discovering a Valuable Asset: Reserve Search and Rescue Units." *Law and Order,* Vol. 47, No. 5, May 1999b, pp. 18–20.

Weinblatt, Richard B. "Holding onto a Knowledgeable Resource: Recruiting Reserves from Full-Time Ranks." *Law and Order,* Vol. 47, No. 6, June 1999c, pp. 127–130.

Weinblatt, Richard B. "Volunteer SPCA Officers." *Law and Order,* Vol. 47, No. 9, September 1999d, pp. 21–22.

Weinblatt, Richard B. "Volunteers Assist in Private/Public Sector Partnerships." *Law and Order,* Vol. 48, No. 1, January 2000, pp. 19–20.

Weisburd, D. *Reorienting Crime Prevention Research and Policy: From the Causes of Criminality to the Context of Crime.* Washington, DC: National Institute of Justice, Research Report, 1997. (NCJ-165041)

Weiss, Jim and Dresser, Mary. "Police Go Waterborne: Tactical Training in a Nautical Environment." *Law and Order,* Vol. 48, No. 1, January 2000, pp. 74–77.

Wexler, Sanford. "Above All Else." *Law Enforcement Technology*, Vol. 25, No. 9, September 1998, pp. 20–24.

Woodyard, Adele. "Volunteers on Patrol." *Law and Order*, Vol. 45, No. 10, October 1997, pp. 179–181.

Wrobleski, Henry M. and Hess, Kären, M. *Introduction to Law Enforcement and Criminal Justice*, 6th ed. Belmont, CA: Wadsworth Publishing Company, 2000.

"Yours, Mine and Hours." *Law Enforcement News*, January 15, 1998, p. 5.

Zappile, Richard Z. and Schmid, William P. "Bicycle Patrols." *The Police Chief*, Vol. LXVI, No. 10, October 1999, pp. 145–146.

16 Performance Appraisals and Evaluation

Excellence is not a standard; it is a frame of reference, a state of mind.

—Anonymous

Do You Know?

- What two basic types of evaluation exist?
- Who can be evaluated?
- What is critical in a successful evaluation?
- Who should conduct an evaluation?
- What purposes are served by evaluation?
- What evaluation's main purpose should be?
- What function job standards serve? In what areas they may be established?
- What a by-the-numbers evaluation is?
- What consequences evaluation should have?
- What common types of evaluation are?
- What the main purpose of a performance interview is?
- How frequently to evaluate performance?
- What problems may occur in evaluations?
- What legal requirements performance appraisals must meet?
- How to evaluate the entire organization?
- What accreditation is and who does it?

Can You Define?

accreditation	descriptive statistics	performance appraisal
automated performance evaluation	evaluate	performance interviews
	evaluation	preevaluation
	formal evaluation	promotability/ assignment factors
behaviorally anchored rating scales (BARS)	halo effect	
	horn effect	standards
by-the-numbers evaluation	inferential statistics	
	informal evaluation	

INTRODUCTION

We are constantly evaluating others and being evaluated ourselves. People evaluate, in varying degrees, every time they meet someone. The opinion they form of others, even in a social situation, is an informal evaluation. People in romantic situations evaluate each other as future partners. In the business world, people are evaluated as possible customers. People who bet on racing evaluate the horse and the jockey before they bet. At election time, people evaluate the candidates for office. Law enforcement is no exception. Kramer (1998, p. 26) states:

> Performance evaluation remains essential to keeping a cadre of dedicated, hardworking employees. Because every organization is unique, law enforcement agencies should create individualized, effective performance evaluation systems. . . .
>   When employees feel their hard work counts for something, they strive to do their best. A carefully constructed evaluation system can make it happen.

This chapter defines evaluation and distinguishes between informal and formal evaluation. Next the chapter discusses the importance of evaluation during field training and on the job as well as specific purposes served by evaluation and the criticality of performance criteria or standards that are clearly job related. Next the chapter examines the type of information sought during evaluations and common types of performance evaluations, including interviews, guidelines for evaluating and problems to anticipate during evaluations.

Performance evaluation is a waste of time unless you use the results. This chapter describes how to translate information gleaned from performance appraisals into performance management. This is followed by a brief discussion of automated performance evaluations, a credit/debit approach to evaluation and some trends in evaluation.

Managers should not only evaluate their subordinates, they should also provide their subordinates the opportunity to evaluate them as managers. This discussion is followed by a look at the benefits of evaluation and the evaluation cycle. The chapter concludes with a discussion of evaluating the teams within a department, evaluating the entire department and the potential role of accreditation in evaluation.

Evaluation Defined

Appraisal and *evaluation* are synonyms. Both refer to measuring on-the-job performance. Decisions should be based on a standardized, objective and structured set of criteria. Appraisals and evaluations are used for both on-the-job performance and promotions. Some jurisdictions use evaluations for step or salary increases. To **evaluate** means to determine the worth of, to find the amount or value of or to appraise.

All these definitions apply to people as well as to objects.

Informal vs. Formal Evaluation

A field training officer provides continuous informal evaluation while helping rookies learn to perform tasks efficiently. The time comes, however, when the rookies will have to pass a test—a formal evaluation of their skills. Both types of evaluation are necessary.

Evaluation can be informal or formal.

Performance evaluations are necessary for both the manager and the officer. Some departments include evaluations of managers by subordinates.

Informal evaluation is thought by some experts to be better than formal evaluation. They do not believe that evaluating on a precise date is how to truly evaluate. It is better to make judgments whenever necessary. Thus, evaluation should be continuous. They also point out that evaluating at the time behavior occurs is more apt to consider the behavior rather than personality. Informal evaluation also saves time because it does not require extensive records. In addition, it reduces the possibility of the **halo effect,** that is, the tendency to allow an employee's performance in one area to unduly influence the ratings in other areas.

Some evaluation experts use a narrower meaning of the halo effect, reserving that term for allowing highly positive attributes in one area to carry over into rating all characteristics positively. When the opposite happens and a highly negative attribute causes other attributes to be rated low, this is called the **horn effect.**

Formal evaluation systems are called efficiency ratings, employee appraisals, service ratings, progress reports, performance appraisal, employee performance review, merit ratings, employee appraisal or appraisal interview. Regardless of what it is called, evaluation is arduous.

Specialists or law enforcement managers devise formal rating forms, and managers at all levels administer them. Employees answer standard questions for individual evaluation and for comparison with other employees. There are various ways of measuring performance: quality of task performance, productivity measurements, attendance records or individual and group testing.

Basically, managers want to know what subordinates are doing, how well they are doing it and how strong performance can be continued and weak areas improved. Evaluation helps law enforcement managers measure past performance, identify important performance areas and set the stage for future development. Of all the methods, seniority alone is probably the least likely to indicate good performance. Regardless of the rating form selected, law enforcement managers must observe subordinates performing their assigned tasks and conduct a **performance appraisal.** They must find some form of comparison and measurement and assess employees' development.

Groups and organizations, as well as individuals, are evaluated.

Law enforcement employees are judged both as individuals and as a group or department. Employees are evaluated by managers and also by the public as they perform community tasks. The public evaluates the law enforcement organization based on personal contacts, how well it suppresses crime or prevents accidents, personal and equipment appearance, local news stories, rumors and other people's opinions and experiences.

Evaluation on the Job

Evaluation exists in every law enforcement organization in some form. Managers must select which form of evaluation to use and who will conduct it. They evaluate subordinates, and they evaluate their own managers. Most informal evaluation is done mentally, without written record, on the spot during a crisis situation and based on reports, opinions of others or other more immediate factors.

Regardless of managers' opinions of performance appraisals, it is their direct responsibility in most law enforcement organizations. Many managers dislike the formal evaluation process. Putting in writing their opinions of their subordinates is not appealing.

Law enforcement managers' attitudes toward evaluation and their ability to evaluate are critical factors for a successful evaluation system.

The importance and usefulness of evaluation depend on what performance appraisals are used. Evaluations are generally done every six months (or more frequently for probationary employees). The formal process should not be so frequent that it becomes burdensome for managers or employees.

Decide how employees will be rated: as individuals, in comparison with other employees doing similar tasks, with the best employee, a selected group of employees, outside employees or national or local standards. Make sure that employees are aware of this.

Managers who provide the most immediate direction of subordinates should do the evaluation.

They can most directly observe employee behavior at the level at which the majority of required tasks are performed. In most cases, the police sergeant evaluates patrol officers, the first-line supervisor for other divisions. The administrative sergeant or lieutenant evaluates dispatch personnel. The investigative sergeant or lieutenant evaluates investigative personnel.

If employees are transferred during a rating period, each responsible manager should put in writing the evaluation for the period of responsibility. A system to establish time periods for evaluation and reminders should be devised, which is often based on the hiring anniversary date. Some type of immediate follow-up and feedback should be provided between formal ratings as needed. Law enforcement managers are motivators, and motivation is one reason for evaluation.

Purposes of Evaluation

Evaluation helps to validate the selection process, satisfy liability and EEO requirements, provide feedback and provide a basis for retention/termination decisions.

> Purposes of evaluation include promoting common understanding of individual performance levels, needs, work objectives and standards; providing feedback and suggesting specific courses of action to improve, including training needs; and setting objectives for future performance. Evaluation may also be used to identify department-wide training needs and to make decisions about promotions, reassignments, disciplinary actions and terminations.

Performance appraisals are not intended to cause undue burdens, criticism or embarrassment to managers or subordinates but rather to provide consistent criteria for improving employee performance. When employees understand how they are doing, know that what they are doing contributes to the organization and know what they are doing correctly, performance levels will justify the evaluation effort.

Some managers claim that evaluations take too much time, that employees resent it or that to do an evaluation is a "pain." The truth is, managers must evaluate employees—either by means of formal rating systems or informally. If managers correct employees on the job, they are in fact evaluating task performance. If they fail to correct a situation that needs correcting, they are not accepting responsibility as managers.

Performance appraisals help managers and employees evaluate work behavior and assess effectiveness and productivity. Most law enforcement organizations use some form of performance evaluation. The criteria for performance evaluation must be related to the required tasks. The position job description should be carefully reviewed, and the evaluation should directly relate performance to the functions listed in the job description.

If, because of management directives or other reasons, an individual is not performing in an area covered by the job description, that person should not be evaluated on that function. If, on the other hand, the individual is performing a function not listed on the job description, either the job description should be revised or the individual should be relieved of that duty. An analysis of the job function and the performance evaluation should reveal such an anomaly.

> The main purpose of performance evaluation is to improve employee performance.

Some other uses of evaluation are to:

- Inform employees where they stand individually and in comparison with the work group.
- Record facts to support promotion or demotion.
- Provide indicators for task improvement.
- Provide a written record of performance.

- Document information against lawsuits.
- Point out an individual employee's potential compared with other employees performing the same tasks.
- Assist managers in assigning and planning human resources use.
- Serve as a basis for merit pay increases.
- Allow managers to state expectations to employees. Employees must have reasonable standards and expectations that are known. These provide stability and a foundation from which to act.
- Provide opportunity for both deserved praise as well as constructive criticism.
- Serve as a basis for termination.
- Identify needs for individual and organizational training.

Performance Criteria

Performance appraisals must be based on clearly stated job descriptions and clearly stated performance standards. If job descriptions change, evaluations must reflect these changes. Evaluation forms and standards MUST fit the job. What tasks are rated? What level of performance is required? As many criteria as possible should be written. A humorous, exaggerated example is presented in Table 16.1. Generally, evaluators must consider what is to be accomplished, the quantity and quality of tasks to be performed and the level of performance required. Regardless of the standards used to evaluate performance, evaluation requires time, effort and money. Figure 16.1 presents a simple *Sergeant's Checklist,* which might be used to evaluate officers' on-the-job performance.

Evaluation information should be related to the standards required of the position and to specific task behavior, not personality. If employees are at a zero

Table 16.1
Guide to Employee Performance Appraisal

Performance Factors	Far Exceeds Job Requirements	Exceeds Job Requirements	Meets Job Requirements	Needs Some Improvement	Does Not Meet Minimum Requirements
Quality	Leaps tall buildings with a single bound	Must take running start to leap over tall buildings	Can leap over short buildings only	Crashes into buildings when attempting to jump over them	Cannot recognize buildings at all
Timeliness	Is faster than a speeding bullet	Is as fast as a speeding bullet	Not quite as fast as a speeding bullet	Would you believe a slow bullet?	Wounds self with bullet when attempting to shoot
Initiative	Is stronger than a locomotive	Is stronger than a bull elephant	Is stronger than a bull	Shoots the bull	Smells like a bull
Adaptability	Walks on water consistently	Walks on water in emergencies	Washes with water	Drinks water	Passes water in emergencies
Communication	Talks with God	Talks with the angels	Talks to himself	Argues with himself	Loses those arguments

Source: Paul R. Timm. *Supervision,* 2nd ed. St. Paul, MN: West Publishing Company, 1992, p.39. Reprinted by permission. All rights reserved.

Sergeant's Checklist*

Date _____

Officer Checked _____

Sergeant _____

Time: From _____ To _____

If answer is Yes, place check mark after statement.

1. ATTITUDE

Is he a willing worker. . . . .   _____

Is he interested in his job. . . . .   _____

Is he satisfied with his assignment . . . .   _____

Is he a clock watcher. . . . .   _____

Does he have confidence in himself . . . .   _____

2. PERSONAL APPEARANCE

Are his shoes shined . . . .   _____

Is his brass polished. . . . .   _____

Is he neat and clean. . . . .   _____

Is his equipment in good shape . . . .   _____

3. HOW DOES HE APPROACH AND CONTACT THE PUBLIC

Is he courteous . . . .   _____

Does he take personal affront at violators. . . . .   _____

Is he positive in his approach. . . . .   _____

Does he use an impersonal business approach . . . .   _____

4. DRIVING HABITS

Does he drive defensively . . . .   _____

Does he observe all regulations. . . . .   _____

Does he check his vehicle at start of shift . . . .   _____

Does he handle car as if it were his own. . . . .   _____

5. OBSERVATION

Does he have good habits of observation . . . .   _____

Does he recognize crime situations. . . . .   _____

Is he on the alert for traffic hazards. . . . .   _____

Does he check his beat thoroughly . . . .   _____

6. BEAT KNOWLEDGE

Does he know his beat and stay on it . . . .   _____

Does he know the people on his beat. . . . .   _____

Do the people on his beat know him . . . .   _____

Does he recognize trouble areas of his beat . . . .   _____

7. TREATMENT OF PRISONERS

Is he polite and courteous when he makes an arrest. . . . .   _____

Is he firm yet kind to prisoner's predicament . . . .   _____

Is he rude and inconsiderate . . . .   _____

Is he friendly and impersonal. . . . .   _____

Continued

Figure 16.1
Sergeant's Checklist

*This checklist might be adapted to use inclusive language (e.g., eliminate male pronouns).

Source: *Police Supervision*, International Association of Chiefs of Police, 1985, pp. 112–113.
Reprinted by permission.

> **8. TRAFFIC CONSCIOUSNESS**
> Does he engage in enforcement activity . . . . _____
> Is he prone to overlook violations . . . . _____
> Does he warn as well as cite . . . . _____
> Is he interested in the traffic problem . . . . _____
> **9. MISCELLANEOUS**
> Does this officer have a sense of humor . . . . _____
> Does he need more experience . . . . _____
> Does he possess and use common sense . . . . _____
> Does he want to be a police officer . . . . _____

Figure 16.1
continued

level of performance, pay should not increase, but opportunity to improve and assistance from the manager should be available. If this does not improve performance, employees should be terminated.

Gather information on improvements as well as failures. The manager's job is to help everyone achieve their level of competence. Although some evaluation systems rank order employees, usually they should not be rated "on a curve" but individually. It is possible to have all excellent employees or the reverse. Employees who meet established standards at the required level should be provided an acceptable rating regardless of how other employees perform. That is why standards or criteria of performance are important to successful evaluation. Evaluation should be positive—not negative.

Standards may involve quality of performance, quantity and meeting established limits, such as time, level of performance, public relations effect or manner of performance. In law enforcement work, quality rather than quantity is often important. Competence and courtesy in handling requests for service are important factors. According to Jones (1998, p. 112):

> Operating without performance standards can doom a department and its officers to work in an energy-draining atmosphere full of inconsistency, bickering and chaos. Operating with performance standards enables supervisors to bring sanity, fairness and consistency to supervisory tasks, enhance performance levels, and make promotions, awards and disciplinary actions fair.

Jones (pp. 109–110) lists the following criteria for a professional performance standard:

- It specifies measurable results of behavior required from an officer.
- It is mission related.
- It is attainable.
- It is nondiscriminatory.
- It is practical to monitor.
- It specifies the line between satisfactory and unsatisfactory results.
- It must be within the officer's classification.

Furthermore, as Jones (p. 110) asserts, a performance appraisal containing the seven points just listed will help supervisors achieve a variety of important goals, including:

- Officers knowing what to expect.
- Minimization of inconsistencies.
- A basis for objective appraisal.
- The removal of personality from ratings.
- The ability of supervisors to factually identify satisfactory work.

Job standards make it easier for employees to meet requirements and for managers to determine whether they have been met.

Obviously, numerical or quantity standards are easier to meet and evaluate, but many law enforcement tasks do not lend themselves to quantitative standards.

When standards are established, they must be made known to employees because they must know what is expected. Managers must accompany subordinates in the field periodically to know what they are doing and how well. They cannot do this from behind a desk.

Reports also measure performance. Activity reports indicate types and numbers of tasks performed. The number of citizen complaints or commendations are also indicators of performance quality.

Setting standards helps subordinates and managers evaluate employees' performance in relation to job tasks and organizational goals and objectives. It identifies areas in which officers need training. It provides a basis for evaluation of physical, mental and emotional qualifications of subordinates. Standards provide a basis for feedback to employees on how well they meet the organizational requirements of their position.

Standards may include areas such as physical energy to perform and emotional stability while performing law enforcement tasks; individual judgment, reliability, loyalty and ability to get along with the public, fellow employees and managers; creativeness and innovation; attitude, knowledge of tasks, competence and amount of required management.

Standards vary considerably among federal, state, county and municipal organizations.

Surveys and Rating Forms

Whether a department creates its own assessment instrument or adopts one from another department, the survey should meet six criteria (Fox, 1999, p. 54): objectivity, comprehensiveness, depth, accuracy, reliability and currency.

The Redondo Beach, California, Police Department extensively reviews both sworn and nonsworn personnel. The form for sworn personnel uses 23 dimensions ranging from knowledge of legal codes and procedures to attitude toward law enforcement work. Five additional dimensions are established for the ranks of officer and agent—driving skills, firearms, interview techniques, investigative skills and radio procedures. Eight additional dimensions are established for sworn supervisory personnel: approachability, budgetary management, delegation, disciplinary control, evaluation of employees' performance, fairness and impartiality, training and instruction and supportiveness of policy and procedure (see Figure 16.2). A separate nonsworn evaluation form contains general performance factors as well as specific tasks related to the job: police services officers, police services specialists, parking enforcement officers, crime prevention specialists and animal-control officers.

By-the-numbers evaluation makes evaluation more objective by using a numerical scale for each dimension.

The Redondo Beach evaluation forms, for example, go from 1 (least proficient) through 7 (most proficient). The values of 1, 4 and 7 are designated as "anchors" with 1 representing *unacceptable,* 4 *acceptable* and 7 *outstanding.* Raters need not comment on any factor unless it is rated 7 or less than 3. **Promotability/assignment factors** attempt to make the evaluation "count for something."

Evaluation should have consequences. Those who rate in the acceptable range might be considered for promotions, special assignments or pay raises. Those who rate below the acceptable range might be given counseling, a demotion, salary reduction, probation or, in extreme cases, termination.

In the Redondo Beach Police Department, a simple mathematical formula is used based on the individual ratings assigned to each factor. The rating counts toward 25 percent of the promotional process and 50 percent of the selection process for special assignments.

In addition, the evaluation has other consequences, with those having acceptable or higher overall ratings being considered for special training. Employees who receive less than acceptable ratings are subject to the following considerations: counseling, training, reprimand, removal from administrative assignment, probation, salary reduction, suspension or termination. Those who receive less than acceptable ratings also have more frequent evaluations.

In the Redondo Beach Police Department, two weeks before their formal evaluation, those being evaluated are given a preevaluation form, as shown in Figure 16.3. **Preevaluation** is a procedure that allows those being evaluated to have input by completing a form outlining their accomplishments. The Redondo Beach Evaluation Manual (p. 17) notes:

> The prime factor in obtaining the best results of the performance evaluation is the supervisor's fair, impartial and sincere desire to help the employee grow and advance. *The performance evaluation process can either be the key link in the supervisor-employee relationship or a periodic source of irritation, depending on the way it is used.* Periodic performance evaluation and counseling is the very best method available in improving relationships with employees and helping them to fulfill their needs for satisfactory recognition and growth.

REDONDO BEACH POLICE DEPARTMENT
PEACE OFFICER PERFORMANCE EVALUATION

NAME (LAST, FIRST, INITIAL)   JOB CLASSIFICATION   SERIAL NUMBER   ASSIGNMENT/DIVISION

EVALUATION TYPE

( ) PROBATION   ( ) SEMI-ANNUAL   ( ) OTHER (SPECIFY) _____

EVALUATION PERIOD: FROM:_____   TO: _____

RATING INSTRUCTIONS: Rate observed behavior with reference to the scale below by using the numeric value definitions contained in the evaluation program guidelines. Specific comments are required for all ratings of "3" or less or "7."

DIMENSIONS RATED   *GENERAL PERFORMANCE FACTORS*   LEVELS OF PROFICIENCY

JOB SKILLS

01. KNOWLEDGE OF LEGAL CODES AND PROCEDURES	1 2 3 4 5 6 7
02. NEATNESS OF WORK PRODUCT, SPELLING, GRAMMAR	1 2 3 4 5 6 7
03. ORAL EXPRESSION	1 2 3 4 5 6 7
04. PLANNING AND ORGANIZING WORK.	1 2 3 4 5 6 7
05. PROBLEM SOLVING/DECISION MAKING	1 2 3 4 5 6 7
06. THOROUGHNESS AND ACCURACY	1 2 3 4 5 6 7
07. WRITTEN EXPRESSION	1 2 3 4 5 6 7

PRODUCTIVITY

08. ACCEPTANCE OF RESPONSIBILITY	1 2 3 4 5 6 7
09. INITIATIVE, RESOURCEFULNESS, AND OBSERVATION SKILLS. . . .	1 2 3 4 5 6 7
10. QUANTITY OF WORK.	1 2 3 4 5 6 7
11. SEEKS TRAINING TO ENHANCE ABILITIES	1 2 3 4 5 6 7

WORK CONDUCT

12. ABILITY TO FOLLOW INSTRUCTIONS.	1 2 3 4 5 6 7
13. ATTENDANCE	1 2 3 4 5 6 7
14. CARE OF EQUIPMENT.	1 2 3 4 5 6 7
15. DEALING WITH CO-WORKERS	1 2 3 4 5 6 7
16. DEALING WITH THE PUBLIC.	1 2 3 4 5 6 7
17. OBSERVANCE OF RULES, REGULATIONS, AND PROCEDURES . . .	1 2 3 4 5 6 7
18. OFFICER SAFETY	1 2 3 4 5 6 7

ADAPTABILITY

19. PERFORMANCE IN NEW SITUATIONS/ACCEPTANCE . . . . TO CHANGE	1 2 3 4 5 6 7
20. PERFORMANCE UNDER PRESSURE	1 2 3 4 5 6 7
21. PERFORMANCE WITH MINIMUM INSTRUCTION	1 2 3 4 5 6 7

PERSONAL TRAITS

22. APPEARANCE.	1 2 3 4 5 6 7
23. ATTITUDE TOWARD POLICE WORK	1 2 3 4 5 6 7

SPECIFIC JOB CLASSIFICATION FACTORS

POLICE OFFICER/AGENT

24. DRIVING SKILL.	1 2 3 4 5 6 7
25. FIREARMS	1 2 3 4 5 6 7
26. INTERVIEW TECHNIQUES	1 2 3 4 5 6 7
27. INVESTIGATIVE SKILL.	1 2 3 4 5 6 7
28. RADIO PROCEDURES	1 2 3 4 5 6 7

RBPD Form 345 11/87

Continued

Figure 16.2
Redondo Beach Sworn Personnel Evaluation Form

Reprinted by permission.

SUPERVISION/MANAGEMENT (SUPERVISORY & MANAGEMENT PERSONNEL ONLY)

29. APPROACHABILITY 1 2 3 4 5 6 7
30. BUDGETARY MANAGEMENT 1 2 3 4 5 6 7
31. DELEGATION 1 2 3 4 5 6 7
32. DISCIPLINARY CONTROL 1 2 3 4 5 6 7
33. EVALUATING EMPLOYEES' PERFORMANCE 1 2 3 4 5 6 7
34. FAIRNESS AND IMPARTIALITY 1 2 3 4 5 6 7
35. TRAINING AND INSTRUCTION 1 2 3 4 5 6 7
36. SUPPORTIVE OF POLICY AND PROCEDURE 1 2 3 4 5 6 7

TOTAL NUMERIC RATING _____

NUMERIC AVERAGE _____   *PROMOTABILITY/ASSIGNMENT FACTOR
(TO SECOND DECIMAL PLACE)   (NUMERIC AVERAGE x 3.58)

*PROMOTABILITY FACTOR TO BE APPLIED AS 25% OF FINAL SELECTION PROCESS SCORE
FOR PROMOTION AND 50% OF THE OVERALL SCORE FOR ASSIGNMENT SELECTION.

Figure 16.2
continued

REDONDO BEACH POLICE DEPARTMENT
PERFORMANCE PREEVALUATION FORM

Name _____

Date _____

You are encouraged to complete this form to provide a more meaningful exchange
of information during the performance evaluation.

If you wish, you may provide a completed copy to your supervisor prior to being
evaluated on your performance.

1. Describe individual accomplishments, noteworthy achievements and/or projects
   that you feel should be considered. Also, discuss those situations you feel
   required special consideration or which involved extenuating circumstances.

2. What personal/professional growth has there been during this time period?
   (a) For yourself?

   (b) For your staff? (Supervisors/Managers ONLY)

3. What additional experiences or training would you like to obtain to enhance
   your professional development and job proficiency?

4. Do you have any ideas or suggestions that would enable you to function more
   efficiently/effectively?

RBPD Form 344 5/86

Figure 16.3
Redondo Beach
Preevaluation Form

Reprinted by permission.

Information for Evaluations

Law enforcement managers responsible for evaluation must record all information as soon as possible after an incident is observed. A form should be retained for each officer the manager rates. It is impossible to remember such information over long time periods. A simple form and notation are all that is required, as Figure 16.4 illustrates. When it is time to complete the formal evaluation form, all the information will be available. This lessens the tendency for information gathered closer to the time of the formal evaluation to overshadow information gathered months before.

The information may be about specific incidents such as a high-speed chase, a shooting by an officer, a kidnapping or a public-relations-type incident. Enter such information immediately after the occurrence while facts are known.

Common Types of Performance Evaluations

Numerous types of performance evaluations are available to managers.

Among the performance evaluations available to managers are the following:

- Ratings by individual traits
- Group ratings
- Critical incident ratings
- Narrative, essay or description
- Behaviorally anchored rating scales
- Overall comparison ratings
- Composite ratings
- Self-evaluation

Opinions vary on the value of each type of evaluation.

Information for Performance Evaluation

City of: _____

Employee evaluated: _____

Date: _____

Description of information: _____

_____

_____

_____

_____

_____

_____

_____

_____

**Figure 16.4
Needed Information**

*Evaluation
of Subordinates
by Managers,
Supervisors
and Others*

Ratings by Individual Traits

The individual trait rating is usually done by the manager immediately above the employee in rank. Various factors concerning individual employees and the job are rated on a scale of 1 to 5 or 1 to 10. For example, a factor such as dependability would be rated from 1 to 10, with 1 being poorest and 10 being outstanding or excellent. It is fairly easy to perform this type of rating.

Differences arise over how to do individual trait rating. Some feel managers should rate the first item only for each employee before proceeding to the second factor. Others feel all factors for one employee should be rated at once before going to the next employee rating.

Unless department policy dictates otherwise, raters should try both ways to decide which is better. The total score is the composite rating. Some feel that poor and excellent ratings should be justified by performance evidence. Trait categories fall into those related to *performance* measured by quantity and quality, accuracy, efficiency and amount of supervision required; *personal qualities,* such as personality, attitude, character, loyalty and creativeness; and *ability,* which involves knowledge of job, mental and emotional stability, initiative and judgment. The traits must be job related.

Group Ratings

Many departments are changing from individual to group ratings, where traits are rated by a group instead of one manager. For example, rather than having a sergeant rate the patrol officers, a group of three or four people of different ranks in the department might evaluate the patrol officers. This might include one officer from the same level as the person rated, overcoming single-rater bias. Varied percentage weights may be applied to different raters according to rank. Or employees could be rated by all members in the organization of the same rank or a section of first-line supervisor, a higher manager, their peers or other group members. Some departments use a member of the personnel department to interview those associated with the employee, and this interviewer makes the rating for the personnel file. This evaluation method involves more time.

Critical Incident Ratings

Most managers keep *critical incident logs* that record all good and bad performances of employees (see Figure 16.5). Keeping such logs is time consuming, but the information is of great value when it is time for the formal performance appraisal. If an officer did an excellent investigation or made an excellent arrest, this would be recorded. If the officer made a bad arrest or a poor investigation, this would also be recorded. All incidents would be discussed with the employee.

Narrative, Essay or Description

In this method, raters use a written description of what they observed rather than a rating scale. It is also possible to combine numerical and narrative in the same form, with words replacing numbers.

```
┌─────────────────────────────────────────────────────────────────┐
│                    CRITICAL INCIDENT REPORT                       │
│  EMPLOYEE:_____│
│  SUBJECT: _____│
│  COMMENTS: _____│
│           _____│
│           _____│
│           _____│
│           _____│
│           _____│
│           _____│
│           _____│
│                                                                   │
│  _____        _____  │
│     SUPERVISOR SIGNATURE                   DATE                    │
│                                                                   │
│  _____        _____  │
│     *EMPLOYEE SIGNATURE                    DATE                    │
│                                                                   │
│  *Employee's signature does not necessarily indicate agreement    │
│  with this report. This form may be used for the purpose of       │
│  preparing performance evaluations.                               │
│  WHITE-FILE            YELLOW-EMPLOYEE          PINK-SUPERVISOR    │
└─────────────────────────────────────────────────────────────────┘
```

Figure 16.5
Sample Critical Incident Report

Behaviorally Anchored Rating Scales

When using **behaviorally anchored rating scales (BARS),** specific characteristics for a position are determined. Employees are then rated against these characteristics by on-the-job behaviors in each area.

Overall Comparison Ratings

Managers review all their subordinates and then rate which one is top and which bottom. They then arrange the others on a comparative scale.

Composite Ratings

Upper-level managers review ratings performed by the first-line supervisors and then prepare a composite rating from the several presented for each employee.

Self-Evaluation

Self-evaluation is becoming more popular. Self-evaluation forms allow subordinates to rate themselves. There is value in people comparing how they perceive themselves with how others perceive them. Self-evaluation assists in getting employees to accept other types of evaluations. In some instances, individuals are more self-critical than external raters, simply because they know things about themselves others do not. These ratings have substantial value if no other evaluation exists.

Evaluation of Managers and Supervisors by Subordinates

One form of performance evaluation has subordinates evaluate their supervisory and administrative personnel. This gives command personnel a new source of information and a reasonably accurate assessment of subordinates' perceptions. A form such as that shown in Figure 16.6 can be used to evaluate first-line supervisory personnel and others who directly supervise field personnel.

Higher level managers and the chief or sheriff might also be evaluated by their subordinates using an instrument that includes management and leadership skills. Although subordinates evaluating managers is not common, it has value. Rating managers could help both managers and the organization, and the same rating method would be used as is used for the subordinate. Subordinates should have as much right to rate their managers as managers have to rate their subordinates.

Performance Evaluation of Supervisory Personnel by Subordinates

This evaluation should be completed by the employee and submitted to the designated proctor for processing. Deviation from this procedure may invalidate this evaluation.

Rated Supervisor: _____

Evaluating Employee:_____

Proctor:_____

Using the graphic scales, rate the performance against the criteria listed. A 10 indicates total agreement or outstanding performance; a 1 indicates total disagreement or unsatisfactory performance. Place a check in the "Not Observed" (N.O.) column if you have not observed performance in that area or if you feel you are not qualified to rate in that area.

Leadership Skills   N.O.
1. Subordinates are encouraged to excel   1 2 3 4 5 6 7 8 9 10 ____
   through the positive, professional attitude
   and action of this supervisor.
2. Innovative ideas are encouraged from   1 2 3 4 5 6 7 8 9 10 ____
   subordinates for improving the
   effectiveness of the unit.
3. Departmental needs, plans, information and 1 2 3 4 5 6 7 8 9 10 ____
   goals are communicated to subordinates.
4. Plans, projects and objectives are consistent 1 2 3 4 5 6 7 8 9 10 ____
   with departmental needs, goals
   and resources.
5. *Composite leadership rating:*   1 2 3 4 5 6 7 8 9 10 ____
                                                              Continued

Figure 16.6
Subordinate Evaluation of Supervisors

Source: Thomas S. Whetstone. "Subordinates Evaluate Supervisory and Administrative Performance." *The Police Chief,* June 1994, p. 62. Reprinted from *The Police Chief,* Vol. LXIII, No. 6, June 1994, p. 62. Copyright held by the International Association of Chiefs of Police, Inc., 515 N. Washington St., Alexandria, VA 22314, USA. Further reproduction without express written permission from IACP is strictly prohibited.

Judgment and Decision Making

1. Makes decisions in a timely manner.   1 2 3 4 5 6 7 8 9 10 ____
2. Demonstrates decisiveness when   1 2 3 4 5 6 7 8 9 10 ____
   faced with options.
3. Decisions rendered are in conformance   1 2 3 4 5 6 7 8 9 10 ____
   with departmental rules and regulations,
   policy and procedure, and all applicable laws.
4. Personnel assignments reflect proper   1 2 3 4 5 6 7 8 9 10 ____
   utilization of manpower resources.
5. *Composite judgment and decision-*   1 2 3 4 5 6 7 8 9 10 ____
   making rating:

Direction of Personnel While under Emergency, Unusual or Stressful Conditions

1. Supervisor is present as appropriate.   1 2 3 4 5 6 7 8 9 10 ____
2. Situation is correctly analyzed, and   1 2 3 4 5 6 7 8 9 10 ____
   appropriate actions are taken to
   control situation.
3. Available resources are properly deployed.   1 2 3 4 5 6 7 8 9 10 ____
4. *Composite stress performance rating:*   1 2 3 4 5 6 7 8 9 10 ____

Application of Departmental Rules, Regulations, Policy and Procedure

1. Sets a good example by adhering   1 2 3 4 5 6 7 8 9 10 ____
   to established policy and regulations.
2. Policy and directives are explained   1 2 3 4 5 6 7 8 9 10 ____
   when necessary.
3. Violations are identified, and timely   1 2 3 4 5 6 7 8 9 10 ____
   corrective action is taken.
4. Rules are applied fairly and impartially   1 2 3 4 5 6 7 8 9 10 ____
   to all subordinates.
5. Subordinates receive evaluation and   1 2 3 4 5 6 7 8 9 10 ____
   counseling in an objective manner
   and in line with established procedure
   with constructive suggestions as to
   how performance can be improved.
6. *Composite application of rules rating:*   1 2 3 4 5 6 7 8 9 10 ____

Training Ability and Communication Skills

1. In-service training needs are identified,   1 2 3 4 5 6 7 8 9 10 ____
   and efforts are made to provide
   proper training.
2. Information given is relevant and timely.   1 2 3 4 5 6 7 8 9 10 ____
3. Ideas are presented in a clear, concise   1 2 3 4 5 6 7 8 9 10 ____
   and understandable manner.
4. Presentations are logical, organized and   1 2 3 4 5 6 7 8 9 10 ____
   in compliance with current policy
   and standards.
5. *Composite training and communications*   1 2 3 4 5 6 7 8 9 10 ____
   rating:

Composite Supervisory Rating

Consider the above criteria and those areas not specifically addressed by this evaluation. Rate the supervisor on overall capability to perform effectively as a supervisor.

Comments

Please use this section to explain any answers and/or address other points not covered that you feel are significant. Attach extra sheets if more room is needed. Your interest and cooperation are appreciated.

Figure 16.6
continued

Performance Interviews

Performance interviews are private, one-on-one discussions of the performance appraisal by manager and subordinate. According to many evaluation authorities, the appraisal or performance interview should be based on comprehensive, accurate records and should focus on employee performance and growth. The appraisal form is the basis for the performance interview. Although rating forms and managers vary, it usually takes two to three hours of preparation time for each person rated. Many managers mark the evaluation forms lightly in pencil in case the interview brings facts to light that change the rating.

Managers should allow 45 minutes to an hour for each performance interview. They should prepare in advance so as not to omit important items. Planning includes the time and place, preventing interruptions and topics to be discussed. A starting point is to review the evaluation form.

Performance interviews open with a statement of purpose and should seek to make the employee feel at ease. Personalize the interview so it does not appear "canned." After rapport has been established, the employee's accomplishments are usually discussed. The appraisal form can serve as the foundation for the discussion. Compare it with the last appraisal. The tone throughout the interview should be positive. Ask employees to indicate what they see as their strengths and weaknesses. Ask what you, as manager, can do to help improve the weaknesses. Encourage participation.

> The performance appraisal interview should help employees do their jobs better and therefore improve individual performance and productivity.

All employee performance interviews should be private. Employees are normally apprehensive about evaluation. They are concerned about the manager's perceptions and how these compare with their own. An interview is a chance for managers and employees to establish rapport. If the interview is conducted properly—inviting input from employees—it will decrease controversy. Emphasize strengths rather than weaknesses.

Interviews of this type may be a discovery technique, identifying conditions, attitudes, ideas, creativity, latent abilities, distractions, lack of resources or equipment to do the tasks required or other obstacles. None of these conditions may have been known to the manager before the interview. Much of this is learned by listening.

A positive approach is likely to produce positive responses. A negative approach normally generates defensiveness and lack of cooperation. This does not mean everything needs to be "hearts and roses." Criticism is necessary for development, but it should be constructive.

Law enforcement managers are employee problem solvers. During performance appraisal interviews, employees will be concerned about any low ratings and individual problems. They should be encouraged to mention perceived problems.

Explain precisely what makes performance unsatisfactory, and do not apologize for discussing the matter. Present yourself positively and forthrightly. As a supervisor or manager, correcting your subordinates is your responsibility. Ask whether the employee understands the problem and has any ideas on how to approach it. Offer help in resolving the problem.

If the problem is resolved at the first meeting, follow up by further monitoring. Congratulate the employee if the problem is corrected.

If the employee's position is one you cannot immediately discuss further or resolve, tell the employee of your next step. Set a time and place to continue the discussion. Explain that in light of what you have been told, you will investigate further and will reach a decision as soon as possible. Follow through within a day or two.

In some extreme cases of intentional misbehavior, it may be necessary to suggest termination if immediate remedies are not available.

Agree on important issues discussed, set future expectations, discuss training availabilities, discuss opportunities available for personal improvement and summarize the entire meeting with a positive ending. If you agree to do certain things, follow through.

The Redondo Beach Evaluation Manual (pp. 14–15) contains the following suggestions, based on both experience and research:

- Plan the appraisal interview in advance. Define your objectives and outline the key points you want to cover.

- Plan and schedule the interview for a time and place that will give you and the employee privacy and allow your undivided attention to be devoted to the subject.

- Get right into the appraisal at the outset, but encourage the employee to speak his/her mind about any portion of the appraisal the employee thinks is incorrect or unfair.

- Listen to the employee during the interview—especially immediately after negative feedback has been given.

Your attitude and interest regarding the employee are more important than any counseling technique you might use. If employees see that your prime objective is to help them do a better job, the appraisal is on its way to a successful result. If you put yourself in the role of a judge and the employee is the defendant, the appraisal will in all likelihood be a waste of time.

The appraisal interview should not be the only time you talk with employees about performance. Appraisal, to be effective, must be continuous.

Most employee rating forms require signatures of the rater and the person rated as evidence the employee has seen the evaluation, not necessarily that he or she agrees with the results, as illustrated in Figure 16.7. Before concluding the performance interview, many managers give the employee an opportunity to discuss their performance as a supervisor. This is done after the formal performance evaluation to increase the likelihood that the person being evaluated will be at ease and discuss more frankly. At the end of the interview, allow for a summary and future action statement. Set objectives for future performance, and also set a date for the next appraisal meeting (opinions vary on how frequently such meetings should occur).

Figure 16.7
Supervisor and Employee Signature Lines and Statement

SUPERVISOR SIGNATURE   DATE

EMPLOYEE SIGNATURE*   DATE

*Employee's signature does not necessarily indicate agreement with this report. This form may be used for the purpose of preparing performance evaluations.

WHITE-FILE   YELLOW-EMPLOYEE   PINK-SUPERVISOR

The most common recommendation for frequency of performance appraisals is twice a year and more frequently for employees who perform below expectations.

When the interview is completed, managers should make appropriate meeting notes immediately. These should be part of the permanent personnel file. Another file should be started with any agreements reached that must be performed before the next appraisal, along with the date of the next appraisal.

Generally, appeals regarding ratings can be made to the next higher manager and on up to the head of the department. There may even be provision for an appeal board. The decision of the appeal board is usually final. Appeals should be required within a specified time and hearings held as quickly as possible.

Guidelines for Evaluating

The following guidelines are summarized from the Redondo Beach Police Department Evaluation Manual:

- Communicate your expectations in advance.
- Appraise performance for the entire period. . . . Critical incidents reports can highlight performance over the entire rating period.
- Keep the appraisal job-related. Don't let your attitude toward individuals or their personal attitudes bias your evaluations.
- Employees should participate. During the appraisal interview, the supervisor may choose to alter his/her appraisal after the subordinate provides additional information and insights regarding performance.
- Avoid the halo effect.
- Use descriptive statements to support your evaluations. Describe the performance on which you base your evaluations.

Problems of Performance Evaluations

Every employee evaluation system has shortcomings.

Some problems of performance appraisals are the following:

- Lack of faith in any appraisal system
- "Late-inning" results count most

- Inaccurate numerical or forced-choice methods
- Unfair percentage ratings
- Rating personality rather than performance
- Rating at the extremes

Lack of Faith in Appraisal Systems

Some managers have a defeatist attitude about performance rating. "It won't work." "Employees should not be compared with one another." "It all depends on the rater." "Managers are not trained to be evaluators." "Employees don't like it." "The seniority system is good enough for me."

A defeatist attitude can arise from excessively high expectations about performance evaluations. Perfection is not the goal; growth and development are. Sometimes choosing the best method is a problem. Any formal performance appraisal is better than no appraisal if it is validated, meaning that the factors rated are job related and the raters are trained.

Late-Inning Results Count Most

When ratings are performed annually, the actions and performance in the last months of the rating period are often remembered and given more weight. This works both ways. Employees may have a good first nine months and a bad last three months or vice versa.

Inaccurate Numerical or Forced-Choice Methods

Numerical ratings do not provide the information needed for improving employee performance because they do not indicate specifics about individuals. Managers who do the ratings are not put to the test of really knowing their employees.

Unfair Percentage Ratings

When raters have to place a percentage of employees in the upper, middle and lower third of ratings scales, they tend to be unfair. The same unfairness exists when raters place all employees at or near the average or middle of the scale. Employees should be rated on the basis of their actual performance, regardless of how many are upper, middle or lower. Some managers do not have the courage or training to do such ratings. In other instances, managers have a problem of being either high, low or middle raters.

Rating Personality Rather Than Performance

Some raters tend to use their personal prejudices to rate employees. Instead of looking at each task or criterion and considering it individually, raters use a personal opinion of the individual based on a single experience. They may also rate on prejudice due to education, race or other factors.

Rating at the Extremes

Some evaluators rate in extremes of too lenient or too strict. This is especially true with marginal employees. Rather than terminate an employee who is liked, managers give a higher rating than the employee deserves. The opposite is true if the rating supports termination because the employee is not a "yes" person but performs other tasks well.

Other rating problems arise when managers rate employees in higher-level positions higher than those in lower-level positions, especially when raters have no training in rating or when raters do not care about the process. Other problems arise when the instructions are unclear or the terms and standards are not clearly defined.

Automated Performance Evaluations

The Cheney Police Department has developed an **automated performance evaluation,** a system to evaluate officers' "production" using a computerized point system. This system assigns points to all possible activities and allows officers to develop their minimum baseline production points any way they wish. Minimum point requirements are set in areas such as parking citations—for example, three points for each traffic citation written. Responding to any type of call is worth one point. Officers are tracked by computer from the time they come to work until they go home. Supervisors can award bonus points for whatever they are focusing on during any given period. Point values can be raised or lowered by the administration as its priorities shift.

Legal Requirements in Performance Evaluation

Performance evaluation rating forms have changed over the last 20 years to meet legal criteria and to make them more directly related to improvement of employees rather than just another form to complete.

To meet legal requirements, performance appraisal criteria must be *job related.*

In times past, fired employees and their families were the only ones to suffer financially, but now it is quite different. Fired employees are suing to get their jobs back—and often winning not only their jobs but also back pay and even damages for emotional injury.

To avoid such lawsuits, any system of performance rating must be based on rating items specific to the tasks performed on the job. For example, law enforcement civilian employees do not use firearms; therefore, the form used for sworn officers is not directly related to civilian employees even though they both work for the same agency.

Fitness-for-Duty Evaluations

Trompetter (1998, p. 97) states: "Common sense, as well as the liability associated with negligent retention, dictates the need for law enforcement officers to be mentally and emotionally stable. . . . Most states have codes or statutes that define a psychological suitability standard for peace officers." Such a standard requires officers to possess a trait that is considered a bona fide occupational qualification. To determine whether officers meet this standard, a fitness-for-duty evaluation (FFDE) may be appropriate. According to Trompetter (p. 98):

> A psychological fitness-for-duty evaluation is appropriate when an officer's behavior calls into question his stability, emotional control, judgment or other psychological functions that create a reasonable doubt as to his psychological suitability to continue carrying out essential job functions in a safe and effective manner.

The IACP guidelines regarding fitness-for-duty evaluation note:

> A psychological fitness-for-duty evaluation is a highly specialized activity within the discipline of police psychology. As such, these evaluations should only be conducted by a qualified mental health professional. . . .
>
> The client in an FFDE is the referring agency and not the officer being evaluated. . . .
>
> An FFDE is not a substitute for supervision or a mode of discipline. . . .
>
> No FFDE should be conducted without either the officer's informed written consent or a reasonable alternative. . . .
>
> An agency is not entitled to any more psychological information regarding an employee than is necessary to document the presence or absence of job-related personality traits, characteristics, disorders, propensities or conditions that would interfere with the performance of essential job functions ("Fitness-for-Duty Evaluation . . .," 1998, pp. 106–107).

Benner (1997, p. 141) notes that such evaluations are expensive, costing anywhere from $1,500 to $5,000, and their usefulness is often limited:

> The issue of mental stability comes under the purview of the Americans with Disabilities Act (ADA), whose primary benchmark is whether or not an individual's condition prevents him from performing "essential job functions." The determination to remove an officer from active duty cannot be reached without addressing how the determination was reached, whether "reasonable accommodations" can be made to allow the individual to function in a different job within the agency and, if not, what "bonafide job requirements" preclude this option.

Benefits of Evaluation

Performance evaluations benefit all levels of a police department. First, they benefit the *organization as a whole* by accurately assessing its human resources so informed decisions can be made about assignments. They provide a permanent written record of the strengths and weaknesses of the department, which can help determine salary changes, promotions, demotions, transfers, court evidence and so on.

Second, they benefit the departments' *supervisors* by giving them a clear picture of their subordinates' abilities and allowing them input into officer development. Areas in which training is needed become more obvious.

Third, they benefit the department's *officers* by letting each know exactly what is expected and identifying areas needing improvement. Once employees come to recognize personal weaknesses, they should be stimulated to set goals for self-improvement. Perhaps most important is that they document officers' good work.

The Evaluation Cycle

Evaluation, like training, should be continuous, and each evaluation should identify areas for improvement. The evaluation cycle is diagrammed in Figure 16.8. Continual feedback, both positive and negative, on each employee's performance is provided throughout the year, giving employees a chance to constantly improve.

Evaluating the Team

Although it might be tempting to think that adding up all the individual performance ratings would be sufficient to evaluate the team as a whole, this is not the case. Periodically, managers and supervisors should formally assess the effectiveness of their teams. A form such as that in Figure 16.9 might be used. Abilities

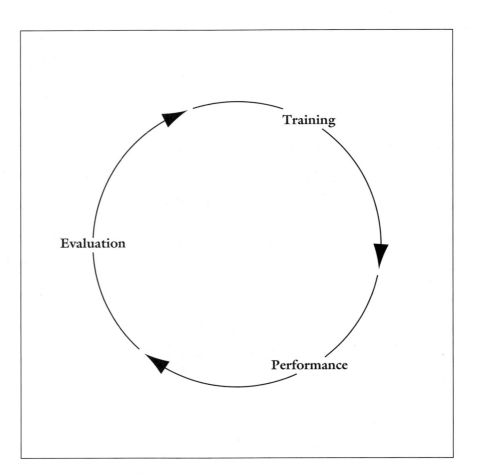

Figure 16.8
The Evaluation Cycle

to evaluate include how the group works together; effective use of individual skills; competence in addressing community issues; ability to engage the citizenry, other city departments, community groups, and so on, in addressing local problems; adaptability to change; ability to function as part of the organization; ability to problem solve and reach a consensus on methods to define solutions; and the quality of solutions produced.

Evaluating the Entire Department

Evaluation must also consider the entire agency and how well it is accomplishing its mission. Again, this cannot be done simply by looking at the performance of individual officers or even of the teams making up the organization.

As managers evaluate the department as a whole, they should remember that people tend to use crime, arrests, and clearance rates to measure how the police are doing. Such measures have several problems:

- Low crime rates do not necessarily mean a police agency is efficient and effective.

- A high arrest rate does not necessarily show that the police are doing a good job.

TEAMWORK ASSESSMENT

Listed below are characteristics of effective, productive work teams. This assessment seeks feedback about (1) how important you feel each characteristic is and (2) how well you feel your team exhibits the characteristic. Please use a rating scale of 1 to 10, with 1 indicating lowest rating and 10 highest rating.

Characteristic	Importance	Performance Rating
Officers work toward common goals, known and understood, that serve both individual officers and the agency.	_____	_____
Officers know their individual responsibilities as well as those of their team.	_____	_____
Officers have the skills and knowledge to accomplish the job.	_____	_____
Team morale is high. Officers are enthusiastic and upbeat.	_____	_____
Productivity is high. Officers work hard and perform to the best of their ability.	_____	_____
Officers have confidence and trust in their team members.	_____	_____
Officers cooperate rather than compete with one another.	_____	_____
Officers can disagree without being disagreeable.	_____	_____
Communication lines are open. Officers can openly discuss their ideas and feelings, and they also listen to their team members.	_____	_____
Officers are not threatened by change. They are eager to try new approaches to routine tasks.	_____	_____
Officers take pride in their team and its accomplishments.	_____	_____
The team frequently evaluates how well it is doing.	_____	_____

Figure 16.9
Team Evaluation

- A high ratio of police officers to citizens does not necessarily mean high-quality police services.
- Responding quickly to calls for services does not necessarily indicate that a police agency is efficient.

Rather than looking at crime rates, number of arrests and response time, evaluation should assess whether the agency is effective in fulfilling its responsibilities to the community and might focus on three areas: organizational, technical and personnel.

When evaluating the effectiveness, efficiency and productivity of the entire department, managers must focus on their mission statement. They must also consider what citizens want and expect from their protectors. Most citizens want to live in safe, orderly neighborhoods. Recall from the discussion of productivity in Chapter 15 that police are considered effective when they produce the perception that crime is under control. Reduction of fear is a very important measure. A fear and disorder index allows police to measure citizens' concerns and also sends a message to citizens that the department is addressing their fear of crime and neighborhood disorder.

Citizen approval or disapproval is generally reflected in letters of criticism or commendation, support for proposed police programs, cooperation in incidents being investigated, letters to the editor, public reaction to a single police-citizen incident or responses to police-initiated surveys.

When officers interact with a citizen, both may be informally evaluating each other. Consequently, positive officer-citizen interaction is extremely important.

Citizen Surveys

One way to assess citizen approval or disapproval is through citizen surveys, which can measure trends and provide positive and negative feedback on the public's impression of law enforcement.

Community surveys are often a win-win situation—citizens are better served and officers receive positive feedback. Community surveys can also be a key in establishing communication.

One citizen survey developed by the Plainsboro Township, New Jersey, Police Department uses a closed-end form (answer yes or no) asking very specific questions to assess the performance of individual officers (see Figure 16.10).

Call-for-Service Contact

We have started a Citizen Response Survey as part of our continuing effort to provide professional and efficient police service to the residents of Plainsboro Township and other individuals with whom our police officers come in contact. Your name has been selected at random from among those who have had recent contact with one of our officers.

Your response will be used internally to help us recognize potential deficiencies, acknowledge officers who continually perform in the manner expected and evaluate our procedures and methods. The feedback you provide will facilitate the improvement of future relations between the police and the public, aid in the evaluation of individual officers and provide an important means of acquiring additional citizen input into how we serve the community.

Please return the questionnaire in the enclosed envelope. It is the policy of this department to follow up unfavorable comments. However, if you do not wish to be contacted, please indicate in the space provided. Thank you.

Sincerely,

Clifford J. Mauler
Chief of Police

Citizen Response Questionnaire

1. Did the officer respond quickly to your call for service?   Y____   N ____
   Approximately how long did it take for the officer to respond
   after being called? _____
2. Was the officer courteous?   Y____   N ____
3. Was the officer neatly attired?   Y____   N ____
4. Did the officer identify himself by name?   Y____   N ____
   If not, do you think he should have?   Y____   N ____
5. Did the officer speak clearly? Were you able to understand him?   Y____   N ____
6. Were you satisfied with the service provided by the officer?   Y____   N ____
7. Did the officer appear knowledgeable?   Y____   N ____
8. Did he obtain all information that would seem pertinent under the circumstances   Y____   N ____
   of this contact?
9. If applicable, did you feel satisfied with the supplemental investigation conducted   Y____   N ____
   by the officer?
10. Upon completion of this police contact, did you feel satisfied with the general quality   Y____   N ____
    of the service rendered?
11. Additional comments:

_____

_____

_____

Signature _____   Date _____

**Figure 16.10
Cover Letter and Citizen
Response Questionnaire**

Source: Elizabeth Bondurant. "Citizen Response Questionnaire: A Valuable Evaluation Tool." *The Police Chief,* November 1991, p. 75. Reprinted from *The Police Chief,* Vol. LVIII, No. 11, November 1991, p. 75. Copyright held by the International Association of Chiefs of Police, Inc., 515 N. Washington St., Alexandria, VA 22314, USA. Further reproduction without express written permission from IACP is strictly prohibited.

Surveys can be conducted by mail or by phone. Mailed surveys are less expensive and reduce the biasing errors in phoned surveys caused by how the person doing the phoning comes across to the respondent. However, they require that the person receiving the survey be able to read, which might not happen. The major problem with mailed surveys is their low response rate.

Phone surveys have a much higher response rate but are also much more expensive unless volunteers can be enlisted to make the calls. In addition, individuals who do not have a phone cannot be included.

No matter which form of survey is used, the expense is small relative to the continued positive police-community relations. Citizen surveys might also help set organizational goals and priorities, identify department strengths and weaknesses, identify areas of improvement and needed training, and motivate employees.

In addition to citizen ratings, the department should also conduct a self-assessment, perhaps through a committee established for this purpose.

As with individual performance evaluation, the department evaluation should be a continuous cycle of evaluating performance, identifying areas to improve, making adjustments and evaluating the results.

Partnerships

Another way to obtain community input is through focus groups, forums or roundtable discussions, which usually take about three hours and have three phases. First, citizens talk and management listens. Second, together they brainstorm ways to work together, using a 10/10 target, that is, coming up with 10 creative ideas in 10 minutes. They then evaluate the ideas and select those with merit. Third, they focus on implementation, setting up teams or task forces to implement and track the ideas.

Groups should be kept small—eight to twelve participants—and should exclude competitors. A facilitator increases effectiveness.

A more formal approach to evaluating the entire department is through accreditation.

Accreditation

Accreditation is a process by which an institution or agency demonstrates that it meets set standards. Schools, colleges and hospitals frequently seek accreditation as recognition of their high quality. Institutions that lack accreditation are often considered inferior.

In 1979, four law enforcement agencies—the International Association of Chiefs of Police, the Police Executive Research Forum, the National Organization of Black Law Enforcement Executives and the National Sheriff's Association—established the Commission on Accreditation for Law Enforcement Agencies (CALEA). The purpose of CALEA was to set national standards against which agencies could evaluate themselves. The program is voluntary but involves a great amount of time and expense. Costs can range from $5,500 for small agencies to $22,000 for larger agencies. According to CALEA, 425 law enforcement agencies are currently accredited ("16 More Join . . . ," 1998, p. 10). Some states have also established standards and a process of accreditation, including California, Colorado, Idaho, Kentucky, New Hampshire, New York and Washington.

Accreditation consists of meeting a set of standards established by professionals in the field authorized to do so. Currently, accreditation may be granted by the Commission on the Accreditation of Law Enforcement Agencies (CALEA) or by some state agencies.

Falzarano (1999, p. 2) asserts: "Accreditation represents perhaps the first step in establishing law enforcement as a profession." He (p. 2) notes accreditation provides a number of tangible benefits, including controlled liability insurance costs, fewer lawsuits and citizen complaints, stricter accountability within the agency, support from government officials, increased community advocacy and recognition for a department's ability to meet established standards. "It represents the culmination of a long, but ultimately rewarding, process."

Intangible benefits of accreditation include pride, recognition of excellence and peer approval. Everyone involved in the process gains a broader perspective of the agency, which ultimately leads to improved management. Sylvester Daughtry, Jr., Chairman of CALEA, states: "Our standards are recognized by the courts as the prevailing professional standards that law enforcement agencies should adhere to" ("A LEN Interview . . . ," 1998, p. 8).

Accreditation is not without its critics, however. In addition to the expense, some feel that local and regional differences in agencies make a national set of standards unrealistic. Many agencies feel the number of standards is simply overwhelming. Smaller agencies must usually meet 500 to 700 standards; larger agencies must usually meet over 700 standards. Other critics contend that accreditation is like having a "big brother" overseeing their activities. Further, most of the standards deal with departmental administration rather than with its mission. Nonetheless, as Falzarano (p. 5) concludes:

> Some administrators may complain that accreditation is costly or time-consuming. Yet, the cost of accreditation becomes insignificant compared to the expense of civil liability or the ill will that develops when citizens feel they cannot trust the police to protect and serve them. Agencies who become accredited can foster the professionalism that citizens expect and deserve.

Accreditation and COPPS

Controversy exists regarding the compatibility of accreditation standards and efforts to implement community policing. According to Cordner and Williams (1999, p. 372):

> Community policing and law enforcement agency accreditation are two of the most significant police reform initiatives of the late 20th century. Whether these two major developments, one primarily operational and the other mainly administrative, are compatible or in conflict emerged as a serious issue in the late 1980s and early 1990s.

After analyzing a variety of data, Cordner and Williams (p. 377) conclude accreditation and community policing are compatible; accreditation does supports community policing to a limited extent; and the two reform strategies do not conflict directly, but there are some indirect tensions and strains in that COP and CALEA compete for resources and attention. Table 16.2 summarizes the degree of support found for various hypotheses regarding the relationship between community policing and accreditation.

Table 16.2 **Summary of Support for 14 Hypotheses about the Relationship between Community Policing and Accreditation**	Hypotheses	Support
	The Anti-COP Hypothesis: accreditation directly conflicts with COP	Little or nor support
	The Anti-POP Hypothesis: accreditation directly conflicts with POP	Little or no support
	The Rigid Bureaucracy Hypothesis: accreditation creates formality which interferes with COP	Some support—mixed opinion
	The Efficiency Hypothesis: accreditation's internal focus deflects attention from substantive problems in the community	Some support—mixed opinion
	The Thin Blue Line Hypothesis: accreditation emphasizes accountability within the organization to the detriment of accountability to the community	Little support
	The Style Over Substance Hypothesis: accreditation focuses attention on process rather than outcomes	Some support—mixed opinion
	The Incident-Driven Hypothesis: accreditation takes an incident-oriented view to the detriment of the problem-oriented approach	Some support—mixed opinion
	The Professional Model Hypothesis: accreditation implicitly favors the professional model over COP	Some support—mixed opinion
	The Scarce Resources Hypotheses: accreditation and COP compete for resources and attention	General support
	The Police Politics Hypothesis: supporters of COP and accreditation compete for status and influence	Little support
	The Support Hypothesis: accreditation directly supports COP/POP	Some support—mixed opinion
	The Neutrality Hypothesis: accreditation is neutral toward COP/POP	Some support—mixed opinion
	The Flexibility Hypothesis: accreditation does not interfere with COP/POP because of the flexibility of the standards	General support
	The Null Hypothesis: no conflict because supporting one or the other (or both accreditation and COP) has no real impact	Some support—but not from chiefs or experts

Source: Gary W. Cordner and Gerald L. Williams. "Community Policing and Police Agency Accreditation." In *Policing Perspectives: An Anthology,* edited by Larry K. Gaines and Gary W. Cordner. Los Angeles: Roxbury Publishing Company, 1999, p. 377.

Evaluation and Research

This chapter has focused on evaluating individuals, teams and entire departments. Sometimes, however, administration wants to evaluate specific problems. In such cases, as Vito (1999, p. 5) notes:

> Research is the key: identifying the problems in more precise terms, assessing the adequacy of the current police response and the existing authority and resources, engaging in a broad exploration of alternatives to present responses, weighing the merits of these alternatives, and choosing among them. This is what the S.A.R.A. (scanning, analysis, response, assessment) method is all about.

Two kinds of statistics are generally helpful in such research: **descriptive statistics** and **inferential statistics,** as Zeller (1999, p. 350) describes:

> There are two reasons for conducting statistical analysis in criminal justice: description and inference. Descriptive statistics focus on simplifying, appraising, and summarizing data; and operate on the assumption that the data set is a census (i.e., a complete enumeration). Inferential statistics focus on making statistically educated guesses about a census from a sample drawn from that census.

At other times administration wants to determine how well a specific program is working. In such instances administrators might want to familiarize themselves with the National Institute of Justice's "Research Partnerships in Policing." As McEwen (1999, p. 3) notes:

> Begun in 1995, the NIJ partnership program in policing currently consists of 41 research projects. The new approach complements the basic premise of community policing: working as partners achieves more than working alone.
>
> A project in Philadelphia exemplifies how the police can establish productive partnerships with researchers just as they establish similar relationships with the community. Philadelphia police worked in concert with Temple University researchers to evaluate the department's community policing initiative. Using multiple methods (surveys, observation, and interviews, for example), the partners documented exemplary community-oriented and problem-solving policing and brought to light factors that facilitated or hindered implementation.

Such research partnerships typically consist of a local police department or other law enforcement agency and a local university and make extensive and effective use of graduate students (p. 4).

Challenging the Status Quo

Research can help evaluate traditional practices that may no longer be productive. Consider the story of the four monkeys and the cold shower:

> In a conditioning experiment, four monkeys were placed in a room. A tall pole stood in the center of the room, and a bunch of bananas hung suspended at the top of the pole. Upon noticing the fruit, one monkey quickly climbed up the pole and reached to grab the meal, at which time he was hit with a torrent of cold water from an overhead shower. The monkey quickly abandoned his quest and hurried down the pole. Following the first monkey's failed attempt, the other three monkeys each climbed the pole in an effort to retrieve the bananas, and each received a cold shower before completing the mission. After repeated drenchings, the four monkeys gave up on the bananas.
>
> Next, one of the four original monkeys was replaced with a new monkey. When the new arrival discovered the bananas suspended overhead and tried to climb the pole, the three other monkeys quickly reached up and pulled the surprised monkey back down. After being prevented from climbing the pole several times but without ever having received the cold shower, the new monkey gave up trying to reach the bananas. One by one, each of the original monkeys was replaced, and each new monkey was taught the same lesson—don't climb the pole.
>
> None of the new monkeys ever made it to the top of the pole; none even got close enough to receive the cold shower awaiting them at the top. Not one monkey understood why pole climbing was prohibited, but they all respected the well-established precedent. Even when the shower was removed, no monkey tried to climb the pole. No one challenged the status quo.

What implications do this story and its lesson hold for managers? The realization that precedents, enacted into policy manuals, and training programs can far outlive the situational context that created them. Simply telling officers, "That's the way it's always been done," can do a great disservice to the organization as a whole. When officers don't know *what* they don't know and, worse yet, aren't even aware *that* they don't know, they are kept from empowerment, and problem-solving efforts are seriously compromised.

Encouraging officers to think creatively, tackle public safety issues through innovative problem solving and question the status quo if necessary has become one of the basic challenges facing law enforcement managers and certainly affects

the future success of their agencies. This is the focus of the next chapter—
managing for the future.

Summary

Evaluation can be informal or formal. Groups, organizations and individuals can all be evaluated.

Law enforcement managers' attitudes toward evaluation and their ability to evaluate are critical factors in whether an evaluation system works successfully. Managers who provide the most immediate direction of subordinates should do the evaluation. Purposes of evaluation include promoting common understanding of individual performance levels, needs, work objectives and standards; providing feedback and suggesting specific courses of action to take to improve, including training needs and setting objectives for future performance. Evaluation may also help identify department-wide training needs and make decisions about promotions, reassignments, disciplinary actions and terminations. Basically, the purpose of performance evaluation is to improve employee performance.

Job standards make it easier for employees to meet requirements and managers to determine whether they have been met. Standards may include areas such as physical energy to perform and emotional stability while performing law enforcement tasks; individual judgment, reliability, loyalty and ability to get along with the public, fellow employees and managers; creativity and innovation; attitude, knowledge of tasks, competence and amount of management required. By-the-numbers evaluation makes evaluation more objective by using a numerical scale for each dimension.

Evaluation should have consequences. Those who rate in the acceptable range might be considered for promotions, special assignments or pay raises. Those who rate below the acceptable range might be given counseling, a demotion, salary reduction, probation or, in extreme cases, termination.

Among the types of performance evaluation available to managers are ratings by individual traits; group ratings; critical incident ratings; narrative, essay or description; behaviorally anchored rating scales; overall comparison ratings; composite ratings; and self-evaluation.

Performance interviews are private, one-on-one discussions of the performance appraisal by manager and subordinate. The performance appraisal interview should help employees do their jobs better and therefore improve individual performance and productivity. The most common recommendation for frequency of performance appraisals is twice a year and more frequently for employees who are performing below expectations.

Some problems of performance appraisals are lack of faith in appraisal systems, late-inning results count most, inaccurate numerical or forced-choice methods, unfair percentage ratings, rating personality rather than performance and rating at the extremes. To meet legal requirements, performance appraisal criteria must be job related.

In addition to citizen ratings, the department should conduct a self-assessment, perhaps through a committee established for this purpose. It might also consider seeking accreditation, which consists of meeting a set of standards established by professionals in the field authorized to do so. Currently, accreditation may be granted by the Commission on Accreditation of Law Enforcement Agencies (CALEA) or by some state agencies.

Discussion Questions

1. What are the advantages and disadvantages of informal evaluation? Formal evaluation?
2. What important things can law enforcement managers do to prepare for employee evaluation interviews?
3. What main change would you recommend for future performance evaluations?
4. Should performance evaluations be used for promotions? Transfers? New assignments? Pay increases?
5. Who should rate subordinates? Single or by group?
6. What type of rating do you like best?
7. What are some uses of performance evaluation?
8. Have you been formally evaluated? What was your opinion of the evaluation? Should such appraisals be retained?
9. What are the advantages and disadvantages of having subordinates evaluate their managers?
10. Do you favor or oppose national accreditation? State accreditation? Why?

InfoTrac College Edition Assignment

Find an article on *evaluation in law enforcement*. You might find it under different names, for example, performance appraisals or assessment. Summarize the article, and include the full reference citation. Be prepared to share your summary with the class.

References

Benner, Alan W. "Determining the Need for Fitness-for-Duty Evaluations." *The Police Chief,* Vol. LXIV, No. 4, April 1997, pp. 141–143.

Cordner, Gary W. and Williams, Gerald L. "Community Policing and Police Agency Accreditation." In *Policing Perspectives: An Anthology,* edited by Larry K. Gaines and Gary W. Cordner. Los Angeles: Roxbury Publishing Company, 1999, pp. 372–379.

Falzarano, Robert J. "Law Enforcement Accreditation: One Department's Experience." *FBI Law Enforcement Bulletin,* Vol. 68, No. 11, November 1999, pp. 1–5.

"Fitness-for-Duty Evaluation Guidelines." *The Police Chief,* Vol. LXV, No. 10, October 1998, pp. 106–107.

Fox, James C. "How to Judge a Survey." *Ventures,* March 1999, p. 54.

Jones, Tony L. "Developing Performance Standards." *Law and Order,* July 1998, pp. 109–112.

Kramer, Michael. "Designing an Individualized Performance Evaluation System: A Values-Based Process." *FBI Law Enforcement Bulletin,* Vol. 67, No. 3, March 1998, pp. 20–26.

"A LEN Interview with Sylvester Daughtry, Jr., Chairman of the Commission on Accreditation for Law Enforcement Agencies." *Law Enforcement News,* June 15/30, 1998, pp. 8–11.

McEwen, Tom. "NIJ's Locally Initiated Research Partnerships in Policing: Factors that Add up to Success." *National Institute of Justice Journal,* Issue 238, January 1999, pp. 2–10.

"16 More Join CALEA Honor Roll." *Law Enforcement News,* March 31, 1998, p. 10.

Trompetter, Phillip. "Fitness-for-Duty Evaluations." *The Police Chief,* Vol. LXV, No. 10, October 1998, pp. 97–109.

Vito, Gennaro F. "Research and Relevance: Role of the Academy of Criminal Justice Sciences." *Justice Quarterly,* Vol. 16, No. 1, March 1999, pp. 1–17.

Zeller, Richard A. "On Teaching about Descriptive Statistics in Criminal Justice: Mean, Variance, and Standard Deviation." *Journal of Criminal Justice Education,* Vol. 10, No. 2, Fall 1999, pp. 349–372.

Chapter 17   Challenges in Managing for the Future

The best way to predict the future is to create it.

—Peter Drucker

INTRODUCTION

Several changes in the law enforcement organization have already been discussed. Among the most important changes likely to affect management in the future are the following:

- Participative management, the manager as a leader
- Flattening of the organizational hierarchy
- The necessity to provide more services with fewer resources
- Better-educated law enforcement officers who are less willing to accept orders unquestioningly
- A shift in incentives, with intrinsic rather than extrinsic rewards becoming more motivational
- Implementing community policing and problem-oriented policing
- An increasingly diverse public to be served
- Privatization of services

This chapter examines global trends and the ways in which they will affect law enforcement, including what the future will demand of the law enforcement manager and the skills a manager will need to meet future challenges. Next, the changing U.S. population is examined, as well as a look at the public's law enforcement priorities of fighting drugs and violence and a discussion of the 1994 Crime Bill. This is followed by a look at how technology is affecting law enforcement, what futuristics is and its potential for managers, and how creativity and innovation are needed for managing law enforcement agencies of the future. The chapter concludes with a revisiting of change and the various ways it might be viewed by progressive managers to positively shape the future of law enforcement.

Megatrends—Looking to the Future

Naisbitt and Aburdene's *Megatrends 2000* (1990) notes the following worldwide trends:

> We are moving from an industrial society to an information society. Children are learning computer skills in school; adults will need special training to catch up to them.
>
> We are moving from forced technology to high tech/high touch. Although technology is stressed, it will not replace the need for human interaction.
>
> We are moving from a national economy to a world economy. To be successful is to be trilingual, that is, fluent in English, Spanish and computer-ese.
>
> We are moving from a short-term orientation to a long-term orientation. We need to pay attention to future trends and engage in long-range planning.
>
> We are moving from centralization to decentralization. More decisions, including major life decisions, are being made at the local level.
>
> We are moving from institutional help to self-help.
>
> We are moving from representative democracy to participatory democracy. Today's leaders need to be facilitators rather than order givers.
>
> We are moving from hierarchies to networks. The old power structure is disappearing, being replaced with teamwork, quality circles and participative decision making.
>
> We are moving (physically) from the north to the south. Spanish is becoming more necessary.
>
> We are moving from an either/or orientation to one of multiple options.

These global trends necessarily have implications for our country, its citizens and those whose job it is to protect and police them.

Law Enforcement for the Future

Significant trends can be seen within law enforcement, most of which have been alluded to throughout this book. Goldstein (1993, pp. 2–5) describes five significant changes in the field:

1. Refining the police function and public expectations. (Becoming proactive rather than simply reactive.)

2. Getting involved in the substance of policing . . . improving relationships with the citizenry. (Implementing community policing and problem-oriented policing.)

3. Rethinking the relationship between the police and the criminal justice system. . . . Police can no longer use arrest, as they so freely did in the past, to deal with a wide variety of ambiguous situations. . . . Police must conserve their use of that system for those situations in which it is most appropriate and potentially most effective.

4. Searching for alternatives. . . . Quite simply, mediating a dispute, abating a nuisance, or arranging to have some physical barrier removed—without resorting to arrest—may be the best way to solve a problem.

5. Changing the working environment in a police agency, including participatory management, total quality management, etc.

These and other trends will significantly affect the ways in which managers will manage in the years ahead. As Goldstein (p. 1) observes: "The policing of a free, diverse, and vibrant society is an awesome and complex task." New challenges and ways of managing police departments will emerge as the United States begins the twenty-first century.

Privatization

One significant trend in law enforcement is **privatization,** that is, either contracting out or working collaboratively with private security agencies, other governmental agencies and other individuals or organizations that can help a police department fulfill its mission. Private laboratories may be used to test seized evidence, and private companies may handle screening applicants or do civilian fingerprinting. Private security officers may be stationed in courthouses, government buildings and airports.

Slahor (1997, p. 31) points out: "This year will see the spending of about $52 billion on proprietary security, access control, armored vehicles, security consultants, forensic experts, employee testing and other segments of the private security sector." She predicts an average annual growth of about 8 percent per year, reaching $104 billion in 2000. Law enforcement, in contrast, is expected to grow in expenditures at a rate of about 4 percent to about $44 billion in 2000. By 2000, 75 percent of protection will come from the private sector, underscoring the need for collaboration between private and public agencies.

Anderson (1999, p. 4) suggests: "Sometimes the gap between the private sector industry and the public law enforcement sector seems hopelessly wide, but if you look closely you can see it narrowing." One good indication of this is the formation of the IACP's Private Sector Liaison Committee (PSLC). According to Seamon (1999, p. 17): "The PSLC was founded in 1986 with the mission to 'develop and implement cooperative strategies for the enhancement of public law enforcement and private sector relationships in the interest of the public good.' " Among the areas the committee is addressing are drugs in the workplace, combatting workplace drug crimes, false alarm perspectives and combatting workplace violence.

One of the committee's projects, the Model States' False Dispatch Reduction Program has been extremely successful. As Reader and Martin (1999, p. 28) report: "This effort has resulted in removing many barriers of distrust between law enforcement and the alarm industry. In addition, it has provided an excellent false alarm reduction program, which can be tailored to the needs of any city."

In addition, Jones and Miller (1999, p. 50) report, public-service partnerships can enhance critical incident planning. Yet another area in which partnerships are working is in crime prevention using interactive security as described by Fotte (1999, p. 57):

> Interactive security is composed of a high-tech system consisting of computer hardware, software, telecommunications and audio equipment that connects an installation site with the remotely located command center. When an alarm is activated, a modem makes an almost immediate connection between the site and command center, sending video images from high-resolution cameras to the intervention specialist's computer screen. If telephone service has been affected, an optional cellular back-up system makes the call to connect the modem and audio system to the command center. . . .
>
> After assessing the situation, the specialist decides whether to intercede (by using a nonthreatening message to the suspects . . .) or to call the police. Because the intervention specialist can be online watching and listening to activities at the site while notifying police, all incidents are witnessed events.

A Basic Change in Needed Management Skills

One reason changes have been so overwhelming in the past decades and will continue to be in the decades ahead is that the required management skills have changed.

Technical competence used to be most important. Now and in the years ahead, "people skills" are most important.

Woodward and Buchholz (1987, pp. 13–14) explain it this way:

> One way to visualize this tactical, people-oriented approach is with a bicycle. The two wheels of a bicycle have different purposes. The back wheel powers the bike; the front wheel steers it. Extending this analogy to an organization, "back-wheel" skills are the technical and organizational skills needed for the organization to function. "Front-wheel" skills are the interpersonal "people management" skills. Corporations tend to rely on their back-wheel, that is, their technical skills.
>
> Typically, however, when change comes, the response of organizations is primarily back-wheel response—do what we know best. But the real need is for front-wheel skills, that is, helping people understand and adapt to the changing environment.

Knowles (1997, p. 43) states: "Winning football coaches know that games are not won or lost in the fourth quarter. The outcome of any game is determined by the amount of preparation prior to kickoff." Knowles asserts that law enforcement managers must possess a combination of technical skills and people skills to successfully guide their departments into the new millennium and provides a "Checklist for the Year 2000" to help managers assess their readiness:

The following checklist will help gauge your level of preparedness for the changes and challenges of the twenty-first century:

- Are you fully aware of the expanded role DNA technology will play in assisting your criminal investigators, now and in the future?

- Have you begun preparing your officers for the enhanced decision-making roles they will assume in the future?

- Have you implemented steps to raise your overall education level and that of your officers and your civilian employees?

- Do you understand DRUGFIRE and CODIS (Combined DNA Index System) and the ways in which each of these national data banks can serve your department in the future?

- Do you know what changes in your department will be necessary in the next few years to sustain a level of excellence?

- What funding sources, other than general revenue, have you identified to assist your department in accomplishing these changes?

- How will you expand your existing resources without an increase in funding?

A Changing Public to Be Served

One of the most significant changes for modern law enforcement is the increasing diversity of the U.S. population. Numerous social changes have affected law enforcement and will continue to affect it in the future.

> The public to be served will include more two-income families, more single-parent families, more senior citizens and more minorities. The educational and economic gap will increase, with those at the bottom becoming more disadvantaged and dissatisfied.

The necessity for two-income families has increased the need for daycare centers, some without security-checked personnel. This has produced problems of child and sexual abuse, which have gained national attention. On the other hand, development of working-at-home programs has helped those who want added income but also want to remain at home to care for their children. Preset performance standards make this possible without regard for when or where the work is actually performed.

The high rate of divorce has changed family relationships. R. Morton Darrow, speaking at the National Press Club, stated: "With growing divorce and remarriage, the United States is moving from a nation in which parents had many children to one where children have many parents. This results in different needs and pressures in the family."

In addition, our population is aging. The baby boomers have turned 50, and by 2010 one-fourth of all Americans will be at least 55 years old. More efforts will need to be spent on crime prevention and on support programs for older adults. Minorities will also increase, requiring law enforcement officers to be able to deal with many divergent social and ethnic groups.

Another change is that the educational gap is increasing, with those at the bottom becoming even more disadvantaged. As the gap widens, economic opportunities dwindle and frustrations increase. The gap between the haves and the have-nots is widening significantly, with the likely result being social unrest. The United States is becoming a **bifurcated society,** with more wealth, more poverty and a shrinking middle class.

The Smokestack America of the early 1900s has been battered by the most accelerated technological revolution in history. Computers, satellites, space travel, fiber optics, fax machines, robots, bar coding, electronic data interchange and expert systems are only the most obvious manifestations. All this has been combined with globalization of the economy, rising competition and many social and cultural changes as well.

Major Crime Problems in the New Millennium

The two greatest crime problems in the 2000s are drugs and violence.

The Drug Problem

The national and international drug problem has placed law enforcement officers on the front line, not only in enforcing drug laws but also in establishing drug undercover operations and participative community programs. The drug problem is of such magnitude that no single individual, segment of society or government can resolve the problem, which means that no segment can move ahead alone. An attack on one segment of society must be accepted as an attack on all.

In 1989 the drug problem was the largest single issue and concern in the nation. The public still expects law enforcement organizations to deal with this problem. Many federal resources will have to be devoted to it, and law enforcement entities must develop new approaches to meet the local challenge. Resolving the problem may involve reducing individual civil liberties in the interest of overall social well-being.

Military measures may have to be instituted to support law enforcement's efforts to control the militant and terroristic tactics of drug lords to protect their huge monetary rewards. This is a war in which all willing and unwilling participants have been losers, either financially or in terms of human distress and suffering. Drastic measures will be necessary to bring about a resolution.

A closely related problem, often linked with drug dealing and gangs, is violence.

Violence

One of the greatest challenges facing law enforcement is increasing violence. The Los Angeles riots following the Rodney King verdict caught the nation's attention. But this was not an isolated event. In Chicago in 1992, for example, after the Bulls won their second NBA title, violence erupted. Two police officers were shot, and more than 90 others suffered injuries.

The national and international drug problem is a major crime issue confronting law enforcement in the twenty-first century. To bring about resolution requires the involvement of law enforcement officials at both the national and local levels.

The nation's tolerance level for violence has been reached, as reflected in the passage of "three strikes and you're out" legislation and the 1994 Crime Bill.

The 1994 Crime Bill

After much agonizing, Congress passed the Crime Bill of 1994, providing billions of dollars to fight crime. One major provision was to put 100,000 more police officers on the street. The snag, however, is that departments must provide 25 percent matching funds—which many departments will find impossible.

The bill also expanded the federal death penalty to cover some 50 offenses and increased or created new penalties for violent crimes such as drive-by shootings and aggravated sexual assault. The bill also banned manufacture of 19 military-style assault weapons. Prevention was also stressed, a focus whose importance is emphasized by James Alan Fox, dean of the College of Criminal Justice at Northeastern University ("Crime Still Ebbs, . . . ," 1995, p. 7): "To prevent a bloodbath in the year 2005, when we will have a flood of 15-year-olds, we have to do something today with the 5-year-olds. . . . But when push comes to shove, prevention programs often fall by the wayside in favor of increased incarceration."

Technology

Technology will continue to enhance law enforcement in communications, records, evaluation and investigation. Rapid availability and dissemination of restricted and confidential information assists investigators and results in increased apprehensions of criminals.

At the same time, technology reduces the need for traditional reports and record keeping. Officers spend less time completing official reports and have more time for field activities.

> Technology will increase in all phases of law enforcement and will greatly enhance efficiency. It will be increasingly imperative for most law enforcement personnel to be computer literate.

Strandberg (1999, pp. 56–60) polled some of the "movers and shakers" in the law enforcement industry about what technological changes they see affecting the profession in the new millennium:

Jose Cerda, special assistant to the President, Domestic Policy Office, White House: "We want to take the COPPS program and shift it from a 100-percent hiring focus to a dramatic focus on technology. . . . We call it the 21st Century Law Enforcement Initiative, and it breaks down like this—$600 million is for hiring and retaining, $350 million is for technology broken into three areas: improved police communications . . . ; developing crime-solving technologies . . . ; and bolstering crime analysis (making sure that departments have the ability to capture real-time crime and arrest data to sophisticated crime analysis)."

Richard T. Garcia, section chief, FBI: "I see more electronic investigating tools for the officers to increase their ability to do reports in the field, and to have those reports search against any known similarities."

"The public may be able to contact [a] law enforcement person quicker, because of technology. . . . I see online crime solving happening, where information to solve a crime can come in over the computer."

"The challenge for law enforcement is that the public will have the sophisticated technical ability as well, allowing the criminal to hide anywhere in the world. Partnerships will be formed internationally, because crime won't be confined to one geographic area."

Larry W. Glick, executive director, National Tactical Officers Association: "Technology will improve and enhance the police officers' ability to respond to those violent criminals. That technology is in specialty weapons, munitions, better protective systems and better communications. . . . Technology is moving very quickly in this area."

Technology allows administration to know better how time is actually being spent and how it should be spent. Tracking officer activities can be more immediate, but it should not be done to the point where officers lose their sense of reasonable freedom and control over decisions.

The application of technology may also bring up ethical issues and challenges regarding the constitutionality of such aids. Strandberg (1997, p. 48) states:

> Imagine you had an instrument that could scan a crowd or a private home and tell, without a doubt, whether there are any weapons present. This would be a great boon for law enforcement. At the same time, however, there are rights issues involved that need to be addressed. Just because law enforcement has the technology, can it legally be used?

This is an issue managers must be aware of.

A Pasadena Police Department chief pilot and investigator checks his helicopter's new tracking system at the Pasadena Police heliport. The new system, called CAATS–Compact Automatic Airborne Tracking System–is an infrared tracking technology similar to the kind used to guide bombs during the Persian Gulf War. Pasadena helicopter crews have been reaping the benefits of a $120,000 tracking system given to them by a Las Vegas-based defense company.

Futuristics

As a profession, law enforcement has relied too heavily on experience and not enough on innovation. Futuristics is a new tool for criminal justice executives. Peak (1994, p. 27) describes how people studying the future use **environmental scanning,** identifying the factors likely to "drive" the environment. He suggests that three categories of change are likely to affect the criminal justice system in and beyond the year 2000:

1. Social and economic conditions (size and age of the population, immigration patterns and nature of employment and lifestyle characteristics)
2. Shifts in the number and types of crimes (including the potential for new types of criminality and for technological advances that might be used for illegal behavior)
3. Possible developments in the criminal justice system itself

Futuristics is the science of using data from the past to forecast alternatives for the future and to then select the most desirable.

Forecasting, a form of futuristics, is similar to the headlights on a car being driven in a snowstorm. The lights provide enough illumination to continue but not enough so the driver can proceed without caution. What lies ahead is still unknown. Futuristics is not something mystical or prophetic. It combines historical facts, scientific principles and departmental values with vision to imagine what could happen in the future. Pettinari and Levin (1999, p. 12) note:

> Forecasting, or futures research, is a central tenet of an organization dedicated to plotting a path to the future of policing—the Society of Police Futurists International (PFI). . . .
> Founded in 1991 by Dr. William Tafoya, . . . PFI is dedicated to futures research in policing, and to stimulating new ideas on a variety of policing theories

and practices. . . . Futures research is, quite simply, a way to plan your route for the long haul instead of groping your way over unfamiliar terrain to get to where you need to go.

Futuristics rests on three basic principles or assumptions about the nature of the universe and our role in it (Tafoya, 1983, p. 13).

The three basic principles of futuristics are as follows:

- The unity or interconnectedness of reality
- The significance of ideas
- The crucial importance of time

The *unity* or *interconnectedness of reality* suggests that we operate in a "holistic universe, a huge mega-system, the activities of whose systems, subsystems, and components interface and interact in synergistic fashion; futurists are very much systems-oriented."

The *significance of ideas,* the second basic principle of futuristics, emphasizes the quest for new and better ways of doing things—exploring divergent new ways to deal with old problems and imagining new ways to anticipate potential problems.

The third basic principle, the *importance of time,* suggests a future focus. Rather than being absorbed with today's problems and holding on to traditions, futurists think five years ahead and beyond. Futuristics often uses the following time frames (p. 15):

Immediate future	Present to 2 years
Short-range future	2 to 5 years
Mid-range future	5 to 10 years
Long-range future	10 to 20 years
Extended-range future	20 to 50 years
Distant future	50 years and beyond

Law enforcement managers tend to focus on the immediate future, dealing with problems that need resolution, trying to stay "on top of things" and "putting out fires." No wonder they do not notice a mere 2–4-percent annual increase in the crime rate. The crisis faced today is probably a minor one that was ignored yesterday. Time is significant. Do not let it be said of the future that it is "that time when you'll wish you'd done what you aren't doing now."

Futurists also operate under three fundamental premises (p. 15):

Fundamental premises of futurists are the following:

- The future is not predictable.
- The future is not predetermined.
- Future outcomes can be influenced by individual choice.

The third premise is critical to managers because the choices that are made today *will* affect law enforcement in the future. As has been said, "The future is coming. Only you can decide where it's going." How can futuristics be used in law enforcement management? Tafoya suggests three primary priorities or goals (p. 17):

Goals of futuristics:

- Form perceptions of the future (the possible).
- Study likely alternatives (the probable).
- Make choices to bring about particular events (the preferable).

If people are to influence future outcomes, perceptions of the future must be formed. . . . be alert to risks as well as opportunities. What is possible is what "could be"; this key role is characterized as *image-driven*. . . . What is required is breaking the fetters of one's imagination. It is the vital, *creative goal* of futuristics.

Once new images have been generated, likely alternatives must be studied. The probable path to the future must be analyzed; quantitatively as well as qualitatively. . . . What is probable is what "may be"; this aim is characterized as *analytically driven*. It is the detached, systematic, and *scientific goal* of futuristics.

Having imagined the possible and analyzed the probable, it is necessary to make choices among alternatives. . . . What is preferred is what "should be"; this intent is characterized as *value-driven*. It is the *managerial, decision-making goal* of futuristics.

Remember: The future never comes. It is like tomorrow. We can only function in today—but what we do today will influence all the todays to come. Managers must be forward looking and willing to accept changes as well as opportunities.

The Need for Creativity and Innovation

Creativity and innovation in law enforcement must continue in the decades ahead. Considerable impetus for innovative projects was provided through past LEAA-funded programs. Much of this impetus has been retained mentally but slowed by decreased funding. Many improvements in law enforcement can be continued or developed within existing budgets and with existing personnel. These programs involve improvements in everyday activities.

One responsibility of managers is to examine and be creative about each task to be performed. Determine how each task can be done better and involve the task doer in the process. Give subordinates input and control over what they do to increase a sense of contribution and well-being on the job and to reduce stress. Many law enforcement tasks generate a high degree of stress. Stress experts state that lack of control on the job is an additional stress producer. Getting the job done better and reducing stress at the same time is one key to future healthy officers.

Management should encourage creativity even at the cost of failures. Experimentation failures must be accepted as part of the process of growth and development. Edison did not fail 25,000 times to make a storage battery. He knew 25,000 ways NOT to make one.

Officers who know that punishment will follow failure will not take the risks necessary for individual and departmental growth. Therefore, managers should encourage reasonable risk taking. They might encourage subordinates to think creatively and take risks by posting slogans such as the following in prominent places:

- Don't be afraid to go out on a limb. That's where the fruit is.
- Don't be afraid to take a big step if one is indicated. You can't cross a chasm in two small jumps.
- If you're made of the right material, a hard fall will result in a high bounce.

Those involved in research understand that failures are the stepping stones to success. "Nothing ventured, nothing gained" remains true for the future and applies to law enforcement managers at all levels and to their subordinates.

Creativity and innovation do not automatically involve large amounts of money. Often they require only the present level of personnel and equipment but provided more efficiently. The future of law enforcement depends on federal financial and research assistance, supported by state and local willingness to support creativity and freedom on the job.

Creativity results from extending, searching into the unknown and trying the untried. It is risky. It may fail. In law enforcement, creativity means viewing a police problem in a new way, having a new idea. No one has a corner on creativity. Everyone can create, but few do. Studies indicate no relationship between high I.Q. and creativity. What is unique about creative people is that they keep trying. In the process they make mistakes but accept them and move on to the next idea. Creative people take time to dream.

Everyone reading this book can be creative. Have you ever said to yourself, "Why didn't I think of that before?" Creativity is nonconformity, not in the destructive sense of being difficult to get along with but in the useful, positive sense.

In police work, every task can be accomplished better. We need police who use their minds to create these better ways. Creativity means thinking of a better technique for handling domestics and, when successfully applied, thinking of an even better way. Creativity is endless.

In the 2000s, failing to be creative can be career suicide. The opportunities for creativity in police work are tremendous. Even though calls for service are categorized, each incident involves different people, circumstances and solutions. To give creativity a chance to work, try some of the following options:

- Take time out to research a specific subject.
- Delay a decision until you have time to think about it and perhaps sleep on it.
- When you feel mentally blocked, take a walk down the hall or outside the building.
- Expand your mental capabilities by going beyond what is known.
- Concentrate on a small part of the problem and deal with that.
- Consider different options and alternatives.
- Instead of everyone sitting down at a meeting, stand up.

- To relieve tension, exhibit some unconventional behavior such as laughing when you want to cry or jumping up and down when you would normally stand still.

Thinking traps and mental locks described in Chapter 4 are relevant as a department strives for innovation. Other obstacles may exist in the form of politics, restrictions mandated by union contracts, local ordinances, special interest groups and so on.

Change Revisited

According to Bentz (1995, p. 14), issues propelling us into the "whirlwind of change" include the following:

- Technological advances
- Changing demographics
- Fiscal constraints
- Fear of crime
- Shifting values
- Global issues (such as environmental concerns and drug trafficking)

"Change," says Rippy (1990, p. 136), "invokes simultaneous personal feelings of fear and hope, anxiety and relief, pressure and stimulation, threats to self-esteem and challenge to master new situations."

Change can occur in one of two ways—changing individuals or changing the organizational structure. The changing process itself involves three phases:

1. Unfreezing of an old pattern or relationship
2. Changing to a new behavior pattern
3. Freezing the new pattern

According to Mulder (1994, p. 55): "The critical issue for today's law enforcement executive (including middle managers) is how to use change to shape a better future for the organization and people within it." He notes several reasons underlying the need for change:

- Severe reductions in fiscal resources while demands for law enforcement services continue to increase (a familiar message)
- Highly publicized incidents of police misconduct or perceived incompetence
- Political simplification of a highly complex profession
- Increasing citizen fear of unabated and ruthless criminal gang violence

Mulder (p. 56) suggests that it often takes a "cataclysmic performance failure," such as seen in the Rodney King incident, to bring about change. Without such an impetus, initiating change may be difficult. Mulder (p. 57) suggests that

Law enforcement must learn to move with the flow of society's needs and constantly improve services. Going against the tide will result in adversity, conflict and frustration. Continual buffeting leads to emotional, mental and ultimately to personal and organizational breakdowns.

people's natural resistance to change can actually be used to bring about change: "Change requires a powerful and unrelenting force, and what could be more powerful than the desire not to change?" To use resistance to bring about change, Mulder (p. 58) suggests:

> First, surface the resistance. Make it as safe as you can. Ask for it all.
>
> Second, honor the resistance. Listen! Acknowledge it. Reinforce that expressing it is okay!
>
> Third, explore the resistance. Is it authentic? What is the objection? What is preferred? Then talk about what is good about the change.

One innovative approach to evolutionary change is to use developmental cells.

Developmental Cells

Lundstrom and Savage (1992, pp. 35–36) note:

> Change in policing generally focuses on superficial, as opposed to substantive issues. Perpetuation of existing organizational systems in a cosmetically new form is common in American policing. Years of inertia lie behind existing philosophy, structure, values and beliefs, whereas substantive change requires risk-taking on behalf of the chief executive.

Lundstrom and Savage suggest that this risk taking can be eased by using **developmental cells.** To begin with, the chief needs to identify one manager as a "champion" of whatever change is desired, whether it is community policing, problem-oriented policing or some combination of the two. The next step is to select one or two units within the department likely to accept the change and have the champion work with these units to develop the skills needed to make the change. Such developmental cells are called "incubators." Lundstrom and Savage (p. 37) caution:

> The challenges for the individual selected as the "champion" to manage the developmental cell are many. He must not only create a new culture for his

subordinates, but must necessarily become the buffer between the classically structured organization and the cell.

As the developmental cell progresses, officers within it will also show leadership abilities and can be assigned to other units in the agency, gradually expanding throughout the entire organization (p. 36): "Over time, the incremental change in culture and values will become self-perpetuating as organizational members of all levels seek out assignments where their value and output is more fully appreciated."

To illustrate how developmental cells can be used to gradually implement change, Lundstrom and Savage use the example of introducing semiautomatic pistols into departments that have been using revolvers. Not everyone is trained at the same time. Officers come in small groups, learn at different rates and are either enthusiastic or sullen about the change. Lundstrom and Savage suggest (p. 37):

> Some people have prior experience that helps them make the change with ease, and some have been doing the same thing for so long that they will never qualify with the new tools. Accept them all and put them in assignments where their particular strengths will contribute most positively to the change process.

They conclude: "Evolution over time is the key to substantive change; developmental cells can be one of the tools for that change." Sparrow (1988, p. 1) makes a classic analogy, comparing changes in policing to driving a 50-ton "semi":

> The professional truck driver . . . avoids braking sharply. He treats corners with far greater respect. And he generally does not expect the same instant response from the trailer, with its load, that he enjoys in his car. The driver's failure to understand the implications and responsibilities of driving such a massive vehicle inevitably produces tragedy: if the driver tries to turn too sharply, the cab loses traction as the trailer's momentum overturns or jackknifes the vehicle.

Police organizations also have considerable momentum. Having a strong personal commitment to the values with which they have "grown up," police officers may find hints of proposed change in the police culture extremely threatening.

Sparrow (p. 2) notes: "A huge ship can . . . be turned by a small rudder. It just takes time." The amount of time needed will vary from agency to agency, but managers should avoid becoming victims of the boiled frog phenomenon.

The Boiled Frog Phenomenon

The **boiled frog phenomenon** suggests that managers must pay attention to change in their environment and adapt—or perish.

The boiled frog phenomenon rests on a classic experiment. A frog is dropped into a pan of boiling water and immediately jumps out, saving its life. Next, a frog is placed into a pan of room-temperature water that is gradually heated to the boiling point. Because the temperature rise is so gradual, the frog does not notice it and sits contentedly in the bottom of the pan. The gradually rising temperature initially makes the frog comfortable but eventually saps its energy. As the water becomes too hot, the frog has no strength to jump out. It boils to death.

*Planning
for the Future*

Richards (2000, p. 8) stresses: "Planning stands not as an attempt to predict the future but as the best chance for survival in a world that is constantly changing." He suggests that: "Administrators should anticipate potential contingencies, continuously prepare for them and regularly review any existing plans." Richards (p. 12) concludes:

> Law enforcement administrators can free themselves from their long-held belief that planning for the future stands as a tedious and formidable task by following some basic procedures. These include developing the plan through defining the problem, gathering relevant facts, developing alternative approaches, and evaluating the effects. Once they have completed these planning phases, administrators can decide on their course of action, develop a written plan, and then test it for potential problems. . . .
>
> Administrators also should encourage and challenge their subordinates to plan for the future. All law enforcement professionals should remember that those who fail to plan, fail to achieve.

Acceptance of Change

Change is inevitable. No person or organization can stop it. Managers must accept that the only constant is change. Whether that change is positive or negative is characterized by Enright (1984) this way:

> . . . a branch floats peacefully down a river whose waters are high with the spring run-off. Although the branch is floating rapidly and occasionally bumps gently into a rock, it is almost effortlessly motionless in relation to the water it floats in. A similar branch has become wedged between some rocks and is thus resisting the swift flow of water around it. This branch is buffeted, whipped, and battered by the water and debris floating past it, and will soon be broken by the pressures against it (unless it dislodges and "goes with the flow"). If branches could experience, the one wedged into the rocks would be experiencing change with intense pain and distress; the floating one would experience ease and, paradoxically, comfortable stability even in the midst of rapid motion.

Change is inevitable. View it as opportunity.

The future is not a result of choices among alternative paths offered by the present but a place that is created—created first in mind and will, created next in activity. Ten two-letter words sum it up: *If it is to be, it is up to me.*

We have trained [people] to think of the future
as a promised land which favored heroes
attain—not as something which everyone
reaches at the same rate of 60 minutes an
hour, whatever he does, whoever he is.
—C. S. Lewis

The future is not some place we are going to,
but one we are creating. The paths are not to
be found, but made, and the activity of
making them changes both the maker and
the destination.
—John Schaar

Summary

The law enforcement career will be a continuous process of everyday learning at a rapid pace. Technical competence used to be most important. Now and in the years ahead, "people skills" are most important.

The public to be served will include more two-income families, more single-parent families, more senior citizens and more minorities. The educational and economic gap will increase, with those at the bottom becoming more disadvantaged and dissatisfied. The two greatest crime problems in the 2000s are drugs and violence.

Technology will be used in all phases of law enforcement work and will greatly enhance efficiency. It will be imperative for most law enforcement personnel to be computer literate. They might also benefit from futuristics.

Futuristics is the science of using data from the past to forecast alternatives for the future and to then select the most desirable. The three basic principles of futuristics are as follows:

- The unity or interconnectedness of reality
- The significance of ideas
- The crucial importance of time

Fundamental premises of futurists are that the future is not predictable, the future is not predetermined and future outcomes can be influenced by individual choice. Goals of futuristics include the following:

- Form perceptions of the future (the possible).
- Study likely alternatives (the probable).
- Make choices to bring about particular events (the preferable).

The boiled frog phenomenon suggests that managers must pay attention to change in their environment and adapt—or perish. Change is inevitable. View it as opportunity.

Discussion Questions

1. What should be law enforcement's role in the drug problem? In the violence problem?
2. Do you think creativity can be learned? Why or why not?
3. What would be the advantages of "flattening" the hierarchy? Disadvantages?
4. What trends do you foresee in the future of policing?
5. What is the importance of innovation and creativity in a law enforcement organization?
6. What do you see for the future development of your law enforcement agency?
7. How would you meet the decline of law enforcement resources?
8. What changes do you think are needed in the selection of future officers?
9. What major changes have you experienced in the past year? The past five years? How well did you handle them?
10. How can you best prepare for the inevitability of change in your life and your career?

*InfoTrac
College Edition
Assignment*

Find one journal article on *the future* in general. Find another article on *the future of law enforcement or criminal justice*. Summarize each article, including the full reference cite. Be prepared to share your summaries with the class.

References

Anderson, Larry. "Partnering with the Public Sector." *Access Control and Security Systems,* Vol. 42, No. 9, August 1999, p. 4.

Bentz, David E. "Leadership with an Eye on the Future." *The Police Chief,* Vol. LXII, No. 2, February 1995, pp. 14–17.

"Crime Still Ebbs in Early '94, But Experts See New Rise Coming." *Law Enforcement News,* January 15, 1995, p. 7.

Enright, John. "Change and Resilience." *The Leader Manager.* Eden Prairie, MN: Wilson Learning Corporation, 1984.

Fotte, Michael B. "Interactive Security: Police and Private Security Join Forces." *The Police Chief,* Vol. LXVI, No. 6, June 1999, pp. 57–61.

Goldstein, Herman. "The New Policing: Confronting Complexity." *National Institute of Justice Research in Brief,* December 1993.

Jones, Radford and Miller, Patricia P. "Public-Private Partnerships Enhance Critical Incident Planning." *The Police Chief,* Vol. LXVI, No. 6, June 1999, pp. 50–54.

Knowles, Terry L. "Meeting the Challenges of the 21st Century." *The Police Chief,* Vol. LXIV, No. 6, June 1997, pp. 39–43.

Lundstrom, Ross and Savage, Michael. "A Tool for Change: Developmental Cells." *The Police Chief,* Vol. LIX, Vol. 4, April 1992, pp. 35–37.

Mulder, Armand. "Resistance to Change." *Law and Order,* Vol. 42, No. 2, February 1994, pp. 55–59.

Naisbitt, John and Aburdene, Patricia. *Megatrends 2000: Ten New Directions for the 1990s.* New York: William Morrow & Co., 1990.

Peak, Ken. "Police Executives as Change Agents." *The Police Chief,* Vol. LXI, No. 1, January 1994, pp. 27–29.

Pettinari, Dave and Levin, Bernard H. "PFI Brings Much-Needed Futuristic Bent to Law Enforcement." *The Police Chief,* Vol. LXVI, No. 11, November 1999, p. 12.

Reader, Lockheed and Martin, Stan. "Public/Private Commitment—Significantly Fewer False Alarms." *The Police Chief,* Vol. LXVI, No. 6, June 1999, pp. 28–31.

Richards, Robert B. "Planning for the Future." *FBI Law Enforcement Bulletin,* Vol. 69, No. 1, January 2000, pp. 8–12.

Rippy, Keith M. "The Politics of Being a Police Chief: The Ins and Outs of Implementing Change." *The Police Chief,* Vol. LVII, No. 4, April 1990, pp. 135–140.

Seamon, Thomas. "Partners in Public Safety." *The Police Chief,* Vol. LVXI, No. 6, June 1999, pp. 17–21.

Slahor, Stephenie. "Partners in Crimefighting: Police and Private Security." *Access Control and Security Systems,* Vol. 40, No. 7, July 1997, p. 31.

Sparrow, Malcolm K. "Implementing Community Policing." *Perspectives on Policing,* November 1988, pp. 20–49.

Strandberg, Keith W. "21st Century Policing." *Law Enforcement Technology,* Vol. 24, No. 10, October 1997, pp. 48–50.

Strandberg, Keith W. "Back to the Future." *Law Enforcement Technology,* Vol. 26, No. 8, August 1999, pp. 56–65.

Tafoya, William L. "Futuristics: New Tools for Criminal Justice Executives: Part I." Presentation at the 1983 annual meeting of the Academy of Criminal Justice Sciences, March 22–26, 1983, San Antonio, Texas.

Woodward, Harry and Buchholz, Steve. *Aftershock: Helping People through Corporate Change.* New York: John Wiley and Sons, 1987.

Appendix A Sample Application Form

DEPARTMENT OF ADMINISTRATION
4801 West 50th Street • Edina, Minnesota 55424-1394
(612) 927-8861   TDD(612) 927-5461

Employment Application

THE CITY OF EDINA WELCOMES YOU as an applicant for employment. Your application will be considered with others in competition for the position in which you are interested. It is our policy to provide equal employment opportunities to all. Individuals are evaluated and selected solely on the basis of their qualifications.

Please furnish complete and accurate information so that the City of Edina can properly evaluate your application.

Be warned that the use of false or misleading information or the omission of important facts may be grounds for immediate dismissal. Also note that information you provide herein may be subject to later verification and/or testing.

You may attach to this application any additional information that helps explain your qualifications. *Please print clearly or type.*

Personal Information

Name	Last	First	Middle	Previous
Present Address	Street	City	State	Zip Code
Permanent Address	Street	City	State	Zip Code
Telephone	Residence	Business	May we call you at work? ☐ Yes ☐ No	

Are you between the ages of 16 and 70? ☐ Yes ☐ No   If "No", state date of birth:

Do you have a Social Security Number? ☐ Yes ☐ No

Work Preferences

Position for which you are applying (or type of work in which you are interested):	*Are you interested in . . .*
	☐ Full-Time ☐ Part Time ☐ Seasonal ☐ Paid on call ☐ Volunteer ■ Date available for work:

General Information

Have you previously been employed by the City of Edina?   If "Yes," Dates   Position
    ☐ Yes   ☐ No

Do you have relatives or in-laws working for the City of Edina?   If "Yes," who:
    ☐ Yes   ☐ No

How did you hear about a job at the City of Edina?

☐ Came in on my own _____   ☐ Other (Specify) _____
☐ City employee _____   ☐ Newspaper (Specify) _____
☐ School (Specify) _____   ☐ Employment Agency _____
(Counselor) _____   (Specify) _____

Have you ever been convicted of a crime for which a jail sentence   Have you ever been convicted of a felony?
of more than 90 days could have been imposed?

    ☐ Yes   ☐ No   ☐ Yes   ☐ No

You may answer "No" to these questions if the conviction or criminal records thereof have been annulled, expunged, sealed, set aside or purged, or if you have been pardoned pursuant to law. Before any applicant is rejected on the basis of a criminal conviction, he or she will be notified in writing and will be given any rights to processing of complaints or grievances afforded by Minnesota Statute Chapter 364. If the answer to this question is "Yes," please attach a separate sheet of paper giving full particulars.

If you are not a citizen of the United States, do you have a valid work permit?   Do you have a valid Drivers License?
    ☐ Yes   ☐ No   Number_____   ☐ Yes   ☐ No
    State:_____   Class:_____

Are you subject to a child support or spousal maintenance order?   If "Yes," are you subject to withholding for child support or spousal maintenance?
    ☐ Yes   ☐ No   ☐ Yes   ☐ No

Education

School Name and Location	Attendance Dates From (mo/yr) To (mo/yr)	Graduate	Type	Degree, Diploma or Certificate and Major/Minor	Academic Standing Grade Average, eg, (3.2/4.0)
High School last attended		☐ Yes ☐ No			
Vocational, technical school		☐ Yes ☐ No			
College or university		☐ Yes ☐ No			
College or university		☐ Yes ☐ No			
Other (skilled trade training, etc.)		☐ Yes ☐ No			

Please list academic honors, scholarships, fellowships, memberships in professional and honorary societies, and any other extracurricular activities:

Special Skills/Training/Licenses

Clerical Skills	What is your present speed per minute?	Typewriter	Shorthand	Speedwriting	Can you operate	Dictating equipment ☐ Yes ☐ No	Computer/terminal ☐ Yes ☐ No
	Other office equipment you can operate (including word processing, database management, spreadsheet and other software):						
	Do you have experience in a skilled trade? If so, please describe the extent/nature of experience.						

Skilled Trade Skills, Licenses, Certifications	Have you completed an apprenticeship in a skilled craft? ☐ Yes ☐ No	If yes,	What craft?		Where did you complete it?		
	List all machines and equipment you have operated:						
	List all current licenses and/or certifications together with an identification of the granting authority:						
	Do you have Advanced First Aid, EMS First Responder, Crash Injury Management (CIM) or EMT certification? ☐ Yes ☐ No						

Employment History

Please give accurate, complete and part-time employment record. *Start with present or most recent employer.*

Company Name	Telephone ( )
Address	Employed (State month and year) From To
Name of Supervisor	Salary ☐ Hourly ☐ Monthly ☐ Yearly $
State job title and list your duties/responsibilities beginning with the duty that consumed the greatest proportion of your time:	Reason for leaving

Company Name	Telephone ( )
Address	Employed (State month and year) From To
Name of Supervisor	Salary ☐ Hourly ☐ Monthly ☐ Yearly $
State job title and list your duties/responsibilities beginning with the duty that consumed the greatest proportion of your time:	Reason for leaving

Company Name	Telephone ( )
Address	Employed (State month and year) From To
Name of Supervisor	Salary ☐ Hourly ☐ Monthly ☐ Yearly $
State job title and list your duties/responsibilities beginning with the duty that consumed the greatest proportion of your time:	Reason for leaving

Company Name	Telephone ( )
Address	Employed (State month and year) From To
Name of Supervisor	Salary ☐ Hourly ☐ Monthly ☐ Yearly $
State job title and list your duties/responsibilities beginning with the duty that consumed the greatest proportion of your time:	Reason for leaving

If you need additional space, please continue on a separate sheet of paper. Be certain to complete both sides of this application.

Public Safety Applicants (Please Respond)

Date and location of POST licensing exam?   Date:

Skills course attended?

Date of graduation from skills course?

Are you currently licensed?   ☐ Yes   ☐ No   If so, License Number

If you are currently licensed, status of license?   ☐ Active   ☐ Inactive   ☐ Part-time   ☐ Other_____

Additional Experience and/or Training

Describe any additional experience or training that qualifies you for this job.

Important facts concerning information on your application

MINNESOTA LAW AFFECTS YOU AS AN APPLICANT with the City of Edina. The following data is public information and is accessible to anyone: veteran's status, relevant test scores, rank on eligibility list, job history, education and training, and work availability. All other personally identifiable information is considered private, including, but not limited to, your name, home address and phone number.

If you are selected as a finalist for a position, your name will become public information. You become a finalist if you are selected to be interviewed by the City of Edina.

The information requested on the application is necessary, either to identify you or to assist in determining your suitability for the position for which you are applying. You may legally refuse, but refusal to supply the requested information will mean that your application for employment may not be considered.

If you are selected for employment with the City of Edina, the following additional information about you will be public: your name; actual gross salary and salary range; actual gross pension; the value and nature of your fringe benefits; the basis for and the amount of any added remuneration, such as expenses or mileage reimbursement, in addition to your salary; your job title; job description; training background; previous work experience; the dates of your first and last employment with the City of Edina; the status of any complaints or charges against you while at work; the final outcome of any disciplinary action taken against you, and all supporting documentation about your case; your badge number, if any; your city and county of residence; your work location and work telephone number; honors and awards; payroll timesheets and comparable data.

Anything not listed above which is placed in your application folder or your personnel file (such as medical information, letters of recommendation, resumes, etc.) is made private information by law. For further information, refer to Minnesota Statute, Chapter 13.

I understand that any false information on or omission of information from this application (including additional information required for Public Safety Applicants, if applicable), or failure to present the required proof, will be cause for rejection or dismissal if employed.

Public Safety Applicants Only: In consideration of being permitted to apply for the position herein, I voluntarily assume all risks in connection with my participating in any tests the City of Edina deems necessary to determine my fitness and eligibility, and I release and forever discharge the City of Edina, its officers and employees from any and all claims for any damage or injury that I might sustain.

Tennessen Warning. The purpose and intended use of the information requested on the application is to assist in determining your eligibility and suitability for the position for which you are applying. You may legally refuse to give the information. If you give the information, that information, or further investigation based on it, could cause your application to be denied. If you refuse to give the information, your application for employment may not be considered. Other persons or entities authorized to receive the information you supply are: Staff of Edina Police Department, Bureau of Criminal Apprehension, Hennepin County Warrant Office, Ramsey County Warrant Office, State of Minnesota, Drivers License Section, Hennepin County Auditor, and other governmental agencies necessary to process your application.

Applicant's Signature

Date

Appendix B Sample Interview Rating Sheet

CITY OF ANYWHERE, U.S.A.
Oral Interview Board
Police Officer

Candidate's Name: _____

Total Score: _____

A. Interview Questions

Instructions: Do not permit candidates to give a "yes" or "no" answer to the following questions. Ask for justification or explanation of candidates' positions.

1. You and your partner have just stopped a driver for speeding. You observe the driver hand your partner some money and drive off. When your partner returns to your police vehicle, he offers you part of the money. What action would you take?

   6   7   8   9   10   _____

2. Give three good reasons why you have become a candidate for the position of police officer.

   6   7   8   9   10   _____

3. Do you feel you could use deadly force, if necessary, to make an arrest? Justify your position.

   6   7   8   9   10   _____

4. What changes do you foresee having to make in your lifestyle to become a police officer?

   6   7   8   9   10   _____

5. What do you perceive is the role of the police in crime prevention?

   6   7   8   9   10   _____

6. When did you decide to become a police officer? What preparations have you made toward that goal?

   6   7   8   9   10   _____

7. Is there anything else you would like to say about yourself with regard to this job position?

NOTATIONS (FOR QUESTION 7 ONLY): _____

_____

_____

TOTAL SECTION "A": _____

B. Personal Characteristics
1. Appearance: Consider the candidate's personal appearance, bearing in mind the requirements of the position. Does the candidate give a satisfactory appearance as a representative of the local government? *(Observe: dress, neatness, posture, sitting position, facial expressions, mannerisms)*

| 6 | 7 | 8 | 9 | 10 | _____ |

2. Voice and ability to use the English language: Consider the quality of the candidate's voice in relation to the subject position. Does the candidate speak clearly and distinctly? Is his/her voice pleasant or harsh? Consider the candidate's choice of words, sentences, phrases, use of slang or needless technical jargon. *(Observe: use of simple and correct English, logical presentation, coherence of thought)*

| 6 | 7 | 8 | 9 | 10 | _____ |

3. Self-Confidence: Consider self-control. Is the candidate nervous or ill at ease? Is he/she poised and relaxed? Does he/she appear to be uncertain or hesitant about his/her ideas? *(Observe: embarrassment, stammering, tension, poise, hesitation, confidence, timidness, over confidence)*

| 6 | 7 | 8 | 9 | 10 | _____ |

4. Ability to get along with people: Consider the candidate's attitude toward the examiners. Does he/she seem over-sensitive? Is there antagonism, indifference, a cooperative attitude?

| 6 | 7 | 8 | 9 | 10 | _____ |

5. Suitability for this position: Consider whether the candidate will work out on the job. Does he/she reply readily to questions asked? Are his/her ideas original? Are statements convincing and appropriate? Is there evidence of leadership? Does he/she speak out voluntarily at proper times? Does he/she have a definite interest in this work? *(Observe: alertness, responsiveness, tact, cooperation, enthusiasm)*

| 6 | 7 | 8 | 9 | 10 | _____ |

TOTAL SECTION "B": _____

GRAND TOTAL: _____

REMARKS:_____

_____

_____

_____

_____

_____

SIGNATURE OF RATER _____

Appendix C Accessibility Checklist for Complying with the ADA Regulations*

Parking Lots

☐ Designated parking spaces should be located near the building, and they should not be occupied by maintenance trucks, employee cars, or the cars of able-bodied guests.

☐ If parking spaces are not close to the building, valet service should be available at curbside.

☐ Verify that access from the parking lot to the building is free and clear. (No gravel or loose impediments.)

☐ The approach should be flat and smooth.

☐ If the weather is bad, is access to the building covered?

☐ Are curbs adjacent to designated parking spaces?

☐ Are the angles on the curbs sharp?

☐ Watch out for open stairs. Are handrails present?

The Building

☐ The approach to the entrance should be a hard surface at least five feet wide.

☐ There should be space for a wheelchair lift to be lowered flat to the ground (not on curb).

☐ Is the doorsill raised?

☐ How heavy is the door?

☐ If there are revolving doors, are the side doors unlocked and easy to open?

☐ Are bell staff available for move in/move out if necessary? What about for late-arriving guests?

☐ A single-door entrance to the building must be at least 32 inches wide (a standard wheelchair is exactly 32 inches wide). The ideal width for a single-door entrance is 36 inches.

☐ A double-door entrance must be at least 48 inches wide.

☐ Once inside, is there signage? What is the height? Is it easily visible from a wheelchair?

The Front Desk

☐ Most front desks are uncomfortably high. If inaccessible for wheelchair users, can registration be moved to the concierge table, or to another table to the side of the front desk, or can the guest use a clipboard to complete registration forms?

The Elevator

☐ Are the control panels low enough to be accessible by wheelchair users?

☐ Are the floor numbers in Braille for the sight-impaired?

☐ Elevators must be a minimum of 48 inches deep and 22 feet square to permit the wheelchair user to turn around and face the door.

☐ The door must be at least 32 inches wide.

The Guest Room

☐ If possible, barrier-free rooms should be located near elevators.

☐ Door handles on the outside door and all inside doors should be levers.

*By January 1993, any major construction required for public accommodations must comply with ADA standards. Both tenants and owners of facilities are responsible for insuring that areas of public accommodation and where public services are offered are accessible. This is a comprehensive checklist for use in site inspections to make sure your site meets ADA standards.

*Note: Although developed for meeting sites, this checklist can be used for any public facility, including police departments.

Source: Cindy Alwood. "Checklist: Does Your Meeting Site Obey the ADA?" *Successful Meetings,* December 1992, pp. 131–132.

Reprinted with permission from the MPI Education Research Foundation Research Center's "Americans with Disabilities Act & Meeting Planning" research subject package.

☐ Once inside the room, all doors and hallways must be a minimum of 32 inches wide.

☐ Mirrors in a guest room should be not higher than 40 inches from the floor.

☐ In rooms with two beds, there should be a space between the beds or along the outside.

☐ Phones, remote controls, and light switches should be located next to the accessible side of the bed.

☐ Maneuverability is important in a guest room, so check for poorly placed furniture.

☐ If the room has a thermostat, it should be no more than 40 inches from the floor.

☐ If the temperature controls are on the heating/cooling unit itself, make sure furniture does not block the unit.

☐ The closet bar should be 40 inches from the floor.

☐ The peephole in the outside door and all locks should be low enough for a person in a wheelchair.

Think about evacuation in the event of emergencies:

☐ Is there a sprinkler system?

☐ Are fire alarms 40 inches from the floor?

☐ Are there flashing lights to alert deaf or hearing-impaired guests?

☐ Is there a voice alarm for guests who are blind or sight-impaired?

☐ The door to the bathroom should open out. If the door does open out, make sure it does not block access to the outside door.

The Bathroom

☐ There should be a cutaway under the sink to allow wheelchair users to roll up to the sink.

☐ There should be space to maneuver along the bathtub.

☐ The bathtub should be equipped with grip bars, ideally with both vertical and horizontal bars low to the tub.

☐ Check for stability of grip bars. Poorly mounted grip bars might not withstand a strong pull.

☐ Towels should be within reach of someone in a seated position.

☐ Toilets should not be higher than 29 inches off the floor, urinals not higher than 17 inches.

Lounge

☐ Is access to the restaurant/lounge a flat surface?

☐ Are there stairs or a ramp?

☐ Is there adequate space between tables for a wheelchair?

☐ Check out table heights.

☐ Is there access to the dance floor?

☐ Are the restrooms accessible by wheelchair?

☐ The upper edge of the drinking fountain should be no higher than 36 inches from the floor.

☐ Phones should feature coin slots that are no more than 54 inches off the ground.

☐ At least one phone should have hearing amplification in the handset.

☐ A phone equipped with TDD (telecommunications device for the deaf) should be available.

Meeting Rooms

☐ Aisles should be a minimum of 32 inches wide.

☐ If you are using a riser, consider its accessibility: Risers require ramps with a slope of no more than one inch vertical to every 12 inches horizontal.

☐ Noisy heating/cooling systems in older facilities can make hearing difficult.

☐ Chandelier and fluorescent lighting are hard on the eyes.

☐ If your meeting has recreation time built into it, recreation facilities—the pool, locker rooms, sundeck—should be accessible.

Staff

☐ Staff should be sensitive to greeting and working with persons with disabilities.
This often requires training. Meeting Planners International (MPI) has members who will conduct Accessibility Awareness Training—call (214) 712-7700.

Appendix D Sample Affirmative Action Questionnaire

The following information is necessary for the city of Anywhere to evaluate its recruiting and hiring practices and to prepare reports required by law for the state and federal governments. We ask your help in filling in the blanks that apply to you. The Civil Rights Act, Title VII, makes it unlawful to discriminate in employment on the basis of race, color, religion, sex or national origin. Federal and state laws prohibit discrimination in employment on the basis of disability or age. This form will be detached from your application and the information will not be used to make any employment decisions which affect you.

_____ American Indian or Alaskan Native (All persons having origins in any of the original peoples of North America.)

_____ Black (Not of Hispanic origin): All persons having origins in any of the Black racial groups.

_____ Asian/Pacific Islander (All persons having origins in any of the original peoples of the Far East, Southeast Asia, or the Pacific Islands. This area includes, for example, China, Japan, Korea, the Phillipine and Hawaiian Islands and Samoa.)

_____ Hispanic (All persons of Mexican, Puerto Rican, Cuban, Central or South American, or other Spanish culture or origin, regardless of race.)

_____ White (Not of Hispanic origin): All persons having origins in any of the original peoples of Europe, North Africa, the Middle East, or the Indian Subcontinent.

Birthdate: _____ Age_____ yrs. Sex: Male _____ Female _____

Do you have a physical, mental or addictive handicapping condition which substantially limits a major life activity?

Yes _____ No _____ If yes, explain: _____

Exact Title of Position for Which You Are Applying: _____

DATE: _____ NAME: _____

Offense	Explanation	Penalties		
		1st Offense	2nd Offense	3rd Offense
1. Failure to carry out assignment/insubordination a. Minor	Deliberate delay or failure to carry out assigned work or instructions in a reasonable period of time.	R.	R. to 5 days S.	R. to D.
b. Major	Refusal to obey legitimate orders, disrespect, insolence and like behavior.	R. to D.	R. to D.	D.
2. Absence without leave a. Minor	Unauthorized absence of 10 hours or less, repeated tardiness, leaving the job without permission.	R.	R. to 5 days S.	R. to D.
b. Major	Unauthorized absence of more than 10 hours (If misrepresentation is involved, see #8).	R. to D.	R. to D.	D.
3. Neglect of duty a. Minor	Unauthorized participation in activities during duty hours which are outside of regularly assigned duties. The offense is usually considered "minor" when danger to safety of persons or property is not acute or injury or loss is not involved.	R.	R. to 5 days S.	R. to D.
b. Major	The offense is usually considered "major" when danger to safety of persons or property is acute or injury or loss is involved.	R. to D.	D.	
4. Careless workmanship or negligence a. Minor	When spoilage or waste of materials or delay in production is not of significant value.	R.	R. to 5 days S.	R. to D.
b. Major	When spoilage or waste of materials or delay in production is extensive and costly; covering up or attempting to conceal defective work.	R. to D.	D.	
5. Violation of safety practices and regulations a. Minor	Failure to observe safety practices and regulations and danger to safety of persons or property is not acute.	R.	R. to 5 days S.	R. to D.
b. Major	Failure to observe safety practices and regulations and danger to safety of persons or property is acute.	R. to D.	D.	
6. Loss of, damage to, unauthorized use or willful destruction of city property, records or information a. Minor	When loss or damage is of small value and such loss or damage is not knowingly perpetrated.	R.	R. to 5 days S.	R. to D.
b. Major	When loss or damage is knowingly perpetrated.	R. to D.	D.	
7. Theft, actual or attempted, in taking and carrying away city property or property of others	Penalty will be determined in part by value of property.	R. to D.	D.	
8. False statements or misrepresentation a. Minor	When falsification, concealment or misrepresentation has occurred, but has not necessarily been done deliberately.	R. to 10 days S.	D.	
b. Major	Deliberate misrepresentation, falsification, exaggeration or concealment of a material fact, especially in connection with matters under official investigation.	R. to D.	D.	

Continued

Note: R. in table means reprimand. The abbreviation S. means suspension. The abbreviation D. means dismissal.

Offense	Explanation	Penalties		
		1st Offense	2nd Offense	3rd Offense
9. Disorderly conduct a. Minor	Rude, boisterous play which adversely affects production, discipline or morale; use of disrespectful, abusive or offensive language; quarreling or inciting to quarrel.	R. to 5 days S.	R. to D.	D.
b. Major	Fighting, threatening or inflicting bodily harm to another; physical resistance to competent authority; any violent act or language which adversely affects morale, production or maintenance of discipline; indecent or immoral conduct.	R. to D.	D.	
10. Gambling a. Minor	Participation in gambling during working hours.	R.	R. to 5 days S.	D.
b. Major	Promotion of, or assisting in, operation of organized gambling.	R. to D.	R. to D.	D.
11. Use of intoxicants a. Minor	Drinking or selling intoxicants or controlled substances on duty or on city premises.	R. to D.	D.	
b. Major	Reporting for duty drunk, under the influence of controlled substances or intoxicated and unable to properly perform assigned duties or to be a hazard to self or others.	5 days S. to D.	D.	
12. Misconduct off duty	Misconduct which adversely affects the reputation of the employee or reflects unfavorably on the city.	R. to D.	R. to D.	D.
13. Failure to honor valid debts	Garnishment of an employee's wages by an appropriate court order.	R. (the first offense requires more than one garnishment before applicable)	R.	R. to D.
14. Discrimination a. Minor	Any action or failure to take action based on age, sex, race, color, religion or national origin of an employee, former employee or applicant which affects their rights, privileges, benefits, dignity and equality of economic opportunity.	R.	R. to 5 days S.	R. to D.
b. Major	If the discriminatory practice was deliberate.	R. to 20 days S.	20 days S. to D.	D.
15. Fiscal irregularity	Misappropriation of city funds which came into the employee's possession by reason of their official position; falsification of payroll records for personal gain.	D.		
16. Political activity	Engaging in types of political activity prohibited by these personnel policies.	R. to D.	R. to D.	R. to D.
17. Violation of code of ethics	Acceptance of gifts or favors influencing discharge of duties; use of position to secure special privileges or exemptions; disclosure of information adversely affecting the affairs of the city; transaction of city business where personal financial interest is involved; deliberately thwarting execution of a city ordinance, rule or official program.	R. to D.	D.	
18. Violation of the city charter or personnel or departmental personnel policies not already covered above. a. Minor	Violation of a policy which has little adverse affect on production, employee morale, maintenance of discipline and/or the reputation of the city.	R.	R. to 20 days S.	R. to D.
b. Major	Violation of a policy which adversely affects production, employee morale, maintenance of discipline and/or the reputation of the city in a direct way.	R. to D.	D.	

Source: City of Boulder City, Boulder City, Nevada, Police Department. Reprinted with permission.

Appendix F Sample Community Policing Implementation Profile*

Complete the profile questionnaire to analyze the degree that different community policing activities are integrated into your police agency and community. For each activity listed, circle a number between 1 ("not implemented") and 5 ("fully implemented") to indicate the degree that you feel the activity is currently implemented.

Build Partnerships with the Community	Not Implemented		Fully Implemented		
1. Police communicate the community policing philosophy through news media, community newsletter or citizen meetings.	1	2	3	4	5
2. Police discuss with citizens what community policing can do and cannot do.	1	2	3	4	5
3. Police at all organizational levels participate in two-way communication with citizens and community leaders.	1	2	3	4	5
4. Police use each neighborhood's own public safety priorities to guide department activity in that neighborhood.	1	2	3	4	5
5. A partnership form documents joint department and citizen group responsibilities concerning specific problem-solving activities.	1	2	3	4	5
6. Police include elected officials in the community policing planning process.	1	2	3	4	5
7. Police involve relevant community agencies in the community policing planning process.	1	2	3	4	5
8. Police coordinate problem-solving activities with appropriate social service agencies.	1	2	3	4	5
9. Police and community agencies track police social service referrals.	1	2	3	4	5
10. Police distribute an information package that gives a realistic picture of community policing.	1	2	3	4	5
11. Top police managers conduct press briefings to explain community policing.	1	2	3	4	5
12. All police personnel are authorized to speak directly to the media about their work.	1	2	3	4	5
13. Police personnel have organized an internal speakers bureau to promote community policing.	1	2	3	4	5
14. Police sponsor public seminars on community policing.	1	2	3	4	5
15. Individual employees participate in civic groups trying to solve crime problems.	1	2	3	4	5

Build Partnerships within the Police Department	Not Implemented		Fully Implemented		
16. Frequent personal communication from top management disseminates community policing philosophy to all personnel, sworn and nonsworn.	1	2	3	4	5
17. All personnel participate in community policing planning processes that affect their own work.	1	2	3	4	5
18. Management recruits people who respect community policing values.	1	2	3	4	5
19. Management seriously considers the merits of all internal suggestions for improvement.	1	2	3	4	5
20. Employees are rewarded for doing community policing activities.	1	2	3	4	5
21. Employees help design their own performance evaluation criteria.	1	2	3	4	5

Continued

Decentralize Police Decision-Making	Not Implemented		Fully Implemented		
22. Management practices emphasize broad-based participation in policy formation.	1	2	3	4	5
23. Problem-solving groups are composed of many different ranks.	1	2	3	4	5
24. Problem-solving groups have the authority to implement their decisions.	1	2	3	4	5
25. The general rules and regulations have been streamlined to emphasize broader guidelines to appropriate action.	1	2	3	4	5
26. Management practices are consistent with the large amount of individual discretion that patrol officers exercise.	1	2	3	4	5
27. Patrol officers accept having increased accountability along with increased decision-making authority.	1	2	3	4	5
28. Management has reduced the rank level of approval required for many decisions.	1	2	3	4	5
29. Management authorizes officers to commit police resources when working with citizen groups to solve problems.	1	2	3	4	5
30. Patrol areas conform to natural community boundaries.	1	2	3	4	5
31. Officers who work in the same neighborhood areas attend frequent meetings with each other to plan their problem-solving activities.	1	2	3	4	5

Restructure Police Training and Education	Not Implemented		Fully Implemented		
32. Management works to change state police academy curriculum to teach more community policing skills.	1	2	3	4	5
33. Department training emphasizes community policing skills.	1	2	3	4	5
34. Management rewards patrol officers who take outside courses that help them to do community policing.	1	2	3	4	5
35. Department policies encourage managers to take outside courses in participatory management skills.	1	2	3	4	5
36. Management uses citizen complaints about police conduct to identify training deficiencies.	1	2	3	4	5
37. Management uses patrol officers who are successful in community policing to help train other officers.	1	2	3	4	5

Go Beyond 911	Not Implemented		Fully Implemented		
38. The department emphasizes using an alternative phone number to 911 for non-emergency police contact.	1	2	3	4	5
39. Citizens are provided a method to directly contact their neighborhood patrol officers.	1	2	3	4	5
40. Police employees have accurate information for correctly referring citizens to other agencies for problem-solving assistance.	1	2	3	4	5
41. The department uses alternatives to automobile patrols.	1	2	3	4	5
42. The method for evaluating the performance of police officers includes monitoring officers' progress on self-generated problem-solving plans.	1	2	3	4	5

Appendix G Sample Goals, Daily Routine, Methods, Responsibilities and Duties of a Community Policing Officer*

The following are examples of goals, daily routine, methods, responsibilities and duties of a community policing officer:

Goals

The following are goals of the Neighborhood Foot Patrol:

1. To decrease the amount of actual or perceived criminal activity.
2. To increase the citizen's perception of personal safety.
3. To deliver to Flint residents a type of law enforcement service consistent with the community needs and the ideals of modern police practices.
4. To create a community awareness of crime problems and methods of increasing law enforcement's ability to deal with actual or potential criminal activity swiftly and effectively.
5. To develop citizen volunteer action in support of, and under the direction of, the police department, aimed at various target crimes.
6. To eliminate citizen apathy about crime reporting to police.
7. To increase protection for women, the aged and children.

Daily Routine

The following is an example of a Neighborhood Foot Patrol officer's *typical* day:

1. Report to roll call.
2. Report to base station.
3. Office call in time, check notes and messages.
4. Establish priority list for complaints received.
5. Make decision as to which complaints would be better handled by another department. For example, garbage complaints would be referred to the Sanitation Department.
6. Start walking beat.
7. Go door to door, make security inspections of home, take complaints of neighborhood problems and concerns.
8. Follow up on written recorded complaints and refer to the proper agency those that cannot be handled.
9. Make person to person contact with residents, including distribution of a personal "letter of introduction" to each home and business.
10. Make contact with families of any juvenile who appears on the juvenile sheet and lives in beat area.

---

*Source: Flint, Michigan, Police Department, "Neighborhood Police Foot Patrol Instruction Manual."

Methods

The Neighborhood Officer

The neighborhood officers themselves are the most important factor in achieving the goals of this program.

The officers who have been selected under this program are operating under a full-service role model, as opposed to the basically narrow, vocational one based primarily on law enforcement alone. A full-service model contains these goals: professionalism, human relations, community relations and law enforcement. The goals are defined as follows:

PROFESSIONALISM: Characterized by independence in decision making which is guided by a code of ethics and the systematic application of a body of knowledge; actions are geared to the needs of the client rather than self-interest; self-monitoring and ultimate accountability to one's own peers.

HUMAN RELATIONS: An awareness of interpersonal dynamics expressed by the utilization of alternatives to physical force; primary focus is on verbal and social interaction skills; a problem-solving orientation in which the police officer becomes a source of support, strength, and authority.

COMMUNITY RELATIONS: A collaborative approach to law enforcement in which liaison with the service community is maximized; cooperation and information flow are enhanced through various attempts to reduce social distance; coordination efforts with community members and resources.

LAW ENFORCEMENT: Characterized by a recognition that the power and authority vested in the police officer is a responsibility to be exercised in consideration of the needs of the individual citizen (victim and criminal alike) and the best interest of society. Law enforcement in the context of "law and order" is feasible only as a *joint effort* of the *police and the citizens of the community.*

The Neighborhood Foot Patrol officer's job is to encourage Flint citizens to work with the Flint Police Department to reduce crime and to develop a community crime prevention network.

The following is a summary of the neighborhood officer's responsibilities and duties:

1. Increase citizen awareness of the problem of crime by analyzing the neighborhood crime patterns and reporting the actual crime problems confronting individuals who live in the target area.

2. Conduct public education programs on crime prevention geared specifically to the various groups in the neighborhoods.

3. Confer with residents and businesses regarding problems relative to the police department, city government and other criminal justice and governmental agencies.

4. Gather and contribute helpful information to the Flint Police Department concerning social problems involving individuals, families and/or neighborhoods.

5. Maintain a high degree of contact with the existing citizen action groups operating within the neighborhoods and involve them in planning, designing and evaluating neighborhood crime prevention programs.

6. Patrol streets to strengthen lines of communication with citizens and prevent crime and delinquency.

7. Attend neighborhood block clubs and services as a resource person relative to crime prevention and police problems, activities and procedures.

8. Attend School Advisory Councils in area assigned.

9. Inspect residential and business premises and make recommendations to improve physical security.

10. Investigate selected crimes against the person or individual and support community education programs to prevent reoccurence.

11. Prepare written crime prevention material for community newsletter.

12. Create an environment of safety for the elderly by encouraging self crime prevention techniques such as direct deposits for income; the use of checks and credit cards instead of cash to decrease chances of monetary loss; and transporting the elderly to banks and shops to further reduce chances of attack by criminals.

13. Maintain an ongoing juvenile delinquency prevention program for our youth through the medium of the Police Athletic League (PAL). This activity will incorporate the traditional sports games that youth enjoy, as well as field trips to museums, art fairs and the theater to culturally enrich those among us who are deprived of such outlets.

14. Inspect the total turf of the beat for any violation of city codes or ordinances. Contingent to the basic concept of the Foot Patrol, the officer has a close personal relationship with all sectors of the populace, both private and commercial. With this in mind, enforcement may be procured on a voluntary basis rather than punitive, thereby not only enhancing the image of the officer, but abating the problem at hand. Areas where the officer may realize this concept in daily activities fall under a myriad of duties.

    The aesthetic beauty of the community is enhanced with the officer's enforcement of abandoned vehicle violations, trash and garbage complaints, and the noncompliance with the sundry animal ordinances.

    In effect, the foot patrol officer becomes a code enforcement officer, and the close rapport established with the public within the beat configuration enables compliance with, and abatement of, ordinances and violations observed through this personal relationship.

    The officer will actively seek out any grievances that the citizenry may have, and seek to alleviate them. Street lights that are inoperative, trees that need to be trimmed, all have an impact on the citizen's view of the environment. The act of actively seeking out complaints such as these and procuring abatement of the problem at hand will improve not only the image of the officer to constituents, but the aesthetic beauty and safety of the assigned area.

15. Work with the elderly to develop programs and activities to help ensure safety and comfort in their living and social environment.

16. Work with youth to develop activities to decrease their opportunities to become involved in delinquent behavior.

17. Routinely review community resources to ascertain what's needed to improve the quality of life in the area.

18. Perform other duties required of a Flint Police Officer.

Glossary

(Number in parentheses is the chapter in which the term is discussed.)

abstract words—theoretical, not concrete, for example, *tall* rather than *6'10"*. (3)

accountability—responsibility for fulfilling tasks. (1)

accounting—the process by which an agency's financial information is recorded, classified, summarized, interpreted and then communicated to managers and other interested parties. (6)

accounting period—the time covered by the income statement and other financial statements that report operating results. (6)

accreditation—the process by which an institution or agency proves that it meets certain standards. (16)

active listening—listening that includes concentration, full attention and thought. (3)

activity-based costing (ABC)—a modern version of the program-budgeting system, except that rather than breaking costs down by program, the approach breaks costs down by activity. (6)

acute stress—severe, intense distress that lasts a limited time and then the person returns to normal. Also called *traumatic stress*. (14)

administrative decision—middle-management-level decision. (4)

administrative services—services that support those performing the field services. Includes recruitment and training, records and communication, planning and research and technical services. (1)

administrative skills—organizing, delegating and directing the work of others; writing proposals, devising work plans and developing budgets. (2)

affirmative action program (AAP)—a written plan to ensure fair recruitment, hiring and promotion practices. (7)

afterburn—the damaging emotional scars on an officer's family as the aftermath of a stressful incident. (14)

agenda—a plan, usually referring to a meeting outline or program; a list of things to be accomplished. (3)

aggressive patrol—patrol that focuses on the prevention and detection of crime by investigating suspicious actions, events and behaviors. Also called *proactive patrol*. (15)

aligned on purpose—having a sense of common purpose about why a team exists and the function it serves. (2)

all-levels budgeting—everyone affected by the budget helps prepare it. (6)

andragogy—the principles of adult learning. (8)

appeal—request for a decision to be reviewed by someone higher in the command structure. (11)

approach-approach conflict—selecting between two positive alternatives. (13)

approach-avoidance conflict—selecting one positive alternative that will also produce a negative consequence. (13)

arbitration—turning a decision over to an individual or panel to make the final recommendation. (7, 12)

assessment center—places participants in the position of actually performing tasks related to an anticipated position. Incorporates situational techniques in a simulated environment under standardized conditions. (10)

assets—items of value owned by an agency. (6)

audit trail—the chain of references that makes it possible to trace information about transactions through an accounting system. (6)

authority—the power to command, enforce laws, exact obedience, determine or judge. The ability to get things done through others by influencing behavior. (1, 2)

Authority/Compliance Management—management system that emphasizes achieving production goals by planning, directing and controlling all work, with good relationships viewed as incidental. It is inner-directed and suppresses conflict through authority. (2)

autocratic leadership—managers make decisions without participant input. Completely authoritative, showing little or no concern for subordinates. (2)

automated performance evaluation—officers are continuously evaluated and awarded points, which are tracked by computer. Supervisors can award bonus points. (16)

avoidance-avoidance conflict—selecting between two negative alternatives, commonly referred to as "the lesser of two evils." (13)

avoiders—people who put things off, procrastinate or physically absent themselves to keep from getting involved. (13)

background check—investigating references listed on an application as well as credit, driving record, criminal conviction, academic background and required professional licenses. (7)

balance of consequences analysis—a grid used to analyze problem behavior and the consequences that follow it in an attempt to understand how the consequences might be changed to alter the problem behavior. (11)

balance sheet—the financial statement of an agency on a specific date, summarizing the agency's assets and liabilities. (6)

"balanced performer" managers—managers who develop subordinates and organization's capabilities. (9)

behaviorally anchored rating scales (BARS)—aspecific characteristics required for a position. Employees are rated against these characteristics by on-the-job behaviors in each area. (16)

bifurcated society—a society in which the gap between the "haves" and the "have nots" is wide; that is, there are many poor people, many wealthy people and a shrinking middle class. (1, 17)

blind self—that part of yourself that others can see but you do not know about yourself. (9)

block grant—a grant awarded by the federal government to the states, who in turn make subawards to state and local government entities. Also called a *formula grant*. (6)

blue flame—the symbol of a law enforcement officer who wants to make a difference in the world. (14)

body language—messages conveyed by gestures, facial expressions, stance and physical appearance. (3)

boiled frog phenomenon—based on a classic experiment, this concept suggests that managers must pay attention to changes in their environment and adapt—or perish. (17)

bona fide occupational qualification (BFOQ)—one that is reasonably necessary to perform a job. It may on the surface appear to be discrimination. (7)

bottom-line philosophy—allows shifting funds from one expense category to another as long as expenses do not exceed the total amount budgeted. (6)

brainstorming—a method of shared problem solving in which members of a group spontaneously contribute ideas, no matter how wild, without criticism or critique. (4)

budget—a list of probable expenses and income during a given period, most often one year. (6)

bullies—people who attack verbally or physically, using threats and demands to get their way. (13)

burnout—a condition that occurs when someone is exhausted or made listless through overwork. It results from long-term, unmediated stress. Symptoms include lack of enthusiasm and interest, a drop in job performance, temper flare-ups, a loss of will, motivation or commitment. (14)

by-the-numbers evaluation—objective evaluation that uses a numerical scale for each characteristic or dimension rated. (16)

capital budget—a budget that deals with "big ticket" items and is usually the responsibility of an agency's fiscal unit. (6)

certified public accountant (CPA)—an accountant licensed by a state to do public accounting work. (6)

chain of command—the order of authority. Begins at the top of the pyramid and flows down to the base. (1)

channels of communication—how messages are conveyed; usually follows the chain of command. (1, 3)

chief executive officer (CEO)—manager at the top of the hierarchy, usually the chief or sheriff. (2)

chronic stress—less severe than acute stress, but continuous. Also called *cumulative stress*. (14)

circadian system—the body's complex biological time-keeping system. (14)

Civil Rights Act of 1964—a law that prohibits discrimination based on race, color, religion, sex or national origin for private employers with 15 or more employees, governments, unions and employment agencies. (7)

civilian review boards—groups of citizens designated to investigate and dispose of complaints against the police. (12)

civilianization—the hiring of citizens to perform certain tasks for law enforcement agencies. (15)

closed shop—a work condition that prohibits management from hiring nonunion workers. (7)

coaching—one-on-one field training. (8)

collective bargaining—the process whereby representatives of employees meet with representatives of management to establish a written contract setting forth working conditions for a specific time, usually one to three years. (7)

command decision—a decision managers make on their own with little or no input from others. (4)

common costs—costs not directly traceable to a segment of an agency such as a department or division. They might include a municipality's insurance costs. (6)

communication—the complex process through which information is transferred from one person to another through common symbols. (3)

communication barriers—obstacles to clear, effective communication, including time, volume of information, tendency to say what we think others want to hear, failure to select the best word, prejudices and strained relationships, judging, superiority, certainty, controlling, manipulation and indifference. (3)

communication enhancers—techniques for reducing or eliminating barriers to communication, including properly encoding messages, selecting the best channel, describing, equality, openness, problem orientation, positive intent and empathy. (3)

communication process—involves a message, a sender, a channel and a receiver; it may also include feedback. (3)

community era—characterized by police authority coming from community support, law and professionalism; provision of a broad range of services, including crime control, decentralized organization with greater authority given to patrol officers; an intimate relationship with the community; the use of foot patrol and a problem-solving approach; 1980–present. (1)

community policing—decentralized model of policing in which individual officers exercise their own initiatives and citizens become actively involved in making their neighborhood safer. This proactive approach usually includes increased emphasis on foot patrol. (1)

complainant—a person or group filing a complaint. (12)

complainers—people who find fault with everything and everyone. (13)

complaint—a statement of a problem. (12)

comprehensive discipline—uses both positive and negative discipline to achieve individual and organizational goals. (11)

conceptual skills—problem-solving ability, planning ability and the ability to see the big picture and how all the pieces within it fit. (2)

cone of resolution—a way to analyze crime rates moving down to increasingly smaller scales of analysis. (15)

conflict—a mental or physical fight. (13)

confrontation technique—insisting that two disputing people or groups meet face-to-face to resolve their differences. (13)

consensus decision—a decision made democratically by a group; a joint decision often made by members of a committee. (4)

consideration structure—looks at the relationship between the group and the leaders. (2)

consultative decision—a decision that uses input and opinions from others, with the final decision still made by the manager in charge. (4)

consultative leadership—employees ideas and input are welcomed, but the manager makes the final decision. (2)

content validity—the direct relationship between tasks performed on the job, the curriculum or training and the test. (8)

contingency funds—monies allocated for unforeseen emergencies. (6)

contingency theory—Morse and Lorsch's motivational theory that suggests fitting tasks, officers and agency goals so that officers can feel competent. (10)

convergent thinking—focused, evaluative thinking. Includes decision making, choosing, testing, judging and rating. The opposite of divergent thinking. (4)

coordination—ensuring that all members of the department perform their assigned tasks and that, together, the department's mission is accomplished. (1)

counseling—one-on-one field training. (8)

Country Club Management—win friends and influence people; sees production as incidental to good relations; supervisors establish a pleasant work atmosphere and harmonious relations between people; very "other" directed; avoids conflict by conforming to the thinking of the boss or peers. (2)

creative procrastination—delaying decisions, allowing time for minor difficulties to work themselves out. (4, 5)

creative talents—applying individual talents and creativity. (2)

creativity—the process of breaking old connections and making new connections; innovation; originality. (4)

crime triangle—a model illustrating how three elements—motivated suspects, suitable victims and adequate locations—are required for crime to occur. (15)

critical incident—an extremely traumatic event such as a mass disaster or a brutally murdered child. (14)

critical incident stress debriefing (CISD)—officers who experience a critical incident such as a mass disaster or large accident with multiple deaths are brought together as a group for a psychological debriefing soon after the event. (14)

crunch—a major problem. (12)

cultural awareness—understanding the diversity of the United States, the dynamics of minority-majority relationships, the dynamics of sexism and racism and the issues of nationalism and separatism. (9)

cumulative stress—continuous, constant, debilitating stress. Also called *chronic stress*. (14)

cutback budgeting—providing the same or more services with less funding. Also called *budget reduction* or *reduced expenditure spending*. (6)

daily values—how people actually spend their time and energy. (9)

decentralization—refers to a department's organizational structure and operations; it is an operating principle that encourages flattening the organization and places decision-making authority and autonomy at the level where information is plentiful—usually the level of the patrol officer. (1)

decision-making process—a systematic approach to solving a problem, for example, force-field analysis, nominal group technique or the delphi method. (4)

decode—decipher a message. (3)

delaying tactics—stalling during negotiations. (7)

delegation—assigning tasks to others. (1, 2)

Delphi technique—a way to have individual input; uses open-ended questionnaires that individuals complete. Answers are shared, and the questionnaires are again completed until consensus is achieved. (4)

democratic leadership—does not mean every decision is made by a vote but rather that decisions are made only after discussion and input of employees. (2)

demonstration—modeling or showing how to do a task, for example, how to administer CPR. (8)

demotion—places an employee in a position of lower responsibility and pay. Often a part of progressive discipline. (11)

dependent—a stage of growth when someone is just learning a job and is very dependent on others—rookie stage. (9)

depreciation—the process of allocating the cost of a long-term asset to operations during its expected useful life. For example, squad cars will decrease in value as they are used. (6)

descriptive statistics—focus on simplifying, appraising and summarizing data and operate on the assumption that the data set is a consensus. (16)

desynchronization—a deviation from the night-sleep, day-wake pattern. (14)

developmental cells—a small unit within an agency where a change is first implemented. From within this unit leaders are selected to implement change within other units. (17)

direct expenses—operating expenses that can be identified specifically with individual departments. This includes things such as salaries and benefits. (6)

disciplinary actions—steps taken, verbally or in writing, to reprimand undesired behavior. Should be done in private. (11)

discipline—training expected to produce a desired, controlled behavior or administering punishment. Also a state of affairs or how employees act, in contrast to morale, which is how employees feel. (11)

discretionary budget—funds available to be used as needs arise. (6)

discretionary grant—awarded based on the judgment of the awarding agency. (6)

discussion—interchange of ideas. (8)

disequilibrium—out of physiological balance. (14)

dismissal—termination of employment. Usually the final step in progressive discipline. (11)

distress—negative stress. (14)

diurnal—day-oriented. Humans are by nature diurnal in their activities. (14)

divergent thinking—free, uninhibited thinking. Includes imagining, fantasizing, free associating, and combining and juxtaposing dissimilar elements. Opposite of convergent thinking. (4)

dog shift/watch—late night, early morning shift, typically from midnight to 0800 hours. (15)

downward communication—messages from managers and supervisors to subordinates. (3)

driving forces—forces that foster goal achievement. (4)

educating—generally refers to academic instruction that takes place in a college, university or seminar-type setting and deals with knowledge and mental skills. (8)

employee assistance program (EAP)—may be internally staffed or use outside referrals to offer help with stress, marital or chemical-dependency problems. (14)

empowered—given legal authority to act on one's own discretion. (1)

encode—place a message into a form to be transmitted. (3)

environmental scanning—identifying the factors likely to "drive" the environment, influencing the future. Includes social and economic conditions. (17)

environmental/instructional variables—refers to the *context* in which learning or training takes place, including physical setting, amount of practice, knowledge of results and incentives. (8)

Equal Employment Opportunity Commission (EEOC)—enforces laws prohibiting job discrimination based on race, color, religion, sex, national origin, handicapping condition or age between 40 and 70. (7)

equilibrium—the problem in force-field analysis—the equilibrium is not where you want it to be. (4)

ethical behavior—that which is "moral" and "right." (9)

ethics—standards of fair and honest conduct. (9)

eustress—helpful stress, stress necessary to function and accomplish goals. (14)

evaluate—to determine the worth of, to find the amount or value of or to appraise. (16)

evaluation—determining the worth of, finding the amount or value of, appraising. May be formal or informal. (16)

executive manager—top management, usually the chief or sheriff. (2)

exonerated—a complaint or grievance in which the investigation determines that the matter did occur but was proper and legal. (12)

expectancy theory—Vroom's motivational theory that employees will choose the level of effort that matches the performance opportunity for reward. (10)

expenses—the cost of providing services. (6)

exploders—people who yell and scream. (13)

external communication—messages sent from within an agency to citizens or other organizations or vice versa. (3)

external complaints—statements of a problem made by a person or group outside the law enforcement organization. (12)

external motivators—see *tangible rewards.* (10)

external stress—tension produced by real threats and dangers, for example, being shot at. (14)

face time—time spent in an agency or a department long after a shift ends and on weekends when not on duty to make sure you are seen putting in extra time by those with the power to promote you. (5)

facilitators—people who assist others in performing their duties to meet mutual goals and objectives. (2)

factual questions—questions that test students' grasp of the concepts presented, for example, "What are the elements of second-degree murder?" (8)

Fair Labor Standards Act of 1938—a law that established the 40-hour week as the basis of compensation and set a minimum wage. (7)

feedback—the process by which the sender knows the receiver has or has not understood the message. (3)

field services—services that directly help accomplish the goals of a department using line personnel. Main division is uniformed patrol. Also includes investigations, narcotics, vice, juvenile and the like. (1)

field training—learning that occurs on the job, usually under the direction of a field training officer (FTO). (8)

field training officer (FTO)—an experienced officer who serves as a mentor for a rookie, providing on-the-job training. (8)

financial accounting—the accumulation of data about an agency's financial transactions and reporting this data to managers and other interested parties. (6)

financial budget—see *budget.* (6)

financial statements—periodic reports that summarize the financial affairs of an agency. (6)

first-line managers—those who supervise the officers actually doing the work—the line staff. Usually called supervisors; usually are sergeants. (2)

fiscal year—the 12-month accounting period used by an agency. A calendar year runs from January 1 through December 31. This may or may not be the same as an agency's fiscal year. (6)

fixed costs—expenses that do not vary in total during a period even though the amount of service provided may be more or less than anticipated, for example, rent and insurance. (6)

flat organization—an organization that has reduced the levels of authority in the organizational hierarchy. (1)

flexible budget—a projection that contains budgeted amounts at various levels of service. (6)

focus groups—groups of people, usually eight to ten, directed by a moderator, who sit around a table and express their opinions about certain products, concepts or companies. (4)

focused on task—keeping meetings or other activities focused on results. (2)

force-field analysis—analysis method that identifies forces that impede and enhance goal attainment. A problem exists when the equilibrium is unbalanced with more forces impeding goal attainment than enhancing it. (4)

formal evaluation—a structured, systematic appraisal of performance. (16)

formal organization—how a group of people is structured on paper, often in the form of an organizational chart. (1)

formula grant—a grant awarded by the federal government to the states, who in turn make awards to state and local government entities. Also called a *block grant*. (6)

Four-System Approach—management system (Likert's) that divides managerial approaches into four different systems going from System 1, a traditional, authoritarian style, to System 4, a participative management style. (2)

free-rein leadership—leaderless, laissez-faire management. (2)

future focused—seeing change as an opportunity for growth. (2)

futuristics—the science of using data from the past to forecast alternatives for the future and to then select those most desirable. (17)

Garrity protection—the employer must guarantee that information sought from an officer during an internal affairs investigation will not be used against the officer in a criminal proceeding. (12)

gender barrier—differences between men and women that can result in miscommunication. (3)

generalists—officers who perform most functions, including patrol, investigation, juvenile, vice and so on. (1)

generally accepted accounting principles (GAAPS)—the rules of accounting used by agencies in reporting their financial activities. (6)

GIGO—computer acronym for "garbage in, garbage out." (4)

goals—broad, general, desired outcomes. Visionary, projected achievements. What business calls *key result areas.* (1)

grapevine—informal channel of communication within an agency or department. Also called the *rumor mill.* (3)

grievance—a formally registered complaint. A claim by an employee that a rule or policy has been misapplied or misinterpreted to the employee's detriment. (12)

grievant—the person or group filing a grievance. (12)

groupthink—the negative tendency for members of a group to submit to peer pressure and endorse the majority opinion even if individually it is unacceptable. (4)

guiding philosophy—the organization's mission statement *and* the basic values to be honored by the organization. (1)

gunny sack approach—occurs when managers or supervisors accumulate negative behaviors of a subordinate and then dump them all on the employee at the same time rather than correcting them as they occur.(11)

halo effect—tendency to rate one who performs above average in one area above average in all areas or vice versa. (7, 16)

hands-on learning—learning by doing. (8)

healthy conflict—challenges the status quo and offers constructive alternatives. (13)

hidden self—that which is secret and which you do not share with others. (9)

hierarchy—a group of people organized or classified by rank and authority. In law enforcement, typically pyramid shaped with a single "authority" at the top expanding down and out through the ranks to the broad base of "workers." (1)

hierarchy of needs—Maslow's motivational theory that people have certain needs that must be met in a specific order going from basic physiological needs to safety and security, social, esteem and self-actualization needs. (10)

high communication—creating a climate of trust and open, honest communication. (2)

highlighting—using a special pen to graphically mark important written information. Should be done *after* the initial reading of the information. (5)

holistic management—views personnel as total individuals who make up their team. (2)

holistic personal goals—includes all aspects of a person's life: career/job, financial, personal, family/relationships, spiritual/service. (9)

homeostasis—the process that keeps all the bodily functions in physiological balance. (14)

horizontal (lateral) communication—messages sent between managers or supervisors on the same level of the hierarchy and between subordinates on the same level. (3)

horn effect—allowing one negative trait to influence the rater negatively on other traits as well. (16)

hot spots—specific locations with high crime rates. (15)

hygiene factors—tangible rewards that can cause dissatisfaction if lacking. (10)

Impoverished Management—don't rock the boat; avoids problems or defers them to others; does not get involved in conflict. (2)

incentive programs—programs designed to motivate. (10)

incivilities—signs of disorder. (15)

independent—a stage of growth where employees can perform a job on their own. (9)

indirect expenses—costs that cannot be easily assigned to a particular department when transactions occur and are recorded. Some indirect expenses, such as depreciation, have a meaningful relationship to individual departments and can be allocated based on this relationship. Other indirect expenses must be allocated on the most logical basis possible. (6)

individual variables—learner characteristics such as age, sex, maturation, readiness, innate ability, level of motivation, personality and personal objectives. (8)

inferential statistics—focus on making statistically educated guesses from a sample. (16)

i**nformal evaluation**—a nonstructured, ongoing appraisal of performance. (16)

informal organization—groups that operate without official sanction but influence department performance. (1)

information variables—relates to *what* is to be learned: knowledge, skills or attitudes. Also called *task variables.* (8)

initiating structure—looks at how leaders assign tasks. (2)

innovation—a new idea or way of doing things. (4)

in-service training—in-house training. (8)

intangible rewards—internal motivators such as goals, achievement, recognition, self-respect, opportunity for advancement or to make a contribution, belief in individual and department goals. (10)

integrity—steadfast adherence to an ethical code. (9)

intelligence—ability. (4)

interactors—those who communicate with other groups and agencies: the press, other local government departments, the business community, schools and numerous community committees and organizations. (2)

interdependent—a stage of growth in which people cooperate, care for, assist and support the team effort. (9)

interfacers—those who coordinate law enforcement agency's goals with those of other agencies within the jurisdiction. (2)

internal communication—messages within an agency or department, whether downward, upward or lateral. (3)

internal complaints—statements of a problem made by an individual or group within the law enforcement agency. (12)

internal motivators—see *intangible rewards.* (10)

intersubjectivity—people's mutual understanding of and respect for each other's viewpoints, a kind of reciprocal empathy. (13)

intersubjectivity approach—uses 3" × 5" cards as a means to get people in conflict to share their most important ideas about a problem and to come to a mutual understanding of and respect for each other's viewpoints. (13)

interval reinforcement—presenting information several times, with breaks between the repetition. (8)

intuition—insight; knowing without using any rational thought process. (4)

jargon—nonsense or meaningless language, often called *legalese,* for example, party of the first part, hereafter referred to as. . . . Also specialized language of a field, for example, *perpetrator.* (3)

job description—detailed, formally stated summary of duties and responsibilities for a position. (9)

job enlargement—assigning additional responsibilities to an existing job. (10)

job enrichment—similar to job enlargement except that in job enrichment the focus is on the quality of the new jobs assigned rather than on the quantity. Emphasizes adding variety, deeper personal interest and involvement, increased responsibility and greater autonomy. Appropriate for any highly routine job. (10)

job rotation—changing the job assignment or shift. (10)

Johari window—a model to illustrate how people can learn more about others and themselves. (9)

just cause—a reasonable, fair, honest reason. (11)

key result areas—the goals of an organization. (1, 9)

killer phrases—judgmental, critical statements that serve as put-downs and stifle others' creativity. (4)

KISS principle—axiom in communication: "Keep it short and simple." (3)

know-it-alls—people who are highly opinionated, speak with great authority, have all the right answers (or think they do) and are impatient with others. (13)

lag time—elapsed time between the occurrence of an incident and its being reported to the police. Often more important than response time. (15)

laissez-faire leadership—involves nonintervention; let everything run itself without direction from the leader; the leader exerts little or no control. (2)

Landrum-Griffin Act of 1959—an act that required regularly scheduled elections of union officers by secret ballot and regulated the handling of union funds. (7)

lateral (horizontal) communication—messages sent between managers or supervisors on the same level of the hierarchy and between subordinates on the same level. (3)

leader—one who influences others by example, guides people, motivates, instills courage and the like. (2)

leadership—influencing, working with and through individuals and groups to accomplish a common goal. (2)

learning curve principle—if you do a group of similar tasks together, you can reduce the amount of time it takes to do them all, sometimes by as much as 80 percent. (5)

lecture—oral presentation of information to a group of learners. (8)

left-brain thinking—thinking that primarily uses language and logic. (4)

line items—specific expense categories, for example, personnel, maintenance, training. (6)

line personnel—those who actually perform most of the tasks outlined in the work plan. (1)

line-item budgeting—budget method that identifies specific categories (line items) and dollars allocated for each. Line-item budgets are usually based on the preceding year's budget and anticipated changes in the upcoming year. (6)

lines of communication—similar to channels of communication. May be downward, upward (vertical) or lateral (horizontal); internal or external. (3)

majority world view—beliefs held by those in the majority. (9)

manage—to control and direct, to administer, to take charge of. (2)

management—the process of combining resources to accomplish organizational goals. (2)

management by objectives (MBO)—management method that involves managers and subordinates setting goals and objectives together and then tracking performance to ensure that the objectives are met. Term first used by Peter Drucker. (2)

management information systems (MIS)—software programs that organize data to assist in decision making. (4, 15)

managerial accounting—an internal reporting system that gives management financial information for use in decision making and long-range planning. (6)

Managerial/Leadership Grid—a management theory (Blake-Mouton's) describing five styles: Task Management, Country-Club Management, Impoverished Management, Middle-of-the-Road Management and Team Management. The "ideal" management style is an integration of high concern for both people and production, resulting in an energetic team approach. (2)

managers—those who control and direct, administer, take charge of. Those who accomplish things through others,

blending resources—human, material and financial—to accomplish organizational goals. (2)

marginal performer—employee who has demonstrated ability to perform but who does just enough to get by. (13)

master budget—a projection that includes both a detailed operating budget and a detailed financial budget. (6)

Mature Employee Theory—management theory by Argyris that views employees and their organization as interdependent. (2)

mediation—bringing in a neutral third party to assist in negotiations. (7, 12)

mental locks—thinking patterns that prevent innovative thinking. Also called *thinking traps*. (4)

mentor—a wise, trusted teacher or counselor. (9)

middle management—those in the middle of the hierarchy, usually lieutenants and captains. (2)

Middle-of-the-Road Management—firm but fair, seeks a balance between high production and sound relations in conflict; supervisors stay neutral and carry out established procedures; samples opinions, manipulates participation, compromises and then sells final solution; deals with surface tensions and symptoms only. (2)

minority world view—beliefs held by those in the minority. (9)

mission—the reason an organization exists. (1)

mission statement—a written explanation of the reason an organization exists. (1)

modified Delphi technique—adapts the Delphi technique by using objective rather than open-ended questions. (4)

morale—a person's or group's state of mind, level of enthusiasm and involvement with work and with life. How employees feel; in contrast to discipline, how employees act. (10)

motivation—an inner or outer drive or impetus to do something or to act in a specified manner. An inner or outer drive to meet a need or goal. (10)

motivator factors—intangible rewards that can cause satisfaction. (10)

narrow eye span—occurs when a reader focuses on one word at a time rather than taking in groups of words or phrases in one look. (5)

National Labor Relations Act of 1935 (Wagner Act)—an act that legalized collective bargaining and required employers to bargain with the elected representatives of their employees. (7)

National Labor Relations Board (NLRB)—the principal enforcement agency for laws regulating relations between management and unions. (7)

negative conflict—destructive disagreements. (13)

negative discipline—punishment or reprimand in an effort to compel expected behavior. (11)

negative reinforcement—punishment following an undesired behavior that tends to decrease the behavior. (10)

negligent hiring—failure to use an adequate selection process resulting in hiring personnel unqualified or unsuited for law enforcement work. Often includes failure to check for prior offenses of misconduct. (7)

negligent retention—failing to terminate an employee when justified. (11)

news media echo effect—occurs when a highly publicized criminal case results in a shift in processing for similarly charged but nonpublicized cases. (3)

nominal group technique—an objective way to achieve consensus on the most effective alternatives by using an objective ranking of alternatives. (4)

nonactor liability—liability that results from this situation: any officer present at a scene where use of force is in question and is obviously excessive and the nonactor officer did nothing to prevent it; that officer is also held liable by the courts. (13)

nonverbal communication—messages conveyed by body language as well as tone of voice. (3)

norms—the attitudes and beliefs held by a group of individuals. (9)

Norris-La Guardia Act of 1932—an act that regulated court injunctions against unions and made yellow-dog contracts illegal. (7)

not sustained—a complaint or grievance in which the investigative facts are insufficient, that is, the evidence does not support the accusations. (12)

objectives—specific, measurable ways to accomplish goals. They are more specific than goals and usually have a timeline. (1)

one minute managing—Blanchard's approach to giving one-minute praises and reprimands. (11)

on-the-job training (OJT)—occurs during field training, in-house training sessions and roll call. (8)

open discussion—issues are debated and resolved in a win-win situation. (7)

open self—what you know about yourself and what you show to others. (9)

operating budget—a budget that contains projections for income statement items as well as expenses. (6)

operating expenses—costs that arise from the normal activities of an agency. (6)

operational decision—first-line supervisor-level decision. (4)

operational stress—the total effect of the need to confront daily the tragedies of urban life; the need to deal with thieves, derelicts and the mentally deranged; being lied to and so on. (14)

opinion-based questions—questions asked to get students to share their personal feelings about topics presented. There are no right or wrong answers, for example, "What type of weapon would you prefer to carry?" (8)

organization—an artificial structure created to coordinate people or groups and resources to achieve a mission or goal. (1)

organizational chart—visually depicts how personnel are organized within the department. Might also depict how the department "fits" into the community's political structure. (1)

organizational stress—tension produced by elements inherent in the paramilitary character of law enforcement agencies, constant adjustment to changing schedules, working at odd hours, requirements that detailed rules and procedures be complied with. (14)

other expenses—costs not directly connected with providing services. (6)

overhead—operating expenses of a department or agency exclusive of personnel. (6)

paradigm—a model, theory or frame of reference; the way the world is viewed. (1)

paradigm shift—a dramatic change in how something is viewed, for example, the shift from an authoritative to a participative style of management. (1)

Pareto principle—20 percent of what a person does accounts for 80 percent of the results. (5)

Parkinson's law—the principle that work expands to fill the time available for its completion. (5)

participative leadership—managers build a team and view themselves as a part of this team. (2)

participatory decision making (PDM)—employees have a say in the decision-making process. (4)

passives—silent, unresponsive people who seldom offer their own ideas or opinions. (13)

people skills—being able to communicate clearly, to motivate, to discipline appropriately and to inspire those within the organization for whom one is directly responsible. (2)

perception—how one views or interprets things. (10)

performance appraisal—formal evaluation of on-the-job functioning; usually conducted annually. (16)

performance budgeting—allocates dollars based on productivity. Budget defines the agency's objectives for the year, the specific activities or programs needed to achieve those objectives and the cost. Also called *planning-programming-budgeting system* or *ppbs.* (6)

performance interviews—private, one-on-one discussions of the performance appraisal by manager and subordinate. (16)

perks—tangible rewards. (10)

perp walk—when suspects are paraded before the news media. (3)

personal stress—tension generated by an officer's racial or gender status among peers. (14)

pessimists—people who always say "no" and see "gloom and doom" in every situation. (13)

petty cash fund—a cash fund of a limited amount used to make small purchases for which it is not practical to write checks. (6)

pinch—a minor problem. (12)

Pinch Model—illustrates the importance of communication in dealing with complaints and the consequences of not communicating effectively. A *pinch,* a minor problem, can turn into a *crunch,* a major problem. (12)

police culture—often described as isolationist, elitist and authoritarian. (9)

police logs—record of requests for services, time, nature of the request and time the incident was completed. (15)

political era—characterized by police authority coming from politicians and the law, a broad social service function, decentralized organization, an intimate relationship with the community and extensive use of foot patrol; 1840–1930. (1)

positive conflict—see *healthy conflict.* (13)

positive discipline—uses training to foster compliance with rules and regulations and performance at peak efficiency. (11)

positive reinforcement—rewards following a desired behavior, which tend to increase that behavior. (10)

posteriorities—tasks that do *not* have to be done, have a minimal payoff and have very limited negative consequences. (5)

post-traumatic stress disorder (PTSD)—a psychological ailment following a major catastrophe such as a shooting or dealing with victims of a natural disaster. Symptoms include diminished responsiveness to the environment, apathy, pessimism and sleep disturbances, including recurrent nightmares. (14)

power—the ability to get things done with or without the legal right. Uses persuasion. (2)

preevaluation—a procedure to allow those being evaluated to have input by completing a form outlining their accomplishments. (16)

prerequisites—necessary background needed to master a given skill. (8)

PRICE method—Blanchard's five-step approach to employee performance problems: *Pinpoint, Record, Involve, Coach* and *Evaluate.* (11)

principled negotiations—pays attention to basic interests and mutually satisfying options. Avoids positional bargaining, which tends to produce rushed agreements that can lead to damaged relationships. (13)

priorities—tasks that must be done, have a big payoff and avoid negative consequences. (5)

privatization—either contracting out or working collaboratively with private security agencies, other governmental agencies and any other individuals or organizations that can help a police department fulfill its mission. (17)

proactive—recognizing problems and seeking their underlying causes, in contrast to being reactive—responding to problems after they have occurred. (1)

problem employee—an employee who exhibits abnormal behavior to the extent that the behavior is detrimental to organizational needs and goals as well as the needs and goals of other law enforcement agency personnel. (13)

problem-oriented policing (POP)—management ascertains what problems exist and tries to solve them, redefining the role of law enforcement from incident-driven and reactive to problem-oriented and proactive. Also called *problem-solving policing.* (4)

problem-solving policing—see *problem-oriented policing.* (1)

procrastination—putting things off. (5)

productivity—converting resources to results in the most efficient and effective way possible. In law enforcement, productivity is achieved through people. Measured by what types of services are provided and how well. (15)

professional model—the reform era style of policing advocated by O.W. Wilson in reaction to the corruption in the political era; the professional model emphasized preventive automobile patrol and rapid response to calls. (1)

program budgeting—see *performance budgeting*. (6)

progressive discipline—uses disciplinary steps based on the severity and frequency of the offense. Steps usually are oral reprimand, written reprimand, suspension/demotion and dismissal. (11)

promotability/assignment factors—an attempt to make evaluation "count for something." (16)

proportionate assignment—area assignments are determined by requests for services, based on available data. (15)

psychological hardiness—the ability to successfully cope with stress. (14)

Pygmalion effect—what managers expect of their subordinates and how they treat them largely determine their performance and career progress; a type of self-fulfilling prophecy. (10)

pyramid of authority—the shape of the typical law enforcement hierarchy, with the chief at the peak and having full authority down through managers (captains and lieutenants) and supervisors (sergeants) to those who accomplish most of the tasks (officers). (1)

Q & A—question-and-answer method of teaching. (8)

quality circle—a group of five to ten employees who volunteer to meet to solve problems in their workplace. (15)

quota—a specific number or proportional share that each officer is expected to contribute or receive. (15)

racial profiling—the practice of using certain racial characteristics as indicators of criminal activity. (9)

random patrol—officers on patrol are unsystematically (randomly) assigned areas to cover. (15)

rapid response—identifying and acting on opportunities swiftly. (2)

rapport—a comfortable relationship, a feeling of mutual understanding and trust. (7)

reactive—responding to incidents after they have occurred, in contrast to being proactive—seeking causes to problems and how to prevent them—an emphasis of community policing. (1)

reform era—characterized by police authority coming from the law and professionalism, crime control as the primary function, a centralized and efficient organization, a professional remoteness from the community and an emphasis on preventive motorized patrol and rapid response to crime (1930–1980). (1)

regression—tendency to look back over previously read material. (5)

reinforcement theory—B. F. Skinner's motivational theory that behavior can be modified by using positive and negative reinforcement. (10)

reprimand—formal criticism of behavior. May be oral or written. (11)

responsibility—being answerable, liable, accountable for. (1)

responsibility accounting—an accounting system designed to evaluate the performance of the various segments of a business, such as departments, and to assign responsibility for financial results. (6)

restraining forces—forces that impede goal achievement. (4)

reverse discrimination—giving preferential treatment to women and minorities, to the detriment of white males in hiring and promoting. (7)

rhetorical questions—questions to which an answer is not expected. The purpose is to get the listener to think about a topic. (8)

right-brain thinking—primarily using images and emotions. (4)

right-to-work laws—laws that make it illegal to require employees to join a union. Established by the Taft-Hartley Act of 1938. (7)

role playing—a learning method that casts individuals into specific parts to be acted out. (8)

roll call—brief period before each shift when officers check in and receive their briefing before going on duty. (2, 8)

rote learning—memorization, not necessarily with understanding. (8)

rumor mill—informal channels of communication within a department or an agency. Also called the *grapevine*. (3)

scanning—reading material rapidly for specific information. (5)

scuttlebutt—one employee complaining to another, uninvolved employee who cannot remedy the situation about an adverse action taken by upper management. (1)

seagull management—when a manager hears something is wrong, flies in, makes a lot of noise, dumps on everyone and flies away. (2)

self-actualization—refers to achievement, to meeting individual goals and fulfilling one's potential. It is fostered by the chance to be innovative and to maximize one's skills and knowledge. (10)

self-discipline—self-imposed rules for self-control. (11)

self-fulfilling prophecy—the theory that people live up to expectations. If people believe they can do a job, they usually can. If people believe they cannot do a job, they usually cannot. (10)

self-motivation—acting from personal choice. (10)

semivariable costs—expenses that have characteristics of both fixed costs and variable costs, for example, utility expense is a semivariable cost. (6)

shared responsibility—a work culture in which all team members feel as responsible as the manager for accomplishing the team's goals and objectives. (2, 9)

shift—time span to which personnel are assigned. Most agencies have three eight-hour shifts. Some agencies call this time span a *watch*. (15)

simulation—an imitation of a process. (8)

single handling—not picking up a piece of paper until you are ready to do something with it. Applies particularly to the daily stack of mail. (5)

situational leadership—leadership viewed as an interplay between the amount of direction (task behavior) a leader gives, the amount of relationship behavior a leader provides *and* the maturity level that followers exhibit on a specific task the leader is attempting to accomplish through the individual or group (Hersey and Blanchard). (2)

skimming—reading information rapidly for the main ideas, usually the first and last paragraphs, the first sentence of all other paragraphs and the captions of any charts or figures. (5)

SMART goals and objectives—objectives that are specific, measurable, attainable, relevant and trackable. (2)

snap decisions—deciding rapidly, making decisions on the spot. (4)

snipers—people who do not attack openly but engage in subtle digs, cheap shots and innuendos. (13)

span of control—the number of people an individual manages or supervises. (1)

special employment groups—groups included in affirmative action programs such as African-Americans, Asians, Eskimos, Hispanics, homosexuals, immigrants, individuals with AIDS, individuals with disabilities, Middle Easterners, Native Americans, religious group members, substance abusers, Vietnam veterans, whites ("reverse discrimination"), women, young and aging individuals. (7)

specialists—those who work in a specific area: investigators, juvenile officers, SWAT officers and so on. (1)

spoils system—members of the prevailing political party were rewarded with immunity from arrest, sought-after appointments and other special privileges; the motto was "to the victor go the spoils." (1)

staff personnel—those who support line personnel. (1)

stakeholders—those affected by an organization and those in a position to affect it. (1)

standard English—language that follows the grammatical rules of American English. (3)

standards—targets to be met, including level of performance. (16)

strategic decision—executive-level decision involving long-range plans. (4)

strategic planning—long-term planning. (2)

stress—tension, anxiety or worry. Can be positive (*eustress*) or negative (*distress*). (14)

stroke approach—using positive "strokes" rather than negative, crooked or plastic strokes. (11)

subconscious self—that part of you neither you nor others have yet discovered. Also called *undiscovered self*. (9)

subvocalization—the contraction of the tongue and other speech-related organs made during learning to pronounce each letter of the alphabet. Becomes ingrained and can slow readers down. (5)

summary discipline—discretionary authority used when a supervisor feels an officer is not fit for duty or for any reason the supervisor feels a need for immediate action. Also called *summary punishment*. (11)

summary punishment—see *summary discipline*. (11)

sunk cost—a historical cost that has already been incurred and is thus irrelevant for decision-making purposes, for example, the purchase of a K-9. Other costs associated with the dog, however, will continue. (6)

supernorms—overriding expectations of a given work group, for example, do not volunteer or do not criticize. (9)

supervision—overseeing the actual work being done. (2)

supervisors—first-line managers. Usually sergeants. (2)

suspension—being barred from a position for a period of time. May be with or without pay. Often part of progressive discipline. (11)

sustained—complaint or grievance in which the investigative facts support the charge. (12)

synergism—condition that occurs when the whole is greater than the sum of its parts; the team achieves more than each could accomplish as individuals. (2, 9)

tactical planning—short-term planning. (2)

Taft-Hartley Act of 1947—an act that balanced the power of unions and management by prohibiting several unfair labor practices, including closed shops, which prohibited management from hiring nonunion workers. (7)

tangible rewards—external motivators such as salary, bonuses, insurance, retirement plans, favorable working conditions, paid vacation and holidays, titles and adequacy of equipment. (10)

Task Management—produce or perish; sees good relationships as incidental to high production; supervisors achieve production goals by planning, directing and controlling all work; "inner" directed, depending on own skills, knowledge, attitudes and beliefs; takes a win-lose approach to conflict, seeking to win its own points. (2)

task variables—relates to *what* is to be learned: knowledge, skills or attitudes. Also called *information variables*. (8)

team—two or more people who must coordinate their activities to accomplish a common task. (2)

Team Management—people support what they create; sees production resulting from integrating task and human requirements; good relationships and high production are both attainable; supervisors attain effective production through participation and involvement of people and their ideas; seeks emergent solutions as the result of debate, deliberation and experimentation; confronts conflict directly, communicating feelings and facts as a basis to work through conflict. (2)

technical skills—all the procedures needed to be a good law enforcement officer, including interviewing and interrogating, searching, arresting, gathering evidence and so on. (2)

technophobia—the fear of using technology because of unfamiliarity or uncertainty as to how it actually works. (15)

termination—being fired from employment. Usually the final step in progressive discipline. (11)

Theory X—management theory (McGregor's) that assumes workers are dull and lazy and need control by coercion, threats and punishment. They want secure jobs above all else. (2)

Theory Y—management theory (McGregor's) that assumes workers are willing workers who can be trusted to do a good job and should share in decision making. (2)

thinking traps—habits people fall into without recognizing what they are doing, including either/or thinking, deciding too quickly, deciding based on personality rather than facts, being a victim of personal habits and prejudices and being unimaginative. Also called *mental locks*. (4)

tickler file system—a set of file folders, organized by year, month and day, into which lists of tasks to be accomplished are placed. (5)

time abusers—activities or tasks that waste time, for example, socializing, drop-in visitors and telephone tag. (5)

time log—a detailed list of how time is spent each day, usually broken into 10- to 15-minute segments. (5)

time management—dividing and organizing time so as to accomplish the most tasks in the most efficient way. (5)

tone—emotional effect of language, for example, an angry tone of voice. (3)

Total Quality Management (TQM)—a management process and set of disciplines that are coordinated to ensure that the organization consistently meets and exceeds customer requirements pioneered by W. Edwards Deming. (2)

touchstone values—what people say is important to them. (9)

training—instruction that often takes place on the job and deals with physical skills. (8)

trait theorists—those who researched special characteristics leaders possess. (2)

traits—personal characteristics. (2)

transformational leadership—treats employees as the organization's most valuable assets. Employee-centered and focuses on empowerment. (2)

traumatic stress—severe, extremely intense distress that lasts a limited time and then the person returns to normal. Also called *acute stress*. (14)

two-factor theory—Herzberg's motivational theory that employees' needs can be classified as hygiene factors and motivator factors. Hygiene factors are tangible rewards that cause dissatisfaction if lacking; motivator factors are intangible rewards that can cause satisfaction. (10)

two-way communication—information is freely exchanged, with feedback occurring during the process. (3)

type A personality—describes people who are aggressive, hyperactive, "drivers" who tend to be "workaholics." (14)

type B personality—describes people who are more laid back, relaxed and passive. (14)

undiscovered self—that part of you neither you nor others have yet discovered. Also called *subconscious self.* (9)

unfounded—complaint or grievance in which either the act did not occur or the complaint/grievance was false. (12)

union—any group authorized to represent the members of an agency in negotiating matters such as wages, fringe benefits and other conditions of employment. (7)

union shop—must belong to or join the union to be hired. (7)

unity of command—every individual in the organization has only one immediate superior or supervisor. (1)

upward (vertical) communication—messages conveyed from subordinates to supervisors and managers or from supervisors to managers. (3)

values—beliefs, principles or standards considered worthwhile or desirable. (1)

variable costs—expenses that vary in total directly with the amount of service provided. For example, personnel costs including overtime. (6)

variance analysis—comparing actual costs against what was budgeted and examining the differences. (6)

verbal channels of communication—one-on-one conversations, phone conversations, radio dispatch, interviews, meetings, news conferences and speeches. (3)

vertical (upward) communication—messages conveyed from subordinates to supervisors and managers or from supervisors to managers. (3)

vicarious liability—the legal responsibility one person has for the acts of another. Managers, the entire agency and even the jurisdiction served may be legally responsible for the actions of a single officer. (7)

videoconferencing—simultaneous, two-way, interactive audio and video communication. (8)

Wagner Act—see *National Labor Relations Act of 1935.* (7)

Wallenda effect—the negative consequences of fear of failure. (2)

watch—see *shift.* (15)

whole-brain thinking—using both the logical left side and the emotional right side of the brain together for best results. (4)

Wolf Pack syndrome—a vestige of primitive male hunting groups within which no weaknesses were tolerated. Deficiencies were attacked by other members of the group. (1)

work plans—the precise activities that contribute to accomplishing objectives. Detailed steps or tasks to be accomplished. (1)

workplace culture—the sum of the beliefs and values that are held in common by those within the organization and that formally and informally communicate what is expected. (9)

written communication—notes, memos, letters, reports, manuals, bulletins, policies and so on. (3)

yellow-dog contract—made union membership illegal under the penalty of discharge. (7)

yes people—super-agreeable people who are vocally supportive in your presence but rarely follow through. (13)

zeitgebers—outside influences to help one keep track of time. (14)

zero-based budgeting (ZBB)—begins with a "clean slate," justifying each expenditure anew. All budget lines begin at zero base and are funded according to merit rather than the preceding year's funding level. (6)

Author Index

Subject Index

posteriorities, 154
post-traumatic stress disorder (PTSD),
    446–447, 459
power, 31–33
praise, 378
predisaster plan, 491
preevaluation, 522, 524
Pregnancy Discrimination Act of 1978, 221
prerequisites, 247
press release policy, 97
prevention, 480–481
preventive patrol, 5, 6
PRICE Method, 377–378
pride, developing, 341
principled negotiations, 428–429
principles of learning, 246–249
printed information, 254–255
priorities, 142, 145, 154–155, 157
Private Sector Liaison Committee (PSLC), 550
privatization, 549–550
proactive, 246
problem behavior (*See also* discipline), 355–382
problem employees, 365–366, 415, 416–419
problem-oriented policing (POP), 23–25, 131–133
problems, 52–53, 107–135
    brainstorming, 128–129
    common mistakes, 130
    creativity, 112–115
    delegating, 116
    Delphi technique, 126–128
    focus groups, 133
    force-field analysis (FFA), 124–125
    indicators, 52–53
    innovation, 112–115
    intuition, 115–116
    management, 52–53
    methods for solving, 115–117
    nominal group technique, 125–126
    not deciding, 116
    SARA process, 131–132
    snap decisions, 116
    solving, 107–135
    systematic approaches to solving, 118–128
    whole-brain research, 110–111
problem-solving policing, 23–25
procrastination, 116, 152–154
    creative, 116, 154
productivity, 164–166, 465–467, 498–509
    defined, 498
    discipline, 506–509
    face time, 164–165
    improving, 501–504
    leadership, 506–507
    measuring, 498–500
    morale, 506–507
    motivation, 506–507
    performance standards, 500

physiology of, 164–165
    problems, 500–501
    quality circles approach, 504–505
    quotas, 500
    technology, 502–504
    work teams, 506
professional model, 5
profiling, 295–297
program budgeting, 178
progressive discipline, 366–370
promises, 340
promotability/assignment factors, 522
promotions, 220, 344–346
proportionate assignment, 475
proposals, writing grant, 193–195
psychological hardiness, 460
psychological support, 457
psychological tests, 209–210, 224
public, 104, 551–552
    relations, 104
Public Safety Officers' Benefits (PSOB), 444
Public Safety Officers' Educational Assistance
    (PSOEA) Program, 445
punishment (*See also* negative discipline), 364–373
    summary, 370
Pygmalion effect, 327
pyramid of authority, 3, 4, 21
Pyramid of Success, 241

Q
Q & A, 251
qualified individual with a disability (QID), 222
quality circles, 504–505
Quartermaster system, 186
question/answer sessions, 251
questions, types of, 251
quid pro quo sexual harassment, 363
quotas, 500

R
racial harassment, 413
racial profiling, 295–297
raises, 326
random patrol, 480–482
Rangers, Texas, 2
rapid response, 5, 6, 69
rapport, 212
rating by individual traits, 526
rating forms, 521–524
rational organization, 13–16
reactions to stress, 449–450
reactive, 24
reading, 162, 163
receiver of message, 83
recognition, 328, 342
recommended basic training curriculum, 260

Photo Credits

Page 24: Associated Press, AP; **45:** Michael G. Bennett/Imagemakers International, Inc.; **70:** © Joel Gordon; **85:** James L. Schaffer; **99:** Associated Press, AP; **119:** ©Michael Newman/Photoedit; **132:** Associated Press, AP; **149:** Michael G. Bennett/Imagemakers International, Inc.; **161:** Associated Press, AP; **164:** Michael G. Bennett/Imagemakers International, Inc.; **176:** James L. Schaffer; **180:** Michael G. Bennett/Imagemakers International, Inc.; **187:** Associated Press, AP; **189:** ©David Eyestone/Minnesota Sun Visuals; **204:** Associated Press, AP; **229:** AP/Wide World Photos; **240:** Associated Press, AP; **257:** Michael G. Bennett/Imagemakers International, Inc.; **263:** ©Michael Newman/Photoedit; **292:** Michael G. Bennett/Imagemakers International, Inc.; **296:** ©Mark Reinstein/Index Stock Imagery; **331:** ©Joel Gordon; **345:** Associated Press, AP; **363:** Associated Press, AP; **367:** AP/Wide World Photos; **387:** ©Index Stock Photography, Inc.; **390:** Michael G. Bennett/Imagemakers International, Inc.; **421:** ©Joel Gordon; **424:** Associated Press, AP; **435:** Michael G. Bennett/Imagemakers International, Inc.; **439:** Michael G. Bennett/Imagemakers International, Inc.; **444:** Associated Press, AP; **458:** A. Ramey/PhotoEdit; **468:** Michael G. Bennett/Imagemakers International, Inc.; **484:** Associated Press, AP; **499:** Michael G. Bennett/Imagemakers International, Inc.; **502:** Corbis; **515:** Michael G. Bennett/Imagemakers International, Inc.; **538:** ©Joel Gordon; **553:** Corbis; **555:** Associated Press, AP; **560:** Michael G. Bennett/Imagemakers International, Inc.; **1:** Associated Press, AP; **29:** ©Joel Gordon; **75:** Associated Press, AP; **107:** Associated Press, AP; **137:** Michael G. Bennett/Imagemakers International, Inc.; **169:** James L. Schaffer; **199:** Associated Press, AP; **237:** ©Michael Newman/PhotoEdit; **279:** Michael G. Bennett/Imagemakers International, Inc.; **315:** ©Joel Gordon; **355:** Associated Press, AP; **385:** ©Index Stock Photography, Inc.; **407:** Associated Press, AP; **433:** Michael G. Bennett/Imagemakers International, Inc.; **465:** Corbis; **513:** Michael G. Bennett/Imagemakers International, Inc.; **547:** Associated Press, AP